ON NATIVE GROUNDS

ON NATIVE GROUNDS

An Interpretation of
MODERN AMERICAN PROSE
LITERATURE

By
ALFRED KAZIN

With a Preface to the
Fiftieth Anniversary Edition

A HARVEST BOOK
HARCOURT BRACE & COMPANY
San Diego   New York   London

Requests for permission to make copies of any part
of the work should be mailed to: Permissions Department,
Harcourt Brace & Company, 6277 Sea Harbor Drive,
Orlando, Florida 32887-6777.

Library of Congress Cataloging-in-Publication Data
Kazin, Alfred, 1915–
On native grounds: an interpretation of modern American prose literature/
by Alfred Kazin.—3rd Harvest ed.
p. cm.—(A Harvest book)
"With a preface to the fiftieth anniversary edition."
ISBN 0-15-668750-X
1. American prose literature—20th century—History and criticism.
2. United States—Intellectual life—20th century. I. Title.
PS369.K39 1995
818'.50809—dc20 94-45100

Printed in the United States of America
Third Harvest Edition 1995
A B C D E

Permissions acknowledgments can be found on pages 539–541
and constitute a continuation of the copyright page.

For

ASYA, GITA, AND CHARLES KAZIN

IN LOVE AND HOMAGE

" . . . sometimes the life seems dying out of all literature, and this enormous paper currency of Words is accepted instead. I suppose the evil may be cured by the rank-rabble party, the Jacksonism of the country, heedless of English and of all literature—a stone cut out of the ground without hands;—they may root out the hollow dilettantism of our cultivation in the coarsest way, and the newborn may begin again to frame their own world with greater advantage."—EMERSON, *Journals*

Contents

Preface to the Fiftieth Anniversary Edition

"The joy of being toss'd in the brave turmoil of these times."
—WALT WHITMAN, *Democratic Vistas*

I began *On Native Grounds* on a kitchen table in Brooklyn, 1938, and completed it in Long Island City, 1942, expecting a call from my draft board at any minute. The dates are essential to any understanding of the book, to its survival for over fifty years and its continued influence. There is no excitement for a writer like that of living in rebellious times. At least before World War II broke out, my work in progress was very much the product of and a response to the social crises of the '30s. The massive breakdown of the American economy in the depression was the greatest national crisis after the Civil War, and I lived in its very midst, tossed up and down in the stormy ocean of the times by the suffering of my unemployed working-class parents, the mass social protests all over the country, the triumph of Fascism in Germany, Italy, and Spain, and the extremism in America itself of Communist and Facist ideologies in violent conflict.

What Whitman wrote about the Civil War in "Drum-Taps" could have been said of the '30s:

> Long, too long America,
> Traveling roads all even and peaceful you learn'd from joys and
>   prosperity only,
> But now, ah now, to learn from crises of anguish, advancing,
>   grappling with direst fate and recoiling not,
> And now to conceive and show to the world what your children
>   enmasse really are . . .

A history of modern American prose literature begun in such a period and continued out of a sense of social crisis during the great global war against Fascism! The literary significance of this is that I believed in what William Hazlitt called the "spirit of the age"— meaning that *this* age we were living in had a character all its own and could be related to other ages and periods, thus constituting a historical scene in which a period was known through its writers and its writers through their period.

Of all my books, *On Native Grounds* was the easiest to write. I felt what I have never felt since 1945—that the age was wholly with me, that I was appealing to "the spirit of the age," that the writers as characters in my book were friends and the most encouraging people in the world to write about. I was writing literary *history,* a genre long abandoned by critics and now suspect (history can no longer be characterized and summed up as confidently as it was in the '30s and early '40s by the young man who wrote this book). This means that I saw connections everywhere between history and literature—between the populism of the 1890s and the realism in Howells, Dreiser, and Wharton; between the first expatriates in the 1890s and the alienation that led the Hemingway generation to what Henry James had earlier called "the conquest of Europe." I saw connections between the writers themselves as fellow-spirits and artists relating to the pressures of American life.

My subject was the emergence of the "modern" in an American literature obviously unsettled by relentless new forces in every sphere: social, intellectual, and religious. My perspective, so natural in the turbulent '30s, was based on a spirit of social protest I shared with almost every writer in my book, from William Dean Howells, whose move in 1891 from Boston to New York opened my narrative, to the Southern Agrarians (Allen Tate and John Crowe Ransom the best known), who in 1938 still thought it possible to create a pre-industrial society on the pre-Jeffersonian model.

There was nothing strange or unexpected in 1938 about my being both critical of "the system" and crazy about the country. What drew me to the serious study of American literature within a historical context was the *narrative* it suggested on every hand. America from its beginnings as "our rising empire" (Washington) embodied a purposeful form of historical movement, unprecedented on such a continental scale, that cried out to be written as a great story. In the background of the particular story I was writing was the sense, which was everywhere at the end of the nineteenth century, of a new age. What struck me from the first was the astonishment with which American writers confronted situations as new to themselves as to the Europeans who were often reading about America for the first time.

What gave me the confidence at twenty-three to begin a book like this? The age, the insurgency of the times, but above all *On Native Grounds* represents my personal discovery of America. The first native son in my immigrant family, brought up in a Brooklyn ghetto by parents whose harshly enclosed lives never gave them a chance even to learn English, I was crazy about the America I knew only through books. And it was such an idealistic, radically Protestant America, defined by its purest spirits, from Audubon and Jefferson to Emerson and Thoreau, to the Lincoln who had saved the Union, to the great democrats of philosophy John Dewey and William James, and to the Willa Cather, Theodore Dreiser, Sherwood Anderson, and Carl Sandburg who brought home the Middle West to me as the valley of democracy and the fountainhead of hope.

There are critical judgments in my book I have long been dissatisfied with. Howells was a realist of great sensitivity and a historically significant novelist, but hardly a great one. I made him altogether too loveable by signifying his instinct for changes in the literary weather and his old-fashioned sense of outrage at the depredations of the iron age in American capitalism.

I was still afraid of Faulkner when I wrote about him in the limiting terms then so conventionally used in discussions about this great artist. My sensitivity to Faulkner's passion—and it is a historical passion both as subject and achievement—was so acute that my style became equally extravagant; I unconsciously imitated a style I pompously disapproved of! Since then, in one essay and book after another, I have written in full appreciation of a man I believe to be the greatest of twentieth-century American novelists—the only "modern" equal to Melville in narrative intensity and philosophic force.

I undervalued Richard Wright, for me the most gifted, honest, and evocative American black novelist. Since I was not writing about poetry, I was hardly fair in describing the Southern formalists and "New Critics," poets most of them and with poetry as their chief interest.

If *On Native Grounds,* for all its youthful brashness and the many brickbats that have been hurled at it, has remained a book hard to get rid of, let me suggest a few things about it as a work of criticism that are still unusual. It was written as a consecutive narrative, and this in the belief that a history of literature can display a pattern evolving from actual historical circumstances. And for all its historical background, it was written out of an old-fashioned belief that literature conveys central truths about life, that it is indispensable to our expression of the human condition and our struggle for a better life.

I wrote about American literature before the study of it became the industry it is today. It was a time when there were almost no separate professorships of American literature, no departments of "American Studies," and above all no belief that American literature constituted a tradition for writers newly coming up. The people in my book still thought, like Emerson, that *they* were creating American literature. It was this lack of what used to be called "a usable past" that made so strong and independent the writers of the first half of the century. They thought they were pioneers and that the rise of the United States in this period was the greatest possible subject for a novelist.

Think now of how much Ralph Ellison and William Styron owe to Faulkner, John Updike to Howells, Jean Stafford (and thousands of others) to Henry James. James and Faulkner knew they had no predecessors. Their relative lack of popular success in their own time was a painful tribute to their arduous originality. No one else before them wrote like Sinclair Lewis or Ring Lardner or Willa Cather— and certainly not like Theodore Dreiser! Like Lincoln and Rockefeller and Debs they were *sui generis* in the old American tradition. Each created his and her own tradition. It is easy for a cloistered translator of Plato like Allan Bloom in *The Closing of The American Mind* to deride Mencken as a "buffoon," but it was rough guys like Mencken, clumsy fellows like Dreiser, terrible spellers like Scott Fitzgerald who created the bold new literature that would soon sweep the world.

I am glad to think that *On Native Grounds* caught the times, the passion, the America that made such writers possible. It is all there for me still as I go back to the book. My subject had to do with the "modern" as democracy; with America itself as the greatest of modern facts; with the end of another century just a hundred years ago as the great preparation. In lonely small towns, prairie villages, isolated seminaries, dusty law offices, and provincial "academies," no one suspected that the obedient-looking young reporters, law clerks, and librarians would turn out to be Willa Cather, Robert Frost, Sinclair Lewis, Theodore Dreiser, and Marianne Moore.

ALFRED KAZIN

New York, New Year's Day, 1995

Preface to the
Fortieth Anniversary Edition

THE YOUNG MAN who wrote *On Native Grounds* between 1938 and
1942 did so in the full confidence that history is the mother of literature and that the insurgent America of the 1930s, connecting him with
our traditions of social criticism and the American scene at large, was
behind his book. He had other advantages (not recognized at the
time). He was not a professor but an entirely free agent, even if this
meant grubbing for a living. And in the midst of depression, his country was still rich enough to afford libraries. The great reading room of
the New York Public Library on 42nd Street, Room 315, was open
every day of the week late into the evening.

His greatest advantage was the nature of his subject, which at the
time was virtually novel. To describe the rise of the modern in American literature, its sensibility, its liveliness, its protest, from the end of
the last century up to the coming of World War II (1890–1940), was
to enter into the fifty years that saw America become a world power,
even the dominant power. It was *the* period of the modern; its ascendency and sudden triumph came in the 1920s, that most abundant
spectacle of successive creativity in our literary history. The period
decisively turned our writers from "the last of the provincials" into
the desperately sophisticated, spiritually rootless satirists and elegists,
like Hemingway and Faulkner, who became dominating influences in
world literature.

The rise of the United States in the first half of the twentieth century,
John O'Hara liked to say, made it the greatest possible subject for a

novelist. O'Hara, flushed with his personal share of American success, never asked the question that a more conscientious imagination, John Cheever, was to ask in two different pieces of fiction: Why, "in this half-finished civilization, in this most prosperous, equitable and accomplished world, should everyone seem so disappointed"? To assume a necessary connection between national power and personal satisfaction is of course dumb. After 1945, when America seemed the only victor on the world scene, an editorial in *Life* magazine churlishly complained of our unpatriotically dissatisfied writers that this nation "is still producing a literature which sometimes sounds as if it were written by an unemployed homosexual living in a packing-box shanty while awaiting admission to the county poorhouse."

But there is in fact a connection between his country's power and a writer's imagination. To pursue this through my chronicle, from the 1890s to the Great Depression, was to take on a supple, endlessly surprising theme, ending in the passionate documentation of the ravaged land and disordered scene with which I ended my book.

I began it with a supposedly antique figure, the early realist William Dean Howells. Howells, an even greater "success" and moneymaker in his time than John O'Hara became in ours, was a writer so complaisant that he managed to be the friend of both Mark Twain and Henry James, who could not even read each other. His most famous pronouncement, alas, is still: "the smiling aspects of life are the more American." But honest Howells was so horrified by the outbreak of savage class war in America and so impatient with the complacent gentility that surrounded his *Atlantic* editor's chair in Boston that he moved to New York. His newfound interest in the wild city, its cosmopolitan flavor and its many "Bohemian" writers and artists, plus the unexpected criticism his novels now made of social injustice, were an obvious prelude for me to the urban realism of his successors. But what, more than his mild Christian socialism and his move to New York, turned this respectable and typical nineteenth-century American success (a perfect example of what he called "the man who has risen") into a pioneer realist of the modern scene? What, in fact, turned an even more successful and prominent writer, Mark Twain, into the raging rebel of the 1890s and later, one who was to leave for *posthumous* publication (the careful little man!) so many violent attacks on Theodore Roosevelt, our horrible treatment of the "liberated" Filipinos, and the hypocrisies of our moral majority?

Forty and more years ago, writing this book, I assumed that excessive power can have an inverse effect on a writer's imagination. I felt myself to be a "literary radical," in the tradition of Van Wyck Brooks and Edmund Wilson. In my long days and evenings of reading at the New York Public Library on 42nd Street, I was surrounded by every possible sign of America's neglect of its people. I felt myself to be one of the people. Everything that the old Mark Twain said about American corruption and selfishness, that was to become the staple of our famous literary "alienation," from James to Hemingway, from Beard, Parrington, and Veblen to Mencken, from Sinclair to Steinbeck, seemed to reverberate from the faces around me during the depression and in the possibility of a more equitable order of society that was being raised (for a time) by left-wing writers.

The alienation that was so much a part of my story was clearly rooted in the abruptly violent changes endemic in American life, which in the nineteenth century made our greatest historian, Henry Adams, feel spiritually homeless, and in the twentieth led Hemingway and so many gifted American writers to a perpetually rootless life anywhere but in America. There was no doubt in my mind, when I began the book, that American writers were to a fault believers in a more equitable human order, and that it was indeed the famous "promise of American life" that made nagging perfectionists of them—of some of them.

Power expanded the imagination, as the greed and audacity of Elizabeth's buccaneers gave more room to Shakespeare's. American "manifest destiny" made possible the brag and vitality of Melville's *Moby-Dick*. But in America, as it seemed to me, our peculiar promise of equality turned so many writers into active critics of the status quo that one of the premises behind *On Native Grounds,* at least early in the book, was what the young Van Wyck Brooks said was incumbent on literary criticism: "impelled, sooner or later, to become social criticism . . . because the future of our literature and art depends upon the wholesale reconstruction of a social life all the elements of which are as if united in a sort of conspiracy against the growth and freedom of the spirit."

That, even in the thirties, was not applicable to many of our boldest and strongest writers, notably Faulkner. Faulkner (I did not altogether realize this at the time) moved in a more significant orbit of tragedy, a more profound awareness of our total human destiny and individual defeat. Nor did I see in my youthful brashness and "hopefully" radical temper that the dissatisfaction of so many American "moderns" was precisely with the "modern" itself. One reason American writers were irritable with America was not that it was socially unjust but that it was spiritually shallow. The arrogant individualism that was encouraged among our writers by Emerson, the "father of us all" (Whitman called him the "actual beginner of the whole American procession"), turned out to be, for many of them, precisely self-limiting.

In any event, the insurgency of the thirties did not even last to the end of the thirties. Before I came to the end of my book in 1942 the moral bankruptcy of many left-wing writers left me, though still radical, less convinced of the "necessary" connection between literature and social criticism. My fierce attachment to the American scene itself, evident in my last chapter, was no doubt written as a protest against ideology. The hope of justice in human affairs had become less important to me, less probable, than undeviating freedom.

The "modern" spirit that was my subject, the "modern" hope in every field of intellectual endeavor from which my book had arisen, closed in on itself with the war, and after the war became an academic matter. This may be one reason why this book, tracing the rise (but not the fall) of the modern spirit in America, became a useful work of reference for so many young people after the war. But the young man who began it in 1938 was not interested in providing a history after the fact. He thought he was living in an age of hope—and he was.

ALFRED KAZIN

New York, May 4, 1982

Preface

TWENTY or thirty years ago, when all the birds began to sing (almost, as it seemed, in chorus), the emergence of our modern American literature after a period of dark ignorance and repressive Victorian gentility was regarded as the world's eighth wonder, a proof that America had at last "come of age." Today we no longer marvel over it; though that literature has become an established fact in our national civilization, we may even wonder a little uneasily at times how deeply we possess it, or what it is we do possess.

This book had its starting point in my conviction that a kind of historic complacency had settled upon our studies of that literature, and that while the usual explanation of it as a revolt against gentility and repression had the root of the matter in it, it did not tell us enough, and that it had even become a litany. It spoke of opportunities and freedoms won; it did not always tell us how they had been used, or whether literature had come with the freedom. It marked off the timidities of the older writers from the needs of the new; we were left to suppose that William Dean Howells was somehow inferior to James Branch Cabell. It made for so arrogant and limited a time-sense that it virtually dated our modern writing from the day of John S. Sumner's collapse. It wrote the history of our early modern literature as a war to the death between Henry Van Dyke and Theodore Dreiser, or between H. L. Mencken and the forces of darkness. It applied mechanically Santayana's well-worn phrase, the "Genteel Tradition," to everything Mencken's iconoclastic generation disliked in late nineteenth-century life. It allowed young people to suppose that *Jurgen* was somehow a great book because it had once been suppressed. It was a serviceable formula, an inevitable formula, the signature in pride

of men who had often fought valiantly and alone for the creation of
a free modern literature in America. But just as it dated time from
1920, the beginning of wisdom from the onslaught against "Comstockery," and confused Mencken with Voltaire, so it too often left
out that larger story in which Mencken's great services were only one
chapter—a story hardly limited to the historic modern struggle against
"Puritanism," the rejection of the old prohibitions, and the attainment
of a contemporary sophistication.

Our modern literature in America is at bottom only the expression
of our modern life in America. That literature did not begin with the
discovery of sex alone, with the freedom to attack ugliness and provincialism, or with the need to bring our culture into the international modern stream. Everything contributed to its formation, but it
was rooted in nothing less than the transformation of our society in
the great seminal years after the Civil War. It was rooted in that
moving and perhaps inexpressible moral transformation of American
life, thought, and manners under the impact of industrial capitalism
and science whose first great recorder was not Dreiser, but Howells—
the Howells who, for all his prodigious limitations, was so alive to the
forces remaking society in his time that he "foresaw no literature for the
twentieth century except under Socialism, and said so"; [1] the Howells
who was so misinterpreted for my generation by some of the light-
bringers of 1920—they saw only his prudery—that we have forgotten
that for him, as for Tolstoy, morality meant also the relation of man
to his society. Our modern literature was rooted in those dark and still
little-understood years of the 1880's and 1890's when all America stood
suddenly, as it were, between one society and another, one moral order
and another, and the sense of impending change became almost oppressive in its vividness. It was rooted in the drift to the new world of
factories and cities, with their dissolution of old standards and faiths;
in the emergence of the metropolitan culture that was to dominate the
literature of the new period; in the Populists who raised their voices
against the domineering new plutocracy in the East and gave so much
of their bitterness to the literature of protest rising out of the West; in
the sense of surprise and shock that led to the crudely expectant Uto-

[1] Mark Van Doren

pian literature of the eighties and nineties, the largest single body of Utopian writing in modern times, and the most transparent in its nostalgia. But above all was it rooted in the need to learn what the reality of life was in the modern era.

In a word, our modern literature came out of those great critical years of the late nineteenth century which saw the emergence of modern America, and was molded in its struggles. It is upon this elementary and visible truth—almost too elementary and visible, so close are we still to its crucible—that this book is based; and it was the implications following upon it that gave me some clue to the patterns of the writing that came after. It was my sense from the first of a literature growing out of a period of dark and confused change, growing out of the conflict between two worlds of the spirit, that led me to begin the book with what is for me the great symbolic episode in the early history of American realism—the move from Boston to New York of William Dean Howells, the Brahmins' favorite child but the first great champion of the new writers. And it was this same conviction that American "modernism" grew principally out of its surprise before the forces making a new world that led me to understand a little better what is for me the greatest single fact about our modern American writing—our writers' absorption in every last detail of their American world together with their deep and subtle alienation from it.

There is a terrible estrangement in this writing, a nameless yearning for a world no one ever really possessed, that rises above the skills our writers have mastered and the famous repeated liberations they have won to speak out plainly about the life men lead in America. All modern writers, it may be, have known that alienation equally well, and for all the reasons that make up the history of the modern spirit; have known it and learned to live with it as men learn to live with what they have and what they are. But what interested me here was our alienation *on* native grounds—the interwoven story of our need to take up our life on our own grounds, and the irony of our possession. To speak of modern American writing as a revolt against the Genteel Tradition alone, against Victorianism alone, against even the dominance of the state by special groups, does not explain why our liberations have often proved so empty; it does not tell us why the light-bringers brought us light and live themselves in darkness. To speak of it only as a struggle toward the modern emancipation—and it was that—does not even hint at the lean and shadowy tragic strain in our modern American writing, that sense of tragedy which is not Aristotle's, not even Nathaniel Hawthorne's, but a clutching violence, and from Dreiser to Faulkner, an often great depth of suffering. Nor does it tell us why our modern writers have had to discover and rediscover and chart the country in every generation, rewriting Emerson's *The American Scholar* in every generation (and the generations are many in modern American writing, so many), but must still cry America! America! as if we had never known America. As perhaps we have not.

No one has told us the whole story; no one can yet weave into it all the many different factors, the rhythms of growth, the subtle effects of our American landscape, the necessary sensibility to what it has meant to be a modern writer in America at all. No one can yet tell us all that F. Scott Fitzgerald meant when he said that "there are no second acts in American lives," or why we have been so oppressed by the sense of time, or why our triumphs have been so brittle. We can only feel the need of a fuller truth than we possess, and bring in our fragment, and wait. So is this book only a panel in the larger story, and not merely because it is limited to prose. It is in part an effort at moral history, which is greater than literary history, and is needed to illuminate it. For the rest, I am deeply conscious of how much I have left out, of how much there is to say that I have not been able to say. It is an intrusion on a living literature, and as tentative as anything in life. But it is clear to me that we have reached a definite climax in that literature, as in so much of our modern liberal culture, and that with a whole civilization in the balance, we may attempt some comprehensive judgment on the formation of our modern American literature.

A few words on critical method. We live in a day when the brilliance of some of our critics seems to me equaled only by their barbarism. In my study in Chapter XIV of the twin fanaticisms that have sought to dominate criticism in America since 1930—the purely sociological and the purely textual-"esthetic" approach—I have traced some of the underlying causes for the aridity, the snobbery, the sheer human insensitiveness that have weighed down so much of the most serious criticism of our day. It may be sufficient to say here that I have never been able to understand why the study of literature in relation to society should be divorced from a full devotion to what literature is in itself, or why those who seek to analyze literary texts should cut off the act of writing from its irreducible sources in the life of men. We are all bound up in society, but we can never forget that literature is not produced by "society," but by a succession of individuals and out of individual sensibility and knowledge and craft. It has been given to our day in America, however, to see criticism—so basic a communication between men—made into either a scholastic technique or a purely political weapon. We have seen the relation of the writer to society either ignored or simplified, though it can never be ignored and is never simple.[1] We have seen the life taken out of criticism, the human grace, the simple all-enveloping knowledge that there are no separate "uses" in literature, but only its relevance to the whole life of man. We have been oppressed by the anemic bookmen, the special propagandists, the scientists of metaphor. Inevitably—see only Van Wyck Brooks's *The Opinions of Oliver Allston*—there has been a reaction through sentimentality, a confusion of the complex relations that must persist between the good of society and the life of art.

True criticism only begins with books, but can never be removed from their textures. It begins with workmanship, talent, craft, but is nothing if it does not go beyond them. An affront when it is not sane, a mere game if it is not absorbed in that which gives it being and is greater than itself—greater even than the world of literature it studies—it can yet speak to men, if it will speak *to* them, and humbly. For its ambition should make it humble, as its humility can make it

---

[1] "A man walked, as it were, casting a shadow, and yet one could never say which was man and which was shadow, or how many the shadows that he cast. Was not a nation, as distinguished from a crowd of chance comers, bound together by this interchange among streams or shadows; that unity of image, which I sought in national literature, being but an originating symbol?"—Yeats, *A Vision*.

useful: it wants nothing less than to understand men through a study of tools. In a letter to a young reviewer who had condescended to like one of his last novels, Sherwood Anderson wrote: "You do not blame me too much for not knowing all the answers." Criticism can never blame anyone too much for not knowing all the answers; it needs first and always to prove itself.

Sections of this work have appeared in the *Saturday Review of Literature,* the *Virginia Quarterly Review,* the *Antioch Review,* the *Sewanee Review,* and the *New Republic.*

This book could not have been written without the fellowship granted me in 1940 by the John Simon Guggenheim Memorial Foundation, and I should like here to express my gratitude to the Foundation and to Henry Allen Moe, its Secretary-General, for his friendly interest in the work, his unfailing understanding and encouragement. I owe also a great debt to the Carnegie Corporation of New York for a grant-in-aid which helped me to complete the book, and to Mrs. Elizabeth Ames and the Corporation of Yaddo.

Various sections of the book in early drafts were read by Carl Van Doren, Henry Seidel Canby, and Newton Arvin; and I should like here to tender my warmest thanks to them for the light they have thrown on various problems, even though I have not always been able to agree with them on matters of interpretation. I am deeply grateful to Oscar Cargill for his very scholarly and helpful reading of the galleys; and for their active aid and criticism, to my friends John Chamberlain, Richard Rovere, Benjamin Seligman, Richard Hofstadter, Dr. Solomon Simon, and Gertrude Berg. To Howard N. Doughty, Jr., and to my sister, Pearl Kazin, I owe a debt beyond all expressing for their scholarship and counsel, and for sustaining me through many difficult periods. There is a debt, so inadequately acknowledged in my dedication, too great for any dedication, that I owe to my wife, Asya Dohn, whose aid on this book was equaled only by her inexhaustible patience with its author.

A. K.

New York,
July 11, 1942.

ON NATIVE GROUNDS

PART I: THE SEARCH FOR REALITY
1890-1917

"Modern times find themselves with an immense system of institutions, established facts, accredited dogmas, customs, rules, which have come to them from times not modern. In this system their life has to be carried forward; yet they have a sense that this system is not of their own creation, that it by no means corresponds exactly with the wants of their actual life, that, for them, it is customary, not rational. The awakening of this sense is the awakening of the modern spirit. The modern spirit is now awake almost everywhere. . . . It is no longer dangerous to affirm that this want of correspondence exists; people are even beginning to be shy of denying it. To remove this want of correspondence is beginning to be the settled endeavour of most persons of good sense. Dissolvents of the old European system of dominant ideas and facts we must all be, all of us who have any power of working; what we have to study is that we may not be acrid dissolvents of it."—MATTHEW ARNOLD

Chapter 1

THE OPENING STRUGGLE
FOR REALISM

"They will have seen the new truth in larger and larger degree; and when it shall have become the old truth, they will perhaps see it all."
—W. D. HOWELLS

WHEN, early in December of 1891, William Dean Howells surprised his friends and himself by taking over the editorship of the failing *Cosmopolitan* in New York, he thought it necessary to explain his decision to one of the few friends of his early years surviving in Cambridge, Charles Eliot Norton.

> Dear Friend: I fancy that it must have been with something like a shock you learned of the last step I have taken, in becoming editor of this magazine. . . . The offer came unexpectedly about the beginning of this month, and in such form that I could not well refuse it, when I had thought it over. It promised me freedom from the anxiety of placing my stories and chaffering about prices, and relief from the necessity of making quantity. . . . I mean to conduct the magazine so that you will be willing to print something of your own in it. I am to be associated with the owner, a man of generous ideals, who will leave me absolute control in literature.

Lowell, for whom Howells had been "Dear Boy" even at fifty, and who had corrected his Ohio ways with gentle patronizing humor down the years—though no one could have become more the Bostonian than

3

Howells—had died that year, and Howells now requested from Norton, as Lowell's executor, a poem on Grant. Six months later Howells suddenly resigned. The experience had proved an unhappy one. It was the climax to a series of publishing ventures and experiments through which he had passed ever since he had left the *Atlantic Monthly* in 1881 and taken the literary center of the country with him, as people said, from Boston to New York.

For ten years after leaving Boston—and Howells was perfectly aware of the symbolic effect of his leaving—he had flitted in and out of New York, writing for the *Century* and *Scribner's,* conducting a column in *Harper's,* supporting himself in part by lectures, and growing older and more embittered than his friends and family had ever remembered him. Leaving Boston had been the second greatest decision of his life, as going to Cambridge in 1866 had been the first; and it had not been easy to tear up his roots in the New England world which had given him his chance and beamed upon his aptitudes and his growing fame. Now he could no longer return to that world even to accept the hallowed chair once occupied by Longfellow and Lowell, though it was pleasant to be asked and exhilarating to learn that the self-educated Ohio printer and journalist had become so commanding a figure in American letters. New York excited and saddened him at once; he once wrote to Henry James that it reminded him of a young girl, "and sometimes an old girl, but wild and shy and womanly sweet, always, with a sort of unitarian optimism in its air." He clung to the city distractedly. "New York's immensely interesting," he had written to a Cambridge friend in 1888, "but I don't know whether I shall manage it; I'm now fifty-one, you know. There are lots of interesting young painting and writing fellows, and the place is lordly free, with foreign touches of all kinds all thro' its abounding Americanism: Boston seems of another planet." To James, whose every letter evoked the great days in Cambridge in the eighteen-seventies when they had dreamed of conquering the modern novel together, he wrote that he found it droll that he should be in New York at all. "But why not?" The weird, noisy, ebullient city, which in his novels of this period resounded to the clamor of elevated trains and street-car strikes, nevertheless suggested the quality of youth; and Howells, old at fifty, delighted in the Bow-ery, walks on Mott Street, Washington Square, and Italian restaurants. He had strange friends—Henry George lived a street or two away, and they saw each other often; he went to Socialist meetings and listened, as he said, to "hard facts"; he even entertained Russian nihilists. Indeed, he now called himself a Socialist, a "theoretical Socialist and a practical aristocrat." To his father he wrote, in 1890, "but it is a comfort to be right theoretically and to be ashamed of oneself practically."

A great change had come over Howells. The eighteen-eighties, difficult enough years for Americans learning to live in the tumultuous new world of industrial capitalism, had come upon Howells as a series of personal and social disasters. The genial, sunny, conventional writer who had always taken such delight in the cheerful and commonplace life of the American middle class now found himself rootless in spirit at the height of his career. *Facile princeps* in the popular estimation, the inspiration of countless young writers—was he not a proof that the self-made artist in America was the noblest type of success?—financially secure, he found that he had lost that calm and almost complacent pleasure in his countrymen that had always been so abundant a source of his art and the condition of its familiar success. To James he could now joke that they were both in exile from America, but acknowledged that for himself it was "the most grotesquely illogical thing under the sun; and I suppose I love America less because it won't let me love it more. I should hardly like to trust pen and ink with all the audacity of my social ideas; but after fifty years of optimistic content with 'civilization' and its ability to come out all right in the end, I now abhor it, and feel that it is coming out all wrong in the end, unless it bases itself anew on a real equality." Never before had he missed that equality in American life; raised upon a casual equalitarianism and a Swedenborgian doctrine in his village childhood whose supernaturalism he had abandoned early for a religion of goodness, he had always taken the endless promise of American life for granted. His own career was the best proof of it, for he had always had to make his own way, and had begun setting type at eight. Now, despite his winning sweetness and famous patience, the capacity for good in himself which had always encouraged him to see good everywhere, his tender conscience and instinctive sympathy for humanity pricked him into an uncomfortably

sharp awareness of the gigantic new forces remaking American life.
Deep in Tolstoy—"I can never again see life in the way I saw it before
I knew him"—he wrote to his sister Anne in November, 1887, that even
the fashionable hotel at which he was then staying in Buffalo caused
him distress. "Elinor and I both no longer care for the world's life, and
would like to be settled somewhere very humbly and simply, where we
could be socially identified with the principles of progress and sympathy for the struggling mass. I can only excuse our present movement
as temporary. The last two months have been full of heartache and
horror for me, on account of the civic murder committed last Friday at
Chicago."

The "civic murder"—stronger words than Howells had ever used on
any subject—was the hanging of Albert Parsons, Adolf Fischer, George
Engle, and August Spies in the Haymarket case. They had been found
guilty in an atmosphere of virulent hysteria not—as the presiding justice readily admitted—because any proof had been submitted of their
guilt or conspiracy, but because their Anarchist propaganda in Chicago
had presumably incited the unknown assassin to throw the bomb
that killed several policemen and wounded several more. Howells,
who was perhaps as astonished that there were Anarchists in America
as he was that legal machinery and public opinion could be mobilized
to kill them, exerted himself passionately in their defense. He sought
the aid of Whittier and George William Curtis, offered himself to
the defendants' counsel, and published a plea for them in the *New
York Tribune* on November 4, 1887. But without avail. "The thing
forever damnable before God and abominable to civilized men," as
he described the execution to a New York editor, shocked him into
furious anger and disappointment. In letter after letter of this period,
he poured out his vexation and incredulity. To his father he wrote,
soon after the execution: "All is over now, except the judgment that
begins at once for every unjust and evil deed, and goes on forever.
The historical perspective is that this free Republic has killed five
men for their opinions." To his sister, a week later: "Annie, it's all
been an atrocious piece of frenzy and cruelty, for which we must
stand ashamed forever before history. . . . Some day I hope to do
justice to these irreparably wronged men." A year later Hamlin Gar-

land, Howells's young Populistic disciple, could joke that Howells had become more radical than he. Garland, who was enthusiastic about Henry George and the single tax, noticed that Howells was luke-warm to it because he did not think it went deep enough. A year after the Haymarket executions, Howells was writing in deep solemnity of the "new commonwealth." "The new commonwealth must be founded in justice even to the unjust, in generosity to the unjust rather than anything less than justice. . . . I don't know yet what is best; but I am reading and thinking about questions that carry me beyond myself and my miserable literary idolatries of the past."

Abused by the pack for his stand in behalf of the Anarchists, Howells suddenly found himself in disfavor for other reasons. In those fateful years, 1886-92, when his social views were brought to a pitch of indignation and sympathy he had never known before and was certainly not to retain after 1900, he was conducting a campaign for the realistic novel in the "Editor's Study" column of *Harper's*. Realism had been his literary faith from his earliest days, his charac-teristic faith ever since he had known that his profession lay in the commonplace and the average. "Unconsciously I have always been," he wrote once, "as much of a realist as I could." He had absorbed realism from a dozen different sources—the eighteenth-century Italian dramatist Goldoni, the Spanish novelists Benito Galdós and A. Palacio Valdés, Turgenev and Tolstoy, Jane Austen (along with Tolstoy a prime favorite), Daudet, Mark Twain, and Henry James. He had been a practising, virtually an instinctive, realist long before the word had come into popular usage in America—was he not the Champ-fleury of the novel in America?—and he could say with perfect confidence that realism was nothing more or less than the truthful treatment of material. Bred to a simple, industrious way of life that accepted candor and simplicity and detestation of the hifalutin as elementary principles of democratic life and conduct, he had applied himself happily for twenty years to the portraiture of a happy and democratic society.

Howells had, as Van Wyck Brooks has said, a suspicion of all romantic tendencies, including his own; his interest in sex was al-ways so timid, his prudishness and modesty so compulsive, that he was as incapable of the romanticist's inflation of sex as he was unconcerned with the naturalist's "scientific" interest in it. His interest was in the domesticities of society, homely scenes and values, people meeting on trains, ships, and at summer hotels, lovers on honeymoon, friendly dinners, the furrows of homespun character, housekeeping as a principle of existence, and the ubiquitous *jeune fille* who radiated a vernal freshness in so many of his early novels and whose dictation of American literary taste he accepted, since men notoriously no longer read novels. Howells had therefore no reason to think of realism as other than simplicity, Americanism, and truth. Painters like Tom Eakins and his friend George Fuller—Howells had a strong feeling for painters, architects, mechanics, careful craftsmen of all types—worked in that spirit and wrought what they saw. Could American writers do any less? Was realism any less exciting for working in the commonplace, or less moving? Like Miss Emily Dickinson of Amherst, Massachusetts, another Yankee craftsman, Howells might have said, "Truth is so rare, it's delightful to tell it." When Matthew Arnold visited America on a celebrated lecture tour to pronounce America lacking in distinction and "uninteresting," William James laughed—"Think of interesting used as an absolute term!" Howells, characteristically, accepted the term gladly. What greater distinction was there than fidelity to the facts of one's lack of "distinction," to the savor and quality and worth of what was abiding and true?

Now, as Howells's views on society deepened, his allegiance to realism, his characteristic feeling for it, took on a new significance. The novel had swiftly and unmistakably, from the late seventies on, become the principal literary genre, and in the wave of renewed interest in the novel which filled the back columns of the serious magazines, Howells's sharp and stubborn defense of realism, seen in the light of his own social novels of this period, made him a storm center. His most ambitious works were disparaged by the romanticists, his judgments as a reviewer ridiculed, and his reputation seriously challenged. Zola, whom Howells had always espoused with lukewarm enthusiasm, could by the middle eighties claim for his work in America a certain tolerance, even a grudging admiration; but Howells, infinitely less dangerous, who never quite understood naturalism and had to the end of his life a pronounced distaste for it, was subjected to extraordinary abuse. One fashionable literary sheet, the *Literary World,* said as late as 1891 that many of Howells's realistic dicta were "as entertaining and instructive as that of a Pawnee brave in the Louvre." When Howells pleaded with young novelists to stick to life in America as they knew it, Maurice Thompson, a leader of the "romanticists," charged that Howells had said that mediocrity alone was interesting, and "a mild sort of vulgarity the living truth in the character of men and women. . . . All this worship of the vulgar, the commonplace and the insignificant," Mr. Thompson whimpered, "is the last stage of vulgarity, hopelessness and decadence."

One reader wrote complainingly to the *Atlantic Monthly* in 1892 that to read the books Howells recommended was "gratuitously to weaken one's vitality, which the mere fact of living does for most of us in such measure that what we need is tonic treatment, and views of life that tend to hopefulness, not gloom." Eminent critics of the nineties wrote bitterly that they were tired of fiction which wrestled with all the problems of life. F. Marion Crawford, the most successful, intelligent, and cynical of the romanticists, laughed that realists are expected "to be omniscient, to understand the construction of the telephone, the latest theories concerning the cholera microbe, the mysteries of hypnotism, the Russian language, and the nautical dictionary. We are supposed to be intimately acquainted with the writings of Macrobius, the music of Wagner, and the Impressionist school of painting." Howells, who did not know that the attacks upon him were more often attacks upon the naturalism to which his disposition was equally alien, was stung when the romanticists in full pack accused him of triviality and dullness. In November, 1889, he wrote bitterly in *Harper's:*

> When you have portrayed "passion" instead of feeling, and used "power" instead of common sense, and shown yourself a "genius" instead of an artist, the applause is so prompt and the glory so cheap that really anything else seems wickedly wasteful of one's time. One may not make the reader enjoy or suffer nobly, but one may give him the kind of pleasure that arises from conjuring, or from a puppet show, or a mod-

ern stage play, and leave him, if he is an old fool, in the sort of stupor that comes from hitting the pipe.

As his popularity decreased, Howells found himself caught between two forces. The young realists and naturalists whom he befriended even when he did not enjoy them—Garland, Stephen Crane, Frank Norris—had made his exquisite cameo studies an anachronism; and by the nineties, when realism had won its first victory, it was being submerged by historical romanticism and Stevensonian gush. Realism had passed silently into naturalism, and had become less a method than a metaphysics. To those younger friends of Howells for whom he found publishers and wrote friendly reviews, but whom he could not fully understand; to the novelists of the Middle Border writing out in silent bitterness a way of life compounded of drought, domestic hysteria, and twelve-cent corn; to the metropolitan esthetes nourished on Flaubert and Zola—to these realism was no longer an experiment or a claim to defend against gentility; it was the indispensable struggle against the brutality and anarchy of contemporary existence. In the first great manifesto of the American naturalists, *Crumbling Idols,* Hamlin Garland wrote exultantly: "We are about to enter the dark. We need a light. This flaming thought from Whitman will do for the search-light of the profound deeps. All that the past was not, the future will be." Yet with the exception of Frank Norris, the younger men were not even interested in the *theory* of naturalism, in the scientific jargon out of Claude Bernard, Darwin, and Taine with which Zola and his school bedecked *le roman expérimental.* Provincial and gawky even in their rebellion (a decade after Henry James had finally and devastatingly disposed of the "moral" purpose of fiction young Garland was still tormented by it), lacking any cohesive purpose or even mutual sympathy, the young naturalists who had drawn the iron of American realism out of social discontent and the rebellion of their generation were united only in their indifference to the simpering enemies of realism and the forces of academic reaction. They loved Howells even if they did not always appreciate him, and like a hundred American critics of the future, regarded him as something of an old woman. They thought of Henry James (if they thought of him at all) as an old woman, too;

but James, the greatest critic of his generation—and theirs—conducted his campaign for the novel on a plane they would never reach. However, never too strong in critical theory, at least defended realism in terms the young men out of the West could assess, develop, or reject.

Yet what the naturalists missed in Howells, as so many others were to miss it for almost half a century after them, was that his delight in reality and his repugnance to romanticism clearly encouraged them to work at the reality they themselves knew. Whatever his personal limitations of taste and the prudery that was so obsessive that it does not seem altogether a quality of his age, Howells's service was to stimulate others and to lend the dignity of his spirit to their quest. Whatever the fatuousness or parochialism that could label "three-fifths of the literature commonly called classic . . . filthy trash" and set Daudet above Zola because the latter wrote of "the rather brutish pursuit of a woman by a man which seems to be the chief end of the French novelist," his insistence that young writers be true to life as they saw it—"that is the right American stuff"—was tonic. For if he was philosophically thin, he could be spiritually intense; he imparted a shy moral splendor to the via media, and though the range of his belief was often narrow, he suffered profoundly for it.[1] Yet despite a disposition to the conventional that was so essential a part of his quality, the amiable old-fashionedness that he displayed from his earliest days, he was wonderfully shrewd, and he could hit hard. "These worthy persons are not to blame," he once wrote of the gentility opposed to realism. "It is part of their intellectual mission to represent the petrification of taste, and to preserve an image of a smaller and cruder and emptier world than we now live in, a world which was

---

[1] To Brander Matthews he wrote in 1902: "*The Kentons* has been fairly killed by the stupid and stupefying cry of 'commonplace people.' I shall not live long enough to live this down, but possibly my books may. I confess that I am disheartened. I had hoped that I was helping my people know themselves in the delicate beauty of their everyday lives, and to find cause for pride in the loveliness of an apparently homely average, but they don't want it. They bray at my flowers picked from the fruitful fields of our common life, and turn aside among the thistles with keen appetites for the false and impossible."

Nor did he ever live it down. His reputation, which began to sink in the middle eighties, reached its nadir soon after. Five years before his death in 1920, he wrote to Henry James: "I am comparatively a dead cult with my statues cut down and the grass growing over them in the pale moonlight."

feeling its way towards the simple, the natural, the honest, but was a good deal 'amused and misled' by lights no longer mistakable for heavenly luminaries." Never less pretentious than in his criticism, Howells could say with perfect justice that the nineteenth century, which had opened on the Romantic revolution, was now closing with equal splendor on the revolution of realism, since romanticism had plainly exhausted itself. "It remained for realism to assert that fidelity to experience and probability of motive are essential conditions of a great imaginative literature." Thus, with all its failings, *Criticism and Fiction,* Howells's little manifesto in behalf of realism, had the ring of leadership in it, and the aging novelist whose tender shoot of rebellion was his last great creative act had a wonderful eagerness for the future. The enemies of realism sigh over every advance, he smiled, but let them be comforted. "They will have seen the new truth in larger and larger degree; and when it shall have become the old truth, they will perhaps see it all."

2

As an idea, as a token of change, as something peculiarly French and unwholesome, but portentously significant, the theory of realism had by 1890 almost gained a certain respectability in America. Even Zola —perhaps because he was Zola—who had, after the American publication of *L'Assommoir* in 1879, been accused of pandering to the wicked, had by 1888 gained a certain tolerance for *La Terre.* In 1882, the *Critic,* a fashionable literary journal of the day, had declared Zola a literary outlaw, and insane. In 1892 it pronounced: "It was a brilliant idea to introduce the scientific spirit of the age into the novel, and Zola set to work upon it with his immense energy and his unshakable resolution. One by one the evils of his time have been taken up by this prodigious representative of Latin realism and laid before the world in all their enormity." By 1900, largely because of his stand in the Dreyfus case, Zola was beginning to be openly accepted almost everywhere and acclaimed a prophet. Yet Howells was not acclaimed much of anything for his stand in the Haymarket affair, and American realists had still to struggle to make themselves heard. By a curious irony, indeed, this had even become more difficult, for as realism in America came of age and passed into naturalism, its very foundations in thought and experience were overrun by the tide of Graustark fiction, the decorative trivialities of the fin de siècle, and the growing complacency of the American middle class in the epoch of imperialism. Where the opponents of realism had once barked at it as immoral, they now patronized it and called it dull. So Howells was told over and again in fashionable literary papers that while he was the noblest of men and his motives indubitably of the loftiest, his novels were a bore. So Eugene Field, who at his Punchinello best liked to josh Garland and other solemn young realists with plotting the destruction of a social order founded on the full dinner-pail and the G.O.P., wrote excessively whimsical papers in his newspaper column, *Sharps and Flats,* on the dreariness of realism.[1] Traditional romanticism, which from the eighties on had flourished in prosperity and yielded dolefully to realism in periods of crisis and panic, was to attain unparalleled confidence in the expansive years after the Spanish-American War; and it was particularly humiliating to compete with Richard Harding Davis and the Gibson girl after twenty years of struggle and devotion.

Yet it was entirely characteristic of the quality and the history of American realism that it should be opposed by the senile and the complacent, by academic reactionaries who feared what they did not understand, and by cynical businessmen of letters like F. Marion Crawford who had made a good thing of superplush fiction. For realism in America, which struggled so arduously to make itself heard and understood, had no true battleground, as it had no intellectual history,

---

[1] Typical of these was an imaginary dialogue between Garland and Tolstoy in a Russian railway train:

" 'From bad humanity goes to worse. Its condition becomes harder and harder all the time. This barren country about us will eventually be cultivated, these trees felled, these mountains quarried, these plains plowed and irrigated.'

'And all involves more labour, more suffering, more sorrow!'

'That will be the harvest of realism,' continued the 'younger genius.' 'There will be more sweat, more sore feet, more lame backs, more callous hands, more evil smells, a greater destitution of socks, and a vaster plenitude of patched pants than the philosophy of veritism even dreams of in these days.'

'And we shall not be here to enjoy these miseries and the telling of them! It is this thought that makes our lot even more wretched!' "—C. H. Dennis, *Eugene Field's Creative Years,* Doubleday, Page and Company, 1924, p. 135.

few models, virtually no theory, and no unity. In France realism and Zolaism had been contested by Ferdinand Brunetière and Anatole France on esthetic as well as moral grounds; it had possessed a school, a program, a collective energy, the excitement that grew out of the modern novelist's sense, as Henry James described it, of his "sacred office"—of being in the direct line of the sages and chroniclers of history. In Scandinavia and Russia the epoch of realism had evoked national energies and ideals, had burst upon a Europe groping its way through the collapse of the old faiths to announce the dignity of art and the recovery of truth. So Zola had written in the general notes to the Rougon-Macquart cycle that he based it "upon a truth of the age: the upheaval of ambitions and appetites." So naturalism, denounced for its crudity and its "atheism," had been founded, whatever its pretentiousness and savagery, upon the logic of science. "I believe above all in a constant march toward truth," Zola had cried. "It is only from the knowledge of virtue that a better social state can be born. . . . My study then is simply a piece of analysis of the world as it is. I only state facts." So the European romantic poet—Shelley, Leopardi, Pushkin—bestriding the world in radiant indignation, became the ubiquitous naturalist reporter, notebook in hand, glorying in the fetid metropolitan air, the mortuary, the sewer, the slum, the prison hospital, convinced that the truth does make men free.

What if naturalism did surrender to the materialism it aimed to expose, and was bogged down too often in the worship of Fact? It had at least shed the rhetoric of romanticism with romantic energy. Henry James saw the matter with almost classic penetration when he wrote in an essay on contemporary fiction that "M. Zola is magnificent, but he strikes an English reader as ignorant; he has an air of working in the dark. If he had as much light as energy, his results would be of the highest value." Yet James knew that the conception of realism of which Zola was at best only an extravagant and even a self-imposed symbol, had in it the seeds of a moving greatness. To the novelist of the future he wrote:

Enjoy [the novelist's freedom] as it deserves; take possession of it, explore it to its utmost extent, publish it, rejoice in it. All life belongs to you, and do not listen either to those who would shut you up into corners of it and tell you that it is only here and there that art inhabits, or to those who would persuade you that this heavenly messenger wings her way outside of life altogether, breathing a superfine air, and turning away her head from the truth of things. There is no impression of life, no manner of seeing it and feeling it, to which the plan of the novelist may not offer a place.

At the moment, however, this was too exalted for an American realism which was still laboring in the nineties to establish elementary principles of candor and seriousness. For how was one to foster those principles when the movement depended upon the business cycle like any industry and was, indeed, principally the by-product of an economic revolution? Everything that is significant in the history of American realism stems from the fact, confirmable over fifty years of subsequent literary experience, that while in Europe realism and naturalism grew out of the positivism of Continental thought and the conviction that one literary movement had subsided and another was needed, realism in America grew out of the bewilderment, and thrived on the simple grimness, of a generation suddenly brought face to face with the pervasive materialism of industrial capitalism.[1] Realism in Europe found its philosophy in mechanism, its cosmogony in the Newtonian conception of the universe, its authority in Comte, Darwin, and Taine, its artistic quintessence in artists like Flaubert and Ibsen, who by their own careers signified the irrepressible movement of the

---

[1] Which is not to say that American realism did not find its characteristic motivations and forms in many sections and for many reasons. *As a doctrine,* realism in America has a suggestive history, but one only passingly relevant to the purposes of this essay. It may, for example, be ascribed to, or linked with, the doctrinal Yankee homeliness of Emerson; the example of Whitman; the appearance of the daguerreotype; the school of nineteenth-century "open-air" painters, notably Thomas Eakins and W. S. Mount. (There is a very rich and illuminating discussion of this aspect in F. O. Matthiessen's monumental study, *American Renaissance.*) It is an interesting commentary on the history of realism in America to remember that one of our earliest realists, Caroline Stansbury Kirkland (d. 1864), began to write her trenchant little sketches of frontier life in opposition to Chateaubriand's *Atala,* which she had taken with her as a bride to her frontier home. Edward Eggleston, who published *The Hoosier Schoolmaster* in 1871, found his spur in a copy of Taine's *Art in the Netherlands,* which showed him "that the artist of originality will work courageously with the materials he finds in his own environment." The history of realism in America after the Civil War is a history of grievances, and the most important thing about it is its cardinal and poignant simplicity—how much audacity it took merely to say: "Write of what you know! Write of your very own!"

literary mind from romanticism to scientific "objectivity" in literature. Realism in America, whatever it owed to contemporary skepticism and the influence of Darwinism, poured sullenly out of agrarian bitterness, the class hatreds of the eighties and nineties, the bleakness of small-town life, the mockery of the nouveaux riches, and the bitterness in the great new proletarian cities. Its primitivism as a literary movement was such that some of the most vigorous pioneer realists—Ed Howe, Harold Frederic, Hamlin Garland—were engaged in precisely the same labor of elementary truth-telling about farm life that had impelled George Crabbe a hundred years before to rebel against Goldsmith's sentimental bucolic elegies. Its leaders were the unhappy sons of prairie families, shriveled New England bluestockings acidly recording the narrowness and meanness of small-town life, romantic academicians like Hjalmar Boyesen, Chicago journalists who enjoyed riddling *le bourgeois*. Realism came to America from everywhere and nowhere ("no one invented it," said Howells, "it came"), and it had no center, no unifying principle, no philosophy, no joy in its coming, no climate of experiment. There was something dim, groping, unrealized in American realism even when it found its master in Dreiser, and long before Dreiser (himself so perfect a symbol of the crudity and emotional depths of American realism) it foundered on a dozen religious and moral taboos. Like so many of the innovations and literary revolutions that were to compose the subsequent history of modern American literature, that pioneer realism utterly lacked a coherent and dynamic orientation. Thus Howells, despite his cultivation, remained something of a provincial to the very end, and as late as 1883 could write to John Hay that Zola's *Nana* was a bad book because "its bad art in one respect arose from the bad French morality." A decade later he was to justify the "purity" of the American novel on the ground that it satisfied the aspirations of the feminine reading audience of America, while in Europe the novel was written principally for "men and married women." So, too, the career of so aggressive a naturalist as Frank Norris was to prove that an American novelist had to grope over Stevenson in order to reach Zola, and that the violence of Wild West stories was the only available introduction to the violence of naturalism—the violence of the modern mind. Indeed, Norris's mind was to suggest that romanticism had not yet even begun to express itself fully in America when it slipped into naturalism.

Yet it is to these primitive realists—to a Joseph and Caroline Kirkland, a Rebecca Harding Davis, an Ed Howe, a Hamlin Garland, a Henry Fuller, as it is to Howells, that contemporary literature in America owes the paramount interests that have dominated it for fifty years, and the freedoms it takes for granted. It is to these lone protestants of their time, who did not always know that they were writing "realism," to Jeffersonian hearts plagued by a strangely cold and despotic America, to writers some of whom lacked every capacity for literature save a compelling passion to tell the truth, that the emancipated and metropolitan literature of contemporary America owes its very inception. It was these early realists, with their baffled careers and their significant interest in "local color," cultivating their own gardens, who encouraged in America that elementary nationalism, that sense of belonging to a particular time and a native way of life, which is the indispensable condition of spiritual maturity and a healthy literature.

It was this insight and this need that Hamlin Garland proclaimed in his naturalist's manifesto, *Crumbling Idols,* when he wrote proudly that the history of literature in America is the history of the slow development of a distinctive utterance. He appealed, at the pitch of Wordsworth's appeal in the Preface to the *Lyrical Ballads,* for that independence of outlook and democratic freedom of mind which signified nothing less than loyalty and affection to native resources. Of what value was the social and political militancy of the West, Garland cried, if it yielded timidly to copy-book maxims and a copy-book art? At a time when colonial antiquarianism and snobbery dominated the respectable imagination, Garland exulted in the candor and bitterness of those young Western writers who, whatever their crudities (not that Garland was particularly aware of those crudities), were devoting themselves to an American, a regional, a democratic art. Garland's regionalism, as it happens, drew him to an exaggerated regional jingoism, but he could claim with perfect justice that the whole school of local color (launched before the Civil War) was an attempt to explore the different resources of the national character.

At the very moment that these pioneer realists marshaled their hopes for a literature appropriate to the new age, however, they were forced into a faltering struggle with the forces of that new age. Out of the first embattled years of the new industrial epoch there developed the abiding quality of an American literature which has ever since been significantly alien to a domineering capitalism and half-nostalgic for a preindustrial society. The cleavage between the artist and capitalist society that runs all through the history of modern Western literature found its first expression in America in people who were themselves, as citizens, stricken by industrial capitalism and frightened by it; citizens who did not so much rebel against the new order as shrink from it. American thought had as traditional a hatred of commercialism and the "cash nexus" as any culture in the world, and had memorialized it imperishably in an Emerson, a Thoreau, a John Humphrey Noyes, in the impulse that had founded a Brook Farm, a Fruitlands, an Ephrata. But the new America that was cradled in the Civil War, baptized by the Bessemer process and married too early in life to the Republican party, the new America that came in rudely through Gettysburg and the Wilderness, stamping across a hundred thousand corpses, blaring its tariffs, sniggering its corruption, crying "Nothing is lost but honor"—that America was so strange, shocking, and new that its impact on the first postbellum generations still reverberates in the American mind. What wonder, then, that the first realists of the period, so many of whom were farmers and small villagers, were almost devastated by it? The only dissent they knew was rhetorical, "Jeffersonian," bound to a preindustrial and precorporate way of life. What was there in Emerson (who now seemed to speak from another world), in any previous tradition of dissent on American soil,[1] by which to oppose or even to understand the Crédit Mobilier

---

[1] Forty years after he had read *Walden,* Howells once confessed that he had never looked at the book afterward. In somewhat the same spirit Charles Eliot Norton wrote, in a letter of 1870: "No best man with us has done more to influence the nation than Emerson,—but the country has in a sense outgrown him. He was the friend and helper of its youth; but for the difficulties and struggles of its manhood we need the wisdom of the reflective and rational understanding, not that of the intuitions. Emerson . . . belongs to the pure and innocent age of the Presidency of Monroe or John Quincy Adams,—to the time when Plancus was Consul,—to the day of Cacciaguida." Howells did, of course, add in the same passage in *Literary Friends and Acquaintance* a famous

and railroad strikes, Pinkertons and Anarchists, trusts and Mark Hanna, or the unforgettable dictum of George F. Baer, the railway official: "The rights of the laboring man will be protected and cared for, not by labor agitation, but by the Christian men to whom God in His infinite wisdom has given control of the property interests of the country"? These pioneer realists, pioneer moderns, in truth, were as unprepared for the onslaught of a capitalist order and its corresponding ethic as European writers implemented by the tireless criticisms of a Marx, a Ruskin, an Arnold, a Tolstoy, a William Morris, were prepared; and they foundered. In their foundering is half the story of their time and of our own.

It is this alienation from the new postbellum order, with its confusions rather than its hatreds, its perplexity rather than its penetration, that marks the beginning of the modern spirit in America. To the historian, as to the revolutionary, the domination of the nineteenth century by the bourgeois mind records a process, a phase of development. To the student who knows that the literary imagination of America has more often been embedded in the Zeitgeist than reflective of it, the anxieties and bewilderment of the distraught folk literature that grew out of the eighties are profoundly significant and moving. The evocation of a new order in literature is to contemporary observers often an unconscious process, but the sense of its presence in the literature of America after 1880 is almost intolerably intense. The conception of the Civil War as "the second American revolution" has already become platitudinous, but the living significance of the contest between Southern plantation owners and Northern manufacturers—between "feudalism" and "capitalism"—was not lost to the postwar mind. John Jay Chapman put it best when he said that the whole history of America after the Civil War was the story of a railroad passing through a town, and then dominating it. So forty years later Sherwood Anderson was to describe in *Poor White* a little town in Ohio whose in-

---

tribute to Thoreau's prophetic criticism of the "unworthiness" of modern civilization—the civilization of industrial slavery. Yet it is significant, as Henry Seidel Canby notes in his *Thoreau,* that it was the nascent British Labor party that used *Walden;* no American social group ever did. American writers admired Emerson and Thoreau; Europeans and Asiastics—Tolstoy and Gandhi are the most famous examples—profited by them.

habitants suddenly knew, one hushed poignant afternoon, "when the stumps had been cleared, the Indians driven away," that they were *waiting* for the new order to overtake them.[1]

When Frederick Jackson Turner told the eighteen-nineties that the era of expansion was over, the frontier forever closed, he told something less than the whole truth; but *The Significance of the Frontier in American History,* whatever its value as a contemporary analysis, had a more direct influence as a contribution to the climate of opinion. Whether writers read Turner or not, the implications of his thesis soon became popular enough, and the image of a closed frontier, of a corporation economy, of a city proletariat oppressed and rebellious, darkened the mind. Even Howells—whose seemingly complacent pronouncement that "the smiling aspects of life are the more American" earned him the contempt of two generations of modernists—added in the same context, however, that while "the sum of hunger and cold is comparatively small in a land where journeymen carpenters and plumbers strike for four dollars a day and the wrong from class to class has been almost inappreciable, all this is changing for the worse." In the first of his Utopias, *A Traveler from Altruria,* he had one character describe the transformation of American life between 1850 and 1890:

---

[1] As early as the eighties, indeed, the concept of superhuman centralization, of vast interlocking combines, so haunted the contemporary imagination that it provoked a remarkably copious Utopian literature which has no parallel in other periods or literatures. *Looking Backward* stimulated hundreds of "Nationalist" clubs to spread its gospel, sold hundreds of thousands of copies a week in the late eighties, and even provoked Morris to write *News from Nowhere*—he had pronounced *Looking Backward* "a horrible cockney dream." The significance of these Utopian novels (even Howells wrote two, and the literary-minded Populist, Ignatius Donnelly, one) lies not only in the startling immediacy of their response to a transformed civilization or the avidity with which the middle class devoured them, but in the simplicity with which Bellamy and his many imitators accepted the industrial era as the herald of a beneficent Socialist totalitarianism. Though they proved themselves as vulgar on occasion as any manufacturer worshiping his machine, and antedated the American advertising mystics of the latest gadget, they were—like all their generation—children playing with fire. Like the late Utopian novelist Bradford Peck, who entitled his thriller *The World a Department Store,* they took the most inane or sinister implications of a profit economy on trust, and asked only to be allowed the destruction of "institutions." So Bellamy, whose state was built like a corporation, unconsciously anticipated the conscripted labor armies of the GPU and the Nazi Labor Front in his suggestion that labor could be organized into an industrial army.

If [in 1850] a man got out of work, he turned his hand to something else; if a man failed in business, he started again from some other direction; as a last resort, in both cases, he went West, pre-empted a quarter section of public land, and grew up with the country. Now the country is grown up; the public land is gone; business is full on all sides, and the hand that turned itself to something else has lost its cunning. The struggle for life has changed from a free fight to an encounter of disciplined forces, and the free fighters that are left get ground to pieces between organized labor and organized capital.

Henry Adams, who invested his life with the dignity of tragedy because, as the legend has it, he had missed the dignity of office, saw the matter now fiercely, now petulantly; but he saw it to its depths when he wrote in an early letter to his brother Brooks: "Our so-called civilization has shown its movement, even at the centre, arrested. It has failed to concentrate further. Its next effort may succeed, but it is more likely to be one of disintegration, with Russia for the eccentric on one side and America on the other." Writing in the *Education* of the new reign of power, of the engineer-statesmen of this new era who were "trustees for the public," he had pointed out that these men were controlled by others, and said:

The work of internal government has become the task of controlling these men, who are socially as remote as heathen gods, alone worth knowing, but never known, and who could tell nothing of political value if one skinned them alive. Most of them have nothing to tell, but are forces as dumb as their dynamos, absorbed in the development or economy of power. They are trustees for the public, and whenever society assumes the property, it must confer on them that title; but the power will remain as before, whoever manages it, and will then control society without appeal, as it controls its stokers and pit-men. Modern politics is, at bottom, a struggle not of men but of forces. The men become every year more and more creatures of force, massed about central power-houses. The conflict is no longer between the men, but between the motors that drive the men, and the men tend to succumb to their own motive forces.

As the little men lost their confidence, admiration for the *novi homines* of the "heroic age of business enterprise" began to wane.

Trust-busting, which was to exhaust so much of the middle-class ardor of the Progressive period, came only *after* the acceptance of capitalism; but it was just at that crucial period when Mark Hanna became one of the great villains of contemporary folklore and Opper's caricatures of barrel-shaped magnates were being scanned with relish, that big business made its boldest bid for power, invaded Washington as a political force, and displayed that ostentatious "reign of gilt" and contempt for society that were to obsess social novelists before the muckraking novel appeared.[1] For at least a decade before the Bryan-McKinley campaign crystallized the social antagonisms of the postbellum era, writers not particularly more sensitive than the great body of the middle class knew that the businessman had become the legendary archetype, even the hero, of the new order. By 1880 there were already a hundred millionaires in the United States (Emerson died only two years later), and the upstarts who built their imitation châteaux pretentiously also built them solidly, as if to signify that they had come to stay.

The age of the individualist was at its height; never before had the commercial mind displayed so much power or so much confidence in its culture, its profits, and its future. Never in the history of business, Miriam Beard has observed, "had such reaches of the earth come into the possession of men of affairs; always, in previous times, the soil had to be taken by the sword, and the merchant, less martial or less interested in the furrow, had not wrested great dominions from feudal chivalry. . . . For the first time, and in America, businessmen acquired territories of regal extent, without lifting a battleaxe." One man owned a million acres alone in the Texas Panhandle; another, Joseph Leiter, offered to buy the Great Wall of China. The father of

[1] "You Americans believe yourselves to be excepted from the operation of general laws. You care not for experience. I have lived seventy-five years, and all that time in the midst of corruption. I am corrupt myself, only I do have courage to proclaim it, and you others have it not. Rome, Paris, Vienna, Petersburg, London, all are corrupt, only Washington is pure! Well, I declare to you that in all my experience I have found no society which has had elements of corruption like the United States. The children in the street are corrupt, and know how to cheat me. The cities are all corrupt, and also the towns and the counties and the States' legislatures and the judges. Everywhere men betray trusts both public and private, steal money, run away with public funds. Only in the Senate men take no money."—Baron Jacobi in Henry Adams's *Democracy*.

William Randolph Hearst, as if to anticipate the exploitation of literary wares that was to make his son's reputation, hired Ambrose Bierce to defame Collis Huntington in a skirmish of the many California railroad wars. In 1896 a stranger asked Mark Hanna if he was not related to Herman Melville, the last the middle name of Hanna's brother. Uncle Mark scratched. "What the hell kind of job does Melville want?" So wild was the extravagance of the new American plutocracy, so mad its pace of acquisition, that even European financiers were shocked by the intensity of its lust. Orgiastic in their greed, the "titans of industry" had become rich so explosively that while they could buy the world's fine art, they themselves could boast no cultivation. In a world of businessmen like Cecil Rhodes, Gustav Stresemann, Walter Rathenau, their only intellectual distinction was James Ford Rhodes's "businesslike" *History of the United States* in seven volumes. They could hardly remember with pleasure the verdict passed by another businessman who also wrote history, Charles Francis Adams. The brother of Brooks and Henry Adams wrote in a famous passage of his *Autobiography:*

> As I approach the end I am more than a little puzzled to account for the instances I have seen of business success—money-getting. It comes from a rather low instinct. Certainly, so far as my observation goes, it is rarely met with in combination with the finer or more interesting traits of character. I have known, and known tolerably well, a good many "successful" men—"big" financially—men famous during the last half-century; and a less interesting crowd I do not care to encounter. Not one that I have ever known would I care to meet again, either in this world or the next; nor is one of them associated in my mind with the idea of humor, thought or refinement. A set of mere money-getters and traders, they were essentially unattractive and uninteresting.

Yet what if the businessman in America had produced nothing of "culture"? In politics he had attained a classic glory when he fostered a Warwick in Mark Hanna; in the arts, a Morgan raiding the Old World of its bibelots, its holograph Bunyan and Milton, its Italian masters. What need had the business mind to apologize for itself? The new commercialism was to become the theme, even the obsession, of a hundred histories, plays, novels, satires; to be analyzed and excoriated and praised with a ferocious interest that was itself the highest flattery. What need had the businessman to scribble or philosophize when he dominated the imagination of his time and the frantic materialism that was his principle of existence had become the haunting central figure in contemporary life?[1]

3

In one of the wittiest of early realistic satires, Henry Blake Fuller's *With the Procession,* a group of Chicago bohemians meet in a restaurant to exchange condemnations of the vulgar herd. The young hero of the novel, whose father had sent him abroad for an expensive education in the arts which had unfitted him for a life in business, asks his mordant companions what consolation they can give him for living in so dreadful a period. "This," responds one sardonic young man, "that we are at last playing the game with all the pieces on the board, with all the cards in the pack; with all the elements, in other words, of a vast and diversified human nature." The realistic conception of life in the new age began, he says, with the terrible railroad riots of 1877, a year after the centennial of American independence.

> The simple hopes and ideals of this Western world of fifty years ago— even of twenty years ago—where are they now? . . . What the country really celebrated at Philadelphia in 1876, however unconsciously, was the ending of its minority and the assumption of full manhood with all its perplexities and cares. The broad life of the real world began for us the very next year . . . and has been going on more fiercely ever since. Take a man who was born in 1860, and who is to die with the century—what would be *his* idea of life? Contention, bickering, discontent, chronic irritation.

"Yes," says another, "a generation ago we thought—poor, pathetic creatures—that our pacific processes showed social science in its fullest

---

[1] "As energetic young Frenchmen in Froissart's day turned to war, as energetic young Englishmen in Elizabethan days turned to exploration, as energetic young Americans of 1800 turned to pioneering, so the young Americans of Rockefeller's day turned to business. They looked to it for distinction, power, and the joys of self-expression."— Allan Nevins, *John D. Rockefeller: The Heroic Age of Business Enterprise.*

development. But today we have all the elements possessed by the old world itself, and we must take whatever they develop, as the old world does. We have the full working apparatus finally, with all its resultant noise, waste, stenches, stains, dangers, explosions."

Another, pointing to Chicago as the symbolic city of the nineties, says that the town "labors under one disadvantage: it is the only great city in the world to which all its citizens have come for the one common, avowed object of making money. There you have its genesis, its growth, its end and object. . . . In this Garden City of ours every man cultivates his own little bed and his neighbor his; but who looks after the paths between?"

"When you see cruelty going on before you," John Jay Chapman once wrote, describing the experience of his generation, "you are put to the alternative of interposing to stop it, or of losing your sensibility." Fuller did not lose his; and it is for such passages of sensibility that he and a few other realists of his generation are to be remembered. Otherwise second-rate craftsmen, they contributed by their passion, their shrewd notations on the transformation of American character, their homely honesty, to the support of realism and its development. Fuller, as it happens, had a more interesting mind than Garland, Ed Howe, Harold Frederic, and the others; but his exquisite soul, and the active moral indignation he was later to display with exemplary courage during the Spanish-American War, were the marks of a graceful and impressionistic artist who was a realist *malgré lui*. There was war in Fuller's members, says Robert Morss Lovett: "He wanted to live and write as a European, and he knew that he must live and write as an American. Undoubtedly his material went sour on him."

Like another Chicago intellectual who was beginning to write "realistically" around this period, Robert Herrick, Fuller loathed Chicago but devoted himself to the study of it, for its packing-house economy, its almost glittering materialism, radiated an atmosphere of pure greed. He could write skillfully, with a lambent touch that mocked his own bitterness; his flip style and loosely sardonic craftsmanship even anticipated the sophisticated novel of the nineteen-twenties; but the gentle little man who abominated Chicago and was obsessed by it, who once wrote to Howells that he had "no great liking for the en-

vironment, and no great zest for life as it is lived," suggested only a
man hopelessly lost in a vulgar time, but determined to record it ac-
curately. Other metropolitan realists, like Hjalmar Boyesen, did not
even succeed so well.

Hjalmar Hjorth Boyesen was a Norwegian and professor of German
at Columbia who had a wide knowledge of the traditions of European
realism and endeavored to emulate the most commonplace of them in
his three best-known novels of American manners—*The Golden Calf,
The Social Strugglers,* and *The Mammon of Unrighteousness.* As early
as 1886, in a famous essay on "The American Novelist and His Public," he ridiculed the "boarding-school" standard of the novel-reading
public. Though he was Howells's protégé and a passionately admiring
friend, he attacked both him and Henry James for not writing of
American politics, as he attacked the fashionable novelist who was
content to satisfy the *jeune fille* taste and the authority of a genteel
tradition that obliged the novelist "to repress that which is best in him
and offer that which is of slight consequence . . . a plight to which
many a novelist in this paradise of women is reduced." He laughed at
novelists who could remain silent "concerning all the vital things of
life," and repeated Goethe's famous adjuration to American writers
to avoid romanticism like the plague.

Though he was a better realist in precept than in practice, even
Boyesen's theoretical studies were mediocre. Like Harry Thurston
Peck, Percival Pollard, James Gibbons Huneker, and so many cos-
mopolites of the fin-de-siècle era, Boyesen's service to the emancipation
and growth of American taste was to expound the work of the great
Continental realists; but despite such valuable pioneer studies as *Essays
on Scandinavian Literature,* Boyesen's mind was not that of a pioneer.
He had an alien's disposition to please, and though Howells liked to
say of him that Boyesen had "outrealisted him," the truth is that the
handsome, kindly, emotional academician did his best work in his
romantic children's stories of Norwegian life. He never found himself
in America, and he never found himself in realism. He took a naïve
pride in the success of the local-color school, exulted in the fact that
by the early nineties all but a dozen states had their "conspicuous
novelist," and exaggerated the quality of their realism, for "local color"
had already become so loose a term that Boyesen seems to have con-

fused sentimental historical fiction with the traditions of Bret Harte and George W. Cable. He wrote an essay on "The Progressive Realism of American Fiction," but he confessed that he was afraid of too rapid a progression. By realism, he insisted, he did not mean

> the practice of that extreme wing of the school which believes only that to be true which is disagreeable, and conscientiously omits all cheerful phenomena. Nor do I confine my definition to that minute insistence upon wearisome detail which, ignoring the relation of artistic values, fancies that a mere agglomeration of incontestable facts constitutes a truthful picture.

Boyesen was, in truth, a unique example in America of the Victorian realist. He rejoiced in realism, particularly the German and the Scandinavian, if it signified the adjustment of taste and belief to the Darwinian world view; he fought nobly for Ibsen at a time when it was dangerous even to expound the dramatist's ideas; he could even say, though with characteristic hesitation, that the "morality" of a realistic novel was less important than its "truth." "The most modern literature, which is impenetrated with the spirit of the age, has a way of asking dangerous questions," he wrote in *Essays on Scandinavian Literature*. ". . . Our old idyllic faith in the goodness and wisdom of all mundane arrangements has undoubtedly received a shock. Our attitude toward the universe is changing with the change of its attitude toward us"— which is Tennyson, and not half so challenging as George Eliot. The worst of Boyesen—or perhaps only his inveterate Victorianism—is seen most clearly in his essay on Georg Brandes, for whom he had the highest praise, but whose Anarchist fling and espousal of "an obscure German iconoclast named Friedrich Nietschke" provoked him to the same ungentlemanly rage provoked in respectable magazine editors of the nineties like R. W. Gilder by the racy passages in the *Yellow Book*.

In a book of essays, *Literary and Social Silhouettes*, Boyesen confessed his reluctance to offend the public that bought his books; his novels confirm it. They are solemn failures, but they fail not only because Boyesen was compromised by "prudence," but largely because, like so many of his daring contemporaries, he was not happy in realism. A facile writer, he was compelled in the manner of his generation to satirize the gross, the squalid, the pretentious; but he had an exceptionally bad ear for dialogue, and his anxiety "to depict persons and conditions which are profoundly American" bogged down in problems of characterization and style for which he simply lacked the necessary skill. His prefatory intentions, as announced in such a novel as *The Mammon of Unrighteousness,* were apparently militant. "I have disregarded all romantic traditions, and simply asked myself in every instance not whether it was amusing, but whether it was true to the logic of reality—true in color and tone to the American sky, the American soil, the American characterization." In practice, however, he displayed a most tepid soul; his very choice of incidents and scale of values prove that though he patronized the romantic commercial novelist, he lacked a necessary flair for the novel. His attempts at dialect moved even contemporary readers to ridicule, but he could please by his gentlemanly airs, his chatty style, and a genuine if reluctant feeling for the happy ending.

Boyesen was not, after all, antediluvian; his realistic novels were published in the nineties at a time when Howells was most deeply under the influence of Tolstoy; when prairie realists like Joseph Kirkland and Ed Howe and Hamlin Garland had already taken realism into the most advanced camp. His mockery of the nouveaux riches in *The Social Strugglers,* or his arraignment of contemporary materialism in *The Mammon of Unrighteousness,* was less comprehensive than Henry Adams's *Democracy.* His distinction was a vigor of conscience. Whatever he lacked, it was not the courage to bring the new gospel of realism to the attention of the public, to fight for it and defend it within the limitations of his intelligence and taste. He contributed a little, a very little, to the realization of the literature of the future; but it was from one little man's courage and another's knowledge that realism drew over the long, difficult years of its apprenticeship the ardor and curiosity that enabled it to survive.

4

Unlike Fuller and Boyesen, who as honest men were attracted by realism but for personal reasons could not give all their devotion to it, the prairie realists who now began to appear in the Middle West had a deeper stake in realism. As Populists or the sons of Populists, as Westerners and farmers, they invested realism with the character of a social movement and saw in it, whatever else they may have lacked, the substance of an authentic literature for democracy. As against the dandy of the Gilded Age who exclaimed, "We are not politicians or public thinkers; we are the rich; we own America; we got it, God knows how, but we intend to keep it if we can," the farmers who had been growling out on the Middle Border ever since they began to clash with the railroads had a movement, a homely democratic tradition of their own making, and a strength of purpose that flowed into the farm-bred novelists who were to describe their grim lives. Half a century before, writing in his journal of 1834, Emerson had worried over the genteelism of American writers and had looked to the West for the necessary challenge to the ingrown conventions.

> I suppose the evil may be cured by this rank-rabble party, the Jacksonism of the country, heedless of English and of all literature—a stone cut out of the ground without hands;—they may root out the hollow dilettantism of our cultivation in the coarsest way, and the newborn may begin again to frame their own world with greater advantage.

So it now proved with the Populist farmers and their literary offspring.

For it was the Populist farmers, not the industrial workers in the East, who first challenged the astonishing and brazen new world of industrial capitalism in the stormy eighties and nineties; and it was farmers or small villagers like the forgotten Joseph Kirkland—author of *Zury: The Meanest Man in Spring County*—Ed Howe and Hamlin Garland and a York State country boy named Harold Frederic, who first created in their primitive fashion a modern literature of protest in America. Though they were not all Populists, they helped, sometimes unwittingly, to express the underlying spirit of Populism; and whatever else the Populists may now represent, they do provide—like Howells's career—a remarkably significant link between nineteenth-century experience and twentieth-century expression in America. For the Populists, speaking for the farmers in the West, were the first great social realists of the new era; the first to speak openly and bravely of the dangers of plutocracy; the first to convey something of the bewilderment and anguish a whole generation felt in the disillusionment that followed the Civil War; the first to influence a folk literature, crude as it often was, based upon common needs and the consciousness of common struggle; the first to proclaim, in a difficult and unhappy period, the enduring worth of the submerged Jeffersonian democracy that was to remain the essential testament of a large section of the American people up to the First World War. In some respects the seeming demagoguery of Populism anticipated the Know-Nothing native Fascists of our own time, for Populism was essentially a groundswell of protest, an amorphous rebellion that caught all the confusions and hatreds of the time. Yet despite its gawkiness and the mountebanks who often seemed to lead it, Populism represented the first great challenge to the modern era. Out of the suffering of the farmers who saw themselves cheated on every hand with the rise of monopoly capitalism streamed a new and aggressive political consciousness in America without which the liberalism of the future would have foundered, and upon which its aggressive drive toward economic democracy had an incalculable influence.

Yet for all its social importance, the significance of the agrarian movement to the growth of a modern literature in America lies beyond the fact that Populism almost frightened Mark Hanna out of his wits, or that a million farmers plagued by the banks and the railroads poked up their heads to listen when Mary Elizabeth Lease or Ignatius Donnelly screamed "Wall Street owns the country!" Mrs. Lease had, as it happens, a most vigorous prose style,[1] and Populist rhetoric became almost a standard vocabulary for native rebels. But the significance of Populism to the slowly forming modern literature is that its protestantism helped partly to shape or to adumbrate the social thinking—

---

[1] "It is no longer a government of the people, by the people, and for the people, but a government of Wall Street, by Wall Street, and for Wall Street. . . . Money rules and our Vice-President is a London banker. Our laws are the output of a system that clothes rascals in robes and honesty in rags. The parties lie to us and the political speakers mislead us. We were told two years ago to go to work and raise a big crop and that was all we needed. We went to work and plowed and planted; the rains fell, the sun shone, nature smiled, and we raised the big crop they told us to; and what came of it? Eight-cent corn, ten-cent oats, two-cent beef, and no price at all for butter and eggs—that's what came of it! The main question is the money question. . . . The people are at bay, and the bloodhounds who have dogged us thus far beware!"

the general and pervasive view of American life—in terms which many writers were to borrow as a matter of course. The whole design of early twentieth-century literature in America, in fact, can be said to rest on the dilemma of a whole generation forced, on the basis of an entirely different experience, to meet the tensions and to seek the prizes of the new capitalism. It is easy enough to acknowledge the political force of Populism, which evoked a mass loyalty and displayed a popular strength greater than any social movement in America up to the New Deal. But in a deeper sense the true importance of Populism is that it represented the slow groping into a new world, the persistent swelling nostalgia for the old, the hurtling passion without direction, that were to be so characteristic of the "new" American literature for years to come. What this means is not only that Populism molded the experience of many writers who came out of the Middle West, but also that the agrarian tradition of dissent in general was the first great force in the modern period to crystallize the over-all conception of a social order in which so many American writers were to feel alien.

Who is there to deny that for fifty years the ethos of American literature at its best has been resignation, attack, escape, but so rarely acceptance? Who is there to deny that the very fame of American writing in the modern era, the very effort to create a responsible literature in America appropriate to a new age, rests upon a tradition of enmity to the established order, more significantly a profound alienation from it? Modern American literature was born in protest, born in rebellion, born out of the sense of loss and indirection which was imposed upon the new generations out of the realization that the old formal culture—the "New England idea"—could no longer serve. Yet for fifty years, through all the progressions of fashion, the welding of America into the world scene, the growth of a modern movement unforeseen by those who helped—stumblingly, like all their generation—to build it, its spiritual history remains curiously the same. Modern American writers have "covered" the country exhaustively, steeped themselves in its reality; but there is a sense in which they have never learned to live in it. The Genteel Tradition, with all its old formal prohibitions and repressions, has become a joke, the old leftover romanticisms have been satirized to death, a tradition of forthrightness and insatiable curiosity and personal freedom has been established, a whole new movement has brought a whole new culture with it; but there is a sense of horror and uncertainty before the reality of American life, of fear and inchoate tragedy, that can be found in equal measure in Harold Frederic and James T. Farrell, in Stephen Crane and John Dos Passos, in Edgar Saltus and William Faulkner, in Howells and Willa Cather, in Frank Norris and John Steinbeck. Emerson could no longer serve the early realists, as the culture Emerson represented seemed only a Biblical ante-world to the world they had to live in and master. Yet if Emerson still seems more curiously modern than many of the moderns, as T. K. Whipple said, was it not because, for all his radiance, he felt something of the uneasiness that has touched them, and was yet lucky enough in his world to rise above it? There have been very few modern writers who have been able to rise above theirs. Instead, they have made their careers out of it—out of their honesty and courage, and out of the pressure of the world upon them.

That is the later story, yet it underscores the whole story of modern American writing. For what is important here is that if agrarian dissent in the eighties and nineties caught the first spirit of revolt in modern American writing, it also made it plain that the learning process for American writers in the new age would be so difficult and laborious, the effort to seek out the truth of their times—and the truth of their relation to them—so exhausting, that they would pass through a series of fragmentary rebellions, of piecemeal elucidations. Thus agrarianism helped to make for what Parrington called "critical realism"; but how significant it is that it should have encouraged simultaneously that indifference to literature as art—*vide* Parrington himself—which was to leave its mark on so many of the early realists! It was already clear from the late eighties on, when so many European influences in art and literature began to be felt here, that American writers were fated to emancipate themselves in one sphere only to be retrogressive in another; to be free of the old "Puritan repressions," but not of their own primitivism of spirit; to run to Europe, in the spirit of Vance Thompson, Huneker, and Mencken, and yet feel no real understanding of the relation between art and society. Yet the contempt for esthetic problems, the living fear of form and craft so marked at various periods in modern American writing, is not something for a few superior esthetes to mock, for nothing is so vivid in the history of that writing as the equivalent narrowness of those whose devotion has been fixed on nothing but "esthetic" problems. Just as Garland and Ed Howe in their day, like James T. Farrell in our own, often wrote badly because they were so preoccupied with telling the fierce bitter truth as they saw it, so nothing so reveals the inveterate provincialism of writers like Cabell and Hergesheimer, or John Crowe Ransom and Allen Tate, as their fond belief that nothing exists but the private cultivation of art.

To many European writers of the period which saw the emergence of realism in America, writers enjoying the advantage of a received tradition in art and literature, the advantage of an unstrained appreciation of artistic truth, writing could mean, as Thomas Mann phrased it so movingly, the fusion of suffering and the instinctive desire for form. In a modern American literature that erupted suddenly into maturity, leaving so many basic problems untouched and unremembered behind it, the need of truth, the need to make manifest the divorce between the old bloodless ideas passed on to the new generation and the new world in which they had to live, came first. The "liberation" came first, and the struggle for that liberation, as was revealed so vividly in the twenties, when the modern writers attained their majority, often became all. It was not only art that seemed a luxury; it was the fundamental belief in it, the conscious knowledge of what its responsibilities could mean. Perhaps there are other reasons by which to explain the curious and often unconscious primitivism that resulted; perhaps too short a period elapsed between Sitting Bull and Henry James. But whatever the reason, the consequences of that difficult struggle for realism are to be seen all through the history of modern American writing—in the crudity of the early social novels; in the sentimentality of the muckraking novels during the Progressive period; in the almost mechanical brutality, from Norris to Farrell, that was to become a fixture in American naturalism; in the simplicity of Vernon Parrington's significant hostility to art that lacked "social purpose"—a

species of bigotry that was to make history in the nineteen-thirties; in
the isolation of craftsmen like Stephen Crane, Henry James, Willa
Cather; in the devotion to a raw intensity of power, a delight in the
grossest possible effects, that were to characterize realistic fiction in the
eighteen-nineties and nineteen-thirties alike; and perhaps most significantly, in the artificial decadence and sickly exaggeration of those
writers, from Edgar Saltus to John Crowe Ransom, who have proved
themselves light-years removed from American life and the most fantastically theatrical of literary aristocrats.

What it has so often come down to is a persistent indifference to art
or a heedless and almost desperate idealization of art as the sole
medium of human understanding; either an indifference to style or a
fanatical devotion to nothing but style. It is as if modern American
writers have had to live at the poles of the world, to start afresh in
every period, to revenge themselves madly on time. And perhaps nowhere as in the modern literary movement in America have men lived
on fragments of the ideal and deceived themselves with fragmentary
victories—victories of style, victories of temporary understanding, victories to write frankly of sex, victories over all the enemies of the
moment's liberation. And nowhere has there been so tumultuous a
subterranean life of the spirit, so much inchoate religion, with so self-
assured a refusal on the part of so many sensitive writers to admit the
reality of a spiritual life. Nowhere has there appeared so appalling a
fear of "emotionalism" and mysticism among the hard-boiled, and
nowhere have there been so many substitutes for them.

Is it strange, then, that in a literature so concerned with realism and
with personal liberation this refusal and impoverishment of the life
of the spirit have always nourished the screamers, the eccentrics, the
pseudo-Whitmans, the calculating terrorists? For whatever else can
be said of that modern literature, of its courage and triumphs and public success, nowhere have writers learned with such difficulty and in
such violent spasms. Nowhere have they led such short lives as writers
or yearned so desperately to be in tune with the age or enraged against
it. Nowhere has there been such an opposition of extremes, so pitiful
a confusion of conformity with taste, so obvious a subjection to the

latest dictum, the contemporary rage, such as have pulled American
literary thought from pole to pole for fifty years.

5

For all these reasons, it is important to remember that the history of
early American realism is a series of documents by men and women
who were not artists but spokesmen. What writers like Ed Howe and
Hamlin Garland and Harold Frederic contributed to realism was their
personal testimony on agrarian life amidst a new order hostile to
agrarian ways and ideals. Wordsworth's plea for peasant poets found
its ironic fulfillment in the person of farmers like Garland who wrote
their first stories at the kitchen table and overworked country editors
like Ed Howe who wrote his one important book, *The Story of a
Country Town,* late at night within sound "of the midnight bell," and
then hesitated to publish it. Like Harold Frederic, a country boy who
spent his life as a foreign correspondent in Europe and wrote bitterly
emotional novels of Mohawk Valley life, Garland and Howe were
bound by their grievances. Frederic had more distinction of mind but
his books were less successful. Novel-writing came too easily; though
he wrote copiously, he never fulfilled himself. He wrote nothing that
was so poignant as his own story, with its record of a talented and
energetic reporter living in the *Yellow Book* society of London in the
nineties, championing the Irish nationalists against England, reporting
cholera epidemics in France and Italy, anti-Semitic riots in Russia, yet
commemorating in his novels the Mohawk Valley of the seventies and
eighties, where farmers lived their narrow lives while the life of the
great cities passed them by. In one of his most passionate novels, *Seth's
Brother's Wife,* Frederic commented on the fact that American humor
grew out of "the grim, fatalist habit of seizing upon the grotesque
side," and his bitterness made the most of it. His most famous novel,
The Damnation of Theron Ware, is a mischievously written museum
piece, persistently overrated because it was among the first American
novels to portray an unfrocked clergyman and to suggest the disintegration of religious orthodoxy. But the unfrocked clergyman was to

become as useful a symbol of the new era as the businessman, whom Howells defined so memorably as "the man who has risen."

The difference between Hamlin Garland and Ed Howe is perhaps that Howe, whose spiritual resources were not superior to a dyspeptic Will Rogers's, did not pretend to be an artist at all. He wrote his dour, lean, savage book without the slightest knowledge that much of its narrative content was puerile romanticism; he would have been indifferent to the fact had he known it. Garland, who was in a sense the victim of his own reputation, gloried in the illusion that he was an "artist," a "veritist." The word flowed easily; he even dedicated his *Crumbling Idols* to "the men and women of America who have the courage to be artists." Yet what a depressing career Garland's was! With his talk of "veritism," his aggressive intensity, his passionate espousal of realism long before the word became fashionable, he performed yeoman labor; but to the end of his life, when he had ceased to write his interminable autobiography and sat in the Hollywood sun composing books on spiritualism, he was essentially a half-writer, a sloganeer of literature who had worked himself so snugly into the formative history of realism that one could barely distinguish between his place in the movement and his palpable contributions to it. He was to an extraordinary degree the Theodore Roosevelt of modern literature, the booster who campaigned so fiercely for freedom, identified himself with realism so completely, that whatever his campaign services, his manifesto, his friendships, his eagerness, one forgot that Garland had a dreary mind and a pedestrian talent.

What gave Garland his importance from the first was the remarkable—and perhaps once justified—extent to which he had dramatized his own life in terms of the battle for realism. To the nineties he became the "realistic young man," the active protagonist of the new spirit, in the fashion in which Byron and De Musset and Pushkin had been the "romantic young men" of the nineteenth-century *Geniezeit*. Garland's work became one long autobiography, and as it became explicit autobiography it lost the explicit intention which lies at the base of art. That is not to say that he contributed less than others in his generation; he contributed more; but his work became increasingly irrelevant to the art of realism and suggested that his service had been to identify himself with the creed and the courage of realism. For Garland's was surely not the imagination of a mature artist; his novels were often embarrassing, and his now famous first short stories painstakingly honest but narrow. He was not a critic, not a polemicist, not a teacher; *Crumbling Idols,* the manifesto of 1894, is one of the windiest critical documents of the new era. Yet precisely because it was hortatory and shrill, Garland acted as the bandmaster of realism. His service was to announce its coming, to suggest its emotional importance and its sterling Americanism, to open the common mind to vistas of nationalism, freedom, and democracy in which Lincoln and Ibsen, Howells and the Declaration of Independence, were somehow commingled.

Unlike Howells and Frank Norris, the other two pioneer theorists of American realism, Garland had very little knowledge of its European counterpart and was not above vulgar references to "imitative English sensationalism and sterile French sexualism." What he saw in realism was utterly remote from its possibilities as a craft, or even as a philosophy of letters. He believed it to be a guide to action, a kind of Utopian literary Socialism, a rhetorical device by which to awaken the dormant energies of writers to the native life they knew. The significance of Garland's career is a nationalistic one; he had an expansive Whitmanesque sense of democratic solidarity in literature. As a young farmer dreaming of literary treasures he had sniffed out the coming Zeitgeist; he now became its official manager. And how simply, in the best tradition of party politics, he put it all! In his mind realism was not a literary counterpart of Populism; it actually was Populism. He reduced the innumerable complexities of taste and form and experience to a class struggle between the burly West and the decadent East. Realism stood for "progress"; romanticism—how much of a romanticist Garland was himself he never knew—for reaction; realism signified democracy, romanticism aristocracy. So the American tyro who had everything to learn from the European example ended by denouncing in vague incendiary belligerence the subtleties and insights he needed most.

But was it not in Garland that American farmers first talked like farmers? Was it not Garland who among the very first dedicated his career to realism? Was it not Garland who, almost alone in the eighties, sat in the Boston Public Library writing out of his loneliness and poverty those first realistic stories that were to guide others to a new literature in America? It is true. He plucked out weeds; to know why he planted them back is to guess at the significance of the modern imagination in America. "We Yankees are a tarnation cute race," runs a verse out of the forgotten stores of frontier folklore; "we make our fortune with the right hand and lose it with the left. . . . We Yankees don't do things like you Britishers; we are born in a hurry, educated at full speed, our spirit is at high pressure, and our life resembles a shooting star, till death surprises us like an electric shock."

6

So one returns to Howells. For in his social novels of the eighties and nineties—*A Hazard of New Fortunes, Annie Kilburn, The World of Chance, The Quality of Mercy, A Traveler from Altruria, Through the Eye of the Needle*—Howells was delineating the new America of industrial capitalism with a felicity, a precision of intention, and a power of emotional suggestion that some of his more robust disciples could not match. He too had staked his career on realism, and if his countrymen looking upon him in his disturbed middle age had but known it, Howells had fought for realism all the more bravely, since the objects of its interest required a new education. He had come to realism on the strength of the very morality that was to constrict his application of it, since it was a morality founded on a simple belief in a simple justice. He had been drawn to it slowly and reluctantly, shedding his lifelong prejudices and his characteristic disposition to please, alienating many of his old friends; but he had come to it because his conscience and his tender regard for humanity were the very springs of his talent. He had experienced the transformation of American life after the Civil War almost as a personal disaster, and his novels now· became the record of that experience.

It was entirely in keeping with the quality of Howells's mind and the very nature of his career that these autumnal novels should not be his best. He was not even to hold to this rebellious mood very long, yet how painful it was for his sunny optimistic nature to acclimate itself to a proletariat and class struggles, to street-car strikes and discussions of Socialism, the pompous banker faces and even more pompous banker prejudices that now entered his novels! For some of these works he reached back into the novels he had written in his forties, for with his feeling for the vast cousinship of American village life Howells liked to use a few favorite characters in novel after novel. He had always thought of American middle-class folk as one family, and forgotten uncles and cousins and aunts and happy young couples grown middle-aged and tired now gathered in his books as at a funeral—the funeral of the romantic and facile promise of the American dream. Yet many of his characters were startling figures. The acquiescent *Atlantic* editor whose social views up to Haymarket had been those of his good friend John Hay, his good friend Lowell, his good friend and coeditor Aldrich, the Wall Street poet-financier Edmund Stedman—the very best gentility of the Gilded Age—now introduced German Marxists and Tolstoyan Communists, speculative intellectuals and hungry radicals who argued out the imperfections of the human race amidst the clamor of New York elevated trains. And with them appeared oil millionaires and hard-fisted village entrepreneurs, workingmen on strike and scabs, commercial-minded unscrupulous journalists, and idealistic young men who thought it degrading to participate in business and finance. The archetypal Silas Lapham, a good fellow despite his crudity, now belonged to another order; the humorous, placid old merchants who had personified the values of another day now yielded to speculators and defaulters and the vulgar new rich. Howells wrote one novel entirely around a defaulter; another dealt with a crooked businessman whose true character became known only after his death; another with the oppression of class distinctions in a placid little village overrun by industrialism; another with Utopian Socialists who had left their colony to study the life of the capitalist cities. And on the piazza of summer hotels, that favorite mise en scène where Howells had once delighted to have young couples meet romantically, he now staged the most devastating scenes of his Utopian satire, *A Traveler from Altruria*.

Howells in these years called himself a Socialist, but he had no social program to espouse, no will toward Socialism; even in his most unhappy moments he could speak with wonted facility of a vague new beneficence that would somehow take care of everything in the end. The characters in these late novels did not revolt against the established order; *they testified against it.* One idealist went mad, a few fled, others compromised—as Howells himself later compromised; but their personal determination to understand the new forces in economic and social life never transcended the dictum of old David Hughes in *The World of Chance:* "The way to have the golden age is to elect it by Australian ballot." Indeed, they rarely spoke of the golden age; and with the exception of Peck, the tragic minister in *Annie Kilburn* who renounced the church to work among the laborers in the cotton mills, they did not even act upon their convictions. They were witnesses to spiritual disorder, observers of social change; their function was to act as a Greek chorus and to furnish the spare but haunting commentary that gave these novels their purpose and texture.

What interested Howells at this period was the education of men of goodwill—the slow and painful growth of a few sensitive minds in the face of materialism and inequality. He went on spinning plots with his gentle, even skill, pulling people together mechanically, staging dinner parties and symposia for no better purpose than to have people talk; [1] but within this fog of discursive amiability and New England twang, people lived "in an age of seeming preparation for indefinite war." It was the element of conscious sensibility that gave these novels their spare, incisive drama. Unlike most of his fellow realists, who described the ravages of the new industrial-technological order in terms of mere victimization—usually their own—Howells presented his stories as parables and quiet homilies. He brooded over his characters as his characters brooded over society, and to the same purpose; for like Tolstoy, he considered it his function to mediate between moral men and immoral society. Each character in these novels now had his representative place in that society, each his characteristic criticism or

---

[1] It must always be remembered, however, that Howells was the first great domestic novelist of American life. In this respect, though Sinclair Lewis would be horrified by the thought, he was rather like Lewis, who more than any other novelist of the postwar period has set average Americans to *talking.*

apology; when they talked together, they represented a whole society in meditation. This stratification of character became so necessary to Howells that by 1894 he even rejected formal realism to write his first Utopia, *A Traveler from Altruria,* a morality play in which Banker Bullion, Novelist Twelvemough, the Altrurian Mr. Homos, the Society Woman, the Professor, the Minister, the Worker, vie with each other in dialectic. The professor mumbles heartless platitudes on "the law of supply and demand," the minister asks naïvely why there are no workers in his congregation, the socialite reminisces on her trivial pleasures, and the Utopian—who acts as a catalyst—asks his half-sorrowful, half-mocking questions.

Like his friend Henry James, Howells now felt a need of a foreground observer, a central intelligence in all these novels. His observers, significantly enough, were usually natives who had returned from a long journey abroad, or had been away in more primitive regions, and who now returned to learn that a new world had destroyed or absorbed the one they had known. Like the heroine of *Annie Kilburn,* who returned from a long sojourn in Rome to discover that Hatboro', Massachusetts, was not the pleasant sleepy New England village she had left, they were dismayed and frightened. "I think there's something in the air, the atmosphere," says Annie, "that won't allow you to live in the old way if you've got a grain of conscience or humanity. . . . It seems to me as if the world couldn't go on as it has been doing. Even here in America, where I used to think that we had the millennium because slavery was abolished, people have more liberty, but they seem just as far off as ever from justice." Acutely conscious of the shame of wealth in a world where so many live in want, she hears the Reverend Mr. Peck say—in a sermon that earns him the hatred of his deacons: "Those who rise above the necessity of work for daily bread are in great danger of losing their right relationship to other men," and she cannot but agree. She discovers that the town grocer, Gerrish, whom she remembers as a mean, narrow little storekeeper, has become a great merchant and Hatboro's symbolic success. She learns that Putney, a lawyer who had always possessed the most cultivated mind and most generous heart among her neighbors, has become an incurable drunkard.

So in *The World of Chance* old David Hughes returns from a
Utopian community with his almost maniacally sensitive son-in-law,
Anselm Denton, to try desperately to struggle against the commercialism around them. In revolt against a materialism to which no sensitive conscience can appeal, Denton destroys a new tool he has invented because it may lose a few workers their jobs, and hopes to
expiate the sins of his greed-laden generation by committing suicide.
A ridiculous and pathetic figure? Even Howells may have thought
so, but he understood Denton. For the values of an earlier day, the
values of Brook Farm, Emerson, and Thoreau, could still press themselves upon the Christian mind with new pertinence against a world
that had passed them by. Surely someone had to say to the whole
capitalist-financial order what Thoreau had said to the imperialists of
the Mexican War: *Non serviam?* Surely one individual soul had to
register itself a conscientious objector in a world committed to profit
and gain?

Even the obligations of traditional morality, Howells now felt, no
longer possessed their sanctioned force in such a society. Capitalism
was a world of chance whose motive power was the rule of the jungle.
In an unsuccessful but curiously haunting novel of this period, *The
Quality of Mercy,* Howells wrote a devastating indictment of hypocritical morality. Northwick, a commonplace but inordinately
greedy businessman of little education, embezzles his company's funds
and runs off to Canada. The village is thrown into feverish excitement, but the son of the industrialist whom Northwick has defrauded
sneers at Gerrish and the vigilante spirit he has aroused. "I don't know
that [justice] isn't any more repulsive than the apparatus of commerce,
or business, as we call it," says Matt Hilary. "Some dirt seems to get
on everybody's bread by the time he's earned it, or his money even
when he's made it in large sums as our class do." Maxwell, the sardonic young reporter, laughs, "Defalcation is the commonest fact in
our society." Even Matt's father agrees: "The defaulter seems to be
taking the place of the self-made man among us. . . . He's what the
commonplace American egotist must come to more and more in
finance, now that he is abandoning the career of politics and wants to
be rich instead of great."

With bitter irony Howells went on to point out that Northwick's real victims, the workers in his mills, had no feeling against him—they were "too tired." The town bourgeoisie, led by the ineffable Gerrish, had refused to suspect Northwick until the facts were made public, and then characteristically sought to evict his daughters from their home. Howells's great moment in this novel, however, came when he portrayed Northwick in flight. Here was the characteristic product of a whole society and its traditional devotion to business; yet when Northwick lay sick and alone in his Quebec refuge, his only occupation was to watch over the money he had stolen. Music, books, conversation, even the obvious attractions of a new land, meant nothing to him; he had, like the businessman Henry Fuller described in *The Cliff-Dwellers,* "never lived for anything but business . . . never eaten and drunk for anything but business . . . never built for anything but business . . . never dreamed for anything but business . . . wrote about nothing but business," and his reward was bleak sterility in exile. It was an amazing presagement of one of the great episodes in American realism: the flight and decline of Hurstwood in Dreiser's *Sister Carrie.*

Howells arrived at the full expression of his social views only in his Utopias. The Altrurian asks the Banker to explain the American ideal of greatness, and the Banker replies:

> I should say that within a generation our ideal had changed twice. Before the war, and during all the time from the Revolution onward, it was undoubtedly the great politician, the publicist, the statesman. As we grew older and began to have an intellectual life of our own, I think the literary fellows had a pretty good share of the honors that were going; that is, such a man as Longfellow was popularly considered a type of greatness. When the war came, it brought the soldier to the front, and there was a period of ten or fifteen years when he dominated the national imagination. That period passed and the great era of material prosperity set in. The big fortunes began to tower up, and heroes of another sort began to appeal to our admiration. I don't think there is any doubt but the millionaire is now the American ideal. It isn't very pleasant to think so, even for people who have got on, but it can't very hopefully be denied. It is the man with the most money who now takes the prize in our national cake-walk.

The Altrurian looks around the grounds of the fashionable summer hotel and asks, "Where are your workers?" The guests are embarrassed. He remarks that ladies of the better class seem to have acquired all the taste and leisure in their class and asks naïvely, "Why are not they in government?" He visits a farmer's family and notices with disgust that his escort, a fashionable lady, regards them with disdain. "We Altrurians," he says quietly, "believe that inequality and inequity are the same in the last analysis." At a characteristically gross dinner party in *Through the Eye of the Needle*, a society woman named Mrs. Strange says to the Altrurian:

> I have come to the end of my tether. I have tried, as truly as I believe any woman ever did, to do my share, with money and with work, to help make life better for those whose life is bad; and though one mustn't boast of good works, I may say that I have been pretty thorough, and, if I've given up, it's because I see, in our state of things, *no* hope of curing the evil. It's like trying to soak up the drops of a rainstorm. You do dry up a drop here and there; but the clouds are full of them and, the first thing you know, you stand, with your blotting-paper in your hand, in a puddle over your shoe-tops. There is nothing but charity, and charity is a failure, except for the moment. If you think of the misery around you, that must remain around you for ever and ever as long as you live, you have your choice—to go mad and be put into an asylum, or go mad and devote yourself to society.

7

In a sense, it was Howells's last word. In the thirteen years of life that remained to him after the publication of *Through the Eye of the Needle* he mellowed into what was, for him, a normal acquiescence. As the rebellions and desperations of the farmers were channeled into the middle-class reform spirit of the Progressive period and the imperialist complacency after the Spanish-American War, Howells, so long the faithful reporter of his countrymen, went with them. The realistic movement had got beyond him, and his ingrained prudishness came to the fore again. When he wrote to the early twentieth-century realists, as he once did to Robert Herrick, it was to chide them, if ever so gently, for their plain speaking on sexual problems. By 1906, as he confessed in a letter to Herrick of this year, he had come to doubt "the art and wisdom of the *crucial* novel," and when he had occasion to write to the Chicagoan again on the publication of the latter's *Together* in 1909, it was to say that he had been profoundly troubled by "its several potential or actual adulteries." Ever since Haymarket Howells had felt himself an old man; now he no longer joked about it. "I am old, old!" he complained to Brander Matthews. "I get tired easily, mind as well as body; I am losing my incentive." As his counsel and experience came to mean increasingly less to the still younger writers who thought even Hamlin Garland an old fogy, he found himself lavished with honors by those worthies of the Genteel Tradition already superseded by the movement he had done so much to establish. He became the first president of the National Academy of Arts and Letters; on his seventy-fifth birthday President Taft honored him by attending a birthday party tendered by some friends. He was grateful for the kindness of a few young writers, for though his official reputation had been restored, he knew that the most vital young spirits in the militant new literature after 1910 had all but forgotten him.

Yet what did it matter what young snips thought and said, since he had at last come back into his own? "I like you, my dear young brother," he wrote Joyce Kilmer in 1915, "not only because you love beauty, but love decency also. There are so many of our brood I could willingly take out and step on." He had never enjoyed the "crucial" novel, the anxiety and the polemics that had attended the campaign for realism. In a generation of realists each of whom was in some fashion a realist *malgré lui,* he was a monumental example of the antiquated nineteenth-century conscience upon whom a new order of society had placed an intolerable burden. He had certainly never meant by realism what his young friends Frank Norris and Stephen Crane had, within the short space of their lives, already shown it to mean. Of that Indiana barbarian, Dreiser, he never spoke at all, though he would have been amused to hear the declaration of an excessively pious disciple, Booth Tarkington, that Dreiser's realism was Russian, while his, Howells's, was true-blue American. From

whom had he learned the dignity and the amplitude of realism if
not from Turgenev and Tolstoy? The satisfaction Turgenev gave
him, he wrote once, "was like a happiness I had been waiting for all
my life, and now that it had come, I was richly content forever." But
at most realism had been for Howells only a method of inquiry and
an acknowledgment of the spiritual realities that bound men—particularly Americans—together. Now, as the new century unleashed
new energies, interests, skills, grievances, realism was to pass altogether beyond him; he was not too sorry. No man had wanted less for
himself and more for his fellow men: it was enough to know that
he had stood at the Great Divide of American literature. He had in
his own person—reluctantly, yet with deep and unconscious ardor—
united the world of Emerson and the world of Zola; he had riveted
his education into the language. Who, indeed, had done as much as
he to unify the traditions of American literature? He was more than
an Elder Statesman of letters; he had been the greatest single force in
the literature of his epoch. Had he read it, he would have enjoyed
John Macy's quip, "for years Howells was the Dean of American letters, and there was no one else on the faculty." It was true. He was
one of the solitary—if minor—architects of the American imagination.

8

Yet . . . what was it he had missed? Howells had missed something,
and he knew it as well as the generations after him were to know it.
It was not frankness in many spheres of conduct, though frankness
would have helped; it was not a different method, a blunter speech. He
had spoken in all the accents of greatness without ever being great himself. What was it that persistently eluded him, that smiled mischievously at him from an old letter of Henry James's—"I regard you as the
great American naturalist. I don't think you go far enough and you
are haunted with romantic phantoms and a tendency to factitious
glosses"? What was it, indeed, but that which James himself possessed
and enjoyed despite the ridicule of the public, the indifference of
editors, the pain of expatriation? For James, with all his "extravagances," his "pose," his "queerness"—"poor dear Harry!" as his brother

William used to write mockingly—had somehow lived the life of a great artist, had held with stubborn passion to the life of art and the dignity of craft. He had made a queer, involuted sort of success of his life; yet it was indubitably a success in the sense that Howells, with all his honors, the happiness of his personal life, the dignity of his position, had never known.

In a world where so much history went into the making of a little literature, James had stood with iron confidence and pride as a writer who had lived for the greater glory of art. One could laugh at him, be bored and vexed with him, but there was that indefinable exultation in him which Howells recognized in Flaubert but never in himself. James irritated the common mind and puzzled the commonplace literary imagination. He was somehow not an American, yet certainly not a European; he was a realist, but somehow not concerned with writing "realism." He had absorbed the problems of realism early in the eighties, had indeed put his finger unerringly on the dilemma of American realism; [1] but he had transcended the commonplace meaning of realism. It was his seriousness that identified James, and to approach him one had in some measure to be equal to that seriousness. But was not Howells serious? Was anyone ever more serious than Hamlin Garland? Nor was it James's cultivation that singled him out, the insatiable curiosity and native shrewdness that had made him the great student of modern letters. It was an inscrutable deceiving intensity, an awareness of all the possible shades and nuances and consequences of art, a phenomenal ability to wind himself deeper and deeper into the complexities of consciousness. Like the Princess Casamassima, James could say: "I don't want to teach, I want to learn; and, above all, I want to know à quoi m'en tenir."

That passion for learning was to make James a comic figure to shallow minds. What was it, presumably, but a persistent excessive verbalization of what he lacked as a novelist, a compensation for the

---

[1] "The only reason for the existence of a novel," James wrote in his essay "The Art of Fiction," "is that it does attempt to represent life." Writing in the *Atlantic Monthly* in January, 1884, he said wih quiet bitterness: "It is not open to us, as yet, to discuss whether a novel had better be an excision from life, or a structure built up of picture cards, for we have not made up our minds as to whether in general life may be described."

dense but "arid" life of his fiction? Did not the richness of James's literary criticism, its almost intolerable intensity of articulation, suggest that James the critic could define in as many registers as a pipe organ what he could not present on the "dramatic" and "representative" level of great art? His own generation, particularly in America, had said that first; yet facilely as one said it, there remained something in James that haunted the mind. "One must be narrow to penetrate," he had one character say. It was astonishing how James's penetration had fastened itself to a hundred different subjects, themes, qualities, events, which by the conventional assessment of James's talent were presumably closed to it, but which, by the slow avid pressure of his perception, he conveyed with devastating lucidity to the inquiring mind. He had no politics, no experience (almost, one would say, no comprehension) of poverty and the poor, no sympathy with social revolution; but he was the only American novelist of his time who, illuminating almost by an artist's instinct what the conscious citizen's mind would never understand, invested the whole atmosphere of revolution and conspiracy in *The Princess Casamassima* with an imperishable significance.

"Are we on the eve of great changes, or are we not?" the Princess asked Hyacinth Robinson. "Is everything that is gathering force, underground, in the dark, in the night, in little hidden rooms out of sight of governments and policemen and idiotic 'statesmen'—heaven save them!—is all this going to burst forth some fine morning and set the world on fire? Or is it going to sputter out and spend itself in vain conspiracies, be dissipated in sterile heroisms and abortive isolated movements?" As he wrote later in his preface to the novel, the very vagueness and the picturesque twilight brooding of the revolutionary spirit described was precisely the effect he had wished to produce: "of our not knowing, of society's not knowing, but only guessing and suspecting and trying to ignore what 'goes on' irreconcilably, subversively, beneath the vast smug surface." What shrewder prognosis of the embattled future was written in James's generation? And if one were limited to shrewdness as the basic quality in American realism, what shrewder portrait had been composed of the type of the new era than that of Christopher Newman in *The American*? If James's protagonists were so often innocent and sensitive Americans lost in a world more complex than any they had known, they were also a parable of the predicament that had given rise to a whole generation of worthy commonplace realists.

More perhaps than he ever knew, James was bound by many ties to the literary history of his generation in America. His expatriation, as Howells wrote in a tender unfinished memoir,[1] was an easy enough matter for his old friends in America to "explain"; nor does it take too much wit to see that James's often ridiculous superrefinement, his habit of enclosing the most commonplace American colloquialisms in quotation marks when the English never did, the density of his style, his often breathless seriousness, had their origin as a kind of protest against the egregious lack of seriousness, critical interest, and discrimination at home. James's great prefaces to the New York edition of his works were written, as he wrote to Howells, "as a sort of plea for Criticism, for Discrimination, for Appreciation on other than infantile lines—as against the so almost universal Anglo-Saxon absence of these things; which tends so, in our general trade, it seems to me, to break the heart."

One could begin to criticize James only at that point where one left off criticizing his contemporaries. He had transcended them, given them an eidolon of greatness; but they could not use him, and he no longer belonged with them. If that isolation was a judgment upon his life and art, it was also a characterization of the generation which struggled to establish a primary sense of realism in American letters. For it was James's essential spirit—not necessarily his temperament or

---

[1] The last thing Howells ever wrote was an essay on James on the publication of the latter's correspondence in 1920. He had learned, wrote Howells, that he "was less a sufferer in Europe than in America. He was better in Paris than in Boston, where he was always suffering and when his brief French sojourn became his English life of forty years it was not mainly because he was better in England, but it was more and more largely so. The climate was kinder to him than ours, and the life was kinder than his native life, and his native land. In fact, America was never kind to James. It was rude and harsh, unworthily and stupidly so, as we must more and more own, if we would be true to ourselves. We ought to be ashamed of our part in this; the nearest of his friends in Boston would say they liked him but they could not bear his fiction; and from the people, conscious of culture, throughout New England, especially the women, he had sometimes outright insult. . . . There is a tenderness in his remembrance of America which does not appear in his public printed criticism of us, but which abounds in the letters which address themselves to more American friends than to English friends."

method or particular interests—that Howells and the others had missed: the consecration of a great career devoted with something more than sincerity to the life of art; the sense that one needed the discrimination, the aspirations, the invincible selfhood of art to live in freedom in a world hostile to the very elucidations of art. What was it James had written long before on the role of the critic? It was a token for all who lived in literature.

> To lend himself, to project himself and steep himself, to feel and feel till he understands, and to understand so well that he can say, and to have perception at the pitch of passion and expression as embracing as the air, to be infinitely curious and incorrigibly patient, and yet plastic and inflammable and determinable, patient, stooping to conquer and serving to direct—these are fine chances for an active mind, chances to add the idea of independent beauty to the conception of success.

To have perception at the pitch of passion. Was it not this that Howells had missed, as so many writers in the tumultuous years ahead were to miss it—even when, more than Howells would ever know, they wanted it eagerly, felt desperately the need of it?

Chapter 2

AMERICAN FIN DE SIÈCLE

"A man is not born in his native country for nothing. I wish I might persuade you."—WILLIAM DEAN HOWELLS to Stuart Merrill

BY THE late nineties, when Howells had gone as far as he would ever go in the direction of realism, his services to the new generation were over. Strange new currents were in the air. Somewhere between Haymarket and the Columbian Exposition of 1893, which proclaimed America's rising industrial and commercial power, the modern soul had emerged in America; and with the remarkable commercial expansion that followed on the technological advance of industry, the way was suddenly cleared for the influx of European modernism into the country. The early nineties, which had seen the establishment of a literature of native realism and protest, were marked by the growth of Populism, severe economic depression, and savage labor struggles in the East; but after the comfort of Bryan's narrow defeat in 1896, the swelling tide of wealth in the country seemed to usher in a brief period of peace and plenty. Populism lost its fire after Bryan had carried it almost into the White House, and the European crop failure of 1897 gave American farmers new markets. The Klondike gold rush and the discovery of the cyanide process for gold extraction helped to dampen the Free Silver agitation; and at the very moment that American writers were now to subject themselves eagerly to the European example, American industry cut loose from its dependence on European capital and turned to exploit the home market as never before.

During the seventies and eighties, as so many historians have pointed out, America's loss of her maritime commerce to England during the Civil War had accelerated the drift of capital investments into railroads and manufactures, into the interior development of the country. As the West was built up, this drift from the old seaboard ports to the prairie towns seemed for the moment to separate American culture from its early nineteenth-century associations with Europe in the period of Ticknor and Longfellow, and emphasized the provincialism of the Gilded Age. But now, as America's industrial power and wealth seemed to run over, there was money enough to encourage exploration in Europe; and in a luxurious postprandial mood the prosperous classes settled down to enjoy their success, while vast numbers of young men, living on the fruits of the new industrial expansion, went abroad to partake of art and culture. Just as in the nineteen-twenties an esthetic revolution in American writing was to be effected by a few postwar expatriates, so cultural history was made in the nineties by the vast numbers (after 1892 the Customs Service could report more than 90,000 American citizens returning each year from Europe) who fled the country only because they could afford to live on it. Like the Wyatts and Howards and Sidneys who helped to shape the Elizabethan Renaissance by their studies in Italy,[1] the many young writers who now turned to Europe were the progenitors of an American Renaissance, the medium through which the new currents in European art and thought began to flow.

Howells himself, thanks to his stay as American consul at Venice during the Civil War, had been deeply influenced by European literature; and his debt to writers like Valdés and Goldoni, Turgenev and Tolstoy, was a great factor in his personal growth. But like so many writers of his generation Howells had absorbed European influences without being submerged by them; the young writers who now began to stream into Europe went there to imitate European examples and to ransack, as it were, the European treasure house.

[1] See Oscar Cargill, *Intellectual America*, Macmillan, 1941.

In the interregnum of conservative complacency that lasted between
Bryan's defeat in 1896 and the upsurge of the Progressive and muckraking agitation under Theodore Roosevelt, the sedulous imitation
of Europe represented a significant reversion to colonialism not much
different from the sudden passion of the upper middle classes for
genealogical charts, family coats of arms, and the historical romances
that now became the rage. The country was prosperous, smug, re-
laxed; prodigal in its generosity, hungry for novelty, ready for any
ostentatious display, and eager for the kind of diversion appropriate
to its new-found wealth. Under the surface there remained all the
terrorism and uncertainty of life in the new epoch, the subterranean
world that Frank Norris was soon to uncover in *McTeague*, Stephen
Crane in *Maggie*, and Theodore Dreiser in *Sister Carrie*. On the surface, in a world busy digesting industrialism and the fruits of the
Spanish-American War, it was the era of Richard Harding Davis
and the Gibson Girl, of the rage for Stevenson and historical confectionery like George Barr McCutcheon's *Graustark* and Charles
Major's *When Knighthood Was in Flower*.

"I find America so cheerful, and so full of swagger and self-satisfaction, that I hardly know it," Henry Adams wrote mockingly in a
letter of 1900. "The change since 1893 is startling. . . . A war or two
seems a matter of entire indifference." Yet the Spanish-American War,
so minor a war and so major in its consequences, had helped to make
the difference; it showed with what carefree romanticism and boundless self-assurance a country beginning to feel its power could em-
bark on the great new adventure of imperialism. This mood of proud
restlessness, of yearning for romance and adventure, became the dominant mood of the time; and it helps to explain why the period that
saw the rapturous apprenticeship of so many young writers to European naturalism and decadence also witnessed so striking a passion
for the synthetic romanticism of the historical novel. For although the
new sophisticates might sneer at the passion of the reading public for
all the dear lost causes, their own indiscriminate delight in Europe
revealed a curiously similar yearning for nouveau-riche trappings.
The country had become rich too quickly, had leaped too suddenly
from the old frontier life; and if it could afford the romance of foreign

travel, it also needed the nostalgic delights of a romantic past. Just as the popularity of historical novels reflected the itch for social distinction and position on the part of a generation that saw the rise of the D.A.R. and ancestor worship, so the writers who now invaded Europe were looking for the romantic splendors—if only in French decadent poetry—that they missed at home. The contemporary scene could afford romance and exoticism, but could not supply them. As Henry Seidel Canby pointed out in *The Age of Confidence,* the good burghers who now had money wanted to forget their own solid but undistinguished ancestry "in a passionate attempt to find émigré great-grandfathers or runaway heiresses from overseas." And the young writers whom they indulged without recognizing felt a similar desire to escape—into the swirl of the European fin de siècle.

2

"Fin de siècle" is a stale phrase today for the ferment of mind that fired the closing years of the nineteenth century with innovation and scandal and has left a train of giggles in its wake. It was an upsurge that never attained the dignity of a movement but was always more effervescent. To intellectual Europe in the nineties it signified a resurgence of that vague sense of liberation in the arts that it had not enjoyed since the supplanting of the romantic generation by scientific materialism. To political Europe it was the noon hour, and to America the dawn, of the imperialist holiday. The yellow press and a yellow literature developed together, and men fell on modern art as Cecil Rhodes fell on South Africa. The end of the century, like the end of many another, saw everywhere in Europe a frenzied search for novelty and an impulse toward slashing independence and "modernism." The "century of hope," which had seen so many intellectual hopes fashioned and dismantled, quickened with life as it drew near to its end. It was as if "the anticipation of the racial birthday," as Holbrook Jackson said, had spurred it on to some last effort. Everywhere in Europe men yearned for the new and turned up with a New Realism, a New Spirit, a New Hedonism, a New Drama, and even a New Socialism. The New Woman, most prominently of all,

wound her way out of the old cocoon. In a loud, coarse voice, a pleasantly mad German Jewish doctor who fancied himself a pathologist
of genius, but was possessed only of a profound moralism and an extraordinary capacity for indignation, thundered his apocalypse at de-
generating humanity. "One epoch of history is unmistakably in its
decline, and another is announcing its approach," shrilled Max Nordau in his *Degeneration,* that long and dull book which is remembered partly as a curiosity and chiefly because it provoked Bernard
Shaw to write *The Sanity of Art.* "There is a sound of rending in
every tradition, and it is as though the morrow would not link itself
with today. Things as they are totter and plunge, and they are suffered
to reel and fall, because man is weary."

In England it was the Yellow Decade, in France the heyday of
Symbolism, in Italy the springtide of D'Annunzio, in Germany and
Scandinavia the last triumphant stand of Wagner and Ibsen, in
Russia the autumnal season that saw Chekhov succeed Tolstoy. In
America, literature had finally, after the Gilded Age, reached its
climacteric. One by one the quavering old voices from the past
ceased. Bancroft died in 1891, and the same year saw the death of a
forgotten customhouse employee named Herman Melville, whose
genius was not to be remembered until after the First World War.
Whittier and Whitman went in 1892, the latter's *Democratic Vistas*
a mournful greeting to the new generation; Parkman in 1893, Oliver
Wendell Holmes in 1894, Mrs. Stowe two years later. The generation
that had fought the Civil War and plucked its first fruits in national
expansion and industrial progress was sinking.

For all anyone could see, literature was in the doldrums, waiting
for the fresh winds that were soon to come. When the *Atlantic
Monthly* published its fortieth-anniversary number in 1897, it had to
boast as its most distinguished offering a paper by the conservative
French critic Ferdinand Brunetière. *Cuba Libre* had meant Hearst
triumphant, and in a sense the outstanding literary event of the day
was the press war between Hearst and Pulitzer. "A blackguard boy
with several million dollars at his disposal," old E. L. Godkin ful-
minated against Hearst in the *Nation,* "has more influence on the use
a great nation may make of its credit, of its army and navy, of its

name and traditions, than all the statesmen and philosophers and professors in the country." To thousands who knew nothing of the literature of protest rumbling in the West, or the exotic importations that were soon to be brought to New York by James Gibbons Huneker and Vance Thompson, Richard Harding Davis was the golden boy of the nineties, the man who personified the union of literature and life. Everyone knew that Hearst had paid him $500 to report a Yale-Princeton football game, knew him for the handsome lad in the Charles Dana Gibson drawings, chuckled over his escapades, his scoop at the coronation of Nicholas II in St. Petersburg, his brashness and reassuring presence at the Spanish-American War. No war was quite first-rate, it was commonly felt, without Davis at it as the lordly correspondent. His "Van Bibber," with its easy sentimentality and metropolitan veneer, was an introduction to life for all those who doted on fancy fiction.

The "daring" note was struck by Richard Hovey in open-shirt ballads in *Songs from Vagabondia.* The Genteel Tradition, which a later generation was to flog long after it had become a dead horse, was a very real thing, however, under the custodianship of such editors as Richard Watson Gilder. Gilder, who liked to call himself a "squire of poesy," wrote sixteen volumes of verse and served as an editor at *Scribner's* and the *Century* for thirty-nine years, was a very amiable man whom some malicious fortune set up as a perfect symbol of all that the new writers were to detest. He wrote once to a reader who had found Mark Twain's works indelicate: "If you should ever carefully compare the chapters of 'Huckleberry Finn,' as we printed them, with the same as they appear in his book, you will see the most decided difference. These extracts were carefully edited for a magazine audience with his full consent." When Robert Louis Stevenson passed through New York, Gilder refused to receive him in the offices of the *Century*. He had heard some rumors about the writer's private life and could not consider him respectable. When the *Yellow Book* (which was, appropriately enough, edited by the American Henry Harland) came his way, he threw up his hands in horror.

The amount of attention that this periodical has attracted is proof, if any were needed, that the mountebank in his motley can call the crowd; but is that all the editors of this quarterly are aiming at? Have they yet to learn that notoriety is not fame? They claim that the *Yellow Book* is the embodiment of the modern spirit. If this is true, then give us the old-fashioned spirit of *Harper's*, the *Century*, and *Scribner's*, whose aim is to please intelligent people and not to attract attention by "tripping the cockawhoop" in public.

As if to mark off for all time the difference between the literature that was passing and the new literature of the twenti. . century, the famous Harvard professor of literature, Barrett Wendell, published in 1900 the last testament of the old school, *A Literary History of America*. As Fred Lewis Pattee said later, Wendell's book should have been called *An Intellectual History of Harvard College;* by its genial assumption that with the decline of New England American literature had reached an impasse, its reluctant and patronizing notes on "modern" writers like Mark Twain and Whitman, Wendell's book signified the end of an era. "The world is passing through experience too confused, too troubled, too uncertain, for ripe expression," he wrote in his last chapter, and added a little sadly, "America seems more and more growing to be just another part of the world." He looked to the future with dread, yet wrote at the last that the nearer "darkness" approached, "the more gleams of counsel and help one may find in the simple, hopeful literature of inexperienced, renascent New England. There, for a while, the warring ideals of democracy and of excellence were once reconciled, dwelling confidently together in some earthly semblance of peace." Wendell's great fear, evidently, was that with the upsurge of the national power in America democracy would go too far, and what he deplored in Whitman was not only the "roughness" attendant upon his "humble origins," but also Whitman's profound devotion to the democratic principles of the French Revolution. Was Whitman truly American, particularly since he had a dangerous devotion to the "ideal of equality"? Wendell was afraid not; he feared that the belief in equality, "carried to its extreme, asserts all superiority, all excellence to be a phase of evil."

Yet though the young writers who now ran to Europe seemed to be opposed to all the orthodoxies Wendell represented, he need not have worried about the extravagance of their devotion to democracy. It was not until the Progressive movement left its mark on the so-called Little Renaissance after 1910 that a democratic humanism became character-istic of the new spirit; in the late nineties and after nothing so charac-terized the movement toward Europe as the affectation of aristocratic decadence and indifference. American letters during this period, as Huneker complained, may have been a backwash of the English liter-ary revolution led by Wells, Shaw, and Kipling, which was itself more than a decade behind that of France, but what now appeared was a sickly exoticism that merely ran after Pater and Huysmans and Oscar Wilde. Significantly enough, there were Americans now working at the center of the international fin de siècle, working together with the immoral creatures, then all vaguely suggestive of Oscar Wilde, who were busy refashioning European literature. Thus the *Yellow Book* it-self, whose yellow covers hid its effete contents so successfully that they have colored all criticism of its period ever since, was edited by an American, Henry Harland. Otherwise unremembered, he was an am-bitious romanticist who spent most of his extraliterary life nagging at other people's reputations. His first novels had been written around Jewish life in New York under the pseudonym of "Sidney Luska," but later he manufactured sugary stories of the British aristocracy, Italian landscapes, and love among the French. After taking on the *Yellow Book* he published a popular success, *The Cardinal's Snuff-Box,* which was genteel enough to please the taste of an audience that wanted sad romances of the nobility against backgrounds reminiscent of Zenda and Graustark. Like so many of his kind, he was more than a literary snob and tried vaguely to pass himself off as a descendant of English aristoc-racy. He tried, at least, to be a good European, and it is said that he composed at his work table in pyjamas, to attain the sagacious industri-ous look of a Renaissance craftsman toiling over his sentences then much admired by young Americans who generously adored both Flau-bert and Pater.

After the death of the *Yellow Book* Harland, like Joris Karl Huys-mans, meditated between the gallows and the cross, and finally found his way to Rome. The great emigration of the American artist had begun; and the abrupt and convulsive movement away from Philistia which saw Stephen Crane die in Germany, James in England, Hearn in Japan, Ambrose Bierce presumably in Mexico, even saw two American poets, Francis Vielé-Griffin and Stuart Merrill, abandon their native tongue to write in French. Stuart Merrill was a New Englander whose father was counselor to the American legation in Paris. Educated in France, he had returned to study law in America by his father's wish, but lived out his life in Paris, writing always in French. An important figure in the French Symbolist movement, he was still a spiritual grandchild of Emerson and Brook Farm, a Christian Socialist who lived in the world of Mallarmé. Attracted by the international avant-garde of the late nineties in Paris, at a time when the new poetry was being written by so diverse a group as the Cuban De Heredia, the Greek Moréas, the German Gustave Kahn, and Renée Vivien, late of San Francisco, he yet thought of himself as a spokesman for the oppressed—particularly in his most famous work, *Une Voix dans la Foule* —but wrote like a pre-Raphaelite. Did America need him; did he need America? William Dean Howells thought so, and only Howells cared to summon him back. "I want you to be an American and to write in English," Howells implored him. "If you must write first in French, reinstate yourself afterwards. A man is not born in his native country for nothing. I wish I might persuade you."

Merrill would not listen, but he contributed to the modern movement in America by translating some of the new French poetry for his countrymen in a remarkably sensitive book, his one book in English, *Pastels in Prose*. Once, visiting Walt Whitman in Camden, he admitted himself profoundly moved by the sight of Whitman in his Socratic old age, "nourished by the purest substances of earth," but beyond that confession he would not go. In his famous salon on the Quai Bourbon he could seem more French than the French; but he could never personify the meeting of two cultures, as Henry James had intermittently done in his exile at Rye. He was a Socialist, with hopes for a co-operative commonwealth half out of Marx, half out of William Morris, whom he adored; and when the war came, it shattered his anticipations of a fraternal humanism and broke his heart.

Pour avoir voulu, ô mon âme affolée,
Monter vers Dieu par l'arc-en-ciel,
Tu pleures au fond de la vallée.

3

Irving Bacheller, then a high-powered publishing executive, could sneer at the "highbrow decade," but the foreign "poisons" now began to seep through. Highbrowism was the compensation of the lonely pioneers of exoticism in the nineties, some of whom, like Percival Pollard, Vance Thompson, and James Gibbons Huneker, were newspapermen with an advantage in European travel to whom talk of the "Gallic spirit" brought the thrill of absinthe. Here and there lone exotics in the universities began to appear, like Harry Thurston Peck and the Harvard impressionist Lewis E. Gates; but Peck is remembered today chiefly because he died by his own hand, symbolically enough, after such a scandal as only the certified depravity of Oscar Wilde could improve upon in England. Peck was the archsophisticate. Anthon Professor of Latin at Columbia, editor all through the late nineties of the *Bookman,* a redoubtable scholar in classical philology, he stood— though chiefly by the power of his personality—squarely for an interest in foreign literature that threatened all the old provincialisms. He insinuated himself into a courageous notoriety by trumpeting such unholy names as Krafft-Ebing, redolent of sex, and Laforgue, still mischievously obscure. Yet his great contribution was his public personality. His energy was limitless; his clothes, thanks to a defective vision that destroyed any color sense, as significant a literary phenomenon as Oscar Wilde's waistcoats; but he was too easily content with shocking guests at dinner by proclaiming Balzac Shakespeare's equal, "and in psychology, Shakespeare's superior." He wrote waspish little essays for his domesticated contemporaries, but in his heart he remained the good New England Puritan whose essential sophistication was confined to the classroom and the dashing costume he wore on the campus. Few men in his generation knew so much and labored so valiantly in the vineyards of criticism, yet it cannot be said that he contributed much to the new movement.

It was in these early years after 1900 that Vance Thompson and James Huneker cut through the fog of provincialism to be the intermediaries between Paris, capital of the new spirit, and America. They were quite different. Huneker made an honest career out of gossip, indirectly wrote criticism, and brought impressionism to America; Thompson merely gossiped, and thought of himself as an aristocrat *manqué*. Thompson's career is, indeed, one of the great comedies of the fin de siècle. At a time when the popular novelists of the day were Robert Barr, Justin Huntly McCarthy, Mrs. Clifford, and Stanley Weyman, when the general notion of a literary gentleman was Brander Matthews, Thompson talked suavely and caressingly of Maeterlinck, with whom he had promenaded the streets of Brussels, and Verlaine, whom he had seen mooning over his drink in a Left Bank café. Educated in the eighties at Jena and Heidelberg after a few boyish years at Princeton, Thompson returned to America early in the decade with a monocle, a talent for publicity, and an extraordinary talent for conveying his immeasurable contempt for his doltish countrymen in trippingly empty prose that was as glazed on the surface as it was bare of ideas. He began as a reporter, was an egregious snob in the city room, and soon became dramatic critic of the *Commercial Advertiser*.

Thompson cultivated a staccato journalese that was enormously effective in displaying his enthusiasm for Italian acting, French symbolism, and Norwegian drama. He was quick-minded, profoundly reactionary, and an epigrammatist of reputed talent, though his most famous quip is his pronouncement on Duse in D'Annunzio's *La Gioconda*—"This hollow-eyed woman is the hasheesh of the stage." His taste in general was sound enough and his appetite for foreign literature prodigious; but he never quite realized, for all his railing at Gilder and Howells, that he was as indifferent to a native literature as they were unable to see beyond it. His world was an upper-middle-class Bohemia in which artists and writers would so enjoy the reciprocal admiration of each other's ideas that they would move the vulgar herd to worship at their feet. A poseur, he addressed himself exclusively to American snobs and rang over and over the changes on the trite decadent formula of Jules Renard: "What I am, I write. What I write is me. It is not art. It is not life. It is myself." The personal pronoun, as Percival Pollard once complained, was never absent from Thompson's writing. But by the theatrical display of his own interests he ushered in the best that had been thought and said in London, Paris, and Copenhagen at least nine months before. Like Pollard, Huneker, Lewis E. Gates, and Edgar Saltus, he was a Service. He introduced Knut Hamsun to the American public, and through his *French Portraits* succeeded in gathering together the first serviceable account in America of the new movements in French poetry.

French Portraits was to be Thompson's best book, but it was never a very good book. He followed the practice of Ernest La Jeunesse, the reigning boulevard critic of the day in Paris, in picturing his subject in some characteristic pose, and succeeded chiefly in retailing malicious gossip. Dedicated to his good friend Huneker, the book was shaped on the belief, then so popular with the New York journalistic critics, that while the ideas of great men are presumably the common patrimony of mankind, cultivated minds would be more directly interested in eccentricity. And Thompson was a very zealous student of eccentricity. He was also very good at celebrating Pierre Louÿs's *Aphrodite* as a "beautiful book—a book frankly non-moral, a paean of the flesh, splendidly eloquent. It is a corrupt book." He spent pages describing Maeterlinck gazing at the moon, or Verlaine as some satanic Pierrot, "a combination of Saint Francis and the Marquis de Sade." But he rarely allowed himself the simple grace of telling his story simply. The occasional charm of *French Portraits* lay in its brushlike effects, but Thompson worked so hard at being a painter in prose that he became a mellifluous bore. He had an exaggerated, but typically provincial, conception of letters as the province of aristocratic amateurs, and wrote simperingly (he much admired the Comte Robert de Montesquiou Fezensac) that in "Young France literature has become more and more an amusement of the brilliant, indifferent aristocrat. 'Tis the only pleasure left him." One of his most memorable utterances was his furious attack upon Prince Kropotkin as "a renegade to the obligations of his royal descent."

The two young Chicago publishers Stone and Kimball had inaugurated a vogue of pamphlet magazines early in the nineties, during the "Purple Cow" period, and Huneker and Thompson now joined to edit the liveliest satiric periodical of them all, *M'lle New York*. Thompson made the most of it, for while the little magazine did not last very long, it gave him an opportunity to play the arbiter elegantiarum in an official role. He sneered in the opening number:

> The public—this grotesque aggregation of foolish individuals—pretends to literary taste. It has its painters, its playwrights, its authors; the part of it which reads the male bluestocking, William Dean Howells, looks down upon that part which reads the female bluestocking, Richard Harding Davis; that part which reads Richard Harding Davis looks down upon that part which reads Laura Jean Libbey (why, in heaven's name?), and the readers of Miss Libbey look down in turn upon the readers of the *Police Gazette*. *M'lle New York* is not concerned with the public. Her only ambition is to disintegrate some small portion of the public into its original component parts—the aristocracies of birth, wit, learning and art, and the joyously vulgar mob.

M'lle New York was faintly bawdy, very self-consciously sophisticated, and distinguished chiefly by the twirling little Beardsleyan cartoons of Tom Powers, who penciled mists of pink and black against which vaguely immoral Parisians were depicted sitting in cafés and devouring *la vie de Bohème. La vie de Bohème,* however, was only a few newspapermen on holiday until their money ran out. Later Thompson adopted "autolotry," the art and religion of the ego, with borrowings from Max Stirner and the as yet unknown Nietzsche. He wrote ferocious articles on the place of women, and finally settled in Paris amidst his fellow expatriates, there to report the sensations of the post-Dreyfus era for the press and to edit the cookbooks, modeled on his wife's recipes, by which he is best remembered.

5

Huneker *was* different: he rushed into the nineties driving a dozen horses and tumbling over between them. He had more energy, knew more people, retailed more gossip, wrote more books, drank more beer, and disseminated more information on the artistic personality, than almost any other journalist of his time. He repeated himself endlessly, told the same anecdotes about Liszt, or Wagner and Cosima, or

Chopin and George Sand, in one book that he told in another, drenched everyone within reach with his enthusiasm; but almost single-handed he brought the new currents in European art and thought to America and made them fashionable. He was the only critic of his time who could introduce the works of Stanislaw Przy-byszewski to the public and not be ridiculed. He knew everything that floated on the surface of the world's thought, and he told everything that he knew over and again in at least a dozen newspapers and too many books. No man who worked so hard to be the Johnny Apple-seed of the arts could help being superficial. He knew it, and it was his most poignant regret. "Life has been the Barmecide's feast to me," he wrote in his autobiography, *Steeplejack*.

> No sooner did I covet a rare dish than fate whisked it out of my reach. I love painting and sculpture. I may only look but never own either. . . . I would fain be a pianist, a composer of music. I am neither. Nor a poet. Nor a novelist, actor, playwright. I have written of many things from architecture to zoology, without grasping their inner substance. I am Jack of the Seven Arts, master of none. A steeplejack of the arts.

Huneker's subject was genius. In one sense he cared for nothing else, and he certainly knew almost nothing of the progressive organization of ideas, the history of forms, the enveloping background of society, that evoke the epiphenomena of individual creation. A hobo of the arts, as Benjamin DeCasseres called him,[1] he also shambled among the monuments like a caretaker in a museum, dusting, admiring, resorting, always relabeling. His mind was fixed on labels: where he could not find the phrase for the man, he could not fix the reputation. Yet it did not matter too much, since his gusto was such that he disseminated ideas as he walked. Intensely rhapsodical, his profound musical sense

---

[1] It was the only good thing Mr. DeCasseres did call him. Mencken was perhaps the one Hunekerite who did not go berserk on the Master's prose: though Huneker goes far to explain Mencken's mind. From De Casseres's tribute to Huneker (a pamphlet published in New York, 1925)—"James Huneker—a perfect furnace of ideas and reading, a groundling who lived on Olympus and an Olympian who could throw the dice with groundlings; a man who could wear the mask of a fool or of Apollo; a fumiste, a living paradox, a revolutionary conservative, an aristocratic anarchist, a patrician of the proletariat, a satyr who never missed mass." This *wort-betrunken* prose is also a guide to the fatty degeneration of style in certain carefree spirits of the twenties, notably Ben Hecht.

gave him the tonal equivalents of literary characteristics, and his essays resound to a symphonic drama of "the modern spirit" in which the life of every subject falls into place. Europe-struck, as Van Wyck Brooks commented, he was at the same time as uncosmopolitan, at bottom, as Mark Hanna. He took an American joy in collecting celebrities and modeling halls of fame; his vivacious geniality of style, his breezy familiarity with everything that had ever been said in the dressing rooms of the great, his delight in pure energy, were not merely typical of the literary journalism of his day; they testified to Huneker's profound attachment to the America he loved to confound. At bottom he was a very humble man. He may have wondered how far he differed from a Jules Lemaître, but he did not confuse himself with Rémy de Gourmont. He had behind him the momentum of a wide and eager provincial audience anxious to learn from Europe, and he satisfied that public at the cost of overreaching himself. The arts jingled in his mind like the tones of a music box, and in his haste he came to judge one art by another.

Yet much of him remains. The only serious contemporary student of impressionism in America, Lewis E. Gates of Harvard, indirectly testified to this when he wrote in his famous essay of 1900, "Impressionism and Appreciation," that "the popularity of impressionism is only one sign more that we are learning to prize, above most things else, richness of spiritual experience." Huneker's impressionism, so facile and instinctive and generous, was not what even a future austere generation could label, in Gates's famous definition, as "the record of a momentary shiver across a single set of possibly degenerate nerves." Impressionism was often nonsense; but it also marked the apprenticeship of the modern critical spirit in America. "The superlative act of the critic," wrote Gates, "is to find in a work of art for the delight of modern temperaments some previously unsuspected implication of beauty." Huneker did that for a whole generation, and he embodied the very quality of his mind in the public taste. In his melancholy moments he liked to say that "a critic is a man who expects miracles," [1] but he believed in them and found them everywhere—his standard be-

---

[1] In his *very* melancholy moments he said, "A critic has no particular importance in the scheme of things."

ing, as Ludwig Lewisohn said, the "sheer ecstasy which he was to continue to seek all his life."

There was a certain basic wholesomeness of temper in Huneker which kept him free from the more bizarre nonsense of the period. At a time of unparalleled affectations and synthetic estheticism, he kept his joy in life. The only genuine exotic of the day, indeed, was Edgar Saltus, who worked so hard at being an élégant that he caricatured himself. Twenty-five years later other exquisites, in the twenties, were to find his fantastically overstylized books interesting; in his own generation he appeared merely desperate. Saltus was something more than a decadent; he was so completely without a core that his fashionable skepticism now seems almost pathological. In most writers who fled from the home shores, one is conscious of the impulse of alienation, of a profound uneasiness, a disenchantment of the mind, that steals through their books to echo the confession of their estrangement. They tried to make up for their loss by laying it to the Ohio or Indiana village; they tried to believe that the mere fact of a foreign excitement, of a more gracious tradition abroad, would supply the words they could not find at home. Saltus was a fantastically pretentious mind, but his tragedy was real—he was homeless by instinct. After composing his exact, acidulous novels of New York society he clung to Europe because he could exploit his unhappiness there with a more dignified irresponsibility. Oscillating between elaborate theories of the unconscious (notably Von Hartmann's) and the bric-a-brac of historical tattle, his stories, poems, translations, and pretentious philosophic manuals became charts through a darkness he could never hope to flee.

Like Poe, Saltus worked in ersatz; unlike Poe, his work everywhere betrays it. In his melodramatic and bibulous imagination the world became a spectacle recounting the flames and terrors of history. His materials were makeshifts for ideas, but he held to them with such stubborn complacence that it is impossible even to infer the most elementary symbolism or moral pattern. Intoxicated by his own prose, he came to a point in which the mania for rhetoric made up for the gnawing emptiness of that sorrow which broods over his works and has weighed them down into obscurity. Yet he was a showman of the "new spirit," which he defined as the "new pessimism." The "new pessimism," he declared grandly in *The Philosophy of Disenchantment,* "holds as first principle that the world is a theatre of misery in which, were the choice accorded it, it would be preferable not to be born at all." He gave his loyalty to the archpriests of pessimism in history, Epicurus, Pliny, Lucretius, Schopenhauer, who had borne witness to the only social idea he really believed in—Leopardi's declaration that "society is a league of blackguards against honest men." As he abandoned the discipline and interests of common literary folk—the claims of even the most genteel American realism, of French naturalism, of idealist German metaphysics—he was left in an extraordinary void of his own, which he confused with a vaguely immemorial standard of international sophistication. There he trumpeted the names of the gods that were discussed in his *Lords of the Ghostland*—Brahma, Ormuz, Ammon-Ra, Bel-Marduk, Zeus, and the "Nec Plus Ultra"; there he compiled his *Historia Amoris;* there he wrote the fantastic *Imperial Orgy* which pleased American sophisticates in the post-Versailles era because it suggested that history is like the political biography of the Romanov dynasty he described—blood and terror and bombast.

5

Out of this welter of enthusiasms that gave so many different clues to the future, there now emerged at the end of the century the one creative artist who sounded the possibilities open to his generation, though he fulfilled so few of them himself. In his day Stephen Crane stood as the "marvelous boy" in the tradition of Chatterton, Keats, and Beardsley—the fever-ridden, rigidly intense type of genius that dies young, unhappy, and the prey of lady biographers. Everything that he wrote in his twenty-nine years seemed without precedent. Before him Harold Frederic and Hamlin Garland had displayed the opportunities for an American naturalism, but their outlook was confined to local grievances and was expressed through a local temper. Frank Norris was still finding his way and was still dependent upon topical issues and the ideas of others. But no conventional background or stimulus explains Crane's disposition to naturalism; neither the depression of the nineties, which never troubled him, nor the classic texts of European naturalism, by which he was generally bored. He was a naturalist by birth, so to speak; but there is nothing in the placid Jersey parsonage of the Reverend Jonathan Crane that explains the grim finality of mind, in its way an astounding capacity for tragedy, that devoured his fourteenth child. Sentimental critics have charged that Crane had a secret disaffection born out of his father's martyrdom in the service of Methodism and its apparent futility in the face of world events, but the surest thing one can say about Crane is that he cared not a jot which way the world went. No one was ever less the reforming mind; revolutions were something foreigners attempted that Hearst would pay good money to report. He accepted the world always, hating it always, plotting his way through it alone with a contempt that was close to pain.

Thomas Beer, who understood him best, hit at the secret of Crane's career when he wrote of a ruthless literary courage possible only to those who are afraid. Life tossed him up and down like a cork. To his last days he was tormented by disease and insecurity, greedy friends and witnesses of his genius who thought him a strangely convivial freak, stupid editors and pristine reviewers, the doltish open mouth of the public, pointing, giggling, and retailing stories. Crane never had a juvenile period, a time of test and error, of sentimental amplitude and human indirection. The hard, fixed boundaries which hold his books were iron clamps which were set early. All through that miserably unhappy life, even in the first days of glory when *The Red Badge of Courage* fell out of the heavens, he was the stricken boy Conrad saw at the end in Brede Place in England, sitting in a baronial pile eating his heart out in hack work, devoured by sycophants, always in some portentous torment, with the suffering eyes and the absurd mustache that fell over his face like the mask of old age.

The world was a ship, he wrote in one of his poems, that God had fashioned and let slip.

> God fashioned the ship of the world carefully.
> With the infinite skill of an All-Master
> Made He the hull and the sails,

Held He the rudder
Ready for adjustment.
Erect stood He, scanning his work proudly.
Then—at fateful time—a wrong called,
And God turned, heeding.
Lo, the ship, at this opportunity, slipped slyly,

.   .   .   .   .   .

Making quaint progress,
Turning as with serious purpose
Before stupid winds.
And there were many in the sky
Who laughed at this thing.

And no more than God could he hope to reclaim it. "I cannot be shown," he said once, "that God bends on us any definable stare, like a sergeant at muster, and his laughter would be bully to hear out in nothingness." He would not appeal against wrong, and he thought it monstrous to complain. Essentially uneducated, his resources lay in his physical senses, which he exploited with an intensity disproportionate to his strength and yet unequal to the fervor of his spirit. He read very little, and nothing surprised him more than when people who read his work condescendingly discovered his debt to Zola or to Tolstoy. *War and Peace,* which he knew, stimulated him to the boyish cockiness that flared at rare instances and was one of his more charming traits. "Tolstoy could have done the whole business in one-third of the time and made it just as wonderful," he laughed. "It goes on and on like Texas." He thought of writing a book entitled *Peace and War,* which would do "the job" better and be an answer to Tolstoy. It was perhaps because he had read so little, as Willa Cather suggested, that he felt no responsibility to be accurate or painstaking in his transcription of common events. Like every sensuous artist, he was a magnificent guesser, and nothing proved how deeply he had imagined the psychology of battle in *The Red Badge of Courage* than his experience as correspondent in the Greco-Turkish War. "*The Red Badge* is all right," he said when he came out of it.

Yet the stark greatness of the novel did grow in part out of his instinctively intimate knowledge of American manners and character.

As Carl Van Doren observed, the verisimilitude of the book testified to Crane's knowledge of the popular memory and authentic legends of the war. One side of him was the local village boy who never quite lost his feeling for the small talk and the casual pleasures of the American town, and it showed not only in the campfire talk of the men in *The Red Badge*, but in the charming little-boy stories in *Whilomville Stories* and the extraordinary transcriptions of Negro speech in *The Monster*. What kept Crane alive, in one sense, was just that feeling; without it his despair might have seemed intolerable and, for an artist of his sensibility, incommunicable. He baited the universe but never those village citizens who are as benign in his work as small-town fathers in the *Saturday Evening Post*. They were his one medium of fraternity, and his strong, quiet affection for them testifies to the unconscious strength of his personal citizenship.

In this sense even the most astonishing effects in *The Red Badge of Courage* reflect Crane's background, for its soldier-hero might have been any American boy suddenly removed from the farm to fight in a war of whose issues he knew little and in which his predominating emotion was one of consummate perplexity and boredom. As a novelist of war Crane anticipated the war studies of the future; he had no palpable debt to Stendhal and Tolstoy, on whom he was supposed to have modeled his realism. Waterloo in *La Chartreuse de Parme* and Austerlitz in *War and Peace* are scenes against which the hero of sensibility enlarges his knowledge of life; but the novelists of social protest after the First World War, from Henri Barbusse to Humphrey Cobb, indicted the morality of war for its assault on the common citizen. Crane's hero is Everyman, the symbol made flesh upon which war plays its havoc; and it is the deliberation of that intention which explains why the novel is so extraordinarily lacking, as H. L. Mencken put it, in small talk. Scene follows scene in an accelerating rhythm of excitement; the hero becomes the ubiquitous man to whom, as Wyndham Lewis once wrote of the Hemingway hero, things happen. With that cold, stricken fury that was so characteristic of Crane—all through the self-conscious deliberation of his work one can almost hear his nerves quiver—he impaled his hero on the ultimate issue, the ultimate pain and humiliation of war, where the whole universe, leering through the blindness and smoke of battle, became the incarnation of pure agony. The foreground was a series of commonplaces; the background was cosmological. Crane had driven so quickly through to the central problem that everything else seemed accessory in its effect, but he was forced to describe emotions in terms of color because the pressure behind so wholly concentrated a force drove him to seek unexpected and more plastic sources of imagery. Often he revealed himself to be a very deliberate tone-painter, as calculating and even mechanical a worker in the magnificent as Oscar Wilde or Richard Strauss. He aimed at picture qualities and he synthesized them so neatly that, like the movement of the hunters and the hunted in a tapestry of the medieval chase, they illustrated a world whose darkness was immensity. "In the Eastern sky there was a yellow patch, like a rug laid for the feet of the coming sun; and against it, black and pattern-like, loomed the gigantic figure of the colonel on a gigantic horse."

Yet for all its beauty, Crane's best work was curiously thin and, in one sense, even corrupt. His desperation exhausted him too quickly; his unique sense of tragedy was a monotone. No one in America had written like him before; but though his books precipitately gave the whole esthetic movement of the nineties a sudden direction and a fresher impulse, he could contribute no more than the intensity of his spirit. Half of him was a consummate workman; the other half was not a writer at all. In his ambitious stories of New York tenement life, *Maggie* and *George's Mother,* the violence seemed almost celestial, but it was only Crane's own, and verbal; both stories suffer from excessive hardness and that strangely clumsy diction that Crane never learned to polish. In a great show piece like *The Open Boat* (drawn from an almost direct report of experiences in the Caribbean in the days when he was reporting the Cuban insurrection for New York newspapers) he proved himself the first great pyrotechnician of the contemporary novel; but the few superb stories are weighed down by hack work. The man who wrote *The Blue Hotel* also wrote more trash than any other serious novelist of his time. Even in buffooneries like his unfinished last novel, *The O'Ruddy,* there is the sense of a wasted talent flowing over the silly improvisation in silent derision.

He had begun by astonishing the contemporary mind into an acceptance of new forms; he ended by parodying Richard Harding Davis in *Active Service* and Stevenson in *The O'Ruddy*. Yet it was not frustration that wore him out, but his own weariness of life. His gift was a furious one, but barren; writing much, he repeated himself so joylessly that in the end he seemed to be mocking himself with the same quiet viciousness with which, even as a boy, he had mocked the universe. An old child, it was not merely by his somberness that he anticipated the misanthropy of the twentieth-century novel. Pride and a fiercely quaking splendor mark his first and last apotheosis: he was the first great tragic figure in the modern American generation.

Chapter 3

TWO EDUCATIONS: EDITH WHARTON AND THEODORE DREISER

"Did you, too, O friend, suppose democracy was only for elections, for politics, and for a party name?"—WHITMAN, *Democratic Vistas*

OUT of the "arrested energies" of the nineties, that great seminal period in modern American life, there now emerged two distinguished novelists whose careers, precisely because they were so diametrically opposed, help to illuminate the spirit of American experience and literature after 1900. Though both did not receive appropriate recognition until the nineteen-twenties, when modern literature received its official "liberation," their best work was largely done by the First World War, and the full significance of their work becomes clear only when considered against the drift of American life between 1895 and 1914.

2

The society into which Edith Wharton was born was still, in the eighteen-sixties, the predominant American aristocracy. Established in New York behind its plaster cast of Washington, its Gibbon and its Hoppner, its Stuart and its Washington Irving, it was a snug and gracious world of gentlewomen and lawyers who stemmed in a direct line from the colonial aristocracy. Though it was republican by habit where its eighteenth-century grandfathers had been revolutionary by necessity, it was still a colonial society, a society superbly indifferent to the tumultuous life of the frontier, supercilious in its breeding, complacent in its inherited wealth. It was a society so eminently contented with itself that it had long since become nerveless, for with its pictures, its "gentlemen's libraries," its possession of Fifth Avenue and Beacon Hill, its elaborate manners, its fine contempt for trade, it found authority in its own history and the meaning of life in its own conventions.

To a writer's mind it was a museum world, delicately laid out on exhibition and impeccable in its sanctuary. To Edith Wharton that society gave a culture compounded equally of purity and snobbery. If no one soared above the conventions, only bounders sought to degrade them. Its gentility boasted no eagles of the spirit and suffered no fanatics. The young Edith Newbold Jones accepted it from the first and admired its chivalry to the end. Its kindliness, its precision of taste, its amenability, were stamped on her. She was educated to a world where leisure ruled and good conversation was considered fundamental. Even in New York, a city already committed to a commercial destiny, ladies and gentlemen of the ancien régime gathered for elaborate luncheon parties. "Never talk about money," her mother taught her, "and think about it as little as possible." The acquisition of wealth had ceased to interest her class. They looked down not in fear, but with an amusement touched by repulsion, upon the bustling new world of frontiersmen who were grabbing the West, building its railroads, and bellowing down the stock exchange. The revolution in Edith Wharton's world, characteristically a revolution of manners, came when the vulgarians of the new capitalism moved in upon Fifth Avenue. For to the aristocracy of New York, still occupying the seats of splendor in the sixties and seventies, the quiet and shaded region just above Washington Square was the citadel of power. There one lived soundlessly and in impeccable taste, the years filtering through a thousand ceremonial dinners, whispering conspiracies, and mandarin gossip. One visited in one's circle; one left one's card; one read the works of Mr. Hawthorne, Mr. Irving, Mr. Edward Bulwer-Lytton. Even as an old woman Edith Wharton was to fill her autobiography with the fondled memory of the great dishes eaten in her childhood, the exquisite tattle, the elaborate service, the births and marriages and deaths of slim patrician uncles and aunts and cousins bestriding time.

It was the way of a people, as its not too rebellious daughter described it in *The Age of Innocence,* "who dreaded scandal more than disease, who placed decency above courage, and who considered that nothing was more ill-bred than 'scenes,' except the behavior of those who gave rise to them." There were standards: the word "standard," she confessed later, gave her the clue her writer's mind needed to the world in which she was bred. Bad manners were the supreme offense; it would have been bad manners to speak bad English, to nag servants. Edith Wharton's first literary effort, the work of her eleventh year, was a novel which began: " 'Oh, how do you do, Mrs. Brown?' said Mrs. Tompkins. 'If only I had known you were going to call I should have tidied up the drawing-room.' " Her mother returned it coldly, saying, "Drawing-rooms are always tidy."

Edith Wharton became a writer not because she revolted against her native society, but because she was bored with it; and that restlessness of the spirit was a primary achievement in such a world as hers. Whatever its graciousness, its almost classic sense of the past, its mildewed chivalry, the gentility which a colonial culture must always impose with exaggerated fervor and weight excluded women from every function save the cultivation of the home. Its distrust of the creative intelligence was as profound and significant as its devotion to the appurtenances of culture and the domestic elevation of library sets and vellum manuscripts. It worshiped literature as it worshiped ancestors, for the politeness of society; and if it distrusted the passions of literature, this was not because its taste was conscious and superior. It had not even that generous contempt for literature so marked in the boorish patronage of the arts by the industrial tycoons of the Gilded Age; it rejected what it could not understand because the creative élan affronted its chill, thin soul. It had already become a lifeless class, rigidly and bitterly conservative, filling its days with the desire to keep hold, to sit tight, to say nothing bold, to keep away from innovation and scandal and restless minds. There was no air in it, nothing to elevate an intellectual spirit; even its pleasures had become entirely ceremonial. To judge it in the light of the new world of industrial capitalism was to discriminate against it, for it offered no possibilities of growth.

By becoming a writer Edith Wharton did discriminate against it; but in the effort she liberated only her judgment, never her desire. She became a writer because she wanted to live; it was her liberation. But what it was she wanted to live for as a writer, she did not know. Unlike her master, Henry James, she did not begin with the conviction of a métier, the sense of craftsmanship and art; she did not even begin with that artist's curiosity which mediates between cultures, that passionate interest in ideas and the world's experiences which stimulates and nourishes the energy of art. She asked only to be a Writer, to adopt a career and enjoy a freedom; she offered nothing in exchange.

Even Edith Wharton's marriage, which might in other circumstances have liberated and matured her, repressed her. Her husband, as she confessed with remarkable candor in her autobiography—and the intensity and poignance of that confession was itself significant in so reticent and essentially trivial a record—was a conventional banker and sportsman of her own class, without the slightest interest in ideas and humiliatingly indifferent to her aspirations. Her greatest desire in youth had been to meet writers, not some particular master, but Writers; her marriage forced her into a life of impossible frivolity and dullness. It was a period in the middle eighties when the younger generation of American aristocracy challenged the vulgar nouveaux riches by emulating their pleasures but soon came to admire them; the aspirant young novelist who had been married off at twenty-three in peremptory aristocratic fashion now found herself dreaming of literary conquests amidst a distracting and exasperating round of luncheons, parties, yachting trips, and ballroom dinners. "The people about me were so indifferent to everything I really cared for," she wrote in later life, "that complying with the tastes of others had become a habit, and it was only some years later, when I had written several books, that I finally rebelled and pleaded for the right to something better." In her earliest years her family had discouraged her; her husband and his friends now ridiculed her. They evidently spoke to her of her work only to disparage it; the young society woman had

now to endure the crowning humiliation of pursuing even spas-
modically a career which her immediate circle thought disgraceful and
ridiculous. Then her husband became ill and remained so for a good
many years. It was not a pleasant illness, and it diverted her from
literature. Significantly enough, it was not until she was able to arrange
for his care by others that she moved to Paris—her true home, as she
always thought of it—where she lived until her death.

3

It is easy to say now that Edith Wharton's great subject should have
been the biography of her own class, for her education and training
had given her alone in her literary generation the best access to it.
But the very significance of that education was her inability to transcend and use it. Since she could do no other, she chose instead to
write, in various forms and with unequal success, the one story she
knew best, the story that constituted her basic experience—her own.
Her great theme, like that of her friend Henry James, became the
plight of the young and innocent in a world of greater intricacy than
they were accustomed to. But where James was obsessed by the moral
complexity of that theme and devoted his career to the evaluation and
dramatization of opposing cultures, Edith Wharton specialized in tales
of victimization. To James the emotional problems of his characters
were the representative expression of a larger world of speech, manners, and instinct—whose significance was psychological and universal.
He saw his work as a body of problems that tested the novelist's
capacity for difficulty and responsibility. To Edith Wharton, whose
very career as a novelist was the tenuous product of so many personal
maladjustments, the novel became an involuted expression of self.

She was too cultivated, too much the patrician all her days, to vul-
garize or even to simplify the obvious relations between her life and
her work; she was too fastidious an artist even in her constricted
sphere to yield to that obvious romanticism which fulfills itself in
explicit confession. But fundamentally she had to fall back upon herself, since she was never, as she well knew, to rise above the personal
difficulties that attended her career. She escaped the tedium and

mediocrity to which her class had condemned her, but the very motivation of that escape was to become a great artist, to attain by the
extension of her powers the liberation she needed as a woman; and a
great artist, even a completely devoted artist, she never became. James,
who gave her friendship, could encourage but not instruct her. Actually, it was not to become such a writer as he, but to become a writer,
that she struggled; what he had to give her—precision of motive, cultivation of taste, the sense of style—she possessed by disposition and
training. James's need of art was urgent, but its urgency was of the
life of the spirit; Edith Wharton's was desperate, and by a curious
irony she escaped that excessive refinement and almost abstract mathe-
matical passion for art that encumbered James. She could speak out
plainly with a force he could never muster; her own alienation and
loneliness gave her a sympathy for erratic spirits and "illicit" emotions
that was unique in its time. It has been forgotten how much Edith
Wharton contributed to the plain-speaking traditions of American
realism. Women wrote to her indignantly asking if she had known
respectable women; Charles Eliot Norton even once warned her that
"no great work of the imagination has ever been based on illicit
passion."

The greater consequence of Edith Wharton's failure to fulfill herself in art was its deepening of her innate disposition to tragedy. She
was conscious of that failure even when she was most successful, and
in the gap between her resolution and her achievement she took recourse to a classical myth, the pursuing Eumenides who will not let
Lily Bart—or Edith Wharton—rest. She was among the few in her
generation to attain the sense of tragedy, even the sense of the world
as pure evil, and it found expression in the biting edge of her novels
and the superficially genial fatalism of their drama. "Life is the saddest
thing," she wrote once, "next to death," and the very simplicity and
purity of that knowledge set her off in a literary generation to whom
morality signified the fervor of the muckrakers and for whom death
as a philosophical issue had no meaning. Spiritually, indeed, Edith
Wharton was possessed of resources so much finer than any contemporary American novelist could muster that even the few superior
novelists of her time seem gross by comparison. It was a service, even

though, like so many artistic services, it was an unconscious one, to talk the language of the soul at a time when the best energies in American prose were devoted to the complex new world of industrial capitalism.

Yet what a subject lay before Edith Wharton in that world, if only she had been able, or willing, to use it! Her class was dying slowly but not painfully, and it was passing on into another existence. To write that story she would have had to tell bluntly how her class had yielded to the *novi homines* of the Gilded Age, how it had sold itself joyfully, given over its houses, married off its acquiescent daughters, and in the end—like all bourgeois aristocracies—asserted itself in the new dominion of power under the old standard of family and caste. It would have been the immemorial tale of aristocrat and merchant in a capitalist society, their mating, their mutual accommodation, their reconciliation. Edith Wharton knew that story well enough; its significance had sundered the only world she knew, and its victims were to crowd her novels. The fastidious college lawyers who had scorned the methods of a Daniel Drew in the seventies would do the work of a Carnegie in the nineties; the Newport settled first by the Whartons and their friends was now to become the great summer resort of the frontier-bred plutocracy; the New York that had crystallized around the houses and reputations of the Livingstons, the Crugers, the Schuylers, the Waltons, now gave room to the Vanderbilts, whose family crest might properly have been the prow of a ferryboat on a field gilded with Erie Railroad bonds, with the imperishable boast of its Commodore founder for a motto: "Law! What do I care about law? Hain't I got the power?" So had the eighteenth-century Dukes of Nottingham developed the mines on their hereditary estates; so would the seedy marquises of France under the Third Republic marry American sewing-machine heiresses. Howells had said it perfectly: the archetype of the new era was "the man who has risen." To tell that story as Edith Wharton might have told it would have involved the creation of a monumental tragicomedy, for was not the aristocracy from which she stemmed as fundamentally middle-class as the rising tide of capitalists out of the West it was prepared to resist?

Edith Wharton knew well enough that one dynasty had succeeded another in American life; the consequences of that succession became the great subject of her best novels. But she was not so much interested in the accession of the new class as she was in the destruction of her own, in the eclipse of its finest spirits. Like Lily Bart, Ellen Olenska, Ralph Marvell, she too was one of its fine spirits; and she translated effortlessly and pointedly the difficulties of her own career into the difficulties of young aristocrats amidst a hostile and alien culture. It is the aristocrat yielding, the aristocrat suffering, who bestrides her best novels: the sensitive cultivated castaways who are either destroyed by their own class or tied by marriage or need to the vulgar nouveaux riches. Henry James could write of revolutionaries and nobility, painters and politicians, albeit all talked the Jamesian language with the same aerial remoteness from plain speech; Edith Wharton's imagination was obsessed by the fellow spirits of her youth. Though she had been hurt by her class and had made her career by escaping its fundamental obligations, she could not, despite all her fertile powers of invention, conceive of any character who was not either descended from that class or placed in some obvious and dramatic relation to it. At bottom she could love only those who, like herself, had undergone a profound alienation but were inextricably bound to native loyalties and taste. Indeed, their very weakness endeared them to her: to rise in the industrial-capitalist order was to succumb to its degradations. "Why do we call our generous ideas illusions, and the mean ones truths?" cries Lawrence Selden in *The House of Mirth*. It was Edith Wharton's stricken cry. She had accepted all the conditions of servitude to the vulgar new order save the obligation to respect its values. Yet it was in the very nature of things that she should rebel not by adopting a new set of values or by interesting herself in a new society, but by resigning herself to soundless heroism. Thus she could read in the defeat of her characters the last proud affirmation of the caste quality. If failure was the destiny of superior men and women in the modern world, failure was the mark of spiritual victory. For that is what Edith Wharton's sense of tragedy came to in the end; she could conceive of no society but her own, she could not live with what she had. Doom waited for the pure in heart; and it was better so.

Is not that the theme of *Ethan Frome* as well as of *The House of Mirth?* Ethan, like Lily Bart or Ralph Marvell, fails because he is spiritually superior and materially useless; he has been loyal to one set of values, one conception of happiness, but powerless before the obligations of his society. It was not a New England story and certainly not the granite "folk tale" of New England in esse its admirers have claimed it to be. She knew little of the New England common world, and perhaps cared even less; the story was begun as an exercise in French while she was living in Lenox, Massachusetts, and she wanted a simple frame and "simple" characters. The world of the Frome tragedy is abstract. She never knew how the poor lived in Paris or London; she knew even less of how they lived in the New England villages where she spent an occasional summer. There is indeed nothing in any of her work, save perhaps the one notable story she wrote of people who work for a living, *The Bunner Sisters,* to indicate that she had any conception of the tensions and responsibilities of even the most genteel middle-class poverty. Sympathy she possessed by the very impulse of her imagination, but it was a curious sympathy which assumed that if life in her own class was often dreary, the world "below" must be even more so. Whenever she wrote of that world, darkness and revulsion entered her work mechanically. She thought of the poor not as a class but as a condition; the qualities she automatically ascribed to the poor—drabness, meanness, anguish—became another manifestation of the futility of human effort.

Edith Wharton was not confined to that darkness; she could hate, and hate hard, but the object of her hatred was the emerging new class of brokers and industrialists, the makers and promoters of the industrial era who were beginning to expropriate and supplant her own class. She disliked them no less fiercely than did the rebellious novelists of the muckrake era—the Robert Herricks, the David Graham Phillipses, the Upton Sinclairs; but where these novelists saw in the brokers and industrialists a new and supreme condition in American society, Edith Wharton seemed to be personally affronted by them. It is the grande dame, not the objective novelist, who speaks out in her caricatures of Rosedale and Undine Spragg. To the women of the new class she gave names like Looty Arlington and Indiana Frusk;

to their native habitats, names like Pruneville, Nebraska, and Halle-lujah, Missouri. She had no conception of America as a unified and dynamic economy, or even as a single culture. There was old New York, the great house in Lenox (from which she gazed down upon Ethan Frome), and the sprawling wilderness that called itself the Middle West, a land of graceless manners, hoary jests, businessmen, and ridiculous provincial speech. It was a condescending resignation that evoked in her the crackling irony that smarted in her prose; it was the biting old dowager of American letters who snapped at her lower-class characters and insulted them so roundly that her very disgust was comic. As the world about her changed beyond all recognition, she ignored the parvenu altogether and sought refuge in nostalgia. Her social views, never too liberal or expansive, now solidified themselves into the traditional views of reaction. After 1920, when she had fulfilled her debt to the past with *The Age of Innocence,* she lost even that interest in the craft of fiction which had singled her out over the years, and with mechanical energy poured out a series of cheap novels which, with their tired and forlorn courtesy, their smooth rendering of the smooth problems of women's magazine fiction, suggest that Edith Wharton exhausted herself periodically, and then finally, because she had so quickly exhausted the need that drove her to literature.

If it is curious to remember that she always suggested more distinction than she possessed, it is even more curious to see how the interests of the American novel have since passed her by. James has the recurrent power to excite the literary mind. Edith Wharton, who believed so passionately in the life of art that she staked her life upon it, remains not a great artist but an unusual American, one who brought the weight of her personal experience to bear upon a modern American literature to which she was spiritually alien.

4

The fortunes of literature can reverse the fortunes of life. The luxury that nourished Edith Wharton and gave her the opportunities of a gentlewoman cheated her as a novelist. It kept her from what was crucial to the world in which she lived; seeking its manners, she missed its passion. Theodore Dreiser had no such handicap to overcome. From the first he was so oppressed by suffering, by the spectacle of men struggling aimlessly and alone in society, that he was prepared to understand the very society that rejected him. The cruelty and squalor of the life to which he was born suggested the theme of existence; the pattern of American life was identified as the figure of destiny. It was life, it was immemorial, it was as palpable as hunger or the caprice of God. And Dreiser accepted it as the common victim of life accepts it, because he knows no other, because this one summons all his resources.

Winter, Dreiser wrote in his autobiography, had always given him a physical sense of suffering. "Any form of distress—a wretched, down-at-heels neighborhood, a poor farm, an asylum, a jail, or an individual or group of individuals anywhere that seemed to be lacking in the means of subsistence or to be devoid of the normal comforts of life— was sufficient to set up in me thoughts and emotions which had a close kinship to actual and severe physical pain." He grew up in the friendly Indiana country of the eighties, in the very "Valley of Democracy" to be rhapsodized by Booth Tarkington and Meredith Nicholson; but he never shared its legendary happiness. His father, a crippled mill superintendent who was unable to provide for the family of fifteen, was a rigidly devout Catholic. The family separated periodically, the father going to Chicago to pick up work, the mother and younger children living in one small town after another. The bugaboo of social disapproval and scandal followed them insistently; at one time the mother kept a boardinghouse and a sister furnished the village gossips with a first-rate scandal. The family poverty was such that the town prostitute, his brother Paul's mistress, once sent them food and clothes, and even arranged for their removal to another city.

Dreiser grew up hating the shabby and threadbare rationale of the poor as only their sensitive sons learn to hate it; he hated his father as much for his repellent narrowness of belief as for his improvidence, and pitied his mother because she seemed so ineffectual in the face of disaster. The shining success in the family was his brother Paul, who became a popular vaudeville artist and composer. It was a painful, brooding boyhood, whose livid scars were to go into the first chapters of *An American Tragedy;* a boyhood touched by the lonely joys of wallowing in Ouida and *Tom Jones,* but seared by the perennial separations of the family and its grim and helpless decline. There was stamped upon Dreiser from the first a sense of the necessity, the brutal and clumsy dispensation of fate, that imposed itself upon the weak. He hated something nameless, for nothing in his education had prepared him to select events and causes; he hated the paraphernalia of fate—ill luck, the shadowy and inscrutable pattern of things that ground effort into the dust. He did not rebel against it as one who knows what the evil is and how it may be destroyed; he was so overpowered by suffering that he came to see in it a universal principle.

As Dreiser wandered disconsolately through the nineties, a reporter and magazine writer in New York and Chicago, St. Louis and Pittsburgh and Toledo, he began to read the pronouncements of nineteenth-century mechanism in Darwin and Spencer, in Tyndall and Huxley. They gave him not a new insight but the authority to uphold what he had long suspected. They taught him to call a human life a "chemism," but they did not teach him the chemical nature of life; they suggested that man was an "underling," a particle of protoplasm on a minor planet whirling aimlessly in the solar system, which for such a mind as Dreiser's was an excellent way of calling man what Dreiser had from his earliest days known man to be—a poor blind fool. The survival of the fittest was not a lesson in biology to be gathered in Darwin; it was the spectacle of the nineties as Dreiser watched and brooded over it in the great industrial cities that had within the memory of a single generation transformed the American landscape. For whatever the middle-class environment of his boyhood had given him, it was not its laissez-faire theology. Capitalism had denied the young Dreiser its prizes, but it had not blinded him to its deceptions. All about him in the convulsive nineties, with their railroad strikes and Populist riots, Dreiser saw American society expanding as if to burst, wealth rising like mercury in the glass, the bitter shambles of revolt, the fight for power. While Robert Herrick was peering anxiously through his academic window and Edith Wharton was tasting the pleasures of Rome and Paris, while David Graham

Phillips was reporting the stale scandals of New York high society for Pulitzer and Frank Norris was eagerly devouring the history of California for *The Octopus,* Dreiser was walking the streets of Chicago, the dynamic, symbolic city which contained all that was aggressive and intoxicating in the new frontier world that lived for the mad pace of bull markets and the orgiastic joys of accumulation. He was not of that world, but he understood it. Who could resist the yearning to get rich, to scatter champagne, to live in lobster palaces, to sport the gaudy clothes of the new rich? It was easy enough for those who had made a religion of their desire; it was easier still for a poor young writer who had been so hurt by poverty and the poor that the call of power was the call of life.

What Dreiser learned from that world was that men on different levels of belief and custom were bound together in a single community of desire. It was not the plunder that excited him, the cheating and lying, the ruthlessness and the pious excuses; it was the obsession with the material. A subtler mind, or a less ambitious one, might have cackled in derision; but Dreiser was swept away by the sheer intensity of the passion for accumulation. In *The Titan* he was to introduce a staggering procession of Chicago buccaneers on 'change with the same frowning, slow, heavy earnestness with which Abraham might have presented his flocks to God. He was fascinated by the spectacular career of Charles T. Yerkes, the most dazzling financier of his day, whose reckless energy and demoniac thirst for money spelled the highest ambition of his culture. Power had become not an instrument but a way of life. The self-conscious tycoons sat a little insecurely before their gold plate, their huge and obvious pictures, giggled perhaps in rare moments at their ostentatious and overdressed wives; but to Dreiser they represented the common soul's most passionate hopes made flesh. The symbols of power had become monumental, stocks and bonds blown feverishly into imitation French châteaux, the luxury of yachts, and conquerors' trips to Europe.

These evidences of success were something Dreiser could neither approve nor disapprove. Secretly, perhaps, he may have admired them for taking the American dream out of the literary testaments and crowning it with a silk hat; but what caught him was the human impulse that stole through the worst show of greed and gave it as natural and simple a character as local pride or family affection. As he wrote the story of Frank Algernon Cowperwood (Yerkes himself) in *The Financier* and *The Titan,* his plan was to build by tireless research and monumental detail a record of the industrial-commercial ethic. Though both novels were published at the height of the Progressive agitation, they have nothing in common with the superficial distaste that ruled David Graham Phillips's books, or with the sensitive homilies of Robert Herrick's. For the muckraking novel of the Theodore Roosevelt era assumed as its first premise that the society it excoriated was a passing condition; the novelists of the period based their values either on the traditional individualism and amenity of an agricultural and small owner's way of life (which was the ideal of the Progressive movement), or on the ideal society of Socialism, as did London and Sinclair. Dreiser would neither tinker with that society nor reject it. It was the only society he knew, the only society he had been allowed to understand; it was rooted in the same rock with poverty and mischance, strength and valor; it was life in which, as he wrote, "nothing is proved, all is permitted."

It was this very acceptance that gave him his strength. Since he could conceive of no other society, he lavished his whole spirit upon the spectacle of the present. Where the other novelists of his time saw the evils of capitalism in terms of political or economic causation, Dreiser saw only the hand of fate. Necessity was the sovereign principle. "We suffer for our temperaments, which we did not make," he once wrote, "and for our weaknesses and lacks, which are no part of our willing or doing." There was in nature "no such thing as the right to do, or the right not to do." The strong went forward as their instinct compelled them to; the weak either perished or bore life as best they could. Courage was one man's fortune and weakness another man's incapacity.

In a lesser novelist this very dependence upon fate as a central idea might have been disastrous; it would have displayed not an all-encompassing intensity but mere ignorance. Dreiser rose to the top on the strength of it. He raised Cowperwood-Yerkes to the level of destiny, where another might have debased him below the level of society.

Cowperwood becomes another Tamburlane; and as one remembers not the cities that Tamburlane sacked, but the character that drove him to conquest and the Oriental world that made that character possible, so one sees Cowperwood as the highest expression of the acquisitive society in which he rules so commandingly. His very spirit may seem repulsive; his ostentation, his multitudinous adulteries, his diabolism, his Gothic pile in Philadelphia and Renaissance palace in New York, merely a display of animalism. But we do not indict him for his ruthlessness and cunning; we despise his rivals because they envy him the very brutality with which he destroys them. When Cowperwood slackens (it cannot be said that he ever fails), it is not because his jungle world has proved too much for him, but because it is not enough. He has exhausted it by despoiling it, as he has exhausted his wives, his partners, his friends, and the sycophantic ingenuity of the architects to the rich. One remembers that poignant episode in which Cowperwood confesses to Stephanie Platow that his hunger for life increases with age but that men have begun to judge him at their own value. He must accept less from life because he has surged beyond its traditional limitations.

5

It was by a curious irony that Dreiser's early career became the battle ground of naturalism in America. He stumbled into the naturalist novel as he has stumbled through life. It is doubtful if he would have become a novelist if the fight for realism in American letters had not been won before he arrived on the scene; but when he did, he assumed as a matter of course that a tragic novel so indifferent to conventional shibboleths as *Sister Carrie* was possible. Frank Norris became a naturalist out of his admiration for Zola; Stephen Crane, because the ferocious pessimism of naturalism suited his temperament exactly. Naturalism was Dreiser's instinctive response to life; it linked him with the great primitive novelists of the modern era, like Hamsun and Gorki, who found in the boundless freedom and unparalleled range of naturalism the only approximation of a life that is essentially brutal and disorderly. For naturalism has always been divided between those who know its drab environment from personal experience, to whom writing is always a form of autobiographical discourse, and those who employ it as a literary idea. The French naturalists, and even their early disciples in America, found in its clinical method, its climate of disillusion, their best answer to romantic emotion and the romantic ideal. Naturalism was the classicism of the nineteenth century. Flaubert, Zola, Stephen Crane, and Frank Norris were all suckled in the romantic tradition; they turned to naturalism to disown romantic expansiveness, lavishness of color, and the inherent belief that man is capable of molding his own destiny. To a Flaubert and a Stephen Crane the design became all; it was the mark of fatality in human life rather than life as a seamless web of imponderable forces that interested them. Much as Pope proclaimed in *An Essay on Man* that

> In human works, though laboured on with pain,
> A thousand movements scarce one purpose gain . . .
>
> So Man, who here seems principal alone,
> Perhaps acts second to some sphere unknown,

so the classic naturalists furnished case histories of suffering to describe the precise conditions under which, as a citizen of the urban industrial world, modern man plans his life, fumbles in the void, and dies.

What Dreiser gave to the cause of American naturalism was a unique contribution. By exploding in the face of the Genteel Tradition, *Sister Carrie* made possible a new frankness in the American novel. It performed its function in literary history by giving the "new" morality of the nineties the example of solid expression; but it liberated that morality quite undeliberately. The young Dreiser, as John Chamberlain has put it, "had not been accepted by Puritan-commercial folk; therefore he was not loaded down in childhood with hampering theories of the correct way in which to live and act and write." The same formless apprenticeship and labored self-education which kept him from the stakes of modern society shielded him from its restrictions. He had no desire to shock; he was not perhaps even conscious that he would shock the few people who read *Sister Carrie* in 1900 with consternation. It would never have occurred to Dreiser that in writing the story of Hurstwood's decline he was sapping the foundations of the genteel. With his flash, his loud talk and fine linen, his rings and his animal intelligence, Hurstwood was such a man as Dreiser had seen over and over again in Chicago. The sleek and high-powered man of affairs automatically became Dreiser's favorite hero. To tell his story was to match reality; and the grossness and poignance of that reality Dreiser has known better than any other novelist of our time.

Dreiser's craftsmanship has never been copied, as innumerable writers have copied from Stephen Crane or even from Jack London. There has been nothing one could copy. With his proverbial slovenliness, the barbarisms and incongruities whose notoriety has preceded him into history, the bad grammar, the breathless and painful clutching at words, the vocabulary dotted with "trig" and "artistic" that may sound like a salesman's effort to impress, the outrageous solecisms that give his novels the flavor of sand, he has seemed the unique example of a writer who remains great despite himself. It is by now an established part of our folklore that Theodore Dreiser lacks everything except genius. Those who have celebrated him most still blush a little for him; he has become as much a symbol of a certain fundamental rawness in American life as Spanish villas on Main Street, and Billy Sunday.

Yet by grudging complete homage to him, Americans have innocently revealed the nature of the genius that has moved them. As one thinks of his career, with its painful preparation for literature and its removal from any literary tradition, it seems remarkable not that he has been recognized slowly and dimly, but that he has been recognized at all. It is because he has spoken for Americans with an emotion equivalent to their own emotion, in a speech as broken and blindly searching as common speech, that we have responded to him with the dawning realization that he is stronger than all the others of his time, and at the same time more poignant; greater than the world he has described, but as significant as the people in it. To have accepted America as he has accepted it, to immerse oneself in something one can neither escape nor relinquish, to yield to what has been true and to yearn over what has seemed inexorable, has been Dreiser's fate and the secret of his victory.

An artist creates form out of what he needs; the function compels the form. Dreiser has been one of the great folk writers, as Homer, the author of *Piers Plowman,* and Whitman were folk writers—the spirits of simplicity who raise local man as they have known him to world citizenship because their love for him is their knowledge of him. "It was wonderful to discover America," Dreiser repeated once after another, "but it would have been more wonderful to lose it." No other writer has shared that bitterness, for no other has affirmed so doggedly that life as America has symbolized it is what life really is. He has had what only Whitman in all the history of the American imagination had before him—the desire to give voice to the Manifest Destiny of the spirit, to preserve and to fulfill the bitter patriotism of loving what one knows. All the rest have been appendages to fate.

Chapter 4

PROGRESSIVISM: THE SUPERMAN AND THE MUCKRAKE

"The political outlook is bright, the brightest thing in sight . . . Politics is the best thing we have. . . . The radical politics, the thinking of men who are giving their minds to social philosophy, is reaching far into the future, and if the ideas of men are an indication of the course of human action, then the future is secure. And it is secure. We are living in a great century, and, after it, there will probably be a still greater era."—LINCOLN STEFFENS, in a letter of 1910

"I feel as fit as a Bull Moose!"—THEODORE ROOSEVELT.

FROM the time Howells took up the cudgels for realism to the time Dreiser published *Sister Carrie* in 1900 only to see it withdrawn, the story of the modern spirit in American literature is a chronicle of lonely and defeated individual ventures, of courageous struggles by a few isolated spirits. With the turn of the century and the coming of a national interest in reform under the Progressive period, however, all the forces that had been pressing on the new literature from the late eighties on were suddenly released in a flood, and a mood of active insurgence seized American writing. The long-awaited reckoning with the realities of the new industrial and scientific epoch was at hand, and a spirit of active critical realism, so widespread in popularity that it seemed to come directly from Theodore Roosevelt in the White House, now swept through politics and journalism, gave a new impetus to young realistic novelists, and stimulated American liberal thought in every sphere.

The significance of the Progressive period to literature is not that it marked a revolution in itself; it simply set in motion the forces that had been crying for release into the twentieth century. It was a catalyst, as Theodore Roosevelt, who seems in retrospect to have given the period so much of his own moral character, was one of its agents. The new spirit of insurgence had been bound to come, as the whole trend of American thought for twenty years and more had been heading in its direction. Yet when it did come, it became less a central movement of insurgence in itself than a medium through which flowed all the borrowed and conflicting European ideas, all the amorphous tendencies toward political reform, all the hopes for a different social order, all the questioning and nostalgia, aspiration and impatience, that had been dammed up so long at the back of the American mind.

The Progressive period of 1904-17 was marked by something more than "progressivism" itself, and it was anything but what a certain sentimental hero worship on the part of those who stood "at Armageddon" with the Progressive party in 1912 have made it out to be: a story of the conflict between liberal righteousness and evil that was written and largely directed by Theodore Roosevelt. By and large, as the social novelists of the period revealed, the Progressive period had no single "progressive" character, and many of its leading intellectual lights were not progressives in their own minds at all. What the period represented fundamentally was an upheaval, a sudden stirring, a breaking of the bonds between the old order and the new. Dominated by the spirit of reform, it was impatient with reform; seemingly revolutionary in mood, it had no revolutionary character. Stanchly middle-class in temperament, it helped to encourage the emergence of Socialism as a political power and saw the rise of proletarian revolutionary groups like the I.W.W. Yet its own Socialist novelists, like Jack London and Upton Sinclair, were the most boyish and romantic writers of the time. The Progressive period was, indeed, so much a repository for all the different influences that were now beginning to press on the American consciousness—Darwinism and imperialism, Socialism and naturalism—that those who think of it as a period devoted solely to muckraking and trust-busting and legislative reform must wonder at its delight in swashbuckling romance and "red-blooded" adventure.

The gusto of American life had not yet died down with the spread of factories and the settlement of the last frontier; and it now welled up in one last tumultuous fling. Everyone had gusto in the period, or tried to catch Roosevelt's gusto. The Wobblies had it, the muckrakers lived on it, novelists like Frank Norris and Jack London and Upton Sinclair had it overwhelmingly. It was this that gave life to the new spirit of insurgence and carried it in all directions. The generation dominated by the dream of reform was a generation fascinated by imperialism; the period of Socialism's greatest growth in America was the same period that saw the worship of brute strength and talk of Anglo-Saxon supremacy. Roosevelt, who attacked the trusts and admired the Kaiser, railed against "malefactors of great wealth" and out of the self-consciousnes of his own search for health preached "the strenuous life," set the tone. Just as Frank Norris, who wrote the most powerful antitrust novel in *The Octopus,* worshiped bigness everywhere else, so even a leading Socialist propagandist like Jack London found no difficulty in preaching Marxian Socialism and Nietzsche's Superman at the same time, and was indeed obsessed with the same imperialist worship of force and conquest that found expression in Kipling and Houston Stewart Chamberlain's glorification of the "great blond beast." That London seems to have thought of the Superman as a Western work-giant like Paul Bunyan, a brawny proletarian eligible for membership in the I.W.W., is another story; a whole generation of modern American writers, from London to Mencken, now began to make its own use of Nietzsche.

It was the shadow of power, of force, that lay over the period, as Frank Norris had forecast in *McTeague* and *The Octopus* and *Vandover and the Brute,* and as Dreiser was now proving in his monumental portrait of Cowperwood in novels like *The Titan* and *The Financier.* Roosevelt and Norris alike were fascinated by "vitality," and it might have been Roosevelt himself, and not Norris, who said: "Vitality is the thing after all. The United States in this year of grace

1902 does not want and need Scholars, but Men." Out of the self-conscious exuberance of a young industrial republic that already was beginning to dominate the world scene, there now emerged a grandiose pride, a thirst after bigness, that was the counterpart of its own fear of bigness. There was a fascination with energy in the Progressive period, with men who did things, *big* men, that was reflected in Dreiser's and Norris's tributes to the massive titans of the time, in Lincoln Steffens's growing impatience with democracy and impending admiration of dictatorship, in the unconscious respect with which the muckrakers described so carefully the immense power of the trusts. Darwinism had already presented Americans with the image of a power world in which the strong were pitiless to the weak, and everything in the world of contemporary industry and finance proved it. In so short a space of years capitalism in America had become a gigantic mechanism, a Behemoth that lay all over the landscape, absorbing everything for itself, brazen in its greed, oblivious to the human society on which it fed. Morgan and Rockefeller, Harriman and Carnegie, may have been bad men; but what big man they were! What a colossus was J. P. Morgan! In a famous cartoon of the period John D. Rockefeller, wearing the death's-head of his old age, was depicted standing over a mound of discarded roses with one exquisitely full-blown American Beauty rose in his hand, the Standard Oil Company—"The American Beauty Rose can be produced in all its splendor only by sacrificing the early buds that grow up around it." No longer were the titans of industry portrayed as lean, grasping men clutching at the bowels of the poor. They were the colossi of the earth, supermen in a supermen's world, titanic Americans appropriate to a titanic America; and if villains, titanic villains.

Significantly, it was the trusts, those dragon's teeth sowed in American individualism, that now came up to haunt the national imagination and that provoked a national effort toward reform. It was monopoly, force, that seemed to have changed American life—a railroad squeezing predatory rates out of small farmers; political bosses imposing their nominees upon the public; state legislatures electing their most powerful members to the United States Senate, that "rich man's club"; steel combines laying down a law of acquiescence or destruction for thousands of small businessmen. It was monopoly—"the curse of bigness," as "the people's attorney," Louis D. Brandeis, called it—that now gave the lie to the traditional American belief that the people enjoyed automatic liberty of economic action in a society of free individuals. For at least a century, as Charles A. Beard and James Allen Smith now began to charge, the American people had confused their political testament in the Declaration of Independence with the economic reality embodied in their class-minded Constitution; and monopoly confirmed that confusion and took advantage of it. Corruption had seemed too long a local evil, unfair trade practices merely a reflection of private greed, central control over political organizations an abstract need. America could no longer be dazzled by the promise of the frontier, the national legend that every man could make his fortune and that only improvidence could unmake it. The national apprenticeship was over, as laissez faire had become something of a joke; and monopoly was the best proof of it.

Despite imperial expansion and the intermittent prosperity of the late nineties, the rebellious spirit had never died out completely among the farmers and landless city workers. But with the realization of the power of monopoly it was the great middle class that now became alive to new dangers, and with the failure of Populism the impulse toward reformism passed from the frontier to the big city, "the hope of democracy," as it was now called. Yet the general trend of Progressivism was not, as revolutionary workmen had hoped for thirty years, one of pure revulsion against the profit system; it was an attack on those who had lived too well on the profit system, on those who had destroyed free opportunity for others. Although often uncertain of what reform could mean, the Progressive spirit was channeled into reform, and it signified from the first a desire to bring the old balance of competition back; to turn, as the young Walter Lippmann said sardonically, even the workers into shopkeepers. For Progressivism had essentially one principle of action: it was nostalgic. Its insurgence was the reflex irritation of a middle class that had suddenly become aware that behind the façade of Commonwealth, with its vaunted institutions and promise of democracy, there lay a new force, "invisible government." Thus the Progressive spirit attacked the abuses of the economic system, the advantage taken by a few; believing itself in nothing so much as the old individualism, it saw the archmenace in monopoly because monopoly threatened the freedom of the will. Everything at the moment, in fact, suggested that the small businessman, like the small farmer before him, no longer had the power to expand, or even to retain, his economic interest.

Yet it was precisely because his economic freedom had been challenged that the American now turned to political reform and regained his optimism through it. For all the power of monopoly, the power of public opinion remained; and it was here that the muckrakers and their fellow spirits in the novel seized their opportunity. Out of the fight against monopoly, the significant belief that monopoly and its attendant abuses could at least be fought, there now emerged that extraordinary spirit of reform—militant in its energy, political in its thinking, political in its literature—that was to carry Woodrow Wilson into the White House and which colored life in America up to the moment when Wilson's New Freedom perished in the war. People were suddenly determined to make a new life for themselves by politics; their heroes were politicians, and some of the politicians were among their best writers. The new liberalism believed in slogans that were good political objectives; its energy had a perennial pre-election zest, and its character was often mirrored in the personalities of its political leaders. And with these anxious strivings toward greater liberty of action went a new spirit that touched everything with its energy. The Progressive spirit was to mean many things before its time was up, but its historic significance is that it stirred up more than it knew. It worked toward economic and social legislation, for greater economic democracy, for women's rights, for more devotion and intelligence in public life; but indirectly it made men conscious of the changes needed everywhere.

The new spirit was abroad; there was change in the air. And everywhere one saw sudden stirrings in the literature that had been waiting for its charter of freedom—in the profound hunger for fresh leadership that fastened on Roosevelt; in the revulsion against ostentatious wealth that united the novelists of the early nineteen-hundreds; in the endless, excited journalism that now flooded the scene and became the tracts of a new time. The technique of the new social novels was not always subtle and the tone was often shrill; but though many of these writers limited themselves to political ends and were deceived by political appearances, they helped to introduce what was virtually a resurgence in all the avenues of American life. The uneasiness, the hesitant half-hopes, remained; but one thing was now clear: The energies of the new century were no longer arrested; American writing had entered upon the Years of Hope.

2

If we think of all the repressed influences that were set loose by the insurgency of the Progressive period, all the exuberant romanticism out of the West that was to find its expression in the adventurousness of the new decade, it is easy enough to see why Frank Norris, who died on the eve of the Progressive period in 1902, must yet seem always so representative of it. For Norris, with his boundless energy and worship of force, his delight in life and willingness to learn from every source, was the perfect child of the Roosevelt era. In fact, if Theodore Roosevelt had had a taste for novels and an admiration for Zola, he might have produced huge transcripts of contemporary life not much different from Norris's. Where Stephen Crane seems so significantly a symbol of the fin de siècle, the last glowing ember of a dying century, Norris, who was his almost exact contemporary, was the counterpart in literature of the tough and muscular new men of the new century—Roosevelt and Big Bill Haywood, Borah and Darrow.

At *McClure's Magazine,* where the first muckrakers were provided with shovels, Frank Norris worked along with Ida Tarbell, Lincoln Steffens, and Ray Stannard Baker. He had been hired on the strength of his early romantic stories, and a romanticist he significantly remained to the end. Norris, who was the most insurgent of the early naturalists and the most reactionary, was the product of many conflicting influences, and he often betrayed them all simultaneously. Born in Chicago of wealthy parents who indulged all his restless early projects, he grew up for a time in San Francisco, then jumped to Paris, where he tried to be a painter, then came back for work at the University of California, where he began to write, and finally spent a year at

Harvard, where he studied writing under the impressionist Lewis E. Gates, and began *McTeague* and *Vandover and the Brute*. In 1898 he was in Cuba, where he reported the Santiago campaign of the Spanish-American War for *McClure's*. At twenty-five he was in South Africa, where he reported the Boer War for *Collier's* and the *San Francisco Chronicle*. He was captured by the Boers, ordered to leave the country, and returned to newspaper work in San Francisco. On the strength of all these influences he was at once a frontier novelist perennially excited by the promise of California, the most devoted follower of Zola in America, and an unhappy child of that fatal marriage between Kipling and Stevenson that ruined many a weaker writer in the nineties. Yet he was stronger than all the forces that composed him, and he had what one never feels in Crane—a capacious gift that he had not even begun to exhaust when he died, an energy almost worthy of the teeming, world-changing forces of the new century. When he died at thirty-two of appendicitis, he had but touched the crucial phase of his ambitious work and was turning slowly in the great circle of his trans-world trilogy of wheat, of which the third volume was never written and the second never corrected.

Norris became a naturalist by that hatred of "pure literature" which developed in Europe after Flaubert into the social studies of Zola. "Who cares for fine style!" he wrote in 1899. "Tell your yarn and let your style go to the devil. We don't want literature, we want life." With a certain boyish opportunism that was characteristic of him, he selected from the naturalist creed chiefly its delight in violence, and accepted its determinism only as it satisfied his dramatic sense. The philosophy behind naturalism in Europe, with its attempt to imitate the studious objectivity of science, its profound tragic sense, he ignored. Studying Zola as the high priest of naturalism, he may, however, have shown a shrewder understanding of Zola, as Franklin Walker has suggested, than of the naturalist creed itself. While still at college Norris wrote:

> Naturalism, as understood by Zola, is but a form of romanticism after all. . . . The naturalist takes no note of common people, common in so far as their interests, their lives, and the things that occur in them are common, are ordinary. Terrible things must happen to the charac-

ters of the naturalistic tale. They must be twisted from the ordinary, wrenched from the quiet, uneventful round of everyday life and flung into the throes of a vast and terrible drama that works itself out in unleashed passions, in blood and in sudden death. The world of M. Zola is a world of big things. The enormous, the formidable, the terrible, is what counts; no teacup tragedies here.

This was hardly what the naturalists had sought in their hope of observing human life under conditions of "clinical objectivity," but it was characteristic of Norris's spirit. He was obsessed by size and violence, and his delight in bigness was a curious blend of his love for the California frontier and an invincible youthfulness that was not exhausted in the thumping romances he wrote as a boy—the autobiographical *Blix* and the red-blooded *Moran of the Lady Letty* so plainly derived from Kipling. Like Roosevelt and Jack London, he had more than his share of the facile Nordicism of his day; yet he believed so passionately in a literature close to the masses that he once wrote that "a literature that cannot be vulgarized is no literature at all." His love of quantity came out most strikingly in the technique of his sprawling novels and particularly in the rhetorical perorations that spoil so many of his books, a trick of piling detail on detail in one grand symphonic swell to suggest the hugeness of Nature. To that overflowing vitality, however, he owed the extraordinary feeling for the common brutality of life that makes his best novel, *McTeague,* one of the great works of the modern American imagination.

For the key to Norris's mind is to be found in a naïve, open-hearted, and essentially unquenchable joy as radiant as the lyricism of Elizabethan poetry, a joy that is like the first discovery of the world, exhilarating in its directness, and eager to absorb every flicker of life. Norris wrote as if men had never seen California before him, or known the joy of growing wheat in those huge fields that could take half a day to cross, or of piling enough flour on trains to feed a European nation. It is out of the surge and greed of that joy that his huge, restless characters grow, men so abundantly alive that the narrow life of cities and the constraints of the factory system can barely touch them. He was the poet of the bonanza, teeming with confidence, reckless in the face of that almost cosmological security that was California to him.

Every object in his books was huge, brought up to scale—the wheat fields in *The Octopus* that are like Napoleonic duchies, the eating and drinking in *McTeague,* the fantastic debaucheries in *Vandover and the Brute* (like a Boy Scout's daydreams of ancient Egypt), the Renaissance prodigality in *The Pit,* and even the back-alley slugging and thievery in an adventure yarn like *Moran of the Lady Letty,* whose heroine, characteristically, is a Viking princess in blue jeans.

When Norris planned his trilogy of wheat, inevitably it became "an idea big as all outdoors." It was to span two continents and, as he boasted to Bruce Porter, deal with the primitive, record man's struggle with nature, depict the conquering of the frontier, the growth of business enterprise, and at the last take in Europe. It was to be the last affirmation of nature's promise in an America rapidly veering away from even industrial promise. The conflict between the railroads and the farmers, as he revealed it in *The Octopus,* was unconsciously conceived in terms of the Biblical legend of evil. It is this fact that explains the book's sentimental mysticism and the shambles he made out of its sequel, *The Pit.* The San Joaquin Valley (rather like Steinbeck's Salinas) is Eden; Magnus and Derrick and his fellows Nature's children; and the Southern Pacific the serpent in the garden. *The Octopus* was, in a sense, the first muckraking novel, and it remains the most confused. Norris was still torn between Zola and Kipling, and though he was already a considerable artist, he was still a boy. He knew that in the society of which he wrote, an agricultural community geared to industry, a railroad could do nothing else; but his appreciation of economic necessity yielded to his desire to pay a last—and majestic— tribute to the frontier. Powerful as the book is, its fervor remains sentimental, its heroes and villains stock figures in a conflict Norris could project passionately but did not comprehensively understand. In the end the rascally railroad agent, S. Behrman, falls to his death amid circumstances reminiscent of the cheapest Victorian melodrama, the railroad takes all the land, and Norris is left to the celebration of the wheat that brings the book noisily to a close.

In *The Pit* Norris intended to tell the second phase of the wheat story, its fortunes on the Chicago market; but he succeeded only in completing a mediocre counterpiece to the stock novel of finance that became popular six years later. Like so many of these novels, it inevitably became a sentimental study in marriage, and proved no more than that the hold of the pit over Curtis Jadwin was exactly like the hold of drink over the good but erring father in a temperance novel. Exciting in its detail, *The Pit* was astonishingly uncritical of the very financial framework Norris had sought to expose in *The Octopus*. Norris's characteristic esteem for pure achievement led him to inflate the commonplace figure of Jadwin into an almost romantic type of adventurer, kindly at times and even magnificently generous, but one hardly typical of his world and certainly never a clue to its morality. As the story of Jadwin and his wife ocupied Norris's mind, the place of the market in the blueprint of his epic obviously lost all significance for him. No one turning to *The Pit* first would guess its purpose in the projected trilogy. There is not even an echo of the struggles of *The Octopus,* for the story rapidly dwindles to a romantic story rooted in one place and centered in one theme. Narrow and compact, it does, however, illustrate that mastery of episode which Norris attained beyond most novelists of his day.

Norris's ambition, it is clear, was to make America equal to the cosmic, to find a literary equivalent for his nation's bigness. Yet it is in *McTeague,* that history of degeneration, that he lives. In his wheat novels he tried to expand local scenes, and that local patriotism which has no parallel in the literature of the frontier, into the cosmic view that fascinated him; it was in this early book, much of which was written before he left college, that he exposed the crude foundations of a whole civilization in his bitterly remorseless drama of one soul's failure. There was a certain coarseness in Norris which was the obverse side of his boyish sentimentality, and if it was sadistic and painfully "literary" in *Vandover,* it lifted Norris's passion for reality to new heights in *McTeague.* "The Dentist," as he referred to the book in letters to his friends, became at once the portrait of a city and the matchless reproduction of its culture. Norris crammed into it the darkness of that world of the poor which always beckoned to him like Nemesis, a world frozen in necessity, merciless to those who lost their foothold, savagely inexorable even in death. It was a melodrama, as all Norris's books were melodramas; but the violence was something more than his usual exhalation of boyish energy; it supported a conception of life. The tragedy of McTeague and Trina was arranged, for once, on a scale of genuine determinism; blindness became the arena and accident the avenging angel; the universe was a wasteland in which men grappled for bread, and life was emptied into the sewers of the city.

Yet perfect an object lesson in naturalism as the book is, despite all its extravagance and crudity, the novel glows in a light that makes it the first great tragic portrait in America of an acquisitive society. McTeague's San Francisco is the underworld of that society, and the darkness of its tragedy, its pitilessness, its grotesque humor, is like the rumbling of hell. Nothing is more remarkable in the book than the detachment with which Norris saw it—a tragedy almost literally classic in the Greek sense of the debasement of a powerful man—and nothing gives it so much power. For McTeague himself, it is safe to say, Norris cared very little; but out of his own instinct for brute force he invested McTeague's own brutality with an imperishable significance. The red-blooded, aggressively tough novelist to the end, he had almost casually improvised a livid modern tragedy out of his own sensitiveness to McTeague's failure; and the tragedy was perhaps more real than he knew. For Norris's gift, to the very end, was a peculiarly indiscriminate one; he was still trying his hand, still the inveterately curious, overgrown boy alternating between Kipling and Zola; still a precocious master of violence whose greatest pride was that he was tough as any in his imperialist generation. "I never truckled," Norris boasted before his death. "I never took off the hat to Fashion and held it out for pennies. I told them the truth. They liked it or they didn't like it. What had that to do with me? I told them the truth."

Shaped to the size of the smaller men who followed Norris, this boast might have been the epigraph of the muckraking novelists who now came on the scene. So far as they could see it clearly before them, they certainly did try to tell the truth; and it was not their fault if they saw a new St. George in Theodore Roosevelt. "Theodore Roosevelt is the ablest living interpreter," Robert M. La Follette wrote in his autobiography, "of what I would call the superficial public sentiment of a given time, and he is spontaneous in his response to it." To Roosevelt, so perfect a child of his time, was it given by Boss Platt, fate, and Czolgosz to enjoy the leadership that stamped his influence on the literature of the Progressive period. As a literary influence he has no parallel in the Presidency. He inspired dozens of political novels that seemed to have been written out of his speeches, invented the militant slogans gratefully received by a generation eager to be militant, gave public opinion something of his own Rough Rider vigor, and set a nation to flexing its muscles, if he did not always set it to thinking. His greatest service lay in his being alive, though Cecil Spring-Rice, the British Ambassador, once wrote in a letter that "you must always remember that the President is about six," and one of his Bull Moose chieftains in 1912 laughed: "Fellows, we must remember that T.R. is great because he understands the psychology of the mutt." Yet what did that matter? Roosevelt so nicely balanced the scales of righteousness that to criticize him was to be either a malefactor of great wealth or a wild-eyed Anarchist. "The Apostle of the Obvious," as Donald Richberg called him, he spoke loudly but he carried a very little stick indeed. "We are neither for the rich man as such nor the poor man as such; we are for the upright man, rich or poor." It took twenty years for the critical intelligence in America to mull over that and realize that he had said nothing at all.

At the moment, however, it seemed a good deal. For Roosevelt talking, Roosevelt grinning, Roosevelt hunting beasts in the jungle and writing about beasts with the same studied bravado, Roosevelt grimacing and thundering at Armageddon, gave the democracy of his day a token of its real or imagined potency. He was a force in a day that yearned after force; he enlivened the air. What did it matter that his antitrust suits had almost no effect upon the earning power of guilty corporations, or that the conservative, slow-moving Taft proved himself a more conscientious, if less spectacular, opponent of the great trusts? What did it matter that Teddy had summoned the Japanese and the Russians after their 1904 war to a peace conference of whose issues he was sublimely ignorant? What did it matter that he excoriated the muckrakers themselves in public and in private admitted the prevalence of corruption more fetid than any they had reported? Genuinely anxious to heal the surface wounds of the American organism, Roosevelt radiated indignation against "wrong" and cheerful encouragement of "right" in terms of such stentorian vagueness that he encouraged and made respectable the whole reform movement. He was blindly ambitious, he did not always have a proper respect for truth, and he worshiped pure energy. Yet because he believed with fierce emotional patriotism, as he proclaimed in *The New Nationalism,* that the history of America was the central event in the history of the world, he made a whole generation believe it. Driving America before him like an errant child, he made people conscious of the great tasks that lay ahead for America; and no one knew it better than the journalists and novelists who were now coming up to the front.

Muckraking, which was to lead from "exposé" journalism to "exposé" fiction, was christened by Roosevelt, though he publicly denounced it. It began almost as an accident, when Lincoln Steffens, who had been demoted from the editorship of *McClure's Magazine* to roam the Middle West on special assignments, found in St. Louis the story of the decade, the corruption of the big cities. It was by a coincidence that Steffens's famous opening report, "Tweed Days in St. Louis," appeared side by side with the first chapters of Ida M. Tarbell's *History of the Standard Oil Company.* McClure, who was shrewd to the point of genius, had no carefully planned policy, but he had long suspected, from the days he had quit peddling pots and pans up and down the Mississippi Valley to sell the housewives sensational journalism, that people wanted something different. As Steffens turned his attention from St. Louis to Minneapolis, and from Pittsburgh ("Hell with the lid lifted") to Philadelphia, he found himself needing assistants; soon the passion for exposure caught on, and muckraking became a major industry. Ray Stannard Baker investigated the railroads; in *Everybody's* Thomas W. Lawton bitterly attacked contemporary financiers; Charles Edward Russell investigated the beef trust and Judge Ben Lindsey existing abuses in criminal law; in *Collier's* Samuel Hopkins Adams published his sensational articles on patent medicines and the press, and David Graham Phillips began those caustic articles on business in government that led to his most famous article, "The Treason of the Senate," and the most popular social novels of the day. Encouraged by the editors of magazines like *Everybody's, Collier's, Cosmopolitan, Pearson's* (even the *Saturday Evening Post* was touched), staff contributors and free-lance writers now scoured the country looking for facts on corruption, and they found it everywhere—stories of franchise steals, pay-roll padding, fraudulent letting of contracts, alliance of police with vice, foul slum dwellings, poverty in the great cities. They visited state capitals and returned with mounting stories of lobbyists at work, of the bribery of legislators, franchise-grabbing, and the working of "invisible government" in machine politics. They examined the conduct of business and exposed worthless stock schemes, dishonest insurance companies, and thieving monopolies.

Muckraking, Roosevelt complained to Taft while still in the White House, was ineffective; at the same time he sensed in alarm that it could go too far. Thus he sneered that most of the muckrakers lacked intelligence; some were Socialists, he felt, and some "merely lurid sensationalists; but they are all building up a revolutionary feeling." In this respect he secretly agreed with Lincoln Steffens, who was trying to prove to him, as the more conservative, that muckraking could never remain on the level of journalistic exposure. "You, who have the democratic sense," he wrote to T. R. in 1907, "know that most of the good done in the last few years has been done by the exposure, not by the conviction of the rascals. . . . You seem to me always to have been looking down for the muck, I am looking upward to—an American Democracy. You ask men in office to be honest, I ask them to serve the public." Ever since he had returned from his graduate studies in Germany to be a reporter in Wall Street, Steffens had seen that "the struggle for existence is very animal-like. The abler the man, the farther he goes over the lines they agree to as the unsafe ones to cross." Now, after two decades of industrious research into the life of the big cities in America, he had a clear insight into the general social pattern. "My gropings into the misgovernment of cities," he wrote in *McClure's* in 1904, "have drawn me everywhere, but always, always out of politics into business, and out of the cities into the state."

The evangelist of the reformer-muckrakers, Steffens had already proved himself a social philosopher—gay, cynical, casually wise, yet growingly impatient with the slowness of reform. The other muckrakers generally had no social philosophy. They had been assigned and encouraged to expose, and they exposed—and how much there was to expose! For the rest, they had little historical curiosity, and the nature of the capitalist state remained as mysterious and inscrutable to them as Melville's white whale. Yet it is too easy to indict them for not transcending the normal boundaries of journalism in their day or in our own. The chief grievance of some contemporary critics against them is that they were "naïve"; that is, that they were not Marxists. Yet if they were "naïve," who was not in their time? Lincoln Steffens, whose growing contempt for democracy led him after the war to become an unashamed admirer of dictatorship, was certainly not less naïve when he found the true religion in Soviet Russia. If any of the muckrakers now deserve censure, it is those who tried to become novelists on the strength of a few facts and a little indignation (rather like some proletarian novelists in the nineteen-thirties); or romantic novelists like Winston Churchill, who set out in "reform" novels like *Coniston* to write truthfully about politics and ended up by sentimentalizing the very political bosses whom they seemed to attack. In the same way some of the early "political" novels, like Alfred Henry Lewis's *The Boss,* Brand Whitlock's *The Thirteenth District,* and Elliott Flower's *The Spoilsman,* were ingenuous transcriptions of newspaper stories—novels exactly as profound, John Chamberlain wrote in his study of the Progressive mind, *Farewell to Reform,* "as the mind of Theodore Roosevelt, no more and no less." It was when muckraking now began to drain into fiction, carrying the romantic subsoil of the period with it, that the essential quality of this second generation of pioneer realists stood clearly revealed. Social realists, they were not yet novelists or even ambitious for the novel; it was enough for them that they had learned some first facts about society in America. With all the essential optimism and energy of their times, they moved exuberantly from journalism into fiction, ready to attack.

The muckraking novel was essentially a reporter's novel; at first it was called the "political" novel and later the "economic" novel, as insurance companies turned out to be as corrupt as Tammany elections, and the trusts as coolly wicked as a Philadelphia district leader. Of all the reporters who turned to fiction, David Graham Phillips soon emerged as the shining example. He was a kind of superior archetype of all the people who went into "reform fiction"—bred and trained in the Middle West, a great reporter, stubbornly honest, prudent, handsome, the dashing ideal journalist in a day when all the great reporters were as romantic as foreign correspondents. He had been born a reporter, as it seemed; enormously prolific, a legend on Park Row before he became the perfect reporter-novelist, his importance to realism lay in his exceptional news sense. One of the most famous of all the muckrakers, his most distinctive contribution was his "Treason of the Senate," but it is in his collection of articles, *The Reign of Gilt,* that the design of his social novels is most clearly seen. Phillips, in whom the nostalgic Jeffersonianism of the Progressive period became a passion, had no higher aspiration than to lay bare the debasement of the old middle-class spirit in the new plutocracy. As it happens, he succeeded only in documenting, out of the overflowing knowledge he had gained as a reporter, the surface corruption in contemporary politics and business. Yet in reading *The Reign of Gilt* one glimpses the hidden intensity of Phillips's essential purpose in the bitterness with which he there described the manners of the new rich and their cheapening of tradition, their comic efforts to found a social caste of their own, their grappling for favors, their monumental bad taste, and their essential cruelty. The rising tide of wealth, most conspicuously displayed in the great trading capitals of New York and Chicago, disgusted him. It was with inexpressible indignation that the small-town Indiana banker's son now recorded it as his authenticated observation that it took no less than three-quarters of a million dollars a year to live at the peak of fashion on Fifth Avenue at the turn of the century.

Like so many in his generation, of course, Phillips knew that to attack the new plutocracy in this spirit was not enough. He was a reformer passionately eager to inculcate a new respect for democracy in

America, and it was with this aim in mind that he wrote until 1908 that group of novels by which he is best remembered. Yet perhaps it is because he tried to do too much that his failure as a social novelist is now so marked. He wanted, as it were, to write the great symbolic epic of what had happened to his country and to his generation; but he wanted to write it from the city room, and he remained so much the reporter in his novels that he succeeded only in dramatizing the headlines of the Progressive era and in packing into his books an unparalleled density of newspaper data. For Phillips was above all a great reporter, and like the great reporters he covered everything: politics in *The Plum Tree,* finance in *The Deluge* and *The Cost,* the "penalties of wealth" in *The Master Rogue,* the insurance scandals uncovered by Charles Evans Hughes in *The Light-Fingered Gentry,* national corruption in *The Fashionable Adventures of Joshua Craig,* municipal corruption in *The Conflict,* state corruption in *George Helm*—twenty-three novels in all. He even wrote an editorial in novel form, *The Second Generation,* that was a general criticism of contemporary industrial ethics.

Yet though Phillips was able to establish precise case histories of stock-juggling and political "fixing," monopoly practice and industrial politics, it was as a novelist of marriage that he tried to give artistic significance to his books. Away from his muckrake, Phillips was a frank romanticist; and like his greater contemporary, Robert Herrick, he seems to have based his criticism of a competitive society on the dangers it presented to the marriage equipoise. He always wrote of Wall Street with loathing, but the great danger of a life on Wall Street for him was that it kept husbands away from home. Though toward the end of his life he began to write eagerly about "the new woman" and published a gusty American *Moll Flanders* in *Susan Lenox,* the women in his "reform" novels were pastel heroines out of Tennyson. What he saw in them, it is clear, was the unburnished old-fashioned idealism that their lovers and husbands had lost on 'change, and by their sweet-smiling patience and fastidiousness they were presented as good examples to their men, enslaved to the industrial or political machine. When a husband and wife are reconciled on the last page of a Phillips novel—and they usually are—you may be sure that the stock market will never see him again. The pattern rarely changed, and was so much like that of the old-fashioned temperance novels that it remains an interesting commentary on Phillips's resources as a novelist. If the hero is essentially a good man, as most Phillips heroes are essentially good, but caught in the toils of the netherworld of corruption, like Matthew Blacklock in *The Deluge* and Horace Armstrong in *The Light-Fingered Gentry*, they must wait until they have broken with corruption to be forgiven by their wives. If the man is good enough to begin with, but hopelessly gone in his greed, an incorrigible rascal like James Galloway in *The Master Rogue*, John Dumont in *The Cost*, or Harvey Saylor in *The Plum Tree*, he dies unshriven and unloved.

Phillips's greatest asset as a novelist of society was his appreciation of the extent to which economic necessity governs middle-class lives, but he was often faithless to his own recognition of that necessity. There is a kind of determinism that reaps its victims in his books as inexorably as in any naturalistic novel, but he always weakened and brought in some deus ex machina at the end to send his characters off in a shower of bliss. Whatever intensity he had sprang out of his deep-felt hatred for ostentation. "Conventionally, it is man's chief business to get rich," he wrote in *The Light-Fingered Gentry*, "woman's chief business to keep young looking." He wrote of "that hungry look, sometimes frankly there, again disguised by a slimy overlayer of piety, again by whiskers or fat, but always there," which he detected on the faces of the new rich. Respectability, as he saw it work out in hundreds of careers that wasted a man's best talents and frustrated his good instincts, often seemed to him a pitiful ambition. It was to the greed for wealth that he laid the corruption of American life, and with equal simplicity, it is by sentimental renunciation in his most positive novel, *The Second Generation*, that men leave the beast world of the big city to build Jerusalem again in Indiana's green and pleasant land. The muckraker's apotheosis was always the same—a vision of small, quiet lives humbly and usefully led; a transcription of Jeffersonian small-village ideals for a generation bound to megalopolis, yet persistently nostalgic for the old-fashioned peace and the old-fashioned ideal.

3

In the eyes of the young Socialist intellectuals who were now beginning to come up, the muckrakers were bourgeois reformers who lacked a comprehensive grasp of the social problem; but they did not always claim that leading Socialist novelists like Jack London and Upton Sinclair were doing a better job. The Socialist intellectuals did not, in fact, seem to have too much respect for the novel, or for their own artistic achievements generally. It was a young Socialist critic named Van Wyck Brooks who commented at about this time on the social conscience in writers like Upton Sinclair which enables them "to do so much good that they often come to think of artistic truth itself as an enemy of progress." The scholars in the movement, such as Brooks and Walter Lippmann, were always a little appalled by the boisterous and raucous and inordinately prolific comrade-novelists like London and Sinclair. Socialists generally were proud that they had novelists of their own, but they must have wondered just how authentically their message was getting across. For the curious thing about these leading Socialist "fictioneers" is that they were the most romantic novelists of their time. London's greatest desire was to slip backwards, away from capitalism, into the lustier and easier world of the primitive frontier; Sinclair, as Robert Cantwell has pointed out, went back to the amiable faddism of a nineteenth-century visionary like Bronson Alcott, and was then, as he remains, the most enthusiastic and angelic of Utopians, a Brook Farmer who gave as much passion to vegetarianism as he did to Socialism and fiction. Indeed, both of these pioneer Socialist writers were amazingly like the romantic archetypes which benighted bourgeois opinion then made Socialist rebels out to be. To the America of Roosevelt and Taft, Socialism was still an exotic mushroom growth, though progressing rapidly—a movement too easily confused with surface phenomena like Sinclair's attempts to set up a Utopian community at Helicon Hall in New Jersey, or Maxim Gorki's expulsion from a New York hotel for living with a lady not his wife. Against this background, London and Sinclair, who lived and wrote in the feverish grand style of romantic revolt, seemed to suggest that Socialism was only a new and wilder romanticism.

Naïve the muckrakers were, but was there ever such a Dick Dare in modern American writing, so incarnate a confusion of all the innocence and lust for power in his day, as Jack London? Grandiloquent without being a fraud, he was the period's greatest crusader and the period's most unashamed hack. A visionary and an adventurer, like no other in his time he now seems cut off from the brave new world of Socialist comradeship to which he called all his life. In a period of "strong men" and worshipers of strong men, London the Socialist was the leading purveyor of primitive adventure tales. His Socialism was his greatest adventure, yet in nothing was he so tragic—and so impatient—as in his Socialism. A leading hero of the movement, he signed his letters with a dashing "yours for the revolution," but he was a prototype of the violence-worshiping Fascist intellectual if ever there was one in America; the most aggressive of contemporary insurgents, he was at bottom the most cynical. Yet like Norris he was pre-eminently a child of the Roosevelt-Kipling age, and his paradoxes were only its own. If he seems to be slipping away even as a boy's hero, he remains significant because his work, with its terror and bombast, is like a feverish concentration of all the adventurous insurgence and obsession with power that came to the fore in the Progressive period.

The clue to Jack London's work is certainly to be found in his own turbulent life, and not in his Socialism. He was a Socialist by instinct, but he was also a Nietzschean and a follower of Herbert Spencer by instinct. All his life he grasped whatever straw of salvation lay nearest at hand, and if he joined Karl Marx to the Superman with a boyish glee that has shocked American Marxists ever since, it is interesting to remember that he joined Herbert Spencer to Shelley, and astrology to philosophy, with as carefree a will. The greatest story he ever wrote was the story he lived: the story of the illegitimate son of a Western adventurer and itinerant astrologer, who grew up in Oakland, was an oyster pirate at fifteen, a sailor at seventeen, a tramp and a "work-beast," a trudger after Coxey's Army, a prospector in Alaska, and who quickly became rich by his stories, made and spent several fortunes, and by the circle of his own confused ambitions came round to the final despair in which he took his life. That story he tried to write in all his books—to depict himself in various phases as the struggling youth in *Martin Eden,* the lonely stormer of the heavens in *The Sea Wolf,* the triumphant natural man in *The Call of the Wild,* the avenging angel of his own class in *The Iron Heel,* and even the reprobate drunkard in *John Barleycorn.* He never succeeded fully, because he never mastered himself fully. That is easy to say, but London knew it better than anyone else. He clutched every doctrine, read and worked nineteen hours a day, followed many directions; in his heart he followed none.

If his Socialism remained longest, it was because its promise of a greater humanity made sense to him in terms of his bitter youth and the life he saw everywhere around him; yet Socialism, which also promised equality, humiliated his vanity. To Cloudesley Johns he once wrote: "Socialism is not an ideal system devised for the happiness of all men; it is devised for the happiness of certain kindred races. It is devised so as to give more strength to these certain kindred favored races so that they may survive and inherit the earth to the extinction of the lesser, weaker races." He never forgot the bitterness of his youth; the leading themes of all his work were to come out of it. Nor, since he could not forget his early sufferings, could he forgive society for permitting them. He determined, with the concentrated passion of the romantic ideal, to revenge himself, quite literally, upon that society. He would hold his place in it with any man, build the largest ranch in California, spend the most money, have the wildest time. He would assert his profound contempt for that society and its necessities by fleeing whenever he chose. His boat, "The Snark," to which he gave so many thousands and so valuable a part of his life, he conceived as grandly as any of his books; it was to be the medium in which he could assert himself as he had always failed fully to assert himself in his books. Instead, it became "London's Folly," and as characteristically mismanaged as his wealth and his loves.

It is the man of power, the aspirant Superman, who bestrides London's books, now as self-sacrificing as Prometheus, now as angry as Jove, but always a "blond beast" strangely bearing Jack London's own strength and Jack London's good looks. His Socialism was in truth an unconscious condescension; he rejoiced in the consciousness of a power which could be shared by the masses, a power that spilled over from the leader, as in *The Iron Heel*. His love for the class from which he sprang was deep enough, but it was a love founded on pity, the consciousness of common sufferings in the past; his own loyalty to it was capricious. What he said of his books he could have said with equal justice of his Socialism: "I have always stood for the exalting of the life that is in me over art, or any other extraneous thing." For one of his most powerful books, *The People of the Abyss,* he lived in London for months as a tramp, searching with the derelicts for food in the garbage thrown by prosperous householders into the mud. After reporting on the half-million and more of those "creatures dying miserably at the bottom of the social pit called London," he quoted with grim approval Theodore Parker's judgment of half a century before: "England is the paradise of the rich, the purgatory of the wise, and the hell of the poor." Yet for all his passionate sympathy with the sufferings of the poor, in England and America, his role as the "first working-class writer" carried no responsibility to the working class with it. He was a working-class writer because the fortunes of that class provided his only major experience; but he had no scruples about cheapening his work when the market for which he wrote compelled him to. Dreiser put it unforgettably when he wrote of London: "He did not feel that he cared for want and public indifference. Hence his many excellent romances."

For if London is remembered as one of the first Socialist novelists of the modern age, he should also be remembered as one of the pioneers of the *Argosy* story tradition. By 1913 he could boast that he was the best-known and highest-paid writer in the world, and he had reached that eminence by cultivating the vein of Wild West romance. Yet in his many novels and stories of adventure he was not always writing as a deliberate hack. He never believed in any strength equal to his, for that strength had come from his own self-assertion; and out of his worship of strength and force came his delight in violence. He had proved himself by it, as seaman and adventurer, and it was by violence that his greatest characters came to live. For violence was their only avenue of expression in a world which, as London conceived it, was a testing-ground for the strong; violence expressed the truth of life, both the violence of the naturalist creed and the violence of superior men and women. Needless to say, it was London himself who spoke through Wolf Larsen, that Zolaesque Captain Ahab in *The Sea Wolf,* when he said: "I believe that life is a mess. It is like yeast, a ferment, a thing that moves or may move for a minute, an hour, a year, or a hundred years, but that in the end will cease to move. The big eat the little that they may continue to move, the strong eat the weak that they retain their strength. The lucky eat the most and move the longest, that is all." So all his primitive heroes, from Wolf Larsen to Martin Eden and Ernest Everhard, the blacksmith hero of *The Iron Heel,* came to express his desperate love of violence and its undercurrent of romanticism: the prizefighter in *The Game,* the prehistoric savages in *Before Adam,* the wild dog in *White Fang,* the gargantuan Daylight in *Burning Daylight,* and even the very titles of later books like *The Strength of the Strong* and *The Abysmal Brute.*

What his immediate contemporaries got out of London, it is now clear, was not his occasional Socialist message, but the same thrill in pursuit of "the strenuous life" that Theodore Roosevelt gave it. No one before him had discovered the literary possibilities of the Alaskan frontier, and he satisfied the taste of a generation still too close to its own frontier to lack appreciation of "red-blooded" romance, satisfied it as joyfully and commercially as he knew how. How much it must have meant, in a day when Nietzsche's Superman seemed to be wearing high boots and a rough frontiersman's jacket, to read the story of Buck in *The Call of the Wild,* that California dog-king roving in the Alaskan wilderness whom London had conceived as a type of the "dominant primordial beast"! How much it must have meant to polite readers, shivering with delight over "the real thing," to read a sentence like: "Buck got a frothing adversary by the throat, and was sprayed with blood when his teeth sank through the jugular"! Socialism or no Socialism, London appeared in his time as a man who could play all the roles of his generation with equal zest and indiscriminate energy —the insurgent reformer, the follower of Darwin and Herbert Spencer, the naturalist who worked amid romantic scenes, and especially the kind of self-made success, boastful and dominant and contemptuous of others, that at the same time appealed to contemporary taste and frightened it. For if it matters to us, it did not matter to London or his time that intensity is not enough. There was an apocalypse in all his stories of struggle and revolt—it is that final tearing of the bond of convention that London himself was to accomplish only by his suicide —that satisfied the taste for brutality; and nothing is so important about London as the fact that he came on the scene at a time when the shocked consciousness of a new epoch demanded the kind of heady violence that he was always so quick to provide.

Yet a romanticist he remained to the end, with all the raging fury of those who live in a hostile universe. The most popular writer of his generation, London was the loneliest; and for all his hopes of Socialism, personally the most tragic. Rejoicing in his adventure yarns, his own day could not see that the hulking supermen and superbeasts in his novels, while as "real" as thick slabs of bleeding meat, were essentially only a confession of despair. His heroes stormed the heights of their own minds, and shouted that they were storming the world. The early nineteen-hundreds read them as adventurers, symbols of their own muscularity; we know them all today—Wolf Larsen and Martin Eden, Burning Daylight and Darrell Standing, Ernest Everhard and Buck himself (London's greatest creation)—as characters in the romance London tried to live all his life. Like so many novelists in his generation, Socialist though he was, London wanted only "to get back," to escape into the dream of an earlier and happier society. The joke is that he reminded that generation—as he has still the power to remind us—only of the call men once heard in the wild, the thrill that could still run down a man's spine when there had been a wild, and life was a man-to-man fight, and good.

Was London the almost great writer some have felt in him, a powerful talent born out of his time? Or was he one of those sub-artists who out of the very richness of their personal experience only seem to suggest the presence of art in their work? It is hard to say, and perhaps, if the irony of his career is forgotten, he will be remembered as one of the last Western adventurers, a "pioneer Socialist" novelist, a name in the books, the friend of all those boys who want to run away from home. Yet it is good to remember that in at least one of his books that are still read today, *The Call of the Wild*, Jack London lives forever in the cold clear light of his life's purpose. For what is it but Jack London's own liberation from the pack of men in their competitive society that Buck, that Nietzschean hound, traces as he runs the pack out to forage alone in the wilderness? There, on the Alaskan heights, was London's greatest burst of splendor, his one affirmation of life that can still be believed.

4

There is a note at the end of the first volume of Lincoln Steffens's correspondence that illuminates the bouncing optimism of the Progressive period as nothing else could. When the war broke out in 1914, Steffens had been preparing to muckrake Europe! Today, when Upton Sinclair actually has been muckraking the Europe of Munich and Hitler in his recent novels with the same combative innocence that he once muckraked the Chicago stockyards, the mining and oil industries, the ways of Hollywood finance, and his own unsuccessful campaign for Governor of California in 1936, it is not difficult to see where he learned the reformer's and historian's passion that has carried him irrepressibly through four decades of American literature and conflict. If Sinclair lives to survive all the bright young novelists of today and to publish a thousand books (and he may yet), he will remain a touching and curious symbol of a certain old-fashioned idealism and quaint personal romanticism that have vanished from American writing forever. Something more than a "mere" writer and something less than a serious novelist, he must always seem one of the original missionaries of the modern spirit in America, one of the last ties we have with that halcyon day when Marxists still sounded like Methodists and a leading Socialist like Eugene V. Debs believed in "the spirit of love."

Sinclair burst into fame with the most powerful of all the muckraking novels, *The Jungle,* and he has been an irritant to American complacency ever since. His life, with its scandals and its headline excitements, its political excursions and alarums, its extraordinary purity and melodrama, is the story of a religious mission written, often in tabloid screamers, across the pages of contemporary history. As a novelist, he has suffered for his adventures, but it is doubtful if he would have been a novelist without them. The spirit of crusading idealism that gave Sinclair his chance inevitably made him a perennial crusader as well, and if his books and career have become hopelessly entangled in most people's minds, they have been entangled in his own from the day he leaped to invest his royalties from *The Jungle* in the single-tax colony of Helicon Hall. That confusion has always given his critics the opportunity to analyze his works by reciting the adventures of his life, and it is inevitable that they should. For what Sinclair had to give to modern American literature was not any leading ideas as such, but an energy of personal and intellectual revolt that broke barriers down wherever he passed. At a time when all the pioneer realists seemed to be aiming at their own liberation, Sinclair actually helped toward a liberation greater than his own by making a romantic epic out of the spirit of revolt. From the first he was less a writer than an example, a fresh current of air pouring through the stale rooms of the past. Impulsive and erratic as he may have been, often startlingly crude for all his intransigence, he yet represented in modern American literature what William Jennings Bryan represented in modern American politics—a provincialism that leaped ahead to militancy and came into leadership over all those who were too confused or too proud or too afraid to seize leadership and fight for it.

Sinclair's importance to the prewar literature is that he took his revolt seriously, he took himself seriously—how seriously we may guess from his statement that the three greatest influences on his thought were Jesus, Hamlet, and Shelley. A more ambitious writer as such would never have been able to indulge in so many heroics; but Sinclair seems to have felt from the first the kind of personal indignation against society which could be quickly channeled into a general criticism of society, and that capacity for indignation gave him his sense of mission. The impoverished son of a prominent Baltimore family, he thought of himself from his youth as a rebel against the disintegration of the South after the Civil War, and he was determined to recite the argosy of his early tribulations for all the world to hear. Even after forty years he wrote with special bitterness, in an autobiography otherwise distinguished only by its immense cheerfulness, of those early days when he had dined with his aristocratic grandmother in great state on dried herring and stale bread, of his father's shambling efforts to ped-

dle the liquor that he drank more often than he sold, of the flight
to New York, his life on the East Side, and the unhappy years when
he worked his way through college as a hack writer of jokes and
stories. In those first years Sinclair was a foreshadowing of the kind of
titanic Weltschmerz which Thomas Wolfe was to personify all his
life, and like Wolfe he became such a flood of words that he began to
write romantic epics around himself. His subject was the young Upton Sinclair and his world young Upton Sinclair's enthusiasms. He
had many enthusiasms—he was intermittently enthusiastic about
chastity, for example—and in that early period before he turned to
Socialism, he gave full vent to his insurgence in lyrical early books like
Springtime and Harvest (later republished as *King Midas*) and *The
Journal of Arthur Stirling.*

These books were Sinclair's *Sorrows of Werther.* Living in great
poverty with his wife and young child, humiliated by his obscurity, he
wrote out the story of his own struggles in *The Journal of Arthur
Stirling,* the furious romantic confession of a starving young poet who
was supposed to have taken his own life at twenty-two. When it was
disclosed that the book was a "hoax" and that Sinclair himself was
Stirling, the sensation was over; but the book was more authentic
than anyone at the moment could possibly know. "The world which I
see about me at the present moment," he wrote there in the character of
Arthur Stirling, "the world of politics, of business, of society, seems to
me a thing demoniac in its hideousness; a world gone mad with pride
and selfish lust; a world of wild beasts writhing and grappling in a
pit." Like the imaginary dead poet who had learned Greek while
working on the horsecars and written a frenzied poetic drama, *The
Captive,* at the point of death, Sinclair was full of grandiose projects,
and when his early romantic novels failed he planned an ambitious
epic trilogy of the Civil War that would record his family's failure
and make him rich and famous. He took his family to a tent outside
of Princeton, where he did the research for the first volume, *Manassas,*
and supported himself by more hack work. But when even his historical novel, a work which he had written with all the furious energy
that was to distinguish him afterwards, fell on a dead market, he found
himself in the very situation that he had portrayed with such anguish

in the story of Arthur Stirling, the epic of the romantic genius who had stormed the heights and failed.

The Jungle saved him. Tiring of romantic novels which no one would read, he had turned to the investigation of social conditions, and in his article on "Our Bourgeois Literature," in *Collier's,* 1904, he exclaimed significantly: "So long as we are without heart, so long as we are without conscience, so long as we are without even a mind—pray, in the name of heaven, why should anyone think it worthwhile to be troubled because we are without a literature?" Although he still thought of himself as a romantic rebel against "convention," he had come to identify his own painful gropings with the revolutionary forces in society, and when he received a chance to study conditions in the stockyards at Chicago, he found himself like St. Paul on the road to Damascus. Yet into the story of the immigrant couple, Jurgis and Ona, he poured all the disappointment of his own apprenticeship to life, all his humiliation and profound ambition. *The Jungle* attracted attention because it was obviously the most authentic and most powerful of the muckraking novels, but Sinclair wrote it as the great romantic document of struggle and hardship he had wanted to write all his life. In his own mind it was above all the story of the betrayal of youth by the America it had greeted so eagerly, and Sinclair recited with joyous savagery every last detail of its tribulations. The romantic indignation of the book gave it its fierce honesty, but the facts in it gave Sinclair his reputation, for he had suddenly given an unprecedented social importance to muckraking. The sales of meat dropped, the Germans cited the book as an argument for higher import duties on American meat, Sinclair became a leading exponent of the muckraking spirit to thousands in America and Europe, and met with the President. No one could doubt it, the evidence was overwhelming: Here in *The Jungle* was the great news story of a decade written out in letters of fire. Unwittingly or not, Sinclair had proved himself one of the great reporters of the Progressive era, and the world now began to look up to him as such.

Characteristically, however, Sinclair spent the small fortune he had received from the book on Helicon Hall, that latter-day Brook Farm for young rebels at which Sinclair Lewis is reported to have been so indifferent a janitor. In his own mind Upton Sinclair had become something more than a reporter; he was a crusader, and after joining with Jack London to found the Intercollegiate Socialist Society, a leading Socialist. "Really, Mr. Sinclair, you *must* keep your head," Theodore Roosevelt wrote to him when he insisted after the publication of *The Jungle* on immediate legislative action. But Sinclair would not wait. If society would not come to him, he would come to society and teach it by his books. With the same impulsive directness that he had converted Jurgis into a Socialist in the last awkward chapter of *The Jungle*, he jumped ahead to make himself a "social detective," a pamphleteer-novelist whose books would be a call to action. In *The Metropolis*, an attack on "the reign of gilt" which Phillips and Robert Herrick had already made familiar, Sinclair took the son of his Civil War hero in *Manassas*, Allan Montague, and made him a spectator of the glittering world of Wall Street finance. In *The Moneychangers* he depicted the panic of 1907; in *King Coal*, the Colorado strike; in *100%*, the activities of a labor spy. Yet he remained at the same time a busy exponent of the "new freedom" in morals, wrote the candid story of his own marriage in *Love's Pilgrimage*, "novelized" Brieux's famous shocker of the early nineteen-hundreds, *Damaged Goods*, and between pamphlets, fantasy plays, and famous anthologies like *The Cry for Justice* ("an anthology of the literature of social protest . . . selected from twenty-five languages covering a period of five thousand years") wrote stories of "the new woman" in *Sylvia* and *Sylvia's Marriage*.

Wherever it was that Sinclair had learned to write millions of words with the greatest of ease—probably in the days when he produced hundreds of potboilers—he now wrote them in an unceasing torrent on every subject that interested him. Like Bronson Alcott and William Jennings Bryan, he had an extraordinary garrulity, and his tireless and ubiquitous intelligence led him to expose the outrages of existence everywhere. He used his books for "social purposes" not because he had a self-conscious esthetic about "art and social purpose," but because his purposes actually were social. Few writers seemed to write less for the sake of literature, and no writer ever seemed to humiliate the vanity of literature so deeply by his many excursions around it. First things came first; the follies of capitalism, the dangers of drinking, the iniquities of wealthy newspapers and universities came first. "Why should anyone think it worthwhile to be troubled because we are without a literature?" His great talent, as everyone was quick to point out, was a talent for facts, a really prodigious capacity for social research; and as he continued to give America after the war the facts about labor in *Jimmie Higgins,* the petroleum industry in *Oil!,* the Sacco-Vanzetti case in *Boston,* Prohibition in *The Wet Parade,* it mattered less and less that he repeated himself endlessly, or that he could write on one page with great power, on another with astonishing self-indulgence and sentimental melodrama. He had become one of the great social historians of the modern era. Van Wyck Brooks might complain that "the only writers who can possibly aid in the liberation of humanity are those whose sole responsibility is to themselves as artists," but in a sense it was pointless to damn Sinclair as a "mere" propagandist. What would he have been without the motor power of his propaganda, his driving passion to convert the world to an understanding of the problems of labor, the virtues of the single tax, the promise of Socialism, the need of Prohibition, a credence in "mental radio," an appreciation of the sufferings of William Fox, the necessity of the "Epic" movement, and so much else? In a day when the insurgent spirit had become obsessed with the facts of contemporary society, and newspapermen could write their social novels in the city room, Sinclair proved himself one of the great contemporary reporters, a profound educative force. He was a hero in Europe, and one of the forces leading to the modern spirit in America; it seemed almost glory enough.

5

It is interesting to recall at this point one of the most serious and neglected pioneer realists of the Progressive era, a novelist whose career was as undramatic as Norris's and Phillips's and Sinclair's were perpetual adventures. One of the most distinguished moral intelligences in the early history of twentieth-century realism, Robert Herrick was neither a Socialist nor a muckraker. He made his living as a professor of English and quietly wrote a series of meditative novels on life in a commercial and acquisitive society that link him with

Dreiser and Norris among the few tragic novelists of the early nine-teen-hundreds. Without their rough genius, however, he seemed to his day, as he does to those who read his books in our own, a peculiarly lonely spirit, a fairly interesting novelist of the reform era whose great-est distinction was his personal cultivation. Yet perhaps more than we know, that cultivation was a great distinction, for Herrick brought to the "reform novel" the resources of an unusual personal spirit, where so many of his companion novelists were dependent for their social philosophy on the speeches of Theodore Roosevelt. A product of Har-vard in the group that included William Vaughan Moody and Robert Morss Lovett, a professor at the University of Chicago for thirty years, Herrick's literary career was like the mission of those young men and women, all master teachers, who had been sent out from Massachusetts before the Civil War to educate the growing new society beyond the frontier. It was his destiny to live out most of his life in Chicago, which had already become the capital of the frontier world of acquisitive energy and was soon to become the center of the new spirit in America, and in Chicago he made his creative life—a spectator from his aca-demic window at the play of business and finance.

Herrick loathed Chicago, but he became an artist by his under-standing of it. In the immediate years before the First World War, when Chicago became the host to the "Little Renaissance," and fore-runners of the new literature like Burton Rascoe and Francis Hackett were leading young writers and artists on to the new European in-fluences, Herrick seemed already old-fashioned and curiously passive in his criticism of society. Overshadowed by the bulking figure of Dreiser, supplanted in part by the keener artistry of Edith Wharton, Herrick naturally seemed to the younger writers only a more fas-tidious David Graham Phillips, only another minor precursor of the modern American novel that was beginning to come in after 1914. Today, ironically enough, he has too long been neglected and penalized for those very qualities of mind that make his work the most sensi-tive analysis of the middle-class life of his time. Yet Herrick deserves to be read and needs to be reclaimed, for if he was anything but a major figure, he had an integrity and a significant tragic imagination that lift him above most of the minor realists of the period.

Read together, Herrick's books seem to form a canon of startling unity, for they are virtually a single chronicle of the emergence of the commercial spirit from the eighteen-nineties on to the First World War. He had a single theme, the corruption of the middle-class soul by commercialism, and despite the diversity of his characters, only a single subject, the businessman: the naïve, pushing, essentially decent common soul raised to the dignity of "heroic enterprise," the business-man as lover and creator, as trickster and victim; the entrepreneur as the most conspicuous symbol, for all the world could see, of a century and a half of American energy, ambition, and spiritual inertia. Precisely written, firm at the core, his books are held together by a solid approach to life that rarely wavered into the easy charity of sentimentalism. Herrick's studies in the middle-class life of his time were a labor dedicated, as he thought, to what was best in the human spirit; but he could never overcome his distaste for the life he de-scribed. Unlike Dreiser, he could never for a moment identify himself with the Cowperwoods; unlike the muckrakers, he had no ambition to reform business as such. He was a fatalist, much as Thorstein Veb-len was in these years proving himself a fatalist; a thinker living on the sufferance of capitalist society, abiding the culture that oppressed him, yet quietly scornful of those who believed that they could make another. This tension gave him his scope for irony, or, when irony failed, to yield to an unresolved mysticism that now seems forlorn in its abstraction. Like every novelist of the day, he felt it necessary to supply some solution, even when he believed in none; and it was char-acteristic of him to propose a change in personal conduct, a vague call for spiritual fellowship among men, that was as remote from the con-temporary code of reformism as it was from the Packing-town morality he loathed.

Yet it was Herrick's fundamental hatred of a business society that kept him going. His novels are like a series of monuments com-memorating, one after another, this man's acquisitive hopes and that man's appointed agony—the hopes being always demolished in his books with wry and conscientious precision. For a novelist like David Graham Phillips the oppression of a commercial civilization had been a romantic problem: for Herrick it could be understood only in terms of slavery or freedom. Slavery to business signified "the curse of egotism," the drive toward success as the sole end in life, the pestilential growth of fashion and greed that had poisoned the spirit. It is precisely in his comprehension of all the spiritual implications of commercialism that one marks Herrick's superiority over the muckraking novelists. The reigning emotion of the "political" and "economic" novelists, those writers over whom even Phillips towers, was shock. They had been shocked out of their instinctive acquiescence and they were determined to shock the public back. Their method was to pile detail upon detail in the style associated with Phillips's glib, surface portraits of the ascendant class on display, with its elaborate documentation of food and dress, rapacity and ugliness. Herrick pierced the conventional spectacle and the conventional indignation to present the trading mind in undress. He sought not its grossness, but its sadness; not its paraphernalia of power, but its emptiness. In that approximation of the tragic sense lies his distinction. Looking back into the past, he could bestow his love and loyalty only upon the first merchants, those "old merchants," solid, bluff, honest, who appear in his novels as examples to their cynical and rapacious sons; or else upon the modern technician, usually as physician and architect, healer and builder, who worked in the spirit of a forgotten craftsmanship and honor— love of the work for its own end.

Between these two classes of men lay the rising class of trust-builders and financiers, monopolists and gorgers, who lived in what Herrick and Henry Fuller before him had called the "cliff-city." These symbolized the achievement and the waste of modern life, for they were men of metal, robbed of all instinct, living in some frozen domain of appearance, their wives robots of fashion, their wills trapped in the endless task of piling money up to no real purpose. Yet Herrick had no great feeling for the class below them. The city proletariat, without land or tools or energy, was to him a sodden mass, commonplace and dull, an immemorial slave class greatly to be pitied, but not even vital enough to characterize in detail. They were the background of the modern tragedy, its silent nemesis, as the upper middle class was its protagonist; but there was nothing to be done for them. "Decay, defeat, falling and groaning; disease, blind doctoring of disease," Herrick brooded upon them in *The Web of Life;* "hunger and sorrow and sordid misery; the grime of living here in Chicago in the sharp discords of this nineteenth century; the brutal rich, the brutalized poor; the stupid good, the pedantic, the foolish—all, all that made the waking world!"

Yet for all his fastidiousness and reticence, Herrick's attack was more intense than it appeared. He went beyond the commonplaces of material reform in the Roosevelt era, but he had an answer of his own. Its limitations were as obvious as its spirit was genteel, but it was astounding in the quality of its purity. As a critic of Philistia, he reminds one of Matthew Arnold, yet Herrick, for all his own devotion to literature, never believed that literature was enough. He saw too much of the world around him to worship what Ezra Pound was later quite properly to parody as *Kulchur*. He took refuge from the machine in the dream of a perfect order, much as Veblen later dreamed of a society of engineers, a society run on skill, through which would course the exuberance of the creative mind. Absurd? Perhaps; but Herrick's projection of a society run by sacrificial intellectuals was no more absurd than the belief, so common in the early nineteen-hundreds, that one had only to pass a law to bring on the millennium. For as in so many novelists of the period, there was a passion in Herrick that was never fulfilled; it clouds his books like the smoke that drifts from the burning Pullman cars in *The Web of Life* over the embattled Chicago of 1894, turning and dissolving in the atmosphere of crisis and impending struggle, spilling the ashes of its eventual failure. In a sense, he was the prisoner of his own conscience and training. He could not place his faith in makeshift laws and the politics of the moment; he believed too completely, out of the fullness of a great sensibility, in individual perfection.

In the end Herrick was caught between the materialism of the age— the materialism of reformers, politicians, journalists, and big business alike—and the ethical standard which oppressed him by its intensity, but which he could not successfully apply. If his novels seem to lack some final excellence, it is not so much because he occasionally compromised, but because his case histories of American business were moralities that he could not resolve plausibly for others. He could suffer with the best spirits in his books, but he could not liberate them; the climax in even his best novels is always a little absurd. One sees it particularly in the bathos of the love scenes between Margaret Cole and Falkner in *Together*, the lovers who have escaped but obviously do not know what they escaped for; in the unreality of John Lane's retreat from Chicago to Arizona, where he is presumably a better man for building up a small railroad than in commanding a large one in Chicago; in the comedy of Adelle Clark's attempts to give away her fortune in *Clark's Field*; in the sentimentality with which Herrick described the backwoods in *The Healer*. Herrick could not rise in his books to a naked *O altitudo!* He had no supermen. The dream is always there, and the reality is always Chicago.

Chapter 5

PROGRESSIVISM: SOME
INSURGENT SCHOLARS

"Free should the scholar be—free and brave. Free even to the definition of freedom, without any hindrance that does not arise from his own constitution."—Ralph Waldo Emerson, *The American Scholar*

With the drift toward realism in letters, the growth of a spirit of experimental inquiry into every department of American life during the Progressive period, there now appeared a group of insurgents in the universities—scholars like Thorstein Veblen, John Dewey, Charles A. Beard, J. Allen Smith, Vernon L. Parrington, and others—who were to have a profound influence on the young writers who were beginning to shape the "Little Renaissance," or, like Parrington, to embody the philosophy of the Progressive spirit in their work. Just as the leading social novelists of the Progressive period were rarely "Progressives" in their own right, so only two of these scholars, Smith and Parrington of the University of Washington, thought of themselves as followers of the Progressive movement. Yet like the novelists of the period, they were all in their different ways symbols of the intellectual unrest that had already affected the novel and was about to transform literary thought. One of their leaders, John Dewey, was to incorporate into his philosophy of experience and education the highest creative idealism of his time, while Thorstein Veblen, who as always went his own way, was soon to seem the Voltairean genius of the "new spirit."

Along with biologists like Jacques Loeb, specialists in jurisprudence like Louis D. Brandeis, Oliver Wendell Holmes, and Brooks Adams, leaders of "the new history" like James Harvey Robinson, the "neo-realists" and "critical realists" in technical philosophy like Ralph Barton Perry, W. P. Montague, and that temporary visitor in America, George Santayana (whom so many praised as a stylist and so few followed as a thinker), these scholars all exemplified the movement toward modern thought in their time.

For at least twenty-five years, from the late eighties on, academic scholarship in America had sought to apply the scientific method learned from Germany, and the naturalism of scientific thought absorbed from Darwin and Comte, to the old disciplines. It was in this period, paralleling the growth of modern industry and of science in America, that there appeared the new graduate schools, beginning with Johns Hopkins; the emergence of a "science of sociology"; the growing domination of the old classical curriculum by physics and chemistry and biology; the transformation of denominational colleges into modern universities; the beginnings of scientific philology and research in literary studies; and the drift from "political economy" into a modern economics. It was a period in which the influence of science-minded university presidents like Eliot of Harvard and Gilman of Johns Hopkins and Harper of the newly founded University of Chicago encouraged the rise of scientific studies and the scientific spirit generally with the same energy that they sought to make their schools wealthy fortresses of learning; a period in which "methodology" in the study of literature was cultivated with the same scientific ardor for historical research that was marked in the development of "historical science" by German-trained leaders of the American Historical Society like Herbert B. Adams; a period in which the whole realm of academic culture, as it seemed in those years, had been suddenly magnetized by the methods and the prestige of science.

Up to the early nineteen-hundreds, however, the notable significance of this worship of science in the universities was that it did not modify the traditional conservatism of academic thought, but rather buttressed it. Although theological studies fell into disrepute, a theological orthodoxy still prevailed, an orthodoxy marked by its acquiescence in the culture of the new industrialism and quick to defend—on the very basis of Darwinism—the dog-eat-dog morality of laissez-faire capitalism. The influence of Herbert Spencer, as a leading Darwinian and apostle of economic individualism, gave new authority to the defense of business and business morality by the classical economists. Darwinism, as Richard Hofstadter has pointed out in his study of Darwinian thought in America, was actually welcomed by conservatives "as a fresh substantiation of an old creed. To some of them the Darwinian struggle for existence seemed to provide a new sanction for economic competition, and the survival of the fittest a new argument in opposition to state aid for the weak."

In the field of scholarship the cultivation of "German historical method" confirmed professors of literature in their contempt for modern literature and literary criticism, and made, in the same period that significantly saw the establishment of the Modern Language Association in 1883, for that worship of purely historical studies and philological method that are associated with George Lyman Kittredge's domination of literary research in America from 1894 on. Generally, in fact, the influence of science made for immense works of "pure" scholarship that were either completely remote from the life of contemporary society, or apologies and rationalizations for the status quo that supported them. It was an era in which academic scholars in America were fascinated by the ponderous "historicism" of German studies, and sought to outstrip each other in industry, in cataloguing, and in methodological analysis. The great works of the scientific spirit, like Francis James Child's notable collection of the English and Scottish popular ballads, William Graham Sumner's *Folkways*, Kittredge's pioneer researches into Anglo-Saxon literature and the history of the English language, Sidney Lanier's *The Science of English Verse*, Herbert B. Adams's studies in the origins of Anglo-Teutonic customs and law, all testified to the great industry and scholarship of the modern universities and were all great monuments of learning; but more than their authors knew, they were monuments to the characteristic spirit of their times.

By 1904, however, when William James published his famous attack on philosophical idealism in "Does Consciousness Exist?" the steady development of scientific research had of itself made for a growing spirit of insurgence against the divorce between scholarship and life in America. Thanks in large part to Charles Sanders Peirce, the precursor of James's own pragmatism, scientific concepts seemed no longer passive reflections of external reality, but logical instruments for the active exploration of a world which could be known only through experience. What Peirce gave to modern American philosophy, in effect, was the realization that abstract ideas, the familiar a-priori dicta of idealism, meant little save as they were tested in action. Peirce called his insight "pragmaticism," a "word so ugly that no one would steal it." By his laboratory-trained insistence on the testing of ideas by active experiment, he led the way for William James, as James led the way for John Dewey, in proposing that life itself be the ultimate laboratory in which theories could be tested, illuminated, and resolved. James's pragmatism, so often misrepresented by those who saw in it only a vulgar imitation of "action at any cost," of business efficiency and amoralism, was actually only a plea to philosophers to take their own ideas so seriously that experience itself would sustain them. With his characteristic distaste for complacency and conservatism, his belief in the essential dignity and necessity of philosophy, he tried to relate philosophy to society, to arouse his academic fellows to the life that lay everywhere around them. Far from losing his faith in philosophical thought, he had so much respect for it that he wished to join it to life itself; far from seeking experience at any cost, he wished to control and ennoble it in the highest spirit of philosophical inquiry. In one of his late books, *The Will to Believe,* he spoke to the younger generation in just those words that they had been waiting to hear from their elders: "If this life be not a real fight, in which something is eternally gained for the universe by success, it is no better than a game of private theatricals. . . . Be not afraid of life. Believe that life *is* worth living, and your belief will help create the fact."

It was this spirit of active experiment and of purpose, so acceptable to the insurgents who were now appearing in the universities, that helped to sever the bonds between scientific research and its devotion to merely descriptive and historical studies. The younger scholars, trained like Veblen and Dewey and Beard in the methods of the new graduate schools, had come to take science so seriously that they now sought to use it toward the concrete analysis of American business, society, and culture. Business had no romance for these men, and they could hardly believe, in the light of society around them, in Herbert Spencer's classic declaration that modern business enterprise represented the highest good—"the rational outcome of the universe, the ideal toward which the course of nature ever tends." Many of these younger scholars, like Beard and Veblen, Smith and Parrington, were Midwesterners; some had even been raised in the atmosphere of Populism; and they had no sentimental loyalty to the status quo. The professional academic class was no longer composed exclusively of genteel scholars and retired ministers. Younger men, trained to poverty like Veblen, farmers' sons rebellious against an order of society which kept them down, were rising everywhere in the schools. There were strange new figures in scholarship like Henry Adams's youngest brother, Brooks, who defied the Brahmin tradition by lecturing in Boston law schools on the prejudice of the courts and wrote salty iconoclastic histories of the Puritan colonists. There were young men like Charles A. Beard, who before he even took his doctorate at Columbia, met with John Ruskin in England and helped to found the first labor college at Oxford; academic rebels like Vernon Parrington, who gaily ran for office on the Populist ticket in Kansas in the nineties; Bryanites like J. Allen Smith, who later became a leader in modern constitutional interpretation and dean at the University of Washington; challenging philosophers like John Dewey, who would not take a post at Chicago until he was promised an experimental school for children to work with. Excellent scholars all, they were now proving themselves interesting rebels as well; and their rebellion was one of the many forces that were helping to shape a modern literature in America.

2

In 1919, when he had come to New York to lecture at the New School for Social Research and to write editorials for the *Dial,* Thorstein Veblen published a characteristic little essay in a professional journal in which he expressed the hope that the Jews would never form a nationalistic movement of their own, since that would be a loss to world culture.

> It appears to be only when the gifted Jew escapes from the cultural environment created and fed by the particular genius of his own people, only when he falls into the alien lines of gentile inquiry and becomes a naturalized, though hyphenate, citizen in the gentile republic of learning, that he comes into his own as a creative leader in the world's intellectual enterprise. It is by loss of allegiance, or at the best by force of a divided allegiance to the people of his origin, that he finds himself in the vanguard of modern inquiry.

For the first requisite for constructive work in modern science, Veblen continued, is skepticism; the Jew, lost between the native tradition he has discarded and the Gentile world he can never fully accept,

> is a sceptic by force of circumstances over which he has no control. . . . He becomes a disturber of the intellectual peace, but only at the cost of becoming an intellectual wayfaring man, a wanderer in the intellectual no-man's-land, seeking another place to rest, farther along the road, somewhere over the horizon.

It was one of Veblen's rare self-portraits. He put the matter a little portentously, as he did everything, half in jest, half because he could not help it (a later generation, discovering that he often affected a witty pomposity, would think his prose nothing but elaborate impersonation); but he exposed the austerity and poignance of his intellectual career as few of his exegetes and literary admirers ever have. He was, in truth, an "intellectual wayfaring man and a disturber of the intellectual peace." His own generation thought him ridiculous or vaguely dangerous, when it did not ignore him; a later generation, having heard that his economic heresies have become commonplace, thinks of him chiefly as an economist who spent most of his time parodying the official prose of other economists and designing lugubrious epigrams for clever intellectuals. As a phrasemonger for critics of the established order, Veblen has become a hero of the intelligentsia. As a Cassandra foretelling the collapse of the economic order in 1929, a satirist of the status quo and the conduct of the middle class, he has even appeared to be one of the most substantial figures in the development of a native radicalism. But that is another phase of Veblen's public reputation and the public legend which delights in his domestic eccentricities and has forgotten that he was one of the most extraordinary and tragic figures in the history of the American imagination.

Professionally Veblen was a leading figure in the destruction of classical economics in America and a post-Darwinian who adapted evolutionary insights and methods in every available social study to institutional economics. But he was also a Western writer with an agrarian background who belonged to Hamlin Garland's generation and shared the problems of Theodore Dreiser's. He was a Norwegian farmer's son who, like so many of his background, was half-destroyed by the struggle to attain self-liberation in the endless conflict with the hostile dominating culture. Veblen was an alien twice over, for he was by every instinct estranged not only from the "pecuniary culture" of the East, but also from the native tradition and speech of his neighbors. He was not Norwegian, but his imaginative sympathies were linked to the parental culture; he was an American scholar and trained exclusively in America, but he spoke English always with a slight accent and wrote it always with more difficulty than his subsequent literary admirers were to know. Until he went to school English had been a foreign language, and the young Norskie who scandalized the denominational world of Carleton College, Minnesota, in the eighties by championing Björnson and Ibsen (and the Greenbackers) spent a good part of his life pottering at a translation of the great Norwegian Laxdaela Saga.

The conflicts in modern society which Veblen was later to describe so mordantly made themselves felt in the tensions of his own life and personality from the first. He was a solitary in every sense: an immigrant farmer's son who was prodigiously brilliant but could not find his way; a child of the equalitarian and Populist ideas of his time and region who had no great love for farmers and only a vast contempt for contemporary provincial ignorance. He was not of the Gentile world of bourgeois culture and intellectual prestige, but he belonged in it; and it was already clear that he would not get too many of the Gentiles' prizes. He was arrogant, lonely, curious, and difficult. When he went to Yale in the late eighties for his doctorate, he saw that the culture he needed was not a culture he could believe in. President Noah Porter, under whom he studied, was intellectually feudal, the exponent of a culture that seemed irrelevant to Veblen's absorbed study of the industrial culture that he had already learned to regard as the enemy of his mind and fortune. Yet when William Graham Sumner, under whom Veblen also studied, railed against Porter's Greco-Latin conception of a gentlemanly leisure-class education, he could not have known that to Veblen the authentic leisure class was the rising business class whose needs Sumner preached so warmly.

For seven years after receiving his degree, Veblen searched fruit-lessly for an academic post and lived among farmers in the Middle West. At thirty-five, after serving as a fellow at Cornell, he was en-gaged by J. Laurence Laughlin to teach at the Rockefeller-endowed University of Chicago. Like Fuller, Dreiser, Herrick, and so many others of his realistic generation, Veblen had finally made his way to the "cliff-city," the great apex of the commercial spirit in America that was to furnish him with so many notes on the institutional habits of a profit society. The newly opened university gave Veblen his chance and introduced him to a gifted group that included Albert Michelson, John Dewey, Jacques Loeb, and George H. Mead among others. With its "oil blessings" from Rockefeller, its Baptist heritage, its gift of an observatory from the notorious traction magnate Charles T. Yerkes (Dreiser's Cowperwood), it was also an abundant source of evidence for a mind like Veblen's. To deck out his university President Harper had robbed the academic halls of America of their best brains and most illustrious reputations; and with his shambling gait, his inscrutable but mocking foreignisms, his air of failure, Veblen was a dubious asset. He was, as the Veblenians forget, a very bad and frequently inaudible teacher; but it is a matter of record that when a friend urged Veblen's promotion (at forty-two he had barely attained the rank of instructor), President Harper replied that Veblen might leave if he wished; he "did not advertise the university." It was not for nothing that when Veblen came to write *The Higher Learning in America* (subtitled *A Memorandum on the Conduct of Universities by Business Men*), he should have written of the relation of university teachers to the businessman: "They have eaten his bread and it is for them to do his bidding." Veblen's bitterness and frustration were now to enter into the composition of his work. It was at Chicago that he composed his first great portrait, written in fury and sardonic contempt, of the business culture, *The Theory of the Leisure Class.*

3

Significantly, the book was immediately picked up by literary people; it was Howells who wrote the review that helped to make it famous. No other economist would have thought of writing the book; not too many economists at the moment troubled to read it. Yet for all its rhetorical tricks and ambitious literary manner, it was a purely professional work from Veblen's own point of view. In his earliest essays, notably, "Why Is Economics Not an Evolutionary Science?" he had attacked classical economics on the ground that it was pre-evolutionary in its method, artificial in its logic, and a "system of economic taxonomy."[1] Drawing upon the radical psychological studies of William James, Jacques Loeb, and John Dewey, which had already destroyed the mechanical antiquated psychology that buttressed classical economics, Veblen had become the principal exponent of a modern and genetic economics. Economics had too long been a pseudo-metaphysical study of Manchester "natural law." At this time he wrote:

> In so far as it is a science in the current sense of the term, any science, such as economics, which has to do with human conduct, becomes a genetic inquiry into the human scheme of life; and where, as in economics, the subject of inquiry is the conduct of man in his dealings with the material means of life, the science is necessarily an inquiry into the life-history of material civilization, on a more or less extended or restricted plan. . . . Like all human culture this material civilization is a scheme of institutions—institutional fabric and institutional growth.

---

[1] It was in this early essay that Veblen, appealing to his fellow economists to modernize the classical doctrine in the light of contemporary science and psychology, wrote of "the taxonomy of a monocotyledonous wage-system and a cryptogamic theory of interest, with involute, loculicidal, tomentous and moniliform variants." This is an early, and exaggerated, illustration of Veblenese.

It was this insight into the need for an economics that would constitute an "inquiry into the life-history of material civilization" that
gave a design to *The Theory of the Leisure Class* and suggested the
imaginative range and depth of Veblen's mind. He had always been
an omnivorous student of anthropology and social psychology, of folk
habit and language (he had once seriously thought of devoting himself to philology). As an evolutionary economist, a student of contemporary material civilization in all its complexity, he could now
freely study the bourgeois Americanus with impunity and in the interests of a modern institutional economics. For as an anthropologist
of the contemporary, an anatomist of society, an evolutionist who had
synthesized the social studies, he could now legitimately describe his
interpretation of the history of civilization—in his eyes a history of
predation, conquest, and ostentatious leisure. Later, in books like *The
Theory of Business Enterprise* and *The Instinct of Workmanship,*
this theory would develop into his famous doctrine that the industrial skill that runs modern technology is opposed to those who draw
their profits from it; that there is an inveterate conflict between engineers and businessmen, efficiency and the profit system, the Veblens
of this world and university trustees in general.

The Veblen who had always been the great outsider, who as a cultural and social alien had always been obsessed by cultural differences,
now found that he could investigate them with propriety. The Veblen
who "loved to play with the feelings of people not less than he loved
to play with ideas" [1] could now adapt his contempt and hatred for the
pecuniary culture to a playful "scientific" scrutiny. As an evolutionist,
Veblen could now prove, as Alvin Johnson once put it, that "the pirate
chieftain of one epoch becomes the captain of industry of another;
the robber baron levying upon peaceful trade becomes the financial
magnate." The introduction to *The Theory of the Leisure Class* fea-
tured a solemn study of leisure-class habits among Eskimos and Japanese and Pacific islanders; the subject was Dreiser's Cowperwood and
Norris's Octopus and David Graham Phillips's Reign of Gilt.

Veblen was, at bottom, not an anthropologist at all, and possibly

----

[1] Wesley Mitchell.

not as learned as his display of neolithic data seemed to indicate; but he could use anthropology as a form of malicious genealogy, and ethnology as a medium of "protective coloration." He had no direct interest in the past; he always despaired of the future; but the material civilization of the present was his subject, even his obsession, and he made the most of it. His great insight, and the one on which he literally deployed his fantastic erudition, was the realization that in the process of human evolution the businessman had become the archetype of modern Christendom. His learning became a series of illustrations by which to "prove" that the warrior of barbarism had given way to the priest and noble of feudalism only to yield in turn to the trader, the financier, and the industrialist. Beneath the ferocious solemnity of manner and the humor that was only an exaggeration of a psychic habit, Veblen could now vent his hatred of modern capitalism on a study of the materialism that sustained it and the elaborate pattern of manners, dress, ritual, education, that illustrated its vulgarity and its greed.

The satiric element in Veblen's book is almost pyrotechnical in its elaboration; but the art in his prose has often been exaggerated. The Veblen legend of a great prose craftsman stems from the fact that Veblen wrote a prose esthetically more interesting than most economists in America (not to forget literary historians, political scientists, and philosophers) have ever written or seem likely to; it has even thrived on the delightful irony that he must always seem imaginatively superior to many American novelists and critics. But the fact remains that he was as much the victim of his material as he was the master of it, and that the pains he took with his prose should not obscure the pain he can still inflict on his readers. If he sought at times to outrage deliberately, he succeeded too often without premeditation; though he loved to parody academic solemnity, it was his natural element. For though Veblen was an extraordinary phrase-maker and even an epigrammatist of superb wit, he was, as John Chamberlain once said, not a good sentence-maker. The peculiar quality of his prose lies, like Dreiser's, in the use he made of a naturally cumbersome and (despite its polysyllabic sophistication) primitive medium. The ironist in Veblen, occasionally mad and often delightful, was always a little ponderous. He succeeded too often, as in his famous passage on "the taxonomy of a monocotyledonous wage-system," by wringing academic jargon to death; but the humor was monstrously grotesque. Veblen's trickery as a writer lay in his use of the "grand" style, but he did not choose it; it chose him.

For Veblen *was* an alien; and like so many alien writers, he had a compensatory need (as he would have said) for formality. The deraci-nated always exaggerate the official tone of the race among whom they are living at the moment, and to no one could dignified circumlocu-tions have been so natural in the nineties as to a Norwegian farmer's son moving in the company of academic intellectuals who did not accept him. Veblen had that certain pompousness of style, largely un-deliberate, which has not yet ceased to be the mark of the professional scholar in America; in his early years it was an article of clothing like the Prince Albert coat, and in many respects resembled it. In a day when wild-eyed Populists wrote like Senators, and Senators talked like Shakespeare's Romans, purity of style demanded a compelling direct interest in diction and rhythm which Veblen did not have. He often parodied the academic style, but with a suffering mischievousness that betrays the intensity of his exasperation. His leading ideas were brilliant intuitions, but he developed their implications slowly, so that the quality of his prose is often characterized by insensitiveness to pro-portion. Every style is an accumulation of psychic habits and records some organic personal rhythm; the Veblen who mumbled in the classroom those "long spiral sentences, reiterative like the eddas," as John Dos Passos called them, also mumbled in his book.[1]

From this point of view Veblen's celebrated irony and prose devices do not appear any less skillful and amusing than worshipful admirers of his style have claimed them to be; they are merely one phase of his temperament and his powers as a writer. He used devices and played with grotesque phrases; he startled the reader into an awareness of the ties that exist everywhere in modern "material civilization" between

---

[1] Nothing illustrates so clearly the effect of his notoriously bad oral delivery as his published lectures on Marxism, which he delivered at Harvard in 1906. "It is no longer a question of whether material exigencies rationally should guide men's conduct, but whether, as a matter of brute causation, they do induce such habits of thought in men as the economic interpretation presumes," etc.

new institutions and the use men make of them, between habits of work and prejudices of thought. But his style was not, as such, a pull-over satiric style like Swift's or the one Goldsmith employed in his Chinese letters. A satiric style is a dramatic characterization, an impersonation; Veblen's verbosity was often painfully ingenuous. When he was ironic, as in a famous passage in *The Theory of the Leisure Class* in which he disclaimed any invidious use of the word "invidious," the humor was almost too palpable for comfort. "In making use of the term 'invidious,' it may perhaps be unnecessary to remark, there is no intention to extol or deprecate, or to commend or deplore. . . . The term is used in a technical sense as describing a comparison of persons with a view to rating and grading them in respect of relative worth or value . . ." and so forth. This type of bearish pleasantry appeared in his definition of leisure as connoting "non-productive consumption of time," which was a hit, a very palpable hit indeed at the jargon of economists, and one that pointed up his satiric interpretation of leisure in modern bourgeois society.

It may be true that Veblen's solemnity of style was a medium of concealing his contempt for the pecuniary culture; but he did not conceal it, and it is an extremely simple and even sentimental criticism which can suppose that Veblen did nothing but play the comedian for thirty years in a world that he found excruciatingly wretched. He had, admittedly, a masquerade; but it was a projection of desperation as well as a disguise. The native self, and the native prolixity, often stole through. For all his labor, he seems to have had a lurking cynicism toward his own work, as if it were only another aspiration that had been disappointed. Veblen's view of the world was not only mordant, it was densely, even profoundly, tragic. As a satirist in *The Theory of the Leisure Class* he could write with almost cheerful irony of the "peaceful," the "sedentary," the "poor," whose "most notable trait" was a "certain amiable inefficiency when confronted with force or fraud"; but his obsession with the forms and honors of property did not, in later books, conceal his despair at their supremacy.

No one before Veblen had realized with such acuteness the monstrous conflict between what he called the instinct of workmanship and the profit motive; the conflict became the design he saw in modern life. In his mind the conflict was not between capital and labor, but between capital and the intellectual élite which ran the profit system for capital and sacrificed itself for capital. He was never interested in the Marxian dream of a revolution by the working class; he had a certain contempt for Marxism, and thought of it as romantic and, in one sense, even unintelligible. The tragedy of that other class struggle, as Veblen saw it, was that it could never be resolved. The engineers, the symbolic protagonists of a harmonious new world, could do nothing about it. In Veblen's view, as Max Lerner has expounded it, "man finds himself ever farther away from the sense of economy and workmanship and social order that his primitive instincts called for. And as if to deepen the irony of his position, every attempt that he makes to adjust himself rationally to the new conditions of life is doomed by the nature of his own institutions." This dilemma had the ruthless severity of Greek tragedy, in which man, like Prometheus, has brought light to the world but must suffer for it. The interests of profit and the community, of industry and business, of skill and greed, were diverse. "Gain may come to" the business classes, Veblen wrote in *The Theory of Business Enterprise,* "whether the disturbance makes for heightened facility or for widespread hardship." Modern life had become petrified in institutional habits of waste and greed. Like Henry Adams, Veblen had a bitter respect for the machine process; but he did not regard it as a literary symbol; it had become the focus of the modern tragedy. The machine, as Veblen was among the first to show, had its own rhythm which it dictated to men and compelled them to live by. The will rebelled, the machine persisted; the critical mind might quarrel with it, the body acquiesced.

Only a thinker who had so pressing a need of social change could have brought so much passion to the doubt of its realization. Veblen's distinction as an American writer of his time was thus uniquely tragic. He saw what so few in his generation could ever see; yet he affirmed nothing and promised nothing. Lonely all through a fairly long life plagued by poverty, alienation, ill-health, he suffered even more deeply from the austere honesty of his vision. Applauded by Marxists for his attacks upon the status quo, he laughed at their optimism; he threw the whole weight of his life into his examination of the pecuniary culture, but bolstered its institutional vanity. He was a naturalist, a more tragic-minded and finely conscious spirit than any American novelist of the naturalist generation; his final view of life was of an insane mechanism, of a perpetual and fruitless struggle between man and the forces that destroy him. Yet though he had what Dreiser and Crane and Norris seemed to lack, he was not their equal as an artist. He knew the rationale of everything where Dreiser, for example, has known only how to identify all life with the poignant gracelessness of his own mind; but he did not have the ultimate humility or enjoy the necessary peace. Veblen was an alien to the end, and the torment of his alienation is forever to be felt in his prose.

4

No thinker of Veblen's stature seems so uniquely free and so thwarted, so much the precursor of the best thought in his time and so isolated from it. He despised the Progressive movement and presciently regarded it as reactionary; he owed nothing and contributed nothing directly to the intellectual ferment that attended Progressivism. Yet his shadow falls everywhere on the period which saw Randolph Bourne's early papers, the Greenwich Village renaissance, the brisk hopeful new magazines, *America's Coming of Age, An Economic Interpretation of the Constitution, History of the Great American Fortunes, The Promise of American Life, The Spirit of American Government,* and the conception of *Main Currents in American Thought.* The intellectual Socialists of the period—the Walter Lippmanns, the John Spargos, the W. J. Ghents—nudged the Progressive mind to become bolder; Veblen was indifferent to it. The J. Allen Smiths and the Charles Beards "muckraked" the Constitution; Veblen ignored it. The Progressives were tinkerers in a middle-class world that Veblen's mind had rejected when the apologists for that world were still unchallenged; the Progressive mind was a lawyer's mind composing a brief against the abuses of capitalism and machine politics. Veblen's evidence had gone beyond the documentary notes of the muckraking school to portray a whole civilization. Everything that characterized the prewar intellectual movement at its best—its optimism, its boyish idealism, its inveterate reformism—Veblen lacked; every principle upon which it rested Veblen had proposed and transcended long before. The Progressive movement needed Veblen; it lacked even his sympathy. It needed fundamental values, and it found what it was ready to take in John Dewey.

Dewey's relation to the Progressive intellectual movement marks only one phase of his career, but that phase is already a historical one: He gave the Randolph Bourne generation its symbolic values— constructive activity, a new conception of experience, intelligence at work. What Thoreau had suggested in *Walden*, "Students should not *play* life or *study* it merely . . . but earnestly *live* it," Dewey raised to a principle. It was he, rather than H. G. Wells, who should have spoken of life before the First World War as a race between education and catastrophe. He created an agent, a moral hero for the times, the progressive teacher; he even proposed a heroic milieu, the new experimental classroom which he had been among the very first to develop at Chicago in the nineties. He so indoctrinated the principle of education and "creative doing" that he became the leader of a group of minds who regarded themselves as teachers and Progressive America as their classroom. He imparted a new freshness, a sturdy and mature optimism, to the best spirits in contemporary society. As a psychologist he opened the mind to new vistas; as a student of ethics, he projected a radiant vision of modern conduct. He was a metaphysician who had found an ultimate principle in the rejection of metaphysics, a thinker whose every thought pointed to a new relation between men and society, even of a society that could become the frame of boundless human fulfillment.

The prewar idealists regarded their America as one vast classroom; Dewey rose to their leadership by projecting in every classroom a miniature society. He did more than give a new philosophy to educa- tion; he transformed the very concept of learning into a new and exciting principle of life. Viewing existence, in Sidney Hook's memo- rable phrase, as "a perpetual open frontier," he had the necessary confidence in men to bring the scientific apparatus of his age and his own arresting conception of logic to bear upon them. His was no literary Emersonian idealism, though he has often appeared to be the last of the great nineteenth-century idealists. He was a child of the revolution of science and common sense, and he had that instinctive confidence in the power of mind to explore and advance its resources, even to chart an illimitable progress, possible only to one born into the world in the great decade of the eighteen-fifties along with Bernard Shaw, *The Origin of Species,* and Havelock Ellis. He believed so deeply in scientific method that he proposed to reorganize society upon its basis and to show that man's realization of his place in society is the beginning of human fulfillment.

"We start not so much with superior capacities," Dewey wrote in *Democracy and Education,* "as with superior stimuli for evocation and direction of our capacities." He was born and raised in a village community in the north of Vermont that bred a democratic faith, even a homely egalitarianism, as a matter of course. It was a homogeneous and industrious little world still remote from the factory system and finance capitalism, a world which believed in the "betterment" that Dewey was later, in *Human Nature and Conduct,* to describe as "a conscious principle of life." It was here, in the last of the handicraft-household age in America, that he undoubtedly first gained his philosophic interest in tools and personal creativeness. He was to write in *The School and Society:*

> We cannot overlook the importance for educational purposes of the close and intimate acquaintance got with nature at first hand, with real things and materials, with the actual processes of their manipulation, and the knowledge of their social necessities and uses. In all this there was continual training of observation, of ingenuity, constructive imagination, of logical thought, and of the sense of reality acquired through first-hand contact with actualities. The educative forces of the domestic spinning and weaving, of the saw-mill, the grist-mill, the cooper shop, and the blacksmith forge, were continuously operative.

"Continuously operative" was to become the mark of Dewey's life and thought. After taking his doctorate at Johns Hopkins, he taught in several Midwestern universities and finally made the great pilgrimage of his generation to Chicago, where he found several decisive influences. He had left a simple, virtually a precapitalist, economy with settled traditions to teach on a border of the frontier that was itself the growing center of American business enterprise; the best of the frontier religion of action now worked itself into his thought. Like Veblen, Dewey was for a number of years a member of the illustrious group at the University of Chicago that did so much to vitalize social studies in America; but where Veblen learned from it only to go his own way, Dewey became its leading experimentalist. He had none of the temperamental difficulties that were to darken Veblen's career, or the felicity and charm that were to give William James so unusual a place in the history of American literature; his view of life was ordered, sensible, generous. Yet in many respects he seemed to be a New England romantic of the Transcendentalist generation, and he was distinguished from the first by a benevolent humanism that was rooted in the instinct of fellowship. Not even Emerson, whose loftiest flights so often marked not the range of his idealism but a poetic capacity to expand upon it, glorified the human will at its best so generously and hopefully. By 1900, when he had ironed out his pedagogical doctrine, Dewey had become supremely the man of goodwill, the prophet of a new society to be transformed by the intelligence and dedicated to it.

It was characteristic of Dewey that the object of his philosophy should be a philosophy of education. With a sublime faith he developed instrumentalism out of pragmatism and put it to work. The act followed automatically from the thought; words like *school, experience, energy,* suddenly became revolutionary even by implication. "The tragic weakness of the present school," Dewey proclaimed in his famous 1899 lecture on *The School and Society,* "is that it endeavors to prepare future members of the social order in a medium in which the conditions of the social spirit are eminently wanting." With superb confidence he therefore projected the theory of a new school. There were to be no bars to human development save those imposed, out of ignorance or fear or special interest, upon the mind itself. Growth and progress were continuous, and if one rejected the static one found fresh goals everywhere. He was to write later in *Experience and Education:*

I am so confident of the potentialities . . . inherent in ordinary experience . . . that the only ground for anticipating failure in taking this path resides to my mind in the danger that experience and the experimental method will not be adequately conceived. . . . Hence the only ground I can see for even a temporary reaction against the standards, aims, and methods of the newer education is the failure of educators who professedly adopt them to be faithful to them in practice.

What could be more splendid, or less disappointing if it failed? If experimentalism failed, the experimenters were at fault; there were always other experimenters and other chances. The human material was everywhere, the prize within every grasp; only a proper patience and a proper respect for experience and intelligent activity were needed to excite the intelligence and to spur society on. Every society was now its own Messiah, as every man was his own liberator.

It was appropriate and moving doctrine for a society untouched by war, not to say Fascism; a society zealous, in the contemporary phrase, for a new republic, a new nationalism, a new freedom. Dewey instantly became the prophet of the new liberation, of the modern ideal that was embodied in material circumstances and could be realized by a reformation of them. His doctrine seemed vague, yet it was anything but superficial in its vagueness. How could one resist a philosophy of creative development so solid in its psychology and one that took all life for its province; one that was so inherently and excitingly democratic? It radiated such an air of health and intelligence and idealistic good sense that to understand it was to yield to it.

But was there not something faintly perplexing and wanting about it? One felt it tentatively in Dewey's prose, in the gracelessness of style that suggested, not prosiness, but an intensity that was curiously monotonous and even naïve. The stress of a great and abundant faith, the satisfactions of a mind that had fulfilled itself genuinely, were in that prose; but it lacked the marginal suggestiveness which in a great writer always indicates those unspoken reserves, that silent assessment of life, that can be heard below and beyond the slow marshaling of his thought. No one ever seemed less provincial than Dewey, less narrow in his conception of life, society, culture; he asked everything of man and nothing less than a universal happiness for his ambition. But Dewey's mind—one saw it again and again—could admit evil only as a problem, a hurdle to be overcome; never as a clue to man and his experience in nature. We begin to live, Yeats once wrote, when we have conceived life as tragedy. Many a less effective and significant writer than Dewey has known that fact too well; he seems never to have admitted it at all.

Breaking with the past, the younger insurgents went to Dewey for fundamental values. But in a sense he had none; he had a principle of creative energy. Radiant in its appeal, Dewey's doctrine made life a little too easy, disposed of human difficulties and mutations too confidently. The attention was focused on processes, tools, activities, means; on discovering the material world and acting upon it. The realization and the final apotheosis were always taken for granted. For this reason Dewey's prose always seemed curiously abstract, despite his profound capacity for realism. His intensity was the intensity of perpetual discovery, of merely naming all the objects and qualities and ultimate satisfactions; only their interior life was forgotten. For Dewey's was a kind of metaphysical sloganeering, a perpetual call to action. Though no other writer ever proved more richly how even art is prefigured in the very processes of living, his perpetual air of falling upon experience suggested, as M. R. Cohen once complained, that the term became equally applicable to everything and served no precise function save as it carried a faint aroma of praise. From a historical point of view Dewey's doctrine was anything but prosaic; in the light of his contribution to the modern spirit in America, it was to seem even the poetry of an awakened self-consciousness. But Santayana was right when he wrote of Dewey's theory of experience that it told a story rather than contained one. Like the young writers of the Progressive generation, Dewey was seeking to awaken men to reality and their responsibility to it; the real—as a slogan, as an issue, as a process of discovery—became all. He recreated the classroom by admitting it to life. In one sense, however, he offered a misleading conception of life by consciously and unconsciously thinking of it as a classroom.

It was this curious paradox in Dewey's instrumentalism—its profound realism of method and subject, its ultimate abstractness of application—that encouraged a few critics after the First World War to see in its emphasis on action a cult of "mere doing," one that lacked an insistence on value and could justify even the rationale of the ambitious business class. It was a false and even vulgar assumption, but the bitterness of Randolph Bourne's attacks upon Dewey during the war gave them the idea. If anything, it was the American tendency to ethical rapture of which Van Wyck Brooks complained in *America's Coming of Age,* the inveterately romantic and overcheerful idealism, that found its noblest expression in Dewey. This was the foundation of Bourne's grievance, and he was right when he complained, in his famous essay of October, 1917, that one could finally see that Dewey's philosophy "has never been confronted with the pathless and the inexorable . . . only dimly feeling the change, it goes ahead acting as if it had not got out of its depth."

It was only a faith equal to Dewey's own that could have made for so profound a disillusionment. Dewey's philosophy had seemed good enough for a society at peace; it had "applied scientific method to 'uplift.'" But that optimism was effective only when there was a strong common desire for social progress. "To those of us who have taken Dewey's philosophy almost as our American religion," Bourne wrote in words that were to become the gospel of the postwar liberals, "it never occurred that values could be subordinated to technique. We were instrumentalists, but we had our private utopias so clearly before our minds that the means fell always into its place as contributory."

5

What the postwar liberals—the disappointed famous "younger generation" which had passed beyond Dewey's influence—forgot, however, was that he could seem disappointing only because he had done so much, and in so many related studies, to define and project the best hopes of the Progressive era. It was the very catholicity and pragmatic humanism of Dewey's work that exposed it to reproach. The other leaders of liberal social thought in America before the First World War were content with special insights in their special fields. Single-handed Dewey virtually gave intellectual Progressivism the dignity of a philosophical movement; the others performed a series of functions. The prewar liberal movement found its counsel in Samuel Untermyer, its muckraker in Lincoln Steffens, its jurist in Louis Brandeis, its crusader in John Reed, its young intellectual in Walter Lippmann, its historian in Vernon Parrington; but it was not a movement, and the best minds that came to its support were unconcerned with it as such. Progressivism, which even at its best had only a casual relation to the Progressive party, was the ferment of a decade, a stirring manifestation of national and intellectual unrest. It was bounded on the left by Socialists who criticized it and Wobblies who despised it; on the right by academic intellectuals and politicians like Roosevelt who soon deserted it. Everyone except the stanch conservatives contributed to it; everyone except the stanch radicals learned from it.

Yet if it represented an accumulation of diverse minds rather than any common activity, Progressivism did popularize one characteristic theme—the economic interpretation of the American past, and one of the great monuments of the period, Vernon Parrington's *Main Currents in American Thought,* owed its very inception to it. Veblen had characteristically used economics as a guide to culture; the Populists, by their campaigns, had made an oratorical transcription of the economic interpretation a common affair in the West; even the common citizen, after the Bryan-McKinley campaign of 1896, could not help thinking of the struggle between opposing economic interests. But when Charles Beard and J. Allen Smith first proposed an economic interpretation of the Constitution, it was the most audacious heterodoxy to expose economic bias as a factor in history. The theologians had been dislodged here and there by the higher criticism, by the new biology and physics; but the conventional histories of America were still as romantic and rhetorically nationalistic as in the days when George Bancroft had viewed the history of the United States as a manifestation of God's special affection for a colonial branch of the Anglo-Saxon race.

It was the new studies of the Constitution, which had so long been regarded as a sacred document, that made it the storm center of the Progressive intellectuals. Up to 1907, when Vernon Parrington's friend James Allen Smith published his *The Spirit of American Government,* constitutional interpretation had been exegetical, and it had become heresy to criticize the Constitution and a patriotic fetish to applaud it.

Public opinion, however it might criticize parties and politicians, had "a fundamentalist belief in the perfection of our system of government-in-the-abstract," Walton Hamilton has written. "In the study of the document there was play for the intellect in neat arrangement, in the sequence of reasons, in deft distinctions and reconciliations, in subtle little problems of logomachy. But, as for the great adventure of the mind, constitutional government was formal and devout and lifeless and dull." The Progressives did not find it difficult to discover in the Constitution a symbol on which to fix their grievances. As it was discovered that attempts to regulate business were restricted by judicial control and the early opposition to an Income Tax law by the Supreme Court made an issue of the conflict, the liberalism of the period came to question the sanctity of the Constitution. "Something had gone wrong with the democratic plans and it was time for the friends of democracy to take stock of the situation," Vernon Parrington wrote of the spirit of those days in his essay on Smith. ". . . Considered historically perhaps the chief contribution of the Progressive movement to American political thought was its discovery of the essentially undemocratic nature of the . . . Constitution."

It was Smith, remembered only by students of constitutional interpretation and because Parrington dedicated his own lifework to him, who led the way. He was a militant Jeffersonian Populist, a Western agrarian whose studies grew out of his feeling for contemporary agrarian doctrines. More than any other insurgent scholar of the time, save Parrington himself, he was profoundly and aggressively radical. Born in Missouri on the eve of the Civil War, Smith had grown up in a frontier atmosphere amid the bitter political and social antagonisms of the war and Reconstruction. He was early influenced by Henry George. Trained for the law, he disliked it, and upon his wife's encouragement, abandoned his practice to do graduate work at the University of Michigan under a liberal economist, Henry Carter Adams. He had a fighting spirit and—in 1896!—characteristically published as his dissertation a theoretical study of money which denied many of the basic contentions of the gold-standard advocates. The study cost him his first university post, but the next year he went to the University of Washington, where he met Parrington and where he remained until his death.

Smith's position in the history of Progressive thought is unique in several respects. With the not too formidable exception of Parrington, who in his youth once ran for town office as a Kansas Populist, Smith remains the lone example of a Progressive scholar active in reform politics; his prestige was such that he could have been nominated for Governor of Washington by the Progressives in 1912. He published only one book in his lifetime; his last work, *The Growth and Decadence of Constitutional Government,* was posthumously published, with an introduction by Parrington. Writing little, Smith seems nevertheless to have been one of those seminal minds which express themselves best in the classroom. By the creative force of his teaching, his quiet and stubborn integrity, he became an example for many Western dissenters in his time. It was an inexpressible debt that Parrington acknowledged when he dedicated the *Main Currents* to him (*"Omnium Amicus erat qui Justiciam amant"*), for Smith's radical interpretation of the Constitution is its cornerstone. Yet it is only as a precursor of Charles Beard's famous study of 1913, *An Economic Interpretation of the Constitution,* and as an influence upon Parrington, that Smith may be remembered. For when Beard documented Smith's thesis of 1907, *The Spirit of American Government,* he supplanted it.

Where Beard was to repeat and extend Smith's argument for purely scholarly motives, Smith seems to have proposed it on the strength of contemporary political feeling. He stated his case boldly and appealed it instinctively to the judgment of contemporary insurgents. The purpose of his book, he said flatly, was "to call attention to the spirit of the Constitution, its inherent opposition to democracy, the obstacles which it has placed in the way of majority rule." He even began his book with a straightforward challenge. "Constitutional government is not necessarily democratic. Usually it is a compromise in which monarchical and aristocratic features are retained." After some examination of the class nature of the English common law, he proceeded in his famous third chapter, "The Constitution a Reactionary Document," to suggest—what Beard later proved so brilliantly—that the conservatives,

Hamilton's "rich and well-born," had destroyed the Articles of Confederation to write a Constitution for their own purposes.

"It is somewhat strange that the American people know so little of the fundamental nature of their system of government," Smith wrote with solemn irony. "Their acquaintance with it extends only to its outward form and rarely includes a knowledge of the political philosophy upon which it rests." In his view the Constitution had plainly taken its form in response to the demands of financial and landed interests for protection against democratic control, and it was for this reason alone that so much power had been given to the judiciary. The highest American judiciary, Smith claimed, was a deliberate body of authority, "politically irresponsible," which the Founding Fathers had set up to combat the powers of a democratically elected Congress. The ultimate power was vested in a Supreme Court which the people neither elected nor controlled; and it was significant that the President's first duty, as proclaimed by the Constitution, was to defend that document rather than to enforce the laws. "It may be said without exaggeration that the . . . scheme of government was planned and set up to perpetuate the ascendency of the property-holding class in a society leavened with democratic ideas." He excoriated the undemocratic two-party system and went on to speak of contemporary municipal corruption, "the real source [of which] is to be found, not in the slums, not in the population ordinarily regarded as ignorant and vicious, but in the selfishness and greed of those who are the recognized leaders in commercial and industrial affairs."

Beard's early work was to open for his generation the whole question of a philosophy of politics, but Smith had a more comprehensive view of society and was by far the more iconoclastic. "The political ideas of our educated classes," he commented sourly, "represent a curious admixture of democratic beliefs superimposed upon a hardly conscious substratum of eighteenth-century doctrines." His book went to the heart of a great American problem:

> A society organized as a political democracy can not be expected to tolerate an industrial aristocracy. As soon, then, as the masses come to feel that they really control the political machinery, the irresponsible power

which the few now exercise in the management of industry will be limited or destroyed as it has already been largely overthrown in the state itself. . . . *Laissez-faire* no longer expresses the generally accepted view of state functions, but merely the selfish view of that relatively small class which, though it controls the industrial system, feels the reins of political control slipping out of its hands.

Smith's challenge thus opened the way to Socialism, but the immediate effect of his book was to arm the Progressive insurgents with the idea that Parrington was to use over and again: that American history represented a conflict between the eighteenth-century idealism of the Declaration of Independence and the economic motives of the small class that had made the Constitution. Beard did not go so far, but quietly and with irrefutable distinction he gave the economic interpretation a new maturity. Smith's interpretation had been rooted in the grievances of Populism and the immediate tasks of Progressive politics; he used the economic interpretation as a political tool, assuming a certain acquiescence in its audacity. Beard's position was that of the disinterested scholar. The history of *An Economic Interpretation of the Constitution* even suggests that its evidence had been forced upon him. Though it was to give certain conservatives apoplexy, he made no claims for his method, but used it experimentally and even, as it seemed, reluctantly. He had no desire to advance the interests of the Progressive party and he remained austerely remote from Smith himself, not to say such Socialists as A. M. Simons and Gustavus Myers, whose notes on the Constitution had preceded his own.

"I simply sought to bring back into the mental picture of the Constitution," Beard was to write many years later, "those realistic features of economic conflict, stress and strain, which my masters had, for some reason, left out of it, or thrust far into the background as incidental rather than fundamental." But "the realistic features, the stress and strain," were immensely interesting and even dramatic. Beard's book has been correctly described as a tour de force of historical research, for despite his fragmentary materials, he set himself nothing less than the task of writing the economic biography of those men who wrote the Constitution, and whose interests as a class were reflected in it. He surveyed the economic background thoroughly, showed how the capital interests that had been adversely affected by the makeshift Articles of Confederation set out ostensibly to "revise" them, but in reality to create a new document that would serve their group needs. He proved that the propertyless had sent no representatives to the convention and that the document had been composed by a group organized by and for the great landholders, and jammed through the ratification process "by a vote of probably not more than one-sixth of the adult males." In sum, "the Constitution was essentially an economic document based upon the concept that the fundamental private rights of property are anterior to government and morally beyond the reach of popular majorities."

Like many another contemporary work of realism, *An Economic Interpretation of the Constitution* was a "shock" book, an attempt to make up for the naïveté and illusions of the past by dispelling them in a body. Beard had been forced by his reading to admit that the conventional interpretation of the Constitution was a mythological one; and when he discovered that economic motives had been written into the document, he inevitably made too much of them. In Beard's own mind there was no desire to advance the theory of economic determinism as a cause; it was simply an appreciation of one factor in history among other factors, a factor that had never been included by presumably objective historians. Yet it was perhaps only because he was employing economic determinism so empirically that critics were to think him narrow and partisan. As Max Lerner pointed out, Beard seemed to suggest that the Founding Fathers "had stood to gain in immediate and personal economic advantage by the outcome of their work," and the suggestion was certainly unfortunate. Yet though Socialist critics have pointed out that Beard had neglected the *class* and group interests, the general attitude toward property as a contemporary force, Beard had advanced their own theory of the state in so early a work as his 1908 pamphlet on *Politics*. For it was there that he first, if ever so cautiously, framed the theory that the state is the product of conquest: "It would seem that the real state is not the juristic state but is that group of persons able to work together effectively for the accomplishment of their joint aims, and overcome all opposition on the particular point at issue at a particular time." To say, in 1908, that a nation was an abstraction, that it was only the groups within the state that gave it character, was a prodigious victory of realism—and for its time in America, an extraordinarily audacious one.

6

It is not strange that Beard's economic interpretation, narrow as it was, had so great an appeal. For the economic interpretation, which at its best gives the historian a new insight and at its worst is mere bigotry and an impediment to thinking, was the highest expression of the Progressive mind. Into it went all the leavings of their nineteenth-century innocence, their brisk dissatisfaction with their own time, their yearning for a simple emancipation, and their fundamental goodness of spirit. Expose evil, the heavens commanded, and it shall vanish; prove the good, and it shall be enacted; we who have stood at Armageddon with T. R., fought the bitter fight with Robert La Follette, and left only Utah and Vermont in the election of 1912 to Big Business, may yet deliver America to virtue.

The reality of America seemed a simple thing in the halcyon year of 1913, with Woodrow Wilson in the White House, reform spreading its wings everywhere, and a new conception of Manifest Destiny based upon the Declaration of Independence and the New Freedom to guide insurgents. There were new tools to work with, new forces everywhere in the arts, in journalism, in the schools; but above all there was the Progressive creed in whose light one could read all American history as a conflict between two sets of ideas—one founded on the right, the other on the wicked zest for predation; one founded on Jefferson's eighteenth-century dream of liberty, the other on the capitalists' Constitution; one founded on republicanism, economic democracy, and clean politics, the other on the ebbing power of plutocracy.

In that spirit one could conceive a new history of American thought and even reinterpret the intellectual past in the light of the convenient Progressive dualism and the radiant Progressive future. While the insurgents had made many new discoveries, they needed a longer view of American culture and an intimate knowledge of their immediate tradition of liberalism. Economic determinism had been put to use by the "new historians"; a social interpretation of letters had been a commonplace in Europe ever since the Romantic period; but the historians of American literature still ignored the relations of that literature to the topical issues and struggles of American life. Tories even when they were occasionally interested in good writing, profoundly conventional and invincibly narrow, they were completely removed from the intellectual resurgence of the period and derived a certain complacency from the fact that their few detractors were mostly journalists. Though the spirit of a new interpretation of American literature was in the air when in 1913 John Macy published his *The Spirit of American Literature* and Leon Kellner his sophisticated *Geschichte der nordamerikanischen Literatur,* the more orthodox literary histories of Richardson and Wendell and Trent still ruled the field. The contemporary Greenwich Village movement and the salutary influence of Van Wyck Brooks's first writings, encouraging as they seemed, were aimed at esthetic maturity. There was yet no effort to revalue the shallow and parochial study of American letters that was so common in the schools.

It was against this background that an obscure university teacher and Western radical named Vernon Louis Parrington began, in 1913, his labors on *Main Currents in American Thought.* The work did not appear until 1927 and became a powerful influence only in the nineteen-thirties. But it represents the most ambitious single effort of the Progressive mind to understand itself, and can be understood only in reference to the idealism, prejudices, and characteristic sentimentality of that mind—all of which Parrington sought almost unwittingly, in the drive of his great idea, to impose upon intellectual history in America. For though Parrington often seemed to go beyond the diverse rebellions of the period, he was astonishingly loyal to them all, and often simultaneously. It was the grass-roots radical, the Populist, the Jeffersonian liberal, even the quasi-Marxist in him, that combined to make him so outstanding a Progressive intellectual. His culture seems to have been wider than that of the others, his education less pedestrian; but these did not show in the indifference to literary values which his book displayed. He differed chiefly in the intensity of his radicalism, for though he was hardly an unusual mind, the militancy of his imagination was such that he had the ambition (a more sophisticated generation would have thought it temerity) to read all American thought in the light of contemporary social struggles and to recover the great tradition of Jeffersonian liberalism for which the Progressives yearned.

It was rebelliousness as a principle that carried Parrington through his work. He was a rebel and a friend to all rebels; he exulted in any aggressive liberalism to a point where he found more crusaders in American life than perhaps ever existed and certainly more rebellion in his worthies than some of them ever displayed; but the secret of his method, his intensity and generosity and marked simplicity of judgment, is that he identified rebellion with the creative impulse, and that impulse with America. "America was founded in rebellion," he wrote of Samuel Adams, "and it should continue in rebellion till every false loyalty was cast off and concern for the common well-being accepted as the single loyalty worthy of respect." It may be said that he even identified himself with Jeffersonian America, since he undoubtedly saw his own image in the rebels of every generation and condition of whom he wrote so glowingly.

Parrington's own family circumstances seem to have been comfortably middle-class, but he was reared in the heart of Kansas Populism and was a radical from his youth. His father, who at various times had been a captain in the Civil War, a judge of probate in Kansas, and a principal of schools, was concerned over his avowed Populism, and Parrington finished his college course at Harvard. He returned as stanch an agrarian dissenter as ever. He seems to have been a lonely student at Harvard and in his two years won no honors, prizes, or scholarships, held no class offices, engaged in no extracurricular activities, and left disliking the college intensely. He always wrote of Harvard and fashionable New England with scorn. If Barrett Wendell's Brahmin *A Literary History of America* has been called an intellectual history of Harvard (with incidental glimpses of minor writers beyond the Charles River), Parrington's may be called an intellectual history of America occasionally directed against Harvard men. In 1918, replying to a questionnaire sent out to members of his class,

'93, Parrington responded that he had spent "the past five years in study and writing, up to my ears in the economic interpretation of American history, getting the last lingering Harvard prejudices out of my system."

On his return from Harvard, Parrington taught for four years in a small Presbyterian school in Kansas, the College of Emporia, where he had begun his college work. He ran for town office on the Populist ticket, studied for one year abroad, and from 1897 to 1909 taught at the University of Oklahoma, which he left as the result of "a political cyclone." For twenty years thereafter, until his death in 1929, he taught at the University of Washington, where his experiences helped to shape the *Main Currents*. Whatever the college administration thought of his outspoken radicalism (he had a characteristic habit of leading graduate seminars in a study of Eugene V. Debs and Robert M. La Follette), his classes found him enchanting. He had a superb talent for teaching, and it was certainly from familiar classroom skill that he learned the dramatic exposition which gives so much vitality to his work. Yet his academic life, despite his popularity and warm friendship with such fellow spirits as J. Allen Smith, Edward McMahon, and E. H. Eby, was not entirely happy. His academic progress was slow and always modest, and though he probably did not miss them, he seems to have been almost entirely removed from the conventional honors and activities of his profession. In 1923 he wrote a little sadly: "Very little happens to a teacher after he has achieved his professorship. He has not made much stir in the world, but he likes to think of himself as more or less a philosophical spectator of the curious ways of men, and discovers satisfaction in an assumed intellectual superiority. Thank God, at any rate, we teachers are not as the Philistines, who believe whatever the newspapers would have them believe."

Up to 1927, when he published his first two volumes and received the Pulitzer Prize in history, Parrington was known for little enough—occasional reviews in Villard's *Nation,* a chapter in *The Cambridge History of American Literature* that was a condensation of material which was to appear in *The Colonial Mind,* a textbook anthology, *The Connecticut Wits,* and essays in encyclopedias. His resources had all gone into the making of his book, yet even that labor of twenty-five years did not reveal certain qualities of his mind. He had a deep love of art and a sympathy with artistic personality that are hardly conspicuous in the *Main Currents,* an appreciation of eighteenth-century classicism that he used with customary facility of definition in his studies of the Federalist mind, but that is suggested elsewhere only in the rigorous symmetry of his work. He wrote verse as a recreation and occasionally permitted himself unfortunate pseudo-poetic flights (notably in the study of Melville in his second volume). His prose was even distinguished for a certain old-fashioned courtliness; but his convictions on esthetic matters, to judge only from his trilogy, were impatient and even a little naïve.

It was unfortunate for Parrington (and equally unfortunate for a later generation that was to use him as an introduction to the study of American literature) that the political traditions which were so strong in him absorbed any taste for esthetic values that he may have possessed. The influences that shaped his mind and dominated the purpose of his book were fundamentally social and economic, always in the direction of patterns and a schematization of American thought in which public documents meant everything and artistic sensibility nothing. His critical method he learned from Taine—Taine's profession of method, but not his exquisite feeling for art. His title he drew from Georg Brandes, from whose profound sensibility he obviously learned little. Yet is it any wonder that as a Western radical and sociologist of ideas Parrington instinctively took the view of the intellectual historian to whom art is nothing but a "reflection" of forces in society? Parrington may have thought that he was following the great nineteenth-century school of historical critics, but his repeated use of the term "belletristic" (usually "narrowly belletristic") was a kind of primitivism, and one that was to have a profoundly injurious effect upon his work.

Parrington's radicalism is not easy to define. He was more radical than he pretended to be and certainly less radical than he always meant to be. In an unpublished letter written to a radical journalist in 1928, he said frankly:

I was a good deal of a Marxian, and perhaps still am, although a growing sense of the complexity of social forces makes me somewhat distrustful of the sufficiency of the Marxian formulae. You were quite
shrewd . . . in commenting on my use of the word liberal. That word
I used deliberately, and for reasons that will be obvious to you. I could
see no harm and some good in using the term, and warping it pretty
well to the left. As a matter of fact, in my first draft I used the word
radical throughout, and only on revising did I substitute the other.

The Populist and the Marxist in him never quite came to terms, and
the partisanship that holds his book together is fundamentally as
vague as it is passionate. It was at bottom a loosely democratic partisanship rather than a class consciousness, an eloquent democratic humanism cheerfully indiscriminate in its allegiance rather than a grim class
loyalty. Parrington often balanced classes against each other, but he
rarely calculated the place of classes in history; his sympathies with rebellious minds in "the propertied classes" were indistinguishable from
his feeling for those who rebelled against institutions of property.
Yet for all his Populist-Jeffersonian rhetoric, the development of his
mature thought went beyond agrarian radicalism. The radicalisms of
his generation were suspended in him and never came to solution.
He responded enthusiastically to them all, since for his purpose they
were all equally vibrant and equally useful. He was seeking "the spirit
of America" in the history of American revolutionary traditions, and
he seems to have found it everywhere.

Drawing upon his sources—his reading of Marx, the influence of
Taine, J. Allen Smith's seminal investigations in the history of early
American class struggles, the works of Jefferson—Parrington soon came
to see all American life in terms of a dualism of interest, taste, philosophy, even of conduct, that had operated in every phase of American experience and was fully as dramatic as the dualism of political
and economic rivalry from which it sprang. His was not a rigorous or
philosophically conceived idea of class struggle; it was the image of
a persistent conflict that had sundered American life neatly in half.
When he wrote in the foreword to *The Colonial Mind* that his point
of view was "liberal rather than conservative, Jeffersonian rather than
Federalistic," he wrote, as he usually did when describing his social

philosophy, in symbols. For as Parrington developed the idea in his own mind, his was to be the first complete history of the whole American imagination, an imagination that had expressed itself most emphatically and traditionally in politico-economic struggles and ideas, and one distinguished by the struggle of a creative democratic equalitarianism (the words always ran loosely off Parrington's pen as indistinguishable counters for the ideal) against landlordism, plutocracy, and injustice. The promise of American life, in Herbert Croly's significant phrase of the time, was thus the great American work of art; all other works were variations upon it and subsidiary to it. Early in his book Parrington wrote, "The foundations of a later America were laid in vigorous polemics, and the rough stone was plentifully mortared with idealism." By his very conception he thus came to view American thought as a perpetual debate in which the opposing sides flung theses, letters, politicians, philosophies, Constitutions, novels, poems, even their respective artists, at each other. At bottom it was only political and economic struggles that had divided American life between them, and they alone illuminated the drift and significance of the American experience.

7

As a young man Vernon Parrington had longed to be an architect, and something of that youthful hope found expression in the elaborate structure of his trilogy. With so dramatic and symmetrical a conception of history, it was natural for him to plan his work on dramatic and symmetrical lines. He had a talent for drawing intellectual equations, and he took an enormous pleasure in drawing the strong, slow march of ideas and marshaling intellectual generalities against each other as if they were armies at war. He began with the neat postulate that the European liberalisms transplanted to America had derived from two primary sources, English Independency and French Romantic theory, and attempted to show that they had developed amidst frontier conditions into a tradition characteristically American. He went on to write of the struggles of the Independents against the orthodox Presbytery in Puritan times that "the principle of religious toleration that was involved in the movement of Independency was the ecclesiastical form of a struggle which, shifting later to the field of politics and then to economics, is still raging about us. The long battle is still far from being won."

From the first days of the Puritan theocracy, Parrington claimed, there had always been two sources of thought that illuminated the basic struggle between freedom and oligarchy. With extraordinary assurance he stated that these "first battles" had been to determine whether the future form of society in New England "was to be aristocratic or democratic." Despite the domination of the religious motive, which he passed over lightly, "the diverse theologies of Luther and Calvin" had fought each other for a similar purpose, as the Puritans had revolted against Laud, the Congregationalists against the Orthodoxy, Levellers against Presbyterians. In his first chapter he wrote:

> Unless one keeps in mind the social forces that found it convenient to array themselves in Puritan garb, the clear meaning of it all will be lost in the fogs of Biblical disputation. . . . If we will resolutely translate the old phrases into modern equivalents, if we will put aside the theology and fasten attention on the politics and the economics of the struggle, we shall have less difficulty in discovering that the new principle for which those old Puritans were groping was the later familiar doctrine of natural rights; and the final end and outcome of their concern for a more equitable relation of the individual to society, was the principle of a democratic commonwealth, established in the conception of political equalitarianism.

In this spirit Parrington went on to trace future struggles between the colonies and the mother country, Loyalists with Revolutionaries, debtors with Federalist merchants, French Republicanism with English Whiggery, agrarians with "the money power," and to sketch the final conflict between a revolutionary proletariat and finance capitalism. *Plus ça change, plus c'est la même chose;* and how conveniently it all added up to the basic conception of ultra-Progressive liberalism! But Parrington did not stop there. Each of his conflicting pairs had its appropriate intellectual tradition, and he was always ready to search it out. Each had its representative thinkers whom he set against each other to fill out the design. Each had intellectual, economic, spiritual, literary "qualities" which illuminated the role of the representative thinkers and thus made for an interesting democratic calculus. So Parrington's passion for symmetry operated on his desire to bring all American liberalisms and radicalisms together, and the result was a clear and dramatic whole.

It was certainly too clear and too perfectly dramatic. The compulsion for balance was so strong in Parrington that he found antitheses where none existed and discovered resemblances in thinkers who had nothing in common but his own affection for them. For a number of years after the publication of Parrington's first two volumes, his scholarship seemed irreproachable enough; but his facility in generalization and an eagerness to take the will for the deed have already exposed him on so many points that he looks considerably smaller than anyone could possibly have foreseen. With the advance of scholarship in American literary history Parrington's prestige will be reduced further, and his critical influence, which reached its peak during the rage of sociological criticism in the nineteen-thirties, may wane altogether. Yet it is impossible to deny the considerable importance of his book as a document, as a stimulus to scholarship, and as a frequently distinguished social portrait of American life. He often made dubious use of his sources, but for all their weakness, they were generally the only sources available to him at the time. His exaggerations and omissions were those of a student who aimed to present America with its democratic tradition, and if he was occasionally overeager, he never denied his partisanship. "Very likely in my search I have found what I went forth to find," he admitted with characteristic honesty, "as others have discovered what they were seeking. Unfortunately the *mens aequa et clara* is the rarest of attributes, and dead partisanships have a disconcerting way of coming to life again in the pages of their historians."

The ultimate significance of Parrington's partisanship can be understood best only in relation to his thinking on literature. In his own mind the scholar could perform no greater service than to write of an America cradled in rebellion in terms of those who had fought most valiantly for the exploited, the weak, the dispossessed, to echo Jefferson's cry that those who labor in the earth keep God's sacred fire. The pride he took in the democratic tradition is manifest everywhere in the trilogy—in his choice of heroes from Roger Williams through Emerson to La Follette, in his blazing scorn for the values and rationalizations of an acquisitive society, in the zeal with which he released so many great figures from the dead hand of sanctimonious approval, or—as with Tom Paine or Jefferson or Wendell Phillips—from the lingering hatreds of the reactionary mind. His pride leaped to exultation when he wrote of Roger Williams—symobl of the faith through three centuries of struggle—that "he lived and dreamed in a future he was not to see, impatient to bring to men a heaven they were unready for. And because they were unready they . . . were puzzled and angry and cast him out to dream his dreams in the wilderness." Parrington knew better than any in his generation that there is a creative greatness in social struggle and the will to a better life, and the ardor of his spirit will always keep his book alive; but in the light of his lamentable chapters on imaginative writers, of his characteristic contempt for the "belletristic," one cannot help wondering, as Lionel Trilling has said so well, "if the literary historian who does not have the perception to understand our best artists understands more than our simplest problems."

Parrington was not, of course, a literary historian as such; but he did try to describe the American imagination, and what one sees in his unfortunate chapters on Poe, Hawthorne, Henry James, and Melville, among others, is that he was not moved by the creative mind save as it revealed itself in the public domain of political and economic polemic. It was not bad taste on Parrington's part that led to his occasional gaucheries; his eulogy of Cabell and his undiscriminating praise of other fashionable writers of the twenties prove only that he was not above the facile enthusiasms of the postwar decade which saw his work brought to an end. Nor was it even a misapplied and overrigorous economic determinism, as some critics have charged, that led him to view individual thinkers and artists exclusively as personifications of the forces behind them. Parrington was hardly consistent or methodical in his use of the economic interpretation. What ailed him, very simply, was an indifference to the problems of art; an indifference that encouraged him to write brilliantly of General Grant but lamely of Hawthorne. Grant had made "history"; Hawthorne merely "reflected" a tradition.

Parrington had his formula, he had his special notion of what "history" and "reality" must be, he had his convenient design. If he could not fit the individual to the design, he sacrificed him to it. Governors, judges, political thinkers, economists, even philosophers (if they had taken sides) illuminated that design and in turn were given meaning by it. But Poe's "problems" (that is, those qualities which had made Poe the artist he was) "are personal to Poe and do not concern us here. . . . He was the first of our artists and the first of our critics; and the surprising thing is that such a man should have made his appearance in an America given over to hostile ideals." There is even a certain vulgarity in his suggestion that Hawthorne was less "realistic" in "mining the Puritan tradition" than Hergesheimer (sic!). On Henry James he permitted himself the flat statement that "the explanation of the curious career of Henry James, seeking a habitation between worlds and finding a spiritual home nowhere, is that he was never a realist."

Reality! In the obsession with that conception Parrington betrayed the fact that, like all his generation, he was only an apprentice to reality. For what manner of liberation was it that admitted the pressure of economic interests, the history of social ideas, the philosophy and practice of politics, the struggles of the masses, yet passed blithely over not merely the need of art in America but that whole world of suggestion and illumination and creative sensibility without which any civilization is only an accumulation of institutions? Parrington was a significant force, but he proved again how slowly men have had to learn in America and how always on one plane; how they could gather a few insights generation by generation, live on the periphery of one moral and intellectual revolution after another, and finally build their creative understanding on fragments. To think of Parrington in his time and place, given the spirit of the age that supported him and the traditions that composed him, is to think of a mind that performed a notable service but was not notable in itself, one that was militant, occasionally moving, and significantly narrow. Yet it is only those who prize his spirit who can seek further than he did, since the great virtue of his book is that those who wish to go beyond it know that they must in some measure build upon it. Like all his generation, Parrington gave a testament to Americans—the testament of their democratic faith, the testament of their hopes for the new age and the new literature that was now beginning to come up out of the ground all about them.

Chapter 6

THE JOYOUS SEASON

"The fiddles are tuning as it were all over America."
—John Butler Yeats, 1912

THE season of great beginnings was at hand. "It is the glory of the present age," wrote Randolph Bourne exultantly in 1913, "that in it one can be young." Out of the unrest of the Progressive period, the European influences that were beginning to flood the literary centers of Chicago and New York, the growth of Socialism and the hopes for "a new republic," the advance of the modern impulse in art everywhere, there now leaped a young generation so dashingly alive, so conscious of the great tasks that lay ahead, that it was ever afterward to think that it had been a youth movement. Slowly, slowly the famous "Little Renaissance" came alive, first in Chicago, where hundreds of young Midwestern writers and artists were championing all the new causes, and then in New York, which the triumphant modernists of the nineteen-twenties were to make their capital. The New Nationalism had been exchanged for the New Freedom, the scholar was in politics, and the Wilsonian rhetoric that was to be so humiliated at Versailles in 1919 now kindled the hopes of a vigorously idealistic generation. "We stand in the presence of a revolution—a silent revolution, whereby America will insist upon recovering in practice those ideals which she has always professed, upon securing a government devoted to the general interest and not to special interests." Revolution it was, if not the silent revolution Wilson thought it to be. Progressivism was at its peak, though the Progressive party itself (or was it only Theodore Roosevelt?) had lost in 1912. Every year now seemed an annus mirabilis; everything seemed possible. Even the wild-eyed hero of Populism, William Jennings Bryan, was an august Secretary of State in 1913.

Everywhere young men and women were coming up who felt themselves the appointed children of the twentieth century. They were given its tools to play with, its developments in power and invention; they talked its liberal language, and saw in the politics of insurgence the counterpart of their own awakening. The joyous season was at hand; new beginnings could be seen everywhere. Suddenly, after 1910, there were new publishers and new magazines, a gay and gifted Bohemian group in Greenwich Village, an eager and growing Socialist movement, experimental little theaters in New England, New York, and the Middle West; experiments in art and photography, even the substantial beginnings of an extraordinary movement in poetry. Everything from the book pages of the Chicago dailies to the *Masses,* from Mencken's explosions against Puritanism to Isadora Duncan, from Burton Rascoe's evangelism for Dreiser and Cabell to Alfred Stieglitz's astonishing new photographs, from Sherwood Anderson's first stories to the gay *Smart Set,* sounded a trumpet call, seemed a standard of unrest, a token of vigorous experiment. Reform had become the necessity of the hour, and modernity was in the air.

Who does not know the now routine legend in which the world of 1910-17 is Washington Square turned Arcadia, in which the barriers are always down, the magazines always promising, the workers always marching, geniuses sprouting in every Village bedroom, Isadora Duncan always dancing—that world of which John Reed was the Byronic hero, Mabel Dodge the hostess, Randolph Bourne the martyr, Van Wyck Brooks the oracle? No other generation in America ever seemed to have so radiant a youth, or has remembered it in so many winsome autobiographies written at forty. "The fiddles are tuning as it were all over America," old John Butler Yeats used to say to his worshipful young admirers at Petipas' in West Twenty-ninth Street, and the promise of great music to come filled the air. In Chicago the enthusiastic literary reporters—Francis Hackett, Burton Rascoe, Floyd Dell—were rejoicing in the discovery of one great European modernist after another. In New York, at 291 Fifth Avenue, Alfred Stieglitz was helping to introduce Cézanne and Matisse and Picasso to America, and one could even see some Postimpressionist paintings before they were shown in Paris. At 23 Fifth Avenue Mabel Dodge, in four ample rooms that always had sunshine in them—she thought them "a refuge from the street"—opened her famous salon. It was the entrance to Bohemia and a preparation for it. Mrs. Dodge proclaimed herself a wind of the future. She propagandized for Gertrude Stein, whose *Three Lives* had been neglected and whose *The Making of Americans* was as yet unpublished; she invoked the post-Freudians at a time when Freud was not yet well known. With equal enthusiasm she campaigned for strikers and Wobblies, for newer systems of "thought control" and the productions of her successive husbands, lovers, and friends. In her eccentric and exhausting way she was almost to the new literary generation what the Princess Mathilde had been to Sainte-Beuve and the Goncourts.

"Looking back upon it now," Mabel Dodge Luhan wrote in her memoirs, "it seems as though everywhere, in that year of 1913, barriers went down and people reached each other who had never been in touch before; there were all sorts of new ways to communicate, as well as new communications. The new spirit was abroad and swept us all together." At the Sixty-ninth Regiment Armory, forever after to be remembered for the great international show of modernist art where a famous nude descended the staircase in cubes, the "new" painting made its first stand in America. "Before it, a painting truly modern was a rumor," Lee Simonson wrote of it later in the *Seven Arts*. And if modern painting had won its charter of freedom, everything seemed possible. New names came to the fore, Stuart Davis and Arthur B. Davies, Marsden Hartley and Georgia O'Keefe, John Marin and Arthur Dove, some of them names that had been linked with the Socialist *Masses* since its establishment in 1911. In Chicago, where the famous prewar renaissance had developed first, though it often seemed, as Burton Rascoe wrote later, that "none of the participators knew about it," the newspapers and bookstores served as the centers of the new spirit. While Harold Bell Wright and Gene Stratton Porter and Winston Churchill went on selling by the hundreds of thousands, young newspapermen like Rascoe and Francis Hackett and Floyd Dell were fighting for the new books that were streaming in from France and Germany and England, and neglected novels like Somerset Maugham's *Of Human Bondage,* D. H. Lawrence's *Sons and Lovers,* Willa Cather's *O Pioneers!* There was a hunger for culture, a culture of America's own, and every new current from Europe seemed to help it along. Even the older publishing houses were issuing translations of Dostoevsky and Chekhov; Macmillan, under Dr. Oscar Levy's direction, was engaged in bringing out a complete translation of Nietzsche's works.

It was about this time that Greenwich Village established itself as Bohemia and ushered in the first great literary society in America since Concord. The rents were low, prices generally modest, ideas abundant, and the heady wind of the New Freedom a stimulus. That freedom was not to become a caricature until after the First World War. In those first years the Village was an exciting community of artists and writers living and working together. Its fanatics and hoaxers were its circus displays, "the Swiss innkeepers and Tyrolese bell-ringers of our mountain health resort," as Floyd Dell later described them. To the true Villagers the circle below Washington Square was an informal academy, audacious and rakish, but dedicated to a solemn belief in literature and art that found its best expression in the *Masses,* the early plays of Eugene O'Neill and the Provincetown Players, the first lyrics of Edna St. Vincent Millay, and the evangelical spirit of George Cram Cook. The Village was nothing in itself; it was a caravansary for young talents seeking the promised land. It was not a state of mind, like the postwar Village, but a center of contagion. It symbolized as nothing else could the successful revolt against provincialism, and provincialism was the Nemesis of a generation claiming its liberation. Yet precisely because the Village throve on mutual sympathy and a sense of common play it seemed not so much in exile from the respectable world beyond it as in preparation to conquer it. On the whole, there was as little of Rolla as there was of Barnum. Garrets had their pretenders, but it was in a renovated stable in MacDougal Street that American drama cast off the dead hand of Clyde Fitch and David Belasco.

The *Masses,* which the masses notoriously never read, became the organ of this community. Calling itself "a magazine with a sense of humor and no respect for the respectable; frank, arrogant, impertinent, searching for the true causes," it had been founded by Piet Vlag in 1911 as a vehicle for the growing co-operative movement, but soon passed into the hands of a gay Socialist group which had no policy, little money, less consistency, but a great capacity for tomfoolery. The *Masses* was a magazine run like a circus wagon. It believed passionately in the class struggle, but though it blew fiercely in its editorial columns, it printed poetry of an almost embarrassing flakiness and illustrations in the style of the comic strip. One wit inquired,

> They draw nude women for the MASSES
> Thick, fat, ungainly lasses—
> How does that help the working classes?

But it could also laugh at itself, and at the garrulous fakery that lurks in every Bohemian group. "Did you know that I am an Anarchist and a Free-Lover?" one artist asked another in a Glintenkampf cartoon. "Oh, indeed!—I thought you were a Boy Scout." Its contributors were as diverse as Gelett Burgess and Amy Lowell, its editors often as conservative in literature as they were radical in their politics. There was little solemnization of Socialism, and only a stabbing reminder of the more violent aspects of the social struggle. The magazine reflected chiefly the antics of its editorial board, a mad, jovial group; and it grew on the spirit of play. "Everybody was playing," Genevieve Taggard recalled later. "And the *Masses* editors were playing hardest of all." The convivial republic Floyd Dell found in the Village, a little nest of artists who worked gaily for the approval of their peers, not for the vulgar Philistines, found its highest and wildest expression in the magazine. It was an organ, as its editors boasted in the very first number, whose ultimate policy was to do as it pleased and conciliate nobody, "not even its readers."

The *Masses* performed many services, but indirectly it served to restore a literary self-consciousness to New York that the city had lost in the heyday of conservative guardians of the old school like Richard Watson Gilder and Hamilton Wright Mabie, both of whom died during this period. After Chicago, New York slowly became the center of the new literary movement, and it was sooner or later in New York that advanced writers gathered to proclaim their "emotional discovery of America"—in the repentant phrase of Stuart Sherman, who remained one of the most bitter opponents of the new writers until he himself came to New York in the twenties. "Within a block of my house," John Reed wrote proudly of New York, "was all the adventure in the world; within a mile was every foreign country."

Yet the new criticism and the new literature were hardly limited at this time to New York. Little magazines were "sprouting everywhere on the tree of dissent," and with them old magazines were being remodeled and new uses for traditionally conservative organs discovered. The same period that saw the establishment in New York of the *New Republic*, the *Masses*, the *Seven Arts*, saw the emergence of Midwestern magazines like Robert J. Coady's *The Soil*, Harriet Monroe's *Poetry*, Margaret Anderson's *Little Review*, and the success of older journals of "the new spirit" like *Reedy's Mirror* in St. Louis. Among the notable little theaters of the time the Washington Square Players and the Provincetown Players in New York caught the public eye, but there were brave ventures like Maurice Browne's Chicago Little Theatre and Sam Hume's theater in Detroit. It was in Chicago, where Harriet Monroe rallied so many of the younger poets, that newspapermen like Rascoe, Hackett, Dell, Lucian and Augusta Cary, Harry Hansen, and others now felt that they were laboring mightily for the freedom of the young writers around them; and it was there that the new spirit had seemed to emerge first. Part of their fight, Rascoe claimed later, was actually against New York and the East, for Rascoe felt that the Easterners were not properly appreciative of the literature growing up in the Middle West.

Whether in Chicago or New York, however, the new spirit was growing by leaps and bounds. It seemed as if new magazines were rising everywhere, and it was significant that so many of them introduced themselves, as the *Dial* did when it passed under new leadership in 1916 from Chicago to New York, in the same spirit of contagious optimism—"to meet the challenge of the new time by reflecting and interpreting its spirit, a spirit freely experimental, skeptical of inherited values, ready to examine old dogmas and to submit afresh its sanctions to the test of criticism." So the first number of the *New Republic,* November 7, 1914, blazoned on its cover the legend—"A Journal of Opinion which seeks to meet the challenge of a new time." George Cram Cook, that Greece-haunted leader in the little-theater movement, spoke for the whole new generation when he dreamed of the great art that would follow out of the Provincetown Players:

> My artistic passion is excited . . . by the idea of showing as vital, as creative a temperament . . . as this of Nietzsche, environed by American society in 1912. . . . An American Renaissance of the twentieth century is not the task of ninety million people but of one hundred. Does that not stir the blood of those who know that they may be of that hundred?. . . I call upon the vital writers of America to attain a finer culture, to develop in themselves and in each other more depth and fire. . . . It is for us or no one to prove that the finest culture is a possibility of democracy.

So Harriet Monroe's *Poetry* carried on its cover Whitman's great cry— "To have great poets there must be great audiences too." So Ezra Pound (*de mortuis nihil nisi bonum*), in the excitement of being its foreign editor, wrote exultantly that the "American Risorgimento" that was coming up would make "the Italian Renaissance look like a tempest in a teapot." So all the new young publishers—Mitchell Kennerley, Alfred A. Knopf, Horace Liveright, Alfred Harcourt, Thomas Seltzer, Ben Huebsch, the booksellers Albert and Charles Boni—were rapturously eager to encourage a younger generation.

It was this spirit that Margaret Anderson carried into her *Little Review,* one of the prime agents of a modern literary culture in America. She had gusto, she was perpetually enthusiastic, and if she was occasionally silly, she was usually a service. "If you've ever read poetry with a feeling that it was your religion," Miss Anderson proclaimed in her opening number, "if you've ever come suddenly upon the whiteness of a Venus in a dim, deep room . . . if you're left quite speechless with the wonder of it all, then you will understand our hope to bring them nearer to the common experience of the people who read us." That aspiration kindled everything she did, and it explained why she was often so prodigious in her enthusiasms and her magazine esthetically a Holy Roller. The *Little Review* turned Anarchist one month when the editor met Emma Goldman, and devoted itself to the Superman another when she read Nietzsche; at one time or another, in fact, it supported twenty-three new systems of art and at all times responded eagerly to every new tremor in the international avant-garde. Yet just as the *Little Review* was later the first to publish *Ulysses* and fight for Hart Crane, so now it sponsored Sherwood Anderson at a time when it required courage to defend his "fleshy" stories. And it was in the same spirit that Willard Huntington Wright, and after him Mencken and Nathan, edited the *Smart Set*. Huneker's children all, perfectly trained in his method or lack of one, they made of their magazine from the first a banner to which all the new writers could rally, and most of them did.

If it seemed to young writers then, as Malcolm Cowley has written, that "the world was going in their direction, the new standards were winning out, and America in ten or fifty years at most would be not only a fatherland of the arts but also a socialist commonwealth," it was in the *Seven Arts,* so soon to die in the war, that these hopes burned brightest. It was here that Van Wyck Brooks first proposed that the slogan of the modern movement in America be a revival of the crusading spirit of the European Romantic movement—"a warm, humane, concerted and more or less revolutionary protest against whatever incubuses of crabbed age, paralysis, tyranny, stupidity, sloth, commercialism, lay most heavily upon the people's life." In the words of its founder, James Oppenheim, the magazine looked forward to a time when "the lost soul among the nations, America, could be regenerated by art," and in the interesting young social critics and artists it gathered together—Brooks, Randolph Bourne, Lewis Mumford, Paul Rosenfeld, Waldo Frank; the significant interest it represented in art and architecture as forces toward a new society—it spoke not only for the ideal of craftsmanship, but also for a new commonwealth. It was these writers who, more than any other in the period, revived the spirit of Whitman as a regenerating force in American thought. Mazzini had had his Young Italy and Sun Yat-sen his Young China: might not Whitman now be the guiding spirit of a Young America? There were aggressive Socialist writers in the *Seven Arts* like Walter Lippmann who protested that "our business is to tear down this mighty structure of words, these imperial will-o'-the-wisps," but the editors, though some of them called themselves Socialists, were not "practical" men; they were the fellow spirits of social-minded architects like Louis Sullivan and Frank Lloyd Wright, planners of the new community like Patrick Geddes and Victor Branford, children of John Ruskin. Their vision was of a universal spirit of craftsmanship and fellowship in which art would give meaning to community life, and society would live by the spirit of art. Thus Brooks, who already seemed their most distinguished spirit, was also a Socialist, but he based his hopes on the spiritual and artistic renascence, as he described it, that would be "a fusing of the race." In the minds of the *Seven Arts* group, a new national self-consciousness was emerging that would be the foundation of a greater America than any nineteenth-century prophet had foreseen. The promise of the future lay everywhere; it needed only art and reason and the co-operative commonwealth to implement it. America now seemed like Turgenev's Russia—*"grande et riche, mais désordonnée."*

2

When, in 1915, Brooks published the significant critical testament of his generation in *America's Coming of Age,* the unrest in criticism was already marked. It was in 1910, following in the wake of the impressionists, that Joel E. Spingarn, the most historical-minded and scholarly student of criticism in America, delivered his famous lecture on "The New Criticism." Spingarn's expressionist doctrine—"Criticism stands like an interpreter between the inspired and the uninspired," in Carlyle's words—had little influence as such, and generally remained a matter of abstract disputation between himself and the conservatives, but it was important for its straightforward challenge of traditional academic standards. Ludwig Lewisohn was right when he complained that Spingarn opposed an empty estheticism to an empty moralism, and the younger critics—save, perhaps, Lewis Mumford—were notoriously unaffected by Spingarn's exquisite rhetoric. But the very violence of his reaction against traditional academic standards of criticism gave him a historical place in the formation of modern criticism. In proposing as the sole critical test "What has the poet tried to do, and how has he fulfilled his intention?" Spingarn blithely waved aside so many problems pressing upon the working critic that he betrayed the naïve pedagogism of his own function. Unconsciously, in seeking an uncluttered and dispassionate study of artistic achievement in itself, he made a cult of beauty at the very moment that he proposed only a more passionate appreciation of it. His famous declaration of revolt ("We have done with all the old rules . . . with the genres . . . with the paraphernalia of Graeco-Roman rhetoric . . . with all moral judgment of art . . .") permitted more tough-minded critics to expose the abstractness of his opinions; but he was inherently a better critic than most of those who appeared in his generation.

Spingarn's misfortune was perhaps no more than a lack of critical vitality, a spirit of gentlemanly connoisseurship that gave him a distinguished place in the history of American scholarship and taste but did not allow him a very wide influence. He was also a signal victim of the conflict between the journalists and the professors that was to make a cockfight out of the critical wars of the twenties. By the very quality of his personal culture Spingarn was remote from the general tastelessness and provincialism of literary scholarship in his day, but he was for corresponding reasons implacably opposed to what he later called "the dilettanti, the amateurs, and the journalists, who treat a work of imagination as if they were describing fireworks or a bullfight (to use a phrase of Zola's about Gautier)." He could not use his scholarship in the service of contemporary literature, and indeed did not seem too deeply interested in the new writers and their books. Spingarn was, in fact, the unusual example of a precursor in modern criticism caught between the world he had rejected and the new world he could not wholeheartedly embrace, and it was significant that there was always something winsomely old-fashioned about his courtly prose. In a day when the most sensitive criticism in America was about to apply itself to the new literature, to encourage its free impulses and work along with it, Spingarn was to find himself caught between the extremes of Mencken and Irving Babbitt.

At the moment, however, the new criticism lacked anything but enthusiasm and vigor. It was in Chicago, where an astonishing group of literary-minded reporters had revolted against the materialism of the "hog butcher for the world," that fighting young men like Francis Hackett, Burton Rascoe, and Floyd Dell made out of their book-review columns a lyceum for all the new American and European books that were coming to mean so much to their literary generation. Dell soon left for New York and the *Masses,* Hackett for the *New Republic,* and Rascoe later to champion his enthusiasms on the *New York Tribune,* but out of their warm belief in the young writers coming up in the Middle West and their contempt for the conservative forces that still seemed to dominate literature in the East, they made a few Chicago newspapers play host to the new spirit. All the famous energy of Chicago, the experience of that life which Rascoe described as a "huge hydroelectric plant," now seemed to go into their literary criticism, and they fought unceasingly for "the moderns" with the proud consciousness that all around them, in forces like "the new poetry" and men like Edgar Lee Masters, Carl Sandburg, Sherwood Anderson, a native literature was arising. Like Huneker, who had long since set the tone for the fighting journalists of the new spirit, they all had extraordinary enthusiasm, an appetite for every novelty, and the kind of bounciness, particularly marked in Rascoe's later career, that made a fetish of energy and could convert energy into the very substance of their criticism. Yet it is easy to understand why they all, and Rascoe in particular, placed so much emphasis on vitality and were so anxious to stir up critical battles. They were evangels, missionaries for anything that seemed fresh and honest and new, and if they drew their sympathies in chortling black and white and even ranted on occasion, it was because they were busy pointing out the differences between a Mr. Dostoevsky and Kate Douglas Wiggin, between Harold Bell Wright and a young man named Sherwood Anderson.

For Burton Rascoe ever afterward, in fact, criticism was to be a battle to the death between what was true, good, and beautiful and the forces of darkness. He fought unceasingly for Dreiser and Cabell and Hergesheimer; he fought against the censors and pompous young academic enemies of the new literature like Professor Stuart Sherman; he fought against those who vulgarized Nietzsche and those who would not read Nietzsche; he fought for every good influence that he thought imperative, and never hesitated to leap in against those who deviated by a hair's breadth from the necessary respect for Greatness. He read enormously, he wrote enormously, and though still in his early twenties when the drama critic and later the literary editor of the *Chicago Tribune,* he proved again, as Huneker had before him, that newspapermen would carry on the passion for ideas as many scholars would not. It was his gusto, always, that characterized him: a gusto in his honesty, a gusto in the insatiable curiosity that carried him everywhere, a gusto so great that he began to live on it. Out of his revolt against the old standards and a mechanical traditionalism on the part of the official custodians of literature, Rascoe came to see in that revolt a principle of existence, and criticism as a perpetual revival meeting for brave spirits; and that was the other side of the story. For Rascoe allowed himself to be carried along by his indignation and his hot idealisms; tremendously absorbed in books, writers, careers, he had, properly speaking, no ideas. It was not that he lacked taste, or humility, or even the necessary respect for scholarship; it was merely that his veneration of literature was at bottom so exclusively energetic, romantic, and boyish that he seemed always to be on the outside looking in.

What Rascoe lacked, as the Socialist Floyd Dell lacked them, was the depth of conviction, the depth of understanding, that arise from something more than courage and enthusiasm. Dell went to New York and the *Masses,* soon to become a leading participant in all the new fashions, and steadily moving away from criticism. Rascoe continued as a kind of *perpetuum mobile,* a living symbol of a day that could welcome Dreiser and Cabell as equally serious artists because both had been neglected; but beyond his struggles for a free native literature and his pride in its emergence, he could not go. "Our renascence," Francis Hackett was writing in one of those book reviews for the *Chicago Evening Post* that were to make his reputation, "promises to be a new understanding of nature, outside priests and kings and pedants. . . . There can be no wise criticism that is unaware of the new world in travail." This insight all the Chicago critics had as a matter of course, but what none of them could do was to invest their criticism with the strength of that conviction, to make their work the solid expression of their faith. For Hackett spoke for them even more significantly when he once wrote casually that "criticism is an art limited by the capacity of the critic for emotion." Like so many in their generation, they were necessarily impressionists, champions of a new literature who concentrated all their forces upon their receptivity to what seemed interesting and new; and if that personal enthusiasm was their distinction and their service, it also became their substance.

Equally enthusiastic but more solid was the now forgotten Socialist critic John Macy. In 1913, the year Parrington embarked on his history of American thought, Macy published the first primer of modern American literary history in *The Spirit of American Literature,* and though it remains a primer, its conclusions were soon to become so conventional in the thinking of the liberal critics that its value has been forgotten. At a time when Carl Van Doren, Stuart Sherman, and John Erskine were preparing their *Cambridge History of American Literature,* that "pre-war history for pre-war readers," Macy based his criticism of the older American writers upon the standards of contemporary realism. His book was, in fact, the first history of American literature to apply all the new ideas—principally from French criticism and the Russian novel—that had been circulating so long among the modern writers. Macy himself, however, was always a spotty writer, as his career was spotty; for all his learning and moral devotion, he never achieved the distinction that seemed latent in him. He had everything to give to the new literature that it needed, but he went his own way and was curiously unrelated to it. At once too old-fashioned for the younger writers seeking the contemporary oracle they found in Van Wyck Brooks, and too radical—he was probably the only literary critic who ever held a card in the I.W.W.—and journalistic to compete with the scholars on their own ground, he was easily passed over. He was among the first who now led the attack on Howells, but with his own devotion to Tolstoy and the old-fashioned Socialism, he was more like Howells than any other contemporary writer. A Tolstoyan, a sometime Wobbly, and always a Socialist; an impoverished scion of the old Pilgrim aristocracy who had to work his way through the American tradition as he had worked his way through Harvard; always in exile from the main groups and contemptuous of the popular prizes—Macy re-

mained a curiously lonely figure, and one whose best work now has to
be recovered in fragments.

Yet up to Brooks and Randolph Bourne, no other critic of the time
possessed in equal measure the humanism and depth of moral understanding that were needed to complement the enthusiastic aggressiveness of the new criticism. For Macy's great distinction, particularly
at a time when in their triumph so many liberal young critics were
to forget that it is not by doctrine that criticism lives, was that he had
rich personal resources. He believed in Socialism as few American
critics since have had the ardor to believe in anything; yet while he
was never tricked by his Socialism into the insensitive thinking on
literature that became so current in the nineteen-thirties, he never
abandoned his hope that the coming new literature in America would
find its base in the hope of a workers' world. He was the kind of
Socialist critic who recognized the greatness of D. H. Lawrence's
spirit from the first, but devoted a large part of his efforts to lecturing directly to workers' groups; yet for all his enthusiasms for modern
European literature, his impulsiveness, and his personal audacities, he
seemed to stand outside the new groups that were coming up.

Macy was, of course, anything but a great critic; but it is significant
that his influence, even in the twenties when he served for a time as
literary editor of the "new" *Nation*, was felt more by workers in
trade-union halls than by the new critics. He did not write enough,
or with sufficient persistence and care, and for many personal reasons,
despite his abilities, could not rise to leadership. Yet there was an intensity in Macy so powerful that he should be remembered as one of
the light-bringers in American criticism. He knew what was going
on so well that with Van Wyck Brooks he was one of the few before
the First World War who forecast the satiric writing of the twenties.
Read today, the essays in *The Spirit of American Literature* seem occasionally overbitter yet startling in their fervor. "The whole country
is crying out for those who will record it, satirize it, chant it," he
wrote in his book, and pleaded for an end of the sweetness and romantic illusions that were choking popular taste. Perhaps the best
of Macy is to be found in his essay on Tolstoy in his collection *The
Critical Game,* an essay which ends: "His work is not done, his books

cannot be outgrown, until every one of us looks at the facts honestly
and cries with him: 'It is impossible to live so! It is impossible to live
so!'" Yet his resolution was not equal to his insight; he whispered
solemn truths, and hoped that the whole country would echo them.
Instead the young generation—that famous "younger generation"
that was to make history in the twenties—now found all its prewar
idealism expressed, its long-awaited affirmation established, in *America's Coming of Age.*

The Van Wyck Brooks who published that work at twenty-nine
had prepared interestingly for it. At twenty-two, just out of Harvard,
he published in London a deceptively languorous dialogue, *The Wine
of the Puritans,* that suggested in an Oxford drawl the main tenor of
the criticism of American materialism that was to make him famous.
"We are all grown-up in America," he lamented, "we are the most
grown-up race in the world." America had never enjoyed a childhood,
and the struggle to survive in a new world had left neither time nor
heart for the cultivation "of those instincts and sensibilities which
produce a genial superiority to the hard facts of life. . . . For most of
us living means getting a living. We never think what life is—we are
continually intent upon what life brings." And in a sensitive study of
John Addington Symonds, published in 1914, he revealed his own preoccupation with the esthetic ideal that he was to oppose—using that
ideal as a symbol of the creative mind—to the tradition of an acquisitive society. Early in life Brooks seems to have become fascinated, out of
his misanthropy before American life, by the great failures, and with
his almost excessive sympathy he was soon to find them everywhere—
first in a tragic dilettante like Symonds, and later, through his translations of Amiel and his books on Mark Twain and Henry James, in
a vast throng of the defeated whom he upheld because they were the
victims of a hostile commercial civilization. But with that same passion
for the ideal standard that he was later to find in Emerson and the
leading figures in the "flowering" of New England, he now opposed
to these failures the lives of the great nineteenth-century prophets—
Ruskin and William Morris, Nietzsche and Tolstoy. The ideal writer,
as Brooks conceived him, was one who neither escaped from con-

temporary civilization nor was acquiescent to it. So in Morris, the leading idol of this young Socialist critic, there was a great example for American writers to follow, for Morris had tried to rise above the new industrial society, to work toward an esthetic commonwealth in which equality and workmanship would bring a new fellowship. Between these two types, the vanquished and the great modern humanists, lay the type of writer whom Brooks found everywhere in the history of modern American life—the unhappy artists who compromised with materialism and in the end sacrificed everything to it.

It was not merely as an indictment of American life, therefore, that Brooks offered his *America's Coming of Age.* His was a call to arms, a call to writers to assert their belief in themselves and their ability to rise above the ensnaring materialism that seemed to dominate American life. He had taken for his own Stendhal's pronouncement—"One is inclined to say that the source of sensibility is dried up in this people [the Americans]. They are just, they are reasonable, but they are not happy"—and more than any other critic of the day, he furnished a concrete analysis of the subjection of American thought to commercialism. American life, Brooks suggested, had fallen too long between the "lowbrow" and the "highbrow," between the entrepreneur who knew nothing but acquisition and the intellectual who in his revulsion or isolation was out of the stream of life in America; between the spirit of Franklin, with Poor Richard's catchpenny ethic, and Jonathan Edwards's glacially cold and remote theology. More, the national history had become a history of commercialism; the strongest and most adroit minds were to be found not in literature, but in business. "In the back of its mind lies heaven knows what world of poetry, hidden away, too inaccessible, too intangible, too unreal in fact ever to be brought out into the open, or to serve, as the poetry of life should serve, in harnessing thought and action together, turning life into a disinterested adventure." The intellectuals had no acquaintance with reality in America; the realists, the businessmen, had made their reality a tyrannical and oppressive force over everyone else.

What Brooks was saying, then, and with all the ardor and "uplift" so characteristic of the Progressive period, was that the acquisitive and creative instincts were at war, and must always remain so. It was not until after the First World War, when the spirit of disillusionment had set in, that the conflict seemed tragic. At the moment Brooks gave his generation not only a more felicitous rendering of the first principles in which they already believed, but the suggestion of a faith to fight for. Literary criticism, as he was to write a little later, "is always impelled sooner or later to become social criticism . . . because the future of our literature and art depends upon the wholesale reconstruction of a social life all the elements of which are as if united in a sort of conspiracy against the growth and freedom of the spirit." *Wholesale reconstruction of a social life . . . turning life into a dis interested adventure.* There spoke all the fine fervent idealism of the new spirit, and by his tone of lofty intensity Brooks gave a new dignity, based upon his own brilliant and seemingly comprehensive analysis of the past, to the long-restive irritation with American capitalist society. He summoned writers eloquently, as only a prewar critic could have done, to a new task based upon a national need. What Brooks called the long baccalaureate sermon of American literature in the past, with its mechanical optimism and its remoteness from the modern problem, had come to an end. Even the tinkering reformism of Progressivism represented a vain compromise. A new possessiveness was needed, a new development of artistic personality in America; and it was to be a possessiveness not of things and wealth, but of the spirit.

Yet what that spirit was to be Brooks left unsaid. He supposed, as so many social critics had supposed before him, that to march forth as to battle against the Philistines was to leave the writer victorious over them. When he complained that American literature had always lacked "a certain density, a certain weight and richness, a certain poignancy, a 'something far more deeply interfused,'" he was brilliantly right; but the very vagueness of his optimism suggests, as his later books were to prove, that though Brooks could be an incandescent critic, he was also a magnificently sentimental one. His great service, like that of all his generation in criticism, was to inspire American writers with the European sense of art; but the directness of his attack on native standards also led him to associate everything at home with an absolute standard of European achievement. He was a Ruskin come alive in New York in 1915, a sensitive, dynamic, brilliant young American who had found his standards in the great Victorian critics of materialism. But if he had Ruskin's elevation, he had also a certain want of toughness and humor that blinded him to the human imponderables that lay beyond theory. It was all very well for Brooks to break sharply with the past and to reveal how little the nineteenth-century writers had served their twentieth-century descendants. But what was that "certain richness"? What did it mean to American literature in terms of a frontier humor which Europe had not known, or a coonskin democracy, or Western agrarianism, or sectional differences? Brooks had established his analysis upon symbols, and he trusted them too well. The Puritan, who was now coming to seem the enemy of the new freedom in art, was his first symbol; his pioneer, coarse and humorless and greedy, was another; the conventional business type, energetic and brazen but only half alive, was still another. Brooks had looked at the nineteenth century in America not as a complex story of a people's growth out of the wilderness, but as a divergence from the European standard. Lowell had failed, but Morris had not; Poe had failed, but Shelley had not. Brooks assumed that the life of the spirit lay everywhere just waiting to be tapped, and that only the brutishness of life had corrupted it. Did a writer, then, need nothing more than hostility to the acquisitive spirit to rise to his own liberation?

Twenty years later Brooks was to remember his first essays with a certain pain that anyone could still be convinced by them in their entirety. Not only had the modern movement long since established itself, but Brooks himself was now turning away from that movement to recite the forgotten greatness of the nineteenth-century writers against whom he had once led the attack. The nineteen-thirties apparently needed Emerson where 1915 could not even locate him. Yet looking back on Brooks's early criticism against the background of that brave new world of Progressive optimism, it is not hard to see why his influence was at once salutary and unfortunate. By his insurgent conception of American culture, Brooks gave the new writers a faith, a standard of reference; he helped them to characterize the world they lived in and to give a character to their ambition. But when the First World War was over, Brooks's complaint against life in America became everything; his summons to action was forgotten, as he himself had to forget it. What happened then was that all that was weakest and most humorless in Brooks's thought became the staple of the new disillusionment. Where he had decried the past, some of his followers now merely wept over it; where he had summoned them to "spiritual pioneering," they now all thought of themselves as a race of Amiels, Symondses, and Henry Jameses—victims and magnificent failures.

If after the war Brooks's grim interpretation of American life became the formula of many nihilists, before the war it encouraged a significant belief in a new citizenship. In Brooks's wake there appeared a new type of critical personality in America—the sensitive social impressionist, like Randolph Bourne, Waldo Frank, Lewis Mumford, who was at once the exponent of a new literature and of a brave new community—that famous "organic" community which was to dazzle Frank in the dream of "wholeness" forever after. Protégés at once of Alfred Stieglitz, who gave them their ideal of craftsmanship, and of Brooks, who gave them their conception of American society, they joined the idealism of the Progressive period to the call to comradeship in Whitman—Bourne's favorite prophet. Here were the new ideas of social planning and architecture that Lewis Mumford was to embody in his early book on the history of Utopias and his later works on industrial techniques and the modern city as a work of art. In these critics, indeed, all the great hopes of the prewar period, the whole drive toward a new functionalism which would take society as well as art for its province, came together; and in no one did "the promise of American life" shine so radiantly as in Randolph Bourne.

Bourne owed less to Brooks, perhaps, than he did to John Dewey and a certain literary idealism in the Progressive period which he personified, but Brooks gave his interest in criticism a direction and influenced it by his technique. Above all Bourne was the perfect child of the prewar Enlightenment; when its light went out in 1918, he died with it. Afterward his story seemed so much the martyrology of his generation that the writer was lost in the victim. Yet even when one goes back to Bourne's books—not merely his bitter and posthumously published collections of essays, but his early studies of contemporary youth, education, and politics—it is not hard to see why Bourne must always seem less a writer than the incarnation of his time. For from his first book, *Youth and Life,* to the *Impressions of Europe* which he wrote on a fellowship abroad and his books on education and the Gary schools, Bourne proved himself so inexpressibly confident of a future established on the evangelicisms of his period, so radiant in his championship of pragmatism, art, reason, European social democracy, and the experimental school, that he now seems a seismograph on which were recorded the greatest hopes and fiercest despairs of his time. No other critic in his period wrote so little about himself, or had, as it were, so little interest in himself. His books were always selfless; they were reports on the great developments of the day. He was not a great writer; he died too young to be even a complete writer; but carried along by his ardent belief in the modern spirit, he made himself an extraordinarily keen and sympathetic observer. Everywhere, as it seems on reading his *Impressions of Europe, 1913-1914,* he found men as eager, as open-hearted, as himself; everywhere he saw "the sense in these countries of the most advanced civilization, yet without sophistication, a luminous modern intelligence that selected and controlled and did not allow itself to be overwhelmed by the chaos of twentieth-century possibility."

Youth alone, he had written in his first book, *Youth and Life,* has all the really valuable experience, for it is youth which has constantly to meet new situations and react to new aspects of life. "It is only the interpretation of this first collision with life that is worth anything." He protested against those who would make youth too humble, who would bind it to conventional traditions; and he protested in the same spirit against those who were so absorbed in their own careers that they missed the gaiety of life and what seemed to him, despite his own crippled body and his poverty, its great promise. "I always have a suspicion of boys who talk of planning their lives. I feel that they have won a precocious maturity in some illegitimate way." When he went to the *New Republic,* he wrote, out of the sublime faith of the instrumentalism that John Dewey had burned into his mind, that "genuine opinion is scientific hypotheses to be tested and revised as experience widens." Two years later the Randolph Bourne who died amidst the fusillades of war, bitterly opposed to what seemed to him the defection of the intellectuals from their own standards, cried "War is the health of the state." But it was not of the state that he was writing with such terrible bitterness at the end; it was the decline and fall of the Progressive ideal. He described in terms of his own experience the fate of the Progressive idealist in a world overrun by war, a world of which the high hopes of 1910-17 had given no warning, a world to which reason and art and the experimental school alone could give no clue. He had spent his life seeking the American promise as his education had prepared him to understand it; and when the war came it seemed to him that his education had betrayed him. "These secular goods, connected with the enhancement of life, the education of man and the use of the intelligence to realize reason and beauty in the nation's communal living," he wrote with what was almost his last breath, "are alien to our traditional ideal of the State. The State is intimately connected with war, for it is the organization of the collective community when it acts in a political manner, and to act in a political manner towards a rival group has meant, throughout all history—war."

In any event, the opening phase in the search for reality was over.

Part II: THE GREAT LIBERATION
(1918-1929)

"It is evident, is it not, that we have risen culturally in the world, as the world indeed has not been slow to admit, and that the golden age of American literature is, happily for us who live in it, the present age?"—LUDWIG LEWISOHN, *Expression in America*

Chapter 7

THE POSTWAR SCENE

"Stabilize America first, prosper America first, think of America first, exalt America first!"—WARREN G. HARDING, 1920

"After such knowledge, what forgiveness?"—T. S. ELIOT, *Gerontion*, 1920

FOR Americans who stayed at home—and for many who did not—the First World War had a certain unreality that has ever since made it seem more remote, and always less interesting, than the Civil War. When the shot was fired at Sarajevo on that quiet summer day in 1914, the United States was at the peak of the Progressive effort. William Jennings Bryan was Secretary of State, but dividing his time equally between Chautauqua and the diplomatic mill. Wilhelm Hohenzollern seemed an absurd and grandiloquent figure in the traditional buffoonery of European statecraft, much given to talking of his special affection for God and his friendship with his Cousin Nicholas of Russia. Carter Glass's Federal Reserve Act loomed larger than the Triple Entente, the Wilson Administration was drawing a deep breath after its first whirlwind year of reform, social workers and reformers were everywhere in government, propagating sweetness and light and the secret ballot. The Europe of immemorial scandals and alarums, of war and aggrandizement, seemed light-years away.

It was somehow Europe's war almost to the very end; and when America entered it, there was a popular suspicion that the government of Imperial Germany bore a marked resemblance to Tammany Hall. In one sense the war was even the last great skirmish in the battle for People's Rights. As the direct primary had been won, the wickedness of the great trusts exposed, so were the bosses in the Wilhelmstrasse to be removed, and all governments everywhere to be restored to the people. The slogans that helped to bring Woodrow Wilson to the White House in 1913 sufficed in part at Versailles in 1919, and if the mapmakers of a new world had never heard of the New Freedom— "Is it Upper or Lower Silesia that we are giving away?" an American journalist reports having heard Lloyd George ask his secretary at the Peace Conference—that fact persuaded many Americans that it *had* been Europe's war after all. It was Europe that had suffered the war, where Americans had merely participated in it; it was Europe that now lay paralytic after four shattering years, where Americans were merely disillusioned by the aftermath; and most significantly, it was Europe that came out of the war only to enter upon the Fascist agony, where America now emerged completely as a dominant World Power.

Everywhere in the Western world now two nations, two communities of men, gazed at each other in silent bitterness and mistrust— those who had known what the war was for, and those who were broken by it; those who had "made" the peace and those who found it difficult to recover from the war. Yet nowhere was that division of interest and belief so marked as in the cleavage between America and Europe. In Europe the war had ended in a general impoverishment and exhaustion, in a despair which, when piled up with so many despairs through the twenties, was to lead straight into the final desperation of Fascism; in the timid ineffectual reformism of one generation, and the catastrophic nihilism of another; in the cynicism and brutality of a culture increasingly skeptical of culture, increasingly scornful of democracy and the democratic hope. To millions of Americans, however, the world of 1920 seemed merely richer and more comfortable, if less naïve, than the world of 1914. With D. H. Lawrence, European writers cried: *"Look! We Have Come Through!"* But as they were to learn soon enough, they had come through only to fight for their survival; they had come through to a growing sickness among men in Europe, a spiritual sickness as well as a social despair, that contrasted strangely with the gaiety and recklessness of society in America and the triumphant self-discovery which dominated the new literature there.

Here, for Europeans too weary to care too much and for Americans too excited to be conscious of all its implications, was the final irony of the war, if any was needed: The period which was marked abroad first by a feverish experimentalism and then by a growing incommunicable sense of the common European tragedy was the same period which saw the public triumph of modern American literature at home. In his bitter war diary for 1917, Randolph Bourne had written darkly, thinking himself a prophet of disaster: "The war . . . or American promise! One must choose. . . . For the effect of the war will be to impoverish American promise." Now the war was over, and if "the promise of American life," as Bourne and his generation had been prepared to understand it, had died in the war, a different kind of promise had come in its place. Something in American life had gone out with the war, as Bourne and all he represented had gone down in it: a contagious idealism, the dream of a new community in America, all the tokens of that brave and expectant fraternalism which had at one period marked the emergence of the modern spirit in America. But the literature of criticism and revolt that Bourne and Mencken had helped to build together before the war, the movement which had proclaimed as its first principle *Place aux jeunes!*—Make way for the Younger Generation!—that movement had not only not died in the war; it had been given a strange new vigor and direction by the restlessness that came after it. In Europe many brilliant young writers had been killed and many older writers morally shattered; in America the heady, booming, half-comic world the war introduced gave modern writers a prominence, a heedlessness, a boisterous pride in their liberation from convention, that was to enter into the very substance of their work. If it was America that "had won the war for Europe," as the popular legend had it, it was the new American literature, seizing the vitality that was left in the world, that made the victory its own.

It was above all this sense of release that came to American writers after the war, the exhilaration of the sudden freedoms they had won with the dissolution of the old order and the proverbial American

colonialism, that now gave so distinctive a tone to the new literature.
It was as if the writers themselves, like so many representative classes
in American society, were for the first time feeling their oats, creeping
out of the old parochial shelters and the old parochial ambitions; and
with their release there came a carefree irresponsibility, a gaiety, a
youthful perkiness, that gave comic undertones to their growling dis-
satisfactions with American society. Never in all history, as Edmund
Wilson said, did a literary generation so revile its country; and never,
as Mencken proved so unforgettably, was the abuse so innocent or so
enjoyable. Fundamentally, of course, they were in their different ways
all enemies of the conventional middle-class order, enemies of convention and Puritanism, members of the "civilized minority," rebels
against all that conspired to keep down the values of art and thought.
But they were at the same time children of the new boom world, the
gay exploiters of a new privilege, provincials intoxicated with their
release from provincialism; and it was this that gave such rollicking
emphasis to their contempt for provincialism.

With the same American concentration, the same sense of having to
revenge oneself on time, that Gertrude Stein brought to the disembodied abstract world of her "perfect sentences," these writers now
tried to make up suddenly for all American writers had missed before,
for all that the American world, seemingly, had denied free spirits
before. Everything now came free in the heady world of the twenties:
all the bitterness of small-town life; all that hunger for richness of
experience that had been repressed so long; all that taste for ineffable
wickedness and dissolution that had never had a chance; all the yearning to prove that American writers could be as ornate or saucy or
satiric as they pleased. If they had a taste for splendor of style, like
Cabell and Hergesheimer and Thomas Beer, they made of their style
a kind of baroque verbal magnificence that was somehow more magnificent than the alleged European magnificence. If they had discovered
the mysticism of sex, like Sherwood Anderson, all life now became
circumscribed around it. If they were contemptuous of the official
myths about great men that had been taught to them in school, they
now discovered, in the luxurious skepticism of debunking, that there
were no great men ever. If they had revolted against their native village

life in the Middle West, all village life in the Middle West now seemed a cesspool of bigotry and corruption and even the very incarnation of joylessness. "Wait and see," Edgar Lee Masters had chortled in 1918, "Spoon River shall be Americee." And so it proved. If the younger generation had emerged from the war, as F. Scott Fitzgerald said, "to find all Gods dead, all wars fought, all faiths in man shaken," all America was now Spoon River, all the deceptions were out, and only the free creative sense of a few remained. But how much fun it was to say so!

2

Everyone now seemed to belong to the Younger Generation, and the Younger Generation seemed to be everywhere. For at least twenty years after their retreat, the forces of the past had lingered on; but the "modern" spirit had finally come into power. Thirty years after the first struggles for realism, ten years after the emergence of the Progressive idealists and the beginnings of an artistic self-consciousness, the first mutterings of literary Socialism, of vers libre and how many manifestoes, the new literature had finally effected its official liberation and conquest. The war had threatened to engulf the new literature of criticism; the gay, rich new era established it. The young writers were in at last, with the new manners and Prohibition and the postwar hangover; after so many years of siege, they had become the latest fashion. The middle-class public was distracted or indulgent, money was high, the literary business was booming, satire had become the order of the day, the custodians of orthodoxy seemed to be in retreat, and a profligate culture refreshed itself on the legend of a rakish youth and the amusements of the new literature. The rebels—a motley so inclusive that Henry Adams and Ambrose Bierce were of it along with Ezra Pound and Sherwood Anderson, Emily Dickinson and F. Scott Fitzgerald—had "won," as they had been emerging slowly ever since the nineties. The future was officially now in their hands.

The younger writers had erupted so suddenly into victory that they were to fancy for at least a decade that modern writing in America had begun with them in 1920. Who cared to remember that Howells had ever fought for realism or that Harold Frederic and Henry Fuller had ever lived? Their histories all began with Dreiser and Mencken. Howells, indeed, had become their bête noir, since he had been afraid of sex, and the Genteel Tradition—how Santayana's clever attack on the unworldliness and frigidity of the Brahmins was to be exploited!— now seemed the last barrier between orthodoxy and freedom. Their heroes were the ghosts of underground reputations—Henry James, who began to come back slowly after his long exile; Herman Melville, whose centenary appropriately fell in 1919, and who was now revived, sentimentalized, acclaimed beyond all belief, an interest stimulated at first—as some modern critics have forgotten—by the revival of interest in the South Seas; Emily Dickinson, who had concealed herself from the Gilded Age for reasons best known to Emily Dickinson, but easy enough to fabricate; Henry Adams, snob, scholar, and misanthrope, whose autobiography became the Younger Generation's primer in history shortly after it was released to the public in 1918 by the Massachusetts Historical Society; Ambrose Bierce, whose war-lacerated mind and addiction to the grotesque endeared him to writers who had revolted against the romance of war.

From the very first moment after the war, as it then seemed, the new writers were riding the crest of the wave. The theories of Sigmund Freud, which had been circulating through the scholarly journals since 1895, suddenly became the indispensable text of the modern personality, and thousands nodded their heads in agreement when Sherwood Anderson soon wrote in *Dark Laughter:* "If there is anything you do not understand in human life, consult the works of Dr. Freud." The *Seven Arts* had died in the war, but Veblen was in New York writing editorials for the *Dial.* The *Nation,* whose literary columns were to become a major influence, suddenly in 1918 veered from its austere and intellectual conservatism and went over to the new writers, as did the *Century.* The "Books" supplement of the *New York Herald Tribune* was soon to be edited by Burton Rascoe and later by the "new" and liberal Stuart Sherman. *Jurgen,* suppressed and then reissued in 1920, became a stormy success, and Eugene O'Neill won the Pulitzer Prize. The "new" books—*Spoon River, North of Boston, Jurgen, My Ántonia, Main Street, This Side of Paradise, Winesburg, Ohio*—some of them formerly published in little magazines or by English publishers, were now available to the "new" public, lauded by the "new" critics, and ready to dominate the literary scene.

The lonely rebels against society, the neglected masters, the "enemies of order," had conquered at last. Victorianism was mocked and parodied to death by the debunkers; and maladjustment, as Van Wyck Brooks was later to say, became a sign of grace. Liberal professors were editing the new magazines, Dostoevsky was a fetish in Bloomsbury, and Gertrude Stein was the inspiration of the "lost generation" in Paris. The solitary, the tragic, the forgotten, all blossomed into fame, and Gauguin and Melville and Rimbaud toppled official reputations from their heavenly chairs. Nothing was so dead in 1920 as the crusading spirit of 1910; but if the victorious moderns looked back with amusement and cynicism on the slogans of the prewar social idealists, their postwar minds now called to other postwar minds across the years and came to rest in the lachrymose terrors of the Gilded Age. One tragic decade needed the moral support of another, and the seeming parallel between life after the Civil War and life after the First World War sufficed to rescue Melville and Henry Adams, Emily Dickinson and Henry James, from the Dreadful Decade, the Mauve Decade, the Tragic Era, the Age of Innocence. Who so nearly resembled Harding, that good-hearted but acquiescent friend of the Ohio Gang, as Grant, the amiable but acquiescent friend of Jay Cooke? Though American writers fled not from the wreckage of a continent, as the European writers did, but from Mencken's "booboisie," from the stranglehold of American Puritanism, from Prohibition and "Comstockery" and A. Mitchell Palmer, what age so closely resembled one's own as the age which had "enjoyed the Great Barbecue, tolerated a Sordid Whiggery, submitted to the Genteel Tradition, suffered from the Pragmatic Acquiescence, failed to outgrow the Colonial Complex"? [1]

Sighing over the ordeal of Mark Twain, the pilgrimage of Henry James, the Calvary Herman Melville had suffered in the New York Customs House, writers in the twenties pointed the moral in their own lives. They, too, were living in a Gilded Age in which the artistic and intellectual energies of a few were obscured or deflected by the bour-

---

[1] W. F. Taylor.

geois mania for wealth, American Puritanism, and the extravagance or insipidity of the masses. Had not Mencken made it all so clear? Did not Van Wyck Brooks attest to it in his studies of the past? To be a writer in the twenties was to be an enemy of the Herd State. "The people still have myth," Ludwig Lewisohn wrote in the *Nation;* the intellectual "has none. . . . What will you say to a man who believes in hell, or that the Pope of Rome wants to run this country, or that the Jews caused the war? . . . How would you argue with a Methodist minister from an Arkansas village, with a Kleagle of the Klan, with a 'this-is-a-white-man's-country' politician from central Georgia?" What Mencken had been saying since 1908 could be said as late as 1930 by Matthew Josephson in the same spirit:

> The dilemma of the artist under mechanism sums up that of a whole (formerly) independent class, all of those who have been detached from the spirit of immediate gain, all who have had the sense of being disinterested—all the prophets, historians, philosophers, pure scientists who have served man so well by their frequent flights from the so-called Practical Realities. . . . The eternal drama for the artist becomes *resistance to the milieu,* as if the highest prerogative were the preservation of the individual type, the defense of the human self from dissolution in the horde.

Mencken would bellow it, Waldo Frank sob it, Van Wyck Brooks intone it tragically; but the chorus was largely unanimous—*We must deliver America to culture!* In a country infested with Comstockery and Prohibition snoopers, monkey trials and women's-clubs prejudices, it was for the new generation to battle for freedom and the rights of personality. "Even as the Russian literature of the nineteenth century was . . . a literature of political revolt," Ludwig Lewisohn was writing, "so our new American literature is one of cultural and moral revolt—a libertarian literature in the broadest sense, urging, imploring, castigating man to live by the monitions of his disciplined soul, not by the dark impulses of his tribal passions." Lewisohn put it a little too grandly, as he put everything, but was he not right? American writers had passed through the first stage of realism and naturalism, the beginnings of "critical realism"; but they had not yet learned to measure their world adequately and they had not yet attained a dynamic confidence in their vocation. Who up to Sherwood Anderson in *Winesburg, Ohio* had written so penetratingly of the undersurface of life in small towns? Who up to Sinclair Lewis in *Main Street* had written with so much necessary bitter truth about the ugliness and timidity of the conventional surface life of that world? Who up to Van Wyck Brooks had pointed with so much moral intensity to the "dualism of American life" which the younger generation could no longer accept as a matter of course? It was not without reason, then, that the new writers regarded all previous experiments in realism as involuntary and spasmodic. The war had transformed life by creating new opportunities, and it was they alone who could perpetuate the life of the spirit in a world suddenly grown odious, deaf, and cold.

"Where is a young man, just out of college," asked Harold Stearns in *America and the Young Intellectual*, "to find the necessary contacts with the national culture?" Blithely he passed over business, politics, reform, the labor movement, music, art, and literature. At the last, "here my hand falters, the picture is too pathetic. Even if he ignores these activities, and wants only to live a gracious and amiable and civilized life for himself, has he a chance in a hundred? . . . Moral idealism is precisely what the institutional life of America does *not* want." In 1922 Stearns edited his famous inquest over American culture, sardonically entitled *Civilization in the United States*. Was there a theater in America? "The American professional theater," replied George Jean Nathan, "is today at once the richest theater in the world, and the poorest. Financially, it reaches to the stars; culturally, with exceptions so small as to be negligible, it reaches to the drains." The intellectual life in America? Controlled by women, the editor volunteered, and stifled by the pioneer, "who must of necessity hate the thinker, even when he does not despise thought in itself. . . . Americans make money because there is nothing else for them to do. . . . One shudders slightly and turns to the impeccable style, the slightly tired and sensuous irony of Anatole France (not yet censored, if we read him in French) for relief." Literature in America? "The chronic state of our literature," replied Van Wyck Brooks, "is that of a youthful promise which is never redeemed. . . . For half a century the American writer as a type has gone down in defeat." Scholarship? "American universities," replied Professor Spingarn, "seem to have been created for the special purpose of ignoring or destroying scholarship." Politics? "Examine the average congressman at leisure," thundered H. L. Mencken, "and you will find that he is incompetent and imbecile, and not only incompetent and imbecile, but also incurably dishonest."

3

"I had not thought"—T. S. Eliot was writing in a poem of that same year entitled *The Waste Land*—*"I had not thought death had undone so many."* But it was precisely because the war had undone so much only to give a new freedom to so many in America that Mencken, now master of the revels, was able to give that freedom the character of a harlequinade. Eliot, having established himself in London during these years, was becoming the exponent of a new traditionalism in a Europe where the decline of culture seemed to threaten the European idea itself. At home, however, Mencken's boisterous attack upon all the vaunted traditions seemed not indecent and irresponsible, but a service. At a time when the seriousness of a profound moralist like Paul Elmer More seemed utterly remote from anything the new writers understood; when an enemy of modern literature like Irving Babbitt could say nothing better of them than that they were the ill-begotten children of Rousseau; when a Stuart Sherman thought of Dreiser only as a "barbaric naturalist," and declaimed pompously that the Younger Generation was following "alien guides," that "Beauty has a heart full of service," Mencken seemed one of the few guides to a necessary culture and civilization. At any other time, it may be, Mencken would have been almost an affront; later, as he proved with all his familiar energy, he could be as tedious and inflexible an old fogy as any he had once demolished. But if Mencken had never lived, it would have taken a whole army of assorted philosophers, monologists, editors, and patrons of the new writing to make up for him. As it was, he not only rallied all the young writers together and imposed his skepticism upon the new generation, but also brought a new and uproarious gift for high comedy into a literature that had never been too quick to laugh. He was just the oracle the new literature

had prepared for itself, the total of the wisdom it was ready to receive; and it was not entirely his fault if, at a time when the loudest noise made the brightest satire and the most boisterous prose recorded the most direct hits, Mencken proved that one could be "a civilizing influence" by writing like a clown.

Mencken belonged so resplendently to the twenties that it is sometimes fancied that he came in with them. The twenties came to him. Much as the thirties passed him by because he did not prove equal to them—was there ever an American writer who seemed to belong so squarely to one period in time?—he was in the prewar years a remotely satiric figure who propounded more than the times were prepared to understand. As a newspaperman from his earliest days, he was taught in the school of Huneker, Percival Pollard, and Vance Thompson, a school not so much of newspapermen as of the bright new esthetic of the nineties which found its shrines in Ibsen, Nietzsche, Wagner, and Shaw. Everything that has been characteristic of Mencken except the scholarly curiosity displayed in *The American Language* was learned in that school; there were times when the monotone of his rasping skepticism suggested that he had learned nothing else. There he absorbed and improved upon his facile style; there he picked up the learning—too often only the marks of learning—that marked the esthetic newspaperman of the period; a learning characterized by its flashing eagerness, its naïve addiction to tags and titles and appropriate quotations from the Latin or the German, its sharp wit and occasional penetration and theatrical superficiality.

What Mencken learned chiefly from the fin-de-siècle mind, however, was a superior contempt for the native culture and manners. The Huneker-Thompson type had all the opportunities of a cosmopolite, and none of the obligations—not even the common emotions, as it then seemed—of a citizen. America was home, unfortunately, but culture was everywhere else. As a newspaperman he was a spectator at the international show, privy to its secrets, appreciative of its color and gossip, and a participant in the gaiety of nations. As a writer he was a dilettante, and in his revolt against the provincial he believed himself a connoisseur. The sexual emancipation that was one of the main props of the renascence of the nineties gave him an added contempt for native American inhibitions; the greater resolution and intellectual distinction of European revolutionaries even provoked a final disgust with the plodding social reformers at home. But Mencken went far beyond Huneker in his contempt for social rebels. For him Marx was always the "philosopher out of the gutter," and Debs was "poor old Debs." Of others in his day one could say that they found Debs's rhetoric soggy because they had been dazzled by Shaw or moved by the nobility of Jean Jaurès; in the brilliance of the European revolutionary tradition, so characteristically European and so pleasingly intellectual, they had found the necessary excuse for their indifference to social problems at home. Mencken needed no excuse. There was a fatal want of generosity in his mind from the first, and his writing was finally corrupted by it.

The gay satire of the American scene that runs all through Mencken's first writings, and which is marked in his editing of the *Smart Set,* was a significantly theatrical revulsion against the American as a type. There was never in it the mark of that quarrel with something one loves that distinguished the best criticism before the war, or the humanity and tenderness of postwar rebels like Anderson and Fitzgerald. Entering into critical journalism at a time when traditionalists and insurrectionists divided the field between them, Mencken began, almost experimentally, with a gay and mocking irresponsibility; and the irresponsibility worked so well that it entered into his constitutional habits as a writer. By 1919, when the *Prejudices* began to appear, this irresponsibility was no longer a trick; it was a facile and pyrotechnical dogmatism which persuaded Mencken himself as easily as it persuaded callow undergraduates in search of a cultural standard. He had no sound opposition; his most articulate opponents were village editors, clubwomen, Fundamentalists, or conservative critics like Stuart Sherman, who called him "pro-German." The times demanded a certain violence of expression and exasperation, and Mencken's appreciation of his sudden notoriety satisfied that demand and encouraged it. If he had not written so brilliantly and recklessly, he would not have been fully understood; but there was no need at the time to know that many of his ideas were cynical improvisations designed to startle and shock. He was an irrepressible force, a stimulant, an introduction to wisdom; when he roared, it was enough to roar with him.

With gay confidence Mencken was thus able to say anything he liked, and he usually did. The American was a lumpish peasant, an oaf, a barbarian in the most elementary matters. His culture was a monstrosity, his manners absurd and indecent, his courage a fiction, his instincts generally revolting. His literature, at best second-rate but usually impossibly mediocre and pretentious, was riddled by impostors, snoopers, and poseurs, dictated to by fakers, criticized by nincompoops, and read chiefly by fools. If there had ever been anything good in it, it had been speedily throttled, since the one thing Americans feared above all else was truth; the worst of it was always ceremoniously glorified. The American was neither a tragic nor a humble figure; he was merely an object of amusement, a figure out of caricature whose struggles for culture were vain, whose heroes were absurd, and whose sufferings were mere drool. To put it gently, he was hopelessly bourgeois, provincial, hypocritical, cowardly, and stupid. Only the lowest representatives of the racial stocks of Europe had congregated to produce him. Everything he possessed was borrowed from the worst of Europe; everything he aped defiled the best of it.

In his own way Mencken thus illustrated perfectly the passage from the America of Randolph Bourne to the postwar America in which he glittered; but it was not entirely his doing. For if he capitalized on the twenties as the period of the Great Silliness, with its profligacy, its vice-snooping in literature, its oil scandals and shady politics, the decade made good use of him. It raised him from a newspaper Petrouchka to the dignity of a social critic; his mockery was prophecy, his very delivery—and what a delivery it was!—became a fashion, and his scorn was almost a benediction. By prodigious skill he managed to insult everyone except his readers. He flattered them by kindling a sense of disgust; his ferocious attacks on Babbittry implied that his readers were all Superior Citizens; his very recklessness was intoxicating. When he proclaimed, with his grand flourish, that all Anglo-Saxons were cowards, his readers were delighted. When he pronounced the Civil War a third-rate war, because no more than 200,000 soldiers had been killed in it, he was believed. When he snickered that Americans drank the beverages of French peasants,[1] played in mah-jong the game of Chinese coolies, wore on state occasions the garb of English clerks, had a melodic taste for the music of African Negroes, and ate in alligator pears the food of Costa Rican billy goats, he was applauded deliriously.

Under such a stimulus Mencken's craving to say the unexpected, as Louis Kronenberger put it, proved stronger than his integrity against saying what was untrue. What he believed and what his readers wanted to be told were soon indistinguishable; his work became a series of circus tricks, a perpetual search for some new object of middle-class culture to belabor and some new habit or caprice of *Homo Americanus* to ridicule. There were no longer divergent American types and patterns; there was only a strange, fur-bearing, highly unpleasant animal entitled the American. Had the American once been a pioneer? "What lies beneath the boldness is not really an independent spirit, but merely a talent for crying with the pack." Were there American farmers in need? "No more grasping, selfish and dishonest Mammal, indeed, is known to students of the Anthropoidea." Did American workers seek higher wages? They were slaves, all of them; any fool could earn enough money in a country where writers grew prosperous by throwing a few pearls before swine. In a commonwealth of third-rate men only morons were ever hungry.

> The Anglo-Saxon of the great herd is, in many important respects, the least civilized of men and the least capable of true civilization. His political ideas are crude and shallow. He is almost wholly devoid of aesthetic feeling; he does not even make folklore or walk in the woods. The most elementary facts about the visible universe alarm him, and incite him to put them down.

Mencken's technique was simple: he inverted conventional prejudices. To a Protestant America, he proclaimed himself a Nietzschean; to a moral America, an atheist; to the Anti-Saloon League mind, a devotee of the fine art of drinking; to a provincial America, a citizen of the world. *His* sphere was that of scholarship, of good manners, and the European graces. It did not matter then that his scholarship, with the

---

[1] In an essay written in collaboration with George Jean Nathan.

exception of his works on language, was as pedestrian as it was showy, or that the translator of Nietzsche and the great apostle of German culture was not a very trustworthy guide to German. Nor did it matter that his scorn for poetry was the manly bigotry of the locker room, or that his conception of the esthetic life, which saw in every great artist the cynicism of La Rochefoucauld, the devotion of Flaubert, the manners of a Hollywood duke, and the liberalism of Metternich, was monstrous in its frivolity and ignorance. Mencken was Civilization Incarnate. Every Babbitt read him gleefully and pronounced his neighbor a Babbitt. Every intellectual blushed for the idiocies of the Bible Belt, and thought Cabell's prose the height of elegance. Good citizens who had forgotten Bryan's significance in the days before he became the absurd figure at the monkey trial thought Mencken's ridicule of him the last word in political sophistication. Under the whip of Mencken's raillery people generally saw the world's folly in their Congressman, the world's wisdom in their scorn of him.

Fortunately, Mencken so parodied the best aspirations of criticism that his most egregious utterances seemed the work of a vigorous comic spirit. What could be more appropriate, in a day when Carol Kennicott dreamed of literary noblemen in velvet jackets and Hergesheimer's butlers came out of the *Almanach de Gotha,* than Mencken's call for an aristocracy? The *Uebermensch* sat on the white steps of Baltimore and invoked the spirits of Dante, Machiavelli, Voltaire, Beethoven, and General von Ludendorff, to come and make America inhabitable. It was to be a community of the rich, the witty, assorted magazine editors, George Jean Nathan, and those who could remember drinking at least one quart of genuine Pilsener. The arbiter elegantiarum was suddenly transformed into a Prussian Junker with a taste for Havelock Ellis. What could be more amusing than an "aristocratic" principle that was fully as provincial as the antics of the "booboisie" Mencken loved to bait, or as romantic and incoherent as Babbitt's search for the dream girl?

Occasionally, of course, Mencken was not amusing at all, and his loose tongue got in his way, as when he said of Altgeld that "his error consisted in taking the college yells of democracy seriously." And it was significant that one of the cruelest things he ever wrote, his essay

on Bryan, was probably the most brilliant. But who in Mencken's heyday could seriously resent a writer who so joyously declared that there
was no real poverty in the United States; or that public schools were a
drag on the community; or "that the ignorant should be permitted to
spawn *ad libitum* that there may be a steady supply of slaves"; or that
war was an admirable institution, and capital punishment an edifying
one?

Mencken's gaiety was the secret of his charm, and his charm was
everything. He seemed so brilliantly alive, so superb a service toward
the advancement of taste and civilization, that it would have been
churlish to oppose him. In a young and growing modern literature
which believed that the revolt against gentility was all, Mencken's
scorn for the Henry Van Dykes and his long fight for Dreiser were
extremely important. In a culture aching for emancipation from the
Prohibition mind, from vulgarity and provincialism and conventionality, Mencken was a source of light and strength. What did it matter
that he was an eccentric and willful critic who celebrated bad writers
and cried down good ones simply because it suited his sense of fun
to do so? What did it matter that he said as many false things about
established writers simply because they were established as he could say
true and urgent things about writers waiting to be heard? What did
it matter that he was not always a sound guide to culture, that he
frequently proved himself cheap and cruel, that his pronouncements on
art and music and books were not always wise and witty, but frequently
glib and malicious? He was the great cultural emancipator, the conqueror of Philistia, the prophet and leader of all those who had been
given their emancipation and were now prepared to live by it.

Chapter 8

THE NEW REALISM:
SHERWOOD ANDERSON AND
SINCLAIR LEWIS

> *"Oh, the briary bush*
> *That pricks my heart so sore!*
> *If ever I get out of the briary bush*
> *I'll never get in any more!"*
> —Verse in FLOYD DELL's *Moon-Calf*

"Cain made things hard for all of us that time he killed Abel at the edge of the field. He did it with a club. What a mistake it was carrying clubs about."—SHERWOOD ANDERSON, *Tar*

IF IT was the first trombone blasts from Mencken's *Prejudices* in 1919 that sounded the worldliness and pride of the new emancipation, it was two stories of revolt against small-town life in the Middle West— Sherwood Anderson's *Winesburg, Ohio* in 1919 and Sinclair Lewis's *Main Street* in 1920—that now brought new life into the American novel by dramatizing that emancipation in terms of common experience. Signalizing "the revolt from the village," as Carl Van Doren described it at a moment when Edgar Lee Masters's *Spoon River Anthology* had already set the tone of the new spiritual migration in the twenties, these two books signalized even more the coming of a fresh new realism into fiction. For up to 1920, the year Howells died and seemed to take what was left of the old realism with him, the fiddles had been tuning, tuning everywhere, but not in the novel. Between the death of Frank Norris and the suppression of *Sister Carrie* at the beginning of the century and the sensational success of *Main Street* in 1920, the realistic novelists had either lived underground or written the perishable social tracts of the Progressive period. When Howells died in 1920 on the eve of the new resurgence in fiction, he had survived himself for so many years that he had long since become a symbol of everything genteel and bloodless that the new novelists detested. Lewis was later in his Nobel Prize speech to use Howells as the measure of that whole "American Victorianism" against which the twenties rebelled; Anderson, growing up in small Ohio villages where the classic New England writers of the past beamed down like amiably remote divinities from their school-wall portraits, wondered whether Howells, the favorite child of the New England school, had ever been a realist at all. So far as they could see, in fact, the new realist had to learn from scratch. They had the example of Dreiser's courage and of Mrs. Wharton's devotion to craft (*Babbitt* was to be dedicated to her); yet though they were realists as a matter of course, they owed their realism more to the current of ideas during the "Little Renaissance" than to the first pioneers of realism in the novel.

The new realism that was ushered in with Anderson and Lewis had, in fact, only a formal relation to that first struggle for realism that had gone on in the eighties and nineties. It was the sudden current of liberation after the war that had set it in motion, and it was a realism, suddenly come free in the indulgent world of 1920, that no longer had to fight for its life. The old challenging rebelliousness remained; but realism had lost its hard, fierce tension. Where Norris and Dreiser had been philosophical naturalists of a sort, men who had taken up a position in defiance of the old traditions, naturalists who had been interested in the struggle for power, men like Anderson and Lewis were essentially as remote from naturalism as they were from the old Pollyanna romances against which they rebelled. For if theirs was a realism of revolt, the revolt was entirely domestic, as it were; it was a realism essentially instinctive, rambling and garrulous, and homespun. It was a realism that had emerged out of the struggle for freedom of conduct, a realism concerned not with the conflict of great social forces that had dominated the first naturalist generation, but with the sights and sounds of common life, with transcriptions of the average experience, with reproducing, sometimes parodying, but always participating in, the whole cluster of experiences which made up the native culture.

Though no two novelists were to prove more different than Lewis and Anderson, it was with them, as with that whole group of modern realists who now came into the twenties—writers so diverse as Floyd Dell, Zona Gale, and Ring Lardner—that the way was opened for the kind of realism that was to dominate American fiction, a realism that neither apologized for itself nor submitted to the despairs of naturalism, a realism that took itself for granted and swept at will over every sector of American life. No longer did the American realist have to storm the heavens, or in the grimness of creation build his books with massive blocks of stone. Realism had become familiar and absorbed in the world of familiarity; it had become a series of homely fabliaux, like the stories grasped out of common life that men had told one another in the Middle Ages; it had become the normal circuit. And though Anderson, and he alone among these realists, was later to learn from Gertrude Stein's literary ateliers in Paris—the learning process did not last very long—the new realists were essentially indifferent to the old dream of a perfect "work of art." For these writers did not usually think of themselves as "artists" in the European sense. They were participants in a common experience, newly liberated from what the young Sinclair Lewis called the "village virus" and writing for others like them. They had no desire to erect artistic monuments as such. They had emerged from the farms, the village seminaries, newspaper desks, with a fierce desire to assert their freedom and to describe the life they knew, and they wrote with the brisk or careless competence —Anderson sometimes did not seem interested in *writing* at all—that was necessary to their exploration of the national scene.

What this meant also, however, was that the new realists, by their very example and instinctive interests, gave the American novel over to the widest possible democracy of subject and theme. It was the homely average type—Sinclair Lewis's Babbitts and Chum Frinkleys, his Rotarians and business-ridden little men and Wheatsylvania farmers; Ring Lardner's dumb baseball players and Broadway producers and Long Island socialites; Zona Gale's unhappy young village couples; Sherwood Anderson's gallery of village librarians, horse-trainers, yearning young poets; even Edgar Lee Masters's farmers—it was these who now brought the savor and pain of common life back into the novel. Where Crane and Norris had gone to the depths to prove their realism, where Dreiser's naturalism had led him to massive realistic characters who were the embodiment of his profound sense of tragedy, the new realists brought into the novel the walking show of American life. For whether they wrote with the photographic exactness of Lewis, the often inchoate exultation of Anderson, or the harsh, glazed coldness of Lardner, they had a compelling interest in people, American people, of all varieties, sizes, temperaments, standards; and the interest was always direct.

It was this feeling for common talk and appreciation of common ways, so marked even in Lardner—perhaps especially in Lardner, though he seemed to hate everything he touched—that gave the new realists their hold over the popular imagination and made them so significant a cultural influence. Indeed, far from having to fight their public, the new realists often seemed to be associated with their readers in a certain camaraderie of taste and humor. Sinclair Lewis, as Constance Rourke said in her *American Humor,* could even in one sense be considered the first American novelist, for in his unflagging absorption of detail and his grasp of the life about him Lewis caught the tone, the speech, of the pervasive American existence; and it was significant that in his sharp attention to American speech—did anyone before him ever catch the American "uh?"—he brought back the comic and affectionate mimicry of the old frontier humor. There had been nothing of that humor in Dreiser, Crane, and Norris; and for all their superior weight, their more profound grasp of human life, nothing of the discovery of American fellowship that made for so significant a bond between novelist and reader in the new novels of the twenties. And even when he seemed to be groping under the surface of life, to be perplexingly "mystical" like Anderson, the new realist made his readers share in the pride of discovering the poignance and the concealed depths to be found in so many prosaic American examples. Anderson more than the others, in fact, gave to a younger generation growing up in the twenties a sense of curiosity, an unashamed acceptance of their difficulties and yearnings, that was to remain with them long after he had come to seem a curiously repetitive and even confused figure. For whatever else men like Anderson and Lewis may have lacked, they gave back, out of their candid and often bitter penetration of American life, a confidence to those who saw in their books the mirror of a common American existence. It was not an impersonal "America" that had stepped finally out onto the world's stage; it was Americans, millions of them—all the Americans who snickered at Babbitt yet knew him for their own; all the Americans who knew how authentic and tender was the world Sherwood Anderson illuminated in *Winesburg;* all the Americans who knew that if Carol Kennicott was not as great a creation as Emma Bovary, she was certainly more real to them, and lived next door. The American was here; he belonged; he was a character in the gallery of the world's great characters even if he did nothing more than sell Ford cars and live in a clapboard house. Even Babbitt inspired a kind of pride by his vividness; even the mean despotic village enemy in Chum Frinkley; and particularly all those Lincolnesque ghosts out of so many different Spoon River anthologies in the novel, village grocers and spinster aunts and thwarted farmers' wives, who addressed themselves so roundly to history, and so well.

2

Under these circumstances it mattered perhaps less that the new realists had turned to explore the national life with a sharp bitterness than that they were the spokesmen of a new liberation. Even a classic of postwar emotion like Masters's *Spoon River Anthology,* which was perhaps not so much a portrait of a representative town as an image of Masters's own bitterness and frustration, posited a new freedom. To know the truth of American life was to rise in some fashion above its prohibitions; to recognize the tragedy so often ignored in commonplace lives was to lead to a healthy self-knowledge. Reveling in the commonplace, the new realists felt that with them the modern novel in America had at last come to grips with the essentials, and the vigor with which they described the mean narrowness and sterility of their world had in it a kind of exuberance. Thus even a writer like Zona Gale, whose early stories up to 1918 had seemed so sentimental, now suddenly burst out with novels like *Birth* and *Miss Lulu Bett* that were almost intolerably intense parodies of everyday American existence. The tone of *Miss Lulu Bett* particularly, in fact, suggested a concentrated dreariness, a high-spirited savagery, that was almost inconceivable in terms of Zona Gale's strong affection for all the small Wisconsin towns represented. Yet the evidence of a sudden disaffection was there, as in Willa Cather's stories of this period; and both of Miss Gale's novels were so harshly written that it was as if concealed depths of repulsion and bitterness in her had suddenly been brought to light.

It was this sense of a personal quest in realism, particularly marked at a time when so many young writers seemed to have endured life in a hundred different Spoon Rivers for the sole purpose of declaring their liberation in their novels, that so clearly distinguished these books from the dark night world of naturalism. And it was this same insistence on personal liberation that made Sherwood Anderson the evangel of the postwar deliverance. For Anderson, so often described as a "naturalist" at a time when any effort at realism was still associated with Dreiser's dour massive objectivity, even appeared to be inadequately conscious of objective reality. His great subject always was personal freedom, the yearning for freedom, the delight in freedom; and out of it he made a kind of left-handed mysticism, a groping for the unnamed and unrealized ecstasy immanent in human relations, that seemed the sudden revelation of the lives Americans led in secret. If Sinclair Lewis dramatized the new realism by making the novel an exact and mimetic transcription of American life, Anderson was fascinated by the undersurface of that life and became the voice of its terrors and exultations. Lewis turned the novel into a kind of higher journalism; Anderson turned fiction into a substitute for poetry and religion, and never ceased to wonder at what he had wrought. He had more intensity than a revival meeting and more tenderness than God; he wept, he chanted, he loved indescribably.

There was freedom in the air, and he would summon all Americans to share in it; there was confusion and mystery on the earth, and he would summon all Americans to wonder at it. He was clumsy and sentimental; he could even write at times as if he were finger-painting; but at the moment it seemed as if he had sounded the depths of common American experience as no one else could.

There was always an image in Anderson's books—an image of life as a house of doors, of human beings knocking at them and stealing through one door only to be stopped short before another as if in a dream. Life was a dream to him, and he and his characters seemed always to be walking along its corridors. Who owned the house of life? How did one escape after all? No one in his books ever knew, Anderson least of all. Yet slowly and fumblingly he tried to make others believe, as he thought he had learned for himself, that it was possible to escape if only one laughed at necessity. That was his own story, as everything he wrote—the confession in his *Memoirs* was certainly superfluous—was a variation upon it; and it explained why, for all his fumbling and notorious lack of contemporary sophistication, he had so great an appeal for the restive postwar generation. For Anderson, growing up in small Ohio villages during the eighties and nineties at a time when men could still watch and wait for the new industrial world to come in, enjoyed from the first—at least in his own mind—the luxury of dreaming away on the last margin of the old pre-factory freedom, of being suspended between two worlds. Unlike most modern American realists even of his own generation, in fact, Anderson always evoked in his books the world of the old handicraft artisans, the harness makers and Civil War veterans like his father, the small-town tailors and shoemakers, the buggy and wagon craftsmen of the old school. It was almost a forgotten America which he brought back out of the simple force of memory—the America of the old slumbering village towns, of the old religious stirrings, of the old village workmen and saloonkeepers and stablemen; an America that could still remember John D. Rockefeller as a bookkeeper in Cleveland and watch a future titan of industry like Edward S. Harkness still running his little "variety" store on Main Street in Anderson's own Camden; and it was an America for whom Anderson, though he helped to lead "the revolt from the village," always, if sometimes unconsciously, spoke.

It was certainly on the basis of his experiences in this world that Anderson was able ever after to move through the world that Chicago now symbolized as if he, and all his characters with him, were moving in puzzled bliss through the interstices of the great new cities and factories. No other novelist of the time gave so vividly the sense of *not* having been brought up to the constraints, the easy fictions, the veritable rhythm, of modern commercial and industrial life. It was as if he had been brought up in a backwater, grown quaint and self-willed, a little "queer," a drowsing village mystic, amidst stagnant scenes; and the taste of that stagnance was always in his work. A certain sleepy inarticulation, a habit of staring at faces in wondering silence, a way of groping for words and people indistinguishably, also crept into his work; and what one felt in it was not only the haunting tenderness with which he came to his characters, but also the measureless distances that lay between these characters themselves. They spoke out of the depths, but in a sense they did not speak at all; they addressed themselves, they addressed the world around them, and the echoes of their perpetual confession were like sound-waves visible in the air.

"I would like to write a book of the life of the mind and of the imagination," Anderson wrote in his *Memoirs*. "Facts elude me. I cannot remember dates. When I deal in facts, at once I begin to lie. I can't help it." The conventional world for him was a snare, a cheat that fearful little men had agreed among themselves to perpetuate; the reality lay underground, in men and women themselves. It was as if the ageless dilemma of men caught by society found in him the first prophet naïve enough, and therefore bold enough, to deny that men need be caught at all. His heroes were forever rebelling against the material, yet they were all, like Anderson himself, sublimely unconscious of it. The proud sons who rebel against their drunkard fathers, like Windy McPherson's son, sicken of the riches they have gained, but they never convince one that they have lived with riches. The rebels against working-class squalor and poverty, like Beaut McGregor in *Marching Men,* finally do rise to wealth and greatness, but only to lead men—as Anderson, though a Socialist in those early years, hoped to lead them—out of the factory world itself into a vague solidarity of men marching forever together. The businessmen who have revolted against their families, like John Webster in *Many Marriages,* make an altar in their bedrooms to worship; the sophisticated artists, like Bruce Dudley in *Dark Laughter,* run away from home to hear the laughter of the triumphantly unrepressed Negroes; the ambitious entrepreneurs, like Hugh McVey in *Poor White,* weep in despair over the machines they have built. And when they do escape, they all walk out of the prison house of modern life, saying with inexpressible simplicity, as Anderson did on the day he suddenly walked out on his paint factory in Ohio: "What am I going to do? Well, now, that I don't know. I am going to wander about. I am going to sit with people, listen to words, tell tales of people, what they are thinking, what they are feeling. The devil! It may even be that I am going forth in search of myself."

"I have come to think," he wrote in *A Story-Teller's Story,* "that the true history of life is but a history of moments. It is only at rare moments that we live." In those early days it was as if a whole subterranean world of the spirit were speaking in and through Anderson, a spirit imploring men to live frankly and fully by their own need of liberation, and pointing the way to a tender and surpassing comradeship. He had left his own business and family to go to Chicago—"there was a queer kind of stoppage of something at the center of myself"— and he would dream, in the tenement-house rooms where he wrote *Winesburg* after working as a laborer or an advertising writer, of the life that went on in those houses, a life that could be heard through thin partitions. "I had thought, then, on such evenings," he wrote twenty-five years later in nostalgia, "that I could tell all of the stories of all the people of America. I would get them all, understand them, get their stories told." Out of his wandering experiences at soldiering and laboring jobs, at following the race horses he loved and the business career he hated, he had become "at last a writer, a writer whose sympathy went out most to the little frame houses, on often mean enough streets in American towns, to defeated people, often with thwarted lives." Were there not people, people everywhere, just people and their stories to tell? Were there not questions about them always to be asked—the endless wonderment, the groping out toward them, the special "moments" to be remembered?

Living in the heart of the "Robin's-Egg Renaissance" in Chicago, as he called it later, it even seemed to Anderson that hardly anyone had ever before him in America asked the questions he needed to ask about people. The novels he knew did not tell their story; their creators were afraid, as the New England writers who had written too many of the fir ᵗ American stories before Dreiser were afraid. Between the people he saw and the books he read, Anderson saw the terrible chasm of fear in America—the fear of sex, the fear of telling the truth about the hypocrisy of those businessmen with whom he too had reached for "the bitch-goddess of success"; the fear, even, of making stories the exact tonal equivalent of their lives; the fear of restoring to books the slackness and the disturbed rhythms of life. For Anderson was not only reaching for the truth about people and "the terrible importance of the flesh in human relations"; he was reaching at the same time for a new kind of medium in fiction. As he confessed explicitly later on, he even felt that "the novel form does not fit an American writer, that it is a form which had been brought in. What is wanted is a new looseness; and in *Winesburg* I had made my own form." Significantly enough, even such warm friends of the new realism as Floyd Dell and H. L. Mencken did not think the *Winesburg* stories stories at all; but Anderson, who had revolted against what he now saw as the false heroic note in his first work, knew better, and he was to make the new readers see it his way.

For if "the true history of life was but a history of moments," it followed that the dream of life could be captured only in a fiction that broke with rules of structure literally to embody moments, to suggest the endless halts and starts, the dreamlike passiveness and groping of life. What Gertrude Stein had for fifteen years, working alone in Paris, learned out of her devotion to the independent vision of modern French painting, Anderson now realized by the simple stratagem of following the very instincts of his character, by groping through to the slow realization of his characters on the strength of his conviction that all life itself was only a process of groping. The difference between them (it was a difference that Gertrude Stein's pupil, Ernest Hemingway, felt so deeply that he had to write a parody of Anderson's style, *The Torrents of Spring,* to express his revulsion and contempt) was that where Miss Stein and Hemingway both had resolved their break with the "rules" into a formal iconoclastic technique, a conscious principle of design, Anderson had no sense of design at all save as life afforded him one. Although he later listened humbly enough to Gertrude Stein in Paris—she had proclaimed him one of the few Americans who could write acceptable sentences—he could never make one principle of craft, least of all those "perfect sentences" that she tried so hard to write, the foundation of his work. Anderson was, in fact, rather like an older kind of artisan in the American tradition—such as Whitman and Albert Pinkham Ryder—artisans who worked by sudden visions rather than by any sense of style, artisans whose work was the living grammar of their stubborn belief in their own visions. Hemingway's bitterness against Anderson, it may be, was as much a recognition of the older man's advantage in his awkwardness as it was a revulsion against his self-indulgence and groping; but it is significant that it was just Hemingway's need of style and a deliberate esthetic in the novel that separated them.

Anderson did not merely live for the special "moments" in experience; he wrote, by his own testimony, by sudden realizations, by the kind of apprehension of a mood, a place, a character, that brought everything to a moment's special illumination and stopped short there, content with the fumbling ecstasy it brought. It was this that gave him his interest in the "sex drive" as a force in human life (it had so long been left out), yet always touched that interest with a bold, awkward innocence. He was among the first American writers to bring the unconscious into the novel, yet when one thinks of how writers like Dorothy Richardson, Virginia Woolf, and James Joyce pursued the unconscious and tried to trace some pattern in the fathomless psychic history of men and women, it is clear that Anderson was not interested in contributing to the postwar epic of the unconscious at all. What did interest him was sex as a disturbance in consciousness, the kind of disturbance that drove so many of his heroes out of the world of constraint; but once he had got them out of their houses, freed them from

convention and repression, their liberation was on a plane with their
usually simultaneous liberation from the world of business. It was
their loneliness that gave them significance in Anderson's mind, the
lies that they told themselves and each other to keep the desperate
fictions of conventionality; and it was inevitably the shattering of that
loneliness, the emergence out of that uneasy twilit darkness in which
his characters always lived, that made their triumph and, in his best
moments, Anderson's own.

The triumph, yes; and the agony. It is a terrible thing for a visionary
to remain a minor figure; where the other minor figures can at least
work out a minor success, the visionary who has not the means equal
to his vision crumbles into fragments. Anderson was a minor figure,
as he himself knew so well; and that was his tragedy. For the significance of his whole career is that though he could catch, as no one
else could, the inexpressible grandeur of those special moments in
experience, he was himself caught between them. Life was a succession
of moments on which everything else was strung; but the moments
never came together, and the world itself never came together for
him. It was not his "mysticism" that was at fault, for without it he
would have been nothing; nor was it his special way of groping for
people, of reaching for the grotesques in life, the homely truths that
seemed to him so beautiful, since that was what he had most to give—
and did give so imperishably in *Winesburg,* in stories like "I'm a Fool,"
in parts of *Poor White* and *Dark Laughter,* and in the autobiographical
Tar. It was rather that Anderson had nothing else in him that was
equal to his revelations, his tenderness, his groping. He was like a
concentration of everything that had been missed before him in modern
American writing, and once his impact was felt, the stammering
exultation he brought became all. That was Anderson's real humiliation, the humiliation that perhaps only those who see so much more
deeply than most men can feel; and he knew it best of all.

I am a helpless man—my hands tremble.
I should be sitting on a bench like a tailor.
I should be weaving warm cloth out of the threads of thought.

The tales should be clothed.
They are freezing on the doorstep of the house of my mind.

"If you love in a loveless world," he wrote in *Many Marriages,* "you face others with the sin of not loving." He had that knowledge; he brought it in, and looked at it as his characters looked at each other; but he could only point to it and wonder. "There is something that separates people, curiously, persistently, in America," he wrote in his last novel, *Kit Brandon.* He ended on that note as he had begun on it twenty-five years before, when Windy McPherson's son wondered why he could never get what he wanted, and Beaut McGregor led the marching men marching, marching nowhere. The brooding was there, the aimless perpetual reaching, that indefinable note Anderson always struck; but though no writer had written so much of liberation, no writer seemed less free. He was a Prospero who had charmed himself to sleep and lost his wand; and as the years went on Anderson seemed more and more bereft, a minor visionary whose perpetual air of wonder became a trance and whose prose disintegrated helplessly from book to book. Yet knowing himself so well, he could smile over those who were so ready to tell him that it was his ignorance of "reality" and of "real people" that crippled his books. What was it but the reality that was almost too oppressively real, the reality beyond the visible surface world, the reality of all those lives that so many did lead in secret, that he had brought into American fiction? It was not his vision that was at fault, no; it was that poignant human situation embodied in him, that story he told over and again because it was his only story—of the groping that broke forth out of the prison house of life and . . . went on groping; of the search for freedom that made all its substance out of that search, and in the end left all the supplicators brooding, suffering, and overwhelmed. Yet if he had not sought so much, he could not have been humiliated so deeply. It was always the measure of his reach that gave others the measure of his failure.

3

It was perhaps only a trick of time and the current of the new freedom after the war that put *Winesburg* and *Main Street* together, since no two novelists could have seemed more different than Anderson and Lewis. Yet it was just by those very differences, at a time when both seemed to be contributing together to the revolt from the old conventions and shibboleths, that they gave the new freedom, in their heyday, a perfect image of itself. For looking at Anderson and Lewis together, the drowsing village mystic and the garrulous village atheist, it seemed as if they had come from the opposite ends of the world (or from the same Midwestern street) to meet in the dead center of the postwar emancipation and be stopped there, wondering what came next. It was as if everything in American life had suddenly conspired to give them a moment's triumph and then betray them with it; to make them light-bringers, spokesmen of a needed modern wisdom, "cultural influences," even, and then leave them hanging pathetically in mid-air. Despite all their differences, Anderson and Lewis did sound in unison just the spirit of that revolt, of that yearning for freedom, which had been awaited; and if they made their triumph out of it, they were to share in the same humiliation—the humiliation of being remembered as "cultural influences" rather than as serious and growing artists; the humiliation of knowing that they had ceased to be significant, or even interesting, after seeing their first works go so deeply into the national mind and bring new words into the national language.

For Anderson, at least, this sense of anticlimax after his first important books in the early twenties was almost a private matter between Anderson and his kind of vision—a private failure to sustain what he had to give. There was always a failure of will in Anderson's books, a slow decomposition that had its source in some fatal stagnance. But Lewis, who enjoyed from the first a sense of public domination such as few novelists have ever known, suffered a different kind of humiliation. For there was nothing obviously "lacking" in him, as in Anderson. All the energy, the hard, bright wisdom, the tireless curiosity, that were in him reached maximum expression; all the public favor and understanding a writer could want he had. Far more than Anderson, far more than any other contemporary novelist, in fact, he had welded himself inextricably into the American scene. But Lewis had done his work so well, fitted the times so perfectly, that he became almost invisible *in* that scene; he had worked over the surface world so thoroughly, and with so contagious a wit and skepticism, that he became part of that surface. A more profound writer would not have had so assured a success; a less skillful one would not have been so influential in his success. But Lewis hit a certain average in art perfectly, as he hit off the native average—or what Americans like to think is the native average—so well in his characters; and that was at once his advantage and his misfortune. As his characters became public symbols, he came to seem more a public influence than a novelist; as his jokes against the old American ways became new American ways themselves, the barrier between his books and life in America came down altogether. George F. Babbitt had entered as completely into the national imagination as Daniel Boone, but with his emergence, as with every new archetype of American life Lewis brought in, some part of Lewis's usefulness seemed to be over.

To say this would seem to pay only the necessary tribute to Lewis's extraordinary place in modern American life and manners; but to define that success is at the same time to define his position as a writer and the resources he brought to the novel. For there is a certain irony in Lewis's career that is now impossible to miss, and one that illuminates it as a whole. Here was the bright modern satirist who wrote each of his early books as an assault on American smugness, provincialism, ignorance, and bigotry; and ended up by finding himself not an enemy, not a danger, but the folksiest and most comradely of American novelists. Here was the young rebel who had begun *Main Street* as his spiritual autobiography, who even wrote dashingly in his foreword that it preached "alien" doctrine and painted that whole world of endless Main Streets where "dullness is made God"—and found that people merely chortled with delight over how well he had hit off the village butcher, the somnolent afternoons on Main Street, the hysterical Sunday-night suppers, and the genteel moneylender's wife, with her "bleached cheeks, bleached hair, bleached voice, and a bleached manner." Here was the crusading satirist who spared none of the hypocrisies by which Babbitt and his group lived, least of all their big and little cruelties, and gave Babbitt back to his people as a friendly, browbeaten, noisy good fellow. Here was the indignant critic of commercialism in science who portrayed the tragedy of Max Gottlieb in *Arrowsmith* and the struggles of Martin Arrowsmith against those who threatened his disinterested worship of truth, yet succeeded even more significantly in making out of Arrowsmith a gangling romantic American hero. Here was the topical novelist, with his genius for public opinion, who tried to describe the nightmare coming of Fascism to America in *It Can't Happen Here,* but really described his own American optimism in the affectionate portraits of Doremus Jessup, that good American small-town liberal.

In the first flush of his triumph in the twenties, when Lewis did seem to be the bad boy breaking out of school, the iconoclast who was Mencken's companion in breaking all the traditional American commandments, it was easy enough to enjoy his satiric bitterness and regard him as a purely irreverent figure. But today, when his characters have entered so completely into the national life and his iconoclasm has become so tedious and safe, it is impossible to look back at Lewis himself without seeing how much native fellowship he brought into the novel and how deeply he has always depended on the common life he satirized. The caricature will always be there, and the ugly terror that Babbitt felt when he tried to break away for a moment from the conventional life of his society. There is indeed more significant terror of a kind in Lewis's novels than in a writer like Faulkner or the hard-boiled novelists, for it is the terror immanent in the commonplace, the terror that arises out of the repressions, the meanness, the hard jokes of the world Lewis had soaked into his pores. But in a larger sense his whole significance as a writer rests on just his absorption of all those commonplaces, for Lewis has seemed not merely to live on the surface of public reality, but for it. It was this that so many critics have felt when they have accused him of living intellectually from hand to mouth, and what T. K. Whipple meant when he so cleverly compared Lewis to a Red Indian stalking the country of his enemies. For Lewis has always led so mimetic an existence that his works have even come to seem an uncanny reproduction of surface reality. Not so much revelations of life as brilliant equivalents of it, his books have really given back to Americans a perfect symbolic myth, the central image of what they have believed themselves to be; and it is this which has always been the source of his raucous charm and his boisterous good-fellowship with the very people and ideas he has caricatured.

For what is it about Lewis that strikes one today but how deeply he has always enjoyed people in America? What is it but the proud gusto and pleasure behind his caricatures that have always made them so funny—and so comfortable? Only a novelist fundamentally uncritical of American life could have brought so much zest to its mechanics; only a novelist anxious not to surmount the visible scene, but to give it back brilliantly, could have presented so vivid an image of what Americans are or believe themselves to be. It was the satire that always gave Lewis's books their design, but the life that streamed out of them impressed people most by giving them a final *happy* recognition. Lewis caught the vulgarity and the perpetual salesmanship, and caught it as effortlessly as he caught the sights and sounds, the exact sound of a Ford car being cranked on a summer morning in Zenith in 1922, the exact resemblance of Chum Frinkley to Eddie Guest and of Sharon Falconer to Aimée Semple McPherson. But he caught also, as almost no one did before him, the boyish helplessness of a Babbitt, the stammering romance of a Martin Arrowsmith on his first day at the McGurk Institute, the loneliness of a great Sam Dodsworth before all those Europeans in Paris. Even his novel on Fascism reminded Americans that when an exiled American Hitler like Buzz Windrip goes to Paris, he yearns only for Lucky Strikes and the smoking-car jokes of his pals. Even his assault on small-town ignorance and bigotry in *Main Street* suggested that if Carol Kennicott was heroically unhappy on Main Street, she was just a little silly with her passion for uplift.

Yes, and for all their sharp thrusts and irritable mutterings, his books also confirmed in Americans the legend of their democratic humility, the suspicion that every stuffed shirt conceals a quaking heart, and the need of an industrial magnate like Sam Dodsworth or a scientist like Martin Arrowsmith to translate the most momentous problems of his craft into the jargon of a manly American fellowship. Lewis's men are boys at heart, living in a world in which boys are perpetually stealing through their disguise as men, and glad to know that a certain boyishness in the native atmosphere will always sustain them. Businessmen, scientists, clergymen, newspapermen, they are forever surprised at their attainment of status and seek a happiness that will encourage them to believe that they are important. They are frontiersmen suddenly ushered into the modern inheritance, and can giggle at themselves, as John Jay Chapman did on his grand tour of Europe in the eighties, by remembering all the derisive ancestors who stand behind them—"Dear old Grandpa, with his old cotton socks; wouldn't he be proud if he could see me hee-hawing and chaw-chawing with Roman princes!" But if Lewis's natives are boys, the Europeans in his books—Max Gottlieb, Bruno Zechlin, Fran Dodsworth's cousins in Berlin—though they are usually crushed by the native barbarians, are older than the rocks on which they sit, older and wiser than life, the sage miracle men of some ancient world of light and beauty and culture. Old Gottlieb in *Arrowsmith,* for example, was not merely a European scientist; he was *the* European scientist, the very incarnation of that indescribable cultivation and fathomless European wisdom—a man on speaking terms with Leonardo, Brahms, and Nietzsche; a scientist whose classic work on immunology only seven men in all the world could understand; a cosmopolitan who advised—sneeringly—his students to read *Marius the Epicurean* for "laboratory calmness," and could prepare exotic little sandwiches for his grubby coworkers.

Martin Arrowsmith himself, be it remembered, had no such skills. In fact, it was not until he came to Chicago (that halfway station to Europe?), shedding the provincialisms of Wheatsylvania and even Zenith, that he heard Mischa Elman, saw a Russian play, and—"learned to flirt without childishness." The Europeans in Lewis's novels never flirted with childishness; they had all the learning of the world at their fingertips; and as Gottlieb, or Bruno Zechlin in *Elmer Gantry,* proved by their inevitable humiliation and fall, they were almost too good to live in the parched American wilderness. Here was only one American folklore legend that Lewis made his own, a legend based on a conviction of native inferiority and subservience to Europe; and nowhere did it show so clearly as in Sam Dodsworth's encounter with Europe, a Europe that was the negation of Gottlieb's, yet cut out of the same cloth—a Europe too charming, too learned, treacherous and sly. Henry James's favorite story of American innocence abroad came back here with a vengeance. Yet it is interesting to note that a character like

Gottlieb succeeded so brilliantly because he was so sentimentally realized a type. Gottlieb suggested so abundantly for Lewis just what many
Americans would have supposed a German-Jewish scientist in Winne-
mac to be that he lived, as it were, precisely because he was a stock
figure; lived because in him banality had been raised to the rank of
creation.

Lewis's characters have often been criticized as "types," and they
are, partly because he memorialized some of them as such, gave people
in George F. Babbitt what seemed the central portrait of a businessman.
But what is really significant in his use of types is that his mind moved
creatively in their channels. With his ability to approximate American
opinion, his lightning adaptability to the prejudices, the fears, the very
tonal mood, as it were, of the contemporary American moment, Lewis
has always been able to invest his tintypes with a careless energy that
other writers would not have been able to understand, much less share,
since they did not work so close to the surface. Lewis restored life;
he did not create it. Yet what that means is that for him the creative
process lay in the brilliance of that restoration—the ability to restore
one Pickerbaugh, with his "he-males" and "she-males," out of the
fledgling Pickerbaughs all over the American scene; the ability to set
his villains or bores—Elmer Gantry, Chum Frinkley, especially Lowell
Schmaltz—so to talking that though they were incredible, they attained
a fantastic representative quality. It is doubtful, in fact, whether Lewis
even wished to make Lowell Schmaltz credible in that long monologue,
The Man Who Knew Coolidge. He wished only to hit him off perfectly, to make Lowell a kind of monstrous incarnate average, just as he
wished to make Elmer Gantry an accumulative symbol of all the
phoniness he hated in American life. With his lonely suffering rebels,
however—Frank Shallard, Erik Valborg, Paul Reisling, Gottlieb and
Zechlin—he attained not an average type but an average myth. For they
are the protestants, the victims of the national life in which his other
characters survive as a matter of course; and though Lewis admired
them and suffered with them, the characters he gives them are just
those which the artist-rebels, the men who are "different," would seem
to possess by average standards.

Just as Lewis has always worked from type to type, embodying in

them now the cruelty, now the sentimentality, now the high jinks, now the high-pressure salesmanship of one aspect of the national life after another, so he has always moved in his books from one topic to another, covering one sector of American life after another—the small town, Rotary, business, medicine, the smoking car, travel, religion, social work. More than any other American novelist since Frank Norris, he felt from the first the need to go from subject to subject that would lead him to cover the entire national scene. He knew that scene in all its range and could characteristically work up any subject; he had concentrated his whole ambition in the national life, and could hit the perfect moment again and again. In fact, like a sailor hitting ducks in a shooting gallery, Lewis gave the impression that he had only to level his aim, seize a new idea, a new flash of life in the American sector, and go after it. Yet this could work only up to a certain point, as the steady decline of his novels after *Dodsworth,* reaching a really abysmal low in *The Prodigal Parents,* has proved. For the ducks in the American shooting gallery soon stopped moving in convenient rotation. In a sense Lewis depended on an America in equilibrium, a young postwar America anxious to know itself, careless and indulgent to his friendly jokes against it, ambitious even to improve its provincial manners in the light of his criticism; but when that America lost its easy comfortable self-consciousness, Lewis's nervous mimicry merely brushed off against it.

It followed also from Lewis's whole conception of the novel that his brisk mimetic energy would become a trick repeating itself long after he had lost his sense of design and purpose. In some of the early brilliant descriptions in *Ann Vickers,* he seemed to be blocking out perfect scene after perfect scene that led to nothing; there is a forlorn flashiness about them that reveals Lewis running over his old technique even when he had little to say. In Lewis's first works his verve had always been able to light up an inconsequential book like *Elmer Gantry* with dozens of hilarious scenes, or, as in *The Man Who Knew Coolidge,* even to make one long monologue out of it; but now, with nothing more substantial to write about than Barney Dolphin in *Ann Vickers,* Ora Weagle in *Work of Art,* or Fred Cornplow in *The Prodigal Parents,* he could keep on bringing in his "trick," his special gift and charm, while the books merely sagged. They were tired, evasively sentimental books, and full of a hard surface irritability and uncertainty. Even *It Can't Happen Here,* for all its attempt to cover the imaginary coming of Fascism to America, was not a really ambitious book and certainly not a careful and deeply imagined one. Responding to the public terror that filled the air out of Hitler Germany as he had responded to a certain public mood he had known so well in the twenties, Lewis could catch only the surface terror, the surface violence; and they erupted mechanically in his book. But he could not really imagine Fascism in America, he had not really tried to; he had tried to hit the bell in 1936 as he hit it in 1920 with *Main Street* and in 1922 with *Babbitt,* to sound off a surface alarm and strike the public consciousness.

What these later works also signified, however, was not only Lewis's growing carelessness and fatigue, but an irritable formal recognition of his relation to American life. Far from even attempting iconoclastic satire, he wrote these books as moralities for a new time; and his new heroes—Ora Weagle, the poetic hotelkeeper; Doremus Jessup, the amiable and cautious liberal; Fred Cornplow, the good solid husband and father betrayed by his erring children—were the final symbols of everything Lewis had always loved best. He had lampooned Babbittry easily enough; but when the Babbitts themselves were threatened, he rushed forward to defend them. From his own point of view, indeed, there were no Babbitts now, or at least nothing to lampoon in them— Fred Cornplow was the mainstay of the times and Doremus Jessup a representative American hero.

Those who had missed Lewis's dependence from the first on the world Fred Cornplow represented, however, could only wonder at Lewis's sentimental tribute to him and his ugly caricature of those who mocked him. The thing didn't jibe; Lewis wasn't supposed to like Cornplow-Babbitt; and how could Doremus Jessup ever seem enough for him? Yet what was it but Doremus, with his fishing tackle and his wise little small-town editorials, that Lewis had ever known and loved? What was it but the Cornplows he had run after for twenty years, trying to catch the warts, the buffoonery up at the lodge on Wednesday nights, the pleasure of the open road on Sunday? The village rebels had all failed, and that was tragic; Gottlieb and Paul Reisling, Frank Shallard and Guy Pollack, had all gone down before meanness and ignorance and terror. But if the Fred Cornplows remained, they were not so bad after all; and Carol Kennicott really had been just a little silly. The village atheist ended his tirade, and sighed, and went on playing a friendly game of poker with the local deacons.

Chapter 9

THE EXQUISITES

"You have such romantic ideas about America. Is there such a thing as a tired business man in America? I suppose so. . . . We try to keep that sort of thing in the background. We try not to be aware of it. It is the smart thing to do nothing, or, at any rate, to appear to do nothing. It is even a trifle démodé *to write or paint. Of course . . . there are people from Chicago who might do."*—Campaspe, in CARL VAN VECHTEN's *The Blind Bow-Boy*

WITH the satire that caught the leading note of the postwar reaction, there now came in a vogue of elaborate decadence and estheticism, very wicked, world-weary, and ornate, that was significantly as much the creature of the boom period as it was the signal of a detached and superior wisdom. In a day when rockets seemed to be shooting up in the air all the time, when small groups of worshipers met to read through Cabell's *Jurgen* again in the hope of finding some saucy bit that John S. Sumner had missed, and met as religiously as taxi-drivers around stock tickers; a day when Carl Van Vechten's discovery of Harlem ranked in the annals of contemporary literature with H. L. Mencken's defiance of the ban on the *American Mercury* in Boston; a day when every Sunday saw the proclamation of some new "authentic masterpiece," and the new literature seemed to be riding on the wave of the new prosperity—in such a day the vogue of sophisticated decadence was not merely a reaction to the Coolidge age, but the very counterpart of it. If the country was on a holiday, the "superior elect,"

227

the writers who belonged to Mencken's "aristocratic minority" and joined with Ezra Pound in celebrating their release from the "bullet-headed many," felt that they were living in a perpetual spirit of holiday —a world in which it was "forever afternoon" in the lotus garden of the twenties.

Just as the pale imitative exoticism of the late nineties had marked not merely the beginnings of revolt against the old parochialism but a leisure-class psychology in an America that had finally attained a leisure class, so the new literature of sophistication that came in with the "James Branch Cabell School" was fundamentally the ambitious baroque luxury of a period that had finally attained a self-conscious splendor of its own. The old barriers were down, down forever; American writers had proclaimed their official emancipation and their entry into the charmed halls of international civilization. But with the final burst of emancipation had come, so very significantly, a literature, or the dream of a literature, as rich and profligate as the postwar world that supported it. The new decadence marked the difference from the status quo ante as nothing else could; it was the very concentration of all the elusiveness and poise, the self-conscious civilization that the modern emancipation demanded. But with the postwar skepticism, the knowledge that the world was so monstrously disorganized that to laugh at it was an elementary obligation, went a luxuriousness of skepticism, a taste for richness and fantasy and "wickedness self-pro-voked," that were the very emblems of a careless joviality. The American writer was free—how free!—with all America before him to report, to satirize, to delight. But if there was a perpetual comedy of American success to laugh at, the very tone of American success had at last got into American writing. "Perhaps historians may yet discover," Thomas Beer wrote in one of the most brilliant and characteristic works of this school, *Hanna,* "that success is just a form of amusement, mostly sacred to those who have not brains enough to attain it." There spoke the half-sentimental, half-cynical apologist for status in all his carefully arranged hauteur. But how strange it was that the taste of money itself was in this prose, and with it all the self-conscious elegance, the elaborate showiness, the arch grandeur of the nouveaux riches!

With the glossiness, of course, went the pose of the aristocratic amateur. Nothing, it appeared, mattered too much; all beliefs were equally vain and just a little crude; life was to be enjoyed, but never respected. In one of the testaments of the Exquisites, "The Code of a Critic," George Jean Nathan took great pains to shock the mob by announcing that on a day when one of the most violent battles in all history had raged during the First World War, he had worked at the preparation of a chapter on esthetics, and then "prepared and drank several excellent apéritifs." Thus did the boy from Fort Wayne, Indiana, tell the Proustian demimonde to move over, just as the boy from Iowa in Thomas Beer always wrote with an elaborate aristocratic cynicism that made Anatole France look callow. "I am constitutionally given," Nathan proclaimed, "to enthusiasm about nothing. The great problems of the world—social, political, economic and theological—do not concern me in the slightest. . . . If all the Armenians were to be killed tomorrow, and if half the Russians were to starve to death the day after, it would not matter to me in the least. . . . My sole interest lies in writing." Soon enough, the masters of estheticism and the prophets of languor rose from the ashes of the fin de siècle. Oscar Wilde lived again. Even old Huneker published a book of exotic fiction, *Painted Veils,* in 1920. The Modern Library, founded in 1918 as a cheap reprint series of books for the new generation, appropriately selected *The Picture of Dorian Grey* as its first choice. The younger publishers, alive to their opportunities, even cultivated a careful air of snobbery in their advertisements. "The dreamer does not attract the obtuse," wrote one. "The secret glory is not vouchsafed the profane. Yet in —————'s more serious novel and in his essays, there is significance for the initiate."

The vogue of the new decadence was to seem shabby and vain soon enough, but it is easy now to see that it had its origin as a protest against the narrowness and poverty of even the most ambitious writing of the day. Like the readers they delighted, the Exquisites were as tired of the evangelical note that had crept into prewar modernism as they were contemptuous of a grubby provincialism and romanticism. They were tired of naturalism, of fiery convictions, of "sentimental American idealism," and they had revolted not merely against meanness and narrowness, like Anderson and Lewis, but against meanness of style, short rations of words, and a view of life which made literature seem as solemn and difficult as life itself. But above all they wanted to prove, in a day when the international American had become a vogue in himself, a citizen of the world, that Americans, too—especially Americans—could write richly and wickedly and idly. They fought no battles, save the great battle of the twenties against Puritanism, against Mencken's Great American Boob, and John S. Sumner. But for a series of happy accidents, and the obvious taste of the new public for majestic writing and a fiction that glittered in epigrams, they might never have enjoyed their triumphant success.

James Branch Cabell had been pursuing his muse with quiet cynical ardor for fifteen years, read by a very few, praised by Mark Twain and Theodore Roosevelt, but trumpeted chiefly by Burton Rascoe. Joseph Hergesheimer had worked alone and unpublished in Philadelphia for fourteen years, confident of his genius and firm in the belief that the ridiculous vogue enjoyed by Booth Tarkington and the literary canaille would pass. Quite suddenly the new public now turned with relief to the one group that had never asked them to believe in anything. Here were the pleasures of life, the veritable Florida Boom Gothic, of America's coming-of-age. Cabell transported them on his golden prose to a lovely Cloud Cuckoo Land of his own, giggled with them over the inanities of history, and raised spicy innuendo to the dignity of an epic. Hergesheimer, the slavish celebrant of the new rich, intoxicated them with endless visions of silver and brocade, introduced them to the very best people, and tittered verbosely on a Cook's tour of colonial America, nineteenth-century Cuba, and the feudal South. Thomas Beer, whose favorite epithet was "drawling," and who drawled very pleasingly himself, wrote sage and oblique comedies of nineteenth-century life in America for them. Carl Van Vechten, fresh from his triumphs as a music critic, narrated and spoofed the adventures of the international literary and artistic demimonde, while Elinor Wylie, their one tragic artist, wrote fantastically rhetorical novels in which eighteenth-century India and London and Venice, the romantic American frontier and Regency England, blossomed like hothouse orchids.

Everywhere, it was soon felt, the Exquisites put all other writers to shame. The critics who usually disagreed with each other now outdid each other in the chorus of praise. The Socialist John Macy and the Populist Vernon Parrington agreed that Cabell was truly incomparable. *Jurgen* was frequently compared to *Tristram Shandy;* Burton Rascoe felt that not *Ecclesiastes, The Golden Ass, Gulliver's Travels,* and *Gargantua and Pantagruel* had a better claim to immortality than *Jurgen.* Sinclair Lewis pronounced Miss Wylie's *Jennifer Lorn* "the first truly civilized American novel," and Carl Van Vechten even organized a torchlight parade through the streets of New York in its honor. For Mencken, Cabell redeemed "an age of oafish faiths, of imbecile enthusiasms . . . of incredible absurdities," and reminded him of Walter Pater and Horace Walpole. *"At last,"* a professor at the Sorbonne proclaimed triumphantly, *"at last* an American novelist with a culture and a style of his own, a conscious artist and a man of letters . . . *at last* we are given a holiday from Theodore Dreiser's triviality, Sinclair Lewis's truculence and Anderson's mystic stammering . . . *at last* an American writer who can think freely and who does not ignore *gaie science.* . . . Praise be to the Lord, *Jurgen* was born in 1919 and the rights of the imagination were restored."

2

It was an interesting legend. Later, of course, when for some obscure reason it became apparent that Cabell and Hitler did not occupy the same universe, some of the panegyrics were frantically taken back. To a younger generation that knew not why Carl Van Vechten had abruptly retired to photography and Hergesheimer to the *Saturday Evening Post,* Cabell could seem quaint, at times even an affront, and was usually unreadable. They did not know that out of the struggle to publish *Jurgen* freely in 1919, Cabell had emerged as a legend rather than a writer—the incomparable Cabell, our own Anatole France, the only living heir of Petronius, Huysmans, and Oscar Wilde. They could not know that the Cabell whose books were so archly romantic had begun his career as an enemy of the old life-denying romanticism, or that there had been a day when Cabell appeared to have brought into American fiction all the gaiety, the taste for fantasy, the urbane sophistication, that had so long been denied it. Least of all could they know, in a period when Cabell published his comic trilogy of *Smirt, Smith,* and *Smire,* that between them the public and the critics had once improvised a faery world all their own in which the very announcement of Cabell's name evoked laughter and applause and the complacent belief that America too had her superior artist. They had made Cabell into an image of all they wanted from the new postwar literature, puffed him up with glory, read their own desires for a *Meister* into his amiable and decorative books; and when the legend collapsed, the writer failed them.

Yet it was only as a legend that Cabell had lived for them, the legend of their own devising. With his flair for literary jokes, his elaborate parody of the apparatus of scholarship, his pleasing grace, his effortless cynicism, his palpable contempt for the mob, Cabell did present the twenties with the homemade portrait of a Major Writer and nothing more. How weary he was! How all the folly of human-kind and the inanity of existence weighed upon him! He was the weary, all-knowing philosophe who had, like his own Manuel, trod through eternity; or, like Jurgen, exhausted the world's sensations and come to the subtle recognition of all life as an illusion and a bore. And life, as Cabell announced mischievously in all his books, was a bore. "I quite fail to see," quoth Felix Kennaston in *The Cream of the Jest,* "why, in books or elsewhere, any one should wish to be re-minded of what human life is actually like. For living is the one art in which mankind has never achieved distinction." Or, as Felix Ken-naston ruminated in Cabell's fanciest prose: "Everywhere, in every age, it seemed to him, men stumbled amiable and shatter-pated through a jungle of miracles blind to its wonderfulness, and intent to gain a little money, food and sleep, a trinket or two, some rare snatched fleeting moments of rantipole laughter, and at the last a decent bed to die in." Life was a bore and only the artist lent it dignity; yet even art, by a curious paradox, did not matter. Like love, it was one of the necessary fictions. Cabell wrote in *Straws and Prayer-Books:*

> It is the privilege of the novelist . . . so to delude mankind that nobody from birth to death need ever really bother upon his, upon the whole, unpromising situation in the flesh. . . . The endeavor of the novelist, even by the lowest and most altruistic motives, is to tell untruths that

will be diverting. . . . His primary endeavor must therefore be to divert not any possible reader, but himself.

Romance, as he developed this thesis in *Beyond Life,* gave literature the quality of a graceful prevarication. "Creative literature would seem to have sprung simply from the instinct of any hurt animal to seek revenge . . . in the field of imagination. . . . [Man] still believes that life is a personal transaction between himself and omnipotence. That is man's dynamic illusion. It was by grace of romance that mankind was endowed with all its virtues and also to romance that man has gone for his vices." And the romancer, as Cabell informed his palpitating middle-class audience, was a rake, a rake by profession and instinct. Languorously he invoked the shades of Villon and Marlowe and Congreve to prove how little a writer need respect his audience or its conscience.

Cabell did not expect his thesis, or even his curious view of literary history, to be taken seriously; he asked only that he himself be taken seriously. And it was difficult not to do so. Under his tutelage literature became a game that rivaled mah-jong in popularity. Sitting in the Harding-Coolidge era, with its ridiculous standards and general dullness, one traveled in armchairs two spaces west to Poictesme, and two south to the Forest of Acaire. One played with tokens marked life, fate, love, which one could arrange in many pleasing and even hilarious combinations, since they were all equally illusory and always a little sad. One dealt with imaginary scholia, giggled over Cabell's cosmogony of a legendary world, and with Jurgen won the ultimate victory over the feigned protests of many a faire ladye. It was a pleasing game: so suggestive of life, and yet so superior to reality; so erudite, albeit so careless.

Unlike that other artificer of the medieval, Thomas Chatterton, Cabell never persuaded himself; and he had no need to persuade his readers. They wanted just what he gave them: the touch of life bereft of life's prosaic sordidness; an easy road to wisdom; a masquerade of the soul in which, by mocking the daydreams of the great herd, one could liberate and enjoy one's own. Cabell did not pretend to be an "escapist"; he was a realist whose cynical appreciation of reality encouraged him to make it ridiculous. By dismissing the superficial world of the present, he illuminated its pathos, lightly and fleetingly. The eagle in *Figures of Earth* was so indisputably a caricature of Woodrow Wilson, Cabell's lyrics to the good red wine of Provence so clever a thrust at Prohibition, that even the absurdities of one's own day gained a final grace.

What Cabell was writing, though no one would have admitted it at the moment, was not allegory but innuendo; the innuendo became tiresome when it became clear that his delight in his own cleverness would inevitably become the final content of his books. Behind their imposing façade, their glossy finish (*gonfalon* was the word then), lay something so stringy in its poverty, so opposed to all that is high, noble, and intense in art, that nothing could long conceal it. The trouble, at bottom, was complacency. Cabell was a keen and amusing ironist, but even his most ambitious satires suggested a perpetual smirk. He did satirize the leavings of traditional romance, but it was not enough to carry him through; after thirty years he was still parodying the Genteel Tradition under the delusion that he was a master of philosophy. A later generation would wonder why, in summing up his critical position in *Beyond Life,* Cabell found only one redoubtable antagonist, Booth Tarkington; but it was clear that Tarkington, not to say Marie Corelli and Robert W. Chambers and Winston Churchill, still represented everything Cabell had ever fought against. His own romanticism was thus only one step from the girlish innocence of the traditional Virginia romance to the charming and elusive demimonde of Poictesme, in which girls were never innocent and men were rarely dull. The critical Babbitts might think Cabell a satanic figure, but he was not even attempting to *épater le bourgeois;* he sought only to amuse him. Reading his books, good middle-class fathers and citizens, like good middle-class undergraduates, enjoyed the luxury of a depravity that was as synthetic as breakfast cereal, and as harmless.

Cabell's great secret, indeed, was that he made almost no demands upon his readers; and since he took such pains to be cute, it was impossible to resist him. He was not a decadent at all, but a mischievous and tryingly whimsical old uncle. The books were all comedies, and they were to be enjoyed for their pleasingly mundane tricks, like that top of a cold-cream jar which Felix Kennaston mistook for a prefatory sigil, or the archness that made the vulgarity of *Jurgen* so picturesque but homely. Yet he had one fatal weakness. He sought so energetically to keep his readers from being bored that he became a bore himself, and when he lost his charm even the famous style seemed ridiculous. "Henceforward you must fret away much sunlight by interminably shunning discomfort and by indulging tepid preferences. For I, and none but I, can waken that desire that uses all of a man, and so wastes nothing, even though it leave that favored man forever after like wan ashes in the sunlight." Could it be that, hiding archly behind his lovely fake ruins, there was nothing but such fantastic rhetoric and the disclosure, so long delayed, that Jurgen was quite a feller? It was a terrible and dismaying thought, a thought that swept away all those lovely ladies, all that mock learning, all the glories of a fabulous satire, and left nothing, nothing at all.

3

Hergesheimer, on the other hand, always had much to say; he was even a born storyteller. He had zeal, a definite talent, and a purpose in life. He composed, over a period of twenty years, an elaborate series of novels in which he detailed with relish the appetites, the dinners, the adulteries, the manners, the fleeting passions, and the clothing of the rich. In a drawling and lacquered prose that was obviously a work of art, he dedicated himself, with a patience that once seemed as inexhaustible as his capacity for affectation, to the pleasures and opinions of the international leisure class. It was no mean achievement, as Clifton Fadiman once said, to have been the Sargent of the modern American novel. Hergesheimer's vision may have been narrow, his scale of values limited; but he had taken his subject for his very own, and one could hardly call him pretentious. He had no society of his own; but he was a court painter to the rich, and the rich were everywhere.

It did not matter where a Hergesheimer character had gained his wealth, or how; he needed only to occupy one of those lush, tropical interiors that marked the true aristocracy of eighteenth-century Richmond or Washington Square or Cuba. Even the Black Pennys, growing poorer despite three centuries of middle-class expansion, preserved their fastidious aloofness to the end. Richard Bale of Balisand had that most signal of virtues in early nineteenth-century America, he loathed Thomas Jefferson. Linda Condon, who would not sell herself in marriage for less than fifty thousand a year, was still the perfect symbol of the perfect lady. Even Charles Abbott of *Bright Shawl*, Hergesheimer's lone rebel, had fought the Spanish oppressors in Cuba not for the Cubans but in defense of chivalry. "All law and order were made for the mob," Savina Grove explained in *Cytherea*. "I don't need the policeman I see on the street." In the Mencken manner, but buoyed up always by his own fine respect for those who had presumably made history, Hergesheimer had an equal contempt for the canaille. *Cytherea* contains an oblique reference to "the undistinguished evils of improvidence." Hergesheimer himself, musing over the delights of building a colonial mansion in *From an Old House,* confessed: "Cypress shingles, cut by a crew of niggers in a Louisiana swamp, hand split and drawn. How was it possible for me to have any other?"

Yet it has to be said that Hergesheimer's passion for the rich was not a vulgar passion. Above all things in this mortal life he loved beauty; the rich had access to it. It was a beauty that flourished in splendor on the faces of their women, the clothes they wore, the silken pursuits of their play; it grew heavily like tropical plants through rooms riotous with color and massive with Hergesheimer furniture. His novels were like a museum devoted to the households of the past. Like Thackeray, he had been a painter before turning to the novel, and he never relinquished a taste for the decorative. The ultimate beauty, however, was the beauty of women, particularly those upper-class women who reflected the chromium-and-gold interiors in which they seemed always to live. He knew them well and celebrated them passionately; to no other American novelist had been divulged in equal measure the secret of their charm. His was frankly a feudal world, and women ruled in it with a fine medieval grace. "They were created," he once wrote of his heroines, "delicate and charming, impracticable in cambric and chiffon, for my personal reassurance and pleasure. I wanted them that way and there they were. Later, when I met delightful women, I discovered a secret they shared with each other and with me: what I had always wanted them to be they wanted to be—delicate and charming in cambric and chiffon, tender and faithful and passionate."

Yet if Hergesheimer was, as even his friend Cabell was once moved to confess, the most insistently superficial of writers, his books were weighed down by a curious melancholy. He sought not merely to pay tributes to beauty, but to imprison it like a genie in his books; and he built so well that his characters suffocated. Everything yielded at some point in every Hergesheimer novel to his passion for decoration, and it was a passion often indistInguishable from snobbery. Even the exquisite and authentic tragedy of *Cytherea* became faintly ridiculous when Hergesheimer wrote sentences like "Savina's bottles were engraved crystal with gold stoppers: it was all as it should be"; or went on to note that "the ice was frozen into precisely the right size; and the cigars before him, a special Corona, the Shepheard's Hotel cigarettes, carried the luxury of comfort to its last perfection. Mrs. Grove smoked in an abstracted long-accustomed manner." His characters all became dolls led up a graveled path by footmen; and the synthetic majesty of the scenes amid which they lived steadily crowded them out of view. The fancy prose, lost in its winding epithets, made movement impossible. Did Clara in *Linda Condon* move to the fireplace and look at her watch? "Clara moved at once to the fire burning in a small open fire-place set in an ornamental Georgian frame of imitation stone. She looked at the minute watch bound on her wrist by a band of platinum and diamonds." Even love waited on "Linda, unresponsive, suffered inordinately." In his world one never turned one's back; one turned a *graceful* back. One did nothing so prosaic as sit down to lunch. "They were at lunch in the Feldt dining-room, an interior of heavy, ornately carved black wood, panels of Chinese embroidery in imperial yellow, and a neutral mauve carpet. The effect, with glittering iridescent pyramids of glass, massive frosted repoussé silver, burnished gold-plate, and a wide table decoration of orchids and fern, was tropical and intense."

"Always the Court," cries Ludowika Winscombe in *The Three Black Pennys,* "do you know what that means? It's a place where women are pretty pink and white candies that men are always picking over. It's a great bed with a rose silk counterpane and closed draperies. Champagne and music and scent and masques." It might have been the world of Hergesheimer's novels itself.

4

A thick and glossy style: a style fit for a thick and glossy world. The desire to build monuments by style which Hergesheimer and Cabell cultivated so lovingly soon developed into a cult of snobism. It was the most obvious of inverted provincialisms, and the most seductive. The new decadence invited a style that became a way of writing studiously away from the object, of pointing one's effects so portentously that indirection became itself a technique. The writer was careful to keep a certain distance between his style and its application, the words and their basic communication. He waved his hand languorously in air, and a vapor settled on his pages, an atmosphere. He lived by his gestures, weaving them together slowly and knowingly; and the gestures were all, since they led to the revelation of his inherent superiority to the material and fixed the attention on himself rather than the book.

Most important, the writer even suggested, with a weary amusement, that the material he worked with was just a little vulgar. As Ben Hecht put it in one of the showiest exhibitions of this school, *Erik Dorn:* "Life is too short for brevities—for details. I save time by thinking, if you can call it thinking, *en masse* . . . in generalities. . . . My wonder is concerned chiefly with the manner in which they [men] adjust themselves to the vision of their own futility." Writing, in fact, was at best an intellectual amusement. Since we are all, these writers would have agreed with Santayana, maniacs held in leash, writing provided a diverting discipline. Art had a place, perhaps *the* place in a world where a few lived to relieve each other of mortal boredom; but it was mischievous, an amiable lie, and doomed: the writer did not ask to be understood; he sought only to be appreciated. Life was optic, pitiful, a welter: the writer could only work away, dream away in his treasure palace, with the comforting reassurance that the world was as irrational as it was vain, and that an epigram provoked, if it did not explain, the sordidness of existence.

It is in this light that one can now understand why Thomas Beer, one of the cleverest writers of his day, found it easier and easier to charm an open-mouthed audience with profundities like "Toussaint L'Ouverture, a superior Negro whose taste in dress was bad." For Beer was an actor; he played a part. Where Hergesheimer reminded one of his own butlers, and Cabell went peacefully ahead spinning his self-conscious little fantasies, Beer at least gave an impression of size, of a large and amused sagacity into which he had fitted perfectly. He had fabricated for himself a style, a manner, an over-all distinction. The part he played was that of a Dr. Johnson, and all the gestures, the imperturbable dogmatism, the hard-breathing obesity, the superior good sense of the part, found majestic expression in his style. He was a Dr. Johnson, pleasantly enough, who had gone to school in the Richard Harding Davis era and picked up its swagger. All the tints of the eighteen-nineties he studied with such sardonic affection in *The Mauve Decade* ("Mr. Whistler said: 'Mauve? Mauve is just pink trying to be purple.' ") were in his prose—the flourish, the archness, the shocking of the bourgeoisie. His style was systematically musical with disdain, carefully draped in artful circumlocutions. "They laid Jesse James in his grave and Dante Gabriel Rossetti died immediately." "The fancy of eternal damnation should be tenderly nursed by American writers on behalf of policemen, who in general are dull, underpaid creatures and frequently fathers." Yet out of that undergraduate archness Beer did attain an oblique irony that he welded into a successful principle of composition; and when he wrote history in it, as in his biographies of Stephen Crane and Mark Hanna and his portrait of the nineties in *The Mauve Decade,* he could sound unutterably wise.

There were moments all through Beer's work, especially in his glossy fiction, when he worked too hard at shocking and dazzling; moments when the glitter turned cold and the writing was pure strain. He always wrote *down;* he turned his wit with cavalier insolence on everything in sight; he puffed with a large and genial brilliance. Yet where Cabell's books now seem merely false and Hergesheimer's forlorn monuments, Beer's histories retain an effect of solidity, of a job clearly seen and cleverly performed. For Beer had an instinct, a great affection, for the late nineteenth-century world to which his books always returned. He might sound all the variations of heresy, the brittle new sophistication of the postwar scene whose flashiest values seemed incarnate in his work. But like Dr. Johnson's, Beer's was a natural orthodoxy: he warmed to status, he enjoyed men of power, he moved serenely through the clubrooms of history. He had worked malice up into a fine art and would seemingly sacrifice anything for an epigram; but for all his bubbling irreverence, he was anything but a debunker. His values were the values of his father, William Collins Beer, a Republican stalwart of Hanna's Old Guard, a businessman and conservative politician; and though they were values tempered by Stephen Crane and by Yale, they were the old values nevertheless. Living, as it were, on the spiritual bounty of his father's success and his father's world, Beer could move effortlessly through that world, the world that Hanna and McKinley and Stephen Crane had known together—laughing at it a little, describing its colored surface with fine zest, yet always returning to its Old Guard complacency as a matter of course.

It was this complacency, the atmosphere of perfect comfort and self-assurance that one felt in Beer's histories always, that actually made his striving for effect so innocent, and the effects themselves frequently so delightful. Veblen would have enjoyed Beer—and put him and his books into the last chapter of *The Theory of the Leisure Class*. For Beer was himself a conscious artist in "conspicuous waste," the perfect example of what a rich, traveled, superior, and comfortable leisure class in America had come to in art. The fathers had been stolid; the sons were wicked. The fathers had lived by the values of the Gilded Age; the sons mocked them. Yet this son mocked but did not contest them at all: he yawned, he found them unpleasantly gross on occasion, but they were the substance of everything on which he thrived. Where wealth had once been a simple faith, it was now a comedy; but wealth remained the subject, the medium along which he moved. "This is the chart of the Gilded Age," Beer wrote in *Hanna*, "a fierce assumption of greatness in a circumfluent weariness. Everyone was tired and wanted to be entertained." No: it was the postwar generation that was tired and wanted to be entertained; and it entertained itself with the

Gilded Age. That was where Beer's opportunity lay. A materialist who thought himself an ironist, he could write brilliant studies in materialism. He was an omnivorous student of detail; he had made antiquarianism into a literary profession; and he had—as chapter after chapter in *The Mauve Decade* illustrated so happily—a positive genius for the surface life, the color and flash, the necessary personal anecdote, the perfect detail about Theodore Roosevelt's trousers. His books were not merely testaments to grandeur; they had a wry authentic grandeur of their own. Cunningly designed and dense with the foliage of the past, they were the elaborate recreations of a mind in love with facts; and they always came back to persons, scenes, characters absolutely seen, a moment grasped unerringly out of the past, the dusk on Fifth Avenue of a summer evening in 1899.

Beer laughed at the ornamental icing on the nineteenth-century cake, but he ate the cake and enjoyed it. So Hanna came back in his brilliant biography not as the wicked and corrupt magnate, the great puller of strings whom millions of simple Americans in the nineties had used as the image of all they loathed and feared, but as a sage and gentle homebody, a dear old character, an interesting nineteenth-century materialist. Was the portrait authentic? It was eminently so, if one saw Hanna from the point of view of Hanna's own class; and Beer had, for all his playful cynicism about the Gilded Age, done just that. He had seen Hanna's power, that is to say, refracted through his own fascination with power. Where Hanna's cynicism had been unconscious, however, Beer's was self-conscious; and there lay the comedy. For Hanna was now sentimentalized as he himself had never sentimentalized anything in his life, and Beer's book, appearing so dramatically just before the crash in 1929, was the last great apology for the old order—from the most sophisticated of postwar sophisticates! In the Appendix he wrote archly:

> I must admit that the morals of leaders in a democracy do not interest me. . . . Morality is an exaltation of personal taste, and taste is something usually sacrificed by leaders of mankind in the mass. . . . Democracy yearns for leadership and accepts many clever dictators before a Julius Caesar declares the ideational ruin of the republic. . . . The characteristic of Hanna's bloodless adventure in government is

this Caesarism, and his charm lies in the candor of his approach to the mass. He appealed to materialists as a materialist; his pragmatism was not draped in virtuous pretenses. He grinned.

This was perhaps not the Hanna that William McKinley knew; it was a titan out of Beer's favorite political philosopher, Oswald Spengler, whose declaration that democracy was only the rule of money pleased Beer and his fellows so much.

But so manner called to manner, and grandeur to grandeur. Wealth was style; style was power. Writers like Cabell and Hergesheimer and Beer had little in common but a manner; but the manner could become all. So even Elinor Wylie joined this group with her four prose novels and exhibited along with them in some of the most fantastically swollen books written in a period rather more like the Gilded Age in its taste for ornament than many could know. Like the others, she felt the contemporary call to build baroque palaces in prose. But where in poetry her intensity had been spectacular, frozen, neat—

> Better to bind your brow with willow
> And follow, follow until you die,
> Than to sleep with your head on a golden pillow,
> Nor lift it up when the hunt goes by.—

in her novels it was feverish and artificial. Unlike the others, she did not have to plot and strain to write well; her feeling for style runs all through her work like a pang. But in her novels she was obsessed by the need to make ornate pictures. Everywhere in them human beings are wrought into marble and ironwork, draped luxuriously like silk dolls, sculptured into a frieze, and given a language so overwhelmingly rapturous as to become meaningless. Like Hergesheimer particularly, she inverted Hemingway's aphorism—"Prose is architecture, not interior decoration." For her prose actually was interior decoration, a pleasure dome in itself. If Hergesheimer carried his frank passion for interior decoration to the point where his world often appeared to be composed exclusively of furniture, she drowned her novels in color. Her aim as a novelist was not "poetic"; it was to give life the surface texture of poetry. To that end she overdressed her characters and their world with a breathless eagerness to find beauty everywhere, or fabricate it. Sacrificing good taste to the dream of elegance, she falsified even her fantasies for the sake of rhetoric. And in the end her novels rested on a profound sense of unreality in which everything was larger than life and totally unrelated to it.

The impulse behind Elinor Wylie's novels, of course, was anything but cynical or vulgar; it was rather desperate. Her despair was so fixed on words, the metallic surfaces and echoes of words, the endless pictures she could draw with them, that her novels were like the clamor of hollow gongs. Just as Hergesheimer was always ready to write a sentence like "Annette and Alice appeared with their wraps turned to exhibit the silk linings, bright like their dresses; and, at a favorable moment, they slipped out into the malice of the wind," so she seemed to be drunk on the pathetic fallacy. Her rhetoric flowered in *Jennifer Lorn,* a nightmare in technicolor which described the impossible adventures in India and London of an eighteenth-century hedonist. When Gerald returned to England, "the weather was like his own sapphire taken out of its ivory box and dissolved in sunlight; he sat on deck, upon cushions of scarlet silk with a snow-white awning like a great cloud between him and the sky, and though the quality of the brandy left something to be desired, he had never enjoyed *Candide* half so much." The very caricature of a sybarite, Gerald was villain enough, too, to whisper "with cryptic sibilance." When he spoke in anger—"in a voice like cracking glaciers"—it was to cry, "Ignore this mummery!" And Jennifer's Oriental lover was "a slim and languid youth of perhaps nineteen or twenty indolent summers."

In *The Orphan Angel* Miss Wylie rescued Shelley from the Gulf of Spezzia, set him on a Yankee clipper, and allowed him to roam along the frontier. It was a boy's book, full of obvious contrasts; but how wonderfully did Shelley talk! "My soul has clothed itself in no rainbow shell; rather has it stifled in something narrow as a coffin and obscure. This was of my own shaping, and by heaven, I have lived withdrawn into its shadows like a tortoise under his horny shield. Often I have felt the outrageous weight of the world upon my back. A sudden cataclysm split that armour. I emerged into a new element, a volatile compound of sun and sea-water and eccentric liberty." But this, of course, was a world in which maple sugar "melted tenderly against his [Shelley's] outraged palate." It was rhetoric in limbo between poetry and prose, the rhetoric of a writer who was not sure at the moment whether she wanted to write poetry or prose, and had taken a subtle refuge in fantasy. It was poignant fantasy, where Cabell's was merely fake; but for all its mountainous splendor it could not hide her confusion, her dream of an elegance that was greater than the words that composed it.

Yet perhaps, as Elinor Wylie's lifelong passion for Shelley suggested and *Mr. Hodge and Mr. Hazard* proved, she was merely fighting out the last battle of the Romantic cause. In that last and most effective of her novels, she came closest to the modern scene. A weary stranger, who might have been Trelawny and should have been Byron, returns from Greece to find England already sinking into Victorianism. The conquering acquisitive middle class had succeeded the great Romantic generation after 1830; Mr. Hodge (Macaulay?) stuttered pontifically where Shelley and Keats had mounted on wings of song. *Vale,* then, the days of glory were over. Yet as she had exhumed Shelley in *The Orphan Angel,* so she would now play out Mr. Hazard's part and smolder on what was left of the romantic ecstasy to the end. Had she not, in a curious little novel published in 1925, *The Venetian Glass Nephew,* resurrected even Casanova? There, among the alchemists of eighteenth-century Venice, her "exquisite monsters" had gathered round for the last time. And the hero—so very appropriately—was made of glass.

CODA

To Carl Van Vechten was granted a less distinguished but more functional role in what threatened, as the twenties ran out, to become a movement. For beginning as its playboy, Van Vechten ended as its historian. He had been a music critic and he had a flamboyant knowledge of the world. It was he who brought the Charleston to literature, took the esthetes on slumming parties through Harlem, retailed the gossip, memorialized the fads, and—a sardonic Punch to the last—

brought one dream of the twenties to a close by writing its obituary in *Parties* before he gave up writing for photography. As a stylist he proved so dexterous that he came uncomfortably close to ridiculing himself. From at least one of his novels, *The Tattooed Countess,* one culls such interesting examples as "The Countess replied, in a conciliatory manner, apparently with morigeration"; "She caught sight of her passerine sister"; "A sciapodous Bohemian girl in a shirtwaist and skirt"; "They had, in a sense, been responsible for his oppugnancy towards his environment." What saved him and gave him his signal importance at the moment, however, was the range of his facile cynicism. As the novelist of the speakeasy intelligentsia, he carried sophistication to its last possible extremity by refusing steadfastly to admit the significance of anything west of Manhattan Island. He represented the Jimmy Walker era in literature as Mr. Walker represented its politics, Texas Guinan its pleasures, and George Gershwin its music. In a series of novels that proceeded with becoming regularity from *Peter Whiffle* (1922) to *Parties* (1930) he meticulously detailed the perversions, the domestic eccentricities, the alcoholism, the esthetic dicta, and the social manners of ladies and gentlemen who did nothing, nothing at all. The world he so amiably described was careless, violently erotic, and cheerfully insane. Written up in Van Vechten's snakelike prose, it boasted an extraordinary appetite for evil; if there was no evil his characters played at being evil. It was a satanism grown weary of being dissolute, a lechery so sated with sex that it took to snake-charmers and hysterical visits to Coney Island.

Like most of the Exquisites, Van Vechten thrived on his own affectations. He began and ended his career as a novelist on a good, heartily satiric note, but there were times—notably in *The Blind Bow-Boy*—when he took such pleasure in his freaks that they seemed to climb all over him. A nudging good sense, of course, never deserted him; he giggled steadily at his own pretensions for eight years. But at last the eroticism became more perverse, the alcoholism more opulent, the lechery for nonsense uncontrolled. It was but a step from the buffoonery of *Peter Whiffle,* in which Van Vechten demolished a whole school of poseurs, to the carnival of idiocy represented in *The Blind Bow-Boy*. There, superintended by the gorgeous Campaspe

("You have such romantic ideas about America. Is there such a thing as a tired business man in America?") Van Vechten's aristocratic perverts and idlers enjoyed their last triumph. The Duke of Middlebottom lived by the Julian calendar, since the herd lived by the Gregorian; Campaspe pronounced Van Vechten's own convictions on literature when she mused: "The tragedies of life were either ridiculous or sordid. The only way to get the sense of this absurd, contradictory and perverse existence into a book was to withdraw entirely from reality." Ineffably bored with their own pursuits, his characters then turned to Harlem, which, as Van Vechten described it in the torrid pages of *Nigger Heaven,* was a place where colored folk slashed each other merrily and had fun.

The final word came in *Parties.* At Donald Bliss's last party "there was Simone Fly, a slim creature in silver sequins from which protruded, at one end, turquoise blue legs and from the other, extremely slender arms and a chalk-white (almost green) face, with a depraved and formless mouth, intelligent eyes, and a rage of cropped hair. Simone Fly resembled a gay death." Unhappily, it was amidst the detonations of a falling stock market and an expiring culture that Van Vechten had gathered his creatures for the last party and the last exquisite sensation of extravagance and futility.

"It's just like the opening chorus of an opera-bouffe," one character laughs. "Somehow it's more like the closing chorus," replies another. "I think we're all a little tired." *Da capo.*

Chapter 10

ELEGY AND SATIRE: WILLA CATHER AND ELLEN GLASGOW

"It's memory: the memory that goes with the vocation."
— WILLA CATHER on Sarah Orne Jewett

THE "new freedom" after the war was not a movement; it was a succession of opportunities for writers who were themselves often in open conflict. To the "middle generation" of writers like Mencken, Anderson, Lewis, Cabell, and Hergesheimer, Willa Cather and Ellen Glasgow, it meant long-delayed triumphs after years of preparation or neglect. To the younger writers who began to come up immediately after the war, like Fitzgerald, Cummings, Hemingway, and Dos Passos, men who felt themselves part of a tougher and disillusioned generation, writing was to seem as much a rejection of what the "middle generation" already represented as it was a testament to their experiences in the war. Layer on layer, emancipation by emancipation, the pattern of a modern American literature took shape out of that simultaneous emergence of so many different educations, talents, and aspirations; and nothing so illuminated the richness and variety of that literature as the fact that everything suddenly seemed to come together in the postwar scene. At the very moment that Fitzgerald was writing his tales of "the flapper age," and Cummings, Hemingway, and Dos Passos were writing their bitterly scornful antiwar novels, Anderson and Lewis were leading "the revolt from the village." At the very moment that the younger writers were going to school to Gertrude Stein in Paris and working away at a new American style, two richly gifted women of an older generation, Willa Cather and Ellen Glasgow, had finally achieved recognition, and. were just beginning to publish their best works. Ellen Glasgow had published her first novel in 1897, when most of the lost-generation novelists were one year old; and there were whole worlds, as it seemed, between *The Sun Also Rises* and *A Lost Lady,* or between *The Great Gatsby* and *The Romantic Comedians.* Yet it was the famous liberation of the twenties that brought them together, and at the time they even seemed to express a common postwar spirit of revolt and—especially with Ellen Glasgow—of satire.

Like the younger writers, both Willa Cather and Ellen Glasgow had a brilliant sense of style and an instinct for craftsmanship. But their feeling for style demanded none of the formal declarations and laborious experiments that Hemingway and Dos Passos brought to theirs. Like so many women in modern American writing from Emily Dickinson to Katherine Anne Porter, they had a certain dignity of craft from the first, a felicity all their own. In a period so marked by devotional estheticism in writing, and one when it was easy to slip into the ornamental fancywork of men like Cabell and Hergesheimer, Willa Cather and Ellen Glasgow stood out as examples of serious craftsmanship; and it is strange how easy it has always been to forget how much more brilliant a stylist Ellen Glasgow is than most of the younger writers, and how much more deeply imaginative an artist Willa Cather proved than Hemingway.

Yet their craftsmanship had no gestures, no tricks, and—this is less true of Ellen Glasgow—no glitter. They were good, almost too serenely good; it was always so easy to put them into their placid niches. Yet if they seemed to be off on their own, it was largely because the experience that became the substance of their books now seemed distant and the hold of the past on them so magnetic. Willa Cather soon became a conscious traditionalist, as Ellen Glasgow satirized traditionalism; but what isolated them both was the fact that they brought the resources of the modern novel in America—and frequently not a little of the bitterness of the postwar spirit—to the persistent exploration and evocation of the past. Unlike so many of their postwar contemporaries, they used modernism as a tool; they did not make it their substance. Sharing in the self-consciousness and freedom of the new literature, their minds persistently ranged below and beyond it. Yet unlike writers like Irving Babbitt and Paul Elmer More, who went directly against the current of the new literature, they were wholly a part of it. Indeed, they testified by their very presence, as writers so diverse as F. Scott Fitzgerald and Anderson, Mencken and Van Wyck Brooks, Hemingway and Cabell, had already testified, to the variety and freedom of the new American literature.

2

Willa Cather and Nebraska grew up together. Born in Virginia, she was taken at eight to a country moving in the first great floodtide of Western migration in the eighties. Within a single decade half a million people—Yankee settlers, sod-house pioneers out of the Lincoln country, Danes, Norwegians, Germans, Bohemians, Poles—pulled up stakes or emigrated from the farms of northern and eastern Europe to settle on the plains of a region that had been "a state before there were people in it." Nebraska was the first of the great settlements beyond the Mississippi after the Civil War, and the pace of its settlement and the polyglot character of its people were such that they seemed to mark a whole new society in flower. The successive stages of economic and social development were leaped quickly, but not too quickly; as late as 1885 the state was mostly raw prairie, and for the children of the first pioneers history began with the railroad age roaring in from the East. Nebraska was a society in itself, a bristling new society, proud of its progress and of values and a morality consciously its own. The prairie aristocracy that was to play as triumphant and even didactic a role in Willa Cather's novels as the colonial aristocracy had played in Edith Wharton's may have been composed out of the welter of emigration; but it was a founding class, and Willa Cather never forgot it.

Her enduring values were the values of this society, but they were not merely pioneer and agrarian values. There was a touch of Europe in Nebraska everywhere during her girlhood, and much of her distinctive literary culture was to be drawn from it. The early population numbered so many Europeans among it that as a young girl she would spend Sundays listening to sermons in French, Norwegian, and Danish. There was a Prague in Nebraska as well as in Bohemia. Europe had given many brilliant and restless young men to the West. Amiel wrote letters to a nephew who died among the Nebraska farmers; Knut Hamsun worked on a farm just across the state line in South Dakota; a cousin of Camille Saint-Saëns lived near by in Kansas. One could walk along the streets of a county seat like Wilber and not hear a word of English all day long. It was in this world, with its accumulation of many cultures, a world full of memories of Grieg and Liszt, of neighbors who taught her Latin and two grandmothers at home with whom she read the English classics, that Willa Cather learned to appreciate Henry James and at the same time to see in the pioneer society of the West a culture and distinction of its own. Her first two years there, she wrote later, were the most important to her as a writer.

All through her youth the West was moving perpetually onward, but it seemed anything but rootless to her; it suggested a distinctive sense of permanence in the midst of change, a prairie culture that imparted to her education a tender vividness. Unconsciously, perhaps, the immigrants came to symbolize a tradition, and that tradition anchored her and gave her an almost religious belief in its sanctity. Growing up in a period of violent disruption and social change, she was thus brought up at the same time to a native and homely traditionalism. Later she was to elegize it, as all contemporary America was to elegize the tradition of pioneer energy and virtue and hardihood; but only because it gave her mind an abiding image of order and—what so few have associated with the pioneer tradition—of humanism. Her love for the West grew from a simple affection for her own kind into a reverence for the qualities they represented; from a patriotism of things and place-names into a patriotism of ideas. What she loved in the pioneer tradition was human qualities rather than institutions—the qualities of Antonia Shimerda and Thea Kronberg, Alexandra Bergson and Godfrey St. Peter—but as those qualities seemed to disappear from the national life she began to think of them as something more than personal traits; they became the principles which she was to oppose to contemporary dissolution.

Willa Cather's traditionalism was thus anything but the arbitrary or patronizing opposition to contemporary ways which Irving Babbitt personified. It was a candid and philosophical nostalgia, a conviction and a standard possible only to a writer whose remembrance of the world of her childhood and the people in it was so overwhelming that everything after it seemed drab and more than a little cheap. Her distinction was not merely one of cultivation and sensibility; it was a kind of spiritual clarity possible only to those who suffer their loneliness as an act of the imagination and the will. It was as if the pervasive and incommunicable sense of loss felt by a whole modern American generation had suddenly become a theme rather than a passing emotion, a disassociation which one had to suffer as well as report. The others were lost in the new materialism, satirized or bewailed it; she seceded, as only a very rare and exquisite integrity could secede with dignity. Later, as it seemed, she became merely sentimental, and her direct criticism of contemporary types and manners was often petulant and intolerant. But the very intensity of her nostalgia had from the first led her beyond nostalgia; it had given her the conviction that the values of the world she had lost were the primary values, and everything else merely their degradation.

It was this conflict, a conflict that went beyond classes and could be represented only as a struggle between grandeur and meanness, the two poles of her world, that became the great theme of her novels. She did not celebrate the pioneer as such; she sought his image in all creative spirits [1]—explorers and artists, lovers and saints, who seemed to live by a purity of aspiration, an integrity or passion or skill, that represented everything that had gone out of life or had to fight a losing battle for survival in it. "O Eagle of Eagles!" she apostrophized in *The Song of the Lark*. "Endeavor, desire, glorious striving of human art!" The world of her first important novels—*O Pioneers! The Song of the Lark, My Ántonia*—was unique in its serenity and happiness. Its secret was the individual discovery of power, the joy of fulfilling oneself in the satisfaction of an appointed destiny. The material Alexandra Bergson and Thea Kronberg worked with was like the naked prairies

---

[1] "Nothing is far and nothing is dear, if one desires. The world is little, human life is little. There is only one big thing—desire. And before it, when it is big, all is little."—Old Wunsch to Thea Kronberg in *The Song of the Lark*.

"Desire is creation."—Godfrey St. Peter in *The Professor's House*.

Jim Burden saw in *My Ántonia* on the night ride to his grandparents' farm. "There was nothing but land: not a country at all, but the material out of which countries are made." It was always the same material and always the same creative greatness impressed upon it. Ántonia was a peasant and Thea a singer, but both felt the same need of a great and positive achievement; Alexandra was a farmer, but her feeling for the land was like Thea's feeling for music. The tenacious ownership of the land, the endless search of its possibilities, became the very poetry of her character; the need to assert oneself proudly had become a triumphant acceptance of life.

Yet even as Willa Cather's pale first novel, *Alexander's Bridge,* had been a legend of creative desire and its inevitable frustration, so in these novels the ideal of greatness had been subtly transformed into a lesson of endurance. Even in *My Ántonia,* the earliest and purest of her elegies, the significance of achievement had become only a rigid determination to see one's life through. The exultation was there, but it was already a little sad. Her heroines were all pioneers, pioneers on the land and pioneers of the spirit, but something small, cantankerous, and bitter had stolen in. The pioneer quality had thinned, as the pioneer zest had vanished. Ántonia might go on, as Thea might flee to the adobe deserts and cliff cities of the Southwest for refuge, but the new race of pioneers consisted of thousands of farm women suffering alone in their kitchens, living in a strange world amidst familiar scenes, wearing their lives out with endless chores and fears.

> On starlight nights I used to pace up and down those long, cold streets, scowling at the little, sleeping porches on either side, with their storm-windows and covered back porches. They were flimsy shelters, most of them poorly built of light wood, with spindle porch-posts horribly mutilated by the turning-lathe. Yet for all their frailness, how much jealousy and envy and unhappiness some of them managed to contain! The life that went on in them seemed to me made up of evasions and negations; shifts to save cooking, to save washing and cleaning, devices to propitiate the tongue of gossip.

By 1920, the stories in *Youth and the Bright Medusa* hinted at a growing petulance, and in stories like "A Wagner Matinée" and "The

Sculptor's Funeral" there was nothing to indicate that Willa Cather thought any better of small-town life than Zona Gale or Sinclair Lewis. Yet by their very bitterness, so much more graphic than the dreary tonelessness of *Miss Lulu Bett,* these stories revealed how sharp her disillusionment had been, and when she developed the theme of small-town boorishness in *One of Ours* into the proverbial story of the sensitive young man, she could only repeat herself lamely. She was writing about an enemy—the oppressively narrow village world—which seemed only one of the many enemies of the creative spirit, but she did not have Zona Gale's inverted sentimentality, or anything like the spirit of Lewis's folksy and fundamentally affectionate satire. *One of Ours* was a temporary position for an artist whose need of an austere ideal was so compelling. Claude Wheeler was only the Midwest *révolté;* her authentic heroes were something more than sensitive young men who "could not see the use of working for money when money brought nothing one wanted. Mrs. Ehrlich said it brought security. Sometimes he thought that this security was what was the matter with everybody: that only perfect safety was required to kill all the best qualities in people and develop the mean ones." The farmer's wife in "A Wagner Matinée" had felt something deeper when, after her few moments of exultation at the concert, she turned and cried: " 'I don't want to go, Clark. I don't want to go!' Outside the concert hall lay the black pond with the cattle-tracked bluffs; the tall, unpainted house with weather-curled boards, naked as a tower; the crook-backed ash seedlings where the dish-cloths hung to dry; the gaunt moulting turkeys picking up refuse about the kitchen door."

The climax in Willa Cather's career came with two short novels she published between 1923 and 1925, *A Lost Lady* and *The Professor's House.* They were parables of the decline and fall of the great tradition, her own great tradition; and they were both so serenely and artfully written that they suggested that she could at last commemorate it quietly and even a little ironically. The primary values had gone, if not the bitterness she felt at their going; but where she had once written with a naïvely surging affection, or a rankling irritation, she now possessed a cultivated irony, a consummate poise, that could express regret without rancor or the sense of irretrievable loss without anguish.

She had, in a sense, finally resigned herself to the physical and moral destruction of her ideal in the modern world, but only because she was soon to turn her back on that world entirely in novels like *Death Comes for the Archbishop* and *Shadows on the Rock*. In the person of a Captain Forrester dreaming railroads across the prairies, of a Godfrey St. Peter welding his whole spirit into a magnificent history of the Spanish explorers in America, she recaptured the enduring qualities she loved in terms of the world she had at last been forced to accept. These were the last of her pioneers, the last of her great failures; and the story she was now to tell was how they, like all their line, would go down in defeat before commerce and family ties and human pettiness.

Only once in *A Lost Lady* did her submerged bitterness break through, in her portrait of Ivy Peters, the perfect bourgeois:

> Now all this vast territory they had won was to be at the mercy of men like Ivy Peters, who had never dared anything, never risked anything. They would drink up the mirage, dispel the morning freshness, root out the great brooding spirit of freedom, the generous, easy life of the great landholders. The space, the colour, the princely carelessness of the pioneer they would destroy and cut up into profitable bits, as the match factory splinters the primeval forest. All the way from Missouri to the mountains this generation of shrewd young men, trained to petty economies by hard times, would do exactly what Ivy Peters had done.

The theme was corruption, as it was to be the theme of *The Professor's House*. It was as explicit as Marian Forrester's dependence on her husband's frontier strength and integrity, as brutal as Ivy Peters's acquisition of Marion Forrester herself. And at the very moment that Willa Cather recognized that corruption in all its social implications, gave its name and source, she resigned herself to it. It had been her distinction from the first to lament what others had never missed; she now became frankly the elegist of the defeated, the Amiel of the novel. The conflict between grandeur and meanness, ardor and greed, was more than ever before the great interest of her mind; but where she had once propounded that conflict, she now saw nothing but failure in it and submitted her art almost rejoicingly to the subtle exploration of failure. In any other novelist this would have made for sickliness and preciosity; now that she was no longer afraid of failure as a spiritual fact, or restive under it, her work gained a new strength and an almost radiant craftsmanship.

The significance of this new phase in Willa Cather's work is best seen in *The Professor's House,* which has been the most persistently underrated of her novels. Actually it is one of those imperfect and ambitious works whose very imperfections illuminate the quality of an imagination. The story of Godfrey St. Peter is at once the barest and the most elaborately symbolic version of the story of heroic failure she told over and over again, the keenest in insight and the most hauntingly suggestive. The violence with which she broke the book in half to tell the long and discursive narrative of Tom Outland's boyhood in the Southwest was a technical mistake that has damned the book, but the work as a whole is the most brilliant statement of her endeavor as an artist. For St. Peter is at once the archetype of all her characters and the embodiment of her own beliefs. He is not merely the scholar as artist, the son of pioneer parents who has carried the pioneer passion into the world of art and thought; he is what Willa Cather herself has always been or hoped to be—a pioneer in mind, a Catholic by instinct, French by inclination, a spiritual aristocrat with democratic manners.

The tragedy of St. Peter, though it seems nothing more than a domestic tragedy, is thus the most signal and illuminating of all Willa Cather's tragedies. The enemy she saw in Ivy Peters—the new trading, grasping class—has here stolen into St. Peter's home; it is reflected in the vulgar ambition of his wife and eldest daughter, the lucrative commercial use his son-in-law has made of the invention Tom Outland had developed in scholarly research, the genteel but acquisitive people around him. St. Peter's own passion, so pure and subtle a pioneer passion, had been for the life of the mind. In the long and exhaustive research for his great history, in the writing of it in the attic of his old house, he had known something of the physical exultation that had gone into the explorations he described. As a young man in France, studying for his doctorate, he had looked up from a skiff in the Mediterranean and seen the design of his lifework reflected in the ranges of the Sierra Nevada, "unfolded in the air above him." Now, after twenty years of toil, that history was finished; the money he had won for it had gone into the making of a new and pretentious house. The great creative phase of his life was over. To hold onto the last symbol of his endeavor, St. Peter determined to retain his old house against the shocked protests of his family. It was a pathetic symbol, but he needed some last refuge in a world wearing him out by slow attrition.

In this light the long middle section of the novel, describing Tom Outland's boyhood in the desert, is not a curious interlude in the novel; it becomes the parable of St. Peter's own longing for that remote world of the Southwest which he had described so triumphantly in his book. Willa Cather, too, was moving toward the South, as all her books do: always toward the more primitive in nature and the more traditional in belief. Tom Outland's desert life was thus the ultimate symbol of a forgotten freedom and harmony that could be realized only by a frank and even romantic submission to the past, to the Catholic order and doctrine, and the deserts of California and New Mexico in which the two priests of *Death Comes for the Archbishop* lived with such quiet and radiant perfection. Her characters no longer had to submit to failure; they lived in a charming and almost antediluvian world of their own. They had withdrawn, as Willa Cather now withdrew; and if her world became increasingly recollective and abstract, it was because she had fought a losing battle that no one of her spirit could hope to win. It was a long way from the Catholic Bohemian farmers of Nebraska to the eighteenth-century Catholicism of the Southwest, but she had made her choice, and she accepted it with an almost haughty serenity. As early as 1922, in "The Novel *Démeublé*," her essay on fiction, she had defined her rejection of modern industrial culture explicitly, and had asked for a pure novel that would throw the "social furniture" out of fiction. Even a social novelist like Balzac, she had insisted, wrote about subjects unworthy of him; for the modern social novelists she had only a very gracious and superior contempt. "Are the banking system and the Stock Exchange worth being written about at all?" she asked. She thought not, and itemized the "social furniture" that had to be thrown out of the novel, among them the factory and a whole realm of "physical sensations." It was now but a step from the colonial New Mexico of *Death Comes for the Archbishop* to old Quebec in *Shadows on the Rock* and the lavender and old lace of *Lucy Gayheart.* Her secession was complete.

2

The significance of Willa Cather's exquisitely futile values was often slurred over or sentimentalized; the felicity of her art was never ignored. Her importance to the older generation—a generation that was now to make room for Hemingway—was a simple and moving one: she was its consummate artist. To critics sated with the folksy satire or bitterness of the village revolt, she suggested a preoccupation with the larger motives; to critics weary of the meretriciousness of Cabell and Hergesheimer, she personified a rich and poised integrity; to critics impatient with the unkempt naturalism of Dreiser and Anderson, she offered purity of style. As an indigenous and finished craftsman, she seemed so native, and in her own way so complete, that she restored confidence to the novel in America. There was no need to apologize for her or to "place" her; she had made a place for herself, carved out a subtle and interesting world of her own. If that world became increasingly elegiac and soft, it was riches in a little room.

Ellen Glasgow, in many respects a much stronger and more interesting talent, presented a different problem. She was even more profoundly a traditionalist than Willa Cather, but her tradition was a subject to be explored, often a very comic subject; it was not an attitude of mind to be imposed upon one's material. Willa Cather made her own tradition and suffered for it; Ellen Glasgow was born imprisoned in a social and physical tradition not of her own making, and made her career by satirizing it. Inevitably, she became a martyr to American criticism. Radical critics ignored her because they could not place her; conservative critics praised her blindly because they could use her as a lesson to irreverent modernists. Critics who wished to prove a thesis were satisfied that she belonged to a "Southern" school, along with James Branch Cabell and Erskine Caldwell and Thomas Wolfe; others were ready to declare her all that was left of the Genteel Tradition. But she always defied facile classification. Like the French historian of English literature who wrote plaintively that Robert Burns "brings an element of complication into what is otherwise the relatively simple evolution of English poetry," critics who need to brand writers like steers must always find Ellen Glasgow disturbing. She began as the most girlish of Southern romantics and later proved the most biting critic of Southern romanticism; she was at once the most traditional in loyalty to Virginia and its most powerful satirist; the most sympathetic historian of the Southern mind in modern times and a consistent satirist of that mind. She wrote like a dowager and frequently suggested the mind of a nihilist; she was at once the most old-fashioned of contemporary American novelists and frequently the wittiest.

Like Tolstoy, who knew only one society and spent his life quarreling with it, Ellen Glasgow knew only the Virginia which to Virginians of her class is not a state but an idea. She did not quarrel with her heritage; she merely coated it with ridicule. Yet her conception of life was bound for her by the feudal tastes, the gracious evasions, the inherent kindliness, and the fierce pride of caste that have marked her class from the first. She grew up to be not so much a Southerner as a citizen of the Old Dominion; and the young Sub-Lieutenant Tolstoy in His Imperial Majesty's Crimean Army could have had no more instinctive loyalty to the concept of Holy Russia than Ellen Glasgow had to the social principles of Virginia.

Thrown back on the defensive after the Civil War, Virginia stiffened in its loyalties and grew more charming and vague as its prejudices grew more rigid. It became a society living perpetually in the shadow of the Civil War, a society curiously lacking in the sense of time, but oppressively fanatical when dealing with contemporary problems; obsessed by principle, but living on pluck; dedicated to "culture" and rapidly suspicious of ideas other than its own. It was a culture that Ellen Glasgow once described as a series of "sanctified fallacies." It believed in the chivalric legends of its history, and practiced a withered gentility. It regarded literature, as Virginius Littlepage confessed in *They Stooped to Folly,* "as a pursuit even less profitable, and scarcely more distinguished than crockery, as a business." Mr. Littlepage even told his errant son-in-law, who aspired to be a writer, that "without posing as an authority, I may express the opinion that there isn't much material in Virginia history that hasn't already been exhausted."

Ellen Glasgow's first problem, unlike Willa Cather's, was thus how to become a writer at all. "I grew up," she confessed in later life, "in a charming society, where ideas were accepted as naturally as the universe or the weather, and cards for the old, dancing for the young, and conversation flavored with personalities for the middle-aged, were the only arts practised." Virginia prided itself on a social philosophy sufficient unto itself, a society that had developed almost a feudal standard of noblesse-oblige neighborliness, of mutual admiration and understanding where feminine virtue set the ideal and complacency was so thick that one could suffocate in it. "From the very beginning of its history," Ellen Glasgow wrote in a preface to *The Miller of Old Church,* "the South had suffered less from a scarcity of literature than from a superabundance of living. Soil, scenery, all the colour and animation of the external world, tempted a convivial race to an endless festival of the seasons. . . . Life was deficient in those violent contrasts that subdue the natural pomposity of man." The natural pomposity of some Virginians, however, became her great subject. Virginia could not stifle her desire to write, but it was necessary for her to hide her first published book from her family and friends.

As a spectator of the disintegration of the feudal South Ellen Glasgow saw so much of what she was later to call "the triumph in Virginia of idealism over actuality" that her first instinct was to quarrel with the facile myths of Southern romanticism. She revolted passionately—the word is her own—"not only from the school of local color, but also from the current gentility of letters, and more especially from the sentimental elegiac tone this tradition had assumed in Virginia." Her first desire as a writer was to tell the truth about Virginia against a setting of those legendary virtues in which she still believed. Her ambition was a whole series of works recording the history of modern Virginia. She aimed to be a realist in behalf of the great tradition, where so many of her compatriots were writing romance for the sake of romance. Significantly, however, she began, even after her first jejune novels, with a conventional Civil War romance, *The Battle-Ground,* on the ground that "one cannot approach the Confederacy without touching the very heart of romantic tradition. It is the single occasion in American history, and one of the few occasions in the history of the world, when the conflict of actualities was . . . the expiring gesture of chivalry."

Written on these lines, *The Battle-Ground* was a superior sword-and-cape romance based on the legend that the Civil War was fought between gentlemen and bounders. Yet for all its girlish sentimentality, it was the first of her many comedies of humors. Her most valuable and characteristic insight into Southern life was to see that the old aristocracy fiercely kept to the illusion that theirs was a truly feudal society; they needed to believe, where once they had claimed it as a matter of course, that life as they knew it was divided by inveterate principles of caste, and that in their caste each man had his place and each gentleman his appointed function. If there were lordly privileges, there were knightly obligations. The comedy of Southern life—Ellen Glasgow was the first realist in her time to see it—was thus the waking difference between illusion and truth. The South lived by a fiction: it rationalized failure with such pompous circumlocution that it could ascribe the most sordid tragedies to a defect of manners, and the most violent to bad taste. The great quality of the life she saw all about her was a simple and astonishing refusal to admit reality. That quality did not always seem wrong to her; she thought it even a little charming, though she knew that it was fundamentally ridiculous and even tragic. But where else in modern American society could one man say to another, as Virginius Littlepage said to his saucy brother Marmaduke, "There are occasions when I should think twice before calling you a Southern gentleman"? Even when the South was cruel— and it could be monumentally cruel, as Ellen Glasgow knew perhaps better than William Faulkner—its addiction to illusion was not something to be destroyed; it was one of those qualities on which a culture is grounded, and without which it perishes. And she was a Virginian, and did not want to see it change; least of all would she admit that it could perish, save in the haunting last pages of *The Sheltered Life*. What remained to her was irony, a crisp and epigrammatic irony that could verge on farce—or an inclination to the despair that is beyond all understanding.

In several of her books—notably *Barren Ground*—Ellen Glasgow wrote about other classes in the South, but her main interest was the aristocracy she knew almost too well. She ignored something far more ominous than the intellectual poverty of her class—its paralytic domination over Southern life—but the modulated bitterness of her wit went far to tell how deep her restiveness, and perplexity, had been. Hers was a wit raised to the dignity of a style, a wit that peered through her affection for the life she described and summed up her exasperation with it. When she discovered about 1913, the year she published *Virginia,* that the comedy of manners was her work, she made it serve what the very best comedies of manners have always served: as an index to the qualities of a civilization, and as a subtle guide to its covert tragedy. From one point of view, of course, her talent was only the highest expression of the society she lampooned; but her attacks on Southern complacency were never complacent in themselves. She belonged to a tradition and lived out her career in it; and her understanding seemed all the more moving because she was so deeply and immovably a participant in the world she scorned.

Virginia, the first of Ellen Glasgow's great tragicomedies, was thus significantly a story of innocence. Of all the chivalric myths she set out to satirize, the most fervid was the religious code of Southern womanhood. It was the crowning unreality. Beneath the hollowed pretensions of the Southern gentleman, the exaggerated and mechanical courtesy, there was sanctimonious cruelty. Pure womanhood, raised in pure ignorance, married off for the purest of motives, came to pure disaster. Young Virginia Pendleton had been educated in the Dinwiddie School for Young Ladies, where Miss Priscilla Batte—"I've always heard that poetry was the ruination of Poe"—indoctrinated the maidenly intelligence. "Just as the town had battled for an idea without understanding it, so she was capable of dying for an idea, but not of conceiving one." In this school Virginia was taught to look for sermons in running brooks and virtue in all men of her class. She ascribed her parents' poverty to their saintliness, her husband's coldness to his superior tastes, and her invincible mediocrity to modesty. Inevitably her marriage disintegrated, while both Virginia and her husband pretended—she out of pure ignorance, he out of loyalty to the genteel code—that proper marriages in their class never failed.

The succeeding novels often kept to this note: they recorded a long succession of frozen and unreal marriages. So Judge Gamaliel Bland, shown burying his wife as *The Romantic Comedians* opens, sighed wistfully over a marriage that was chiefly polite conversation, and straightway outraged his code and himself by falling madly in love with a flapper. So Virginius Littlepage in *They Stooped to Folly,* the very model of a Virginia gentleman, found himself smothered by the massive and imperturbable respectability of his wife. The classic wife in Ellen Glasgow's novels is a woman perfect in energy and grace, rich in quiet affection, a successful hostess, an admirable mother; but never a lover. She thwarts her husband as energetically as she inspires him to rise in their world; she preserves his place in the community and keeps him from enjoying it; she is so good that she bores him, and so possessive that she absorbs him. Beneath those ceremonial and inviolate marriages, frozen into the established order by an endless round of social duties, supported by a tradition capable of destroying any threat to its security, respectable lawyers dream of a world adolescent in its pleasures and overwhelming in its subterranean desire. Like Virginius Littlepage, they may even come to dislike their own children; but their emotion is little more than exasperation.

The scene of Ellen Glasgow's first postwar novels may seem at first to be only the comfortable upper-middle-class world of the twenties; in reality it is the last and most tragic phase of Southern feudalism. "In Queenborough," she wrote in her preface to *The Romantic Comedians,* "where lip-homage was still rendered to the code of beautiful behavior, the long reverberations of violence were felt chiefly under the surface. An increased momentum, a shriller vehemence, a wilder restlessness—these were the visible manifestations of a decayed . . . social order. The comic spirit, an enemy to unreason in any form, was still urbane, though its irony was suddenly spiced with malice." This was the society she described in the text of the novel as one which "had never outgrown an early stage of arrested development." Like Chekhov, she needed to describe a world that seemed to be dying slowly at the roots. Chekhov, who did not know that his world was prerevolutionary, sensed its coming disintegration; Ellen Glasgow, who never believed that the South would be revolutionary, knew that its great tradition was already dead. In the twenties her novels remained comedies, since the illusions by which her characters lived seemed private and vain; but when those illusions became something more than the winsome futility of tired old men like Littlepage and Judge Bland, they came to suggest a sick horror. It was the subtle development of this idea that became the subject of her most moving and penetrating novel, *The Sheltered Life.*

Like Chekhov's *The Cherry Orchard,* which it closely resembles in spirit, *The Sheltered Life* became a haunting study in social decomposition. Its characters were an archetypal gallery of Ellen Glasgow's society: Judge Archbald, married for thirty years to a woman he did not love simply because he had "compromised" her in their youth by being found alone with her in a carriage after midnight; Aunt Etta, the painfully indomitable spinster gentlewoman, the last of that procession of women who stream through Ellen Glasgow's novels quarreling with life and protected from it; George Birdsong, married to a beautiful woman whom he idolized but could not remain faithful to; Isabella, the coquettish rebel against Southern chivalry; and Eva Birdsong, in whom Ellen Glasgow had her triumph. For Eva was the last and the purest embodiment of ideal Southern womanhood, and her agony bespoke the ultimate agony of her tradition. Intelligent enough to grasp the disastrous implications of her code, she was blindly committed to it. Her powerlessness in the face of her husband's philandering, the rigid genteel resignation by which she was condemned to poverty, became the parable of her class in its final distress. Under the impact of the depression the gentility of its traditional manners turned in on itself, and Eva, who had been the town belle, was now the subject of its busiest gossip. She had once been an image of the ideal, and she was now being used to kill it.

Behind the livid tragedy of Eva's invalidism, her sweet-smiling and grotesque patience, the world of which she was so perfect a symbol was now going under. The old families were being smoked out by the nouveaux riches and factories in the countryside. George Birdsong's poverty, which in the first years after Appomattox might have been almost a badge of honor, was now only an inconvenience. "Here they had lived, knit together by ties of kinship and tradition, in the Sabbath peace that comes only to those who have been vanquished in war. Here they resisted chance and adversity and progress; and here at last they were scattered by nothing more tangible than a stench." Reduced by George's poverty, the Birdsongs now live too close to the factory, and their tragedy—emphasized by George's helpless philandering—is only a cold and forlorn indignity. Like the cry from that other world which closes *The Cherry Orchard,* that first ax breaking into the twilight darkness, *The Sheltered Life* ends as the new society that the South has denied and patronized so long encroaches on the old. "After living here all our lives," cries George Birdsong, "shall we at last be driven out by a smell?"

Chapter 11

LIBERALS AND NEW HUMANISTS

"The men of our age of critical realism, goaded by mass-stupidity and mass-tyranny, have protested against the common people to the point of losing all direct knowledge and vision of it. . . . And perhaps—strange that it should be left for me to make this observation—they have not affected their folk more profoundly because they have not loved it enough."—LUDWIG LEWISOHN

"Fighting a whole generation is not exactly a happy task."
—IRVING BABBITT to G. R. Elliott

IT WAS the liberal critics, from Howells and Garland to Van Wyck Brooks and Mencken, who had paved the way from the first for the new literature that was streaming into the twenties, and it was in liberal criticism, triumphant after the war, that the significance of the new literature and the liberations it preached were now fought out. Dominating the criticism of the period, the liberals found themselves attacked at its end, however, by the followers of two conservative critics, Irving Babbitt and Paul Elmer More, who had themselves from the late nineties on opposed the emergence of a modern literature in America. The New Humanism was perhaps less significant as a critical movement than as a portent of the disaffection and sense of crisis which so many writers were to feel at the end of the twenties; but its agitation for new standards marked the end of the postwar decade, as the triumph of the liberal critics marked its beginning. Be-

tween these two groups, save for the purely esthetic criticism of magazines like the *Dial* and the organs of the expatriates abroad, a large
part of the criticism written in the twenties was ranged.

If the liberal critics had proved courageous and independent before,
the critics who led the modern movement now performed great services. In scholarship, in cultivation, in appreciation of the creative sense,
they were to make the criticism of other periods seem thin, arid, and
crude. Yet there was a comic element pervading their labors which
Mencken, their great showman, was quick to see and ready to exploit. For the state of the country after the war, sigh as one will over
its dreariness and ugliness, was such that the great middle-class public,
the politicians, the "Old Guard," were actually on the defensive.
Never perhaps in any country had "advanced" writers commanded so
large a public and so wide an influence. Where the rebels of other literary movements had often worked in isolation and contempt to the
end, even the liberal critics now enjoyed a public prestige and position which afforded them unusual cultural influence and an intoxicating sense of their own power. Much as the conscious fashion of people
everywhere after the war was fixed on being "young," so the sudden
vogue of the new writers—and particularly the presence of the vocal
and enthusiastic public which doted on them—could be traced to the
effectiveness of the postwar liberation. Soon, very soon, the established
academies were to be open to the rebels, the official prizes—even two
Nobel Prizes—to be tendered to them; but their most immediate and
most significant victory lay in their extraordinary domination over the
public many of them now scorned.

It was here that the postwar reaction was felt in criticism. Mencken's
need to say the unexpected, the ironic complacency with which intelligent people lisped the saturnine convictions of *The Modern Temper,*
the widespread disrepute of traditional orthodoxies (how significant it
is that the traditionalism of Babbitt and More was felt most deeply on
the eve of the great changes in the thirties, not after the war), were
but the public evidences of this success. More suggestive and even a
little ominous was the carefree irresponsibility and the fashion of
"shock" statements—anything to beat the past—in intellectual matters.
Freudianism, in its inception a clinical method for carefully trained

and imaginative students, became—often quite unconsciously and un-scientifically—the laziest kind of sophisticated small talk in criticism and a technique by which writers armed with nothing more than the debunking spirit as such could expose the conflicts between the apparent and the real in every sphere. Debunking—America's journalistic Dadaism—was perhaps urgent, certainly juvenile, and always obvious; but debunking on the strength of a little reading in Freud, Jung, and Adler left extraordinary consequences in the criticism of a period which finally saw criticism reach its majority in America. For though the new criticism after the war stimulated new insights, new declamations, new tools of analysis commensurate with the needs of a growing modern literature, it also corrupted, more than a little, the best traditions of criticism.

Even the most progressive minds in America have always been victims of the liberations they have brought, and the sense of reality after the war, as is common to people suffering from hangovers, was slightly defective. The occasionally hysterical generalizations and assumptions that began to come into American criticism after the war were not altogether adventitious. Nothing, in one sense, so graphically distinguishes some of these critics in history as the solemnity which allowed one of the most sensitive of them to refer in all seriousness to the "cast-iron purity of the late 19th century," or another to the "essential sexlessness" of the same period. Mencken's flip ability to define love as "a minimum of disgusts" set the tone; but Mencken was hardly alone in a day when monstrous perversions of fact were taken for wit, or the self-confidence of the emancipated for a philosophy of history. The liberal critics had become fascinated with science, and they brought to the general chorus of doom the comforting misanthropy of a science that had plainly bereft man of his dignity. Criticism became not scientific in intention, as in the thirties, but science-fascinated: a method of analysis which laid no claims to scientific value and was even arrogantly antirationalist, but soaked up the fashionable jargon of science. In a world of postwar tremors, aches, and pains, of psychic disorders and neurasthenia, a criticism which used psychoanalysis almost absent-mindedly from time to time was but one of the obvious techniques by which all the lost generations exercised their bitterness against the secret diplomacy of the mind. Even as the revolutionary new governments in Russia, Hungary, and Germany had thrown open their archives, so many of the new critics opened up their subjects' souls and believed that they, too, were revenging themselves on the illusions of the past. Criticism necessarily lives by speculation, but it now became increasingly easy to speculate about glands and to evaluate artistry by amateur diagnosis. Dr. Freud, so brilliant a writer himself, regarded literature with awe, but for some of the critics literature became less important than the divagations of artistic personality itself. And it was but a step from the increasingly irresponsible use of such amateur diagnosis in criticism to the significant contempt with which literary men like Max Eastman were soon to patronize the literary imagination itself.

As in all periods, criticism illustrated its inveterate disposition to be something other than itself, and the critics had something of a holiday. The debunkers, as Bernard De Voto has said, destroyed Parson Weems, but paved the way for the sensation-mongering of MacFadden's *Daily Graphic*. Even the most sensitive and cultivated liberal critics of the time were not always able to disassociate the contemporary rage of debunking from their necessary need to comprehend the personal motivation of works of art. For some—this was a point that the opponents of psychoanalysis missed altogether—psychoanalysis did aid toward a modern transcription of Sainte-Beuve's desire to write criticism as "the natural history of souls"; for others, however, the superstition persisted that to have proved one's subject impotent was to have made a critical statement.

Yet this is but a fragment of the story, and to miss the intention and crusading force of liberal criticism in the twenties is to miss the fact that it established the place of criticism in America, and that, most significantly, it encouraged, defended, and often stimulated the new writing. For as innovators and sponsors of the new poetry and drama and fiction, the liberal critics were all engaged, as Van Wyck Brooks particularly had been since 1910, in establishing a taste for modern literature in America; and their gusto and sympathy were indispensable to the very growth of an adult literature. Like Carl Van Doren, who watched over many of the new writers from his offices at the *Nation*, they asked elementary questions in revolutionary language; but the questions seem elementary now only because they had been so rarely asked before. The very pitch at which Van Doren demanded that a book be *alive* was a sufficient measure of the urgency of vitality in 1920. Van Doren's esthetic theory never went beyond that, and fifteen years after he had written that "the measure of the creator is the amount of life he puts into his work. The measure of the critic is the amount of life he finds there," the statement seemed banal. In 1920, however, it meant the very creation of a public for Dreiser and Frost, and stressing the difference in the *Nation,* as Ludwig Lewisohn put it, between Sherwood Anderson and Zane Grey.

It was out of many of the new magazines that had been established before the war, and others that had been established after it, that liberal criticism now streamed in triumph. But though it was hardly alone in leading the new literature, it was in the literary columns of the *Nation* —"the newspaper of a passionate minority clamoring for justice"— that many of the liberal critics first became famous. Despite a limited circulation, its influence was immense. The magazine caught, as Van Doren later wrote in his autobiography, "the spirit of youth, as the younger generation caught the leading note of the twenties," and Van Doren himself carried that influence into his teaching of American literature at Columbia, his lectures and anthologies, and his editorship of the *Century.* The *Nation* became the spearhead of the revolt against the professors, but its offices and reviews were crowded with frocked and unfrocked professors. Van Doren, who alternated between Columbia and the *Nation,* was the prototype of the contemporary scholar in literary journalism and the leader of an increasing number of college teachers who were eager to adapt the freshness and insights of the new writing to literary research and pedagogy. He was passionately interested in literature, but a very empirical critic; much of his own success was that of a mediator between the public and the new literature. As a scholar he was not the most challenging of the *Nation* group, but thanks to his precision in matters of fact and a fundamental neutrality, usually the most sensible. In *The Roving Critic* he wrote:

> Those novelists and dramatists who now hate our provinces most are nearly all dissatisfied men lately escaped from stodginess and devoted

to getting their revenges. . . . But the truly emancipated spirit no longer has time for recrimination and revenge. He knows that familiarity with mankind comes partly from affection for it, and that the truth is therefore not unrelated to affection. How then shall he tell the truth about the provinces so long as he feels nothing but animosity for them?

Except in literature, however, too many of the *Nation* critics were content with the age that had given them their place in it, and their social criticism was often not more thoughtful than Mencken's. They were liberals by acquiescence, and their conception of social forces was either curiously decadent or frankly conservative. Van Doren and Lewisohn (the latter in those early years when he was still smarting from the social indignities of his experience during the war) had a conscious interest in democracy; but their liberalism was often couched in capital letters reminiscent of the casual benevolence of humane scholars and honestly cautious in the tradition of nineteenth-century liberalism. Lewisohn, at least, could claim a conscious devotion to the memory of John Morley at a time when most of his colleagues picked up their history from Spengler and Count Hermann Keyserling, the favorite postwar doctrinaires of aristocratic pessimism. To write glibly of the "unthinking herd" in the *Nation* was, perhaps, to be less in the style of Mencken than in the tradition of Matthew Arnold. As enemies of Philistia, the *Nation* critics were not consciously enemies of the "booboisie"; like so many writers of the time they were merely detached from its common life and fashionably superior. They were revolutionaries, yes, but not by habit or intellectual profession, and certainly not out of any profound revolutionary convictions; they were protagonists of culture. They usually believed, as Lewisohn once wrote in a *Nation* review of John Galsworthy, that they had "tested the political and moral pretensions of mankind and found them a blunder and a shame," but their understanding of social necessity was at bottom as sentimental as Galsworthy's, or even neo-aristocratic in the fashion of Cabell and Hergesheimer. They all approved Lewisohn's dictum— though without sharing his characteristic excitement in the matter— that "man is a metaphysical animal even more profoundly than he is a political one," but if some philosopher had charged that they had no philosophy, they would have thought him queer; if a radical had accused them of timidity, they would have been offended. Were they not all against Irving Babbitt, and did they not all have in some measure the modern view of life? If they were nihilists, it was for the sake of literature; if they were liberals, it was because conservatism had become a joke.

Philosophically, therefore, the liberal school reached its apogee when it encountered philosophy in Joseph Wood Krutch's *The Modern Temper*. In it a whole postwar generation found its primer, and by seizing upon it avidly, revealed its purpose in the image of a universe without purpose. What was remarkable about Krutch's felicitously written essay in futility was not its iconoclasm, since philosophical materialism had already won its major battles in America, but the self-contentment of its pessimism. It was an exercise in superior nihilism written exclusively for nihilists, that their indifference and skepticism might have a "scientific"—or philosophical—authority. With a cavalier detachment that would have stupefied any of the world's great philosophical naturalists, Krutch blithely took it for granted, as did his readers, that to prove the universe no longer anthropocentric was to prove life nothing more than a vain spectacle. "To understand any of the illusions upon which the values of life depend inevitably destroys them. . . . At bottom, life is worth living only because certain of our conscious activities allowed themselves to be regarded as though they were possessed of some importance or significance in themselves." Even more suggestive was Krutch's neo-Darwinism, which, equating the power to survive with brute animalism, proceeded to assert that since contemplative minds were always found at their rarest pitch in societies at the point of death, melioration was the enemy of thought. The modern intellectual, in short, was the very orchid of civilization, and by the nature of his preciosity of soul removed from society's rude purposes and hence not responsible to its mass values. A perfect society was therefore nothing but an ant pile; the vigor of the great eras in literature, Periclean and Elizabethan, Krutch ascribed to the supremacy in them of "adolescent man," man still capable of some harmonious world-view, as opposed to the world-weary, exacerbated intellectual of the modern era.

Much of what Krutch said in *The Modern Temper* was true, but its significance was not that of a philosophical document at all. It was an attempt to justify an absolute skepticism to a generation which took frigidity for detachment and sophistication for contemplative wisdom. The very animus of Krutch's essay was an attempt to bolster the provincial superiority of the intellectuals by proving the universal inferiority of human life. "A [truly] tragic writer does not have to believe in God, but he must believe in man," wrote Krutch. The critics of the Mencken age, armed with what must now seem a capsule metaphysics, did not choose to believe in man. What Krutch was summing up in his little book was not the bankruptcy of human standards but the predicament of his contemporaries, and he admitted as much when he wrote that literature at the present time could "tell itself no stories except those which make it still more acutely aware of its trivial miseries."

Unwittingly, perhaps, Krutch also hinted at the growing sickliness and sentimentality of a literary criticism that was ready to see failure, failure everywhere, and to ascribe it to everything in life and society save the inadequacy of the writer's personal resources and imagination. That there were creative spirits at home and abroad who, though conscious of the sickness of the age, were able to meet it with their gifts, their capacity for life, their need to convert, as André Malraux put it, the largest possible quantity of experience into conscious thought, did not concern those who found in the *taedium vitae* of *The Modern Temper* an extenuation of their unimportance. To talk plainly of talent and personal resources, of sensibility and imagination, was becoming the rarest note in American criticism. Postwar hypochondria, real enough, had made determinism convenient and attractive, but this determinism consisted of studies in victimization; it was not an interest, like Sainte-Beuve's, or Taine's, or even Vernon Parrington's, in the sub-structural relations between art and society, literature and belief. It was a conception of criticism which had begun with the need to characterize society and to define the artist's place in it, but soon exhausted itself by bewailing the fate of the artist in a hostile world; a criticism self-consciously aristocratic and unwittingly sentimental. The critic rarely asked the writer he studied: What have you to declare?

The writer, it seemed, had everything to declare; only the stupidity of the mass and the thinness of life in America kept him from greatness. Few people were now ready to venture the platitude that a writer is only the sum of his abilities and no more significant than his conception of existence. No, one blamed Life, and went on baiting the American Pioneer, the American Puritan, and Mencken's Great American Boob.

2

Ludwig Lewisohn was among the very few who did venture, and the passion with which he insisted upon the elementary facts of the creative process singled him out immediately at a time when cynicism and apathy could so easily be taken for the tragic sense. This is not to say that he was averse to the extravagances and inanities of contemporary critical thought. On the contrary, he was the most frenzied apostle of them, since he carried the postwar discovery of sex and the growingly bitter calumny of the past to the point of self-ridicule. But Lewisohn was never a "simple" figure, and his worst qualities represented the exaggerations of a mind which was in itself indispensable to the growth of a mature criticism in America. Few critics in America have ever, indeed, had so moving an ideal of the critic's function or kept to it so stubbornly. It was merely unfortunate that the very intensity with which he insisted with an almost religious conviction upon the nobility of art and the universal significance of creative expression— "Art is the life-process in its totality"—tricked him into saying too much.

The climate of opinion in the twenties was largely responsible, for it was deceptively friendly to Lewisohn. Criticism in the twenties— and not only then—needed to be told that it had "neither passion nor vision." Our critics "are very able, very honest, very well-informed, and very witty. But, to put it mildly and yet correctly, they don't care enough." Lewisohn told them—rather often. Inevitably, he conceived a function for his criticism that was oracular rather than didactic. More strikingly than any other in a generation of critics who wished to write like artists, he was a tormented and imaginative writer who carried over into his criticism the tensions of his novels. At the same time he was an oversensitive alien who had been lacerated by Know-Nothingism in the Middle West during the war, a Jew who raised the immemorial loneliness of the Jewish mind to a historical principle, and a humorless lover-hero of the Freudian epoch who translated his domestic difficulties into pompous dicta for everyone at large. As the future was to prove, Lewisohn's criticism was thus not merely creative, but also a form of martyrology.

The extent to which Lewisohn interpreted his temperamental qualities as absolutes, and his personal prejudices and superstitions as critical dicta, was unique only in its frankness; but the imperturbable gravity and messianic confidence with which he refused ever to look beyond his own ideas were extraordinary. When the war was over and Oswald Garrison Villard called him from his unhappy university experiences in the Middle West to review plays for the *Nation,* Lewisohn took his liberation as a call to arms. Two liberations—Lewisohn's and that of American literature—had plainly coalesced; and with his passionate devotion to Goethe, his superior scholarship, his lofty taste, he instinctively took 20 Vesey Street for Weimar and "the unthinking herd" for a race of doltish Eckermanns. Born a German and a Jew, he had been educated in a genteel Southern Episcopalian environment which gave him his florid style but cheated him, as he was later to feel, of his true heritage. He was an exile and unwanted; and with his sensibility, a self-indulgent rhetoric formed by passionate reading in the English romantic poets, and the Latinisms of Southern gentility, it was inevitable that he should remember his unhappiness bitterly and phrase it grandly. When he was refused a fellowship at Columbia in his youth, it was because "they"—the Calvinist enemies of freedom and truth—"felt in me the implacable foe of the New England dominance over our national life." "I was beaten, broken, breadless," he wrote in his autobiography. "I was a scholar and forbidden to teach, an artist and forbidden to write. Liberty, opportunity. The words had nothing friendly to my ear." Compelled to teach German rather than English literature, his isolation during the war confirmed in him the sense of a spiritual mission in America. Later his unhappy marital experiences proved to him that the artist had no freedom in America and that "the Nordic Protestant masses" had no conscience and no delicacy; "they know only superstition or a whip."

To a literary generation which saw all the wisdom of life in the passion for individual freedom and a hatred of provincialism, Lewisohn's passionate interpretation of his sufferings became the emblem of its own purpose. His conception of art as autobiography became infectious at a time when to regard oneself as an artist was to talk of oneself as a victim. Where the ego had once been a figure of speech, it was now a banner, and Lewisohn's esthetic gave the self-conscious individualism of the day a new solidity and impressiveness. For with all his faults, he was no mere rhapsodist, no secondhand Rousseau. He had greater cultivation than any of his fellow critics save Van Wyck Brooks; he knew the principal European literatures at first hand, and not merely for the purposes of quotation; he was devastatingly, irrepressibly in earnest. The Hebraic genius which he was so sentimentally to misinterpret did reveal its scriptural attributes in him. He believed, as very few students of literature in America have ever believed, with a sense of pressing, driving, irresistible need, in the highest purpose of expression.

It is in *The Drama and the Stage,* a selection from his drama reviews published in the *Nation,* that Lewisohn's exciting contribution to the postwar renaissance is seen at its best.[1] He did not delude himself that the new American theater on Broadway that emerged in the wake of the early experimental theaters was as sustained and imaginative as the great experiments in the modern drama at the Théâtre Libre in Paris and the Freie Bühne in Berlin.

> No one can understand the theatre who sees it too intently from within; no one can serve it who does not, as it is today, hold it a little cheap. . . . Revolving stages, subtle lights, elaborate scenes are

---

[1] Before coming to the *Nation* Lewisohn had done yeoman pioneer labor in adapting modern European literature to American criticism: in 1915, his essays on the modern European drama; in 1916, his Wisconsin lectures on modern German literature; in 1918, his book on modern French poets. His greatest service at the time was his masterly editorship and partial translation of the Hauptmann plays. It was characteristic of Lewisohn that his valuable early anthology of modern criticism, *A Modern Book of Criticism* (1919), included more of his own criticism than that of any of the other twenty-four French, German, English, and American critics represented. Yet it was entirely in keeping with the progress of American criticism at the time that Lewisohn should have been among the first to present such an anthology.

in their right order beautiful and useful things. They become a menace when they cause it to be forgotten that the platform is the platform of the eternal poet struggling with the mysteries of earth. This is not fine language; it is the plain and sober truth. But who will admit it?

Who did, indeed? Lewisohn's style, usually a little too oily, always too intent upon the rolling period, the ceremonious, vaguely celestial epithet, had not yet expanded into the purely magisterial splendors of *Expression in America*. Nor did it conceal his sober good sense and salutary passion for that conception of criticism as spiritual scrutiny which Jules Lemaître would have understood, but never George Jean Nathan; Alfred Kerr, but never Percy Hammond. Nathan, he remarked,

> wants to sit quietly in his aloof and faun-like elegance and glance at the exquisite form and glow of the petals and forget annoying things. . . . Never was the theatre less likely than today to become a gentleman's Paradise . . . We must cast in our lot with the world process and seek to bring the gravest and most stirring of the arts nearer in its true character to an ever-increasing number of men.

In those first great days of liberal criticism Lewisohn was more than a working critic; he was a force for progress. He aimed his reviews at the public, "the contented middle classes . . . who will endure physical but not moral suspense." He corrected superficial journalists and told them to read the *Poetics*. He satirized academic snobs given to desiccated piety to the past by reminding them of the contemporary and topical problems discussed in the Greek and Elizabethan theaters. He kept himself aloof from dramatic shoptalk and the jargon of the Broadway reviewers. "You do not understand the theatre," he had a manager say in an imaginary dialogue. "And you," Lewisohn replied "wearily," "understand nothing else." And that was certainly true. Yet Lewisohn's criticism soon began to defeat its own purpose. Over and again he wrote in the *Nation* that "the poet, the experiencing one, is a poet at every moment, in every relation. He cannot become an average man at a feast or in a church or in a jury box. His vision is his constant self. His material is not stone or iron or market values or laws; it is love and aspiration and ecstasy. His business is with fundamentals."

But the lofty tones, at first so portentous, soon lost their flavor and became a mechanical rhetoric of exaltation. It was true, as Carl Van Doren said in one of those necessary tributes to Lewisohn that are now never heard at all, that Lewisohn's merit always lay in his power to enlarge and elevate the matters before him; but Lewisohn's conception of those "matters" became increasingly patronizing and even irresponsible. His own master, Goethe, had said it best: *Im Anfang war die Tat.* As Lewisohn became fixed in his special enmity to the American scene, he increasingly showed a curious disinclination to look at Fact and a positive incapacity to look at the objects of his criticism fairly and dispassionately. Criticism was expression; it was autobiography, usually Lewisohn's own; it was lyrical, confessional, religious, "scriptural." But was not a critic's first duty to the simple homely truth?

In his own mind, and in his eloquent declamations on the high duty and austere function of criticism, Lewisohn agreed that it was. No critic in America save Paul Elmer More had gone so studiously to the whole history of criticism for guidance. No critic had ever insisted so strenuously on the need of precise study of the basic facts underlying a philosophy, an art, a spiritual vocation. Abstractly, indeed, Lewisohn was the most admirable of critics: a naturalist of great imaginative perception and with a salutary insistence on form; a scholar of great sensibility and seemingly the very type of the discerning and generous critical intelligence. In practice, for all his contempt for impressionism and the empirical methods of most American critics, he began more and more to write the history of literature as the history of Ludwig Lewisohn. By one of those summary psychic equations and emotional transferences that contribute so much to imaginative art but can corrupt the necessary poise of criticism, Lewisohn solemnly reasoned out his critical position to a point where he could evaluate literature in America solely in terms of his own character, his own sense of race, his own vicissitudes, and his own private aspirations as citizen, lover, and artist. He had begun, quite properly, by treating his European education and sense of "difference" as a personal advantage. His service, frequently valuable, was to leaven the lump, to talk the language of Goethe and Sainte-Beuve to the parochial, the superficial, and the complacent. Yet it is not too much to say that Lewisohn ended by defrauding himself, and the process was all the more gross because it rested on a lofty idealism and superior pretentions.

Out of the code of what Lewisohn repeatedly called "selfhood"—the artist against the world—he came to interpret almost sadistically the basic qualities of the literature he sought so passionately to elevate. It was not enough for him to write in his autobiography that "the Jewish problem is the decisive problem of Western civilization. By its solution this world of the West will stand or fall, choose death or life." Nor was it enough to say, as many were eager to agree, that "the relations between the sexes constitute the deepest and sorest problem of American life." For Lewisohn did not stop there. If he did not, like Mencken, consciously exploit the foibles of the postwar period, he became intoxicated with them. Where Mencken continued to proclaim his most egregious convictions on the level of pure comedy, Lewisohn began to write criticism at the heroic pitch of Wagnerian Volk metaphysics. In a world of intellectuals who adhered to nothing but themselves, he had suddenly recovered his race, his natal Hebraic culture, his place in the Judaic tradition. In a world of skeptics who chafed under their own skepticism, he had found a Moses in Freud and the whole meaning of life—not merely a method—in Vienna.

Lewisohn had, then, at least two seeming advantages over his rootless and empirical fellow critics when he sat down to compose the interpretation of American literature he had planned ever since he had been a graduate student at Columbia in 1904; and to them he now added a spiritual exaltation of psychoanalysis. For most of his contemporaries literary psychoanalysis was an interesting postwar experiment, a dissection of dead authors who could not defend themselves for the titillation of contemporaries who would not object. For Lewisohn it was a method of salvation. "Is it not but natural," wrote a friendly psychoanalyst, "that he use this science as a yardstick to measure the shortcomings of American literature? What applied to himself, and he often insisted that his case was a paradigm for the world, must equally apply to others. Psychoanalysis gave him his freedom for objectified creation; can it not provide the insight into what hampered or made for success of other contributors to American literature?" Since Lewisohn's "healing-process" was now complete, his study of the American tradition became, quite deliberately, a vindication of his talent and his due, a reversal of traditional standards. Where he had been the victim of the Gentiles, he was now their arbiter; and his creed was monstrous in its simplicity: "If ever there was a civilization in which evil, in the utterly questionable sense of sin, has been emphasized to a destructive and corrupting extent, it was and is America."

"Historic explanations are not statements of cause," Lewisohn had written in *Mid-Channel,* one of his autobiographies. "They are only rationalizations after the fact." In this light his *Expression in America* was truly, as Ernest Sutherland Bates said, an attempt to write a history of American literature from a completely unhistorical point of view. For Lewisohn felt no need to examine individual types and particular works disinterestedly or in the light of contemporary philosophies, social compulsions, the climate of opinion, the complexities of the national culture, the weaknesses of mortal flesh: he *knew.* For all his power, his sensibility to esthetic quality, he promptly revealed that he had very little curiosity—a critic's most obvious excuse for existence —in minds different from his own. With his thesis and his nostalgic idealization of an abstract European standard which Americans could never, never hope to emulate, he refused to understand, and lacked even the will to investigate, anything upon which his ubiquitous and tireless "selfhood" could not fasten. What had ailed American writing from its dark colonial infancy on had been the baneful influence of the Puritan mind and the Calvinist tradition of repression. How could one doubt it in the face of what he himself had suffered, in the face of Prohibition, John S. Sumner's snoopers, the Anti-Saloon League mind, and the pious banalities of Professor Stuart Sherman?

It has to be said of Lewisohn, of course, that he could be incandescent even when he was irrelevant and moving even when he was wrong. Yet it is indisputable that the man who wrote of Emerson and Thoreau "That they were chilled under-sexed valetudinarians, deprived of helpful and sympathetic social and intellectual atmosphere, renders their achievements only the more remarkable," lacked something indispensable to the comprehension of the American imagination. Emerson, it may be, would have understood Lewisohn as he would not have understood some other critics of the day, and Lewisohn did appreciate a basic quality in Emerson that Irving Babbitt never did when he wrote that the professors so given to celebrating Emerson would have been shocked to see his ideas in practice. It was this Hebraic humanism in Lewisohn, the belief he held, with William Blake, that "truth cannot be uttered so as to be understood and not be believed," that enabled him to appreciate Paul Elmer More's quality at a time when the modernists and traditionalists merely suspected each other.

Lewisohn was, indeed, one of the few critics of the day who talked good sense during the New Humanist controversy. No one in the liberal camp saw so clearly into the superficial estheticism of the twenties and inveighed so passionately against its nihilism. Yet for all his frequent brilliance of judgment, his own esthetic was not a directive. One could understand, even if one could not approve, the lofty neo-Goethean patronizing of Mark Twain as "our one American example of the bardic type of artist and sayer . . . one whom the common people can understand because he is theirs." Common people, forsooth! But what was one to say of a student of American literature who could in all sobriety declare that a "thousand *voluntary* delusions and repressions still afflicted" American writing after the Civil War? Or that "Franklin's eighteenth-century shop-keeping attitude toward the moral life . . . has survived in America and in America alone"? His highest praise, always, was "not ignoble." Not ignoble! It was the pure distillation of his fear of the enemy—Mencken's "booboisie" armed with pitchforks against truth and expression—and of his contempt for him.

3

Though Lewisohn lacked to a remarkable degree the ability to look beyond his own ideas—to hold them, as it were, in human suspension —he had at least one paramount service to perform, and he failed in it as much for reasons beyond his control as through his own rigidity of mind and supreme lack of humility. For what Lewisohn was always declaiming, out of his self-consciousness in America and his Hebraism, was what Van Wyck Brooks had said out of his Socialism before the war, and was now to apply negatively in his biographies of Mark

Twain and Henry James and Emerson—that if a writer is not rooted in a native culture, if he does not belong or find happiness in his belonging, he is nothing. It was the truth that Brooks had propounded in his first book, *The Wine of the Puritans,* when he had written at twenty-two with all the ardor of his characteristic spirit that "a man's work is more the product of his race than of his art, for a man may supremely express his race without being an artist, while he cannot be a supreme artist without expressing his race." Lewisohn *suffered* this truth; his own example was not enough to persuade others of it. Brooks, on the other hand, had lived by it from the first, and was now, as one of the leading spokesmen of the postwar school, to become the historian of its defeat. He became, that is to say, the historian of the negative and repressive aspects of American culture before he turned completely away from postwar nihilism in his *Life of Emerson.* In his *The Ordeal of Mark Twain* particularly, he gave the twenties the image of the Gilded Age that lies at the heart of that whole sentimental-pathetic conception of the artist in America which dominated the critical opinion of the time.

In composing *The Ordeal of Mark Twain, The Pilgrimage of Henry James,* and *The Life of Emerson,* Brooks illustrated many of the qualities that he brought to his first seminal essays and was later to exemplify so richly, even too richly, in his loving studies of the nineteenth-century mind in New England. The twenties marked his transition. He was moving slowly away from the polemics and blighted aspirations of the prewar Enlightenment, with its elementary definitions and forgotten sense of purpose, toward his final and affirmative recognition of the American heritage; inevitably, the Twain-James-Emerson triptych testifies to a retreat. Yet the example of his work was such that he did more than influence the liberal criticism of the time; he gave sophisticated opinion a whole new set of prepossessions. As a biographer his half-hearted Freudian analyses and self-indulgent lyricism directly encouraged less gifted "interpreters" in biography to mistake their prejudices for facts and to write bad poetry when they meant to write biography. As a historian his dramatic misanthropy furnished a dangerous model for those emotional followers who were eager to lament the past, never to study it. As a critic he was moving, eloquent,

stimulating—and monstrously inexact. Had Brooks merely sought to
be as cleverly irreverent as Lytton Strachey or Philip Guedalla in the
fashionably meretricious intention of the time, his faults as a biographer
would have seemed as trivial as their ambition for biography. But his
biographies, particularly his studies of Mark Twain and James, were
essays in tragedy. More, he had picked up from a French biographer
of Thoreau, Léon Bazalgette, a trick of incorporating quotations into
his text without acknowledgment, of pasting together his impressions
and borrowed quotations into a sickly lyrical "soul-portrait," and this
melancholy portrait-painting was to confuse criticism with the kind
of "artistic" representation that could become merely fictional in others.

Like so many of the younger critics who found themselves after
1920, Brooks often seemed to be grappling for something in criticism
that was simply not there—an exaltation, a secondhand ecstasy and
poetry. In Lewisohn's misuse of criticism there was no such conflict
of mind; he wrote his novels and critical essays with the same florid
hand. But Brooks's greater insight and tension invested his books with
a curiously tragic force. What John La Farge once said of Henry
Adams's feeling for history could be applied to Brooks's feeling for
criticism: it amounted to poetry. And if it was not good poetry, it was
because, as Ezra Pound once said of writers, more of them fail from
lack of character than from lack of intelligence. In Lewisohn and even
in some members of Brooks's own "school," notably Waldo Frank,
one saw criticism that was counterfeit poetry or synthetic "expression,"
criticism so illicitly creative and derivative that it was chiefly introspec-
tion. In Brooks, whose lifelong interest in the writer as failure became
at this period an obsession, one saw many unusual gifts for criticism
deflected, primary resources frustrated, through some inveterate personal sentimentality and weakness, some obscure personal failure of
the will. Whatever the cause, his work became marked by so ardent
and even morbid an interest in sensibility as such that his work lost
the toughness and fine edge it had possessed. It was Waldo Frank,
one of his most sympathetic admirers, who spoke of "a petulant delight
in pain." Brooks had lost his interest in difficulty, but he did not lose
his interest in criticism; the criticism now appeared as a series of
lamentations.

The Ordeal of Mark Twain and *The Pilgrimage of Henry James* were so different in style that they might have been written by different hands; but they served a common purpose by giving literary opinion in the twenties a conveniently misanthropic image of the Gilded Age to take comfort in. It was curious to note, however, that Brooks's influence as a historian of the moral life in America was always greater than his instructiveness as a critic. What he had to give most to the awakening of sensibility in America was passed over in silence; his solemn denigration of life after the Civil War made the Gilded Age a figure of speech, as facile a literary association as the Freudian Ego. Brooks's long lament over Mark Twain's tribulations came at a time when the revolt against Victorianism was being led by the debunkers, and in their own way the intellectuals read his book as they read Claude Bowers's *The Tragic Era, The Education of Henry Adams,* and the many fictional studies of Emily Dickinson—for solace and malicious amusement. Very few shared his feeling for Mark Twain, his lofty indignation at the repression of a great artist, his characteristic and moving insistence on the spiritual importance of great art. They were content to applaud his solemn attack on Olivia Clemens and Elmira, New York; the "brutish" frontier and the parochialism and vulgarity of contemporary taste. That Brooks's history took no account of the vitality of American thought during the Gilded Age, that his psychoanalytic flights were a subtle form of wish fulfillment, that his humorless condemnation of a whole period in American life was a little absurd, did not matter to them. Out of his profound conviction of Mark Twain's unhappiness and failure Brooks had written a brilliant study of the meanness and poverty against which artists had to rebel in America; and it was enough.

What is so significant about *The Ordeal of Mark Twain* today, despite Bernard De Voto's long and heated refutation of Brooks's complaints against the frontier, is not so much its simplicity of interpretation as its effort to draw an analogy between the Gilded Age and the postwar scene; an analogy between the "ordeal" of Mark Twain, which was dubious, and the self-consciousness of Brooks's literary generation, which was palpable enough. Brooks had from the first realized more deeply and illustrated more vividly than any other Amer-

ican critic just what the degradations of living in an acquisitive society
were; but where he had earned his reputation by discovering that fact,
he now sentimentalized it—and his sentimentality, in a word, was to
attribute the whole experience of his own generation to Mark Twain's.
It was inevitable that writers after the war should be obsessed with
the fate of writers in the eighties and nineties; as inevitable as that
they should simplify the correspondences between them. Both periods
were distinguished by an outrageous materialism; both saw a vulgar
boom society in full flower, a tawdry popular culture, dismal and
selfish statesmanship; both found writers in flight from their native
culture and tradition. But there was at least one difference between
them, and it was the failure to see that the worst qualities of the
Gilded Age represented an excess vitality, the almost primitive sensationalism of a young and growing society, that caused Brooks to miss
Mark Twain's physical verve and joy in life, the rough vigor of frontier life and the frontier mind. He complained that Mark Twain was
a boy; he forgot that his own generation was full of old young men,
caught by the disillusionment after the war and more than a little
exhausted by it.

Brooks's conception of the Gilded Age was not false; it was a great
literary myth, like Henry Adams's glowing interpretation of twelfth-
century culture, or Nietzsche's Dionysian portrait of Greek drama
—one of those primary hypotheses by literary men that give a design
to history and awaken the imagination. But as he applied it to Mark
Twain it rested on a curious amalgamation of social history and a
literary psychoanalysis that was so dazzling and new in 1920, still so
fundamentally a challenge to the old conventions, that it was at once
unconvincing and incontestable. Brooks did not say of his book, as
Joseph Wood Krutch said in his interesting psychoanalytic biography
of Poe, "Whatever a critic can convincingly read into a work may be
said to be actually there, even though it be thought of as the creation
of the critic rather than of the author criticized." Whatever else could
be said of Krutch's interpretation of Poe, it had been thought through,
and even possessed a logical coherence within the Freudian scheme.
Brooks was more ambitious and less logical; he was writing as
both artist and critic, and the worst that could be said of his psycho-

analysis was that he did not seem to believe strongly enough in it himself. His use of it was at once declamatory and sporadic; it played both ends against the middle. In Krutch's *Poe* one could legitimately criticize its thinking by analyzing the Freudian view of personality, the validity of its application to a particular subject, the assumption of literary Freudians, as Lionel Trilling has said, that the "meaning" of a work lies solely in its intention, not in its effect. Like the Freudians, Brooks was writing to a thesis; but it was not a Freudian thesis. His aim was to dramatize a great artist (Mark Twain) degraded by a narrow, prudish, greedy, hostile environment (the Gilded Age, Olivia Clemens, the frontier, and so on). In that aim, certainly, he succeeded brilliantly, and by his own sensibility and seriousness invested the whole context of late nineteenth-century letters in America with a tragic and unforgettable force. He even "proved" many things in the interest of criticism; what he could not prove was that his lay psychoanalytic interpretation of Mark Twain's somnambulism, or Mark's famous boyhood promise to his mother to eschew all evil, was anything more than another weapon in his armory, an indictment of Mark Twain's age that quickly passed into an indictment of everything Brooks and his contemporaries disliked at the moment.

In *The Pilgrimage of Henry James* Brooks went even further. He not only postulated an even more doubtful thesis—James's need to "escape" from the Gilded Age; he attempted to persuade the reader by impressionistic portraiture what he had in the Mark Twain at least marshaled evidence to prove. Aiming at criticism, he wrote biography like a novelist. He incorporated into his text a pastiche of quotations from James's novels, essays, letters, memoirs, with the intention of lulling the reader into the belief that what he had James say in a specific passage was what James had actually said at a specific time, or what James had felt in the recesses of his soul at a specific moment. Whatever one might think of Brooks's thesis—which in itself was another lamentation on the artist in American society and even less applicable to so complex and cosmopolitan a mind as that of James—his procedure was an unhappy one. His reading of James's novels was often evocative and shrewd, but the setting in which he placed it was sentimental and false.

In one passage, for example, Brooks sought to present one of the most poignant, but of itself hardly decisive, episodes in James's career, his disillusionment with the Flaubert *cercle* and the chilling of his first enthusiasm for the French literary mind.

> Was it possible that he had come to Paris too late, that he would have been more at home there in the old romantic days? If he had grown up in France . . .[1] if he had been still in his twenties. . . . It was impossible now; and besides, there was something so harsh and metallic about these naturalists, who dissected the human organism with the obscene cruelty of medical students, to whom nothing, or rather everything, everything but art, was common and unclean, whose talk savored only of the laboratory and the brothel. Ah, one's tender dreams of Europe, the soft illusion, the fond hope—was *this* what lay behind the veil? Perish the profane suggestion!

Not only did Brooks in such a passage—and there were many of them—misrepresent James's own notes on the matter, which were less insistent and more complex than Brooks ever suggested, but its images were so compiled that his lacquering of the surface produced something grotesquely unrepresentative of James's style and mind. It was a kind of "artistic" criticism which aimed so palpitatingly at an artistic effect that its critical substance was false.

Brooks reduced James's personal problem to such dimensions that only a consecutive and pointed argument could have supported him. Instead he offered pretty pictures, exquisite shades, operatic melancholy. His own distinguished style became painfully soft, clinging, humble. "Let us seek merely to observe our author at his writing table," he exclaimed in one passage, "to experience a few of the sensations that animate him, to share some of the thoughts that ascend from the obscure regions of his inner being." What wonder is it that Brooks consequently missed as much in James as he misrepresented in the imaginary soliloquies? James's own letter of 1872 was a reprimand. "It's a complex fate, being an American, and one of the responsibilities it entails is fighting against a superstitious valuation of Europe." In at least one passage Brooks revealed that he was restive under that "super-

---

[1] The dots of elision are in the text.

stitious valuation," but for general purposes he insisted upon it. Quoting Renan's beautiful tribute to Turgenev—"The silent spirit of collective masses is the source of all great things"—Brooks went on to declaim on James's failure to evoke that silent spirit:

> The great writer is the voice of his own people: *that* was the principle, the principle of which every European novelist of the first order has been a living illustration, and James had been too intelligent not to perceive it. . . . A fixed idea had prevented him from throwing himself into the life that he feared, and that life, which he had never challenged, had grown more formidable every day. Was it a choice between losing one's soul and losing one's senses; between surviving as a spiritual cripple and not surviving at all? In any case, principle or no principle, there was only one course open to him: he must escape.

There it was again: the obsession with the artist in society. Why had James fled? Obviously because his America offered no place for an artist. Why had James "failed"? Because no one can be an international pilgrim of art; the highest expression of the artistic will and the mark of its greatest success consist in the creative evocation of one's own culture, society, and tradition. But was not James a great artist? Yes, but he vitiated his art. He withdrew into the limbo of art for technique's sake; he became "a passionate mathematician of art." After writing *Washington Square* and *The Bostonians*, *The Pupil* and *Brooksmith*, *The Author of Beltraffio* and *The Beast in the Jungle*, he began to adapt himself to the foreign world he had once criticized and needed to satirize, and in his last period lost all common sense and human values. "The great thing had always been," he had James say, "to be saturated with something—in one way or another with life; and his own saturation had given out, had run short. He had scarcely scraped the surface of Europe; he had been too old to attach himself to another country." Hence Brooks's final indictment: James had become more interested in "manners" than in "morals." And the case was complete. James had failed to meet the social critic's test of "life"; he had wronged himself by failing to meet the demands of his "time"; his end was poignant but inevitable.

The professional Jacobites were not altogether wrong when they

insisted that Brooks did not understand James. For whatever their own
sickly worship of James, there was just enough understanding in
Brooks's criticism to make the staggering finality with which he presented his thesis unfortunate. Brooks's fault was not merely that he
virtually falsified passages from James's own books to "prove" what he
wished to believe;[1] it was the blend of sympathy and myopia, of sensitive appreciation and stern denunciation, that made his own sentimentality so painful. He was again writing criticism as allegory, and
his interest was fixed not so much on the quality, the density, the vivid
living penetration, of James's perception, as on the moral another nineteenth-century "failure" had for postwar exacerbation and sterility.
Brooks missed in James something so obvious as the effect of an international education upon an artist's sense of nationality. He missed
the very real ambiguity in James's own mind of his relation to America.
He missed, for all his sympathy, the unconscious divergence of a great
artist's loyalties and interests. By simplifying James's mind, Brooks
reduced the significance of his labor; and the deep earnestness with
which he pointed the parable of James's "escape" did not conceal his
own failure to comprehend the multiform intention and devotion
which gave James's career the appearance of a consecration. What
Brooks missed most strikingly was the extent to which James, for all
his elephantine slowness, his lack of invention, his detachment from
the speech and pace and movement of ordinary life, had burned his
curiosity into the secret innermost core of everything he touched. *That*
was James's success, and success enough—the defiance which had given
his monumental integrity a touch of greatness in the modern epoch;
the devotion to his craft which had imparted as much moral significance to his art as his art had illuminated hidden meanings in human
life.

When Brooks completed his Twain-James-Emerson triptych with
The Life of Emerson in 1932, the whole design became clear, and
Brooks entered upon a third phase in his portrait of America. Mark
Twain had been broken by nineteenth-century materialism in America;
James had fled from it; Emerson became the oracle and radiant first

---

[1] There is a devastating array of evidence on this point by Edna Kenton in the *Bookman*, October, 1925.

citizen of that springtime Concord world before the Flood whose greatest spirits had known a plenary happiness no other writers would know. After almost twenty-five years of quarreling with the national character, Brooks suddenly fell in love with it. This metamorphosis, adumbrated in the soft clouded impressionism of the book on James and Brooks's evident restiveness under formal criticism, was to lead him straight into his ambitious and loving rewriting of New England history. *The Life of Emerson* was a preliminary idyll, an unabashed prose poem so mellifluous in its infatuation that it could almost be set to music. Brooks had sloughed off with an imperturbable serenity all his early bitterness against the Emerson who had been only a ventriloquist in *America's Coming of Age.* Ralph Waldo was now a Voice: "the Hesiod of a dawning Nation, the Ennius, the Venerable Bede, up so early before the break of day." What greater marvel had ever been known than that village Athens in antebellum Massachusetts? It was, indeed, "a world of marvels," and Emerson was its Philosopher-King. What writers and thinkers so delightful as Alcott and Margaret Fuller, so quaint and brave as Thoreau, so pure as Channing, so reverent as Dr. Ripley? Brooks's happiness in them was moving in itself, so passionate and unclouded was his delight in Concord Pond and Concord streets, Concord books and houses, Concord talk and religion. Radiant in his exposition of Emerson's radiance (as of the young David: this Emerson was Biblical, he communed with Jehovah and instructed kings), Brooks sought only to restore him to the world. He had no wish to criticize, to evaluate, to blame; he had found himself in finding Emerson, and he now tried to hide himself in Emerson. His book was not biography, not history, not criticism; it did not seek to describe Emerson's growth, to evaluate his message, to place him in relation to his time; it wished solely to dramatize with loving care the Master's Soul. The book was a poem in which every cadence was a suggestion and every other word, culled with laborious delicacy from Emerson's own text, set with a jeweler's craft into the design. It was a poem decked with flowers from Emerson's own garden; even the most casual images were horticultural, and their fragrance calculated to delight.

Only rude unbelievers have wondered at the sudden incandescence, the startling contrast between the brisk irritated eloquence of the Mark Twain, the moody lushness of the Henry James, and the trancelike cheerfulness of the hymn to Emerson. Brooks's sentimentalization of America before the Civil War had always been implicit in his work; it was the necessary assumption of all his thinking and a principal article of faith for a writer whose quarrel with America had always been a lover's quarrel. He had exhausted his bitterness against one phase of the past, and he now turned with almost radiant simplicity to the celebration of another. And he was not alone. A conviction of the increasing futility and barrenness of the whole postwar experience seized writers everywhere as the twenties ran out and international panic and war lent a new significance to the sickness of the Western world. One saw the drift to some new affirmation—often any positive affirmation—in the frantic haste with which writers turned to the New Humanists and Marxism, Anglo-Catholicism and Thomism, social credit and even Fascism. T. S. Eliot's famous declaration of principles in the foreword to *For Lancelot Andrewes* had long since shown which way the wind was blowing. Writers might follow the path of Moscow rather than of Lambeth, but the postwar nihilism was outmoded, the wasteland was a battlefield, and the need of some positive loyalty was urgent. Brooks rapturously gave himself to the American tradition. Where he had once expounded America's enmity to the creative spirit with eloquent bitterness, he now became the most eloquent contemporary apostle of the genius of America. A decade after he had set down his conviction in *The Pilgrimage of Henry James* that one of the greatest of modern literary minds had fled from his homeland in loathing and terror, Brooks was to send an unqualifiedly patriotic emotion tingling down the national spine with *The Flowering of New England*. Skepticism had quietly dissolved. The last word had come in 1931, when Lewis Mumford wrote in *The Brown Decades,* "The desecrators [of the Gilded Age] are aware of epithets, but impervious to realities." The American patrimony had been claimed at last; the younger generation was now a middle generation, and had come home.

4

It was at this point, with liberal criticism going out on the ebb tide of the twenties and writers everywhere turning to new faiths on the eve of the thirties, that the violent counter-reformation against modern literature and thought which called itself the New Humanism made itself felt. The enthusiasm and rancor which the followers of Irving Babbitt and Paul Elmer More were able to stir up on the eve of the thirties now seem almost as remote as Babbitt and More always did themselves from the modern scene in America. Some of these followers have logically followed their yearning for authoritarian principles into the camp of Fascism; others have lapsed into a sadly hopeless disapproval of modern literature, where once they hoped to convert it, and emerge from time to time only to proclaim that something of the conservative wholesomeness they admire can be found in modern writers like Willa Cather, Robert Frost, and Lewis Mumford. The New Humanists helped to shape the traditionalism of certain esthetic critics in the thirties, much as the liberal critics influenced the Marxists; but the doctrine itself, with all the polemical excitement and ambitious grandeur it evoked, has passed into history along with that whole postwar carnival of freedom and disillusionment against which it was brought. Even Babbitt and More, so markedly different in their approach to orthodoxy and their understanding of traditionalism, so different in talent and imagination, seem fated to be remembered by smaller and smaller groups of academic admirers, and may yet go down merely as the twin elder saints of the old school.

Yet nothing now so clearly reveals the growing atmosphere of tension at the close of the twenties as the sudden revival of interest in the doctrines of these two scholars. It was as if everything that had been rejected by modern writers had suddenly come back to expose their own insecurity, as if everything that had been denied and leaped over so quickly by them in their haste to escape the fetters of the past now asserted itself in the face of their growing doubts. More's monumental series of *Shelburne Essays* had stood since 1904 as a solemn reproach to modernism in all its forms. Babbitt's first book, *Literature and the American College,* a furious attack on modern literature, politics, education, and conduct, had been published at the height of the Progressive agitation in 1908. They had been the "enemy" for almost thirty years and had been welcomed by Charles Eliot Norton early in the century as a bar to modern anarchy and democratic vulgarity, but they now came significantly to seem the spokesmen of a traditionalism which was itself the newest challenge. In the first flush of the triumph of the younger generation after the war, when Babbitt's favorite pupil, Stuart Sherman, had himself gone over to the modern camp and the *Nation,* which More had edited, became one of its chief organs, it seemed as if their opposition to modern naturalism and "romantic laxness" was futile, as indeed it was. They had been defeated time and again; More could even refer to himself as "the least read and most hated author in existence." The Mencken age enjoyed as one of its most fashionable jokes the complete extinction of the two "birchmen" who almost alone still attempted to impose discredited orthodoxies upon it. But though their influence was to pass almost as quickly as it had been revived, they were now called forth as prophets of the modern despair and doctrinaires of a new order.

Ironically enough, the New Humanists spoke only for a few conservative critics and teachers of literature. Their great contribution to letters was More's *Shelburne Essays,* but they had no share in contemporary imaginative literature, were completely out of sympathy with the modern age, contemptuous of democracy, and distrustful even of the poetic achievements of a fellow traditionalist like T. S. Eliot. But they had, if not an applicable standard, a *sense* of standards, a conviction of the necessity of order, a belief in some exterior authority and discipline; and it was the assurance with which they inveighed against naturalism in literature and impressionism in criticism, the deliberation with which they propounded the need of a literature based on human responsibility and aristocratic dignity, that gave them their importance. The social doctrine behind the New Humanism has, of course, a special significance today, in view of the new unhumanism in Europe that has also based itself on authority and discipline and a hatred of "degenerate" modernism. But that is only one aspect of the New Humanism in America, and even one of its many paradoxes. For the movement was a summons to order of all who were in revolt against the disorderliness of modern life, its drift and despair. To some of the older men, like Babbitt and More themselves, and Norman Foerster, it was in part a return to the dignity and gentility of other days; to the Oswald Mosleys of the time, like Seward Collins, it was an invitation to a Fascism run by gentlemen; to younger writers just leaving the colleges, men who had read Benda and Eliot and Maritain, and who were fascinated by the rigor and philosophical substance of Neo-Thomism or Marxist dialectics, it meant an end to the easy ardors and genialities of liberal American criticism. Whatever else Babbitt and More may have lacked, they had waged a lifelong war against facility and triviality and were solid and philosophical scholars; and it was their solidity more than anything else that now gave them their appeal.

From their first meeting at Harvard in 1892—when they had composed the entire class in Sanskrit that semester under Professor Charles R. Lanman—Babbitt and More had been united by a common passion for ancient languages and literatures, a profound capacity for learning, and an articulate contempt for conventional academic standards. At a time when Greek and Latin were already passing out of the curriculum and it was soon to require as much determination to acquire a classical education as it had once been to evade one, their devotion to the classic texts was their first distinction. To that devotion and their respect for each other's gifts, they added a disinclination to work toward the doctor's degree and a distaste for what it represented. They saw that university education in America was being rapidly driven in two extreme directions—one toward laborious pedantry in the worst tradition of the German graduate schools, the other toward a momentous cheapening of humanistic values and studies, a process which had already begun with the substitution of sociology for Latin and would end with the introduction in some universities of courses in plumbing and hog-calling. Science and the prestige of scientific authority already dominated the universities, while the humanities were being steadily robbed of their importance and their power to elevate the mind. The materialism of American life, Babbitt and More felt, was corrupting every last citadel of cultivation and taste; and while the gentlemanly

traditions of honor, morality, self-control, the summum bonum of
decorum, were being destroyed from the inside, they were being
threatened from the outside by Populism and Socialism and the creeds
of the new emancipation.

Though both had been born in the Middle West, Babbitt and More
were the spiritual, if not the intellectual, children of the last Brahmins
in New England at the opening of the twentieth century. Lowell's
gentlemanly orthodoxy was to speak in them, and Thomas Bailey
Aldrich, and the Barrett Wendell who liked to boast that he had never
pronounced a liberal sentiment in all his life. But where it had been
enough for a Charles Eliot Norton to denounce the modern age, the
problem before Babbitt and More was a curious and difficult one.
They were the heirs of a tradition of polite conservatism which they no
longer possessed, but which they had to establish and to apply against
the modern age in which they lived and wrote. There were a few
traditionalist young men like them in every intellectual society in
Europe, the spiritual descendants of de Maistre and Lamennais and
Newman, royalists and classicists and clericalists whose detestation of
the modern "heresy" was stronger than their differences among each
other. But the Europeans were part of a counter-revolution that had
itself been a tradition in Continental politics and philosophy since the
French Revolution. What Babbitt and More hated in all their young
austere zeal was something they were unable to define and to meet,
much less to eradicate: a loose American system of democratic life and
thought that had been rooted in the eighteenth-century Enlightenment
and had grown out of the economic compulsion to exploit a continent. Babbitt and More admired clericalism, but there was no hierarchical tradition in America to follow. They were profound scholars,
but they would neither follow the conventional path of scholarship nor
accept the democratic code of pragmatism. They were classicists who
abominated the whole conscious and unconscious course of romanticism since Rousseau, but they had to work in an American literature
that owed all its humanity and vigor to a "romanticism" as elemental
as folk poetry, and as natural.

Had Babbitt and More been merely as commonplace as most of their
followers, however, they would have been only another manifestation

of the bankruptcy of reaction in America and their labors would have been reduced to the tragicomic exhibitionism of so much academic learning and pride. But if they were passionately reactionary, they were hardly conventional. From any respectable point of view, indeed, their careers were a solemn defiance of academic self-contentment, a challenge to the sort of conservatism which is merely unconcerned. Narrow and censorious and even patronizingly vulgar as they were on occasion, Babbitt and More did bring so unusual a moral conviction to their effort that its very power will always distinguish them in the history of criticism. They were "the enemy" for thirty years, the Old Guard that stood in the way of every humane impulse in modern thought; but more than they ever knew they were themselves an almost monumental example of the rootlessness of American writers in the twentieth century. This was the poignance of their effort—not their abomination of modernism, but their ambitious opposition to historic tendencies of which they were the signal victims. They were traditionalists without a tradition, neoclassicists in a plutocracy, reactionaries who found themselves almost alone in their effort to impose standards of order upon a literature for which they had no sympathy. And the last bitter joke is that, standing between the nineties and the thirties, between James Russell Lowell and Hemingway, they were the center of a revival on the eve of the thirties that was itself a manifestation of the modern desperation—a manifestation of the disintegration even of those who believed themselves superior to contemporary disintegration.

5

For the New Humanism, that predepression fever glow, was itself soon extinguished; and if anything remains of it, it is the different stories of Babbitt and More, whom their followers usually linked together so piously. Babbitt and More recognized that difference from their first meeting, when they learned that their religious differences were as great as their common devotion to traditionalism and self-discipline. Babbitt was profoundly, even rigidly, traditionalist, but a commonplace skeptic. More, who had been trained in a severe Calvinist regime, had long since broken away from ancestral orthodoxy and was just extricating himself from a confusion of Herbert Spencer and German romanticism, both cold comfort to an unusually sensitive religious personality desperately eager for some satisfying illumination of life. Save for a boyish revolt against his father's addiction to spiritualism, Babbitt had no religious history. If he disliked radicalism and "laxness" (his father was also a parlor Socialist), his positive and athletic opinions forbade any sympathy with religious struggles. At twenty-five he seems to have adopted with crushing finality the fundamental principles he was to expound with increasing passion all his life, and he was already a dogmatist.

More's entire intellectual progress, on the other hand, was a series of religious discoveries. Both young men were conservatives by instinct; but where Babbitt's hatred of modern "tendencies" expressed itself in a rasping intolerance, More's was provincial, meditative, timid. They were both intensely bookish, but while More was already ashamed of his susceptibility to romanticism, Babbitt at nineteen had sternly condemned his friends at college for reading novels. His conservatism, from earliest youth, was not a philosophy but an emotion. He never yielded to false temptation. When More and he began their studies in the literature of India, More naturally gravitated toward the Upanishads and "the elusive mysticism" of Hindu poetry. Babbitt immediately absorbed himself in the Buddhistic tradition and the Pâli language and literature, which More described as "hard, cold, stressing endlessly the necessity of the will."

In later life Babbitt, encouraged by overzealous admirers, liked to think of himself as another Dr. Johnson, an archpriest of Toryism furiously lashing at the weakness and sentimentality of mankind. But he never knew anything of Johnson's profound religious sensibility. One saw the marks of an ancestral Puritanism in Babbitt's austerity, his delight in difficulty, his hatred of sham, his contempt for the sensuous pleasures of life; but he was as blind to the Puritan's craving for God as More's whole life was to be racked by it. All cosmologies, Babbitt once declared in his dogmatic fashion, "were only illicit pryings of the inquisitive mind into the unknowable, intellectually pompous rather than edifying." Buddhism pleased him because it propounded the extinction of desire; the classics delighted him because they stimulated his robust mind; but one could hardly imagine him reading Homer over and over again for the love of the music, as More did every summer on the Maine coast. Babbitt was in love with order; he had a positively romantic lack of moderation in his insistence upon it; but it was a love of order for the sake of order, a delight in difficulty that satisfied some pressing personal need, a veneration of classical purity and serenity as unquestioning as devotion to family tradition.

"What might have happened," More mused in his memoir of Babbitt, "if he had spent his energies expounding a literature to which he could have given his positive allegiance?" For Babbitt's failure to obtain a post in the Classics Department had forced him into French, a subject which he pursued, in More's words, "chiefly to annihilate." He felt an almost sadistic malevolence against everything in French literature that did not correspond to his standards of order. Few people in the history of scholarship have ever spent so much learning and effort on a subject to which they were so temperamentally alien. "The French language," he once declared to his department chairman at Harvard, "is only a cheap and nasty substitute for Latin." But there was method in his choice and a dramatic logic to his career. He was not a consecrated classicist in the tradition of Bentley or Porson or Housman; one could hardly imagine him devoting his life to the preservation and correction of the classical texts or the zealous elucidation of their meaning. His veneration of classicism was part of his orthodoxy, like his belief in the political principles of Alexander Hamilton. His conservatism was as political as it was moral, but not, like More's later contempt for democracy, political because it was moral. Spiritually Babbitt was not superior to Mark Hanna; he was in almost every respect save one pre-eminently a successful middle-class citizen of his generation, and that distinction—a voracious intelligence —did not conceal the limitations of his imagination. His conservatism was that of Andrews Norton rather than Charles Eliot Norton, of Henry Cabot Lodge rather than Henry Adams, of Thomas Bailey Aldrich rather than Howells, of Elihu Root and John Hay—a conservatism that had never doubted the sanctity of its principles or compromised with "sentimental" liberalism, a conservatism that was as little curious to understand the motive of others as it was to question its own. By his herculean energy and his talent for domination, he belonged to the age of "heroic enterprise." Even More once confessed that there was something "almost appalling in the immobility of his central ideas." Babbitt acquired vast stores of erudition, but he never, confessed More, doubted or varied the convictions to which he applied his learning. The robust young graduate student who railed at everything that was "effete" or "decadent" and could talk anyone down, was only a more vivacious reflection of the professor who for almost forty years waged unrelenting war on Romanticism and never once wondered why the human soul is so frail that it will occasionally yield to it.

As an example of American personality Babbitt remains one of the few exceptions to the young Van Wyck Brooks's complaint that the most energetic talents in America have gone into business and politics. He was a Force, as tough and majestic a nineteenth-century American character as Collis Huntington or Grover Cleveland. There was a hard-fisted prosiness to Babbitt's mind that sets him off completely not only from all the yearning little people who offered literature nothing but their sensibility, but also from so monkish and incorrigibly sensitive a mind as Paul More's. One saw the difference between the two men most clearly in their styles. More's prose was often distinguished, but it was fundamentally a provincial prose, slightly affected in diction while portentously severe in tone, and always a little too courtly. Babbitt's was eminently a tool for combat; not an excuse, as he would have said, sneeringly, for the expression of his soul. Its greatest distinction was its overt contempt for appearing distinctive. It was aggressively a prose with no nonsense about it, the prose of a hard-headed, absorbed, and stubborn man; it went like a motor. More, who was something of a rhetorician, could write now like a deacon, now like an Oxonian born in Missouri, now like a Neo-Platonic poet; even his most passionate passages were self-consciously florid, and his occasional interposition of a Midwestern turn excessively arch. Babbitt wrote all his life in the same rhythm, which was often no rhythm at all, but a plain and aggressive solemnity. By a curious irony some of his more ambitious esthetic students—notably T. S. Eliot, it is said—picked up his style and put it to new use when a more precise and chastened English became current after the war. But where the distinction of Eliot's critical style was a verbal simplicity as calculated as Mallarmé's, one which even more than Hemingway's bore the overtones of an inexhaustible disillusion, the severe line of Babbitt's prose bespoke a lack of self-consciousness and the assumption of authority.

Babbitt belongs "to the great race before the Flood." His style, like his philosophy, was not a compensation for anything save as all conservatives, in Emerson's biting phrase, "are such from personal defects." He knew what he knew so absolutely and insisted upon it so inflexibly that the very passion which gave him such moral authority exposed his temperamental rigidity. He never defended his basic propositions, he illustrated them; he never explained his reasoning, he enforced it. Traditionalism was good because all history testified to it, but he could never say, as More did in an essay on Cardinal Newman, "that to be deep in history is to cease to be a Protestant." Without permanent standards there was no criticism, and self-control was necessary because man was inherently expansive and weak. "Human nature," as he once remarked in *The Masters of Modern French Criticism*, "is an endless series of false bottoms." Had Babbitt believed in original sin, his conviction of man's depravity would have been contestable, and therefore coherent; but his hostility to religion and metaphysics suggest that his conservatism was a requirement of his nature, not an ethical conviction. When More defended the priority of property in *Aristocracy and Justice*,[1] his arguments were dubious, but they rested upon the elaborate rationalization that where property is unsafe, society is in danger, and where society is insecure, culture is impossible. When Babbitt, publishing his *Literature and the American College* during the Progressive agitation, prepared to demolish the "new morality," his excoriation of social liberalism was a snarl: the rascals want to destroy society! He admitted that "a few more Harrimans, and we are undone," but went on to say that "our real hope of safety lies in our being able to induce our future Harrimans and Rockefellers to liberalize their own souls, in other words to get themselves rightly educated." His defense of the robber barons was characteristic:

---

[1] "The rights of property are more important than the right to life."

The evil principle is represented in society nowadays by the wicked capitalist, much as it was in the old revolutionary times by the wicked king and priest, who were also deemed to be of a different species from the rest of humanity. As a matter of fact, Messrs. Rogers and Rockefeller are not only human beings but representative Americans, who have done with superior capacity what a multitude of the business men of their time would have liked to do.

That was certainly true; but did it follow that all criticism of the religion of property rested upon envy? Soames Forsyte was no more generous, or Jay Cooke.

One could be persuaded by Babbitt, as were so many of his pupils, through the authority and strength of his delivery, the stark intensity of his conviction. He was so powerful a teacher that the very presence of him, the slow stubborn consecration to his ideal, was moving. In the face of so much inertia, cynicism, and triviality in others, the total absence of anything like his force in American criticism, his moral effectiveness was profound. Yet what he once wrote of Désiré Nisard was peculiarly applicable to him: "He succeeds at times . . . in so defending the traditional general sense as to affront the general sense of his contemporaries." Babbitt knew everything about the history of criticism save that unquenchable curiosity and interest in human intelligence which is the very life of criticism. Though no one could quote the noblest maxims of criticism so eagerly or phrase his own so nobly,[1] his judgments on others were often tragically wrong because he lacked elementary tolerance of their needs. His narrowness fed his intensity and despoiled it. What gave him his vocation and his distinction was the terrible earnestness with which he insisted that the criticism of literature is ridiculous if it does not stem from an ethical comprehension of life. But of what use was that earnestness when it spent itself crying *Ecrasez l'infame?* "Modern literature has been more or less sentimental since Petrarch, and a morbidly subjective strain has existed in it since Rousseau, while of late a quality is beginning to appear which we cannot better describe than as neurotic." True, true; but how did that dispose of a significant native writer like Dreiser, or the

---

[1] "Criticism is such a difficult art because one must not only have principles but must apply them flexibly and intuitively."—*Rousseau and Romanticism*, p. xvii.

America which made Dreiser possible? What was the ultimate justification of a criticism which would not distinguish between the "infamy" in Rousseau and the provincial sex-haunted romanticism in Sherwood Anderson; that would grant no ethical distinction between the primitive evangelicism of Tolstoy, struggling against an ecclesiastical dictatorship, and the naturalism of a self-educated writer like Dreiser; that dismissed with equal contempt Shelley's phenomenal sensibility and Mencken's journalistic irreverence? They were all "romanticists" and committed to the same sin. *Ecrasez l'infame!*

Babbitt's opponents often charged that his conception of Romanticism was so narrow as to be grotesque, and it was. Yet in one sense he knew better than any of them that Romanticism was not a sudden corruption of the artistic sensibility but an epoch in the history of Europe. He was perfectly aware that it encompassed Napoleon as well as Victor Hugo, Beethoven along with Keats. His misfortune—it was the very point of his career—was that where so many of his fellow neoclassicists in Europe were able to trace their hatred of romanticism back to their opposition to the French Revolution and even the Protestant Reformation, he remained a Yankee Republican and a Tory materialist. He was under the illusion that his formal allegiance to a conservative republicanism, his dislike of the Catholic-Royalist turn of classicism in twentieth-century France, proved that he was not a reactionary. The truth is that he confused his racial and ancestral ties with a positive liberalism. He once complained naïvely (in the preface to *The New Laokoön*) that in France bookstores often displayed together works of neoclassic criticism and Royalist politics, and begged his readers not to infer that the New Humanism was—un-American. But, mutatis mutandis, he was himself the peer of any reactionary in Europe; his failure to admit the political implications of his wholesale rejection of modern democracy was as characteristic as his Yankee disinclination to join an authoritarian and supernaturalist church. In that international Vendée which boasted a Charles Maurras, a Hilaire Belloc, a Nicholas Berdyaev, Babbitt remained, for all his intellectual distinction, a characteristically provincial American who would not see that his abomination of modern "heresy" had become so uncontrolled that he could no longer identify it with the politics of Alexander Hamilton or the criticism of Matthew Arnold. To believe in standards of order is hardly reactionary in itself and need not lead to reaction; but Babbitt's thinking was so inherently reactionary in every sense that there was something poignant in his failure to see, as so many of his shrewder and less "old-fashioned" disciples rapidly did after 1929, that he stood between two worlds. As he grew increasingly irascible toward the end of his life he once confessed that had he to choose between Jesuits and Bolsheviks, he would willingly have chosen Jesuits; but he never believed that the choice was urgent. The world from which he had drawn his first inspiration, that world whose antipodes were Charles Eliot Norton and Nelson W. Aldrich, had never heard of Fascism; and though Babbitt led some of his followers to Fascism, he still belonged to a generation that had no "need" of it.

"No one in his generation," wrote Babbitt of Ferdinand Brunetière, "so emphasized the relationship between literature and thought, the relationship between thought itself and life. It is a pity that the needed example he sets in this respect should be compromised by the reactionary trend of his thinking; that men who are his inferiors in the scholarship of ideas and even in the scholarship of facts should yet have the advantage, in attacking him, of at least seeming to be champions of the modern spirit." This was Babbitt's own case, and he was even less fortunate than Brunetière. For the conservative French critics moved in a world trained to the use of ideas, while their opponents felt the need of ideas even when they had none. The enemies of naturalism might think Zola a pig, but even Zola, with his zest for the sewers of Paris, could defend naturalism on historical and scientific grounds. Babbitt's misfortune was that his opponents would not admit the moral drive of Humanism, while he would not even admit Dreiser's right to exist. Had he, like More, integrated his classicism within a religious system —or what is sufficiently distinctive in a period of skepticism, felt the need of religious principles—he would have stood outside the age and hence have preserved a certain spiritual superiority to it. But with his air of an Increase Mather strayed into modern letters, he was at once the most striking example of the desiccation of traditionalism and the most vociferous apostle of it. While the younger writers were perplexed and even a little frightened by More, they recognized in Babbitt only a more forceful voice out of the past they had rejected; and the debate became comic when Babbitt thought he could dispose of their "heresy" by tracing it solemnly to Rousseau, to Shaftesbury, and to Bacon.

A subtler or more generous mind than Babbitt's would have at least granted that grievance against modern capitalism in others which, like a good Humanist, he felt in himself; it was entirely in keeping with his character and the nature of his criticism that he should have missed it. He devoted his life to the conviction that a great literature is possible only to those possessed of their full humanity, and—by the highest principles—consistently ignored or misrepresented the humanity of others. More's taste was narrow enough, but he could write with moving eloquence of what he loved and even with great acuteness of what he was prepared to detest. Babbitt carried his inflexibility to the point of fanaticism, and his range of perception was suffocating. He admired Emerson, and at least one of his devoted followers, Stuart Sherman, once liked to believe that Babbitt was in the Emersonian tradition; but was there ever an American who had less in common with Emerson's fraternity and curiosity? Quoting Emerson in one passage of *The Masters of Modern French Criticism,* Babbitt went on to say:

> Emerson says that we descend to meet. This is no doubt true of certain kinds of meeting, of the kind that takes place at an afternoon tea, let us say; and Emerson probably did not mean much more than this. But the phrase may evidently have another and, from the humanistic point of view, far more sinister meaning. Instead of disciplining himself to some sort of perfection set above his ordinary self, a man sinks down from the intellectual to the instinctive level, on the ground that he is thus widening his instinctive sympathies.

It was this tireless insistence upon the will—a kind of abstract spiritual manliness—which became the content of Babbitt's morality, and he defeated himself in the end by mistaking it for a bludgeon. He had worked himself into a rage too early in life, and deceived by the submission of those who found him a Major Force, he allowed himself to be caught in it. He knew that he stood virtually alone, but his vituperation had become a habit, and when he began to moralize at will all over history his obiter dicta seemed merely gross. It was one thing for a respectable citizen in 1908 to complain that coeds were being allowed to read the Restoration dramatists, or even for a Back Bay professor to sneer at folk poetry, since "to look for poetry at all among gondoliers and the like is, under existing conditions, at least to chase an Arcadian dream." But he fancied himself a Savonarola. He censured Renan for advocating a reduction of the French Army in 1869 on the ground that "a real statesman would have sacrificed his humanitarian vision of peace, in case he happened to have one, to the actual danger of war which was already patent to a careful observer." His highest praise for Joubert—one of his few admirations—was that "[he] is far removed from a man like Coleridge who retired from his actual obligations into a cloud of opium and German metaphysics." With characteristic amenity he pronounced the crudest possible verdict on Diderot and his generation: "The great discovery had been made that man is naturally good and that the proper way for this goodness to manifest itself is to overflow through the eyes." In *Rousseau and Romanticism* he was faced with the "paradox" that the "lawless" romantics were devoted to careful workmanship, and exclaimed with heavy irony that he could make no sense of it. "But if a man is to be a romantic genius in the fullest sense he must, it should seem, repudiate even the discipline of technique as well as the discipline of culture in favor of an artless spontaneity." Quoting a charming and perfectly innocent little passage from Sainte-Beuve on the pleasures of reading, in which the French critic lamented that the modern scholar had become a laborer rather than "a delicate amateur," Babbitt must needs reprimand him: "A humanism that hopes to act upon the world cannot afford to decline even with Horace and Gray. It must take hold on the character and will and not be simply Epicurean." Even Edmond Scherer, one of the most disciplined of conservative critics, offended him. "Does not criticism consist above all in comprehending?" asked Scherer. "No," reproved Babbitt, "but in judging." Criticism on such principles, however effective it may have been in pointing out the weakness and confusion of others, became not rigorous but rigid, and could go no further, save to catalogue with hollow fury the lusts and follies and "romanticism" of world literature.

Like Babbitt, More was a formidable anachronism; unlike him, he had a profound sensibility to literature and more than a little of that "romantic" imagination which he came to abhor in others. From their first meeting More had seemed less assertive and admitted to being timidly fond of Heine, given to the writing of mawkish verse, and troubled with religious doubts. It was those religious doubts—doubts at first of his ancestral Calvinism, persistent doubts to the end of the Catholic dogmas whose history he later wrote—that made More so zealous an ethical critic of literature. For he suffered all his life the disintegrations and upheavals of his time on the level of spiritual experience; and unlike most of his fellow traditionalists, his interest in literature was formed by compulsions beyond the reach and even the sympathy of most writers in his time. Where Babbitt's orthodoxy was instinctive, More's was the clinging to order of a religious spirit haunted by the world's corruption. Babbitt looked upon all modernism as a revolt against the proper standards, and it was characteristic of his outlook that he never doubted that his theories had only to be understood to be adopted. That primitive confidence was impossible to More. For Babbitt sought to correct an "aberration" which he did not understand; More, with his quicker sensibility to literature, rejected in modernism its disbelief and its sensuousness. Babbitt opposed "weakness"; More abominated skepticism and every departure from that perfect Christian order in which he tried to dwell.

To understand More's craving for a spiritual ideal and a spiritual order is to penetrate the massive surface of his learning to that Platonism which fascinated him all his life. For the world of pure essence and spiritual authority which he found in Plato, with its pervading dualism and lofty contempt for the material, was the very image of More's idealism and of his orthodoxy. The world was disorder and error; the spirit alone was life. The flesh was corruption; only a craving for the higher truth that was immanent in man's relation to God provided an understanding of human perfection and order. Out of his lifelong fear of disorder and change—perhaps the timorousness of a shy romantic soul—of modern "anarchy" and pluralism, More made for himself a creed of order as abstractly and glacially perfect as the Platonic forms, a dream of order as the very incarnation of the Christian truth. He wrote the doctrinal history of the early Christian Church, in his volumes on *The Greek Tradition,* as a study in Platonism, and he made himself a critic of modern society and literature on the same terms. Anything but an aristocrat himself, he was ambitious for an aristocratic Christian Church; a child of the modern age who persistently questioned himself and his own Protestant education, he felt only a profound horror in the face of contemporary agnosticism and "relativism." His Christ, as Christian Gauss once hinted in a little joke, was very, very remote from men; he himself was even more remote still. There is a strained and unconscious cruelty in More's philosophy of society, for example, that is not even aristocratic, but merely a sedulous worship of the status quo, an adoration of legality for its own sake. Yet to understand why More thought it "Rousseauistic selfishness" for workingmen to ask for higher wages, or virtually criminal to encourage Jane Addams's social-settlement work among the poor, is to understand how far his passion for a disembodied orthodoxy carried him.

There was, as his opponents always claimed, something preternaturally cold about More; but his forbidding austerity was only the surface of his lifelong struggle for discipline, and had many cracks in it. For what lay behind his famous rigor was not an instinctive repugnance to "romanticism" like Babbitt's, but a hunger for system. His classicism had the iron exultation of Calvinism in it, where Babbitt's was a cold distrust. Babbitt, indeed, always approached literature from the outside and considered it an erratic form of philosophy; More could write with great sympathy and penetration, or with penetration even when he had no sympathy, of all world literature up to Proust and Joyce. He had a natural love of literature, where Babbitt thought most modern writers merely willful and even a little mad; and though he always discussed writing within an ethical framework, his appreciation of it was often passionate and, in the great passages of the *Shelburne Essays,* even moving. "I was too much addicted to literature to be accepted by the philosophers," he wrote in *Pages from an Oxford Diary,* "and too fond of interpreting art by an ethical criterion to find favour among the literary. And by an odd mischance I, whose life has been a passage through storms of emotion, am regarded as a cold and heartless intellectual."

From the time he had left his graduate studies at Harvard, More had modeled his ambition as a critic on the example of the great nineteenth-century historians and moralists, and when he took up his "exile" as a young man at Shelburne, New Hampshire, he planned his work on a scale as majestic as Sainte-Beuve's. Turning slowly against his early romantic writings and a career in creative literature, he centered his whole energy in criticism; and criticism indeed became for him, as it has for few men, a consecration. For thirty-two years, from 1904 to a year before his death in 1937, he steadily built away at the monument of the *Shelburne Essays,* and the fourteen volumes are in truth a monument—a monument to More's profound absorption in world literature and to a search for salvation and a craving for the ideal that are without precedent in the modern literature of criticism. Begun in his hermitage, when he felt himself lost in the modern world and had come under the influence of Thoreau, the essays remain the record of his own lifelong spiritual hermitage; and for all their lapses in taste and frequently extreme narrowness, have an absolute integrity, a devotional tone, as it were, that is like the silent radiance of the Puritan divines.

Yet More's quality as a critic, so mechanically praised by his admirers and as mechanically condemned by at least two generations of modernists in America, is not easy to define. There was something persistently small in him, something curiously provincial and strained, that lies like a shadow over his ambition, his stupendous learning, and his so carefully wrought essays in human failure. He had a great ambition and was certainly not unequal to it; he had profound imaginative sympathy, if not particularly imaginative insight, and was a distinguished student of ideas. But though he loved literature as he loved nothing else in life, he was always a little suspicious of it, suspicious of its testimony to human frailty and disorder. To say that he was merely cold and bigoted is to forget with what ardor and conviction he could write of Thoreau and Sir Thomas Browne, of figures so different as George Gissing and Shelley. Compared with Babbitt, More seemed to roam easily and sympathetically over the whole range of world literature, and he did write with great acuteness of dozens of writers repellent to his taste. But there was a lack of some final personal distinction in More, a crabbedness, a fundamental want of generosity and ease, that make his ambition to be an American Sainte-Beuve just a little preposterous. Catholic in his learning, catholic in his yearning for absolutism and dogma, he yet lacked more than some of the little men who mocked him so facilely a simple catholicity of human interest and curiosity. Even the courtly old-fashioned tread of his style, so solemnly careful and formal a scholar's style, revealed the struggle he always waged with himself. It was certainly one of the most self-conscious styles ever brought into criticism, and for all its intensity and dignity, a kind of magnificent patchwork, the style of a man at once passionate in conviction and hungry for what he did not have in himself. It was not merely a great bookish style; it was an uneasy style, the style of an enormously learned man who had worked too hard to get himself a style, as he had worked too hard all his life to attain a perfect faith and spiritual repose.

The experience of the *Shelburne Essays* today, even to one properly appreciative of the solidity of More's approach to criticism, is therefore likely to be a curious one. He had a pronounced tendency to take tradition as a value in itself, as when in Volume XI he praised Henry Vaughan over Thoreau, the Thoreau for whom he had so much feeling, because Vaughan had been "in" a tradition, and Thoreau not. He tried to dispose of Freudianism by saying smugly that "pretty much all the truth of Freudianism can be found in the Platonic and Stoic theory of dreams." His distrust of all modern tendencies carried him so far that he could even, in his essay welcoming the revival of Humanism, describe contemporary "novelists and poets of discontent" as men "deliberately preying on the intellectual defeat and spiritual dismay of the times, as vultures fatten themselves on carrion." What is particularly striking about More's ethical criticism of literature, however, is the formalism of his ethical values. Although he declared, out of his characteristic faith, that "there can be no great and simple and sincere art without ideals of greatness and simplicity and sincerity prevailing in society," he usually associated those ideals with the established values of the society in which writers lived. He

was interested in writers themselves, that is to say, only up to a certain
point; for closely as he studied their works for signs of a spiritual
history and discussed their significance, he invariably disapproved of
them if their individualism as writers became a questioning of orthodoxy. Where another conservative would merely have patronized the
American Utopians, for example, More had to call the colonists at
Fruitlands "altruistic humbugs"; where another critic would have
sought to understand the intention behind John Morley's liberalism,
More bitterly berated Morley because, though he owed his education
to Oxford, he helped to "undermine its religious traditions."

More's curious essay on Morley, which ends by being an attack on
the whole progress of English liberalism since the Reform Bill of 1832,
is a microcosm of his fantastic legalism. What no modern English
conservative would dare to uphold, he upheld as a first principle of
existence. The perfect colonial in this respect, he was always more
Royalist than the King, more worshipful of Oxford than any Oxonian,
and a perfectly gratuitous defender of aristocracy. Only More would
have thought of accusing Viscount Morley—that good Victorian liberal
—of "duplicity" because "he sought to undermine" the English aristocracy while moving in its company. Only More, for all his passionate
love of Milton's poetry, could have approved and repeated Dr. Johnson's strictures on Milton's politics. Orthodoxy was all, law was all,
tradition was all; and if the writer, like Thoreau, "cut himself off from
the Church and State" and did not move in "the greater currents of
tradition," so much the worse for him. For if More believed in anything, he believed in that iron legality which he propounded in his
famous ninth volume, *Aristocracy and Justice*:

> We are bound, in any clear-sighted view of the larger exigencies of
> the relations of man with man, to fortify ourselves against such a per-
> version of the institutions of government as would adapt them to the
> nature of man as he ought to be, instead of the nature of man as he
> actually is, and would relax the rigour of law, in pity for the degree
> of injustice inherent in earthly life. . . . Looking at the larger good
> of society, we may say that the dollar is more than the man, and that
> *the rights of property are more important than the right to life.*

It was this code, perhaps more than More's equal insistence on individual moral responsibility, that was the center of his ethical criticism of literature. What one felt in his essays was his own passionate sense of moral responsibility, not his sympathetic attention to the dilemma or struggles of others. For that reason the weakest feature of his criticism was always his lack of psychological penetration. He recited the careers of his subjects with a certain formality, and occasionally with a certain self-righteousness, as when he announced that the story of Sainte-Beuve's love for Victor Hugo's wife "is of a kind almost incomprehensible to the Anglo-Saxon mind"; but there is a sense in which he was not interested in them as subjects. He did not go as far as Babbitt in regarding literature as an interlocking system of ideas, but for all his devotion to literature, he was not interested in seeing how moral values get *into* literature.[1] There is a command of philosophical ideas in the essays, even an ability to get to the depths of writers he admired, such as Newman and Sir Thomas Browne, that is profound, as More was often profound. But rarely has a good critic interested himself so little, at bottom, in esthetic problems.

The final irony of the New Humanist adventure is that More's own devotion to religion was the thing his admirers were least interested in. When the New Humanism became current after 1928, he pleaded earnestly with them to see that their doctrine was futile without religious faith; but T. S. Eliot knew what was wrong better than More when he described the movement acidly as "a tardy rear-guard action which attempts to arrest the progress of liberalism just before the end of its march; an action, besides, which is being fought by troops who are already half-liberalized themselves." Some of them, it must be said, were rather half-Fascist; but theirs certainly was a "rear-guard action." Portents of the crisis, they were themselves the first victims of it. Yet if their protest against modern literature in America has a memorial, it is not to be found in their ambition for a movement, or in their wrangling controversy with opposing critics, or in the pages of Seward Collins's authoritarian *American Review,* which so easily

---

[1] Yvor Winters originally said this of Babbitt.

went from Irving Babbitt to Mussolini. It is the story of Paul Elmer More, both Christian and Pharisee, scholar and moralist: so ambitious a Christian, so inadequate a prophet, alone with himself in the modern American wilderness.

Chapter 12

INTO THE THIRTIES:
ALL THE LOST GENERATIONS

"What do you think happens to people who aren't artists? What do you think people who aren't artists become?"
"I feel they don't become: I feel nothing happens to them; I feel negation becomes of them."—E. E. CUMMINGS, Introduction to *The Enormous Room*

"All right we are two nations."—JOHN DOS PASSOS, *U.S.A.*

WHEN Paul Elmer More denounced one of John Dos Passos's early novels, *Manhattan Transfer,* as "an explosion in a cesspool," he was yielding to his familiar rage against the whole trend of realism and naturalism in America rather than expressing a judgment on Dos Passos. Yet as the tradition of that realism, so uniformly abominable to More and his fellows, passed on to the younger writers of Dos Passos's own generation, it became clear that it was not uniform at all, and that with these writers, for whom life and literature had begun with the war, a fateful new influence had entered American writing.

In 1920 and 1921 their first novels, *This Side of Paradise* and *Three Soldiers,* had been among the leading testaments of contemporary revolt and had come in with the stream of new novels like *Winesburg, Main Street, Jurgen,* and *My Ántonia.* The Hemingway character dominated the imagination of the twenties as easily as the Mencken irreverence, and the "flapper generation" which found its historian in Scott Fitzgerald was the most obvious of postwar phenomena. But where the writers of the "middle generation," like Lewis and Anderson, Cabell and Mencken, had been released by the new current of freedom after the war, had been given opportunities and themes in the postwar scene, the young writers who had been through the war made it and its aftermath their very substance. Born in the middle nineties, when modern American writing was just beginning to emerge as a positive force, they arrived on the scene just at the moment of triumph; and they seemed from the first not merely the concentration of all that the modern revolution had brought to America, but its climax. Standing at the center of the whole modern literary experience in America, writers like Fitzgerald, Hemingway, and Dos Passos were significantly the evangels of what had been most tragically felt in the American war experience. They were "the sad young men," the very disillusioned and brilliant young men, "the beautiful and the damned," and counterparts of all those other sad and brilliant young men in Europe, Aldous Huxley and Louis Aragon, Ernst Toller and Wilfred Owen, who wrote out of the bitterness of a shattered Europe and the palpable demoralization of Western society. Between Hemingway and Sherwood Anderson, between Fitzgerald and Sinclair Lewis, there was as wide and deep a gulf as there had been between Stephen Crane and Howells. And it was in that gulf, something more for these young writers than the familiar disassociation of the American generations, that they lived and wrote—proud and stricken in the consciousness of their difference from their predecessors, from all those who had not shared their intimacy with disaster, from all those who spoke out of an innocence the young writers no longer knew, or through a style that seemed to them conventional.

It was the war, of course, that had made that difference primarily, even for a writer like Scott Fitzgerald, who had not been abroad to the war at all, and had written the first of the lost-generation novels, *This Side of Paradise,* under army lanterns at an officers' training camp. The war had dislodged them from their homes and the old restraints, given them an unexpected and disillusioning education, and left them entirely rootless. They were—in the slogan Gertrude Stein gave to Hemingway—the lost generation, the branded victims, the generation that had been uprooted and betrayed, a generation cast, as one of them wrote, "into the dark maw of violence." Life had begun with war for them and would forever after be shadowed by violence and death. *"The only place where you could see life and death, i.e., violent death now that the wars were over, was in the bull ring and I wanted very much to go to Spain where I could study it."* But it was not only the war that had at once isolated them and given them their prominence; it was also their sense of an artistic mission. Alone in their disenchantment and famous by it, they were at the same time the appointed heirs of modernism, the new American pilgrims of art, closer to James Joyce than to Mencken, and more familiar with Gertrude Stein's revelations than with Warren G. Harding's blunders. It was their enforced education in the international community of war and art, their impatience with an art that did not express *them*, that separated them so persistently from the older writers who had become famous in the twenties with them. They had leaped at one bound from the Midwestern world of their childhood into the world of Caporetto, of Dada, of Picasso and Gertrude Stein, and their detachment from the native traditions now became their own first tradition.

Mencken and Lewis and Cabell spoke for them in the sense that they spoke for all young people after the war, but in the greater sense they did not speak for them at all. What had Hemingway, the Hemingway who, it is said, had been left for dead on the Italian front and was now dreaming away in Verlaine's old room in Paris of a new style, to learn from the older writers save Sherwood Anderson's honest simplicity? What had Scott Fitzgerald, the golden boy of the twenties who moved through them like a disenchanted child, to learn from the complacent satirists of a society that he at once enjoyed more lustily and held more cheaply than they? What had the very sensitive and romantic and conscientious Dos Passos to learn from writers who could mock everything save the essential cruelty and indignity of the industrial culture he hated? In its own mind the lost generation was not merely lost in the world; it was lost from all the other generations in America. It was a fateful loss and perhaps a willing loss, no tragedy for them there; but it was part of the general sense of loss, the conviction by which they wrote (and experienced the world, as with different senses), which gave them so epic a self-consciousness.

Lost and forever writing the history of their loss, they became specialists in anguish; and as they sentimentalized themselves, so they were easily sentimentalized. "It was given to Hawthorne to dramatize the human soul," John Peale Bishop once wrote. "In our time Hemingway wrote the drama of its disappearance." No other literary generation could have commented on itself with such careless grandeur. Had Hemingway really recorded the disappearance of the human soul "in our time"? Had Dos Passos's America, so symmetrical a series of hell pits, as much correspondence to America as his inclusive ambition promised? No: but what was so significant about these writers from the first was that they were able to convince others that in writing the story of their generation, they were in some sense describing the situation of contemporary humanity. It was the positiveness of their disinheritance, the very glitter of their disillusionment, the surface perfection of a disbelief that was like the texture of Hemingway's novels, that made them so magnetic an influence, in manners as well as in literature. They had a special charm—the Byronic charm, the charm of the specially damned; they had seized the contemporary moment and made it their own; and as they stood among the ruins, calling the ruins the world, they seemed so authoritative in their dispossession, seemed to bring so much craft to its elucidation, that it was easy to believe that all the roads really had led up to them—that a Hemingway could record "the disappearance of the human soul in our time."

Indeed, it was even easy to believe that they were not merely a group of brilliantly talented young writers enjoying a special prominence, but major voices, major artists.

2

Beyond this point, of course, these writers differed very strikingly. Hemingway and Dos Passos were as essentially unlike each other as two contemporaries sharing in a common situation can ever be. Fitzgerald, who never underwent the European apprenticeship that the others did, always stood rather apart from them, though he was the historian of his generation and for a long time its most famous symbol. For Fitzgerald never had to create a lost-generation legend or apply it to literature—the exile, the pilgrimage to Gertrude Stein, the bull-fighters at the extremity of the world, the carefully molded style, the carefully molded disgust. The legend actually was his life, as he was its most native voice and signal victim; and his own career was one of its great stories, perhaps its central story. From the first he lived in and for the world of his youth, the glittering and heartbroken postwar world from which his career was so indistinguishable. Living by it he became for many not so much the profoundly gifted, tragic, and erratic writer that he was, a writer in some ways inherently more interesting than any other in his generation, but a marvelous, disappointed, and disappointing child—"a kind of king of our American youth" who had long since lost his kingdom and was staggering in a void. He became too much a legend in himself, too easily a fragment of history rather than a contributor to it. And when he died in his early forties, the "snuffed-out candle," dead in that Hollywood that was his last extremity, with even one of his greatest books, *The Last Tycoon,* unfinished like his life, glittering with promise like his life, he served the legend in death as he had served it by his whole life. *Eheu fugaces!* Scott Fitzgerald was dead; the twenties were really over; the waste and folly had gone with him.

It was almost impossible, of course, not to discount Fitzgerald in some such spirit, for he was as much a part of the twenties as Calvin Coolidge, and like Coolidge, represented something in the twenties almost too graphically. He had announced the lost generation with *This Side of Paradise* in 1920, or at least the home guard of the international rebellion of postwar youth, and the restiveness of youth at home found an apostle in him, since he was the younger generation's first authentic novelist. Flippant, ironic, chastely sentimental, he spoke for all those who felt, as one youth wrote in 1920, that "the old generation had certainly pretty well ruined this world before passing it on to us. They give us this thing, knocked to pieces, leaky, red-hot, threatening to blow up; and then they are surprised that we don't accept it with the same attitude of pretty, decorous enthusiasm with which they received it, way back in the eighties." As the flapper supplanted the suffragette, the cake-eater the earnest young uplifter of 1913, Fitzgerald came in with the modernism that flew in on short skirts, puffed audaciously at its cigarette, evinced a frantic interest in sport and sex, in drinking prohibited liquor, and in defying the ancient traditions. In 1920 he was not so much a novelist as a new generation speaking; but it did not matter. He sounded all the fashionable new lamentations; he gave the inchoate protests of his generation a slogan, a character, a definitive tone. Like Rudolph Valentino, he became one of the supreme personalities of the new day; and when his dashingly handsome hero, Amory Blaine, having survived Princeton, the war, and one tempestuous love affair, stood out at the end of the novel as a man who had conquered all the illusions and was now waiting on a lonely road to be conquered in turn, it seemed as if a generation ambitious for a sense of tragedy had really found a tragic hero.

Like Alfred de Musset's Rolla, Fitzgerald might now have said: *Je suis venu trop tard dans un monde trop vieux pour moi*—and he did, in all the variants of undergraduate solemnity and bright wisdom. With its flip and elaborately self-conscious prose, *This Side of Paradise* was a record of the younger generation's victory over *all* the illusions. The war, Amory Blaine confesses, had no great effect on him,

> but it certainly ruined the old backgrounds. Sort of killed individualism out of our whole generation. . . . I'm not sure it didn't kill it out of the whole world. Oh, Lord, what a pleasure it used to be to dream I might be a really great dictator or writer or religious or political leader—and now even a Leonardo da Vinci or Lorenzo de Medici couldn't be a real old-fashioned bolt in the world.

Knocking loudly and portentously at the locked doors of convention, Fitzgerald had already become the voice of "all the sad young men." With a sly flourish, he announced that "none of the Victorian mothers —and most of the mothers were Victorian—had any idea how casually their daughters were accustomed to be kissed." Mothers swooned and legislators orated; Fitzgerald continued to report the existence of such depravity and cynicism as they had never dreamed of. The shock was delivered; Fitzgerald became part of the postwar atmosphere of shock.

But though it was inconsequential enough, *This Side of Paradise* had a taste of the poignance that was to flood all Fitzgerald's other books. To tell all was now the fashion; flaming youth was lighting up behind every barn; but of what use was it? Behind the trivial irony of Fitzgerald's novel, its heroic pose, its grandiose dramatizations ("Amory was alone—he had escaped from a small enclosure into a great labyrinth. He was where Goethe was when he began 'Faust'; he was where Conrad was when he wrote 'Almayer's Folly'") lay a terrible fear of the contemporary world, a world young men had never made. Freedom had come, but only as a medium of expression; while some of the young men licked their war wounds, others sought certainty. "We *want* to believe, but we can't." The problem was there for all men to ponder, and for "the beautiful and the damned" to suffer. But how did one learn to believe? What was there to believe in?

Fitzgerald never found the answer, yet he did not mock those who had. In those first years he did not seek answers; perhaps he never did. As Glenway Wescott said in his tribute at the end, he "always suffered from an extreme environmental sense." He commented on the world, swam in it as self-contentedly as the new rich, and understood it sagely—when he wanted to; he had no innerness. His senses always opened outward to the world, and the world was full of Long Island Sundays. This was what he knew and was steeped in, the procession and glitter that he loved without the statement of love, and he had the touch for it—the light yet jeweled style, careless and knowing and affable; the easiness that was never facility; the holiday lights, the holiday splendor, the twenties in their golden bowl, whose crack he knew so well. He was innocent without living in innocence and delighted in the external forms and colors without being taken in by them; but he was pre-eminently a part of the world his mind was always disowning. The extravagance and carnival of the times had laid a charm on him, and he caught the carnival of the world of his youth, and its welling inaudible sadness, as no one else did—the world of Japanese lanterns and tea dances, the hot summer afternoons in *The Great Gatsby,* the dazzle and sudden violence, the colored Easter eggs whose tints got into his prose, the blare of the saxophones "while a hundred pairs of golden and silver slippers shuffled the shining dust.

At the gray tea hour there were always rooms that throbbed incessantly with this low, sweet fever, while fresh faces drifted here and there like rose petals blown by the sad horns around the floor."

Inevitably, there was a persistent tension in Fitzgerald between what his mind knew and what his spirit adhered to; between his disillusionment and his irrevocable respect for the power and the glory of the world he described. "Let me tell you about the very rich," he wrote in *All the Sad Young Men.*

> They are different from you and me. They possess and enjoy early, and it does something to them, makes them soft where we are hard, and cynical where we are trustful, in a way that, unless you were born rich, it is very difficult to understand. They think, deep in their hearts, that they are better than we are because we had to discover the compensations and refuges of life for ourselves. . . . They are different.

He was fascinated by that difference, where a writer like Hergesheimer merely imitated it; none of the others in his generation felt the fascination of the American success story as did Fitzgerald, or made so much of it. ("The rich are not as we are," he once said to Hemingway. "No," Hemingway replied. "They have more money.") This was the stuff of life to him, the American achievement he could recognize, and hate a little, and be forever absorbed by. And from Amory Blaine's education to Monroe Stahr's Hollywood in *The Last Tycoon,* Fitzgerald's world did radiate the Cartier jewel glints of the twenties— the diamond mountain in "The Diamond as Big as the Ritz," Anson Hunter in "The Rich Boy," Jay Gatsby's mansion and dream, the prep-school princelings who swagger through so many of his stories, the luxurious self-waste of the last expatriates in *Tender Is the Night,* and finally Monroe Stahr, the Hollywood king, "who had looked on all the kingdoms, with the kind of eyes that can stare straight into the sun."

Fitzgerald did not worship riches or the rich; he merely lived in their golden eye. They were "different"; they were what the writer who lived forever in the world of his youth really knew; and they became for him what war became for Hemingway, or the anarchy of modern society for Dos Passos—the pattern of human existence, the artist's medium of understanding. His people were kings; they were imperious even in their desolation. They were always the last of their line, always damned, always the death-seekers (there are no second generations in Fitzgerald). Yet they were glamorous to the end, as the futilitarians in *Tender Is the Night* and Monroe Stahr were iridescent with death. For Fitzgerald always saw life as glamour, even though he could pierce that glamour to write one of the most moving of American tragedies in *The Great Gatsby*. Something of a child always, with a child's sudden and unexpected wisdom, he could play with the subtle agonies of the leisure class as with a brilliant toy; and the glamour always remained there, even when it was touched with death. In one sense, as a magazine writer once put it, his books were "prose movies," and nothing was more characteristic of his mind than his final obsession with Hollywood. In the same way much of his writing always hovered on the verge of fantasy and shimmered with all the colors of the world. Just as the world swam through his senses without being defined by him, so he could catch all its lights and tones in his prismatic style without having to understand them too consciously. What saved his style from extravagance was Fitzgerald's special grace, his pride in his craft; but it was the style of a man profoundly absorbed in the romance of glamour, the style of a craftsman for whom life was a fairy world to the end.

To understand this absorption on Fitzgerald's part is to understand the achievement of *The Great Gatsby*, the work by which his name will always live. In most of his other work he merely gave shallow reports on the pleasures and self-doubts of his class, glittered with its glitter. He tended to think of his art as a well-oiled machine, and he trusted to luck. Rather like Stephen Crane, whom he so much resembled in spirit, the only thing he could be sure of was his special gift, his way of transfusing everything with words, the consciousness of craft; and like Crane he made it serve for knowledge. But like Crane in another respect, he was one of those writers who make their work out of a conflict that would paralyze others—out of their tragic moodiness, their troubled, intuitive, and curiously half-conscious penetration of the things before them. And it is this moodiness at the pitch of genius that lights up *The Great Gatsby*. For Fitzgerald was supremely a part of the world he there described, weary of it but not removed from it, and his achievement was of a kind possible only to one who so belonged to it. No revolutionary writer could have written it, or even hinted at its inexpressible poignance; no one, perhaps, who was even too consciously skeptical of the wealth and power Jay Gatsby thought would make him happy. But for Fitzgerald the tragedy unfolded there, the tragedy that has become for so many one of the great revelations of what it has meant to be an American at all, was possible only because it was so profound a burst of self-understanding.

To have approached Gatsby from the outside would have meant a sacrifice of Gatsby himself—a knowledge of everything in Gatsby's world save Gatsby. But the tragedy here is pure confession, a supplication complete in the human note it strikes. Fitzgerald could sound the depths of Gatsby's life because he himself could not conceive any other. Out of his own weariness and fascination with damnation he caught Gatsby's damnation, caught it as only someone so profoundly attentive to Gatsby's dream could have pierced to the self-lie behind it. The book has no real scale; it does not rest on any commanding vision, nor is it in any sense a major tragedy. But it is a great flooding moment, a moment's intimation and penetration; and as Gatsby's disillusion becomes felt at the end it strikes like a chime through the mind. It was as if Fitzgerald, the playboy moving with increasing despair through this tinsel world of Gatsby's, had reached that perfect moment, before the break of darkness and death, when the mind does really and absolutely know itself—a moment when only those who have lived by Gatsby's great illusion, lived by the tinsel and the glamour, can feel the terrible force of self-betrayal. This was the playboy's rare apotheosis, and one all the more moving precisely because all of Gatsby's life was summed up in it, precisely because his decline and death gave a meaning to his life that it had not in itself possessed.

Here was the chagrin, the waste of the American success story in the twenties: here, in a story that was a moment's revelation. Yet think, Fitzgerald seems to say to us, of how little Gatsby wanted at bottom—not to understand society, but to ape it; not to compel the world, but to live in it. His own dream of wealth meant nothing in itself; he merely wanted to buy back the happiness he had lost—Daisy, now the rich man's wife—when he had gone away to war. So the great Gatsby house at West Egg glittered with all the lights of the twenties, and there were always parties, and always Gatsby's supplicating hand, reaching out to make out of glamour what he had lost by the cruelty of chance. "Gatsby believed in the green light, the orgiastic future that year by year recedes before us. It eluded us then, but that's no matter— tomorrow we will run faster, stretch out our arms farther. . . . And one fine morning—" So the great Gatsby house, Gatsby having failed in his dream, now went out with all its lights, save for that last un- expected and uninvited guest whom Nick heard at the closed Gatsby door one night, the guest "who had been away at the ends of the earth and didn't know that the party was over." And now there was only the wry memory of Gatsby's dream, left in that boyhood schedule of September 12, 1906, with its promise of industry and self-develop- ment—"Rise from bed. . . . Study electricity . . . work. . . . Practice elocution and how to attain it. . . . Read one improving book or maga- zine per week." So all the lights of Fitzgerald's golden time went out with Jay Gatsby—Gatsby, the flower of the republic, the bootlegger who made the American dream his own, and died by it. "So we beat on, boats against the current, borne back ceaselessly into the past."

Gatsby's was Fitzgerald's apotheosis, too. As the haunting promise of *The Last Tycoon* testifies, he did not lose his skill; there is a grim poetic power in his unraveling of Monroe Stahr greater in itself than anything else in his work. But something in Fitzgerald died concur- rently with the dying of his world. His fairy world decomposed slowly, lingeringly; and he lived with its glitter, paler and paler, to the end. Writing what he himself called "the novel of deterioration" in *Tender Is the Night,* he kept to the glow, the almost hereditary grace, that was so natural for him. But he lavished it upon a world of pure emptiness there; he was working away in the pure mathematics of sensation. The subtlety of his last books was a fever glow, a neurotic subtlety. He had always to return to the ancient dream of youth and power, the kings who always died in his work but were kings nevertheless—the dominating men, the ornate men, the imperials in whose light he lived because they were the romantic magnifications of the world of his youth. And reading that painful confesssion of his own collapse, the essay smuggled away in *Esquire* which he called "The Crack-Up," one felt how fantastic it was, as Glenway Westcott put it in his tender tribute to Fitzgerald, "that a man who is dying or at least done with living—one who has had practically all that the world affords, fame and prosperity, work and play, love and friendship, and lost practically all—should still think seriously of so much fiddledeedee of boyhood." But Fitzgerald was a boy, the most startlingly gifted and self-destructive of all the lost boys, to the end. There is an intense brooding wisdom, all Fitzgerald's keen sense of craft raised and burnished to new power, in *The Last Tycoon* that is unforgettable. To see how he could manipulate the emergence of Stahr's power and sadness, the scene of the airplane flight from New York to Hollywood and the moment when the earthquake trembled in Hollywood, is to appreciate how much closer Fitzgerald could come than most modern American novelists to fulfillment, of a kind. But what is Monroe Stahr—the Hollywood producer "who had looked on all the kingdoms," who died so slowly and glitteringly all through the book as Fitzgerald did in life—but the last, the most feverishly concentrated of Fitzgerald's fairy-world characters in that Hollywood that was the final expression of the only world Fitzgerald ever knew? Fitzgerald could penetrate Hollywood superbly; he could turn his gift with the easiest possible dexterity on anything he touched. But he did not touch very much. With all his skill (it is odd to think that where he was once too easily passed off as the desperate Punch of his generation, he may now be rated as a master craftsman in a day worshipful of craftsmanship), Fitzgerald's world is a little one, a superior boy's world—precocious in its wisdom, precocious in its tragedy, but the fitful glaring world of Jay Gatsby's dream, and of Jay Gatsby's failure, to the end.

3

After Fitzgerald, much of the story of his lost generation is the story of the war he never saw, the craftsmanship which became so great an ideal for his generation, and the blistering new world of the thirties and early forties in which he died.

In 1922, two years after F. Scott Fitzgerald had first propounded the idea of the lost generation in *This Side of Paradise,* a young artist and poet, Edward Estlin Cummings, published the record of his unique war experience in a narrative entitled *The Enormous Room.* It was not the first of the American war novels—John Dos Passos, like Cummings a Harvard graduate and a volunteer in the Norton-Harjes Ambulance Service, had already published *One Man's Initiation* in 1920 and the better-known *Three Soldiers* in 1921—but it showed a new kind of sensibility, as *This Side of Paradise* had announced a generation. Unlike Fitzgerald, Cummings had seen the war at first hand, and his book was something more than Fitzgerald's defense of a generation that "had grown up to find all Gods dead, all wars fought, all faiths in men shaken." *The Enormous Room* was one of those works that break so completely with one tradition that they mechanically inaugurate another. The book seemed to be an exercise in violence; it rumbled with an indignation that was as livid as the experience it described. Its language, more radical in spirit than the buck-sergeant profanity of *What Price Glory?,* was less obvious, and suggested a philosophy of war compounded equally of resignation, hatred for all authority, and an almost abstract cynicism. America had possessed no Barbusse or Sassoon or Wilfred Owen during the war; the irreverence of its war literature, like its bitter reaction against the war spirit, came much later. Cummings's harsh book was thus almost the very first to express for America the emotions of those artists, writers, students, and middle-class intellectuals who were to constitute the post-mortem war generation, and whose war experience was to transform their conception of life and art.

Cummings's war experience had not been typical. Serving as a volunteer in the gentlemanly Norton-Harjes Ambulance Service, he had been arrested by French military police because of some indiscreet letters written by his friend Slater Brown. Jaded with the war spirit, he gave flippant answers at his hearing and was shipped off to a foul and barnlike "preliminary" prison in the south of France, where he spent months in the company of international spies and suspects, thieves, eccentric vagrants from every corner in Europe, prostitutes, and profiteers. The enormous room was his theater of war: he fought no battles, followed the progress of the war through rumor, and spent most of his time trying to keep sane, to get a little food, and to escape. Yet huddled together with the flotsam of war, living on the grudging patronage of a government too busy with routine to be kind, and too suspicious of its prisoners to be fair, Cummings experienced the indignity, the brutality, and the mechanical cruelties of war as a personal disaster. He lived the war through on a lower level, where the slogans seemed farcical, the reality more oppressive, and the great movements of the armies almost unreal. The enormous room concentrated the war. Living on dirty mattresses, humbled by a succession of punishments and insults, deprived of freedom though not confined to "jail," thrown together without common loyalties or even a common purpose, its inmates consciously parodied the war ideals and the war mind. They lived in a perpetual state of mutiny, but there was nothing to protest except life and the French state, no one outrage on which to fix their indignation save the general outrageousness of existence. The enormous room, by its very remoteness from war, mirrored and intensified its inherent meaninglessness; it became a maze in which men clawed each other to escape or to keep their reason. And the central theme of their imprisonment was chaos.

The enormous room was a cell-like sliver torn from life, and its character, as Cummings saw it, was sheer monstrousness. It was a world so profoundly irrational that anger was wasted on it. It was so atrocious that it was comic; it mingled a perverse horror with hysterical exaltation. It was like a surrealist vision of the universe, for it seemed to caricature the conventional dimensions and emotions with such a contempt for order that the very effort to express its horror ended in jollity. *C'est de la blague.* "Who is Marshal Foch?" the Dadaists used to ask in 1921. "Who is Woodrow Wilson? What is war? Don't know, don't know, don't know." War, Cummings proclaimed in this spirit, was the history of decomposition. It was reflected in the tubercular German girl, interned for the greater protection of the French Republic, who was choking to death in solitary. It was the tragic life of Jean Le Nègre, the great dumb beast playing with war as a child plays with blocks. It was the living corpses on their mattresses, the gamblers whispering of European stakes, the lechery and the gossip.

> The doors opened with an uncanny bang and in the bang stood a fragile minute queer figure, remotely suggesting an old man. The chief characteristic of the apparition was a certain disagreeable nudity which resulted from its complete lack of all the accepted appurtenances and prerogatives of old age. Its little stooping body, helpless and brittle, bore with extraordinary difficulty a head of absurd largeness, yet which moved on the fleshless neck with a horrible agility. Dull eyes sat in the clean-shaven wrinkles of a face neatly hopeless. At the knees a pair of hands hung, infantile in their smallness. In the loose mouth a tiny cigarette had perched and was solemnly smoking itself.

The enormous room was a Black Bourse of all the war emotions.

To describe this procession of horrors Cummings needed a prose that was as nervously mobile as jazz, as portentously formal as a document, and as crisp and precise as his own poetry. He developed a style as far removed from declamation as possible, but one that parodied the pompous undertones of declamation, a style that took its pace and weight and diction from the unspoken resources of war cynicism. The essential character of this prose was its self-conscious originality. In a world nerve-lacerated by the prevailing sense of defeat, riddled with pretensions and platitudes that were grisly in their unconscious irony, it offered none of the conventional courtesy that a young writer can tender to standard rhetoric. It was a rebellious prose, defiantly new, and contemptuous of conventional patterns. And though it scattered its effects carelessly, the motive behind it was austere: Cummings's great desire was for a prose that should be, beyond everything else, completely and inexorably true; a prose that would express, as Hemingway later said in a celebrated statement of his own purpose, "the truth about his own feelings at the moment when they exist." It was to be a prose as ruthless, as impolite, as sharp, as consciously and even elaborately bitter, as the world it described. It was to be a prose so contemptuous of conventional standards that no one could doubt its purpose or the depth of the experience behind it.

Cummings's prose was not the hard and deliberately plain prose which Hemingway and later Dos Passos established as their own. Like theirs, it was a prose of inverted lyricism, but more frankly emotional and self-assertive. What he had rejected in his novel was the tonelessness, the machinelike patter, of conventional writing, its implicit submission to the objective world and lack of personal force. With the same passionate individualism that he was soon to bring to his poetry—an individualism not unrelated, as some critics have observed, to the Emersonian and New England tradition that has always been so strong in Cummings—he sought to impose a new conception of reality. Like so many in his generation, he had returned to an elemental writing, as writers often do in periods of social crisis; but his "simplicity" was a form of grotesquerie and not, like Wordsworth's realism or Whitman's, a serene faith that his fellow men would approve a democratic language and purpose. As Cummings saw it, the world was composed of brutal sensations and endured only by a fiercely desperate courage and love; it was so anarchical that all attempts to impose order were motivated by either ignorance or chicanery. What remained to the artist, who was always the special victim of this world, was the pride of individual self-knowledge and the skill that went beyond all the revolutionary and sentimental illusions of a possible fraternity among men and gave all its devotion to the integrity of art.

A parallel code of fatalism developed in Ernest Hemingway's hands into the freshest and most deliberate art of the day. What Cummings had suggested in his embittered war autobiography was that the post-war individual, first as soldier and citizen, now as artist, was the special butt of the universe. As Wyndham Lewis wrote later of the typical Hemingway hero, he was the man "things are done to." To Hemingway life became supremely the task of preserving oneself by preserving and refining one's art. Art was the ultimate, as it was perhaps the only, defense. In a society that served only to prey upon the individual, endurance was possible only by retaining one's identity and thus proclaiming one's valor. Writing was not a recreation, it was a way of life; it was born of desperation and enmity and took its insights from a militant suffering. Yet it could exist only as it purified itself; it had meaning only as it served to tell the truth. A writer succeeded by proving himself superior to circumstance; his significance as an artist lay in his honesty, his courage, and the will to endure. Hemingway's vision of life, as John Peale Bishop put it, was thus one of perpetual annihilation. "Since the will can do nothing against circumstance, choice is precluded; those things are good which the senses report good; and beyond their brief record there is only the remorseless devaluation of nature."

The remarkable thing about Hemingway from the first was that he did not grow up to this rigid sense of tragedy, or would not admit that he had. The background of his first stories, *In Our Time,* was the last frontier of his Michigan boyhood, a mountainous region of forests and lakes against which he appeared as the inquisitive but tight-lipped youth—hard, curt, and already a little sad. With its carefully cultivated brutality and austerity, the sullen boy in *In Our Time* revealed a mind fixed in its groove. These stories of his youth, set against the superb evocation of war monotony and horror, elaborately contrived to give the violence of the Michigan woods and the violence of war an equal value in the reader's mind, summarized Hemingway's education. Their significance lay in the number of things the young Hemingway had already taken for granted; they were a youth's stricken responses to a brutal environment, and the responses seemed to become all. Just as the war in *A Farewell to Arms* was to seem less important than the sensations it provoked, so the landscape of *In Our Time* had meaning only as the youth had learned from it. For Hemingway in his early twenties, the criticism of society had gone so deep that life seemed an abstraction; it was something one discounted by instinct and distrusted by habit. It was a sequence of violent actions and mechanical impulses: the brutality of men in the Michigan woods, the Indian husband who cut his throat after watching his wife undergo a Caesarian with a jackknife, adolescent loneliness and exaltation, a punch-drunk boxer on the road. And always below that level of native memories, interspersed with passing sketches of gangsters and bullfights, lay the war.

> Nick sat against the wall of the church where they had dragged him to be clear of machine-gun fire in the street. Both legs stuck out awk-

wardly. He had been hit in the spine. His face was sweaty and dirty. The sun shone on his face. The day was very hot. . . . Two Austrian dead lay in the rubble in the shade of the house. Up the street were other dead. . . . Nick turned his head carefully and looked at Rinaldi. "Senta Rinaldi. Senta. You and me we've made a separate peace."

The glazed face of the Hemingway hero, which in its various phases was to become, like Al Capone's, the face of a decade and to appear on a succession of soldiers, bullfighters, explorers, gangsters, and unhappy revolutionaries, emerged slowly but definitively in *In Our Time*. The hero's first reaction was surprise, to be followed immediately by stupor; life, like the war, is in its first phase heavy, graceless, sullen; the theme is sounded in the rape of Liz Coates by the hired man. Then the war became comic, a series of incongruities. "Everybody was drunk. The whole battery was drunk going along the road in the dark. . . . The lieutenant kept riding his horse out into the fields and saying to him: 'I'm drunk, I tell you, mon vieux. Oh, I am so soused.' . . . It was funny going along that road." Then the whole affair became merely sordid, a huddle of refugees in the mud, the empty and perpetual flow of rain, a woman bearing her child on the road. "It rained all through the evacuation." By the sheer accumulation of horrors, the final phase was reached, and the end was a deceptive callousness.

> We were in a garden at Mons. Young Buckley came in with his patrol from across the river. The first German I saw climbed up over the garden wall. We waited till he got one leg over and then potted him. He had so much equipment on and looked awfully surprised and fell down into the garden. Then three more came over further down the wall. We shot them. They all came just like that.

Hemingway's own values were stated explicitly in the story called "Soldier's Home," where he wrote that "Krebs acquired the nausea in regard to experience that is the result of untruth or exaggeration." The Hemingway archetype had begun by contrasting life and war, devaluating one in terms of the other. Now life became only another manifestation of war; the Hemingway world is in a state of perpetual war. The soldier gives way to the bullfighter, the slacker to the tired revolutionary, the greed of war is identified with the corruption and violence of sport. Nothing remains but the individual's fierce unassailable pride in his pride, the will to go on, the need to write without "untruth or exaggeration." As a soldier, he had preserved his sanity by rebelling quietly and alone; he had made the separate peace. Mutiny was the last refuge of the individual caught in the trap of war; chronic mutiny now remains the safeguard of the individual in that state of implicit belligerence between wars that the world calls peace. The epos of death has become life's fundamental narrative; the new hero is the matador in Chapter XII of *In Our Time*. "When he started to kill it was all in the same rush. The bull looking at him straight in front, hating. He drew out the sword from the folds of the muleta and sighted with the same movement and called to the bull, Toro! Toro! and the bull charged and Villalta charged and just for a moment they became one." The casual grace of the bullfighter, which at its best is an esthetic passion, is all. And even that grace may become pitiful, as in the saga of the aging matador in "The Undefeated." For the rest, defeat and corruption and exhaustion lie everywhere: marriage in "Cross-Country Snow," sport in "My Old Man" ("Seems like when they get started they don't leave a guy nothing"), the gangrene of Fascism in "Che Ti Dice la Patria?" The climax of that first exercise in disillusion is reached in the terse and bitter narrative called "The Revolutionist," the story of the young boy who had been tortured by the Whites in Budapest when the Soviet collapsed, and who found Italy in 1919 beautiful. "In spite of Hungary, he believed altogether in the world revolution."

> 'But how is the movement going in Italy?' he asked.
> 'Very badly,' I said.
> 'But it will go better,' he said. 'You have everything here. It is the one country that every one is sure of. It will be the starting point of everything.'

4

When Hemingway published those first stories in 1925, he was twenty-seven years old, and the rising star—"the surest future there," Lincoln Steffens recalled in his autobiography—in the American literary colony in Paris. Unlike most of the writers in the "lost generation," he had not gone to a university; after completing a round of private schools he had gone to work, still in his teens, for the *Kansas City Star,* a paper famous for its literary reporters. He had driven an ambulance on the Italian front before America entered the war, been wounded gloriously enough to receive the Croce di Guerra, and after 1921 had traveled extensively as a foreign correspondent. "In writing for a newspaper," he reported seventeen years later in the rambling prose of *Death in the Afternoon,* "you told what happened, and with one trick or another, you communicated the emotion aided by the element of timeliness which gives a certain emotion to any account of something that has happened on that day. But the real thing, the sequence of motion and fact which made the emotion and which would be as valid in a year or ten years or, with luck and if you stated it purely enough, always, was beyond me and I was working very hard to get it."

Hemingway's intense search for "the real thing" had already singled him out in Paris before he published *In Our Time.* In those early years, guided by his interest in poetry and his experiences as a reporter of the European debacle, he seemed to be feeling his way toward a new prose, a prose that would be not only absolutely true to the events reported and to the accent of common speech, but would demand of itself an original evocativeness and plasticity. What he wanted, as he said later in *Death in the Afternoon,* was a prose more intensely precise than conventional prose, and hence capable of effects not yet achieved. He wanted to see "how far prose can be carried if anyone is serious enough and has luck. There is a fourth and fifth dimension that can be gotten. . . . It is much more difficult than poetry. It is prose that has never been written. But it can be written without tricks and without cheating. With nothing that will go bad afterwards." Yet what he was aiming at in one sense, F. O. Matthiessen has pointed out, was the perfect yet poetic naturalness of a Thoreau. Hemingway's surface affiliations as a prose craftsman were with his first teachers, Gertrude Stein and Sherwood Anderson, who taught him the requisite simplicity and fidelity and—Gertrude Stein more than Anderson—an ear for the natural rhythms of speech. But his deeper associations went beyond them, beyond even the Flaubertian tradition of discipline and *le mot juste.* He did not want to write "artistic prose," and Gertrude Stein and Anderson, equally joined in their hatred of display and their search for an inner truth in prose, had certainly taught him not to. But he wanted not merely to tell "the truth about his own feelings at the moment when they exist"; he wanted to aim at that luminous and imaginative truth which a writer like Thoreau, on the strength of a muscular integrity and passion for nature very like his own, had created out of a monumental fidelity to the details of life as he saw them. What he wanted was that sense of grace, that "sequence of motion and fact" held at unwavering pitch, that could convey, as nothing else could, the secret fluid symbolism in the facts touched and recorded.

It was this that separated him essentially from Gertrude Stein and Anderson. Anderson was not fundamentally interested in *writing;* Gertrude Stein, who could help everyone in the world but herself, was interested in nothing else. The Hemingway legend, which Hemingway himself fostered in the twenties, encouraged the belief that he was only a pure nihilist and coldly assimilative, even brutish in imagination. But nothing could have been more false. He brought a major art to a minor vision of life, and it is as important to measure the vision as it is to appreciate the art. But his seeming naïveté was really an exemplary straightforwardness and a remarkable capacity for learning from every possible source. As a practicing artist he had the ability to assimilate the lessons of others so brilliantly that he seemed to impart a definitive modern emotion to everything he touched. He learned so brilliantly, indeed, that the extent of his borrowing has often been exaggerated. What is significant in Hemingway's literary education is not that he learned prose rhythm from the Gertrude Stein of *Three Lives,*[1] the uses of simplicity from Sherwood Anderson, the sense of discipline from Ezra Pound and the cosmoplitan literary ateliers of postwar Paris, but that they gave him the authority to be himself. Despite his indebtedness to Mark Twain's *Huckleberry Finn*—the

---

[1] Style Hemingway learned from many sources; even, as John Peale Bishop has suggested, from the bullfighters. He learned much from T. S. Eliot, as he was later to learn from the smooth, luscious purr of Archibald MacLeish's poems, where the words lie clustered like grapes on the vine. And when the young priest speaks of Abruzzi in *A Farewell to Arms,* there is even the tone of the King James Bible.

greatest book in all American writing for him—he had no basic relation to any prewar culture. Byron learned from Pope, but Hemingway learned to write in a literary environment that could not remember 1913. Even the literary revolution that found its appointed heir in him, an avant-garde forever posing under its Picasso, and talking modernism with a Midwestern accent, could not long claim him. Once Hemingway had learned the principles and tricks of his art, made a literary personality out of the Midwestern athlete, soldier, and foreign correspondent, created a new hero for the times in the romantically disillusioned postwar dandy, he went his own way in his search for "the real thing."

It was in his unceasing quest of a conscious perfection through style that Hemingway proclaimed his distinction. To tell what had happened, as he wrote later, one used "one trick or another," dialogue being the supreme trick. But "the real thing," the pulse of his art, was to Hemingway from the first that perfect blending of fact into symbol, that perfect conversion of natural rhythm into an evocation of the necessary emotion, that would fuse the various phases of contemporary existence—love, war, sport—and give them a collective grace. And it was here that style and experience came together for him. Man endured the cruelty and terror of life only by the sufferance of his senses and his occasional enjoyment of them; but in that sufferance and enjoyment, if only he could convey them perfectly, lay the artist's special triumph. He could rise above the dull submissive sense of outrage which most men felt in the face of events. By giving a new dimension to the description of natural fact, he could gain a refuge from that confusion which was half the terror of living. What this meant was brilliantly illustrated in the association of the worlds of peace and war in *In Our Time;* the theme of universal loneliness in the midst of war that was sounded in the very first paragraph of *A Farewell to Arms* and attained its classic expression in the retreat at Caporetto, where the flowing river, the long grumbling line of soldiers, the officers who are being shot together by the carabinieri, seem to melt together in the darkness; the extraordinary scene in *The Sun Also Rises* where Robert Cohn, sitting with Jake and his friends at the bullfight, is humiliated a moment before the steer is gored in the ring. In each case the animal in man has found its parallel and key in some event around it; the emotion has become the fact.

If "the real thing" could not always be won, or retained after it had been won, there were other forms of grace—the pleasures of drinking and making love, the stabbing matador dancing nervously before his bull, the piercing cry of the hunt, the passionate awareness of nature that would allow a man to write a sentence like "In shooting quail you must not get between them, or when they flush they will come pouring at you, some rising steep, some skimming by your ears, whirring into a size you have never seen them in the air as they pass." If art was an expression of fortitude, fortitude at its best had the quality of art. Beyond fortitude, which even in *For Whom the Bell Tolls* is the pride of a professional integrity and skill, there was the sense of nature paralyzed, nature frozen into loneliness or terror. No nature writer in all American literature save Thoreau has had Hemingway's sensitiveness to color, to climate, to the knowledge of physical energy under heat or cold, that knowledge of the body thinking and moving through a landscape that Edmund Wilson, in another connection, has called Hemingway's "barometric accuracy." That accuracy was the joy of the huntsman and the artist; beyond that and its corresponding gratifications, Hemingway seemed to attach no value to anything else. There were only absolute values or absolute degradations.

The very intensity of Hemingway's "nihilism" in his first stories and novels proved, however, that his need for an ideal expression in art was the mark of a passionate romanticist who had been profoundly disappointed. The anguish of his characters was too dramatic, too flawless; it was too transparent an inversion. The symbols Hemingway employed to convey his sense of the world's futility and horror were always more significant than the characters who personified them, and they so often seemed personified emotions that the emotions became all. The gallery of expatriates in *The Sun Also Rises* were always subsidiary to the theme their lives enforced; the lovers in *A Farewell to Arms* were, as Edmund Wilson has said, the abstractions of a lyric emotion. Hemingway had created a world of his own

more brilliant than life, but he was not writing about people living
in a real world; he was dealing in absolute values again, driving his
characters between the two poles of an absolute exaltation and an
absolute frustration, invoking the specter of their damnation.

After that, *Death in the Afternoon* and the Hemingway legend.
There had always been a Hemingway legend, and with good reason;
like Byron, he was in part the creation of his own reputation. But
the legend became ominous and even cheap only when Hemingway
chose to treat it as a guide to personal conduct and belief; when,
in truth, he became not only one of his own characters but his own
hero. After *Death in the Afternoon,* Hemingway's work became an
expression of the legend, where the legend had once been a measure
of the world's response to his work. The sense of shock, the stricken
malaise of his first stories, were now transformed into a loud and
cynical rhetoric. "Madame, all our words from loose using have lost
their edge," Hemingway tells the Old Lady in *Death in the Afternoon;* and proves it by his own example. "Have you no remedy then?"
she asks. "Madame, there is no remedy for anything in life." The
pose, pretentious in one scene, becomes merely gluttonous in another.
The high jinks of the wastrels in *The Sun Also Rises* had suggested
a tragic self-knowledge, an affirmation of life as they saw it; Hemingway's own tone was now giggly and a little frantic. "So far, about
morals, I know only that what is moral is what you feel good after
and what is immoral is what you feel bad after." It was on a plane
with the famous parody of Marx in "The Gambler, The Nun, and
the Radio":

> Religion is the opium of the people. . . . Yes, and music is the opium
> of the people. . . . And now economics is the opium of the people;
> along with patriotism the opium of the people in Italy and Germany.
> What about sexual intercourse; was that an opium of the people? Of
> some of the people. Of some of the best of the people. But drink was a
> sovereign opium of the people, oh, an excellent opium. Although some
> prefer the radio, another opium of the people. . . . Along with these
> went gambling, an opium of the people if there ever was one. . . .
> Ambition was another, an opium of the people, along with a belief
> in any new form of government.

As the years went by, one grew accustomed to Hemingway standing like Tarzan against a backdrop labeled Nature; or, as the tedious sportsman of *Green Hills of Africa,* grinning over the innumerable beasts he had slain, while the famous style became more mechanical, the sentences more invertebrate, the philosophy more self-conscious, the headshaking over a circumscribed eternity more painful. Most of the lost generation had already departed to other spheres of interest; Hemingway seemed to have taken up a last refuge behind the clothing advertisements in *Esquire,* writing essays in which he mixed his fishing reports with querulous pronouncements on style and the good life. Then, eight years after the publication of *A Farewell to Arms,* when the Hemingway legend had already lost its luster with the disappearance of the world that had encouraged that legend with emulation and empty flattery, Hemingway wrote *To Have and Have Not.* It was a frantically written novel, revealing a new tension and uncertainty in Hemingway; but for all its melodrama, it was not cheap, and it was strange to note that it was the first novel he had written about America. The dry crackle of the boozed cosmopolitans eating their hearts out in unison, the perpetual shift of scene to Malaga or Paris or the African jungle, seemed to have been left behind him. The America of *To Have and Have Not* was Key West, like the Paris of 1925 an outpost of a culture and its symbol. It was by Key West that Hemingway had come home, and it was Key West, apparently, that became a working symbol of America for him, a cross-section: the noisy, shabby, deeply moving rancor and tumult of all those human wrecks, the fishermen and the Cuban revolutionaries, the veterans and the alcoholics, the gilt-edged snobs and the hungry natives, the great white stretch of beach promising everything and leading nowhere.

The Hemingway of *To Have and Have Not* was not a "new" Hemingway; he was an angry and confused writer who had been too profoundly disturbed by the social and economic crisis to be indifferent, but could find no clue in his education by which to understand it. Inevitably, he lapsed into melodrama and sick violence. To the Hemingway who had gained his conception of life from the First World War only to crash into the Second by way of international panic and the Spanish Civil War, mass suffering had always been a backdrop against which the Hemingway hero persisted by dint of his Byronic pride, his sense of grace. But this new crisis had to be endured with something more than artistic fortitude; every generation was caught up in it, every phase of contemporary culture and manners was transformed by it, as even his beloved Spain was being devastated by it. It was like Hemingway, of course, to pick for his new hero in the thirties the pirate of *To Have and Have Not* and the international secret agent of *The Fifth Column:* the two men left in the era from Black Friday to Munich who could remain casual about annihilation! He was reaching for something in these two productions that he could not identify satisfactorily or project with confidence, and it was inevitable that both Harry Morgan and Philip should represent a tormented individualism passionately eager for human fellowship and contemptuous of it. The Hemingway hero was now a composite exaggeration of all the Hemingway heroes, yet nothing in himself. He was the *Esquire* fisherman and an OGPU agent in Spain who found that he had to choose between the Spanish Republic and a Vassar girl; he was a murdering gangster who killed only because Hemingway wanted to kill something at the moment, and a sentimental sophisticate who, when he heard the militia sing *"Bandera Rossa"* downstairs in the shell-battered Hotel Florida, cried: "The best people I ever knew died for that song." Yet Philip in *The Fifth Column* was not one of the best people; he was Jake Barnes making up for his impotence by murdering Fascists, and the Fascists were as unreal as the sick wisdom he and the perennial Lady Brett mumbled at each other in the midst of a civil war that was shaking Western society.

Whatever it was Hemingway tried to reach, however, he found in some measure in Spain; and he found it first in an extraordinary little story, "Old Man at the Bridge," that he cabled from Barcelona in April, 1938. "It will take many plays and novels to present the nobility and dignity of the cause of the Spanish people," he wrote in his preface to *The Fifth Column,* "and the best ones will be written after the war is over." "Old Man at the Bridge" was more than an introduction to the retrospective wisdom of *For Whom the Bell Tolls;*

it was a record of the better things Hemingway had learned in Spain, an intimation of a Hemingway who had found the thwarted ideal clear and radiant again through the martyrdom of the Spanish masses. In the retreat of the Loyalist forces a Spanish officer encounters the last refugee from San Carlos, an old man who has been taking care of eight pigeons, two goats, and a cat, but has been separated from them and from his own people by the advancing Fascist armies. "And you have no family?" the Loyalist officer asks. "No," replies the old man, "only the animals I stated. The cat, of course, will be all right. A cat can look out for itself, but I cannot think what will become of the others." "What politics have you?" the officer asks. "I am without politics," replies the old man. "I am seventy-six years old. I have come twelve kilometers now and I think now I can go no further."

It was in something of this spirit that Hemingway wrote *For Whom the Bell Tolls,* the work of a profound romanticist who had at last come to terms with the ideal, and who had torn down the old charnel house with such ardor that his portrait of the Spanish war was less a study of the Spanish people than a study in epic courage and compassion. The idealism that had always been so frozen in inversion, so gnawing and self-mocking, had now become an unabashed lyricism that enveloped the love of Robert Jordan and Maria, the strength of Pilar, the courage and devotion of the guerrillas, the richness and wit of Spanish speech, in a hymn of fellowship. "All mankinde is of one Author, and is one volume. . . . No man is an Island, intire of it selfe." Nothing could have been more purely romantic than the love story of Robert and Maria, and no love story ever seemed so appropriate an expression of a writer's confidence in life and his overwhelming joy in it. Hemingway had apparently gained a new respect for humanity in Spain, an appreciation of the collectivity that binds all men together; and in the spirit of the Catholic devotion by John Donne which gave him his title, it seemed as if his long quest for an intense unity, the pure absolute fortitude and grace, had become a joyous unison of action and battle and love.

Yet *For Whom the Bell Tolls* is among the least of Hemingway's works. Its leading characters are totally unreal; as a record of the human and social drama that was the Spanish Civil War, it is florid and never very deep. And if one compares this work of his ambitious conversion, with its eloquence, its calculation, and its romantic inflation, with the extraordinarily brilliant story of this late period, "The Snows of Kilimanjaro," it is clear that the attempted affirmation of life in the novel, while passionate enough, is moving only in itself, while the concentrated study of waste and death in the story is perfectly dramatic, perfectly Hemingway's own. Hemingway's world is a world of death still, even in *For Whom the Bell Tolls;* and the great things in it, like the battle scenes or the pillage of the Fascist town, flow with a carefully contrived violence and brutality from him. But the Spanish war is essentially only Robert Jordan's education—"It's part of one's education. It will be quite an education when it's finished." The Hemingway "I" is still the center of existence, as only he could alternate between the war and Maria in the sleeping-bag so easily; as only he could seem less a man entering into the experience of others than the familiarly damned, familiarly self-absorbed lost-generation Byron playing a part beside them. Yes, and the Hemingway hero is still "the man things are done to"—the war is something happening to Robert Jordan—still the brilliant young man counting the costs of his own life among the ruins. *For Whom the Bell Tolls* is thus an unsatisfactory novel, certainly unsatisfactory for Hemingway, because it is a strained and involuntary application of his essentially anarchical individualism, his brilliant half-vision of life, to a new world of war and struggle too big for Hemingway's sense of scale and one that can make that half-vision seem significantly sentimental.

The will is there, the reaching hope; nothing could be more false than the familiar superstition that Hemingway wanted to go round and round in the old nihilist circle. But as Robert Jordan lived and fought the war so curiously alone, so he dies alone, waiting for the enemy to come—the Hemingway guerrilla dying a separate death as once he made a separate peace, the last of the Hemingway heroes enjoying the final abnegation, and now the least impressive. That separate death and abnegation were all there before, and they were very good before. Good when the hunter was alone in the hills, the matador before his bull, the quail skimming through the air. Good when Gertrude Stein could teach a young man fresh from war to write perfect sentences, and the triumph of art was equal to the negation of life. Good when the world could seem like a Hemingway novel; and the "I" was the emblem of all the disillusionment and fierce pride in a world so brilliant in its sickness; and the sentences were so perfect, spanning the darkness. It did not matter then that the art could be so fresh and brilliant, the life below its superb texture so arid and dark. For Hemingway's is one of the great half-triumphs of literature; he proved himself the triumphal modern artist come to America, and within his range and means, one of the most interesting creators in the history of the American imagination. But if it did not matter then, it matters now—not because what is supremely good in Hemingway is in any way perishable, but because his work is a stationary half-triumph, because there is no real continuity in him, nothing of the essential greatness of spirit which his own artistic success has always called for. It matters now that Hemingway's influence has in itself become a matter of history. It will always matter, particularly to those who appreciate what he brought to American writing, and who, with that distinction in mind, can realize that Hemingway's is a tactile contemporary American success; who can realize, with respect and sympathy, that it is a triumph in and of a narrow, local, and violent world—and never superior to it.

5

Technically and even morally Hemingway was to have a profound influence on the writing of the thirties. As a stylist and craftsman his example was magnetic on younger men who came after him; as the progenitor of the new and distinctively American cult of violence, he stands out as the greatest single influence on the hard-boiled novel of the thirties, and certainly affected the social and left-wing fiction of the period more than some of its writers could easily admit. No one save Dreiser in an earlier period had anything like Hemingway's dominance over modern American fiction, yet even Dreiser meant largely an example of courage and frankness during the struggle for realism, not a standard of craftsmanship and a persuasive conception of life, like Hemingway's. Hemingway is the bronze god of the whole contemporary literary experience in America. Yet in a sense he marks an end as clearly as he once marked a beginning. If we consider how the whole lost-generation conception of art and society reached its climax in him, and how much that conception was the brilliant and narrow concentration of the individualism and alienation from society felt by the artist in the twenties, it is clear that Hemingway's stubbornly atomic view of life is the highest expression of the postwar sequence, not a bridge to the future. Despite his will and formal conversion to "the interests of humanity," the "I" and society do not meet imaginatively for him. The writing that came after him in the thirties had only the surface of his brilliance, when it had that at all; but by its absorption in the larger concerns of society, its conviction that no man is alone today, it reveals a departure from Hemingway as much as its toughness reveals his association with it.

A chapter in the moral history of modern American writing does come to an end with Hemingway and the lost generation, and nowhere can this be more clearly seen than in the work of John Dos Passos, who rounds out the story of that generation and carries its values into the social novel of the thirties. For what is so significant about Dos Passos is that though he is a direct link between the postwar decade and the crisis novel of the depression period, the defeatism of the lost generation has been slowly and subtly transferred by him from persons to society itself. It is society that becomes the hero of his work, society that suffers the anguish and impending sense of damnation that the lost-generation individualists had suffered alone before. For him the lost generation becomes all the lost generations from the beginning of modern time in America—all who have known themselves to be lost in the fires of war or struggling up the icy slopes of modern capitalism. The tragic "I" has become the tragic inclusive "we" of modern society; the pace of sport, of the separate peace and the separate death, has become the pounding rhythm of the industrial machine. The central beliefs of his generation, though they have a different source in Dos Passos and a different expression, remain hauntingly the same. Working in politics and technology as Fitzgerald worked in the high world and Hemingway in war and sport, Dos Passos comes out with all his equations zero. They are almost too perfectly zero, and always uneasy and reluctantly defeatist. But the record of his novels from *One Man's Initiation* to *Adventures of a Young Man,* whatever the new faith revealed in his hymn to the American democratic tradition in *The Ground We Stand On,* is the last essential testimony of his generation, and in many respects the most embittered.

Dos Passos's zero is not the "nada hail nada full of nada" of Hemingway's most famous period, the poetically felt nihilism and immersion in nothingness; nor is it the moody and ambiguous searching of Fitzgerald. The conviction of tragedy that rises out of his work is the steady protest of a sensitive democratic conscience against the tyranny and the ugliness of society, against the failure of a complete human development under industrial capitalism; it is the protest of a man who can participate formally in the struggles of society as Hemingway and Fitzgerald never do. To understand Dos Passos's social interests is to appreciate how much he differs from the others of his generation, and yet how far removed he is from the Socialist crusader certain Marxist critics once saw in him. For what is central in Dos Passos is not merely the fascination with the total operations of society, but his unyielding opposition to all its degradations. He cannot separate the "I" and society absolutely from each other, like Hemingway, for though he is essentially even less fraternal in spirit, he is too much the conscious political citizen. But the "I" remains as spectator and victim, and it is that conscientious intellectual self that one hears in all his work, up to the shy and elusive autobiography in the "Camera Eye" sections of *U.S.A.* That human self in Dos Passos is the Emersonian individual, not Hemingway's agonist; he is the arbiter of existence, always a little chill, a little withdrawn (everything in Dos Passos radiates around the scrutiny of the camera eye), not the sentient, suffering center of it. He is man believing and trusting in the Emersonian "self-trust" when all else fails him, man taking his stand on individual integrity against the pressures of society. But he is not Hemingway's poetic man. What Emerson once said of himself in his journal is particularly true of Dos Passos: he likes Man, not men.

Dos Passos certainly came closer to Socialism than most artists in his generation; yet it is significant that no novelist in America has written more somberly of the dangers to individual integrity in a centrally controlled society. Spain before the war had meant for Hemingway the bullfighters, Pamplona, the golden wine; for Dos Passos it had meant the Spanish Anarchists and the Quixotic dream he described so affectionately in his early travel book, *Rosinante to the Road Again*. Yet where Hemingway found his "new hope" in the Spanish Civil War, Dos Passos saw in that war not merely the struggle into which his mind had entered as a matter of course, the agony of the Spain with which he had always felt spiritual ties, but the symbolic martyrdom of Glenn Spotswood, the disillusioned former Communist, at the hands of the OGPU in Spain in *Adventures of a Young Man*. Hemingway could at least write *For Whom the Bell Tolls* as the story of Robert Jordan's education; Dos Passos had to write his Spanish novel as the story of Glenn Spotswood's martyrdom. And what is so significant in Dos Passos's work always is individual judgment and martyrdom, the judgment that no fear can prevent his heroes from making on society, the martyrdom that always waits for them at its hands. That last despairing cry of Glenn Spotswood's in the prison of the Loyalists—"I, Glenn Spotswood, being of sound mind and emprisoned body, do bequeath to the international working-class my hope of a better world"—is exactly like the cry of the poilu in Dos Passos's callow first novel, *One Man's Initiation*—"Oh, the lies, the lies, the lies, the lies that life is smothered in! We must strike once more for freedom, for the sake of the dignity of man. Hopelessly, cynically, ruthlessly, we must rise and show at least that we are not taken in; that we are slaves but not willing slaves." From Martin Howe to Glenn Spotswood, the Dos Passos hero is the young man who fails and is broken by society, but is never taken in. Whatever else he loses—and the Dos Passos characters invariably lose, if they have ever possessed, almost everything that is life to most people—he is not taken in. Hemingway has "grace under pressure," and the drama in his work is always the inherently passionate need of life: the terrible insistence on the individual's need of survival, the drumming fear that he may not survive. Dos Passos, though he has so intense an imagination, has not Hemingway's grace, his need to make so dark and tonal a poetry of defeat; he centers everything around the inviolability of the individual, his sanctity. The separation of the individual from society in Hemingway may be irrevocable, but it is tragically felt; his cynicism can seem so flawless and dramatic only because it mocks itself. In Dos Passos that separation is organic and self-willed: the mind has made its refusal, and the fraternity that it seeks and denies in the same voice can never enter into it.

It is in this concern with the primacy of the individual, with his need to save the individual from society rather than to establish him in or over it, that one can trace the conflict that runs all through Dos Passos's work—between his estheticism and strong social interests; his profound absorption in the total operations of modern society and his overscrupulous withdrawal from all of them; the iron, satirical prose he hammered out in *U.S.A.* (a machine prose for a machine world) and the youthful, stammering lyricism that pulses under it. Constitutionally a rebel and an outsider, in much of his work up to *U.S.A.* a pale and self-conscious esthete, Dos Passos is at once the most precious of the lost-generation writers and the first of the American "technological" novelists, the first to bring the novel squarely into the Machine Age and to use its rhythms, its stock piles of tools and people, in his books.

Dos Passos has never reached the dramatic balance of Hemingway's great period, the ability to concentrate all the resources of his sensibility at one particular point. The world is always a gray horror, and it is forever coming undone; his mind is forever quarreling with itself. It is only because he has never been able to accept a mass society that he has always found so morbid a fascination in it. The modern equation cancels out to zero, everything comes undone, the heroes are always broken, and the last figure in *U.S.A.*, brooding like Dos Passos himself over that epic of failure, is a starving and homeless boy walking alone up the American highway. Oppression and inequity have to be named and protested, as the democratic conscience in Dos Passos always does go on protesting to the end. Yet what he said of Thorstein

Veblen in one of the most brilliantly written biographies in *U.S.A.* is particularly true of himself: he can "never get his mouth round the essential yes." The protest is never a Socialist protest, because that will substitute one collectivity for another; nor is it poetic or religious, because Dos Passos's mind, while sensitive and brilliant in inquiry, is steeped in materialism. It is a radical protest, but it is the protest against the status quo of a mind groping for more than it can define to itself, the protest of a mind whose opposition to capitalism is no greater than his suspicion of all societies.

In Dos Passos's early work, so much of which is trivial and merely preparatory to the one important work of his career, *U.S.A.,* this conflict meant the conflict between the esthete and the world even in broadly social novels like *Three Soldiers* and *Manhattan Transfer.* But under the surface of preciosity that covers those early novels, there is always the story of John Roderigo Dos Passos, grandson of a Portuguese immigrant, and like Thorstein Veblen—whose mordant insights even more than Marx's revolutionary critique give a base in social philosophy to *U.S.A.*—an outsider. Growing up with all the advantages of upper-middle-class education and travel that his own father could provide for him, Dos Passos nevertheless could not help growing up with the sense of difference which even the sensitive grandsons of immigrants can feel in America. He went to Choate and to Harvard; he was soon to graduate into the most distinguished of all the lost generation's finishing schools, the Norton-Harjes Ambulance Service subsidized by a Morgan partner; but he was out of the main line, out just enough in his own mind to make the difference that can make men what they are.

It is not strange that Dos Passos has always felt such intimate ties with the Hispanic tradition and community, or that in his very revealing little travel book, *Rosinante to the Road Again,* he mounted Don Quixote's nag and named himself Telemachus, as if to indicate that his postwar pilgrimage in Spain was, like Telemachus's search for Ulysses, a search for his own father-principle, the continuity he needed to find in Hispania. It was in Spain and in Latin America that Dos Passos learned to prize men like the Mexican revolutionary Zapata, and the libertarian Anarchists of Spain. As his travel diaries and particularly the biographical sketches that loom over the narrative in *U.S.A.* tell us, Dos Passos's heart has always gone out to the men who are lonely and human in their rebellion, not to the victors and the politicians in the social struggle, but to the great defeated—the impractical but human Spanish Anarchists, the Veblens, the good Mexicans, the Populists and the Wobblies, the Bob La Follettes, the Jack Reeds, the Randolph Bournes, all defeated and uncontrolled to the last, most of them men distrustful of too much power, of centralization, of the glib revolutionary morality which begins with hatred and terror and believes it can end with fraternity. So even the first figure in *U.S.A.,* the itinerant Fenian McCreary, "Mac," and the last, "Vag," are essentially Wobblies and "working stiffs"; so even Mary French, the most admirable character in the whole trilogy, is a defeated Bolshevik. And it is only the defeated Bolsheviks whom Dos Passos ever really likes. The undefeated seem really to defeat themselves.

The grandson of the Portuguese immigrant was also, however, the boy who entered college, as Malcolm Cowley has pointed out, "at the beginning of a period which was later known as that of the Harvard esthetes." The intellectual atmosphere there was that of "young men who read Pater and 'The Hill of Dreams,' who argued about St. Thomas in sporting houses, and who wandered through the slums of South Boston with dull eyes for 'the long rain slanting on black walls' and eager eyes for the face of an Italian woman who, in the midst of this squalor, suggested the Virgin in Botticelli's Annunciation." Dos Passos went to the slums; and he could find the Botticelli Virgin there. The *Harvard Monthly* was publishing his first pieces: a free-verse poem, an editorial, and an essay on industrialism entitled "A Humble Protest." "Are we not," asked the young author, "like men crouching on a runaway engine? And at the same time we insensately shovel in the fuel with no thought as to where we are being taken." It was but one step from this to *One Man's Initiation,* published in England in 1920, and significantly subtitled *1917.* For this first of his two antiwar novels made no pretense to the hard-boiled realism of *Three Soldiers.* It was the very boyish and arty memoir of a young architect-poet whose chief grievance against the war, in a way, seems to have been that he could not admire the Gothic cathedrals in France for the clamor of the guns in his ears. The hero, consciously posing himself against a Europe ravaged by war, was a pale imitation of all the pale heroes in fin-de-siècle fiction, a hand-me-down Huysmans torn between a desire to enter a monastery, a taste for architecture, and a need to write a ringing manifesto for all the embittered artist-revolutionaries in the world. "God!" exclaims Martin Howe in the trenches, "if only there were somewhere nowadays where you could flee from all this stupidity, from all this cant of governments, and this hideous reiteration of hatred, this strangling hatred."

By 1921, with *Three Soldiers,* the esthete had become something more of the social novelist. The rhetorical petulance of *One Man's Initiation* had given way to a dull, gritty hatred. No longer could Dos Passos write a sentence such as "Like the red flame of the sunset setting fire to opal sea and sky, the old exaltation, the old flame that would consume to ashes all the lies in the world, the trumpet-blast under which the walls of Jericho would fall down, stirs and broods in the womb of his grey lassitude." He was a realist whose odyssey of three buck privates—Fuselli from the West, Christfield from the South, John Andrews the musician from New York—was an attempt to tell in miniature the national story of the A.E.F. Yet for all the grimness of *Three Soldiers,* the sounding in it of the characteristically terse and mocking tone of Dos Passos's later social novels, it was essentially as flaky and self-consciously romantic as *One Man's Initiation.* There are three protagonists in the book, but only one hero, John Andrews; and it is his humiliation and agony in war that finally dominate the book. It is interesting to note that in this first important novel Dos Passos had already shown that interest in the type, the mass as central protagonist, that would distinguish *U.S.A.;* and certainly nothing is so good in the book as his ability to suggest the gray anonymity, the treadmill, the repeated shocks and probings of the private's experience, the hysterical barroom jokes and convulsive brothel loves, the boredom and weariness.

Yet it is even more significant that Dos Passos did sacrifice his inclusive design to John Andrews. For Andrews is what he cares most for; Andrews is a sadder and older brother to Martin Howe, the shy and esthetic and fumbling Dos Passos hero, and like the hedonists of *1919,* he survives the war only to die—at least symbolically, at the hands of the military police—in the peace. Where the enemy in *One Man's Initiation* was abstract, the society at war in *Three Soldiers* is a bureaucratic horror. But the war does exist still only as something oppressive to John Andrews; the artist is against the world, and when Andrews speaks out of his full heart at the end of the book, it is to say to Jeanne: "We must live very much, we who are free to make up for all the people who are still . . . bored." The artist has no place in war, as in a sense he has no place in the industrial mass society Dos Passos has not yet discovered; war seems only the last brazen cruelty of the enemy, the outrage inflicted upon those who would live bravely and be passionately free—for art. The army is the public self (Dos Passos can never accept the public self); the artist can only conceal himself in it or die by it. "This sentient body of his, full of possibilities and hopes and desires, was only a pale ghost that depended on the other self, that suffered for it and cringed for it." And the public self wins; it always will in Dos Passos. So John Andrews, who deserted to write a great orchestral poem (around the Queen of Sheba), is captured after all; and when the police take him away, the sheets of music flutter slowly into the breeze.

Thirteen years after he had completed *Three Soldiers,* Dos Passos wrote that it was a book that had looked forward to the future. For all its bitterness, he had written it as an epilogue to the war from which men in 1919 seemed to be turning to reconstruction or even revolution. "Currents of energy seemed breaking out everywhere as young guys climbed out of their uniforms . . . in every direction the countries of the world stretched out starving and angry, ready for anything turbulent and new." He himself had gone on to Spain, Telemachus looking for the father and teasing himself because he was so callow. Spain was where the old romantic castles still remained; Spain had been neutral during the war; in Spain one might even be free of the generation "to which excess is a synonym for beauty." In Spain there were the Anarchists, and tranquillity without resignation, and the kind of life that would develop a Pio Baroja, physician and baker and novelist of revolution. "It's always death," cries the friend in *Rosinante to the Road Again*, "but we must go on. . . . Many years ago I should have set out to right wrong—for no one but a man, an individual alone, can right a wrong; organization merely substitutes one wrong for another—but now . . ." But now Telemachus is listening to Pio Baroja, whose characters, as he describes them, are so much like the characters in *Manhattan Transfer* and *U.S.A.*—"men whose nerve has failed, who live furtively on the outskirts, snatching a little joy here and there, drugging their hunger with gorgeous mirages." Baroja is a revolutionary novelist as Dos Passos only seems to be, but as Dos Passos reports Baroja's conception of the middle-class intellectual, one can see his own self-portrait:

> He has not undergone the discipline which can only come from common slavery in the industrial machine, necessary for a builder. His slavery has been an isolated slavery which has unfitted him forever from becoming truly part of a community. He can use the vast power of knowledge which training has given him only in one way. His great mission is to put the acid test to existing institutions, and to strip the veils off them.

By 1925, when he published *Manhattan Transfer*, Dos Passos had come to a critical turn in his career. He had been uprooted by the war, he had fled from the peace; but he could not resolve himself in flight. More than any other American novelist of the contemporary generation, Dos Passos was fascinated by the phenomenon of a mass society in itself; but his mind had not yet begun to study seriously the configuration of social forces, the naturalism and social history, which were to become his great subject in *U.S.A.* Like so much that he wrote up to 1930, *Manhattan Transfer* is only a preparation for *U.S.A.*, and like so many of those early works, it is a mediocre, weakly written book. He had as yet no real style of his own; he has not even in *Manhattan Transfer*. But he was reaching in that book for a style and method distinctively his own; and just as the Sacco-Vanzetti case was two years later to crystallize the antagonism to American capitalist society that is the base of *U.S.A.*, so the experimental form of *Manhattan Transfer*, its attempt to play on the shuttle of the great city's life dozens of human stories representative of the mass scene (and, for

Dos Passos, the mass agony), was to lead straight into the brilliantly original technique of *U.S.A.*

Yet the achievement in style and technique of *Manhattan Transfer* is curiously inconclusive and muddy. The book seems to flicker in the gaslight of Dos Passos's own confusion. Out of the endlessly changing patterns of metropolitan life he drew an image that was collective. He was all through this period working in expressionist drama, as plays like *The Garbage Man, Airways, Inc.,* and *Fortune Heights* testify; and as in the expressionist plays of Georg Kaiser and Ernst Toller, he sketched out in his novel a tragic ballet to the accompaniment of the city's music and its mass chorus. Most significantly, he was working out a kind of doggerel prose style completely removed from his early lushness, full of the slangy rhythms he had picked up in *Three Soldiers* by reproducing soldier speech, and yet suggestive of a wry and dim poetry. This new style Dos Passos evidently owed in part to contemporary poetry, and like his trick of liquefying scenes together as if in a dream sequence and fusing words to bring out their exact tonal reverberation in the mind, to James Joyce. But what this meant in *Manhattan Transfer* was that the romantic poet, the creator and double of Martin Howe and John Andrews and the novel's Jimmy Herf, had become fascinated with a kind of mass and pictorial ugliness. The book was like a perverse esthetic geometry in which all the colors of the city's scenes were daubed together madly, and all its frames jumbled. What one saw in *Manhattan Transfer* was not the broad city pattern at all, but a wistful absorption in monstrousness. The poet-esthete still stood against the world, and rejected it completely. Characteristically even the book's hero (*U.S.A.* was to have no heroes, only symbols), Jimmy Herf, moons through it only to walk out into the dawn after a last party in Greenwich Village, bareheaded and alone, to proclaim his complete disgust with the megalopolis of which he was, as the Dos Passos poet-heroes always are, the victim.

So Dos Passos himself, though torn between what he had learned from Pio Baroja and his need to take refuge in "the esthete's cell," was ready to flee again. The conflict all through his experience between the self and the world, the conflict that he had been portraying with growing irony and yet so passionately in all his works, was coming to a head. And now the social insights he had been gathering from his own personal sense of isolation, from his bitterness against the war, from Spain, were kindled by the martyrdom of Sacco and Vanzetti. More perhaps than any other American writer who fought to obtain their freedom, it can be said, Dos Passos was really educated and toughened, affected as an artist, by the long and dreary months he spent working for them outside Charlestown Prison. For many writers the Sacco-Vanzetti case was at most a shock to their acquiescent liberalism or indifference; for Dos Passos it provided immediately the catalyst (he had never been acquiescent or indifferent) his work had needed, the catalyst that made *U.S.A.* possible. It transformed his growingly irritable but persistently romantic obsession with the poet's struggle against the world into a use of the class struggle as his base in art. The Sacco-Vanzetti case gave him, in a word, the beginnings of a formal conception of society; and out of the bitter realization that this society—the society Martin Howe had mocked, that John Andrews had been crushed by, that Jimmy Herf had escaped—could grind two poor Italian Anarchists to death for their opinions, came the conception of the two nations, the two Americas, that is the scaffolding of *U.S.A.*

Dos Passos knew where he stood now: the old romantic polarity had become a social polarity, and America lay irrevocably split in his mind between the owners and the dispossessed, between those who wielded the police power and the great masses of people. He began to write *The 42nd Parallel,* the first volume in *U.S.A.,* after the Sacco-Vanzetti case; and the trilogy itself draws to its end after Mary French's return from their execution in *The Big Money.* The most deeply felt writing in all of *U.S.A.* is Dos Passos's own commentary on the Sacco-Vanzetti case in the "Camera Eye," where he speaks in his own person, an eloquent hymn of compassion and rage that is strikingly different from the low-toned stream-of-consciousness prose that is usually found in the "Camera Eye" sections, and which lifts it for a moment above the studied terseness and coldness of the whole work.

they have clubbed us off the streets   they are stronger
they are rich   they hire and fire the politicians the newspapereditors the old judges the small men with reputations the collegepresidents the wardheelers (listen businessmen collegepresidents judges America will not forget her betrayers) they hire the men with guns the uniforms the policecars the patrolwagons

     all right you have won   you will kill the brave men our friends tonight

     America our nation has been beaten by strangers who have turned our language inside out who have taken the clean words our fathers spoke and made them slimy and foul

     their hired men sit on the judge's bench they sit back with their feet on the tables under the dome of the State House they are ignorant of our beliefs they have the dollars the guns the armed forces the powerplants

     they have built the electricchair and hired the executioner to throw the switch

     all right we are two nations

All right we are two nations. It is the two nations that compose the story of *U.S.A.* But it was the destruction of two individuals, symbolic as they were, that brought out this polarity in Dos Passos's mind, their individual martyrdom that called the book out. From first to last Dos Passos is primarily concerned with the sanctity of the individual, and the trilogy proper ends with Mary French's defeat and growing disillusionment, with the homeless boy "Vag" alone on the road. It is not Marx's two classes and Marx's optimism that speak in *U.S.A.* at the end; it is Thorstein Veblen, who like Pio Baroja could "put the acid test to existing institutions and strip the veils off them," but "couldn't get his mouth round the essential yes." And no more can Dos Passos. *U.S.A.* is a study in the history of modern society, of its social struggles and great masses; but it is a history of defeat. There are no flags for the spirit in it, and no victory save the mind's silent victory that integrity can acknowledge to itself. It is one of the saddest books ever written by an American.

6

Technically *U.S.A.* is one of the great achievements of the modern novel, yet what that achievement is can easily be confused with its elaborate formal structure. For the success of Dos Passos's method does not rest primarily on his schematization of the novel into four panels, four levels of American experience—the narrative proper, the "Camera Eye," the "Biographies," and the "Newsreel." That arrangement, while original enough, is the most obvious thing in the book and soon becomes the most mechanical. The book lives by its narrative style, the wonderfully concrete yet elliptical prose which bears along and winds around the life stories in the book like a conveyor belt carrying Americans through some vast Ford plant of the human spirit. *U.S.A.* is a national epic, the first great national epic of its kind in the modern American novel; and its triumph is not the pyrotechnical display that the shuttling between the various devices seems to suggest, but Dos Passos's power to weave so many different lives together in narrative. It is possible that the narrative sections would lose much of that power if they were not so craftily built into the elaborate framework of the book. But the framework holds the book together and encloses it; the narrative makes it. The "Newsreel," the "Camera Eye," and even the very vivid and often brilliant "Biographies" are meant to lie a little outside the book always; they speak with the formal and ironic voice of History. The "Newsreel" sounds the time; the "Biographies" stand above time, chanting the stories of American leaders; the "Camera Eye" moralizes shyly in a lyric stammer upon them. But the great thing about *U.S.A.* is that though it sweeps up so many human lives together and intones their waste and illusion and defeat so steadily, we seem to be swept along with them and to see each life perfectly at the moment it passes by us.

The brilliance of the structure lies therefore not so much in its external surface design as in its internal one, in the manifold rhythms of the narrative. Each of the various narrative sections has its dominant musical mode, as it were; each of the characters is encased in his characteristic prose. Thus at the very beginning of *The 42nd Parallel,* when the "Newsreel" blares in a welcome to the new century, while

General Miles falls off his horse and Senator Beveridge's toast to the new imperialist America is heard, the story of Fenian McCreary, "Mac," begins with the smell of whale-oil soap in the printer's house in Middletown. That smell, the clatter of the presses, the political arguments, the muddy streets and saloons, give the tone of Mac's life from the first, as his life—Wobbly, tramp, working stiff—sounds the emergence of labor as a dominant force in the new century. So the story of Eleanor Stoddard begins with "When she was small she hated everything," a sentence that calls up the thin-lipped rebellion and superciliousness, the artiness and desperation, of her loveless life before we have gone into it. *The 42nd Parallel* is a study in youth, of the youth of the new century, the "new America," and of all the human beings who figure in it; and it is in the world of Mac's bookselling and life on freights, of Eleanor Stoddard's rebellion against her father and Janey Williams's picnic near the falls at Georgetown, of J. Ward Moorehouse's Wilmington and the railroad boarding house Charley Anderson's mother kept in North Dakota, that we move. The narrator behind his "Camera Eye" is a little boy holding to his mother's hand, listening to his father's boasts (at the end of the book he will be on his way to France); the "Newsreel" sings out the headlines and popular songs of 1900-16; the "Biographies" are of the magnates (Minor C. Keith, Carnegie), the wonder men of the new century (Steinmetz, Edison, Burbank), the rebels (Bryan, Debs, Bob La Follette, Big Bill Haywood).

We have just left the world of childhood behind us in *The 42nd Parallel,* but we can already hear the clatter of the conveyor belt pushing all these lives along. Everyone is sparring hard for position; the fences of life are going up. There is no expectancy in this youth, not even the sentimental poetry of adolescence. The "Newsreel" singing the lush ballads of 1906 already seems very far away; the "Biographies" are effigies in stone. The life in the narrative has become dominant; the endless pulsing drowns everything else out. Everything is hard, dry, and already a little outrageous. Johnny Moorehouse falls in love only to learn that the socially prominent girl whom he needs for his ambition is a whore. When Eleanor Stoddard's father announces his plan to marry again, he tells her it will be to a "Mrs. O'Toole, a widow with five children who kept a boardinghouse out Elsden way." Mac, after his bitterly hard youth, leaves the Wobblies with whom he has found comradeship and the joy of battle to marry a girl who drives him almost insane; then leaves her and is thrown into the Mexican revolutions of the period. Janey Williams's life has already taken on the gray color of the offices in which she will spend her life. There are no refuges in this world, no evasions, and above all no second starts. The clamps have been laid down early, and for all time.

Yet we can feel the toneless terror of all these lives, the oppression and joylessness that seem to beat down upon us from the first, only because every narrative section is so concrete and every sentence, as Delmore Schwartz pointed out, "can expand in the reader's mind to include a whole context of experience." *U.S.A.* is perhaps the first great naturalistic novel that is primarily a triumph of style. Everything that lives in the book is wound up on the spool of that style; from the fragments of popular songs in the "Newsreel" and the clean verse structure of the "Biographies" down to the pounding beat of the narrative, the book seems to be propelled by one dynamic rhythm. The Dos Passos prose, once so uncertain and self-conscious, has here been whittled down to a sharpness that can kill; but it has by no means lost its old wistful rhetoric in *U.S.A.*, which is particularly conspicuous in the impressionist "Camera Eye" sections, and generally gives a kind of secret and mischievous color to the severely reportorial prose. Scrubby, slangy, with a kind of grim straightforwardness, it is the style of a very cunning artisan who seems to be working in these human materials as another might work in stone or wood—forever carving away, forever whittling, but never without subtle turns and a loving sense of design. It is never a "distinguished" style, beautiful in its own right; never as prismatic as Fitzgerald's or as delicately molded as Hemingway's, and there is always something fundamentally mechanical about it. But it is the style Dos Passos needs to turn the motor of the conveyor belt; it is the reportorial and satiric style needed to push along and circumscribe all these lives. With *The 42nd Parallel* we have entered into a machine world in which the rhythm of the machine has become the primal beat of all the people in it; and Dos Passos's hard, lean, mocking prose, forever sounding that beat, calling them to their deaths, has become the supreme expression of his conception of them.

Perhaps nowhere in the trilogy, save in the descending spiral of Charley Anderson's life in the first half of *The Big Money,* is Dos Passos's use of symbolic rhythm so brilliant as in the story of Joe Williams in *1919.* For Joe, Janey Williams's sailor brother, is the leading protagonist of the war and the early postwar period, as J. Ward Moorehouse's ambitiousness marked the pattern of *The 42nd Parallel.* Joe's endless shuttling between the continents on rotting freighters has become the migration and rootlessness of the young American generation whom we saw growing up in *The 42nd Parallel;* and the growing stupor and meaninglessness of his life became the leit-motif of the waste and death that hold everyone in the book as in a ghostly vise. The theme of death, of the false optimism immediately after the Armistice, are sounded immediately by the narrator behind his "Camera Eye" reporting the death of his mother and the notation on the coming of peace—"tomorrow I hoped would be the first day of the first month of the first year." The "Biographies" are all studies in death and defeat, from Randolph Bourne to Wesley Everett, mutilated and lynched after the Centralia shootings in Washington in 1919; from the prose poem commemorating the dozens of lives the Unknown Soldier might have led to the death's-head portrait of J. P. Morgan ("Wars and panics on the stock exchange,/ machinegunfire and arson/ . . . starvation, lice, cholera and typhus"). The "Camera Eye" can detect only "the almond smell of high explosives sending singing éclats through the sweetish puking grandiloquence of the rotting dead." And sounding its steady beat under the public surface of war is the story of Joe Williams hurled between the continents—Joe, the supreme Dos Passos cipher and victim and symbol, suffering his life with dumb unconsciousness of how outrageous his life is, and continually loaded and dropped from one ship to another like a piece of cargo.

> Twentyfive days at sea on the steamer *Argyle,* Glasgow, Captain Thompson, loaded with hides, chipping rust, daubing red lead on steel plates that were sizzling hot griddles in the sun, painting the stack from dawn to dark, pitching and rolling in the heavy dirty swell;

bedbugs in the bunks in the stinking focastle, slumgullion for grub, with potatoes full of eyes and mouldy beans.

All through *1919* one can hear death being sounded. Every life in it, even J. Ward Moorehouse's, has become a corrosion, a slow descent. Richard Ellsworth Savage goes back on his early idealism and becomes a cynical but willing abetter in Moorehouse's schemes. Eveline Hutchins and Eleanor Stoddard lose all their genteel pretense to art and grapple for Moorehouse's favor. "Daughter," the Texas girl Savage has betrayed, falls to her death in an airplane. Even Ben Compton, the New York radical, soon finds himself rotting away in prison. The war for almost all of them has become an endless round of drink and travel; they have brought nothing to it and learned nothing from it save a growing consciousness of their futility. And when they all slip into the twenties and the boom with *The Big Money,* the story of Charley Anderson's precipitate rise and fall becomes the last mad parable of their existence, a carnival of greed and corruption. Beginning with Dick Savage's life on ambulances and trains over France and Italy in *1919,* the pace of the trilogy has become faster and faster; now, as the war world empties into the pleasure world of *The Big Money*—New York and Detroit, Hollywood and Miami at the height of the boom— it has become a death ride. There is money in the air, money and power for Charley Anderson and Margo Dowling and Dick Savage; but as they come closer to this material triumph, their American dream, the machine has begun to spin them too rapidly. Charley Anderson can kiss the bright new century notes in his wallet, Margo can rise higher and higher in Hollywood, Dick Savage, having sold out completely, can enjoy his power at the hands of J. Ward Moorehouse; the machine has begun to strangle them; there is no joy here for anyone. All through *The Big Money* we wait for the balloon to collapse, for the death cry we hear in that last drunken drive of Charley Anderson's and his smashup.

What Waldo Frank said of Mencken is particularly relevant to Dos Passos: he brings energy to despair. Not merely does the writing in the trilogy become richer and firmer as the characters descend into the pit, but Dos Passos himself seems so imbued with an almost mystical conviction of failure that he rises to new heights in those last sections of *The Big Money* which depict the last futile efforts of the liberals and radicals to save Sacco and Vanzetti, and their later internecine quarrels. The most moving scene in all of *U.S.A.* is the scene in which Mary French, the only counterpoise to the selfishness of the other characters in *The Big Money*, becomes so exhausted by her labors for Sacco and Vanzetti that when she goes to bed she dreams that her whole world is forever coming apart, that she is climbing up a shaky hillside "among black guttedlooking houses pitching at crazy angles where steelworkers lived" and being thrown back. The conflicting hopes of Mary French, who wanted Socialism, and of Charley Anderson, who wanted the big money, have brought two different kinds of failure; but it is failure that broods over them and over everyone else in *U.S.A.* in the end—over the pompous fakes like J. Ward Moorehouse, the radicals like Ben Compton, the grasping little animals like Eleanor Stoddard and Eveline Hutchins, the opportunists like Richard Ellsworth Savage. The two survivors are Margo Dowling, supreme for the moment in Hollywood, and the homeless boy "Vag," who stands alone on the Lincoln Highway, gazing up at the transcontinental plane above winging its way west, the plane full of solid and well-fed citizens glittering in the American sun, the American dream. *All right we are two nations*. And like the scaffolding of hell in *The Divine Comedy*, they are frozen into eternity; for Dos Passos there is nothing else, save the integrity of the camera eye that must see this truth and report it, the integrity and sanctity of the individual locked up in the machine world of modern society.

With *The Big Money*, published at the height of the nineteen-thirties, the story of the twenties comes to a close; but even more does it bring the story of the lost generation to a close, that generation which has stood at the peak of modern time in America as no other has. Here in *U.S.A.*, in the most ambitious of all its works, is its measure of the national life, its conception of history—and it is a history of struggle that is vain, of failure that is irrevocable, and of final despair. There is strength in *U.S.A.*, Dos Passos's own strength, the strength of the craft that can weld so many lives together and make them live so intensely before us as they pass. But for the rest it is a brilliant hecatomb, and one of the coldest and most mechanical of tragic novels. By the time we have come to the end of *U.S.A.* we begin to feel what Edmund Wilson could detect in Dos Passos before it appeared, that "his disapproval of capitalistic society becomes a distaste for all the human beings who compose it." The protest, the lost-generation "I," has taken all of them into his vision; he has given us his truth. Yet if it intones anything affirmative in the end, it is the pronouncement of young Orestes Brownson—"There is no such thing as reforming the mass without reforming the individuals who compose it." It is this conviction, rising to a bitter crescendo in *Adventures of a Young Man,* this unyielding protest against modern society on the part of a writer who has now turned back to the roots of "our storybook democracy" in works like *The Ground We Stand On* and his projected life of Thomas Jefferson, that separates Dos Passos from so many of the social novelists who follow after him in the thirties. Where he speaks of sanctity, they speak of survival; where he lives by the truth of the camera eye, they live *in* the vortex of that society which Dos Passos has always been able to measure, with hatred but not in panic, from the outside. Dos Passos is the first of the new naturalists, and *U.S.A.* is the dominant social novel of the thirties; but it is not merely a vanished social period that it commemorates: it is an individualism, a protestantism, a power of personal disassociation, that seem almost to speak from another world.

Part III: THE LITERATURE OF CRISIS
(1930-1940)

"Each time the human mind puts itself to a difficult task, it begins its conquest of new fields and especially of its proper spiritual universe by bringing with all this a certain amount of disturbance, of disaster. The human being seems to become disorganized; and sometimes in fact it happens that crises of growth end unhappily. But there are, in any case, *crises of growth*."—JACQUES MARITAIN, "Poetry's Dark Night"

Chapter 13

THE REVIVAL OF NATURALISM

"Naïveté in art is like a zero in a number: its importance depends on the figure it is united with."—PAUL OVERT in Henry James's "The Lesson of the Master"

THE crisis of the nineteen-thirties, which opened for Americans as a financial panic and as a sudden stop to the gluttony of the boom period, marked the opening phase of a revolution in world society more comprehensive but no more significant than the transformation it effected in American life. From the first shock of some sudden and indefinable dissolution to the enforced world citizenship which finally related it to the progressive disintegration of the European order, it took its place among the prime experiences of the American mind and even suggested a climax to them. For whether interpreted as a breakdown of capitalism or a visitation from on high, a temporary failure of institutions or the epilogue to America's participation in the First World War, the crisis imposed with catastrophic violence what other national experiences had induced slowly and indirectly—a new conception of reality. In the light of this sudden collapse, this material failure which could not be understood in material terms alone, this economic disaster that was so manifestly something more that it was as bewildering as it was oppressive, the very conception of responsibility seemed unique. Life seemed at once so different in tone, in the very consciousness that sustained it, that all conventional values were suddenly uprooted and many of them seemed cheap. Society was no longer a comfortable abstraction, but a series of afflictions; the crazy rhythms of dissolution gave one the sense that people, like their most cherished illusions, were submitting without direction, submitting in a collective stupor of the will.

It was the depression of the mind that from the first gave significance to the depression of society, for the impact of the crisis on culture was far more violent than its transformation of the social order. Something happened in the thirties that was more than the sum of the sufferings inflicted, the billions lost, the institutions and people uprooted: it was an education by shock. Panic, a panic often significantly disproportionate to the losses of those who were most afraid, became the tone of the period. No longer was it true, as Santayana had said in *Character and Opinion in the United States,* that the "moral materialism" and "love of quantity" in the American character were inconclusive because the American had never yet faced the trials of Job. They had erupted suddenly and with a vengeance; and it was the shock to that moral materialism and love of quantity that so brutally deprived men of their security and left them impotent in the face of disaster. In the world after 1932, where everything seemed to be breaking up at once, the American had at first neither a sense of history nor the consolation of traditional values. He was oppressed by forces that were meaningless to him in operation and hence all the more humiliating in effect. His sense of leadership, his bourgeois vanity that America was "different," disappeared when he saw the effect of his own failure upon European morale and the mounting catastrophe that led directly to Fascism. He had been in "panics" before—1857, 1873, 1893, 1907; but this was more than an economic stoppage. At the very moment that it marked the close of a period of expansion and revealed the impossible complication of the world economy, it isolated him before the world precisely because he had been so proudly the agent and the symbol of that expansion. When he betrayed his fears as a creditor and helped to topple the jerry-built structure of postwar loans and reparation payments, he seemed to lose his function, his legend, and a condition of his existence.

In Europe, the Austrian economist Peter Drucker has written, the characteristic feature of the crisis was the sudden collapse of all rational values. When the individual was deprived of his social order, his world was deprived of a rational existence.

> He can no longer explain or understand his existence as rationally correlated and co-ordinated to the world in which he lives; nor can he co-ordinate the world and the social reality to his existence. The function of the individual in society has become entirely irrational and senseless. Man is isolated within a tremendous scene. . . . This disintegration of the rational character of society and of the rational relationship between individual and society is the most revolutionary trait of our times.

The American, however, did not lose his social order, nor did he experience the full agony of that predicament which invited Fascism in Europe: the sense of living in a world which has entirely lost its meaning. If he experienced a sense of terror—at least in the opening years of the crisis—that suggested a dissolution far more brutal than that which had occurred, it was because he had no defense against it, as even writers—Ezra Pound's "antennae of the race"—had no defense against it. Like so many of the great American social experiences, the crisis represented an almost fantastic acceleration of reality, a sudden and complete break that could be grasped in terms of an oppressively intense superficiality, a welter of emotions, but never as something that had to be thought through as well as suffered.

Suddenly, as in the years after the Civil War or in the post-Versailles period, one saw the emergence of a new sensibility—sullen, aggressive, and confused, the signal of the familiar instantaneous break with other types and other needs, yet for all its pride—the equally familiar pride of the perennial American "realist"—making its substance out of fear and struggling for expression rather than deliverance. One saw again the recurrent loneliness of the American writer in each new generation and the tragicomic kaleidoscope of a culture where every five years, as the literary joke ran, saw a new "generation" addressing itself combatively to a "new" experience. Yet what had other experiences been when measured against the violence of this crisis? Where the American had once needed only to adapt his life to the external development of society, he was now directly menaced by society and physically victimized by it. The crisis was not, like so many events in the history of American development, a disenchantment that was at once a half-promise of delightful things and the urgent, ferocious conquest of nature: it was a sickening paralysis. Like the great Charles Schwab, the common man after 1929 could only say: "I'm afraid, every man is afraid. I don't know, we don't know, whether the values we have are going to be real next month or not." What he could not understand was confused by his despair, since he could only throw himself headlong upon life or appeal to abstractions to comfort him. His traditional rootlessness was no longer merely poignant, and never had he less chance of evading it; the brutality and sentimentality that composed his response to the catastrophe became, in a period of collective sensations, the very expression of his need to survive.

2

The impact of the crisis upon American writing was obvious from the first, obvious as an earthquake, a breadline, or the living proof of Thoreau's observation that one generation abandons the enterprises of another like stranded vessels. In a world in which institutions and states now began to fall with such passive regularity, the succession of the literary generations that marked the opening of the decade seemed as inevitable to the departing celebrities of the twenties as it was urgent to the Marxists, tough-guy naturalists, sociologists, and documentary reporters who were so eager to take over. The sensation that an era had passed became so widespread, and entered so contentedly into the literature of the new period, that it soon became tedious. Yet it was emphasized by the self-pronounced obsequies of those older writers who, with an almost embarrassing solicitude for the simplicities of history, resigned not merely from their posts but from literature itself. Like Sinclair Lewis in Stockholm in 1930, they were suspiciously ready to acclaim their own generation—*O Pioneers!*—as worthy but tired. From the first the crash had a too-perfect symbolic utility, and it was not the Marxists alone who felt—though only a certain type of Marxist intelligence could have put it so grandly—that "1929 brought clarity out of existing confusion."

One now saw enacted against a portentous setting—the crisis of a traditional order—the drama of a literary revolution that would, for once, work simultaneously toward a social revolution: a new generation armed with fresh purpose, fresh thoughts, ready to sweep away the follies and tinsel glamor of the twenties and to fulfill the perennial promise of the American commonwealth. The crisis, everyone now felt, had marked the end of a long apprenticeship. From their first thwarted and poignant efforts to understand and to live with an industrial society in the eighteen-eighties and nineties, American writers had passed through a succession of major experiences; but seen against the larger and more tragic pattern of European history their work had always seemed a delayed reaction, the evidence of an approximate maturity—troubled, formless, satiric. The year 1929—so ran the legend from almost the first moment of the crisis—had brought all that to an end: the depression generation had finally caught up with history. It alone had restored the sense of reality, for measured against the terrors and obligations of the thirties all previous experiences seemed trivial and even the literary victories a little cheap. The twenties, that halcyon experience in literary rebellion, now seemed no more than a boisterous version of the Continental fin de siècle, a struggle against provincialism and for personal freedom that was no more than the counterpart to the Flaubert period in France and the Bernard Shaw period in England. Writers in the past had won a certain number of rights, but only writers in the thirties, it was now felt, would exercise them properly.

In the face of general dissolution the writer of the thirties personified a transformation of sensibility, of style, of the very nature of the American literary character, that seemed unprecedented. There were now two orders of prose: one that included Van Wyck Brooks along with Howells, Sinclair Lewis as easily as Hamlin Garland; and another, profoundly influenced by Hemingway and Dos Passos, that already seemed as remote from Lewis and Anderson as they had once from Howells. Although the post-1929 period was to be characterized as much by nostalgia as by the contagious naturalism which revealed the nature of its social interests, the very act of writing in the thirties seemed to impose new obligations. The obsession with society was much more than an influence; it often became the content of the new literature. Writing was no longer an exercise of personality testing the range of the writer's strategy and powers; it was an expression of belief, a participation at once so urgent and so vague that unusual sensibility seemed almost immoral in a world where mediocrity could conceal itself by the assumption of a political faith that compensated for the lack of perceptions by decrying the need of them. The political faith was not always the literary man's Communism, that *sanctus simplicissimus* possible only in countries with some tradition of liberty. It was at bottom the political gesture, the political compulsion, which revealed the fear of society and preserved the fiction of the writer's free will. Armed with a political concept, the writer felt that his "realism" had a new foundation and literature itself a new dimension; and if what he produced was not always literature, his militancy and compassion augured a finer and riper humanity.

It was not for nothing, then, that the documentary and sociological prose of the depression period often proved more interesting than many of the new social novels.[1] Everyone was writing documentary prose in the depression period, but novelists were writing it under a psychological handicap. In a period of unparalleled national self-assessment the sociologist writing as a sociologist enjoyed the liberty and revealed the candid freshness of the explorer, the social reporter. He investigated the process of change and described his results; his values were often as obvious as his method, but what he produced had the strength of his knowledge and curiosity. The authors of the La Follette Committee report, *Five Cities, Deserts on the March, The Trouble I've Seen, Industrial Valley, These Are Our Lives,* had only to say, like Casy in *The Grapes of Wrath:* "Somepin's happening. I went up an' I looked, an' the houses is all empty, an' the lan' is empty, an' this whole country is empty. I can't stay here no more. I got to go where the folks is goin'." This was the spirit of the new prose written in the thirties, and it satisfied the country's need to know what had happened to it, a demand that aroused interest in the oppressive *facts* of change, such as migratory workers, silicosis, the emotions of people on relief, and the personality of Adolf Hitler.

There were many novelists who wrote on that level, but they were

---

[1] See Chapter XVI.

not the best novelists of the period. The ambitious imaginative writer and critic of the thirties had to give meaning to the crisis at the very moment that he was forced to defend his writing against it. He had to justify his writing by a social sanction and to give a social purpose to it, to persuade his readers that he was helping to direct society, though he may only have been drifting along with it and catching his themes from the headlines. Never before did he feel with such force the writer's alienation from modern American society; yet never before had it seemed so dishonorable or so difficult for him to admit it. The common victim of the depression, who lost his identity when he lost his job, his function when he lost his home, saw the dissolution around him as a primary fact because his literal conception of security was literally destroyed. Writers, who must adopt a convention, a personality, to exist at all, who must by the very nature of the literary act display more certainty than they feel, could not afford such candor. They were moved by an unconscious conflict between their desire to reorganize society and their struggles to survive in it; between the revolutionary subjects they often employed and their frightened and even sadistic use of them; and it was this that gave so many of the social novels in the thirties their rancor. The new social novelists had to rise above their own fear of society, yet expose society's fear of itself; to announce their revolt against capitalist society and yet satisfy their crisis-begotten sense of violence, that significant disposition to hate and to destroy which grew out of the pervasive atmosphere of panic, and often entered into the very texture of contemporary style and speech.

It is the presence of a vast subterranean life under all the slogans, the formal militancy, the busy literary activity, that explains the quality of so much of the writing of the thirties. Never were writers so militant in their challenge or so conscious of what was wanted, so anxious to participate in society and to liberate it; never were they so much at the mercy of all the social pressures and so driven by public events. In a period of many ironies none was so glaring as this, for like the growing domination of American literature in a world increasingly forbidden by Fascism to read and write at all, it suggested a reality beneath the appearance that was without consolation and almost a mockery. For no longer could the European ask, like Sydney Smith,

"Who reads an American book?" Who, after 1933, could afford not to read an American book? The literature that was too long a maiden cousin to English literature, a provincial forever gawking at the literatures of the world, that had apologized for itself and doubted its strength since the Civil War, now seemed the only free literature left in the world. While American writers had been trying to come of age longer than it seemed decent to remember and to meet the standards of Europe, Europe was trying desperately to stay alive; and the long and humiliating submission that had been growing weaker ever since the nineties now seemed the last phase of American colonialism. In Hemingway, Dos Passos, Faulkner, Farrell, Wolfe, there had been synthesized a new and original type, gifted, as one English critic wrote so admiringly, "with the bold power to shock that is so strong in modern American literature." In a moribund world he seemed a phenomenon of energy—reckless, aggressive, inventive, the symbol of a world, as the Russians saw it in Henry Ford or the Germans in Thomas Wolfe, that had learned the secret of production and would remain vigorous and new. To some the retrogression of the American literary type from Mark Twain to Frank Norris, from Norris to Mencken, from Mencken to, say, James T. Farrell, might have suggested some subtle disintegration of personal distinction and style; but *autres temps, autres mœurs*: the American writer, like American business, had become a Force, and one that dominated the Western world.

Such, at least, was the reversal of the American writer's reputation, his legend, in less than fifty years, a process which began with the half-patronizing delight in the "Western romances" of Mark Twain, and ended with Europe's youth eagerly reading Sinclair Lewis and Dos Passos. Yet was the success of the new writers in Europe anything more than the success of Hollywood pictures or Ginger Rogers? The American verve and toughness were refreshing, but did they not hide some secret sickness perceptible at closer range? Yes, the American writer had certainly come of age; but if one looked carefully into this violent naturalism which slick Broadway reporters and proletarian novelists now adopted with the same half-naïve, half-cynical fatalism, a naturalism that embodied the discovery of Hollywood as well as the docks and the logging camps, the tabloid murder along with the sharecroppers, he seemed almost overripe. What held the naturalists together, with a few honorable exceptions who differed only in the selection and weight of their ideas, was an emotional protest that became the very substance of their social attitude. This was not the cult of violence as one saw it in Faulkner's delight in monstrosity or Robinson Jeffers's disgust with the human species in toto; it was a naturalism, as Edward Dahlberg wrote when he revolted against it, of "matter in motion loathing itself." In Faulkner one saw the use of naturalism toward quasi-philosophical ends, and a type of mind, though lush and rhetorical, that was profoundly interested in craft and ambitious to convey the quality of a dissolution hardly limited to capitalist economy and morals. The naturalists—a company that included passionately honest talents like Farrell, realists out of the sharecropper country like Caldwell, hard-boiled reporters like John O'Hara, pedestrian realists, and most of the proletarian novelists—were more commonplace and more aggressive. They were the writers in whom the literal significance of the crisis had aroused a literature of literal realism, mechanical prophecy, and disgust. Their violence was in some respects the familiar realistic savagery of the American novelist in bad times, but what distinguished it from preceding naturalisms was the knowledge that they were obeying a common impulse and that the need to shock, so compulsive that it went into their every conception and even the language of their minds, was the most intense literary "equivalent" of contemporary disorder.

3

It was the abject surrender to naturalism on the part of so many vigorous young novelists in the thirties that gave the new social novel its basic character. In America, as one saw the type emerging in Dreiser, there had appeared after 1900 a succession of naturalists who had almost nothing in common with Zola's classic desire to impose the mechanism of nineteenth-century science upon the novel, but who had at least remembered the origins of naturalism and preserved some feeling for its philosophical design. After Dos Passos, perhaps the last naturalist in American prose who had a conscious conception of naturalism as a philosophy of life, naturalism was no longer a creed or even a method: it became a reflex. The typical young naturalist of the thirties, whatever his personal experience—it was usually bitter enough—liked to think that he had been born tough and without "literary" pretensions; and he convinced himself as easily as he convinced the public. He believed in determinism well enough—there is a question whether he believed in anything else—but it was the determinism of the class struggle, the policeman's night stick, love without money, and the degradations of a society in which so many men were jobless and hungry. Believing in that, he could be anything else he pleased: a maker of comic grotesques like Erskine Caldwell; an autobiographer like James Farrell; a Broadway reporter like John O'Hara; a novel-writing Communist declaiming the party line; an impressionist of contemporary horror, like Edward Dahlberg or Benjamin Appel; an apostle of his race, like Richard Wright. In novelists like these the classic interests and the equally classic hardness of naturalism were instinctive, for they all saw life as an experience in oppression; and the hard, loud vocabulary of naturalism, its energy and passion, its mechanical technique and methodical simplicity, were all taken for granted.

Explicit, murderous, profane, this contemporary naturalism expressed so vigorous a reaction to the crisis and provided so facile a mastery of common speech and incident that it gave young writers a unique sense of release. By throwing "pure art" overboard, as George Orwell has observed, they freed themselves from many artistic scruples and vastly "enlarged" their scope. Precisely because this naturalism retained and even exaggerated the rawness of American realism from Ed Howe to Dos Passos, and could call upon the familiar American tradition of literary horror and sadism in Poe and Bierce, it spoke to the depression mind and evaded literary responsibilities. Naturalism has always thrived on the appearance of power and gross, heavy effects; but in the thirties even the most transparent vulgarity—*vide* the stories of some of the more egregious party-liners like Edwin Seaver and Isidor Schneider—had social significance: shall not the truth make you free? It did at least make one bold, for social truth was social evidence. In the interests of that truth the most pitiful impotence, the crassest philistinism, the cheapest pretensions, could be obscured by the exploitation of Engels's declaration that freedom is the recognition of necessity. Everything in this naturalism gave the appearance of social criticism even when it did not rest upon the slightest understanding of human values; everything except an elementary knowledge of form, a sense of balance, or a conscious idea of selection, satisfied its needs.

"When you are actually *in* America," D. H. Lawrence had written in his *Studies in Classic American Literature,* "America hurts, because it has a powerful disintegrative influence. . . . The very commonsense of [white] Americans has a tinge of helplessness in it, and deep fear of what might be if they were not common-sensical." Under the bravado of depression naturalism lay something more than the familiar and almost standard disillusionment of the postwar mind: it was an obsession with pain and cruelty that was oppressive in the intensity of its expression or revulsion. The young naturalist of the thirties was afflicted by that "destructive element" which Stephen Spender has defined as "the experience of an all-pervading Present, which is a world without belief"; but that was all, and hence more than he could bear. Even the most talented of the new writers had usually nothing in common with Hemingway's psychological interest in fortitude or Dos Passos's moral condemnation of contemporary life; and he was certainly light-years removed from Lawrence's passionate condemnation of materialism or Joyce's interest in craftsmanship. His own values were not always conscious ones; when they were, they were either as vaguely prophetic and mechanical as a literary Communist's, or brutish. Exulting in his freedom and power to shock, the young naturalist deceived himself by mistaking his desire to write violently on violent subjects for a criticism of society. And a good many people were mistaken with him.

4

Up to 1930, when writers began to stream into the Communist party and its numerous affiliates with an impetuous and submissive eagerness that astonished the party leaders themselves, proletarian literature was an abstraction that had meaning only as a political weapon. A working-class literature in America, which had once meant the Wobbly songs

of Joe Hill and the poems of Arturo Giovannitti, the novels of Jack
London and Upton Sinclair, had been reduced in the twenties to the
Marxist criticism of Michael Gold, V. F. Calverton, and Joseph Freeman, and was frankly a method of indoctrination rather than a literary
movement. During the twenties, corresponding to the period in Russia
between Lenin's death and Stalin's final seizure of control, the Communist party in America was itself rent by opposing groups struggling
for power, and the wistful literary Socialism of the Greenwich Village
period soon became a tender memory. The *Masses* had expired in 1918,
the *Liberator* in 1924, and when the *New Masses* was founded in 1926
it was still possible to number among its official and contributing
editors so diverse a group as Michael Gold, Louis Untermeyer, Freda
Kirchwey, John Dos Passos, and Edmund Wilson. Save for a few
political writers and young literary rebels, Marxist and quasi-Marxist
writers in the twenties talked mostly to themselves. The Socialist poet
of 1912, writing Spenserian hymns to May Day and the liberation of
womanhood, had given way to the Bolshevik journalist, and a few—
but a very few—middle-class liberals who still kept a "social accent"
in their work. The Sacco-Vanzetti case had done much to encourage
radical sympathies, but many writers, like Edna St. Vincent Millay,
picketed the Boston State House and returned home to write, after
the first excitement had lapsed, on their usual subjects. The New
Humanists, by their rigorous insistence on standards of belief and
taste, had challenged the liberals to seek firmer ground for their
opinions; but the Humanist debate was itself a phase of the decline
of literary skepticism in the twenties, and the Marxist writer was
usually a party pamphleteer.

In the twenties the Communist leaders were too busy seeking out
revolutionary "situations" and fighting among themselves to encourage
and to direct a working-class literature that was insubstantial. They
wished for the support of middle-class writers but distrusted them; and
since the proletarian arts in the Soviet Union had followed no clear
design, more than one professional Marxist agreed with Trotsky—in
the days when it was still possible to agree with that literary Beezlebub
—that proletarian art "will never exist, because the proletarian regime
is temporary and transient. The historical significance and the moral

grandeur of the proletarian revolution consist in the fact that it is laying the foundations of a culture which is above classes and which will be the first culture that is truly human." But by a curious irony— one that was to have interesting consequences—the sudden prestige of the Communist party as an influence upon writers became a force just at that moment in the history of international Communist politics when the increasing narrowness and totalitarianism of Stalinist theory and practice revealed a characteristic contempt for the individual mind. In Russia the Lunacharskys and Mayakovskys had already given way not only to men like Mikhail Sholokhov but also to party hacks, "shock-brigadiers of literature," adulators of the All-Highest, and sentimental historical novelists like Alexey Tolstoy who could be depended on to wring a tear and point a moral. Where the typical Soviet writer had once been a man of eager literary culture, and as ready to keep up with international literature as he was to honor his country's revolu-tionary purpose, he was now too often a cynical intellectual anxious to please the State Publishing House or an Uzbek primitive singing Beowulf hymns of Lenin's resemblance to God.

Soviet letters, in the new era of "Socialist realism," encouraged simple chronicles about the making of a new society; how much better if the writer himself were simple! Even in America, despite the eager interest in a working-class literature, local Communist politicians did not hesitate to denigrate writers who objected to an occasional display of Stalinist defamation and violence. Proletarian literature was impor-tant, but political correctness was more important still; in the Stalinist cosmogony writers, like people, were notoriously cheap. When the Communists found themselves leading a literary movement—and no one knew better than they how little conspiracy had gone into it at first —they were only too anxious to help it grow and to point it in the "correct" direction; but considerations of orthodoxy outweighed all lit-erary considerations.

As it happened, however, too many writers were very happy to submit, particularly if up to the moment of their conversion they had thought of Karl Marx as a dull nineteenth-century German with a beard. They were so shell-shocked by the crisis and so plaintively eager for some new and positive conception of change that the manifest poverty or despair of alternative creeds brought them directly to the Communists. Bolshevism had iron in it, militancy, spirit, and a Program. Proletarian literature—though the proletarians rarely heard of it and would certainly never enjoy it—had in it the promise of a new society, not to say a new literature that would put all other periods in American literary history to shame. In the face of the world-wide breakdown of capitalism even a literary middle-class Socialist ardor sounded the mighty diapason of salvation. The clean prophetic lines of Marxist theory, so overwhelming in their relevance to all phases of contemporary demoralization, provided an inexhaustible assurance of victory. A working-class philosophy aroused all the native democratic instincts of American writers and strengthened them within a pattern of ideas that made sense and had urgent international significance. What did it matter that H. L. Mencken sneered or that few good writers ever remained very long in the Communist camp? To be a Marxist writer in the early thirties was to give one's work a new dignity and ennobling seriousness. It needed only a few lusty plays and poems of revolt, critical essays that saw failure, failure everywhere in the bourgeois past, for one to say, even before proletarian literature became a fashion, that "it grows in richness and maturity, while bourgeois literature slips from casualty to casualty."

The poignance of the Communist literary adventure for so many writers in the thirties lay in the confusion of two distinct entities: their hopes for greater social and economic democracy at home, and the influence of a country that had never known democracy. This fact became tragic enough after the Nazi-Soviet Pact and the Great Disillusionment; but it was clear after 1935, when the Communist party, seeking a united front against Fascism, allowed proletarian literature to wither away and became interested, as Philip Rahv has said, in authors rather than in books. But who of these writers could see it in the early thirties, when the Communists prophesied and worked toward an imminent revolution, and the raw zeal of the converted found its expression in a literature of *New Masses* covers, declamations, garish satire, and intense hopefulness? It did not matter then that the sum of their radicalism was only a literary Populism; a new and warmer sensibility seemed the order of the day. Lincoln Steffens had seen the

Future, and it worked. In the period of the great optimism Russia seemed more than a great social "experiment"; it was a new form of literary therapy. Steffens wrote to Ella Winter when she was in Russia:

> Get it all; all but the details. Get it as a whole. Let it lift and clear your mind. It is better to be a revolution than to see one, and Russia can put you forward centuries in civilization. It can jerk you up to where it has got, and then show you the future. . . . Russia is just what Dorothy Parker, Hem, Dos Passos and all the Youth school of writers lack and need. They seek it in drink and get it in cynicism. You can take it, as it is, in the living form of a people on the job, in a religion. Faith, hope, liberty, a living,—Russia doesn't need to drink.

Writing in the *New Masses* in 1930, Dos Passos addressed a moving appeal to writers to arouse themselves to the plight of humanity, and to slough off the cynical irresponsibility that had proved so fashionable in the twenties. "It's as if the carnage of the European war and the years following it and the rapid mechanization of life had entirely dulled the imaginative response (putting yourself in the other man's place) that's biologically at the bottom of feelings of mercy and compassion." To Dos Passos, who was no convert and who had a passionately scrupulous sense of human values, the depression seemed to call as a matter of course for a militant social literature; but too many of the writers now uprooted by the crisis found also in the Russian example the consolation and protective monism of a system. Literature became something more than literature, and hence did not always have to be literature at all. In the general excitement of submitting to the Future That Worked, writing itself became a significantly new experience. Superficially the hysterical joy with which so many writers embraced the revolutionary cause proved only that they were men of goodwill, which was perhaps as true of Ezra Pound in the arms of Mussolini as it was of Henri Barbusse in the arms of Stalin; and superficial or not, it was a plain fact. Yet it is clear that writers could be "attracted by a form of Socialism that makes mental honesty impossible" [1] only because they had little interest in literature and were even a little contemptuous of it.

---

[1] George Orwell.

Proletarian literature, as Philip Rahv has said, was the literature of a party disguised as the literature of a class; and it was dangerous to forget it, as too many disillusioned writers learned to their cost. But whatever one may say of the political interests that at first guided and later destroyed that literature as a movement, it is important to remember that the tropism toward Communism represented only a symptom rather than a cause of what happened to so many writers in the thirties. The influence of Communism explains dozens of cheaply tendentious political novels and much of the more simple-minded and party-minded Marxist criticism. Yet only the disorganization and demoralization of the crisis period explain why so many sincere writers yielded so worshipfully to the Russian example, the marked coarsening and opportunism of literary standards, and the characteristic savagery of writers who, often mediocre enough in imagination, delighted in hitting back at life in their books as violently as life had hit them. As early as 1934 Horace Gregory, one of the most sensitive of left-wing critics, already noted the moral crudity of much Marxist writing on literature, and protested against the muckerism of a *New Masses* reviewer who had objected to the use of the word "honor" in one of Stephen Spender's poems. It was not that most left-wing writers lacked honor themselves or were tolerant of cynicism in others. What they lacked, what the atmosphere of the time lacked, was that measured consideration of literature as a human need which is possible only in periods when the writer does not have to live in an atmosphere of violent social pressures. In such an atmosphere the belief in literature, the necessary respect for it, waned perceptibly; simplicity of a kind seemed not merely inevitable, but necessary; and the writer's energy, which so often became a mechanical ferocity and a grim delight in ugliness, sufficed to explain his purpose and to provide the necessary defense for his work.

It must be said too that the left-wing writer who had himself been a worker or had been brought up in a working-class atmosphere, like Farrell, Caldwell, Dahlberg, Cantwell, and many others, also brought to his work the pride of that first victory against middle-class society which had given him the freedom to become a writer at all. This was something conservative critics ignored and *New Masses* editors sentimentalized when they wrote about "novelists writing after long days in shops and offices, poets polishing their verses as they stand in bread-lines"; but it made for a powerful and often deeply moving literature of confession and autobiography. "A first book like yours, of a young working-class author, cannot be regarded merely as literature," Michael Gold once wrote to Jack Conroy in the *New Masses*. "To me it is a significant class portent. It is a victory against capitalism. Out of the despair, mindlessness and violence of the proletarian life, thinkers and leaders arise. Each time one appears it is a revolutionary miracle." At the very least, certainly, it made for revolution-minded novels; and a generation of novelists who had been toughened in alleys, orphanages, logging camps, and mills proved not only that the democracy of author-ship was strong in America, but that the compulsion of these men to write of the life of the working class was rooted in the memory of their own life in it.

It was this which united writers so diverse as Dahlberg and Farrell, Caldwell and Richard Wright, in that fellowship of proletarian natu-ralism which went beyond temperamental and political differences and was based on the significant personal need of catharsis by terror, if not by pity. For writers like these the act of composition was truly, in terms of T. S. Eliot's famous insight, an escape from personality rather than an expression of it, a continual sacrifice of the writer's self in and through his book. The more intense the writer's disgust with the environment from which he sought release, the more ferocious his obsession with its details. In many Communist novelists this be-came what Edward Dahlberg later described as the "yea-saying com-munistic rite. . . . The guilt is the proletarian populace, the ritual bull that must be killed and eaten so that society, the cadaver-flesh of the masses, can be reborn." Yet this was only a more deliberate and programmatic exposition of the cult of violence that became a familiar style in others. One saw it in Caldwell's necrophilism and Farrell's inexhaustible interest in brutality; in the sort of writing in minor novelists like Benjamin Appel which invested the most trivial observations with fantastically disproportionate intensity and saw every conversation between an employer and a worker as a "rape"; in the diseased impressionism, really a prose of hysteria, of Edward Dahlberg's novels; in the calculated brutality of dozens of proletarian short stories, the authors of which took so much moral pleasure in scenes of murder, suicide, rape, abortion, and starvation that the violence evidently provided some effective release. These stories were certainly as naïve artistically as the often-ridiculed "conversion" epics which always ended with the hero raising his fist amidst a sea of red flags; but their temper had really very little to do with politics, as such critics as Granville Hicks learned when they protested against energetic exercises in horror that had no obvious relation to Socialism.

The two most formidable left-wing naturalists, Erskine Caldwell and James T. Farrell, brought a zest to their documentation of "capitalist decay" that was strangely irrelevant to Socialism, but actually the very secret of their power. Caldwell's twisted comic sense was defended on the strength of a suspicion that he really belonged to the tradition of Southern frontier humor, and it was sgnificant that when he was not energetically grotesque, he was merely cute. His delight in cruelty and outrage, in sharecroppers being devoured by hogs and little girls sold into prostitution for a quarter, was as gamin in its quality as his delight in the sexual antics of his poor whites, and equally reflective of a primitive, sly, and stuttering romanticism. But Farrell was hardly a naïf, and certainly never a purveyor of Gothic tidbits for the delectation of urban sophisticates who thought Jeeter Lester a representative Southern citizen, but amusing. Passionately honest and passionately narrow, he brought to his novels the intensity of an autobiographical mission as tortured and complex in its way as Proust's. Like Proust, Farrell seems to have endured certain personal experiences for the sole purpose of recording them; but he also desired to avenge them, and he charged his work with so unflagging a hatred of the characters in them, and wrote at so shrill a pitch, that their ferocity seemed almost an incidental representation of his own. Like Caldwell, he wrote with his hands and feet and any bludgeon within reach; but where Caldwell's grossness seemed merely ingenuous, or slick, Farrell wrote under the pressure of certain moral compulsives that were part of the very design of his work and gave it a kind of dreary grandeur. He had the naturalist's familiar contempt for style, but his gracelessness seemed so methodical that it became a significant style in itself—not awkward, as in Dreiser at his worst, or grandiose as in Frank Norris, but an automatic style, a style rather like a sausage machine, and one whose success lay in the almost quantitative disgust with which Farrell recorded each detail.

Farrell was perhaps the most powerful naturalist who ever worked in the American tradition, but the raw intensity of that power suggested that naturalism was really exhausted and could now thrive only on a mechanical energy bent on forcing itself to the uttermost. There is a total and moving design unfolded in his conflicting histories of Studs Lonigan and Danny O'Neill—the history of the South Chicago world out of which both sprang; the history of these two careers, one descending and the other ascending, with the ascendant Danny O'Neill giving back the life that had almost crushed him as a youth—*giving it all back*. But scene by scene, character by character, Farrell's books are built by force rather than imgaination, and it is the laboriously contrived solidity, the perfect literalness of each representation, that give his work its density and harsh power. As an example for novelists Farrell was as much a blind alley as Dreiser, but where Dreiser remained a kind of tribal poet, a barbaric Homer who exercised a peculiar influence because of his early isolation and his place in the formation of naturalism, Farrell, so much less sentient a mind, grew out of the materialism of the early thirties. For while Dreiser was the epic recorder of the American tragedy in the first great period of naturalism, his awkwardness seemed merely a personal trait, and one that did not conceal the great depths in his work. Farrell was the archetypal novelist of the crisis and its inflictions, and the atmosphere of crisis supported his work as appropriately as his own conception of life satisfied the contemporary need to shock and to humiliate. It is not only that all the rawness and distemper of the thirties seem to live in Farrell's novels; though written as the story of his own education, they are at the same time the most striking example of that literalness of mind which showed all through the depression literature in the surrender of imagination and in the attraction to pure force and power.

It is this literalness, this instinctive trust in the necessity of violence, which make Farrell's practice in fiction so livid a symbol of the mind of depression America. In his hands the cult of violence was something different from Faulkner's overstylized Gothic, which had to be seen through a maze of confused lyricism and technical legerdemain, or Caldwell's pellagra Frankenstein, which was wryly comic. It was naturalism proving its bravado to itself, and expanding by the sheer accumulation of sensations. The technique was a kind of arithmetical progression, notably in such furious scenes as the famous New Year's Eve bacchanal in *The Young Manhood of Studs Lonigan*, the nightmare initiation scene in *Judgment Day*, and that apocalyptic passage in *No Star Is Lost* which portrayed Aunt Margaret O'Flaherty, drunk to the hilt, thrown out by her latest lover, sitting on the steps and counting her fingers in a devouring rush of the D.T.'s Farrell's style was like a pneumatic drill pounding at the mind, stripping off the last covers of the nervous system. Primitive in their design, his scenes aroused a maximum intensity of repulsion by the sheer pressure of their accumulative weight. If one submitted to that pressure, every other consideration seemed irrelevant or falsely "literary," like Farrell's tone-deafness, or the fact that he improvised his scenes within so narrow a range that the final impression was black unrelieved dullness. This was Life, or at the very least the nerve-jangled and catastrophic life the thirties knew.

What gave Farrell his edge over other left-wing naturalists, many of whom perished singly even before their movement did, was his complete confidence in his material and gifts, in the very significance of his literary existence. Cantwell gave up after two novels; Dahlberg was exhausted by his own sensibility; Caldwell, as Kenneth Burke once said, became so repetitious that he seemed to be playing with his toes; Gold wrote nothing after *Jews without Money*, which expressed all he had to say, except his *Daily Worker* twaddle; Schneider, Seaver, Rollins, Conroy, Burke, Lumpkin, were all unable to follow up their early novels. Of the host of younger writers who seemed to promise so much to Marxist critics in the early thirties—the Tillie Lerners, the Arnold Armstrongs, the Ben Field—only Richard Wright and Albert Maltz went on writing at all. But Farrell's will to endure gave him the energetic faith to write a trilogy and to launch one of the most expansive autobiographical epics in literary history. If his grimness often became the very tone of his work, it also served as a rationale, a formal conception as grandiose as Jules Romains's. Farrell's very need to write along a line of single concentration was, like his complete dependence upon his own resources, a kind of spiritual autarchy—there was only one subject in his work, and the spirit with which he pursued it soon became one with it. For Farrell was not "making" subjects out of proletarian life, like those occupational novelists whose books reflected their special knowledge of automobile workers, textile hands, relief supervisors; or those nationality novelists who were as crude as the Communist party's program for a "black belt" in the South to be composed exclusively of Negroes. He never wrote about his fellow Irish in that fake sociological spirit; Studs Lonigan's gang, the Flaherty and O'Neill families, the priests and nuns, were all dramatis personae in the story of Danny James Farrell O'Neill, whose story *was* his will to endure, to be free of the influences that had threatened to stifle his spirit.

Farrell's distinction was thus a very real one: in a period of moral collapse, he believed in himself with an almost monumental seriousness. Far more than Dreiser, whose career was spotted with failure, who wrote his books by intermittent and devastating exertions, Farrell represented the supremacy of the naturalist's imagination in, rather than over, a period of tormented materialism. He did not rise above the hazards of writing, he was fiercely unconscious of them; his personal victory over the first enemies of his freedom—the Church and Studs Lonigan and the slums of Chicago—became a literary victory by the sheer force of his remorseless attack upon them. If all writers remember longest what they learned in their youth, Farrell's work suggests that he remembered nothing and learned from nothing but his youth. Unlike all the little people in left-wing letters who loved the working class to death but could never touch them, Farrell was joined by every instinct to men and women who have never known the barest security, who have clawed the earth to live from one day to the next. What more was needed in *Studs Lonigan* than the literal transcription of the Irish Babbittry's inhuman yammering, with abysmal cruelty banging against animal insolence, where only Celtic blood could get back at Celts with so much grisly humor? What more was needed in *A World I Never Made* and after than the toneless saga of drink, of a new child every year, of meat once a week, of endless, life-shattering recrimination, of a little boy named Danny O'Neill who wanted baseball and a quiet table, but who could never forget, though his grandmother took him away, that at home his parents and brothers and sisters were slowly dying together?

Unlike some sentimentalists, Farrell certainly never defended his work by calling it "sociology." Although he quickly became a convenient symbol to cultural historians who saw in him a student of the American city, to sociologists and social-settlement liberals and literary anthropologists of the lives and morals of the poor, Farrell insisted, with the traditional justice and something more than the traditional vehemence of the naturalist, that his work had the self-sufficient form and self-justifying power of a solidly written and precise literary record. And it was not the Marxist critics alone—who, indeed, were often cold to Farrell's work because it was not formally "revolutionary"—who supported this view; it was a kind of collective esthetic simplicity, or paralysis, of men of goodwill in the thirties who, having rejected genteel objections that *Studs Lonigan* was sociology, decided that it must be art—and obviously very powerful art. These genteel objections, which occurred only to those who feared the widest possible democracy of subject in the novel, were, as John Chamberlain wrote in his introduction to the Lonigan trilogy, "an incantation designed to exorcise the uncomfortable memory of Studs and his frightening palsy-walsies, with their broads, their movies, their pool, their alky, their poker and their craps. . . . Like all incantations, it masks a real respect. People don't usually bother to spin fine distinctions between documentary and artistic excellence when they are not disturbed by a book." Whereupon one asked, as Mr. Chamberlain did, impatiently, "What in hell is art, anyway?"

What was it indeed? To a democracy slowly arming against Fascism and conscious of its latent forms in the United States, *Studs Lonigan* did, at the very least, rank as a brilliant exposure of brutality and ignorance and corruption. If a healthy literature, as the Marxists insisted, meant an aroused concern with social analysis and the pressure of class forces in capitalist society, *Studs Lonigan* was a dynamic naturalism whose depth of insight and furious vitality gave it the stamp of creative power. To an America obsessed by the atmosphere of dissolution, proud of its "realism" and urgently in need of stimulation, Farrell's violence was salutary—a vigorous demonstration that art had to respond, at some stage of human development, with as much vigor as the strident life that gave it birth. "When a book has depth and pace," John Chamberlain wrote of *Studs Lonigan,* "when it continually flashes with meanings, when it coördinates one's own scattered and spasmodic experiences and reflections, when it mounts to climaxes that suddenly reveal by artistic mutation what has been imperceptible and latent in a character, then aren't we justified in calling it art, no matter how 'photographic' the realism?"

Yes; but in these terms art became only another abstraction, a hypothetical end-product as unreal as the famous "withering away of the state" in Leninist theory. For what if the realism was as brutal in its way as the brutality it exposed? It was not that Farrell's work was "amoral"; on the contrary, the moral judgment Danny O'Neill was forever making on his world—though familiarly mechanical as in most books of the kind, forever declaiming *J'accuse!*—was the most pervasive element in his work. It was art, powerful and vital art; but it was also a perfect example of that unconscious and benevolent philistinism which believes that one escapes from materialism by surrendering to it; that the principle of action, for writers as well as for revolutionaries, is to gain freedom for oneself by denying it to others. In the Marxist-Leninist theory of the state, one began as a terrorist and ended theoretically as a free man living in a more "human" world that had never practiced a conscious humanity. In the left-wing theory of literature, which was so riddled with determinism that it employed only half one's mind and soul, spiritual insight was to be won only by proving how little there was of it in life.

5

Farrell's success proved how easily these considerations could be "evaded" if the writer imposed himself with sufficient force. The failure of so many other left-wing naturalists, however, suggest that their movement came to end because it had no real hold upon them. The revulsion against Stalinism after the Nazi-Soviet Pact was the most significant factor in the decline of left-wing letters, but literary convictions which could suddenly become unfashionable because of an agreement between two foreign dictators exposed their own barrenness. Yet Stalin or no Stalin, the social problems left-wing literature exposed and explored were still problems with which a democratic literature had to contend. The folly of so many left-wing minds was to assume that artistry was something one *added* to the concern with those problems, and that what one added to it was nothing more than the quality of one's knowledge and energy. In the end this primitivism sapped both knowledge and energy, for it compelled writers to rely too much upon their emotional resources and thus cheated them. The energy was lost in declamations and that hoarse strident irony which became a traditional feature in left-wing style; the knowledge became less an aroused awareness of the pain of life than a need to arouse others by shocking and indoctrinating them.

The violence of left-wing writing all through the thirties, its need of demonstrative terror and brutality, relates that writing to the slick, hard-boiled novel which, in the hands of writers like John O'Hara, James M. Cain, Jerome Weidman, and many others, became a distinctive contemporary fashion. The vogue of such a novel as Richard Wright's *Native Son* may suggest that the novel of "social significance" had at last entered into the thinking of the middle class, that the people who read it with bated breath or applauded it on the stage felt a deep compassion for, and even some solidarity with, the oppressed Negro masses; but that is an illusion. It is precisely because Wright himself was so passionately honest and desired to represent the sufferings of his race as forcefully as possible that the unconscious slickness of *Native Son,* its manipulation of terror in a period fascinated by terror, seems so sinister. For Wright was only the child of his generation, and his resources no different in kind from the resources of naturalism and the left-wing conception of life and literature to which, like many Negro writers, he surrendered his thinking because of the general indifference or hostility to Negroes and Negro writing. If he chose to write the story of Bigger Thomas as a grotesque crime story, it is because his own indignation and the sickness of the age combined to make him dependent on violence and shock, to astonish the reader by torrential scenes of cruelty, hunger, rape, murder, and flight and then enlighten him by crude Stalinist homilies. Bigger Thomas "found" himself in jail as Wright "found" himself, after much personal suffering and confusion, in the Communist party; what did it matter that Bigger's self-discovery was mechanical and unconvincing, or that Wright—from the highest possible motives—had written "one of those books in which everything is undertaken with seriousness except the writing"?[1] In his work one felt, as in Gold's *Jews without Money,* in the livid stories of Albert Maltz, in the desperate pedestrianism of Josephine Herbst's saga of the declining middle class, in Farrell's novels, the reverberation of the struggle of millions in America to survive disaster; and it did not matter that once the point had been made, the reader's apathy destroyed, the moment's urgent release effected, there was nothing left but to go round and round in the same vindictive circle.

In the more fashionable kind of hard-boiled writing, like John O'Hara's, one saw the same confusion of means and ends operating in reverse. The left-wing naturalist surrendered his craft to what seemed ultimate considerations beyond literature. Literature, in the Communist jargon, was a "front," and each militant writer a guerrilla fighting in his own way for a common purpose. In O'Hara and less-talented Broadway-Hollywood novelists one saw the rejection or corruption of all conscious values. For these writers virtuosity became an end in itself, and a stunning precision in the recording of the national talk and manners, a "shrewd eye" and a "sharp ear," the very substance of the cynical and elaborately amoral literary personality. Like many left-wing naturalists (whom they resembled more closely than moralistic Marxist critics ever knew or confessed), they took a huge delight in the indiscriminate vulgarity, the temptation to shock, which provided contemporary readers with an image of the times and a factitious sophisticate's superiority to it; but their delight was primitive cunning. The "poets of the tabloid murder," as Edmund Wilson called them,

[1] R. P. Blackmur.

they were frankly technicians of sensation, opportunists who learned from every native source—Hemingway, Ring Lardner, Dorothy Parker, Hollywood, radio, the slick new journalism, the trickery of smooth-paper fiction—but always to their special purpose: the need to startle and thrill the reader by a series of exhibitions in which competence became so brisk and mechanical that it lost all relation to a mature art.

The obsession with pure competence, tricky or amusing as that competence became in the hands of novel-writing journalists who never stopped thinking in journalistic terms, reflected something more than the familiar addiction to "technique" on the part of commonplace writers of fiction in America. One could trace the mannerisms of the hard-boiled school back to the Hemingway tradition of the literary dandy, the stricken, reserved postwar observer whose nihilism had left him only the sensual pleasures of life and the joy of craftsmanship. But it is significant that they exploited what was most obvious and showy in Hemingway, made an article of commerce out of that "nihilism," at the very moment that he renounced it. In order to reach their public at all, they had to titillate it by introducing forbidden subjects and soothe it by keeping it away from most of the common problems of its own experience; to outrage it mischievously, but never to perplex its mind. In a writer like James M. Cain this practice was indirectly a pandering to the same taste which enjoyed the synthetic violence of the murder mystery and drugstore treatises on lesbianism; but it also involved a superficial representation of contemporary disorder, a kind of jazz allegory which muffled the heartbreak and bewilderment of contemperary experience in such energetic cynicism that it pointed coyly to its reticent decency and compassion. But for this familiar masquerade of the Tin Pan Alley soul, rather like the concealed "seriousness" of swing, the fundamental mindlessness of these writers would have exposed itself, and the lust for depravity, for toughness in every paragraph, would have seemed merely cheap. On the strength of it they appeared to be "realists" in the contemporary fashion.

In these terms one could say of the best of the "hard-boiled" novels, John O'Hara's *Appointment in Samarra*, that it was a very serious book indeed, its seriousness consisting in the exactitude with which O'Hara portrayed the disintegration of an upper-middle-class soul like

Julian English. And was not the agony of English's life the agony of his class, an implicit denunciation of its frivolousness, its hunger for sensation, its callousness toward others, its essential joylessness? O'Hara had been a reporter before he turned to the novel, and he managed, with quiet and exciting grace, to bring the very special and elaborate technique of metropolitan reporting into the novel and even to improve upon it. He wrote with such neat dexterity and cleverness that the sheer perfection of his ear, the casual precision with which he reproduced the manners of the country-club set, a bootlegger eating his Christmas dinner alone in a roadhouse, the mocking modesty of two lovers going to bed, the rhythm of a dance, the subterranean hysteria of a boring dinner-party, seemed remarkably good and staggeringly true. And to his gift for realism, his intimate knowledge of what he was writing about, he brought a boyish zest which gave it added vigor. He was neither superior to his subject nor afraid of it; his cleverness stemmed from a perfect confidence in his material and his personal relation to it. His book was even, if one liked, a folk tale for contemporary folk minds, as appropriate and cheerful in its idiom and urban tone as any other.

Yet the curious thing about O'Hara's work—one saw it especially in books like *Butterfield 8* and *Hope of Heaven*—was that despite his cleverness and wry modesty he seemed to be less a novelist than an interesting introduction to the novelist's craft. He seemed to know precisely what he was doing, and he had certainly been unpretentious enough in marking the limits of his work; but the final effect was of a virtuosity that had no relation to anything but the drive and weight of its own skill. It would be easy to say that O'Hara's virtuosity was so glittering that he believed it self-sufficient; but the trouble was that he relied upon a criticism of life which he did not fully understand. Unlike those left-wing novelists who felt the significance of more than they were able to describe or even to suggest, O'Hara could characterize everything and anything; but the sophistication that gave him his air of professional verve, his reporter's authority, compelled him to name things and assess relations of whose substance he was essentially ignorant. His writing was anything but false; it was merely excessively knowing and energetically superficial in the fashion of that metropolitan journalism which relies so much upon irony as a rhetorical device that it can finally communicate nothing but its irony. A genial, boyish, and commonplace mind like O'Hara's could therefore easily slip into an acquiescence that was almost indistinguishable from callousness, and a freedom to comment and satirize at will that suggested his disgust with the life he described. But no writing was ever more remote from satire, and the disgust was not O'Hara's own.

In the cheaper variety of hard-boiled writing one felt a complacency, a surrender to conventional prejudice, that would have been sinister if there had been any seriousness of intention behind it; but O'Hara's cynicism revealed his failure to understand the larger significance of the life he described rather than any disinclination to study it. If his perceptions were always reduced to mimicry, it was because mimicry provided a facile solution to his problem and a way of evading it. It is true, of course, that O'Hara genuinely enjoyed his night-club touts, Park Avenue wastrels, Hollywood bawds, and hard-boiled automobile salesmen. It was the normal admiration of the small-town doctor's son—the O'Hara self who always lurks in the background of his own novels as James Malloy—for the careless prodigality and sensationalism of a class he was fated to observe from the outside, first as an Irish Catholic boy in a small Pennsylvania town whose socially elect were of Anglo-Saxon Protestant descent and later as a reporter in New York. But with this characteristic and secret delight in Café Society *luxus* and dissolution went a very significant resentment and hostility. In his own way O'Hara had his share of the Dreiserian emotions so traditional with young novelists in America, and the biting zest with which he recorded Julian English's downfall evidently had its origin in the dislike of old Doctor Malloy's son for old Doctor English's son, who was a snob, a drunkard, and a lecher. "Why are you talking about you people, you people, your kind of people, people like you" Jimmy Malloy's girl friend asks him in *Butterfield 8*. "I want to tell you something about myself that will help to explain a lot of things about me," Jimmy replies. "First of all, I am a Mick. I wear Brooks clothes and I don't eat salad with a spoon and I probably could play five-goal polo in two years, but I am a Mick. Still a Mick . . . James Cagney is a Mick, without any pretense of being anything else, and he is America's ideal gangster. America, being a non-Irish, anti-Catholic country, has its own idea of what a real gangster looks like."

The light, fleeting tenderness of O'Hara's personal references, notably in the background of his novels and in some of the stories in *The Doctor's Son,* throws more light on the place of this personal motive in his work; but it is evident that the resentment was never too deep. In another novelist—Farrell's case is notable—the bitterness would have worked its way into the very texture of the prose and become the familiar allegory of the vengeful young artist-Hamlet. Resentment, however, is not bitterness, and few novelists have ever been less consciously disposed than O'Hara to think of themselves in grandiose terms. O'Hara may have wanted to "get back," as he did in his portrait of "Gibbsville" society in *Appointment in Samarra;* but beyond that he was only the buoyant young reporter enjoying his job. It is significant that the corruption of Julian English seemed less portentous to O'Hara than the degeneration of Gloria Wandrous in *Butterfield 8.* Although his own interpretation of Gloria's character was crude and evasive—he seems to have thought of her as a Vassar girl *manqué* —she provided him with a clue to the speakeasy era he described; and it is this which makes this novel his most ambitious venture. In *Appointment in Samarra* he was a social novelist only by courtesy; in *Hope of Heaven* and *Pal Joey* he lapsed into pure mimicry. In *Butterfield 8* he was writing a Proustian epic of metropolitan society in monosyllables; and though the writing was often adolescent in its cruelty and bright irrelevancies, it was as indisputably serious a criticism of contemporary society as *Native Son* or *Studs Lonigan.*

The effect of the novel, however, was of a final incoherence peculiarly representative of O'Hara and the Broadway-Hollywood cult of violence. He portrayed all the details in his foreground brilliantly—the speakeasy atmosphere of frantic conviviality, Gloria's drinking and adventures, Liggett's talk and seductions, the brilliant cocktail scene between Mrs. Liggett and the Farleys—as he always did in his foregrounds. But despite his brisk commentary and ready information, he could see Gloria's behavior only in terms of her depravity and the incommunicable sensationalism of the speakeasy era. His need to get that sensationalism down with mimetic accuracy made for a clever and energetic foreground, but he was baffled by its communicable significance. The pathos was there, the waste and boredom and the bootlegged emotions; but they were like a geographical marking, a clue to space and time; they were everywhere under and hovering about the story, but never in it. In the end O'Hara's casual truculence, his bright, hard confidence, were his undoing; they exposed his uncertainty and fundamental naïveté and proved that the structural line of his book, so clean in execution, had reference to nothing but his adroitness. The episodes, taken together, remained only a series of episodes; the mimicry had only an entertainment value; the story moved everywhere, and ultimately revealed nothing.

"He had developed an appetite for profound emotion," John Steinbeck wrote of a character in *The Pastures of Heaven,* "and his meagre imagination was unable to feed it." This was O'Hara's case. What remained was the naturalist's familiar desperate energy in the face of an experience which he could devour, mimic, attack, but never project; an experience that had proved to be too much and yet not enough to produce a healthy, poised, and contemplative fiction. In Caldwell and Farrell this had meant the recourse to a sadism of the word, a recapitulation in emotional terms of what the imagination could not satisfactorily possess and convey. In O'Hara, equally thwarted but less ambitious, it meant a vulgar comedy of New York manners, a stabbing journalistic brilliance, and unconscious moral surrender of his own.

> Seated directly across the room was Mrs. Noel Lincoln, wife of the famous sportsman-financier, who had had four miscarriages before she found out (or before her doctor dared to tell her) that a bit of bad luck on the part of her husband was responsible for these misfortunes. Mrs. Lincoln was sitting with pretty little Alicia Lincoln, her niece by marriage, who was the source of cocain supply for a very intimate group of her friends in society, the theater, and the arts. Alicia was waiting for a boy named Gerald, whom she took to places where girls could not go unescorted.

And so on. Beyond this point the hard-boiled novel could become an article of commerce, as in James M. Cain, or even bring the Weltanschauung of the Minsky Brothers into literature. Sensationalism of this kind, living on sensationalism, could go no further, save to parody its own mindlessness.

6

There were a few social realists in the period who did promise something different from the automatism of contemporary naturalism and the cult of the hard-boiled, notably John Steinbeck; but his case has always been a curious one. Steinbeck's approach to the novel was interesting because he seemed to stand apart at a time when naturalism had divided writers into two mutually exclusive groups, since the negation of its starved and stunted spirit came more and more from writers who often had no sympathy with realism at all, and were being steadily pulled in the direction of surrealism and abstractionism. Naturalism had made for so drearily uniform a conception of the novel, so mechanical an understanding of reality, that it is not strange to find many writers, and particularly so many young writers, revolting entirely against realism to work in *Innerlichkeit*. Just as the literary criticism of the crisis period was marked by the conflict of two groups of absolutists, one absorbed in "social significance," the other in technical problems, so it is significant to note the polarization in fiction between a grim surface realism and a literature of private sensibility. Inevitably, in a world where the public reality can seem so persistently oppressive and meaningless, while the necessity for new means of communication is so pressing, the more sensitive artist is steadily withdrawn into himself, into those reaches of the unconscious where "one can make a world within a world." But in this conflict between the outer and inner worlds of reality, between the fragmentary realizations that each represents, the patterns of contemporary desperation can nullify one another.

Steinbeck, standing apart from both the contemporary naturalists and the new novel of sensibility that one finds in Faulkner and Wolfe, brought a fresh note into contemporary fiction because he promised a realism less terror-ridden than the depression novel, yet one consciously responsible to society; a realism mindful of the terror and disorganization of contemporary life, but not submissive to the spiritual stupor of the time; a realism equal in some measure, if only in its aspiration, to the humanity, the gaiety, the wholeness, of realism in a more stable period. It is the failure of so many contemporary American novelists to suggest even the urgency of such an achievement that marks their unconscious submission to the demoralization in contemporary life. Yet it cannot be said that Steinbeck's work, which has become more and more tenuous and even sentimental, has really answered to that need. With a writer like Farrell, oppressively narrow as his world is, one at least knows where he stands—his integrity, his materialism, the full range of his belief. Steinbeck is a greater humanist, and there is a poetry in some of his best work, particularly *The Long Valley* stories and *The Pastures of Heaven,* that naturalists of Farrell's stamp have never been able to conceive. But there is something imperfectly formed about Steinbeck's work; it has no creative character. For all his moral serenity, the sympathetic understanding of men under strain that makes a strike novel like *In Dubious Battle* so notable in the social fiction of the period, Steinbeck's people are always on the verge of becoming human, but never do. There is a persistent failure to realize human life fully in his books, where the characters in many American naturalistic novels have simply ceased to be human. After a dozen books Steinbeck still looks like a distinguished apprentice, and what is so striking in his work is its inconclusiveness, his moving approach to human life and yet his failure to be creative with it.

Steinbeck's moral advantage as a realist in the depression era was to be so different in his region—the Salinas Valley in California—his subject, as to seem different in kind. It was his famous "versatility" that first earned him his reputation—his ability to follow a *Tortilla Flat* with *In Dubious Battle, Of Mice and Men* with *The Grapes of Wrath*—but this was the least noteworthy thing about him and has come more and more to suggest not versatility but a need to feel his way. His great possession as a writer was not an interest in craft or an experimental spirit; it was an unusual and disinterested simplicity, a natural grace and tenderness and ease in his relation to his California world. Artistically, notably in early works like *To a God Unknown* and *The Pastures of Heaven,* these appeared as a shyly artful primitivism reminiscent of Sherwood Anderson, and in its boyish California mysticism, of Frank Norris. But at bottom Steinbeck's gift was not so much a literary resource as a distinctively harmonious and pacific view of life. In a period when so many better writers exhausted themselves, he had welded himself into the life of the Salinas Valley and enjoyed a spiritual stability by reporting the life cycles of the valley gardeners and mystics and adventurers, by studying and steeping himself in its growth processes out of a close and affectionate interest in the biology of human affairs. Steinbeck's absorption in the life of his native valley gave him a sympathetic perspective on the animal nature of human life, a means of reconciliation with people as people. The depression naturalists saw life as one vast Chicago slaughterhouse, a guerrilla war, a perpetual bombing raid. Steinbeck had picked up a refreshing belief in human fellowship and courage; he had learned to accept the rhythm of life. In one of the most beautiful stories in *The Long Valley,* "The Chrysanthemums," the heroine asks:

> Did you ever hear of planting hands? . . . It's when you're picking off the buds you don't want. Everything goes right down into your fingertips. You watch your fingers work. They do it themselves. You can see how it is. They pick and pick the buds. They never make a mistake. They're with the plant. Do you see? Your fingers and the plant. You can feel that, right up your arm. They know. They never make a mistake. You can feel it. When you're like that you can't do anything wrong.

It was this "unpanicky questioning of life," as Edmund Wilson put it, that gave Steinbeck's work its unusual tenderness, gave his valley-bred simplicity an advantageous perspective on contemporary social problems. With his deep amateur interest in biology, it gave him the necessary detachment and slow curiosity to approach the modern social struggle as a tragicomedy of animal instincts, which, as the best things in *The Grapes of Wrath* and *In Dubious Battle* testify, meant an aroused compassion, an understanding of the pain that the human animal can suffer and the mistakes he can make. The Doctor in *In Dubious Battle,* speaking for Steinbeck, disputes the Communist organizer's instinctive terrorism, and says quietly:

> My senses aren't above reproach, but they're all I have. I want to see the whole picture—as nearly as I can. I don't want to put on the blinders of "good" and "bad," and limit my vision. If I used the term

"good" on a thing I'd lose my license to inspect it, because there might be bad in it. Don't you see? I want to be able to look at the whole thing.

Later he adds reflectively: "Group-men are always getting some kind of infection."

This was the spirit of *The Long Valley*, the spirit of the old pioneer grandfather in "The Leader of the People," who, reminiscing of the westward migration, described it as "a whole bunch of people made into one big crawling beast. . . . Every man wanted something for himself, but the big beast that was all of them wanted only westering." People in Steinbeck's work, taken together, are often evil; a society moving on the principle of collective mass slowly poisons itself by corrupting its own members. But beyond his valley-bred conviction of the evil inherent in any society where men are at the mercy of each other's animalism, Steinbeck knew how to distinguish, in works like *The Long Valley, In Dubious Battle,* and *The Grapes of Wrath,* between the animal processes of life and social privation. Out of his slow curiosity, the strength of the agrarian tradition in him, Steinbeck was able to invest the migration of the Joads, if not his monochromatic characters, with a genuinely tragic quality precisely because he felt so deeply for them and had seen at first hand the gap between their simple belief in life and their degradation. He did not confuse the issue in *The Grapes of Wrath;* he was aroused by the man-made evil the Okies had to suffer, and he knew it as something remediable by men. And where another social realist might have confused the dark corners he described with the whole of life, Steinbeck had the advantage of his Western training, its plain confidence in men. The old pioneer grandfather in *The Long Valley,* remembering the brutality of men on the great trek, also remembered enough of its glory to say:

It wasn't Indians that were important, nor adventures, nor even getting out here. . . . When we saw the mountains at last, we cried—all of us. But it wasn't getting here that mattered, it was movement and westering. We carried life out here and set it down the way those ants carry eggs. And I was the leader. The westering was as big as God, and the slow steps that made the movement piled up and piled up until the continent was crossed.

It was these associations that contributed to the success of *The Grapes of Wrath* and made it the most influential social novel of the period. Though the book was as urgent and as obvious a social tract for its time as *Uncle Tom's Cabin* had been for another, it was also the first novel of its kind to dramatize the inflictions of the crisis without mechanical violence and hatred. The bitterness was there, as it should have been, the sense of unspeakable human waste and privation and pain. But in the light of Steinbeck's strong sense of fellowship, his simple indignation at so much suffering, the Joads, while essentially symbolic marionettes, did illuminate something more than the desperation of the time: they became a living and challenging part of the forgotten American procession. Though the characters were essentially stage creations, the book brought the crisis that had severed Americans from their history back into it by recalling what they had lost through it. It gave them a design, a sense of control, where out of other depression novels they could get only the aimless maniacal bombardment of rage. The lesson of the crisis, so often repeated in the proletarian novel and yet so lifeless in it, was suddenly luminous: it was an event in history, to be understood by history, to be transformed and remembered and taught in history. It was as if Steinbeck, out of the simplicity of his indignation, had been just primitive enough to call men back to their humanity, to remind depression America that a culture is only the sum total of the human qualities that make it up, and that "life can give a periodical beating to death any time," as a contemporary poet put it, "if given a chance and some help."

It was this tonic sanity in a bad time, his understanding of the broad processes of human life, that gave Steinbeck his distinction among the depression realists. But no one can pretend, particularly after a book like *The Moon Is Down,* that it tells the whole story about him. For Steinbeck's primitivism is essentially uncreative, and for all his natural simplicity of spirit, there is a trickiness, a stage cunning, behind it that has become depressing. Though his interests have carried him squarely into certain central truths about the nature of life, he has not been able to establish them in human character. Nothing in his books is so dim, significantly enough, as the human beings who live in them, and few of them are intensely imagined as human beings at all. It is obvious that his mind moves happily in realms where he does not have to work in very complex types—the *paisanos* in *Tortilla Flat*, the ranch hands in *Of Mice and Men*, the Okies in *The Grapes of Wrath*, the strikers in *In Dubious Battle*, the farmers in *The Long Valley*, the symbolic protagonists of democratic struggle and Nazi power in *The Moon Is Down*. But what one sees in his handling of these types is not merely a natural affection for this simplicity, but a failure to interest himself too deeply in them as individuals. It is not their simplicity that makes Lennie and George in *Of Mice and Men* into furry little animals, or the Joads into stage creations, or the characters in *The Moon Is Down* into manikins; it is Steinbeck's simplicity of characterization. It is not their paganism that makes the *paisanos* in *Tortilla Flat* so hard to take from one point of view; it is their undiluted cuteness. Steinbeck's perspective on human life always gives him a sense of process, an understanding of the circuits through which the human animal can move; but he cannot suggest the density of human life, for his characters are not fully human.

It is in this light that one can understand why Steinbeck's moral serenity is yet so sterile and why it is so easy for him to slip into the calculated sentimentality of *Of Mice and Men* and *The Moon Is Down*. In writers of a certain natural awkwardness, like Dreiser and Anderson, there is a sentimentality, an impurity, that follows from exaggeration and lack of control; but one is always conscious of the amplitude through which they move. Steinbeck is not awkward, no; but he is not ample. He is a simple writer who has acquired facility, but though he is restive in his simplicity, his imagination cannot rise above it. And it is that simplicity and facility, working together, a tameness of imagination operating slickly, that give his work its surface paradox of simplicity and trickiness, of integrity of emotion and endless contrivance of means. This does not mean a lack of sincerity; it does mean that Steinbeck is not so simple that he does not know how to please; or to take, as it were, advantage of himself. It is, after all, the cunning behind the poignant situation in *Of Mice and Men*, a certain Woollcott-like ambush of the heartstrings, that makes his little fable meretricious in its pathos, a moment's gulp; and it is the same air of calculation in *The Moon Is Down*, so much more glaring because of its subject, that makes this allegorical drama of the struggle of free men today merely depressing.

The Moon Is Down, published after Pearl Harbor, was heartily disliked by many people; but chiefly, as it would seem, because Steinbeck had not been tough and violent enough, had not portrayed his Nazis in Norway as the brutal gangsters that Nazis in Norway, as elsewhere, have been. But this demand for absolute realism was too shrill with war tension, and missed the root of the book's failure. What is really striking about the novel—so openly written, like *Of Mice and Men,* for the stage—is how fantastically simple the whole anti-Fascist struggle appeared to Steinbeck even as an allegory, and yet how easy it was for him to transcribe his naïveté into the shabbiest theater emotions. There is credulity here, even an essential innocence of spirit, and the kind of slow curiosity about all these war-haunted creatures that has always made Steinbeck's interest in the animal nature of life the central thing in his work. He does not appeal to the hatred of Hitlerism, no; he has never appealed to any hatred. The Doctor, with his patient wisdom, speaks for him here as another doctor, a student of human affairs, spoke in *In Dubious Battle.* But it is not the student's detachment that one remembers here; it is the facility that can turn this greatest of contemporary themes into a series of contrivances. We hear the affirmation of nobility Steinbeck wanted to make, as we hear it in all his work; but we cannot believe in it, for though it is intended to inspire us in the struggle against Hitlerism, there are no men and women here to fight it. . . . And Europe under Hitler, even a representative stage Europe, is not Monterey, where the *paisanos* had their fun; and it is not the Salinas Valley; and the people locked in its supreme struggle today are not Steinbeck's familiar primitives, only seeking to be human. No, they are not primitives at all. But Steinbeck's world is a kind of primitivism to the end—primitive, with a little cunning.

Chapter 14

CRITICISM AT THE POLES

"People who are engrossed with their pet 'values' become habitual killers. Their game is the images, or the things, and they acquire the ability to shoot them as far off as they can be seen, and do. It is thus that we lose the power of imagination, or whatever faculty it is by which we are able to contemplate things as they are in their rich and contingent materiality."—JOHN CROWE RANSOM, *The World's Body*

THE crisis in criticism that paralleled the social and economic crisis of the thirties was only one of many profound transformations felt in American society and thought, and considering the relative isolation of critical opinion at all times in America, hardly the most distinctive. Yet it had from the first a symbolic significance for the times, a dramatic interest, for as a field nominally concerned with values and responsive by its very nature to social and intellectual change, criticism in the period symbolized a vast overhauling of ideas in America, an unusual tension and resolution, growing out of a world revolution in values.

This striking transformation in critical values and critical personality, which began with the collapse of liberal criticism in the late twenties, was not merely, as it seemed, a change to "social" interests in criticism. What had criticism in America usually been if not predominantly social, even political, in its thinking? From Emerson and Thoreau to Mencken and Brooks, criticism had been the great American lay philosophy, the intellectual conscience and intellectual carryall.

It had been a study of literature inherently concerned with ideals of citizenship, and often less a study of literary texts than a search for some new and imperative moral order within which American writing could live and grow. Never more than incidentally concerned, save for men like Poe and James, with problems of craftsmanship and style, it had always been more a form of moral propaganda than a study in esthetic problems. It had even been the secret intermediary—read and practiced though it was by so few—between literature and society in America. Just as the main tradition of American letters for a century and more had been the effort to create a truly national literature, a literature of broad democratic reality, so criticism had usually sought —now as a midwife to talent, now as a common scold of the national manners—to unite American writers in the service of one imperative ideal or another.

What gave so much criticism after 1930 its distinct character, however, was the remarkable intensity and narrowness with which it gave itself over entirely to the subject of contemporary crisis. Criticism became not merely a more passionate debate of literary values in the light of social responsibility, a more intense preoccupation with the importance and function of literature in society; it became a search for fulfillment by the word, a messianic drive toward social action bent on liberation by conquest and extermination. A significantly predominant section of serious critical opinion (this at a time when "seriousness" significantly became the badge of critical honor) was divided between two groups of extremists, each of which became increasingly narrow as time went on, absorbed in its pet values, passionately contemptuous of any other, and insistent that only its particular loyalties were a valid guide to the understanding of literature. Whether written on the extreme left or the extreme right (how significent it is that even opposing political extremisms often seemed to pre-empt the field), whether propounded as a series of Marxist judgments on the bourgeois past or used with great technical skill and subtlety and elaborate hauteur by the new "Formalists" in the analysis of poetry—criticism became a totalitarianism in an age of totalitarianisms, rather characteristic of the times in its rigidity and pride, and not the easiest to live with. Where the first "modern" critics in America had been crusaders against Puritanism and materialism, latter-day Victorians, as it were, seeking to find a place for literature in America, the more aggressive critical minds in America now became religious crusaders, as of a world to be saved or lost. It would be easy to say, for it was often true, that they subordinated the consideration of literature as a distinct element in human experience to the service of their creed. Yet what was most remarkable about them was the extent to which they vented so much passion upon literature while betraying their essential remoteness from it. The Marxists, who never ceased to proclaim their devotion to literature and never proved it, steadily drove criticism into a corner of sociology, where it became either a purely political weapon or a sub-literary calculus concentrated on classes and social functions. The Formalists—many of them quasi-religious traditionalists and passionate devotees of a limited modern poetry—began, from a variety of motives, at the opposite extreme. To them literature became not merely a great moral and intellectual activity; it became the only activity. They reduced all human discourse to literature, all literature to poetry, all poetry to the kind of poetry they cared to write and study, and like Talmudists reduced all critical discourse to the brilliant technical exegesis of a particular text. Between so doctrinaire a sociological criticism and so rarefied an esthetics there would seem to be nothing in common; but the search for an absolute that each represented brought them together in spirit.

The tone of this new criticism, heard in the work of T. S. Eliot, the New Humanists, and prophetic European critics ever since the close of the First World War, suggested that criticism had become a crucial battleground of world values. It was the spirit in which T. E. Hulme had called for a new classicism based upon a return to philosophical dualism; the spirit in which Julien Benda had so bitterly attacked "the treason of the intellectuals"; the spirit in which Eliot, writing "Thoughts after Lambeth" in 1931, concluded solemnly with the warning that the world was entering upon the new Dark Ages, and that only the Faith could "renew and rebuild civilization, and save the World from Suicide." It was the spirit in which Irving Babbitt had concluded his fighting career with a last passionate adjuration to the moral intelligence in America to recover discipline and control and to stand against the encroaching forces of naturalism and democracy. It was the spirit in which many of Babbitt's young disciples, ambitiously applying his principles in the light of contemporary conditions, embraced authoritarian principles for the sake of authority and soon became open Fascists. It was the spirit in which Ezra Pound ceased to be the Johnny Appleseed of the "Little Renaissance" and eventually found his way to Mussolini's corporate state and corporate intelligence. Everywhere in criticism as the twenties drifted to their end in panic, there had been, as the bitterness of New Humanist controversy significantly proved, a tightening of intellectual tension, a desperate search for some primary and inclusive article of faith. The indispensable but fundamentally amiable and discursive liberal criticism of the twenties had proved brittle enough. It had guided the victory of the modernists, but having done so much, it collapsed. The key figures in the movement did not all stop writing, but they hastily removed themselves from criticism.

The drift to new standards—often to any standard—and the new "seriousness" in criticism were thus something more than the passage from one fashion to another. It was above all a domestic episode in the history of contemporary dissolution, in the breakup of the international social order that became synonomous with the thirties. At once something less and something more than criticism, it symbolized above all the absolute break with the old laissez-faire order toward which American writers had been moving for half a century and more. Yet the transformation in criticism—paralleling the crisis in every literature of the democratic West—was something more than the effort to make criticism an arbiter of a changing world, and its symptoms were deeper and more far-reaching than the popularity of Communism among the intellectuals. For it was at this moment that every modern problem that had weighed upon criticism for a century and more, above all the steady retreat of literature before science and the inroads made into criticism by laboratory psychologists, now became a central problem in the light of the international crisis. "The poet finds himself balanced," Allen Tate was writing at this time in words that were equally applicable to the critic in the period, "upon the moment when a world is about to fall." And at the same time he found himself balanced upon a moment when criticism itself had been thrown upon the defensive; a moment when the world's traditional, if unconscious, indifference to criticism or contempt for it had yet raised exigent questions as to its purpose as a form of inquiry.

It was in 1931, significantly a year of fateful changes in critical opinion, a year when manifestoes and challenges were pouring out by the bushel and critics in every camp were preparing to raise criticism to new heights, that Max Eastman published *The Literary Mind: Its Place in an Age of Science*. The subtitle told all: literature had no place. Eastman's book was not, like I. A. Richards's epoch-marking *Principles of Literary Criticism,* a bombshell thrown at critics from the psychologist's laboratory; it was a literary man's contemptuous valedictory to literary men, and particularly caustic on the subject of criticism. It told writers in general, and literary critics in particular, that their day was over, that all the "emotional" and "psychological" problems traditionally the property of literature could be dealt with better by neurologists, and all the social and economic problems by "scientific revolutionists" and engineers.

> Where our own parents consulted the poets for direct guidance in the unmanageable crises of their lives, we consult the nerve-specialist, or some technical expert in education. . . . To "know the best that has been thought and said in the world" rings false to the ardent spirits of our day; we want to know what, if anything, has been found out to be true . . . in our time the Pavlovs and Freuds and Marxian Lenins are driving poetry out of the books which convey knowledge of man. And to them we are turning for guidance. That is why the poets have ceased to try to tell us anything about life—because they have gradually and fully been compelled to realize that *as poets* they don't know anything about life. That is not their business.

On these lines Eastman satirized the modernist poets, laughed at the New Humanists, hacked away at the critics and university teachers jealous of their traditional prerogatives, and pronounced criticism an anachronism—the last illusion of nonscientific mentality in a world increasingly dominated by science. Science took care "of every problem that arises," and would sooner or later dispose completely of literature.

Unlike Richards, who had proved his own devotion to art and whose later books partly retracted his first contempt for "empirical" criticism, Eastman spoke not as a trained scientist, but as a lay brother in the scientific priesthood; in fact, as a literary critic speaking for the enemy. He "proved" nothing that had not been proved before, and he could not convince literary men jealous of the honor, not to say the vested interests, of their profession. But his attack—in itself particularly unworthy of him and significantly a critic's tour de force full of the harsh wit and irascible intensity that were to be so characteristic of a new age of critical polemic—had a topical significance. By bringing to a head a general suspicion of the validity of criticism, Eastman leveled his attack upon its studies at a time when criticism had come to think of itself as a mediator between two worlds, as an exercise of intelligence that could help bring a new society into being. The "crisis in criticism" of which critics were speaking so confidently at the turn of the decade was for them really a crisis in the whole moral order of civilization, a crisis in which critics, seeking and applying new standards, illuminating the necessary social forces, helping to create a brilliant new literature, would play a leading role.

Defending itself against those who challenged its validity as a form of knowledge, criticism now significantly proclaimed itself a central moral activity, a beacon in an age of confusions. It was precisely because Hitler, almost as his first move in power, had ordered the burning of the books, precisely because an easy-going materialism had proved so disastrous and the disruption of the social order threatened the foundations of thought, that criticism now came to think of itself as a central office. "It is likely," I. A. Richards had written prophetically in *Principles of Literary Criticism,*

> that modes of mental organisation which are at present impossible or dangerously unstable may become possible and even easy in the future with changes in social structure and material conditions. This last consideration might give any critic a nightmare. Nothing less than our whole sense of man's history and destiny is involved in our final decision as to value.

And however neglected and ancillary criticism had been, it had concerned itself with value. Indeed, looking about them, the critics could even assume that criticism had become a primary modern concern with value, as science and the new "progressive" education and modern politics had not. The world was in panic and disorder, laboring in agony toward some new birth which it feared and could not envision; and in such a world, where the most elementary intellectual activities were being threatened, where Fascism had uncovered so much social disorganization and capacity for evil in men, criticism had become a philosophical front where the great central forces seeking to rebuild the world were locked together in battle.

It is only in the light of this high purpose, this encompassing ambition, that one can understand the messianic drive, the quarreling factionalism, the intensity and narrowness, that now became characteristic of so much criticism in the crisis period—not merely a "serious" criticism, but rather a seriousness applying itself in criticism. What so often distinguished this contemporary criticism was the formality and rigor of its responsibility, its insistence on necessary values, its tough austerity and sense of discipline; but too many of the new critics, even the Formalists who brought so many great technical insights into the contemporary study of literature, emerged through the years as a race of conscientious fanatics, working in fragmentary elucidations, stifling in their narrow zeal. Yet they were always sustained and uplifted by the conviction that they were not merely fostering their own necessary kind of literature, but helping to save the whole domain of culture as well. Too much of their work seems now to have had a high, solemn futility; but it is significant to remember that both the Marxists and the Formalists were united in their contempt for the whole existing order and their confidence that they could help make another. The Marxist, speaking in the person of V. F. Calverton, could say in 1932:

> At the present time . . . the artist is faced with an environment which is in a stage of dissolution, an environment in which the tentacles of the past have lost their grip, in which the old traditions have broken down. . . . An old America . . . is in the process of dying, and a new one, still in the chrysalis state, is struggling to be born.

The Formalist, speaking as a Southern traditionalist in the person of John Crowe Ransom, could say at about the same time in *I'll Take My Stand*:

The South is unique on this continent for having founded and defended a culture which was according to the European principles of culture; and the European principles had better look to the South if they are to be perpetuated in this country.

Beyond this point, of course, the typical Marxist who persistently subordinated esthetic values to a rigid social doctrine and the Formalist who subordinated everything to his esthetic values were as far removed as the poles and at times did not even seem to occupy the same universe. But extremities always meet, as it is in the literature and politics of extremity that our time has found its key symbols of power and disaster.

2

From a historical point of view, as Jacques Barzun pointed out, the sudden popularity of Marxism among intellectuals in the thirties represented an international resurgence, the third great wave of Marxist influence in modern times. And it was in criticism—an activity notoriously easy to counterfeit at all times, and particularly in a revolutionary mass movement where energy becomes slogans and the slogans tend to become everything—that the radicalization of the intellectual middle class made itself most deeply felt. Inevitably the sudden efflorescence of Marxist thought had often little to do, even nominally, with serious criticism. The critical patter and performance became the property of party functionaries, fellow travelers, fellow travelers to the fellow travelers, and often nothing more than the articulation of the revolutionary attitude or will. The theory of Marxism, for all its elaborate structure, can easily be "reduced" to a series of simplicities; and just as Marxism often became formula-mongering in conversation, so conversation often became a form of criticism. Few world systems were ever hammered together with so much ardor and rigor and persistence as Marxism; no other philosophy has lent itself so easily to arrogance, superficiality, or idle malice. If Marx and Engels had a vision of history not unequal in grandeur to Dante's, the literary Marxist's vision was all too often a refraction of his own pettiness. The limitations and vast arid stretches of the Marxist doctrine help to explain the limitations and aridity of

Marxists themselves, but for much in the course of the left-wing adventure in criticism in the thirties Marx and Engels and Lenin bear little enough responsibility.

It was almost exclusively in conversation and polemic, in casual book reviews, programs for action, and speeches at writers' congresses, that the body of Marxist criticism was produced. The most astonishing thing about it in retrospect, and perhaps the most significant, is how little there was of it. After 1935, with the inauguration of the People's Front, aggressive Marxist criticism was discouraged, and left-wing literature itself was certainly short-lived enough; yet looked at as a whole Marxist criticism was important only as an influence, and it was always less a movement than a tendency. That influence, full of a vague atmospheric pressure, *was* its content. Save for the mass of periodical journalism, most of which rapidly became a museum of monstrosities, the body of Marxist criticism in the period comes down to exactly four systematic books, two of which were produced at the end of the period, and the earliest of which, though overtly condemned for its palpable grossness, suffered chiefly because its author had fallen into the heresy of anti-Stalinism: V. F. Calverton's *The Liberation of American Literature,* Granville Hicks's *The Great Tradition* and *Figures of Transition,* and Bernard Smith's *Forces in American Criticism.* In one way or another the Marxist doctrine influenced the thinking of some of the ablest critical minds of the time, notably Edmund Wilson; it served to bring out a few literary biographies, notably Newton Arvin's *Whitman,* that were sensitive and valuable. But for the most part Marxist criticism consisted of speeches and autobiographies, polemics, a rare essay in Marxist self-evaluation like James T. Farrell's *A Note on Literary Criticism,* political disputes, and congresses. The characteristic production of Marxist criticism in the thirties was a polemic written in answer to a polemic in last Saturday's *New Masses* that had in turn been written as a polemic in answer to someone's ineffable book review in the *Daily Worker* of a week before; and its characteristic tone usually was militancy that came out as rancor and prophecy trumpeting itself as disgust.

The imperative consideration in any understanding of the nature and influence of Marxist criticism in the thirties is the fact that it was the product of many diverse forces that operated toward one—and frequently unhappy—effect. The cant that weighed down Marxist criticism, so often meaningless in itself and representative of nothing but posturing bad taste, was the result of a melancholy synthesis into which went the worst of the Marxist tradition in polemic, the worst of the Russian example in criticism, the political influence of Stalinism, and a general mediocrity of local talent. No single element will explain why the general course of Marxist criticism was so sad and so dull. Something more and something less than a literary movement, it was however the most spectacular phase of the radicalization of the intellectual middle class, and from one point of view has more interest as a sociological fact than as an example in criticism. Left-wing novelists and poets themselves had little enough respect for it, as a famous symposium in the *New Masses* proved what everyone knew; and the polemics in which opposing radical critics engaged untiringly—generally in an effort to learn by what presumption the other group called itself Marxist at all—were so fratricidal that they dismembered each other far more effectively than they did the enemy.

The forces of disintegration that launched Marxist criticism in the thirties remained its constituent parts to the end; and it is as an eruption, a literary excitement, that it is to be remembered. Yet it is significant to note that there had been no tradition of historical criticism in America for the native Marxists to apply, and that it is not strange that in the first red glow of the thirties they fell upon the new criticism as they fell upon Marxism itself, seeing in it not an instrument that required the greatest care and imagination, but a series of trumpet calls, an infallible scientific barometer that could be used alternately as a bludgeon. Marxist critics were generally recruited from two groups: academic teachers of English literature, who had little critical practice and were trained to investigate the origins and background of literary works in the literal and quasi-scientific tradition of the graduate school; and influential journalists, sometimes in the service of the Communist party or happy to submit to its influence, who enjoyed their responsibility in an age of unprecedented publicity and thrived on the atmosphere of perpetual crisis and change. To those urban intellectuals who found themselves groping for any positive standard of belief, any positive assurance of their survival and purpose, however, Marxism became what it had long since ceased to be to the European masses: the only counterpoise to capitalist chaos, a world view that was at once an infallible guide to history and an immediate, "scientific" program of action. After its great victories and decisive defeats in the universities and parliaments and trade-union halls of western Europe, intellectual Marxism, "theoretical" Marxism, came to roost in New York publishing and editorial offices and in an army of writers who, often beginning from scratch, made careers for themselves on the strength of the Marxist canon and the religious inspiration of the Soviet example.

The perennial appeal of Marxism to modern intellectuals, with its inexhaustible militancy and knowingness, falling upon such ground and at so opportune a moment, now became a contemporary American phenomenon; and a phenomenon, rather than a body of critical thought, it remained to the end. Looking at it against the background of the times, the sudden paralysis of traditional ideas, the overpowering sense of change felt everywhere at the time, it is not difficult to see why Marxism attracted the middle-class intelligentsia and why a succession of public "literary events"—chiefly Michael Gold's attack upon Thornton Wilder and the "leisure-class" writing of the twenties—should have stimulated so much fervor. For whatever the truth or falsity of Marxism as an interpretation of history; whatever the soundness or myth of the dialectic, the grandeur of Marx's career and the pettiness of his relations with other men; whatever the heroism and cruelty of the Marxist tradition, the creative idealism that belies its materialism, the stultifying dogmatism that belies its pretensions to science—Marxism has always preserved the fascination of a great modern world-view, in its way one of the few world-views of seemingly universal relevance and historical grandeur to have moved men's minds since the stormy beginnings of capitalism in the Protestant Reformation. It was not for nothing that Henry Adams, the almost classic example of the modern intellectual dispossessed of his status and office under capitalism, complained bitterly in the nineties of the German revisionists of Marxism that they were preaching "the bankruptcy of the only idea our time has produced." For it is the confidence that Marxism is and must always remain the central idea of our time, the confidence that it is at once an interpretation of history and an incontrovertible program of action, at once the heir of the best thought of the past and the only valid transmission of it, that explains why Marxism has always presented certain modern imaginations with a vision operating on scientific principles, and why it has always produced so inexpressible a conviction of certitude and resolution in the lives of those who submit to its doctrine.

Considered as an event in modern history, the theory of Marxism may even seem one of those primary efforts in science, like Harvey's discovery of the circulation of the blood or Darwin's theory of biological evolution, with which modern thought begins rather than ends. Many of the constituent parts of the Marxist theory have again and again been shown to be demonstrably false, or mystical, or vague; but just as the first propositions of Marxism have influenced the thinking of the West, with many of its leading assumptions operating, however unconsciously, in the minds of those who believe themselves most bitterly opposed to it, so Marxism has always been far more than the sum of its parts. The appeal of Marxism to writers in the thirties was rarely founded upon their conscious and intelligent acceptance of it as a doctrine; rather it found converts and stimulated zeal by setting up an image in their minds, by giving their thinking a new sense of order and their everyday lives the excitement of a liberation. It did not always produce the sense of incipient revolution that it did in the mind of the European working class up to the First World War; but it did give them an indefinable yet inexhaustible assurance of the significance of their thought, an assurance of their function as intellectuals; and that was enough.

Hence the curious paradox that pervades the history of Marxist thought. As a body of doctrine, a radical interpretation of human experience, Marxism often appears rigid and programmatic; but there is something almost too prehensile about it—it lends itself to too many different uses. In its own mind it knows absolutely the nature and function of all human society, and its laws appear to it as the primary foundation all other thought must build on. The dialectic is a great hollow vessel into which anything can be poured, for as Engels wrote so confidently in *Anti-Dühring*, it is an extremely general—and for this reason extremely important—law of development of Nature, history and thought; a law which . . . holds good in the animal and plant kingdoms, in geology, in mathematics, in history and philosophy. . . . Dialectics is nothing more than the science of the general laws of motion and development of Nature, human society and thought.

General laws. Yet Marx and Engels did not claim more than that, and Engels himself wrote in the same passage:

> I do not say anything concerning the *particular* process of development. . . . When I say that all these processes are the negation of the negation, I bring them all together under this one law of motion, and for this very reason I leave out of account the peculiarities of each separate individual process.

Marx and Engels propounded general laws; the Marxists who follow them seek to prove these laws, or rather to apply them in different fields, by studying the "peculiarities"—what a word for the density and complexity of human thought and experience! Thus it is not strange that there are great empty wastes in the theory of Marxism, great as all human civilization itself; yet it is in those empty wastes, where they seek to apply the general laws, that so many Marxists have had to live and think. And it is in the great empty wastes of Marxist literary theory particularly that the Marxist criticism of the thirties struggled for the light and drooped without it.

For Marx and Engels laid down almost no literary theory as such; profoundly cultivated men both, they merely presented an example of scholarship and cultivation, and trusted to the cultivation and good sense of their followers. Laying the groundwork for the greatest single event in human history as they saw it—the Socialist revolution that would eventually bring in a superperfect harmony and humanity among men—they automatically, in sketching out the naturalistic and economic foundations of all human experience, subordinated literature and art under the general heading of culture, and studied culture itself as a process reflecting various economic and class struggles. For them culture was a body of human activity grounded, as they thought all human activity to have been, in the material relations of production. But they did not believe that works of art come into being through mechanical causation, nor did they anticipate that in speaking of culture as the "superstructure" above the main groundwork of economic relations—a trunk on the central tree—their imagery would be taken to mean that literature, for example, is nothing but a by-product of material activity. The economic factor is not "the *sole* determining factor," Engels wrote in a letter toward the end of his life. "The production and reproduction of real life constitutes in the last instance the determining factor in history." What this "last instance" was to mean, Edmund Wilson has pointed out, was confusing enough, since it could mean either the last in time or the last in the sense of being the fundamental motive of human behavior and culture. But it has been confusing only because Engels and Marx took it for granted that their radical insistence on the material foundations of art and literature would not be seized on to confuse the social origins of art with its esthetic values. Toward the end of his life Engels himself came to deplore the unthinking use so often made of historical materialism, and wrote sharply to a correspondent:

> I must tell you from the very first that the materialist method is converted into its direct opposite if instead of being used as a guiding thread in historical research it is made to serve as a ready-cut pattern on which to tailor historical facts.

"Marx and I," Engels once wrote significantly to Franz Mehring, "both placed and *had to place* the chief weight upon the *derivation* of political, legal and other ideological notions . . . from fundamental economic facts. In consequence we neglected the formal side, *i.e.,* the way in which these ideas arose, for the sake of the content." For all their understanding of the social origins of art, Marxist critics, if they seek to be critics, begin at that point. To an extraordinary degree Marxism becomes a vast filing-cabinet with the compartments indexed and waiting to be filled with appropriate and illuminating studies in every field of human activity and culture. Since he has accepted the doctrine as a guide to his own research, the responsibility of the Marxist scholar or critic is thus peculiarly great. The filing-cabinet stands waiting for him, but what he puts into it is the sum of his own intelligence, knowledge, and general good sense. And what the Marxist critic particularly is faced with—since no field of criticism makes so many demands on the active imagination as the study of literature in its relation to society—is the obligation to show just what those relations are and just what values emerge from a study of them. Condemning the esthete, who seems to believe that art exists in a vacuum, he must yet show that art is something more than the "ideological" representation of class forces in society. Patronizing the genteel impressionist who does not know to what extent works of art themselves have often acted as social forces, battlegrounds of ideas, he must yet show that the significance of any art work begins with its immediate success and fulfillment as art, its fulfillment of esthetic need and pleasure. Fighting the reactionary ideologue, who holds that art is aristocratic and the property of a few exquisite sensibilities, he must yet admit (precisely because he is confident that it is only with the advent of Socialism that human energy will be great enough, human fellowship broad enough, to make great works possible again) that without individual talent and humility and discipline, without its immediate origin in exceptional persons, no art is possible at all.

It is thus precisely because the Marxist critic believes himself to be at once a historian, an expert analyst, and an agitator; precisely because he appears to be salvaging the best culture of the past and establishing the requisite foundations under Socialism for a literature of unparalleled human fellowship and dignity; precisely because he seeks what critics have always sought, yet seems to go beyond them in his understanding of the whole social context of culture, that his responsibility is so great. Criticism under Marxism usually becomes a form of *Kulturgeschichte,* but a study of literature in its relation to society is not a feather bed for minds seeking cozy formulas; it is, presumably, a rousing-up of the best intellectual energies and a stimulus to the richest structural imagination that criticism affords. It was with a whole new perspective on literature, with the confidence that they saw the whole course of human development in a fresh and promising light, that the Marxist critics of the thirties went forth to battle and create.

3

The results are notorious. The excitement of the early thirties remained a public excitement; the slogans filled and darkened the air; and the end was a failure rooted in the shock of the crisis and the disposition of so many critics to subordinate everything to it. A social critic is not merely a critic, he is a kind of demiurge; if he turns out to be an inadequate or foolish critic, he does not merely fail the people; he may even mislead and betray them. One laughed, as indeed many Communists laughed, when a Michael Gold declared: "When a Nazi with hands dripping with the blood of workers begins to sentimentalize over Wagner, or an ex-Czarist officer who has hung and flogged peasants tells us that Dostoevsky shakes him to the very soul, one is perhaps justified in suspecting both Wagner and Dostoevsky." But Gold was only exaggerating with crude native force what more sophisticated literary intelligences held as a prime critical superstition. What happened, as was clear soon enough in the thirties, was that too many people set themselves up as critics on the strength of their devotion to the Communist cause, and translated the militancy of the class struggle into a verbal militancy, a slashing political attack, that was more arduous than serviceable even to their own cause. They did not go so far as to state dogmatically, like the English left-wing critic Edward Upward, that "Literary criticism which aims at being Marxist must . . . proclaim that no book *written at the present time* can be 'good' unless it is written from a Marxist or a near-Marxist viewpoint," but by their example they showed often enough that they were thinking in these terms.

The more fantastic examples of Marxist criticism in action were written by official party doctrinaires—but not always. A Communist official, A. B. Magil, once wrote in the *New Masses* that whereas "bourgeois realism" was merely objective, proletarian realism,

> expressing the interests and the fullest consciousness of that class which is destined to do away with all classes and class limitations, can rise to the historic height, the mountain-top of dialectic materialism, where not only a truer and deeper picture of the objective world is possible, but for the first time the development of art *as science*.

In theory the dialectic gave the critic an insight into the concrete development of historical epochs; it showed him just what reality lay beneath the prevailing social-political-ideological forms. In practice it merely provided him with a bludgeon with which to attack the past. Bukharin, who was so notoriously "undialectical" as to attack Plato for not being more of a modern progressive than he was, was surely not more foolish than the Marxist critics who attacked one writer out of the past after another for not being adequately conscious of the class forces of his time—or joining up on the "progressive" side. The average critic did not mean to confuse his analysis of the class nature of art—its famous "social determination"—with his judgment of particular books. Nor did he mean to use the dialectic as a religious canon by which to read the literature of all preceding epochs in the single light of the impending Socialist revolution, or set up, as Granville Hicks did at one period, arbitrary conditions for the creation of revolutionary masterpieces. But he did. And what emerges from the record of Marxist criticism—not the manifestoes, the declarations of high purpose, but the actual criticism as it was written—is an unconscious *contempt* for the past, for all that history which must seem "prehistory" with the advent of Socialism. The manifestoes prove nothing, as even the example of the great Marxists availed so many left-wing critics nothing. Marx and Engels loved literature passionately, had exemplary taste, and defended the "reactionary" Balzac against some of their followers. Lenin wept over *Camille,* adored Beethoven and Tolstoy, and thought always of the revolution as an opportunity for the Russian people, so long kept in darkness under Czarism, to share in the best of human art and culture, and to use it as the starting-point for their own development. But just as Lenin's political example was more dangerous than he knew, so the optimism, the messianic drive that lies at the heart of the dialectic, became a norm by which to judge the literature of past and present.

Yet it is not the intellectual legerdemain, the totalitarian control inherent in Bolshevism, that explains the course of left-wing criticism; it is ineptitude. The Marxist critics were not all of them party-line journalists; they were merely betrayed by their confusion of Socialism with the Communist party, as they confused Socialism with their desire to whip literature into an ideal order preparatory to Socialism. Just as the Communist equates humanity with the proletariat, the proletariat with the party, the party with the central committee, the central committee with the top bureaucracy, the bureaucracy with Stalin, so the left-wing critics equated their own notion of what was wanted in literature with the dialectic and Socialism. The critic, having accepted the Marxist doctrine, found himself lost just where he needed guidance most. For the crucial question that followed upon the dialectic, the central problem for Marxist critics, became this: What is to be salvaged from the "bourgeois past" and what is to be rejected? If literature in any period is fundamentally only the reflection of the great social-economic realities of that period, what is "progressive" and serviceable to the Cause, and what is to be condemned? Though they rarely attacked the problem so directly, this was in reality the only question Marxist critics ever asked themselves. And it was upon their solution to that problem that their success or failure depended. Had they handled it well, they would have kept a proper relation in their minds between the demands of taste and the demands of "class analysis," and they would not have underestimated the "backwardness" of the past or overestimated the zeal and sloganeering of their own revolutionary literature.

It is easy now to see why the Marxist critics fell into so many involuntary confusions. If one looks at so typical a specimen of leftist criticism as Joseph Freeman's introduction to *Proletarian Literature in the United States,* it is interesting to note that though he begins with several perfectly valid propositions, he sooner or later falls into a trap. Like every Marxist critic, Freeman distinguished between literature and social action; like many Communist officials, he even announced solemnly that "no party resolution, no government decree can produce art, or transform an agitator into a poet." He offered a valid, even a necessary, defense of the life of the masses as a subject for writers, and asked eloquently for the widest possible democracy of subject in literature. But beginning with a defense of proletarian experience, he now lapsed into a condemnation of every other. The formula was to become all too familiar: Our experience is a proper subject became Only our experience is a proper subject. Thus the invidious distinction drawn between a dynamic social consciousness, and "nightingales, the stream of the middle-class unconscious, or love in Greenwich Village." This was the central superstition of Marxist criticism and the most illuminating one. The other side always wrote of nightingales; the Marxists alone were high and purposive. Sooner or later almost every leftist critic slipped into making these distinctions; and in proportion to his fealty to the Communist party, could dismiss—now in the light of Bolshevik arrogance, now on the strength of the seemingly unimpeachable and exclusive validity of Marxist theory—anything that did not conform, that did not point in a "progressive tendency," that could be labeled with indiscriminate contempt as escapist, bourgeois, petty-bourgeois, aristocratic, decadent, sentimental, Trotskyite, ultra-leftist, not leftist enough, and so on.

What this meant, as the record shows, was that the left-wing critics, beginning with the commendable desire to show how firmly literature had always been planted in human experience, ended on the assumption that as scientific Marxists they alone understood the history of literature and knew the way to its possible salvation. From this followed all the dogmatic cant, the fantastic political judgments that masqueraded as literary judgments, and the fatal wordmongering. Wrapped in the vestments of his office, a Marxist critic could say *anything*. And he usually did. He had the norm, and the norm became everything. Like V. F. Calverton, he could write a history of American literature that did nothing but spell the changes on the epithet "petty-bourgeois," a term applied so freely to every writer from John Smith to Eugene O'Neill that it became meaningless. Like Granville Hicks, he worried whether Proust should be read after the revolution, yet confessed that while "no novel as yet written perfectly conforms to our demands . . . it is possible that a novel written by a member of the bourgeoisie might be better than a novel written by a member of or a sympathizer with the proletariat." Like Edwin Berry Burgum, he could define the bourgeois novel as

> either (1) a novel of escape written under the influence of idealistic philosophy or (2) a novel of despondency written under the influence of pragmatism or (3) a novel combining elements of both. An example of the first is Thornton Wilder's *The Bridge of San Luis Rey*, of

the second William Faulkner's *Sanctuary,* and of the third Thomas Wolfe's *Of Time and the River.* These three types exist in time: *i.e.* the first tends to be supplemented by the second, and the third reflects the rise of fascism; *i.e.* in the third type certain aspects of contemporary society are recognized with disgust and then distorted by the optimism of an idealistic (Nietzschean) interpretation.

It was zeal—raw converts' zeal, headlong zeal, the zeal possible only to those seeking some security for the mind in a time of blind panic and disorder, a zeal fastening itself on slogans and petty formulas, a zeal that brought energy to mediocrity and militancy to fear—that explains the course of this thinking. And from the first it was afflicted with a profound uneasiness, a perpetual atmosphere of challenge and mutual recrimination, that became its very content. Its ranks were filled with little people, caricatures of the literary revolutionist at all times, as its leaders were little people. And it is only when seen against this body of criticism that had no criticism, this critical movement that subsisted on polemical journalism, meetings of the John Reed Clubs and speeches at the League of American Writers, endless manifestoes and a vague excitement in academic halls and publishers' offices, that one can understand the very nature of its leadership and why left-wing criticism crumbled long before the Nazi-Soviet Pact drove many writers away and significantly alienated some from social criticism entirely. What one studies in this criticism is not a series of critical productions, but a public event, a social phenomenon, an episode in the history of New Deal America; and it is not strange that Marxist criticism, whatever its indirect influence, came chiefly to mean the use of the Marxist vocabulary, and that the public excitement was soon dominated by the few who had enough ambition and patience and scholarship to apply its dicta on some scale.

A writer like Granville Hicks, whatever his virtues or limitations, became the central figure in Marxist criticism, the dean of a faculty whose members spent most of their time grading papers, only because he was actually one of the very few critics on the left to assume a critic's responsibility. Assuming so much, his very energy and labor cost him dear; and when he resigned from the Communist party at the time of the Great Disillusionment, he found that he had retired from criticism and that the movement which he had led was largely a history of failure. *The Great Tradition* was not so much a bad book as a book of monumental naïveté, the work of an intelligent if not exceptional scholar on whom Marxism worked like strong drink; but it would not have been so blindly praised or so savagely attacked had it not been the only attempt made after Calverton's ill-fated *The Liberation of American Literature* to apply Marxist principles to a systematic interpretation of American literature. As literary editor of the *New Masses* Hicks said many foolish things, and as literary editor his pronouncements were more ambitious but hardly more judicious than the general run of pronouncements in the *New Masses*. But Hicks soon found himself, to a degree he little realized at the time, a symbol—a symbol of the Marxist critic who had written a book of Marxist criticism; a symbol of the Marxist critic who had the courage of his beliefs; a symbol of the Marxist scholar actively at work in his field and the repository of whatever scholarship his school could boast; a symbol above all of the influence of Marxism upon young writers and scholars in the universities at a time of unprecedented interest in the study of American literature. Inevitably he became the battleground on which Marxists and anti-Marxists fought—the rather inordinately aggressive young *doyen* of the left-wing critics who, though he believed that he was leading a critical movement, actually came more and more to bear the responsibility for left-wing criticism in the thirties.

Yet what the militiamen of the left never realized, perhaps, was that while Hicks was a symbol, he was also the unconscious representation of much that had made their movement possible and guided its course. He symbolized the tragicomedy of a movement, an atmosphere of challenge and excitement, in which a profoundly earnest but essentially unimaginative scholar, a patient and careful scholar too often lacking in sensibility, could rise to critical leadership. He symbolized a race of young men, lost in the tides of change and vaguely hostile to traditional forms, who submitted to Marxism so hungrily that their ambition overreached itself in the spell of the absolute. They had found a new purpose for themselves in the light of the Marxist purpose; but in them one saw the working of that absolute on minds never supple or imaginative enough, never talented or sensitive enough, to write significant criticism. It was this conventionality, aroused and militant in Marxist battle dress, a conventionality moving briskly but with metallic ardor through a period of confusion, that betrayed Hicks in the end and gave his resignation from the Communist party—so significantly a resignation from Marxism and perhaps even from criticism itself—such melancholy bitterness. Superior to the superficial encyclopedism and gross taste of a Calverton, the disingenuous partisanship of the local campfollowers, the village carnivalism that spoke through a Joseph Freeman, the hoarse and coy emotionalism of a Michael Gold, Hicks was still painfully limited—and his limitations all arose from his effort to apply his seriousness as a judgment of sensibilities immeasurably subtler and deeper than his own. His great gift was seriousness, a quality of moral intelligence that burrowed anxiously in the works of others; inevitably he fell into a shrewish moralism, a tension, that he had not intended.

From this disproportion followed the petty dogmatism and narrowness that so often made Hicks appear the little Calvin of the left, scourging the frivolous and the weak of will. Yet it was not bad taste or ignorance that one felt in his most flagrant utterances; it was an evangelical urge forced back on itself, a moral idealism that became rasping and hard for lack of subsidiary personal curiosity and wit. The range of his aspiration was wide; but he never understood, as Yvor Winters once said of Irving Babbitt, how the moral intelligence actually gets into literature. Hence the prevailing note in Hicks's criticism was querulousness, a moralism that more than once proved itself suspicious of sensibility, a moralism, as John Strachey once noted, that was conscious of esthetic differences but had no talent for conveying the necessary discriminations between them. In discussions of critical problems Hicks often showed that he knew what was wrong, as when he criticized Calverton for thinking exclusively in economic terms, or confessed in a Communist symposium:

> We make too little effort to understand the writer's problems; we look too seldom through his eyes. . . . Moreover, we remain almost purely negative; we seem unable to evoke positive literary achievement as the great bourgeois critics of the past sometimes succeeded in doing. We

not only fail to give anything directly to the writers; we rarely contribute to the creation of the kind of audience that inspires greatness.

In his own practice, however, he persistently took a mechanical interpretation of these problems, and as the leading Communist critic even became notorious for a habit of outlining categories into which he expected comradely novelists and poets to fit.

It was the intensity of Hicks's naïveté that made too much of his work seem so stiff and demanding and empty. He composed blueprints for ideal revolutionary masterpieces; he scolded writers for excessive "pessimism"; he had a picture in his mind of the perfect Communist writer, and always wondered a little sadly why no one fitted the picture; he issued edicts for contemporary writers and saw failure, failure, everywhere in the past. Reading one of the few distinguished revolutionary novels of the thirties, André Malraux's *Man's Fate,* he complained that there were not enough proletarians in it. The proletarian novelists, he declared at another time, had discovered a new way of looking at life and would certainly create an unprecedented literature in the light of that conception, whereas "there is no bourgeois novel that, taken as a whole, satisfies me. I am not merely conscious of omissions and irrelevancies; I feel within myself a definite resistance, a counter-emotion, so to speak, that makes a unified esthetic experience impossible." Yet no proletarian novel ever really satisfied him either; in a sense, nothing ever did. Above the mechanical note of Marxist prophecy and expectancy, there was always heard in Hicks's work a tone of disappointment and secret perplexity, a suggestion that he wanted something that he could not name but must pursue with unflagging zeal. His vision was always of some final excellence, but that excellence was curiously unrelated to the major problems of art and artistic sensibility. It was a vision of some ineffable fusion of the perfect revolutionary attitude and the perfect revolutionary talent; and since he could never project it clearly or provocatively, save in formulary terms, his judgments and supplications were, for all their terrible earnestness, always a little hollow to the ear. It became a naked moral entreaty, a search for some moral perfection worthy of the Marxist world-view; but Hicks could define it only in his own terms, and they proved to be the terms of a critical mind never responsive enough to literature to save them from incantation.

In a work like Calverton's *The Liberation of American Literature* one saw a fixation on the Marxist vocabulary, a gross carelessness that lumped social and literary problems together and discussed them in interchangeable terms. In *The Great Tradition* Hicks made the distinction between them, kept them separate in his mind, but persistently subordinated literary values to the Marxist social values. It is only a very rare type of social critic in America—notably Brooks and Edmund Wilson—who has been able, like Brandes or Michelet, to write with such abundant sensibility of literature in its relation to civilization that for the first time one really sees writers moving through the stream of time, a view in which not only a new sense of history is grasped, but also the pang of individual experience. Writing literary history, Hicks's thinking revolved around social attitudes, and became a judicial examination in which a study of the operation of social forces upon individual writers slipped into a demand that they express the one imperative attitude toward those forces. Where a more imaginative critic would have seen his problem as a series of discrete human situations, a problem of personality and character and will expressing themselves in form, a problem of talent moving against the pressures of a particular age, a problem of the subtle and multiform relations through which a writer moves in order to write at all, Hicks fell into a censorious Marxist puritanism that allowed him to condemn writers a little too mechanically. Dozens of writers were marched into court, questioned roundly on what position they had taken, lectured on their personal behavior, their sloth or sinful melancholy, their indifference or cynicism, and sentenced. Yet with it all went the beseeching attitude and the baffled disappointment at their cynicism or indifference or escapism, as who should say: *I beseech you, believe, in the bowels of the dialectic, that you may be mistaken!*

Are good writers "indivisible," as Hicks was later to write of Hardy in *Figures of Transition,* or are they not? Hicks believed that they were, but he showed over and again that, with the best intentions in the world, he could not make the fact of that indivisibility vivid in his analysis of a writer's work. The pressure of the Marxist world-view was too much for him, as it was too much for all his school; but there was a certain poignance in his zeal. For he *knew,* as too many of his fellows in the Marxist camp never allowed themselves to know; and knowing, he could protest that he had kept the balance straight, though his practice often belied him. This showed particularly in his most ambitious critical work, *Figures of Transition,* a carefully detailed study of English literature at the end of the nineteenth century. He had dropped the narrow tone of *The Great Tradition,* and with sober discrimination described the lives and works of the late Victorians against the social problems and forces transforming Victorian society. Yet for all its quiet reasonableness, its clarity and many valuable insights, the book was essentially a study in social change rather than in literature. He did not slight artistic problems and achievements; he merely, and almost unconsciously, as it were, treated them in an offhand manner, much the same manner in which a liberal culture-historian like Harry Elmer Barnes will note "literary notables and achievements" in a study of civilization from the Ape Man to Hitler. The Marxist obsession with the social background revealed in Hicks a biographer of minds, a historian of broad intellectual tendencies. With the best will in the world he could illuminate at every point what was happening to writers and writing in England as the century ran out, where literature was going, what forces influenced and directed it, what its main concerns were; he did not show what that literature was. For all the revolutionary philosophy behind it, it was essentially an academic work and representative of the failure in imagination that has too often characterized the academic study of literature—a study of origins, currents and cross-currents, attitudes and influences, the kind of study that has always rooted works of art in everything save the facts of their own creation.

Hicks's book, as it happened, appeared at a time when left-wing criticism had become a thing of the past; and it was greeted either with vast apathy, or, thanks to his sensational departure from the Communist ranks, with the malice or political partisanship that had always attended the history of left-wing criticism. The last word came with Bernard Smith's *Forces in American Criticism,* an industrious and prosy history of literary criticism in America which, ending upon a confident dismissal of every school of criticism save his own, was an ironic dénouement to the whole period. Hicks's discovery that the Nazi-Soviet Pact had invalidated "a great deal, though by no means all" of Marxist criticism at least revealed the extraordinary confusion of Russian politics and American literature that had operated in certain Marxist minds; but like Smith's wistful military metaphors, as of a whole army still going forth to battle, it was merely an anticlimax. No one needed now to be told, as Hicks wrote in a memorial to "The Fighting Decade," that "throughout the thirties, the faults of left-wing writers have been attributed to political dogmas, when, even if the faults existed, they should have been attributed to ignorance, failures of insight, literary competence, or weaknesses of that order." It was true, and as always, it was something less than the whole truth.

4

The arts may die of triviality, as they were born of enthusiasm.
—GEORGE SANTAYANA

It was an involuntary fanaticism that characterized Marxist criticism to the end, and it was an involuntary fanaticism fully equal to it, if immeasurably more gifted and more directly concerned with literature, that characterized the fashionable new esthetic school of criticism. Taken together, both schools lend a new perspective on the moral and intellectual retreat that made them possible; and it is perhaps as a commentary on the Ice Age of the thirties and after that they are to be understood. Each of these polar extremes in criticism was the symbol of some tragic disassociation, the mark of an obsession with pet values that became a cult; and in each case the fixation upon these values signified a sacrifice of everything that seemed to interfere with a particular conception of necessity. Among the Marxists literature became a function of politics and as such no more significant than any other. Among the Formalists—which was less a cohesive group than a loose association of poets, university teachers, traditionalists aching for lost symbols of authority, professional reactionaries brought together by a common contempt for a democratic society—the study of literature became the property of a few brilliant but narrow minds who prided themselves on their isolation and were increasingly ravaged by it. At the Marxist extreme all consideration of literature as a distinct element in human experience was ignored or corrupted; at the other extreme there emerged a forbidding neoclassicism that combined strangely with estheticism and fulfilled itself in traditional reaction. Between the zealots and the *précieux* fanaticism had a holiday, but criticism almost starved to death.

"The kind of poetry which interests us," John Crowe Ransom wrote in *The World's Body,* "is not the act of a child, or of that eternal youth which is in some women, but the act of an adult mind; and I will add, the act of a fallen mind, since ours too are fallen." This, with all its pride in a private greatness and private spiritual tragedy, became the tone of what Ransom was to celebrate as "the new criticism"—a criticism absorbed in studying "the structural properties" of poems, finely contemptuous of the romanticism and crudity with which inferior minds fulfilled themselves in the grosser disciplines, and even tampered with the inviolable purity of poetry. The fine grace and cozy self-satisfaction of the esthetic cult at all times were in this criticism, but with them went an extraordinary resignation, the knowledge of their defeat before the forces of vulgar commercialism and naturalism and liberalism, that gave these critics a new character among the *précieux* of history. Their preciosity was not an "escape" from anything; it was a social pressure, subtle and enraged and militant in its despair, working against the positivism of the age and sustained by a high contempt for it; a despair in the face of contemporary dissolution and materialism and irreligion that found its locus in the difficulty of modern poetry and prized that difficulty as the mark of its alienation and distinction. What gave meaning to their obsession with technique, their religious veneration of "form," their attempt to read out of literature everything but the "poetic strategy" of a Donne or a Dante or an Eliot, was a humiliating sense of exile, a loneliness of the spirit and even the political intelligence. The Marxists thought of literature as a military weapon in a planetary war, but ultimately treated it as a game. The Formalists gave their textual analyses the character of a game, but they were always playing for higher stakes than most people knew.

What was this "humiliating sense of exile"? Primarily, as all the critics of this school proved, it was rooted in the isolation of modern poetry and in the example of poetic sensibilities like Poe and Baudelaire, Rimbaud and Valéry; but it was rooted also in the growing revolt against democratic liberalism and its culture, a revolt which easily found expression, thanks to the Southern leadership of this school, in the Southern grievance against capitalism and the dominant North. It was the aggrieved traditionalism of critics like Ransom and Tate, coming to life at a time when traditionalism had proved a major literary force in the postwar world, that attracted a whole school of young esthetes seeking some positive affirmation in the "wasteland" of modern experience. It was a traditionalism that went hand in hand with the passionate but synthetic traditionalism of Eliot and Pound; a traditionalism that recaptured everything writers contemptuous of the laxness and easy ardors of liberalism had found in Babbitt and More; a traditionalism seemingly more attractive, indeed, than the New Humanists', since it combined artistic sensibility with discipline and order. It was a traditionalism that gave poets and critics a magnetic field of authority, a centrality and order of belief, superior to that which Marxism assumed for itself and degraded. It was an eclectic traditionalism, a literary man's traditionalism that found its resources in half a dozen ill-assorted orthodoxies; but its mainspring was a passionate revolt against capitalism and the popular mind under capitalism, and as such fell upon any standard worthy of itself to fix against the anarchy of the day. It was the passion for orthodoxy that brought these orthodoxies together; and as such it found its leadership in the South and its own assumptions in the contempt of Southern philosophy for Northern materialism and egalitarianism.

The publication in 1930 of *I'll Take My Stand,* a collective statement in favor of agrarianism by Southern writers, teachers, and publicists, was thus as significant a revolutionary document for the times as the *Culture and the Crisis* pamphlet prepared by the Communists and their fellow travelers for the 1932 election. Unlike any Communist statement that was ever prepared, however, there was a desperate optimism about it, a conviction of impending defeat, that gave it a kind of lonely grandeur appropriate to the lonely grandeur of the Southern cause.

"We fight rather to keep something alive than in the expectation that anything will triumph," Eliot was later to confess in behalf of traditionalists; and it was this conviction of heroic defeat, of an unimpeachable private distinction and purity of aspiration in persons of superior cultivation and taste, that was to dominate the criticism of this school. There was challenge in Ransom's declaration that "the South is unique on this continent for having founded and defended a culture which was according to the European principles of culture, and the European principles had better look to the South if they are to be perpetuated in this country," but the challenge was merely wistful and aggrieved. The prevailing note, in all its contempt and rage, was heard in Allen Tate's protest that the Southern intellectual, to win out, "must use an instrument which is political, and so unrealistic and pretentious that he cannot believe in it, to re-establish a private, self-contained, and essentially spiritual life." Like Hilaire Belloc, these writers thought of themselves as "sufferers who will probably fail"; but in the fact of their suffering lay their claim to distinction, the necessary clue to the profundity and courage of their break with a system bred in materialism and inextricably bound to it.

It is not difficult to see why the new traditionalism found a home in the South, much as the new traditionalism in England found its way into the Established Church, or the new traditionalism in France became associated with Royalism and a kind of superior intellectual Fascism. The South of which Ransom and Tate spoke was certainly not the South of Gastonia and Birmingham, or the South for which thousands of Confederate boys had once fought under the leadership of the plantation aristocracy, or the South which Ellen Glasgow satirized. Yet whatever its unrepresentative character, that South became the convenient symbol of an aristocratic tradition based upon moral order, a tradition in which the sense of race and community and the soil had supported a culture and proved the distinction of its aspiration and integrity to the end. Allen Tate's South was remarkably like Michael Gold's Russia—an ideal embodied in a culture, a community to be used as a standard of order and fellowship against the Enemy. Each was a great literary myth, to be appreciated in its own terms only by the literary intelligence. But with one difference, the vital difference between a culture believed by its adherents to be alive and militant, the very center of moral energy in a changing world, and a culture whose grandchildren mourn it in the country of their enemies—"a buried city," as Tate once wrote—yet one they must defend and whose example they are ready to apply in the face of all those forces that once destroyed it.

It is the difference between these two myths that explains why Marxist criticism was so often only a summons to political action, and why the example of these Southern critics fostered a criticism of great subtlety and moral self-consciousness, yet one remarkably parochial, tense, and forbidding. For while the transformation of Marxist politics into Marxist criticism was always as obvious as that criticism itself, the process by which the traditionalist yearning for orthodoxy fostered a curiously Alexandrian criticism was tortuous, and in itself most revealing testimony as to the use of literature in the thirties and after. The Southern traditionalist began with a powerful moral critique of the superficiality and debasement of letters under capitalism, and ended, like John Crowe Ransom, by declaring art to be "post-ethical." He began by excoriating naturalism and positivism, yet ended by affirming that the analysis of the "structural properties" of poems was the main business of criticism. "I suppose our modern critics have learned to talk more closely about poems than their predecessors ever did," Ransom wrote contentedly in *The World's Body*. "The closeness of Mr. Eliot in discussing a text may well be greater than anybody's before him, and he in turn may now be even exceeded in closeness by Mr. Blackmur, and perhaps others. These are close critics, and define our age as one of critical genius." Where, then, did the barbarism of the world end and this "age of critical genius" begin? Or had they no relation to each other? The answer is that this new criticism, based on a vicarious orthodoxy and textual analysis of advanced poetry, seemed to these men the only answer to the havoc of the times. Like George Gissing, they were ready to say: "Keep apart, keep apart and preserve one's soul alive—that is the teaching for the day. It is ill to have been born in these times, but one can make a world within a world."

On the obvious level this criticism resulted in a literature of decadence, a literature specializing in isolated ecstasies, a literature cut off from the main sources of life and floundering in the sick self-justifications of estheticism. But its estheticism was bound up with a primary disgust; it was a defense against modern life rather than a conventionally decadent evasion of it. Underneath all the trappings of neoclassic snobbery and the obsession with form as an ideal end in itself, it was a profound and impotent disaffection that moved in this criticism. There was in it always a defeated responsibility, a sense of loss, of an enforced narrowness and inversion, that needed some exterior authority upon which to fall and replenish itself. If the critics of this school, as Ransom admitted indirectly, were of a kind "who are incapable of remarkable catharses, who make the little and precious effects their virtue, who are without dimensions," it was because in their own minds they represented the last stand of the intelligence in a world that had forced the intelligence back on itself. Even more, they represented the last stand of sensibility in an age that had, by their own testimony, no belief in itself, no literature worthy of themselves, and no satisfying belief in the importance of literature as a guide to life. Hence their obsession with Form and their curious and desperate hypothesis that poetry, as the quintessence of literature and the repository of value, was the product of "poetic strategy." For the strategy by which a poem was composed, the strategy by which its every element was then tirelessly analyzed and weighed, had become the last exercise of the intelligence in defeat. Strategy is for those who attack because they mean to win; strategy can become an end in itself, a grammarian's paradise, for those who mean to go on fighting though they never hope to win.

On the surface, of course, this "new criticism" seemed to represent only a protest against the looseness and impressionism of so much American criticism, a necessary protest against the perpetual degradation of criticism to history or propaganda or sociology. As Flaubert once wrote to George Sand: "When will critics be artists, only artists, but really artists? Where do you know a criticism? Who is there who is anxious about the work in itself, in an intense way?" An anxiety "about the work in itself, in an intense way," was certainly the great contribution of this school to American criticism. Yet this criticism was as partisan a social criticism as any other, and there was a rigidity of mind about it from the first that suggested that the passion of these critics for form had made a fetish of form and had become entirely disproportionate to the significance of form in the artistic synthesis. Form had, in a word, become a sentimental symbol of order in a world that had no order; it had become the last orthodoxy in the absence of all other orthodoxies.

What one saw in the work of critics like Ransom and Tate, Blackmur and Yvor Winters, was the use of form as a mysterious ultimate value, form as a touchstone, a kind of apotheosis in a void. On the basis of it they could analyze and mock, always with great brilliance, the confusions and limitations of one writer after another; but form always meant to them something more than structure and proportion and inner logic, the palpable execution of a writer's particular sense of necessity. At bottom their form was always an indeterminate vision of some secret ideal, an ideal fundamentally vague and incommunicable, and therefore in the service of every personal association of snobbery, eccentricity, rigidity, malice, or plain ignorance the critic might reveal. Like the Marxist dialectic, which is also a religion of form (form in history), this conception of form was always an image of some perfect discipline and harmony, some perfect assemblage of movements, which gave the critic the advantage of a personal sense of order, a primary conception by which to read the world's folly and error. But like the dialectic, it was more an image than an idea; and one the critic could use with the willfulness and irresponsibility that attach themselves to all monisms.

The result of all this was an extreme neoclassicism; a neoclassicism toward which certain serious critics had been aiming ever since T. E. Hulme and T. S. Eliot, but one that was to make Eliot look like an unashamed romanticist. For this was a neoclassicism that began with a purely professional snobbery and ended, as in Ransom, by outlawing the emotions in favor of a poetry of cognitions; a neoclassicism, as I. A. Richards complained, that repeated the worst excesses of its predecessor and showed "a fascinating versatility in travesty." Yet unlike most modern attempts to play the neoclassic game, it was not purely reactionary or pontifical in tone; it was always an exercise in fragmentary perceptions rather than an assumption of authority. Without robustness or the moral devotion to supreme examples that has always marked the neoclassic mind, without even the very conception of great models to follow, there was a willfulness about it, a disjointedness, a profound weariness, that represented its own inner sense of defeat. Expert in textual analysis, it was a marginal wisdom that seemed to dwell in odd corners of the mind—a criticism supreme in local apprehension, feline in strategy, petulant rather than authoritative in dogma, and curiously boneless. Despite its academic seriousness, there was an air of eccentric and almost furtive intensity about it, a nervous hauteur; and despite its dour professionalism, an unrelieved bitterness and rage and contempt that were to find expression in a tensely emotional prose.

It was a neoclassicism of attitudes, a neoclassicism resting on an incommunicable distaste for the world and a desperate satisfaction with itself. The new critics, as Van Wyck Brooks said, doubted the progress of everything save criticism—their own criticism. And the tone in which Ransom could proclaim that "in depth and precision at once it is beyond all earlier criticism in our language" was rather like the tone in which Edgar Allan Poe had written of his day that "this is emphatically the thinking age; indeed, it may very well be questioned whether man ever substantially thought before." It is in this self-satisfaction, the pride these critics took in their own distinction and the significance they gave to their isolation, that one may see the outlines of their curious literary creed. A critic like John Crowe Ransom, for example, would seem to have been interested only in the professional problems of poetry. Yet it was an interest which enclosed him so tightly in a world all his own that he could suggest, in an essay on Shakespeare's sonnets, that they were inferior, since there is

> no evidence anywhere that Shakespeare's imagination is equal to the peculiar and systematic exercises which Donne imposed habitually upon his. None, and it should not really surprise us, if we remember that Donne's skill is of the highest technical expertness in English poetry, and that Shakespeare had no university discipline, and developed poetically along lines of least resistance.

What Ransom meant by this became clear enough in his patronage of poor Shakespeare, who

> was not an aristocrat, did not go to the university and develop his technical skill at once, got into the rather low profession of acting,

grew up with the drama, and never had to undergo the torment of
that terrible problem: the problem of poetic strategy; or what to do
with an intensive literary training.

As a critical pronouncement such a statement betrayed the critic far
more pointedly than it said anything about Shakespeare; yet it was
entirely in keeping with Ransom's proposal that "the critic should regard the poem as nothing short of a desperate ontological or metaphysical manoeuvre." In Ransom's forbidding but perfectly coherent
interpretation of literature and experience, a poet was never, as the
Romantic prejudice in Wordsworth had it, "a man speaking to men—a
man who rejoices more than other men in the spirit of life that is in
him." That was the prejudice of a democratic simplicity, the mark of
a sentimental ingenuousness, and one that might conceivably today,
mirabile dictu, rank Tolstoy over Rimbaud, and Wordsworth with
Wallace Stevens. With his air of gentle cynicism, of a special and
ironic disillusionment, Ransom proposed an esthetic rooted in a philosophy of civilized resignation and a poetry so perfect in texture and
structure that it alone would be worthy of the "adult fallen mind."
The modern poet, as he wrote proudly, was above the sentimental
glorification of poetry as a guide to life, though the modern reader had
as yet "no general recognition of the possibility that an esthetic effect
may exist by itself, independent of morality or any other useful set of
ideas." The modern poet "has disclaimed social responsibility in order
to secure this pure esthetic effect. He cares nothing, professionally,
about morals, or God, or native land. He has performed a work of dis-
sociation and purified his art."

For all its fin-de-siècle swagger, this was something more than the
exaggerated preciosity with which the American esthete has usually
fallen into one heresy in an attempt to destroy another. In Ransom's
view art itself existed as a technique of restraint; the pleasure it gave
was bound up with its regulation of the vulgar passions. The great
European communities of the past had sought to humanize man, not to
confirm him "in his natural objects." And this meant, "so far as his
natural economy permitted, to complicate his natural functions with
sensibility, and make them esthetic." In the ideal community, therefore,
art and manners and religion operated toward the same end, since

religion was more important for its rites than for its doctrines, and "the object of a proper society is to instruct its members how to transform instinctive experience into esthetic experience." The modern poet and critic lacked the foundation of religion and manners, the necessary background of a traditionalist society; but no matter. In so far as he was estranged from them, he was a fallen mind; and by exercising the sense of discipline in his art, by proving the validity of his own discipline in devotion to form and craft, he was secure from the ravages of disorder. This was the modernism Ransom recognized and approved, the modernism appropriate to a period, as he wrote with characteristic shrewdness, when "the modern mind achieved its own disintegration and perfected its faculties serially."

Was there something wanting in this view? Ransom knew it perfectly well, and accepted its limitations as proudly as he accepted distastefully the world which enforced such a position. "Style is the thing which the Russians have not wanted but which Western writers have developed so lovingly; the symbol of personality which is precious to our battered civilization and worth all its fury and expense." He was not content to say, as the most commonplace student of esthetics knows, that "poetry has to be a technical act, of extreme difficulty, when it wants only to know the untechnical homely fullness of the world." The difficulty had become a prize in itself, and it stimulated so many associations of honor and pride and style that it became a world of supreme felicity and grace in itself. The poet lived only for the perfection of his poem, as criticism lived only for the elucidation of that perfection. Hence Ransom's unforgettable remark on Wallace Stevens's *Sea Surface Full of Clouds:* "The poem has a calculated complexity, and its technical competence is so high that to study it, if you do that sort of thing, is to be happy." Hence his notation on the Macbeth soliloquy: "I do not know why *dusty death;* it is an odd but winning detail." Criticism had become expert at last; it had finally turned its full attention upon the poem in itself; it missed nothing; it was stainless in motive, happy only to study the calculated complexity of those few poems whose technical competence was "high." It had become "a sort of thing," a game of devotions by knightly grammarians, and it made one happy.

5

The proudest boast of these new critics was that by their concentration on textual analysis, they had, in the words of Cleanth Brooks, "done much to enlarge our view of the imagination, indicating how complex, how elastic it is and what diverse and intricate matters it can accomplish." To a certain degree this was clearly true, yet it explains the nature of their influence—at a time when there has been less and less literature in the world—even more than it marks their contribution to technical criticism. For one of the most significant things about this school of textual analysis is that it found a home in the universities and has now become almost an academic property. The last essay in Ransom's *The World's Body* had been a call to university teachers to take over criticism professionally, a call for "a Criticism, Inc., or Criticism, Ltd." "Criticism must become more scientific, or precise and systematic, and this means that it must be developed by the collective and sustained effort of learned persons—which means that its proper seat is in the universities." Just as psychology and sociology, studies sharing in the limitations of literary criticism, had improved immeasurably "since they were taken over by the universities," so criticism now looked for its grounding in scientific method and assumption of authority to the university. What Ransom meant by science and scientific method came out clearly in his praise in *The New Criticism* of Cleanth Brooks, who "prefers poetry to science because he judges that poetry is capable of the nicer structures," and of Yvor Winters, "the critic who is best at pouncing upon the structure of a poem." But despite its curious *pastiche* of estheticism and "scientific method," this was a criticism eminently appropriate under academic auspices.

With the growing decline of criticism its leadership did now pass to the universities, and Irving Babbitt's dream of a school of scholar-critics who would hold the field against the forces of liberalism and naturalism seemed to be on the way. It was significant that at a time when critical organs were dying off rapidly, brilliant and indispensable new critical quarterlies like the *Kenyon Review* and the *Southern Review* were established under academic sponsorship, while even a challenging new publishing venture like *New Directions* became, for all its little-magazine surrealism, a center for academic critics and young poet-teachers. For this was a new criticism of unique background and prestige: it appealed to native conservatisms, yet stood at the very center of experimental poetry; it had all the solid advantages of academic discipline and method, yet put them at the service of a radical esthetic. It was an eminently respectable criticism, a "scientific" criticism, a criticism as solid in documentation as any paper in *P.M.L.A.*, yet one that brought a tested scholarship to the service of contemporary letters, and even exercised its own leadership over them. With its faint air of academic snobbery, its cold objectivity and rigor, its scrupulousness and professional cast, it did stand for "Criticism, Inc." Hitherto the dissatisfaction of young teachers with traditional academic interests had usually left them helpless, or susceptible to idle impressionism. Now there lay at hand a critical method, a vocabulary, a sense of standards, that called upon all their training, yet put it to fresh use.

As a development in the history of critical activity in America, this was all to the good, and particularly heartening at a time when the pressure of events and the dominance of scientific positivism in the universities would seem to have driven criticism and the academic study of literature to the wall. It was this foundation in textual analysis, for example, that made possible a work of extraordinary academic distinction like F. O. Matthiessen's *American Renaissance,* though the book would have been less notable without Matthiessen's particular distinction among these critics: his strong democratic faith and feeling for democratic minds and ideas. Yet for all the influence and prestige of this school, it *was* a criticism driven to the wall; and it was as a criticism now pretentiously "scientific" and neoaristocratic, as with Ransom, or written in a tense new jargon, as with Blackmur, or shrilly moralistic, as with Winters, that this criticism slipped into leadership. As the influence of Marxism waned, as critical activity became rarer and rarer in America, criticism suddenly seemed to be divided between the textual analysts and the "commodity critics" who found a new masterpiece in every Sunday's book supplement. It had been easy enough to escape from the Marxist cult, but the Formalist cult had about it a professional prestige, an aura of vague solidity, that in the absence of worthy opposition easily carried the day.

In this new age of international convulsions and mass psychosis, literary criticism became again the property of bookmen and gentlemen. Save for Allen Tate, the only philosophical mind among these critics, they suggested just that fundamental apathy toward leading ideas, that curious secret cynicism, which could burrow in its haughty isolation and fasten upon textual analysis in a period when society needed a fresh and virile intellectual leadership as never before. These critics made readers conscious of "the integrity of a work of art," but they did this at the expense of withdrawing literature itself into chill and airless corners of human life. And it was for this reason, above all others, that their claim that they had done much "to enlarge our view of the imagination" was so grotesquely untrue. For their conception of the imagination was such that they could understand it only in terms of technical analysis: the level on which the imagination gets into a particular poem and is to be studied there. To them the imagination was not the summation and projection of a writer's resources, the very distinction of them; it was rather a kind of machine which did its work in poetry, and only in poetry of acceptable tension and difficulty. They made a fetish of Dante and the "structural properties" of his poetry; yet lacking any structural imagination of their own, they never understood the rage in exile, the sickness and pain of his alienation from his own country and people, that went into Dante's conception of the poetic mission. They made a fetish of Donne's difficulty and strategy, but they never suggested that the difficulty and hazardous poise of Donne's poetry arose from something more than an ambition to write perfect poems. Of Goethe and Tolstoy, Mark Twain and Whitman, Emerson and Dickens, they never spoke at all. Their heroes were the tutelary divinities of the modern sensibility—James and Rimbaud, Kafka and Proust, Joyce and Rilke—great artists all, but writers whom they often reduced to *problems* of sensibility, writers whom they brought down to their own size and read as masters of craft.

In a critic like Yvor Winters this cult was allied to a cold and savage moralism and resulted in a critical system so rigorous and ungenerous that it was paralytic. Winters, of whom William Troy properly said that he wrote like a combination of a medieval scholastic and a Puritan divine, was admittedly an extremist, and one who handled his fellow Formalists as roughly as he handled almost everything else. But his traditionalism, it must be said, was not a desperate improvisation for the times, a patchwork of religious orthodoxy without religious convictions. He had become a traditionalist long before it became fashionable for literary men to play the chevalier in rude exile, and could very properly say that his objection to T. S. Eliot (almost no one pleased him) was not that Eliot was a reactionary, but that what he found in Eliot's work was only the "illusion of reaction." If Winters had clerical venom, he had the apostolic passion. There was always in his work a searching for so supreme a perfection of form that his earnestness became theological; yet because of his extreme isolation, there remained a fundamental background of incoherence, a strained and lofty self-satisfaction, that made his ideas curiously unapproachable. A work like *Primitivism and Decadence,* for all its many brilliant technical insights, was so venomous an attack on modern poetry that many Formalists uneasily detected a Torquemeda in their midst. In *Maule's Curse,* a study of "obscurantism" in American literature from Hawthorne to James, Winters even went to the extreme of saying that a definition of the novel would be "neither difficult nor illegitimate" that would exclude Melville entirely, a definition that left Henry James as the greatest novelist in English.

Nothing was so characteristic of these critics as the attempt to study Henry James in their own image, the attempt to transform James into a pure disembodied intelligence who had written perfect novels for their instruction. The most extraordinary example of this—in its way one of the most extraordinary phenomena in contemporary literature—was the attempt of R. P. Blackmur to write critical essays in much the same manner in which James had in his last period studied human character in books like *The Sacred Fount* and *The Golden Bowl.* To Yvor Winters, James was merely a uniquely successful writer, and how well he had understood James's background and spirit is best revealed in his praise of "this greatest novelist in English" as one whose father was "elegantly Bohemian," and who himself, for all his greatness of form, seemed to Winters an example of great moral confusion and obscurantism, a writer who vented his gifts of psychological analysis on trivialities. Blackmur, however, modeled himself on James almost too well. It is perhaps not too much to say that this critic, formed by an exclusively literary culture, became the sedulous shadow of James in criticism—though this was a pupil raised on Eliot and Pound rather than on Turgenev or George Eliot; though this was a pupil who would never understand why the master of his soul had admired Howells so warmly and had worshiped Turgenev's great spirit in envy, as he had admired in Flaubert only his devotion to form.

Blackmur's unique style, which often read like an unconscious travesty of James's density and circumlocutionary wisdom, is one of the most revealing emblems of his school. It was a style such as perhaps no other critical period could have fostered, a style so harried and strained in its tireless salvage of technical insights, so sharp in appearance and so bodyless as a whole, so curiously furtive and tormented and "deep," that it suggested a violent narrowness of spirit. "Here," as he said of Laura Riding in *The Expense of Greatness,* "meanings beat against each other like nothing but words; we have verbalism in extremis; and end-product of abstraction without any trace of what it was abstracted *from.*" No one carried the passion for textual analysis, the weighing of the poetic processes, to such lengths as did Blackmur; no critic ever lived, as it seemed, who could measure the range and depth of a poem with such confident exactitude, dissect a poet's language and craft with such grappling fervor.

> If we may say that in Shelley we see a great sensibility the victim of the early stages of religious and philosophical decay in the nineteenth century, and that in Swinburne we see an even greater poetic sensibility vitiated by the substitution of emotion for subject matter, then it is only a natural step further to see in Hardy the consummate double ruin of an extraordinary sensibility that had been deprived of both emotional discipline and the structural support of a received imagination.

Could anything be more "shrewd"—and more unhappy in its shrewdness? This, as John Crowe Ransom said so proudly, was a criticism "in depth and precision beyond all earlier criticism in our language," and for an excellent reason. For this was a criticism possible only in an age that has no literature and no confidence in literature; a criticism, as Blackmur wrote of T. E. Lawrence, that lacked the power to "make, or even to see, character complete; but had inexhaustibly the power to make a willed substitute for it." It was a criticism that sat on the hazardous peak of human experience and sensibility in the Hitler age, and *knew*—knew from the depths of its own sick torment, knew as only marginal minds can know, that Shelley had been the victim "of the early stages of religious and philosophical decay" and that Hardy's had been "a consummate double ruin." It was a criticism that displayed so devouring an intensity of mind, so voracious a passion for the critical process in itself, that it became monstrous—an obsession with skill, a perfection of skill, that made criticism larger than life ... and never touched it. It was a criticism so *driven* to technical insights that it virtually conceived the literary mind as a sensibility machine—taste, conscience, and mind working as gears, levers, and wheels. To no one else but Blackmur would it have occurred so to exhaust all the possible considerations of T. E. Lawrence, or Henry Adams, as an artist that one lost him as a human being living in a society where social tensions involved something more than the familiar—and for Blackmur so readily defined—tensions of the literary mind. But Blackmur *had* to see his every subject as an artist, as he had to see every artist as a technical problem and a study in ruins. What was criticism for?

6

As textual analysis and estheticism became increasingly "pure," it began to occur to various philosophers of science that since criticism was seeking so arduously to become a science, it was about time that the "real" scientists—semanticists and logical positivists with no literary nonsense about them—took over. Only one of the Formalist critics, Allen Tate, had the wit to see what was happening, and he countered by withdrawing literature from the scientists and from "the rich and contingent materiality" of life itself. In Tate's system "the integrity of a work of art" was not merely something to be understood and appreciated for its own sake; it was to be prized because it was relevant to nothing save "that unique and formed intelligence of the world" which literature alone could provide. To save criticism from the scientists, Tate disengaged literature itself from society and men, and held up the inviolate literary experience as the only measure of human knowledge. Literature in this view was not only the supreme end; it was also the only end worthy of man's ambition. Critics who saw in works of literature "not the specific formal properties but only the amount and range of human life brought to the reader" were vulgar expressionists. Critics who studied literature as "expressive of substances" beyond itself were only historical scholars aping the positivism of science and remote from the crucial spiritual values to be derived from literature. Thus only Formalist criticism remained, to elucidate those "high forms of literature [which] offer us the only complete, and thus the most responsible, versions of our experience."

What one saw in Tate's system was a fantastic inversion of the Marxist system; and in him the extremities met as in no other critic of the time. The Marxist critic could study a work of art only in terms of its social relations; Tate would study literature—that is, only poetry of a certain intensity and difficulty—precisely because it had no social relations at all. A form like the novel could be despised because it was so much like history. Could anything be more illuminating of the contemporary mind in criticism? As fanatical as the Marxists, Tate never admitted for a moment that one could study both the specific formal properties of literature and its relation to civilization. The Marxists would have only the history, and he would have only the literature. "The true paradox," as Blackmur once wrote, "is that in securing its own ends thought cannot help defeating itself at every crisis. To think straight you must overshoot your mark." And how Tate overshot the mark! Overshot even Matthew Arnold's wistful faith that poetry could be "a criticism of life"! In his reaction against "our limitation of the whole human problem to the narrow scope of the political program," he gave literature so self-sufficient and austere a character that almost everything that went into the making of literature and its significance for men was driven out. The Marxists made life and literature indistinguishable; Tate made life indistinguishable in literature. In a desperate effort to save literature from science and criticism from mere history or impressionism, he transformed the experience of literature into what I. A. Richards had called a set of "isolated ecstasies." The positivism was removed, the history forgotten, all extraneous vulgarities of circumstance disengaged. Only the poem remained, and its incommunicable significance; and before it the critic worshiped as at a mystic shrine, since in it was all human knowledge and all spiritual insight.

Here, at last, was the tragicomic climax to the long and often unconscious history of American pragmatism. In his revolt against the positivists and efficiency experts and progressive educators, against those who sought in literature only the paraphrase of poems and a doctrine of action, in education only a training for a business civilization, in politics only the good life of materialism, Tate based his faith on dualism and a traditionalism dedicated to religion and hierarchy and ontology. Like so many American traditionalists, of course, he himself had no religion; but religion, like the cult of form, was now a necessary symbol of order, and as such the necessary framework of any traditionalist and reactionary society. Yet Tate's bitter hatred of pragmatic liberalism was something deeper than the effort of a Mortimer Adler to move at one step from John Dewey to St. Thomas Aquinas. The most aggressive and intransigent of all the Southern traditionalists, his animus against the culture of capitalism was rooted in a formal philosophy of Southern regionalism, and thus expressed itself in an opposition to everything the dominant North represented in business, culture, politics, and education. More than most Southerners, in fact, he raised that whole cluster of loyalties and convictions which had once been the abstract community faith of the South to the dignity of a philosophical position, and he now used it with great point and skill as a basis of attack. "The South clings blindly," he wrote approvingly in *Reactionary Essays on Poetry and Ideas,* "to forms of European feeling and conduct that were crushed by the French Revolution and that, in England at any rate, are barely memories. . . . Where, outside the South, is there a society that believes even covertly in the Code of Honor?"

It was just the baffled pride of this position that gave Tate so curious a philosophical leadership in the South and his criticism the character of an absolute philosophy of society. What one saw in his work was a rage, so profound and superior a hatred of science and positivism, not to say democracy, that it was almost too deep for words. There was, of course, a certain irony in his position, since the very textual analysis he defended was an aping of scientific method and rigor. But Tate never saw that, as he never saw how presumptuously his plantation aristocrat's philosophy represented the subordinate classes in the South. In his biographies of Jefferson Davis and Stonewall Jackson, in critical works suggestively titled *Reason in Madness* and *Reactionary Essays,* there was fashioned a literary apotheosis of the South, the negation of whose ambiguous splendors in modern experience he explored with pyrotechnical bitterness in his poems. It was an affirmation so much more Royalist than the King's, so much more hierarchical than any hierarch's, that the view of American society which emerged was as false to the South as it was a travesty of its own idealism.

Yet there was method in this apotheosis, and a kind of tragic satisfaction to be derived from it. For everything Tate wrote proved the abundance of his talent and his own modern and sophisticated powerlessness to use it. His orthodoxy was so palpably a convenience, a foothold, a margin of security, that it made a joke of the historic legends it ran after, and belied them. This was the perfect manufactured traditionalism, the apex of desire: it called for faith, but it had no faith; it called for order, which it could find only in poetry; it summoned men to the tasks of philosophy as if philosophy were a dignity of mind rather than the relation of ideas to the human situation. A Southern writer like Ellen Glasgow could find her release in satire, but Tate had no release. The South haunted him and he beseeched it to live again; but it was not a South that even plantation owners had ever known—it was a historical idyll appropriate to a modern poet's absence from community, the modern writer's longing for a society in which literature belonged, as writers must belong, to the forward urge of life itself. How transparent a makeshift this traditionalism was stood revealed on every page of Tate's books; yet he never gave himself away more clearly than when he wrote in *Reactionary Essays* that while slavery was wrong, it was wrong because the master gave everything to the slave and got nothing in return; that the "moral" wrong of slavery meant nothing, since "societies can bear an amazing amount of corruption and still produce high cultures." *High cultures!* Here lay the ultimate significance of Tate's plea for moral philosophy, for discipline, for hierarchy. It was in the quest of high cultures that the modern poet lived at last; alone with his poem, alone with its ecstasy, withdrawn in its exclusive and superior knowledge; weighing the poem in all the contentment of textual analysis, dreaming in embittered resignation of a time when there had been order, order, order in the world.

7

Meanwhile the semanticists were ready and waiting to take over. Whatever Tate might say, the textual analysts had opened the gates wide to the lay scientists of letters, all of them ready with their geologists' hammers, slide rules, and thermometers; all of them firm in the conviction that the deterioration of the contemporary world could best be studied in the deterioration of its language.[1] In the new *International Encyclopedia of Unified Science,* begun as a serial publication at the University of Chicago, there was developed the theory of "semiosis," or the functioning of language as "signs." This, as a professional study of the various functions of human discourse, put even semantics in its place, since it distinguished sharply between the semantical, which was scientific discourse; the syntactical, which covered esthetic discourse; and the pragmatical, which was technological. Since language could be understood in terms of *signs,* referents, objects to be connoted or denoted, language had obviously to be studied in scientific terms. This was appropriate doctrine for a scientific age, since it proved that criticism was not merely subject to all the pressures of science but a particular manifestation of them. At a time when the field scientists of metaphor, from an R. P. Blackmur busily dissecting poetic diction to a William Empson discovering "seven types of ambiguity," promised a substitute for the loose chitchat of nonscientific minds, this augured well. Empson, as one admiring professor said, had reached "the farthest periphery of criticism," and in Kenneth Burke,

---

[1] Or even exclusively studied in it. As a dictum frequently repeated among semanticists has it, "The crisis of today is a crisis of language."

who discussed literature as "symbolic action" and saw it as "the adoption of various strategies for the encompassing of situations," American criticism found a textual analyst of great acuteness and psychological insight. In all this, as John Crowe Ransom said, there was confidence that "literary studies must very soon develop by policies like those that have served science so well: by a series of close and small efforts rather than by some single great push."

One danger, of course, remained. Though the scientists and textual analysts had between them made a new spectrum analysis out of criticism, what if the scientists became tired of literature (only one field of discourse among many), and the textual analysts, weighing every poem down to its last atom, became tired too? This was science, excellent science, and its many insights were certainly of the highest importance; but the scientist of letters, for all his technical prowess, his indispensable interest in the complexities of human inquiry, had a curious disposition to get so far away from literature that, as Kenneth Burke's breathlessly brilliant studies revealed, he might have been talking about the household customs of Brazilian Indians. The Marxist critics were scientists and these new critics were scientists; but this was a science perpetually talking all around the object, a science that could disclose every insight relevant to the making of literature save why it was important to men. It betrayed itself by betraying its fundamental lack of interest and faith in literature, and as a consequence it made literature so algebraic that in giving its elucidation in criticism to a Veblen caste of experts, a corps of engineers, it raised the professional prestige of criticism at the expense of every human need of literature as prophecy or history or sustenance. Albert Einstein once returned a Kafka novel to Thomas Mann with the protest: "I couldn't read it; the human mind isn't that complex." Reading Ransom on form, or Empson on the seven types of ambiguity, or Kenneth Burke on the strategies of poetic form, that protest raised a still small voice of compassion for their presumption and contempt for their ignorance: *the human mind isn't that complex*. Only difficulty was complex, and the self-fascinated puzzles, and the work sheets of scientists, and the baffled aridity of poets without poetry and critics without literature. "The poem is a bird that threatens to escape the net of analysis," Mark Van Doren wrote of these critics; "so the net grows wider, and tougher with inwoven semantic threads." And in the end the critic was caught in the net himself, threshing and probing, reduced to counting the strands; and so had his happiness.

Yes, criticism had become a science at last, as all the critics had become engineers. Yet how strange that for all their expertness they were idle, and busiest when measuring each other! Criticism had become a science, but while the science flourished literature gasped for breath. As criticism was withdrawn into smaller and smaller pockets of the human mind—withdrawn, one dared to think, by smaller and smaller minds—it became so purely professional a game among the cognoscenti that a general apathy settled over it. The traditional indifference to criticism in America was no longer a feeble complaint by critics against Philistia; it had become a leading phenomenon among critics themselves. Nothing now so distinguished criticism as the distaste for it, the weariness and contempt; whatever its supposed need, the critics seemed happiest when they deserted it. It had become even unfashionable, as the work of Bernard De Voto testified, to refer to oneself as a critic at all. If criticism was not science, De Voto thought, it was nothing; whereupon it became nothing. What remained, as De Voto said so positively, was literary journalism, with no nonsense of *any* kind about it. The journalists and the engineers would divide the field between them; and the critics were only too happy to leave it to them. The criticism that had been launched with so many quaking hopes and ardors in the early thirties had finally disposed of itself in disposing of its illusions. A planet locked in war had no room for it; the critics, it seemed, were only bored with it.

8

Only a few were not. Despite the pretense and impotence of criticism, despite the atmosphere in which so gifted and sensitive a student of poetry as Mark Van Doren publicly proclaimed his disgust with contemporary criticism and said farewell to it, a tiny handful of writers—Edmund Wilson, Stark Young, Morton Dauwen Zabel, Louise Bogan, Lionel Trilling; younger writers like Harry Levin and Philip

Rahv and Delmore Schwartz—continued to believe in criticism and to practice it—between times. Criticism could now be practiced only between times. It had become a luxury trade, so many minds being dedicated to more imperative considerations; a delicate luxury for the inquiring mind, a prodigality that needed a certain illusion and pride to sustain it; and it lived by smuggling. Yet nothing proved how much criticism was still wanted as the warmth and gratitude with which Lionel Trilling's brilliant study of Matthew Arnold was greeted, or the hunger for critical leadership, for active insight and stature and vision, which so often fastened upon Edmund Wilson because there were so few others like him. In these writers criticism lived as securely as it had ever lived in America, but it lived underground; it lived by fits and starts; and, as one saw particularly in many young critics, it paid a subtle price in generosity and breadth of insight. Their reviews and notes were often extraordinary in perception, but there was a tightness, a sullen wisdom, about them that told how far the diminution of critical energy had gone.

It was the relative freedom from this special tension, as much as his abundant and moving talent, that gave Edmund Wilson so unique a place in contemporary writing. At a time when so many writers had either wearied of criticism or corrupted it, a time when the very exercise of criticism seemed peculiarly futile and isolated, Wilson continued to write criticism as a great human discipline, a study of literature in its relation to civilization that sacrificed nothing to closeness of observation, yet kept its sights trained on the whole human situation. This, in a sense, was peculiarly the effect of his criticism rather than its intention; for in an age of analysis Wilson stood out as a great elucidator, the expert reader whose ability to tell what a book was about, as Morton Dauwen Zabel said, remained his great distinction, the mark of his distinction among living students of literature. It was always as a reader of fascinating resourcefulness, a reader in whom the best qualities and leading doctrines of a naturalistic age had converged to throw every possible light on the book under examination, that Wilson excelled. A tougher and more adventurous mind than Van Wyck Brooks, he had none of Brooks's primary moral force, the spiritual conviction that had been so indispensable to the modern movement in America. In Sainte-Beuve's phrase, Wilson was rather a "naturalist of souls," a critic in whom judiciousness and sympathy became illumination, the kind of critic who can exploit every auxiliary field of knowledge and become the partisan of none. As a critic, therefore, he became associated with no particular doctrine, canon of taste, or normative zeal. His was the fluid, catholic, supple mind that gives itself to criticism as observation and causerie, the criticism that was the gift of the great market-place critics of genius, like Brandes and Sainte-Beuve, rather than the moral intensity of a Hazlitt or the supreme historical vision of a Francesco de Sanctis. Quiet in tone, pragmatic and skeptical, marvelous in the apprehension of a book, a career, a contemporary pattern, it was a criticism that passed easily from one incidental conquest to another.

Wilson called himself a historical critic in the tradition that stems vaguely from Vico and Herder through Taine and Marx, but his distinction was hardly a distinction of doctrine and method. What gave him his place of honor, rather, was the fact that he seemed to embody so much of the sanity lacking in other contemporary critics. F. Scott Fitzgerald once called Wilson his intellectual conscience; but Wilson was, even more, the conscience of two intellectual generations. A modernist and a scholar, he was the best example of the richness and exactitude that criticism in America had always missed in its modernist critics. In an age of fanaticisms and special skills, he stood out as the quiet arbiter, the private reader of patience and wisdom whose very skill gave him a public importance. In an age of avant-garde scholarship, of febrile enthusiasms, of inadequacies that were posed as assets and ignorance that passed for taste, he remained the adventurous critic who brought Proust and Joyce to a wide audience, but found lessons of the spirit for absolutists in Sophocles' *Philoctetes;* unraveled *Finnegans Wake* with great skill and excessive reverence, but discussed A. E. Housman's classical scholarship in a way that threw new light on a tragic personality. He worked in the foreground of contemporary literature, with Gertrude Stein and Rimbaud, Shaw and Yeats, Steinbeck and O'Hara; but he was the translator of Pushkin, the student of Marxism who had gone back to Vico and Michelet and had read Marx on

Democritus, the guide through Axel's castle and the portraitist of Dickens, the reporter of the depression scene in America and the historian of Symbolism. By the catholicity of his interests, the freshness and directness of his performance, he seemed more than any other critic in America the experimentalist who worked with the whole tradition of literature in his bones.

It was this sense of balance, of resourcefulness and quiet strength, that gave Wilson his place. Not a critical leader but a superlative interpreter, a mediator rather than a great teacher, he gave new emphasis to the inquiring mind, the exemplary modern student's mind that had passed through every movement and fashion in the twenties and thirties and become the victim of none. He was above all the spectator, the bookman of active humility and detachment, the kind of mind, as he once wrote in an autobiographical sketch, that seeks not to acquire but "quietly to understand." It was this distaste for the acquisitive spirit, with its emphasis on inquiry and detachment, that gave Wilson's Socialism so humanist and meditative a character, and his book on Marxism, *To the Finland Station,* so rich and sensitive an appreciation of the primary moral urge behind Marx's apocalyptic vision. For Wilson's personal background was not, like that of so many writers in his generation, a vague and treacherous preparation for life in a capitalist society; it was, rather like Edith Wharton's or Robert Herrick's, deeply anticapitalist, with a distaste for the values and exhibitions of an acquisitive society that went back to a family tradition of scholarship and cultivation, of gentlemen's politics and community. In the thirties particularly, Wilson was a spiritual anachronism, a writer whose reaching for Socialism was rather like the yearning for a new spiritual order which so many writers of the early 1900's had made familiar—a reaching not frantic or explicitly political, but based upon a deeply ingrown alienation from the culture and prizes of capitalism; a reaching that was as Arnoldian as Robert Herrick's, and as quick to turn to literature as a record of society and a criticism of life.

Without Herrick's mysticism or Mrs. Wharton's cold scorn, Wilson became, like them, a spectator in the social sense, a spectator between two worlds. It was for this reason that one always saw the density of the past in his work, the underground sense of history and curiously aloof sympathy with the present. As a leading figure in the Heming-way-Dos Passos-Fitzgerald generation, he seemed to be at the center of the modern scene, yet seeking only to inquire into it. His student's mind was something more than an aptitude and a gift of balance; it was the exercise of his sense of history, the very groundwork, as it were, of that open-mindedness and elegiac resignation which gave his best essays, like the study of Proust in *Axel's Castle,* of Housman in *The Triple Thinkers,* of Dickens and Kipling in *The Wound and the Bow,* of Michelet and Marx in *To the Finland Station,* so extraordinary an effect of sympathy with the great outsiders, the spiritual aliens, in art and thought. And it was always this heightened personal conscious-ness, the response to a personal design in every writer he touched, that made Wilson so supremely the modern student of literary origins. In every subject he saw a career, a personal leit-motif, some primary ten-sion. This appeared most explicitly in *The Wound and the Bow,* where the study of writers so diverse as Dickens and Joyce, Casanova and Kipling, Mrs. Wharton and Hemingway, revolved around some child-hood wound in each writer which led him to become the writer he was. Yet this curiosity as a "naturalist of souls" was dominant in everything he wrote, and it gave a new freshness to intellectual history in *To the Finland Station,* where Vico and Michelet, Marx and Lenin, arose like living men from under the coffers of their doctrines to re-mind the world of the ardors and accidents, the personal exultations and defeats, that had gone to fashion belief in a new human society.

In another critic, needless to say, this curiosity would have become only biography; but nothing so distinguished Wilson as the subtlety with which he saw the career in the work and turned the career as a new point of illumination upon the work. Above everything else, he was always the observing reader, the vibrant critical intelligence in whom everything joined toward dispassionate understanding. His great gift always was an ability to get into the body of the work discussed, and his capacity for exposition was such that as he presented it the mere summary of a novel seemed to draw light at every point. Unlike most critics, he seemed even to be taking the part of the reader rather than talking at him; thinking with the reader's mind and even, on occasion, at the reader's pace; and this humility and absorption in the work

helped to persuade as much as his evidence did. In the end the utter
lack of aggressiveness created his triumph, for it was a critical exposition so homely and studious, so full of Gallic lightness and ease and
thrust, that it was as far removed from impressionism as it was from
formal analysis. It was a criticism in the best tradition of causerie, the
open mind luminously at work everywhere; a criticism that sought
not to be esthetic criticism or social criticism per se (that fatal either/or
in modern criticism), but a felicitous blending of the two in the interest of the fullest possible understanding of the work as a fact *in*
civilization, a repository rather than a symbol. Seen in these terms,
the civilization was something more than a "background," the work
under consideration something less and something more than an object
to be discussed for its own sake. The value was apprehended, the
civilization gave it meaning; the book lived in the mind, yet perhaps
only because every association in society and circumstance and intellectual history had been used to understand it.

What one missed in this criticism, of course, was a positive affirmation, the intensity of a great conception. It was an immensely satisfying criticism, a criticism of inquiry and elucidation and clarity; but
the nobility in it was incidental, and the wisdom, as it were, was always
a little incidental too. More than any other American writer of his
time, Wilson gave meaning to the service of criticism and the honor
of integrity and taste. But he excelled by preserving an example in a
bad time, by illuminating the margin of greatness that keeps the spirit
alive. The great liberators hovered for a moment in his interpretation,
but he was no companion to them. An exemplary modern student always, the best expression of contemporary skill and aspiration, he was
still poles removed from what Yeats had meant when he wrote that
"Belief makes the mind abundant." Ernest Renan had said it for all
time: *"La paix n'habite que les hauteurs. C'est en montant, montant
toujours, que la lutte devient harmonie, et que l'apparente incohérence
des efforts de l'homme aboutit à cette grande lumière, la gloire, qui est
encore, quoique l'on dise, ce que a le plus de chance de n'être pas tout
a fait une vanité."*

Yet to have come up to this point, if not to meet it, was distinction
enough. What Wilson had to give, always, stood best revealed in his

own words, as when he said in a lecture that the object of any intellectual activity is to give meaning to experience—"that is, to make life practicable; for by understanding things, we make it easier to survive and get around them." This, as he said, was the great achievement of the historical interpretation of literature; it was certainly his special triumph. In his beautiful essay on Housman, he reflected upon the type of genius that went into *A Shropshire Lad,* and thought of the university monastic minds—Housman and Lewis Carroll, Thomas Gray and FitzGerald and Pater—whose "works are among the jewels of English literature rather than among its great springs of life." *The great springs of life.* Few other critics of the time could turn the mind to them; in no other critic was a fundamental remoteness from them something to be missed.

Chapter 15

THE RHETORIC AND
THE AGONY

"The terror of which I write is not of Germany, but of the soul."
—EDGAR ALLAN POE

ON THE surface much of the prose literature of the thirties was an attempt to study and to meet the crisis on a literal plane of social realism. But there were great secret depths in it, depths of individual terror and sensibility; and in those depths strange new sea-monsters lived.

When William Faulkner published a first novel in 1926 entitled *Soldiers' Pay,* no one could possibly have known that the ghost of the Gothic novel had appeared to record a new and portentously macabre view of contemporary dissolution. Cheerfully slapdash in its structure and rather poignantly overwritten, *Soldiers' Pay* was no more than what it appeared to be—a weary epilogue of the peace to the already familiar lost-generation autobiography of the war; a turgid and roughly composed story of postwar disillusionment by a Southern gentleman who had an obvious taste for romantic rhetoric and plainly betrayed a neatly inverted romantic view of life. What distinguished it from almost all the other lost-generation novels, however, was the extraordinary verbal resources which its author exhibited with such pretentious and melancholy defiance. It was the work of a poet who was not sure that he wanted to write poetry and of a novelist whose use of the novel was at once irritably contemptuous and frantically bold. Yet the confused and opaque bitterness of the book also hinted mysteriously at a disillusionment that was somehow more elusive and profound than the fashionable arbitrary disgust with war standards and a war world. *Soldiers' Pay* was the work of a writer who was so regional that he was almost parochial; and he had tasted the ultimate bitterness of the war at home, in that South which was forever after to provide him with an image of existence and a concept of tragedy.

Unlike his international-minded contemporaries—Hemingway, Cummings, Dos Passos—Faulkner was the creature of a tradition and completely, if restively, submissive to it. Born into a distinguished Mississippi family that had once played an important role in state politics, he had lived in Oxford—the seat of the state university—from early childhood, been educated at the university, and had returned to the town (the "Jefferson" of his future sagas) after his experiences in the Canadian and British Air Forces. He had worked in a bookstore in New York and written descriptive sketches for newspapers while living with Sherwood Anderson in New Orleans; but his life was in Oxford, where he wrote pastoral verse, recovered from a war wound, and worked at odd jobs as a carpenter, a roof-painter, and a postmaster at the university. He was a Southerner, but hardly a Southern university intellectual, and his associations and interests were not overtly esthetic. He might write novels, like his great-grandfather, Colonel William Falkner, author of the popular romance *The White Rose of Memphis;* he even published a book of his pastoral verse in 1924 and sold most of the copies to a local bookstore at ten cents each; but he was not a Writer in the sense that Hemingway, Cummings, Fitzgerald, Dos Passos, and so many writers of his generation were.

Superficially and publicly Faulkner did not, in those early days, appear to be consciously "literary." He liked to write, as he liked to drink beer with the boys after an afternoon painting roofs; but he wrote too fluently to think too much about it, and he practiced his writing with the same apparent fatalism with which he worked at hard-laboring jobs and was soon, when *Sanctuary* had been rejected by the New York publishers, to support himself by shoveling coal in a power plant. He was an impoverished Southern gentleman who had run away to war as a boy, been wounded and matured in it, and had returned to seek his place in the only tradition he had ever known. The bitterness of being a Sartoris (the Southern aristocrat *manqué*) in a Snopes world (the world of the small, mean traders and expropriators and ambitious poor whites) was very real, and became one of the foundations of his thought; but he could project it idly, as it seemed, only because his disenchantment was a vague and expansive moodiness. Despite the terror-stricken atmosphere that was to fill his novels, and an almost ferocious misanthropy, Faulkner was essentially a boyish mind for all his complexity, a mind humorous in the broad country fashion, and given to lazy improvisations; and a certain slyness, an indirectly comic view of life, at once racy and tormented and ambiguous, appeared in his work from the first. His sophistication was secret and violent. He had returned from the war, as Warren Beck has commented, "with an enlarged perspective which discerned the decadence of his native region while still holding to his associations with it," and this, along with the shock of his war experiences, was the source of the tension in his work which was ever after to show itself as nervous power. But his bitterness with the South was only one phase of a generally romantic and even self-complacent pessimism, and one which life in the South, enclosing him on all sides, illustrated in dramatic and fertile symbolism.

It was long ago realized that Faulkner was anything but a "Southern realist," that silly tag applicable to George W. Cable and Thomas Wolfe alike; but his relationship to the South, even his conception of that relationship in his novels, has never been understood. In any other age Faulkner would have been one of the world's great romantic novelists, as in one sense he still is. But his ability to invest his every observation of Southern life and manners with epic opulence and profligate rhetoric and Poe-like terror concealed the fact that he had no primary and design-like conception of the South, that his admiration and acceptance and disgust operated together in his mind. He was at once a fallen aristocrat and a fantasist, a quasi-philosophical critic of the South's degradation and a native son in whom its antics and institutions excited a lazily humorous disgust that was often indistinguishable from cynical acquiescence. He admired the South, loathed it, wept for it, enjoyed it, lived in it; but he could not imagine an order of experience fundamentally different from it. If he thought of it as the jungle in *Sanctuary,* it could also become the gracious manor house in *Sartoris,* the seat of the gracious feudal mind in *The Unvanquished.* If it was a neighborhood full of racy farmers and sly village yokels in *The Hamlet,* it was also the cesspool of *As I Lay Dying;* the futile, corrupt, festering village world of *Soldiers' Pay* and *The Sound and the Fury;* the maniacal traditionalism, epic in scale, of *Absalom! Absalom!.* If the South was a repository of a great frustrated tradition and charming memories, it was also—as he proved almost too well to be convincing—a symbol of all the hatred and terror in the world. In Faulkner's mind the association was instinctive and violent: life *was* the South, and what he saw and remembered or was told of it exhausted the imaginative range and depth of the human mind for him. Like a Homeric battlefield, it was not only the center of the world's stage, the polar symbol, but the very periphery of existence, that barrier of the imagination beyond which life could not be said to exist at all.

It was because he was so completely bound up in this tradition and yet hardly subject to it that Faulkner's extraordinary intensity, the superabundance of which has often seemed profligate and mechanical, was turned directly upon the South in a hot and confused fury. In one sense, of course, his love and hatred for his native region were so inextricably fused that his passion became the struggle of the will against itself, the interlocked anguish and complacence and joy with which a man may hate the earth he stands on, yet hate himself most for his enmity. But another expression of his divided will, even the suspension of will which went so far to explain his luxurious incoherence and euphuism, his need of a facile magnificence in rhetoric, was a driving and really fantastic vitality of mind, a virtuosity and ready inventiveness unsurpassed in modern American writing. As a thinker, as a participant in the communal myth of the South's tradition and decline, Faulkner was curiously dull, furiously commonplace, and often meaningless, suggesting some ambiguous irresponsibility and exasperated sullenness of mind, some distant atrophy or indifference.

Technically he soon proved himself almost inordinately subtle and ambitious, the one modern American novelist whose devotion to form has earned him a place among even the great experimentalists in modern poetry. Yet this remarkable imaginative energy, so lividly and almost painfully impressed upon all his work, did not spring from a conscious and procreative criticism of society or conduct or tradition, from some absolute knowledge; it was the expression of that psychic tension in Faulkner which Sherwood Anderson had observed when they were living together in New Orleans, and which, as his almost monstrous overwriting proves, was a psychological tic, a need to invest everything he wrote with a wild, exhilarated, and disproportionate intensity—an intensity that was brilliant and devastatingly inclusive in its energy, but seemed to come from nowhere.

The problem that faces every student of Faulkner's writing is its lack of a center, the gap between his power and its source, that curious abstract magnificence (not only a magnificence of verbal resources alone) which holds his books together, yet seems to arise from debasement or perplexity or a calculating terror. It is the gap between the deliberation of his effects, the intensity of his every conception, and the besetting and depressing looseness, the almost sick passivity, of his basic meaning and purpose. No writer, least of all a novelist so remarkably inventive and robust of imagination, works in problems of pure technique alone; and though it is possible to see in his books, as Conrad Aiken has shown, the marks of a writer devoted to elaboration and wizardry of form, who has deliberately sought to delay and obscure his readers so that the work may have a final and devastating effect, Faulkner's "persistent offering of obstacles, a calculated system of screens and obtrusions, of confusions and ambiguous interpolations and delays," seems to spring from an obscure and profligate confusion, a manifest absence of purpose, rather than from an elaborate but coherent aim.

For while Faulkner has brought back into the modern American novel a density of perception and elaboration of means unparalleled since Henry James, his passion for form has not been, like James's, the tortuous expression of an unusual and subtle point of view; it has been a register of too many points of view, and in its way a substitute for one. It is precisely because his technical energy and what must be called a tonal suggestiveness are so profound, precisely because Faulkner's rhetoric is so portentous, that it has been possible to read every point of view into his work and to prove them all. To a certain type of social or moralist critic, his work seems at once the product of some ineffable decadence and a reluctant commentary upon it. To certain sympathetic Southern readers, such as George M. O'Donnell, Faulkner has even seemed a traditional moralist, not to say a belated neo-Humanist, devoted to the "Southern social-economic-ethical tradition which [he] possesses naturally as a part of his sensibility." To many critics and graduate students (no novelist has ever been so rich in citations), he has even seemed a new and distinctive philosophical voice in the novel. For Faulkner's fluency, even his remarkable fecundity, has been such that it is almost impossible not to take his improvisations for a social philosophy, his turgidity for complexity, and even his passivity for a wise and reflective detachment. It is not strange that he has appeared to be all things to all men, and often simultaneously—a leading exponent of the cult of violence and a subtle philosophical force in the novel; a calculating terrorist and (as in *Sartoris*) a slick-magazine sentimentalist of the gladiola South; the most meticulous and misanthropic historian of the South's degeneration and a country-store humorist; an Edgar Allan Poe undecided whether to play Bret Harte or Oswald Spengler. He has been all things to himself. Like Tolstoy at Yasnaya Polyana, he has in one sense been a provincial fastening upon universality, a provincial whose roots are so deep that the very depth and intensity of his immersion have made for a submarine cosmopolitanism of the spirit. His imagination is of itself so extraordinarily rich and uncontrolled, his conscious conceptions so few and indifferent, that he has been able to create an irony of a higher order than he himself shares. For his imagination is not merely creative in the familiar sense; it is devastatingly brilliant, and at the same time impure; it is a kind of higher ventriloquism, a capriciousness at once almost too self-conscious in its trickery and inventiveness, yet not conscious enough, not even direct or responsible enough, in its scope and deliberation.

" 'I want you to tell me just one thing more,' " the young Canadian, Shreve McCannon, says to Quentin Compson in *Absalom! Absalom!*: " 'Why do you hate the South?' 'I dont hate it,' Quentin said quickly, at once, immediately; 'I dont hate it,' he said. *I dont hate it,* he thought, panting in the cold air, the iron New England dark; *I dont. I dont! I dont hate it! I dont hate it!*" By identifying all life with the South, by giving himself so completely to it, Faulkner showed why he could see all things in it and at the same time draw no clear design from it. His absorption was too complete; it was almost a form of abnegation. Accepting the South, hating it, memorializing it, losing himself in it, Faulkner was forced into a series of improvisations; and his need for pyrotechnics and a swollen Elizabethanism of rhetoric, his delight in difficulty and random inventiveness, became the expression of his need to impose some external intensity, an almost synthetic unity, upon his novels. The nerve-jangled harshness and self-conscious grandeur of his work show only one elaboration of that inner confusion, that compulsion to brood always at polar extremes. More significant has been his need to present almost all his characters at the unwavering pitch of absolute desperation and damnation, to expand everything to a size larger than life and ambiguously more tragic, to represent everything—every life, every thought, every action—as something unutterably lost and doomed.

There is a pillar of darkness that moves between the Faulkner characters and the world—blotting out the sun, blotting out our simple and confident knowledge of their qualities and relations to each other, blotting out their normality. But if this darkness is in one sense the equivalent atmosphere of Faulkner's misanthropy and bitterness, it is also a mechanism, a stage apparatus, that provides an artificial medium within which his people move, and it suggests some secret and harried compensation for his failure. For what one always feels in even Faulkner's greatest moments is not a lack or falsity of achievement; it is a power almost grotesque in its lack of relation to the situation or characters; it is a greatness moving in a void. From this point of view the mechanical damnation of his characters is not a valid projection of some conception of damnation which must include everything that draws breath in the South; it is a simple lack of flexibility, some cardinal stiffness or agony of imagination. It is significant to note that while Faulkner's ability to create character has always been superb, his characters are not so much a succession of individuals freshly, directly visualized and created, as molds into which the same fantastic qualities have been poured. They live, they live copiously and brilliantly; but they live by the violence with which Faulkner sustains them, by the sullen, screaming intensity which he breathes into them (often with all of Faulkner's own gestures, fury, and raging confusion of pronouns), by the atmospheric terror that encloses them. They live because they are incredibilities in action, because they have been scoured by death before they reach the grave, so that one sees them always in the posture of some fantastic relinquishment and irrevocable agony, the body taut and the soul quivering with death. And if they seem forever to be watching and waiting in their own stupor, to be accumulated sensations rather than people having sensations, to be even the same extreme sensations (the doctor in *The Wild Palms*, Quentin Compson and old Mr. Coldfield in *Absalom! Absalom!*, young Bayard in *The Unvanquished*, the young teacher in *The Hamlet*, Joe Christmas and almost everyone else in *Light in August*), is it not because they are personifications rather than human beings, and is not their astounding capacity for unhappiness and perdition a confession of some final awkwardness in Faulkner—his need to write and think in monotones?

Nervously alive, his characters are fundamentally not alive at all, not acting out individual parts, but seem rather to be pure fantastic aggregates. They are multiform qualities acting out, participating in, that general myth of Faulkner's creation, the jungle South, and it is significant that the darkness in which they live, the darkness through which they must always be grasped and pieced together, makes them appear curiously distant, refractions of refractions. In the end we seem always to be reading the same story, following through the familiar formula of damnation, conscious of the same mysterious submission— extraordinarily abject—to perdition. Yet though the energy that drives them along is torrential, we do not see *them* intensely; we see everything under *conditions* of intensity. It is precisely because Faulkner's characters are charged with a vitality not their own that he is able to do everything with them except make us believe instinctively and absolutely in them. And it is precisely because Faulkner does not know too much about them himself, does not believe in them with sufficient consciousness of purpose, that he is forced into those leaping improvisations of language and incident, that nervous magnificence, which invests everything with epic grandeur that is suspiciously grandiose, that plots and strains and leaves us all too often with the mere fact of tumultuous exaggeration.

"It is with fiction as with religion," Herman Melville wrote in *The Confidence Man;* "it should present another world, and yet one to which we feel the tie." Even at its best, as in the portrait of old Mr. Coldfield in *Absalom! Absalom!,* Faulkner's extraordinary nervous achievement seems rooted in something purely arbitrary, not to say synthetic. Old Mr. Coldfield had barricaded himself *against* the Civil War, had locked himself up and stolidly starved to death because he disapproved of the idea of waste—"of wearing out and eating up and shooting away material in any cause whatsoever." The scene, the image created, is magnificently original, but it is grotesque. Faulkner carries it off with his usual high exhilarated energy, but while it is "convincing" on its own terms, it is an improvisation of pure fantasy and basically unreal. So with the lyrical record of the love of the idiot Snopes in *The Hamlet* for his neighbor's cow. The long dithyramb is clever mimicry and wry, gleeful sentimentality, an idealization that is mostly parody; yet though the mood is sustained almost too well, it is a caricature that mocks itself, a tour de force so calculating that it is corrupt. So with the extraordinary last scene in *The Sound and the Fury,* Faulkner's greatest achievement; the famous—and more than a little cheap—coffin scene in *As I Lay Dying,* the whole scheme of *Sanctuary* (admittedly a deliberate shocker), the flight of the Negro slaves in *The Unvanquished* when the Confederate armies are broken, the flood scene in *The Wild Palms.* There is always in Faulkner some final obsessive exaggeration, some half-careless, half-cynical grotesquerie, that spoils. And even when he opens upon a scene of complete sincerity and power, as in *Light in August,* with its unforgettable image of Lena Grove, pregnant, walking from Alabama to Mississippi, shoes in her hand, looking for her lover, everything is soon engulfed in boiling rhetoric and the impossible plot. Yet though Faulkner's over-writing is usually a striving for total effect, for a kind of over-all intensity that springs from the abundance and confusion of his extraordinary resources, he can caricature his best efforts by some unwilling inflection, as in the scene in *The Hamlet* (admittedly a scene of high comedy) where Mrs. Varner, vexed with her errant daughter and puritanical son, rages: "I'll fix him. I'll fix both of them. Turning up pregnant and yelling and cursing here in the house when I am trying to take a nap!" Not always unwillingly, of course; the fantastic duel between Charles and Henry in *Absalom! Absalom!* at the most critical juncture of the Civil War (love conquers all!), like so much else in Faulkner, suggests an element of protruding bad taste, often mere carelessness or indifference extending itself into vulgarity. And it suggests what almost every reader of Faulkner must feel at one time or another, his inability to choose between Dostoevsky and Hollywood Boulevard.

In the end one must always return to Faulkner's language and his conception of style, for his every character and observation are lost in the spool of his rhetoric, and no more than they can he ever wind himself free. That rhetoric—perhaps the most elaborate, intermittently incoherent and ungrammatical, thunderous, polyphonic rhetoric in all American writing—explains why he always plays as great a role in his novels as any of his characters to the point of acting out their characters in himself; why he has so often appeared to be a Laocoön writhing in all the outrageous confusions of the ineffable; why he has been able, correlating the South with every imagined principle and criticism of existence, writing in many styles, to project every possible point of view, every shade or extremity of character, and to persuade us of none. In one sense, of course, Faulkner has sought to express the inexpressible, to attain that which is basically incoherent in the novel and analogous only to the most intense mysticism in poetry, where sensations contract and expand like tropical flowers. Yet his novels are not poetry or even "poetic"; they are linked together by a sensational lyricism, itself forever in extremis and gasping for breath, that, as Yeats said of rhetoric, "is an attempt of the will to do the work of the imagination." For what one sees always in Faulkner's mountainous rhetoric, with its fantastic pseudo-classical epithets and invertebrate grandeur, its merely verbal intensity and inherent motor violence, is the effort of a writer to impose himself upon that which he cannot create simply and evocatingly. It is the articulation of confusion rather than an evasion of it; force passing for directed energy. With all its occasional felicity and stabbing appropriateness of phrase, Faulkner's style is a discursive fog, and it is not strange—so clever and ready is his style the advantage taken over confusion itself—that his extremities should seem intimations of grandeur and the darkness within which his characters move an atmosphere of genuine tragedy.

"By April," we read of the idiot Snopes's infatuation with the cow in *The Hamlet,* "it was the actual thin depthless suspension of false dawn itself, in which he could already see and know himself to be an entity solid and cohered in visibility instead of the uncohered all-sentience of fluid and nerve-springing terror alone and terribly free in the primal sightless inimicality." Or Varner's trip to Ab Snopes's farm:

> When he passed beyond the house he saw it—the narrow high frame like an epicene gallows, two big absolutely static young women beside it, who even in that first glance postulated that immobile dreamy solidarity of statuary (this only emphasised by the fact that they both seemed to be talking at once and to some listener—or perhaps just circumambience—at a considerable distance and neither listening to the other at all) even though one of them had hold of the well-rope, her arms extended at full reach, her body bent for the down pull like a figure in a charade, a carved piece symbolising some terrific physical effort which had died with its inception, though a moment later the pulley began again its rusty plaint.

The point made, the evocation sought, have passed into endless convoluted variations; and even the incredibility of the scene (who was it saw "that immobile dreamy solidarity of statuary"—a mean backwoods trader like Jody Varner?) seems less fantastic than the mechanical elaboration of the image. Faulkner's perpetual need for some verbal splendor, a merely illustrative richness, always suggests some self-fascinated energy, not the moving intensity of a writer who throws the weight of his body into each word; and it is not strange that his most magnificent effects should so often seem pointless. So in *The Sound and the Fury* Quentin Compson ruminates on a classmate sculling on the Charles River alone:

> Gerald would be sort of grand too, pulling in lonely state across the noon, rowing himself right out of noon, up the long bright air like an apotheosis, mounting into a drowsing infinity where only he and the gull, the one terrifically motionless, the other in a steady and measured pull and recover that partook of inertia itself, the world punily beneath their shadows on the sun.

Jody Varner, taking his sister Eula to school, "had a vision of himself transporting not only across the village's horizon but across the embracing proscenium of the entire inhabited world like the sun itself, a kaleidoscopic convolution of mammalian ellipses." Or Faulkner will begin with one of those perfect and tangential perceptions that light up his books, that perfect talent for incidental perception, and crush it to death, as when Flem Snopes's metallic bow-tie becomes

> a tiny viciously depthless cryptically balanced splash like an enigmatic punctuation symbol against the expanse of white shirt which gave him Jody Varner's look of ceremonial heterodoxy raised to its tenth power and which postulated to those who had been present on that day that quality of outrageous overstatement of physical displacement which the sound of his father's stiff foot made on the gallery of the store that afternoon in the spring.

Yet why must everything in Faulkner's novels be raised to its tenth power? Why must the idiot Snopes's love agony become "starspawn and hieroglyph, the fierce white dying rose, then gradual and invincible speeding up to and into slack-flood's coronal of nympholept noon"? Why must Rosa Coldfield's hatred of men become "that fond dear constant violation of privacy, that stultification of the burgeoning and incorrigible I which is the meed and due of all mammalian meat, become not mistress, not beloved, but more than even love. I became all polymath love's androgynous advocate"? Why is it that the Faulkner country must always appear as "a shadowy miasmic region," "amoral evil's undeviating absolute," a "quicksand of nightmare," "the seething and anonymous miasmal mass which in all the years of time has taught itself no boon of death"? For the same reason, as it must appear, that despite his extraordinary talents no writer has ever seemed so ambitious and so purposeless, so overwhelming in imaginative energy and so thwarted in his application of it. A fanatic, as Santayana once said, is a man who redoubles his effort when he has lost sight of his aim; and even if it be admitted that Faulkner's effort has been to express the inexpressible, to write the history of the unconscious, to convey some final and terrifying conception of a South that seems always to exist below water, the impression one always carries away from his novels is of some fantastic exertion of will, of that exaggeration which springs from a need to raise everything in Yoknapatawpha County, Mississippi, to its tenth (or its hundredth) power because there is not sufficient belief, or power, or ease in his conception of Yoknapatawpha County, or the South, or human existence in general.

It is not strange, then, that his scene should always be some swamp of the spirit, or that his subject should always be murder, rape, prostitution, incest, arson, idiocy (with an occasional interpolation of broad country humor almost as violent as his tragedies); or that the country of his mind should be a Mississippi county larger than life, but not visibly related to it. Faulkner's obsession has been agony, as his art has been the voice of that agony—the agony of a culture, his culture; but it has been even more the agony of his relation to that culture, the tormenting disproportion between his immersion in the South and his flinging, tumultuous efforts to project it. It has been the agony inherent in any effort to transcend some basic confusion by force of will alone. Faulkner's corn-fed, tobacco-drooling phantoms are not the constituents of a representative American epic, protagonists in a great modern tragedy; they are the tonal expression of Faulkner's own torment, the walking phantasmagoria, sensation beating against sensation, of his perpetual tension. No writer ever made so much of his failure; in no writer of his stature is the suggestion of some cardinal failure so ambiguous and yet so penetrating.

2

From another point of view, however, Faulkner's example has a significant historic interest. He represents, as almost everyone has felt, the perpetuation of a seemingly inveterate Southern romanticism, the tradition of the weird tale and the grotesque, the florid Southern chevalier defying the heavens by sheer force of rhetoric; but he stands also as a forerunner, and along with Thomas Wolfe and a writer like Henry Miller, as a prime example of a new school of sensibility in the contemporary American novel. Few writers, certainly, have ever exploited so many of the devices of naturalism and remained so basically different in kind from naturalism; and it is curious but significant that Faulkner, one of the patron saints of the cult of violence, a writer who has presented younger novelists with a veritable patrimony of brutality and calculated terrorism and the technique of shock, should actually represent a rejection of naturalism—even of the conventional scheme of realism—that is as marked in contemporary American writing as the passionate social consciousness and materialism of so many left-wing and hard-boiled novelists.

For the violence of Faulkner's novels is, at bottom, not the violent expression of a criticism of society, but the struggles of a sensibility at war with itself, just as the emotionalism of Thomas Wolfe's novels suggests the efforts of a sensibility to comprehend itself, and Henry Miller's the sense of outrage inflicted by society upon the individual soul. The frantic ubiquitous "I" in their books, its manifold agony and susceptibility to rhetoric, marks something more than the explicit rejection of the characteristic mechanisms of realism found in the formalism and preciosity of distinguished craftsmen like Elizabeth Madox Roberts, Kay Boyle, and Katherine Anne Porter. It marks the rise of a school of agony, of romantic sensibility, that is perhaps unconscious in its negation of realism. This "school" is not in any sense a school at all; it does not even stem from a common tradition, save as Henry Miller has acknowledged his debt to Whitman, and Wolfe continually betrayed his; save as Faulkner insistently recalls a whole gallery of American romanticists from Poe through Melville to Ambrose Bierce. Few writers have ever seemed so different in intelligence, or clashed so irreconcilably on so many vital points; yet for all their presumable lack even of common sympathy, Faulkner and Wolfe particularly represent a tormented individualism in the contemporary novel, a self-centered romanticism, a vitality expressing itself in and through rhetoric, that is one of the most significant phenomena in the moral history of contemporary literature.

Different as Wolfe and Faulkner are, the common note one hears in them is one of pure terror. They represent, like the surrealists, like the anxious and moving search for spiritual integrity in so much contemporary poetry, the loneliness of the individual sensibility in a period of unparalleled dissolution and insecurity; and they represent even more vividly a reaction against a literature of surface realism that merely records the facts of that dissolution. Like Melville's Captain Ahab, they could both say, "that inscrutable thing is chiefly what I hate," for their violence is the expression of their obsession with the evil that lurks under the surface of contemporary society and thought. In that sense they may be said to represent the subterranean life of the spirit in a society too pressed to preserve, much less to foster, an extreme type of sensibility. Yet what so many have felt even in so cultist and avant-garde a writer as Henry Miller, his essential commonness of spirit—"a naturally genial American," as Philip Rahv said, "who has been through hell"—is in a sense true of Faulkner, for all of his technical virtuosity, and of Wolfe, an ego-centered boy. All these writers seem remote from average men only because of the intensity of their self-exploration; but it is just their capacity for expressing all the fever and exacerbation and gnawing humiliation of average men today that identifies them. They are not great religious spirits or mystics or poets, examples of the inviolate private intelligence that fashions an arbitrary and purely individual conception of existence and compels others to believe in it. Nor are they—not even Faulkner, for all his legerdemain—technicians of the novel, great craftsmen who attempt to mold the novel into a new form of inquiry. They are materialists flying in the face of contemporary materialism; and it is always the agony of common life—the commonness raised "to the tenth power"—that identifies and torments them, for their sensibility is the expression of their reaction against the indignity and violation suffered by men like them. Like D. H. Lawrence, they could say, and with equal ardor: "The only thing unbearable is the degradation, the prostitution of the living mysteries in us. Let man only approach his own self with a deep respect, even reverence for all that the creative soul, the 'God-mystery' within us, puts forth." But it is of degradation, not of the God-mystery, that they speak. There is no religion in these writers; there is only the religious intensity brought to the understanding of men's alienation from each other today.

It is their rhetoric, a mountainous verbal splendor, that holds these writers together; and it is a very American rhetoric. Just as Trollope said of Hawthorne's weird tales that he believed them to be not manufactured in the Gothic tradition, "but something indigenous, something inescapably there," so it is impossible not to feel in Faulkner and Wolfe and Miller an indiscriminate vitality, a pride in their fresh and overflowing power, that goes back to Whitman, to Melville, to the creators of the great mass-myths of Davy Crockett and Paul Bunyan, Johnny Appleseed and Mike Fink. In Faulkner and Wolfe the extravagant and ornamental tradition of Southern rhetoric is manifest, but like Henry Miller (and is there anything more American than the picture of this last and most violent of the expatriates, hating America and all its deeds in torrential profanity, yet worshiping Whitman in the slums of Paris?), they are all big men in the colloquial tradition of American demigods—living big, writing big, exuding a power somehow more than their own, a national power in which they share. Colossal even in their extreme neuroticism, they retain all the epic force that went into the making of the great legends of American power and the American promise. Just so did Wolfe burn himself out trying to bring all the rivers, sights, sounds, pleasures, torments, books in America within the compass of the one long novel he wrote all his life. Just so did he express his final contempt, in *You Can't Go Home Again,* for "the world's fool-bigotry, fool-ignorance, fool-cowardice, fool-faddism, fool-mockery, fool-stylism, and fool-hatred for anyone who was not corrupted, beaten, and a fool." Just so has Faulkner invested his every observation of Southern life and manners with epic grandeur, epic hints and portents, Aeschylean darkness and primeval rage. Just so has Henry Miller seen in the contemporary crisis the intimations of an absolute doom, a world dying in pandemonium, "the earth moving out of its orbit," and written with significant exhilaration, in *Tropic of Cancer,* that

THE RHETORIC AND THE AGONY   469

> Art consists in going the full length * * * The task which the artist implicitly sets himself is to overthrow existing values, to make of the chaos about him an order which is his own, to sow strife and ferment so that by the emotional release those who are dead may be restored to life.

The significance of these writers thus lies in the subject of their energy. They are the epic recorders of demoralization and collapse, specialists in doom, as Whitman was the first great voice of American nationality, or Mark Twain of the frontier legends, or Melville of the exuberant myth-making prowess of the imaginative mind in America. In *Tropic of Cancer* Henry Miller wrote:

> It may be that we are doomed, that there is no hope for us, *any of us;* but if that is so then let us set up a last agonizing, blood-curdling howl, a screech of defiance, a war-whoop! Away with lamentations! Away with elegies and dirges! Away with biographies and histories, and libraries and museums! Let the dead bury the dead. Let us living ones dance about the rim of the crater, a last expiring dance. But a dance!

Miller's extremism, however, gives itself away by the sheer exhilaration of his own energy, just as Faulkner's monotonal despair has always seemed the ironic negation of his extraordinary imaginative vitality, and Wolfe's herculean boyishness always the expression of some uncontrolled power expending itself on every object in view. There is a native strength in all these writers, a comic exaggeration, that always makes a theme of its own prodigality. And it is precisely because their resources are so overwhelming and so uncontrolled, precisely because their vitality is tumultuous and self-fascinated and desperate, that they embody a perpetual *mal du siècle,* a furious sickness and rage. It is as if the long and deep estrangement of the modern American writer from his society—the inveterate air of crisis which he bears within it— had reached a climax, found some extreme symbol in them. Seeing their unhappiness, or the unhappiness of their relations with the world, in gargantuan terms, they have made epics and historical chronicles and quasi-philosophical systems out of that conflict; but the theme has always been the individual, their own individualism, and their strength the intensity—majestic and all-inclusive in its rhetoric—possible only to a type of sensibility that hears the reverberations of the world's collapse in the fever ecstasies and desperations of its own isolation. That isolation, expressing itself in many different forms and rhythms and themes, is the central thing in Faulkner, and it tells the story, directly and lividly, of Thomas Wolfe.

3

At twenty-two, when he was studying dramaturgy under Professor Baker at Harvard, Wolfe wrote to his mother:

> I know this now: I am inevitable, I sincerely believe. The only thing that can stop me now is insanity, disease, or death. . . . [Life] is not all bad, but it is not all good; it is not all ugly, but it is not all beautiful; it is life, life, life—the only thing that matters. It is savage, cruel, kind, noble, passionate, generous, stupid, ugly, beautiful, painful, joyous—it is all these and more—and it's all these I want to know, and BY GOD I shall, though they crucify me for it. I will go to the end of the earth to find it, to understand it. I will know this country when I am through as I know the palm of my hand, and I will put it on paper and make it true and beautiful.

When he died in September, 1938, not yet thirty-eight, he was what the world calls a leading novelist; but no one would have called him a prodigy. There have been writers, like the twenty-five-year-old Keats whose last letters are moving in their very profundity, who compressed all maturity into their boyhood, and even transcended it. Wolfe was always a boy, a very remarkable boy; and his significance as a writer is that he expanded his boyhood into a lifetime, made it exciting and important, even illuminated many of the problems that give life its common savor, without ever transcending the alienation and pain of his boyhood. "All this hideous doubt, despair, and dark confusion of the soul a lonely man must know, for he is united to no image save that which he creates himself," he wrote in "God's Lonely Man," a frankly autobiographical essay which he composed and recomposed many times; "he is bolstered by no other knowledge save that which he can gather for himself with the vision of his own eyes and brain."

This feverish dependence upon himself, a fantastically uninhibited innocence, was his torment and his advantage. Naïve, self-absorbed, full of homespun mysticism and adolescent grandeur, he cut his way blindly and noisily to achievement; by his passionate insistence on the importance of self, that self is the very center of existence, he gave his fever and uncertainty a remarkable scope and something more than the dignity of the conventionally mature understanding. Believing in nothing but his own power, he infected the world of his novels with it. He made his characters larger than life without suggesting that they were superior to, or removed from, it. He lived in a world in which man was forever haunted by his own promise and deflected from it. Inevitably, there were no half-tones in that world, as there were few gradations and nuances in Wolfe's own mind; man lived by compromises with fate, or conquered (as perhaps only the artist spirit could conquer) by a supreme contempt for it. Believing so completely in the possibility of happiness, he gave human ambition, human valor, human expression, a rooted strength in nature, the quality of primeval fact.

"I believe that we are lost here in America, but I believe we shall be found," Wolfe wrote in his last letter to "Foxhall Edwards" in *You Can't Go Home Again*. ". . . I think that the true discovery of America is before us. I think the true fulfillment of our spirit, of our people, of our mighty and immortal land, is yet to come." Seemingly, then, it was not only life as an idea, but life as victory, that possessed him; the very callowness of his more expansive flights persuades one of that. In a world of endless possibilities and limitless power—that is, a world seen refracted through such a mind as Wolfe's—every object, properly understood, possessed an incredible radiance, and every function had its heroic purpose. He wrote one book all his life, as all the volumes he produced were chapters in it; and his hero—now Eugene Gant, now George Webber, now Orestes, now Faust, now Telemachus in search of the father and Proteus in the sea world of the city, now Jason on the eternal voyage and Antaeus back to earth, now Kronos dreaming of time and Faust gazing at Helen—was able to bestride cities, to hear in every love urge the detonations of "fate," to feel every twinge as a blow, every yawn as a snicker, to hear as from his own heart the music of multitudes, to read a hundred books and guess at the contents of a thousand, to eat like a regiment, to bellow at the universe and hear it whimper submissively back.

That persistent yearning, that ambiguous universal victory, is Wolfe's most palpable memorial, the testimony he gave to the world in a raging torrent of words, the thing he wished most to believe true of himself. And it was, in a sense, the real Wolfe, as every facet of his mind and impulse of his tumultuous consciousness represented the "real" Wolfe. Yet it is impossible to appreciate his achievement, as it is impossible to understand what constituted his literary mind and character, if one misses the extraordinary deliberateness of his total conception, and the self-consciousness (in the best sense a self-understanding) of his life and purpose. For to an extent that seems almost unreal Wolfe did embody the conflict between the modern individual and society; he even found his central theme in that conflict, where so many different and certainly more interesting talents have merely moved in its atmosphere. The feverishness and wayward exultation of his novels mark only one aspect of that conflict, for he had a keen, if seemingly eccentric, social intelligence, an insight into the pattern of events and societies seemingly beyond him, that became part of his subject as much as his rhetoric supported it. He was not a novelist *of* society; he was a refraction of everything in society that he saw in some vital relation to his own individuality. Yet his native innocence and romantic self-trust were such that his mimicry (much of Wolfe's "objective" realism is strained, if powerfully successful, mimicry) attained the level of satire and a sweeping symbolic tragedy. "His aim," as John Peale Bishop has written, "was to set down America as far as it can belong to the experience of one man." In no other writer in America after Whitman could that aim have been realized; in no other, not even Whitman, was the sense of that need so apparently voracious and insistent.

Describing "Eugene Gant" at twelve, Wolfe wrote in *Look Homeward, Angel*: "He had learned by now to project himself mechanically before the world, an acceptable counterfeit of himself which would protect him from intrusion." From the very first the long epic of self to which he devoted his life became the history of his tribulations, a history of his self's struggle against all the manifold threats, humiliations, paralyzing cautions and frustrations, which composed his outer experience—the enemy which he had to destroy in order to conquer—that is, to live truly, at all. The theme, then, was the conflict between the "I" and the world, that first person in which he began to write *Look Homeward, Angel,* and which slipped, like a Freudian gamin, through the rough disguise of Eugene Gant in *Of Time and the River.* In his first novel the enemy was the world narrowed to the first horizon of a child's sensations, and found its abundant representation in his mother Eliza, her greed and lovelessness and talk, the burning acquisitiveness which found its symbol in the boardinghouse that supplanted their home, the family's slow disintegration, his newspaper route in the early winter mornings—a mother in whom he recognized a fateful source of his torment, as he saw its theatrical reflection in his father. And struggling against his mother and the experience she at once represented and imposed upon him, Wolfe was struggling with even more painful ardor and bewilderment against those in his own family—Ben and Helen particularly—who had submitted and been defeated. Or, in making his newspaper rounds in the Negro quarters, he was rebelling simultaneously against the hysterical "success" of his brother Luke, the frenzied Oliver Optic mind stammering its way to the forlorn middle-class victory of money and status.

"Lost, lost, forever lost," he wrote of his kind in the anguished little prose lyric that became the leit-motif of his work. *"Naked and alone we came into exile. In her dark womb we did not know our mother's face; from the prison of her flesh have we come into the unspeakable and incommunicable prison of this earth."* Doomed as they all were, they represented even more the threat of his own doom, the enemy made symbol, the symbol made flesh. Even the very young Eugene, describing himself as a child at the fair, became the Romantic Self. "His mind, just emerging from the unreal wilderness of childish fancy, gave way completely in this Fair, and he was paralyzed by the conviction, which often returned to him in later years, that his life was a fabulous nightmare and that, by cunning and conspirate artifice, he had surrendered all his hope, belief, and confidence to the lewd torture of demons masked in human flesh." In the light of that con-

viction, so remarkably unchanged to the end as to seem the very principle of Wolfe's existence, his every experience became an encounter
with the Enemy, a measure of defeat or apotheosis. With the same
ingenuous grandeur with which he wrote the story of his trip from
Asheville to Harvard on a scale larger than that which Homer had
permitted himself in the *Odyssey,* Wolfe went on to describe the enemy in all its subsequent manifestations—Harvard and "The School
for Utility Cultures" in New York, the "Rock City" and the Jews; the
Hudson River gentry and Brooklyn and the New York intellectuals;
Esther Jack, the Jewish mistress who became associated in his mind
with all that was opulent and proud and corrupt in the metropolitan
culture; his old neighbors and relatives and friends in "Altamount"
and "Libya Hill," who had read their own portraits in his first book,
and hated him for it.

In this struggle between two absolutes, the "I" and the Enemy world,
Wolfe found the theme of his rhetoric, and the source of the imagery—swollen and turgid, yet curiously dramatic—that illuminated the
struggle in his own mind and sustained it by symbols. The prime
symbol, always, was the image of the Father, the gate that would open
the doors of the prison house for him. "The deepest search in life, it
seemed to me, the thing that in one way or another was central to all
living," he wrote in *The Story of a Novel,* "was man's search for a
father, not merely the father of his flesh, not merely the lost father of
his youth, but the image of a strength and wisdom external to his need
and superior to his hunger, to which the belief and power of his own
life could be united." The image of the Gate that recurred in his works
(*"Where shall the weary rest? When shall the lonely of heart come
home? What doors are open for the wanderer? And which of us shall
find his father, know his face, and in what place, and in what time,
and in what land? Where?"*) thus became the theme of his pilgrimage,
the gateway to reality and happiness. But with it was united in Wolfe's
mind the sense that this was somehow related to the American loneliness, the perpetual American migration, the loneliness of the artist-
spirit in America that could so easily become the loneliness of all its
young men and ardent spirits. Lost, lost, forever lost. "We are so lost,
so naked and so lonely in America," he wrote over and again. "Im-

mense and cruel skies bend over us, and all of us are driven on forever and we have no home." The Romantic "I" he remained to the end, consciously writing the story of his life and of all existence within the framework of that personal epic struggle; but the "I" became more than Thomas Eugene Gant Wolfe, or Thomas George Webber Wolfe. It became (with the same facile incandescence with which Whitman had associated himself with the hero of *Leaves of Grass,* and *Leaves of Grass* with all America) the moral history of the Young American, even of modern American life. For the second of his primal symbols was the Rock, the city world and the city darkness, the flowing river of time that absorbed and dissipated life; and as the Father image represented the yearning for freedom, and the Rock the waste and chagrin of experience, so only the artist's "I" could mediate between them and conquer the Enemy.

In this light Wolfe's perpetual recourse to America as an idea, the seeming paradox between his frenzied self-interest and his assumption of a moral authority in which he spoke for all the lost young men in America, even for all America itself, was not a paradox or a sentimentally expansive gesture at all, but the necessary consequence of his situation and his understanding. For though he used his life and art interchangeably in this quest (so that the relations between them were perhaps as dark and radiantly confused as they are to us), they were, taken together, a reflection of Wolfe's conviction that he himself was a prime symbol of American experience and of a perpetual American ambition. In his quest for grandeur, his very thinking in terms of grandeur, his self-trust and self-absorption announced that he had found America in himself, and that if he was alone in America, America was alone among the nations of the world, and incomparable in its range and fervor, its spiritual quality and aspiration. Hence the further significance of his need to set all of America down on paper, as Whitman had done. Hence his recurrent effort (always using his life and art interchangeably, always using his life not as the material of art but as the very voice of his art) to capture America as an idea and to master it as one, since in his own mind he was a spiritual agent, speaking and acting for others, and always in the name of nationality and destiny.

It was in this spirit, certainly, that Wolfe sought to make monuments, to "set down America as far as it can belong to the experience of one man." He was not "celebrating" America, as Whitman had done; he was trying to record it, to assimilate it, to echo it in himself. This, the very quality and turn of his abundant energy, was the source of his frenzied passion for American details, of his need to reproduce them exactly for the substance of his art. Sitting in a Paris café, he would remember the railing on the Atlantic City boardwalk, an iron bridge across an American river, the clink of a milkman's horse going slowly up the morning street. He set down with agonizing precision the look on the face of an old teacher, the mountain coldness and Appalachian heights back home, the tone of boys playing one-o'-cat in the sleepy twilight. In *You Can't Go Home Again* he wrote of George Webber:

> He spent weeks and months trying to put down on paper the exactitudes of countless fragments—what he called "the dry, caked colors of America"—how the entrance to a subway looked, the design and webbing of the elevated structure, the look and feel of an iron rail, the particular shade of rusty green with which so many things are painted in America. Then he tried to pin down the foggy color of the brick of which so much of London is constructed, the look of an English doorway, of a French window, of the roofs and chimney pots of Paris, of a whole street in Munich—and each of these foreign things he then examined in contrast to its American equivalent.

This passion for accumulation was not, however, a sentimental habit or even the mere reflex of his energy. He was offering America, or the possible idea of America, as a standard and as a reaction against all the sloth, degeneration, weakness, and cynicism which he saw in that Enemy which had become the symbol of everything he hated and feared. It is precisely because he was not merely "celebrating" America, in Whitman's sense, that he thought of his own struggle and of the necessary moral struggle in contemporary life in the same terms. Believing rapturously in the Romantic "I," he extended that faith, as he extended almost everything else, into a counterpoise to chaos. As Whitman had come at the beginning, when America was shapeless and nascent, so Wolfe thought of himself as coming at the climacteric, when the choice between the promise and its disillusionment, between life and death even, summoned all a man's resources—his own resources above all. From one point of view, of course, this was the most monstrous of his confusions, for he was not thinking, like Whitman, of a new conception in terms of a new subject ("the Promise of These States"). He was not, that is to say, a moral intelligence working itself out exhilaratingly and indiscriminately, a powerful romantic spirit who caught fire from every phase of contemporary experience, an antebellum Everyman who had absorbed his own personality in his countrymen and found his values in their celebration. Where Whitman had identified himself with his America out of a supreme act of fellowship, the radiant confidence possible only to him and his time, Wolfe made his self equal to the communal tragedy he saw and wished to describe; he kept to the "I" as Whitman never did. This, perhaps, is the larger significance of his inveterate self-interest, and the reason why he became the least interesting character in his work, and certainly the character in all his books one knows least. He could prove himself a striking realist of contemporary society, but at bottom his sense of tragedy was always a personal complaint, an imperial maladjustment. For if he knew the significance behind "the malady of the ideal," knew it with an excruciating pain and intensity and livid precision unmatched by his contemporaries, it was always, at bottom, because his experience was what sustained and afflicted *him;* it was because he wanted, consciously and dynamically, more of America than it was prepared to give him. He thought of himself as writing the last great epic of American nationality, certainly the last great American romance, as perhaps he did; but the epic was a personal quarrel, and the romance a vast inchoate yearning to the end.

That Wolfe proved himself the most self-centered and most inclusive novelist of the day is thus no paradox. His imagination was a perpetual tension between his devotion to himself and his devotion to his self's interests and symbolism, and he made his art out of the equation he drew. It is this that explains why Wolfe, in no real sense an objective novelist, was yet one who incorporated the best methods of American realism and passed beyond them; and it is this that explains why, though he often seemed determined to prove himself the sickliest of romantic egotists, he was, ironically enough, the most alert and brilliant novelist of depression America, and an extraordinarily imaginative analyst of American types and the social disorganization of the thirties. Though the feverish surface of his work hardly suggests it, he did write on several levels. Just as his imagination had presented his own situation and the American situation as coeval, so he was not always the stricken child wailing through thousands of pages of epic unhappiness—lost, lost, forever lost—but a prophetic voice who brought the same shattering intensity to his studies of contemporary demoralization, the climate of Fascism in Europe and America, the confusion and rout of the masses, that he did to his self-torment and yearning for personal freedom and redemption; brought it, indeed, with a conviction of absolute harrowing need and sense of achievement that made him seem the richest in spirit of contemporary American novelists. Though what he saw in society was always refracted through his own self, was always tangential to his own situation and his private agony, the force behind that agony broke through, enveloped and absorbed the life of contemporary society, as no social realist of the time, not even Dos Passos, ever did. He had come to believe that the Enemy was as much the nemesis of his America as it was of himself; and in that identification lay half his strength, and as has too often been forgotten, something as representative of his spirit as his lack of artistic discipline.

In one sense, then, there were two forces in Wolfe, mutually accommodating, springing from the same source, yet different in tone and effect. One was the mountaineer's son who wrote with a hard, driving force of the people he had hated as a child, who described the death of Old Gant, the peregrinations of Bascom Hawke, his mother's haggard kitchen sourness and scolding old age—the Wolfe who poured into the first third of *The Web and the Rock* a beautiful and haunting chronicle of mountain legends and mountain life, the Wolfe who composed a whole gallery of titanic American portraits and, almost with his last breath, sketched the decomposition of the German soul preparing itself for Fascism in *You Can't Go Home Again*. It was the Wolfe who proved himself a richly comic novelist, with an ear for dialogue, a sense of timing (consider the reproduction of the gasping, stammering Gant speech in the first chapter of *Of Time and the River*, the fantastic montage of New York in all his last works, the Brooklyn scenes in *You Can't Go Home Again*) that were remarkable in their nervous power. It was the Wolfe who wrote the unforgettable sketch of the New York poor huddling in the City Hall latrine for warmth in the depth of a depression winter, the creator of Nebraska Crane and "Lloyd McHarg" and Ben Gant and Grover. He saw them always —Hitler Germany and the baseball players out of his boyhood, the Jewish students at "The School for Utility Cultures" and Esther Jack, the mountain folk and Foxhall Edwards—as segments of that outer world that had significance only in its relation to Eugene Gant-George Webber, saw them often with a disproportionate intensity and strident wit that were literally fantastic in their excess; but he saw them always with great acuteness and wit, and they became, for all their stridency or angularity, as vivid and true as he had seen them in his mind.

The "other" Wolfe, always the centripetal Wolfe who related everything to the dead center of his own fate, was the Asheville, North Carolina Hamlet who dramatized himself perpetually in pride and suffering, rose in his books above the world he was trying to discover and redeem, and could never save himself. For at the bottom of all his frenzy, his herculean misery, the millions of words that spurted out of his pen without drawing him closer to the salvation, the answer he needed so desperately, lay an extraordinary fear of himself and the world he lived in. He was proud of his passion, he even gloried in its energy; but it could not satisfy him. Jason and Kronos, Orestes and Faust, as he proclaimed himself in *Of Time and the River,* he was also a gangling overgrown boy with seven brothers and sisters whose mother kept a boardinghouse in Asheville, and whose father was a stonecutter with a taste for rhetoric. He had been mocked as a child, had been awakened on cold winter mornings to deliver newspapers (lost, lost, forever lost), and had suffered like a million other American boys (but so much more than they) because his parents were dull, his gifts unrecognized, and his teachers stupid. The stonecutter's son had gone on to college, self-conscious before the middle-class campus nobility; he was no good at baseball, he had a taste for Elizabethan prose, and he was vaguely rumored to be queer. Later he went to Harvard, wrote plays, and came to New York to dazzle the stage. Instead, he became a college instructor. His classes were full of gossipy, hungry, loud, and superficial children who stared at him, who did not love the best that had been thought and said, and whose greatest ambition was to become Certified Public Accountants.

Wolfe raged and suffered; he was lonely, he prowled the streets of New York, hated the beast-city and the beast-people, wept, and thought himself a failure. At night he wrote savagely in old ledgers, and wrote always of himself; he would reclaim the dream of time lost in the Rock City, he would make himself a monument. *"Could I make tongue say more than tongue could utter! Could I make brain grasp more than brain could think! Could I weave into immortal denseness some small brede of words, pluck out of sunken depths the roots of living, some hundred thousand magic words that were as great as all my hunger, and hurl the sum of all my living out upon three hundred pages!"* That Wolfe was the Tarzan of rhetoric, the noble lover, the antagonist of cities, the spear of fate, the Wolfe whose rhetoric, swollen with archaisms out of the English classics, can be as painful to read as a child's scrawlings. His rhetoric, pilfered recklessly from the Jacobeans and Sir Thomas Browne, James Joyce and Swinburne, Gilbert Murray and the worst traditions of Southern oratory, was a gluttonous English instructor's accumulation. He became enraptured with the altitudinous, ceremonial prose of the seventeenth century, with the vague splendors of a dozen assorted romanticisms, and united them at the pitch of his father's mountain oratory. Yet it is significant that the more Wolfe sank into the bog of "lost, ah forever lost," "the fairest fame of praise," "a thousand barren and desolate places, a thousand lights and weathers of the soul's gray horror," "he was the Lord of life, the master of the earth, he was the city's conqueror," the more did he seek refuge not in what he felt but in celebrating his own uncertainty, in giving epic grandeur to his own frustration. He wrote his private rhetoric because he had no faith in that writing; he repeated himself, rang endless euphuistic variations on the same phrase, embossed it. As he wrote on and on, he yielded to his confusion and embraced it; it came to hold a music for him, for in the very statement of his wretchedness, with its emotion and nervous clamor, he found the tonal equivalent of his spaceless and inchoate ambition.

In his first works, notably *Look Homeward, Angel,* this rhetoric was almost cheerfully self-conscious, a facile clouded magnificence, and transparently bookish—"Holding in fief the storm and the dark and all the black powers of wizardry, to gaze, ghoul-visaged, through a storm-lashed window-pane, briefly planting unutterable horror in grouped and sheltered life." The two most obvious influences upon the book, curiously enough, seem to have been Sinclair Lewis and James Joyce, and it is the tension of this divided loyalty that makes the novel seem the most cheerfully "objective" of Wolfe's novels, full of a folksy, quasi-poetic braggadocio in the worst and best style of Lewis, and yet the most confusedly romantic. At one point he even inserted a literal reproduction of the Joycean stream-of-consciousness soliloquy, and much of the bad poetry of the book came from his desire to imitate the silken mellifluousness of Joyce's prose lyrics in *The Portrait of the Artist as a Young Man.* Yet for all its tense imitativeness and mawkishness, that first novel seems in retrospect to have been Wolfe's least harried production, and curiously "objective," if only because he was attempting to describe a period in his life that he felt completely behind him. Later, for all his more significant achievements, the prose became more obviously expansive, and even mechanical, in its self-indulgence; it seemed to be fixed in perpetual attitudes of defiance and supplication, where the author of *Look Homeward, Angel,* describing his earliest youth, was commemorating his adolescent exaltations with a certain detachment and what was almost passing good humor.

For by the time he had completed and published *Of Time and the River,* six years after the publication of his first novel, Wolfe had caught up with his life, or rather had not caught up with it at all. His books and his life became so indistinguishably confused that his novels and stories became the living record of every phase in his experience and formed his journal. When, as it was frequently announced toward the end of his life, he "changed" in the direction of a greater maturity and objective comprehension, he never ceased to portray everything in American (and European) society as an accompaniment to, or a variation upon, the rhythm of his psychic life; he had reached that point in his novel-journal where the events of his own life had become contemporaneous with the depression and the impending Second

World War. It was at the moment of his greatest agony, therefore, that he found himself reporting the contemporary crisis between Black Friday, 1929, and Munich; and reporting it as that larger history of national and international disintegration of which he felt himself a part. For though he did grow in power, grew to the very end, he never attained certainty or the simple confidence that he had found his place in the world and could enjoy some basic relation to it. The great dissolution in America had begun the year he published his first book, 1929, the year of his emergence and reputation; yet his sudden fame crystallized his unhappiness, set up new tensions in his life, as nothing else had. He suddenly realized, in those years when he was wandering in Germany and England, suffering his affair with the Esther Jack in whose world he could not believe, that the publication of his book, the literal proclamation of his self, had not destroyed the old enemy or given him an advantage over it, but had rather caused it to react with a formidable directness and violence against him. He had forgotten, in his basic self-absorption, how cruelly and even selfishly he had described the world of his childhood and youth, as he had forgotten the external significance of his relation to the world at all; and it all came back—at a time when bitterness and hate were rising in the atmosphere like mercury in the glass.

You Can't Go Home Again, his last novel, was pieced together out of fragments he left at his death; but for all its gaps and editorial interpolations it did represent this last and most fateful period in Wolfe's life faithfully. He had reached the end, as in his mind America and the world had reached the end, and for all his talk of "going on," of writing "greater and greater," he almost unconsciously told what he wished most to tell when he wrote into the fragments of the book a long study in dissolution. For *You Can't Go Home Again,* a climax to the one long book he wrote all his life, was rooted in a conviction of decline and fall, of emptiness and dissolution—George Webber himself, Lloyd McHarg, the depression atmosphere in Brooklyn and "Libya Hill," the symbolic party given by Esther and her husband (a bacchanal disturbed by Wagnerian fire), the smashup of his affair with Esther, Germany on the eve of Hitler, the days he spent in a Munich hospital after a brawl. And since he was writing with something more than his old fury, with what seemed almost a new sense of prophecy and scorn, he was able to invest the poverty of New York, the crash back home, the bitterness his family and old neighbors felt against him, the very boom psychology of business itself as he saw it rotting away before him, with a terrible and incandescent loathing.

Something of the old romantic naïveté, always implicit in the absolute conflict he posed between the world and himself, remained to the end, as when he wrote of the sudden humiliation of the middle-class "successes" at home that "he had found out something about life that he had not known before." Yet that naïveté, as always, was the source of half his power. "They were always talking about the better life that lay ahead of them and of the greater city they would build," he wrote of the ruined business people in his old town after the first shock of the depression, "but to George it seemed that in all such talk there was evidence of a strange and savage hunger that drove them on, and there was a desperate quality in it, as though what they really hungered for was ruin and death. It seemed to him that they *were* ruined, and that even when they laughed and shouted and smote each other on the back, the knowledge of their ruin was in them." Discovering the external world afresh at every moment, he discovered what more mature writers had known perhaps almost too well to say. A raging naïf to the end, Wolfe had the naïve curiosity as well as the naïve credulity and bombast; and that curiosity enabled him to see the depression and its atmosphere as a type of universal experience, a cataclysm not merely rooted in the facts of social change but inexpressibly more significant than them. He was discovering the mass agony as he had hitherto explored only his own, and though that larger world was still only a reflection of his own, he proved, almost by the depth of his self-absorption, that his romantic conception of a world that seemed to exist only to oppress Thomas Wolfe *had* actually led him somewhere, had justified his stricken devotion to Thomas Wolfe and his fate.

The two worlds had converged at last, if only in that last projection of himself which he offered to the world and the Enemy. And having achieved that much of the essential victory, he proved—it seems at once so little and so much—that in making his "I" equal to all America, he could speak for that essential truth in it which only a certain spirit could know, and suffer. "I believe that we are lost here in America, but I believe that we shall be found. . . . I think that the true discovery of America is before us. I think the true fulfillment of our spirit, of our people, of our mighty and immortal land, is yet to come." The failure and triumph went hand in hand to the end, the nonsense and grandeur; and more than he knew—was not *this* his distinction?—they were his alone. He went roaring through a world he had never made and which he never fully understood; a gargantuan boy (they had told him he was different, and he believed it; they told him he was queer and alone, and he affirmed it), begging, out of that loneliness and secret defeat—*Believe! Believe!*

Chapter 16

AMERICA! AMERICA!

"Do you know that European birds have not half the melody of ours?"—ABIGAIL ADAMS to John Adams

UNDERLYING the imaginative life in America all through the years of panic, depression, and the emergence of international civil war was an enormous body of writing devoted to the American scene that is one of the most remarkable phenomena of the era of crisis. That literature has hardly run its course, and it may even dominate the scene for many years to come; but for all its shapelessness and often mechanical impulse, it is a vast body of writing that is perhaps the fullest expression of the experience of the American consciousness after 1930, and one that illuminates the whole nature of prose literature in those years as nothing else can. For that literature of nationhood, beginning with the documentation of America in the depression and reaching a thunderous climax in an effort to seek out the American tradition, is largely the story of the American people as they came to understand it for themselves in a period of unprecedented crisis. It is the story of that now innocent, now calculating, now purely rhetorical, but always significant experience in national self-discovery which had its origin in the same obsession with society that led to the social novels of the period, but went on to create original or to reclaim traditional forms in a passionate effort to make a living record of contemporary American experience. It is the story of a vast new literature in itself, some of it fanatical or callow, some of it not writing at

all, much of it laboriously solid and curious and humble, whose subject was the American scene and whose drive always was the need,
born of the depression and the international crisis, to chart America
and to possess it. It is the story of a literature of collective self-
consciousness, a people's and a nation's biography; a story of physical
and human geography, composed under pressure, often testifying only
to the immediacy of that pressure, yet for all its occasional opportunism or naïveté, never without some fundamental joy in the study
of America and the pride taken in its aroused self-comprehension.

Whatever form this literature took—the WPA guides to the states
and roads; the reaction against the skepticism and now legendary
"frivolity" of the twenties; the half-sentimental, half-commercial new
folklore that manufactured or inflated comic demigods out of the
reclaimed past; the endless documentation of the dispossessed in
American life—it testified to so extraordinary a national self-scrutiny,
signified so widespread and insistent a need, that all other considerations of it seem secondary. As if it marked a release of energies more
thwarted in the past than anyone had suspected, a release of powers
of affirmation crying for expression, whole divisions of writers now
fell upon the face of America with a devotion that was baffled rather
than shrill, and an insistence to know and to love what it knew that
seemed unprecedented. Never before did a nation seem so hungry for
news of itself, and not since those early years of the nineteenth century when the American had been the world's eighth wonder to
European observers did America—if only the very texture of the country—seem so magnetic a subject in itself to so many different minds.
The question now was no longer posed from afar—"What is an
American?" Here the intelligence was native, as the subject was its
very self, and by that very token a moving and always astonishing
hunger for self-knowledge, since it seemed to express a profoundly
innocent unanimity of spirit.

On the eve of this new nationalism, in 1932, Albert Jay Nock published a sardonic paper, "Return of the Patriots," in which he foretold
that the "license of indiscriminate negation" during the twenties
would be followed by "a license of indiscriminate affirmation" in the

thirties. He saw ahead a literature of mechanical patriotism modeled upon the worst of the old—"it will be turgid, superficial, unintelligent, truculent." Yet though the spirit of the new nationalism did result in unprecedented affirmation, it was not at all what anyone in 1932 could have expected, for at its center lay a devotion to the heroic example, a need to question contemporary failure and demoralization, that had its roots in the same impulse which drove so many writers to report on the country all through the thirties. Obviously, of course, much of this writing represented the reflex patriotism and hungry traditionalism of a culture fighting for its life as it moved into war. Obviously, too, Hitler made nationalists out of many American writers almost as easily as Mencken had once made them scornful of the most commonplace national allegiance. The nationalist trend was marked here and there by a sentimentality that found its appropriate expression in the historical romance, and a certain comfortable smugness that showed in even ambitious histories and biographies and documentary studies. In a period when Hollywood found it so necessary to take a flyer on the Spirit of '76, a period when too many people thought they were writing history when they were only searching their attics, a period in which wistful souls who had in the twenties revenged themselves on their fathers now sought only the solid comfort of their grandfathers, the need to reclaim the past made for a certain complacency and swooning antiquarianism.

Often exploited, this new nationalism was, however, something profoundly more than a fashion, and to understand the spirit in which so many writers turned to recover America and to understand it is to appreciate how compelling was the drive toward national inventory which began by reporting the ravages of the depression and ended by reporting on the national inheritance. In his sequel to *The Flowering of New England,* a prime example of this new nationalism, Van Wyck Brooks rejoiced that "the goldenrod rises again in its season, and the folk-poem recovers its meaning, when the heart of a nation, grown old, returns to its youth." But as Brooks's own passionate attacks on certain modern "misleaders" later proved, his kind of devotion to the past was reminiscent with a purpose beyond reminiscence. For whatever the elegiac piety of this new traditionalism, its longing for the past was curiously in agreement with what André Malraux had meant when he said that a cultural inheritance does not consist in works which men must respect, but in works which help them to live. Nothing proves how well the leaders of the new nationalism believed that as the fury with which writers like Brooks and Archibald MacLeish, Howard Mumford Jones and Lewis Mumford, now began to excoriate so much of the modernism that had flowered between two world wars. Theirs was the rhetoric of haste, but in their own minds their haste was that of the demiurge; and the most significant aspect of the new traditionalism, whatever its inevitable narrowness or bigotry, was always its insistence upon reclaiming the past for the strengthening of the present.

So far from being merely a blind and parochial nationalism, this experience in national self-discovery was largely shaped by the sudden emergence of America as the repository of Western culture in a world overrun by Fascism. America may have been cut off from Europe after 1933, but the migration of so many European intellectuals to America meant, as John Peale Bishop said, that the European past was now confided to us, since we alone could "prolong it into the future." This was a profound influence on the reawakening to America's own tradition, since it meant a study of the national past conducted in the light of the European example in America, in the light of a new—if frantically enforced—sense of world responsibility. In an America which had either received or enrolled among its own so many of Europe's finest spirits from Thomas Mann to Jacques Maritain, from Albert Einstein to Sigrid Undset, the pride of helping to breed a new cosmopolitan culture gave a healthy stimulus to the searching of our own culture. To believe, as one German émigré wrote so wistfully, that "in America the word still has real value; in Europe it is only make-believe" was to give an unprecedented importance to the consciousness of the word in America and an appropriate dignity.

For better or worse this new nationalism was a pervasive force, a new historic consciousness that gave new meaning to contemporary experience and thought, and to appreciate that is to see something in the experience of the times that we are perhaps not now fully prepared to understand. For here, in the revealing—especially revealing because it was so often mechanical—effort of so many American writers to seek out the reality of America in times of crisis, is an authentic and curiously unconscious characterization of a tragic period. Here, in the vast granary of facts on life in America put away by the WPA writers, the documentary reporters, the folklorists preparing an American mythology, the explorers who went hunting through darkest America with notebook and camera, the new army of biographers and historians—here, stocked away like a reserve against bad times, is the raw stuff of that contemporary mass record which so many imaginative spirits tried to depict and failed to master. What we study here is all too often only a sub-literature, perhaps only a preparation for literature—evidence of a nostalgia too easily content with the trappings of sentimental autobiography and romance; evidence of a need to retreat into the solid comfort of descriptive facts, of a social awareness that found its appropriate expression in photographic details and sociological captions. Yet in that signal literature of empiricism which embodies the failure of so many to discriminate between the pen and the camera, between the need for the past and the comforting surface of that past, is the record of what most deeply interested the contemporary imagination.

Here, in this body of writing, is evidence of how deeply felt was the urge born of the crisis to recover America *as an idea*—and perhaps only thus to build a better society in the shell of the old; only thus to prepare a literature worthy of it. Out of the decade of unrelieved crisis and failure, of fumbling recovery and tension and war; out of the panic and extremism of so many of its finest talents; out of the desire to assess what could be known and to establish a needed security in the American inheritance, came the realization of how little, for all its now world-famous triumphs, American writing had served the people and how little it had come to grips with the subject that lay closest at hand—the country itself.

2

There is a profound significance in the fact that this need to search out the land, to compile records, to explain America to itself, found its most abundant expression in a literature of formal social exploration and descriptive journalism. The novel, as Allen Tate said just a little contemptuously, may be an impure literary form because it is so much like history; but in a period when society is changing too rapidly and too violently for literature even to command the necessary detachment for imaginative truth, the serious novel itself will suffer in its effort to dominate what is not yet really known. In times of crisis people prefer to take their history straight, and on the run; and the documentary journalist who writes it on the run will give them history in terms which they are prepared to understand. If we ask why so many documentary journalists did more with their material than the social novelists who seemed to be working with the same material, the fact seems inescapable that because of the very nature of the crisis and the explosive strains it imposed, too many contemporary imaginations were simply not equal to it. Nothing proves that so well, perhaps, as the readiness of so many novelists today to desert the novel altogether, or the palpable fact that so many writers enjoyed a greater certainty and ease when they no longer felt it necessary to impose an imaginative unity upon their work.

For what emerges so unmistakably from the enormous descriptive and historical literature of our day is how unready so many writers have been to seek its imaginative truth, how lacking they have been in the requisite confidence or detachment to dominate as artists what they suffer as citizens seeking to survive. Why is it, as so many have felt, that a job of straight left-wing reporting like Ruth McKenny's study of the rubber workers in Akron, *Industrial Valley*, is so much a better study (so much better a proletarian novel, as Malcolm Cowley said) than most proletarian novelists achieved? Why is it that so sensitive and scrupulous a work of reporting the depression scene as George Leighton's *Five Cities* is so much richer and more authentic than most novels of the period? Why is it that in a period of unprecedented literary interest in the South, a period when the sharecropper haunted the imagination, the most moving and illuminating testimony of life in the South came from a WPA record of case histories, *These Are Our Lives?* Why is it that so much of the literature of the thirties and early forties must seem in retrospect a literature of Fact—one of those periods in which, despite the emergence of so many brilliant individual sensibilities, the chief effort of many writers seemed bent only on reporting, reporting; on running not too far behind the phenomena of the times?

The decline of the novel all through the period, a moral and physical decline, tells its own story in this respect. In so curious and difficult a revolutionary period as our own, so peculiarly hazardous a period, no one needs to be told how difficult it is for the imaginative spirit to command a necessary poise. Yet while the preponderance of descriptive nonfiction can be attributed partly to those who can appreciate reality only in terms of public events, there is an advantage the typical social reporter of the period enjoyed that explains why, as it happens, he often did succeed brilliantly within his sphere. For there is a sense in which the reality of our time *has* been composed of public events—a series of shattering shocks and tremors that has pounded away mercilessly at the mind. In such a period, marked by so pervasive and unexampled a sense of insecurity, the social reporter did not have to affect certainty; he was only a spectator of the passing show, a taker of notes. And because of the very nature of those repeated shocks, the moral and intellectual climate of the time seemed to call for nothing more than so passive (at most passively indignant) and even sardonic a spirit as the documentary literature of the thirties provided.

Like the effect Henry James sought in *The Princess Casamassima,* the reporting mind that opened the way for this new nationalism might be described as one "of our not knowing, of society's not knowing, but only guessing and suspecting and trying to ignore what goes on irreconcilably, subversively, beneath the vast smug surface." The surface was now anything but smug and, far from trying to ignore what went on beneath it, the world of contemporary opinion was haunted by its subterranean revolution. Yet that conviction of "our not knowing, of society's not knowing," was the field in which the documentary reporter and traveler now operated with ease and a certain serene humility that in that "not knowing" lay his usefulness as an observer and his ability to satisfy his readers on the same level.

We don't know
We aren't sure
We wonder
We're asking

In that "not knowing, of society's not knowing," indeed, was the test of his participation in the great contemporary experience, for society, which knew only that it did not know, would respond to and believe in only those writers who pressed it on—not too hard, certainly—to grasp the first facts about itself.

The two great associations of this literature of social description—the New Deal and the camera—help to illuminate its character in this respect. For rather like the New Deal itself, which opened so many new fields of investigation for this documentary school and even subsidized the WPA contributions to it, this new literature symbolized the effort of the inquiring mind, living in a period when the New Deal represented all the manifold adjustments of crisis government, to approach the problem of democratic survival. And just as the New Deal was weakest in philosophy, most transparently lacking in some centrality of direction and belief, so this documentary literature of the New Deal era represents a profound yet significantly indirect process of education. It was, indeed, a literature just as profound as the New Deal, no more and no less; a plastic literature, with all America for its subject, that became, as Dixon Wecter said of President Roosevelt, "a rare seismograph for all the social tremors of his time"; a crisis literature moving by an explosion of quick yet uncertain starts within the framework of the established order; a literature in which the sense of movement and of perpetual search was always more dynamic than any conception of the ends toward which it moved.

Franklin Roosevelt, considered as one national leader among others, may seem distinctive enough, since he was the leader of a mass movement greater than any Jackson, Lincoln, T. R., or Wilson led. But what is significant here—it may yet seem a fact of the first importance to future students of New Deal America—is not the power or resourcefulness of his leadership, but the extent to which his famous malleability, his "statesmanship as adjustment," was the focus of the great national experience under the New Deal. Everyone was learning in the thirties (well, nearly everyone), learning and groping at a time when the learning process had become a major experience in itself; and H. G. Wells's description of Roosevelt—"a ganglion for reception, expression, transmission, combination, and realization"—expresses one of the great truths of a time that found its appropriate expression in a literature of responsive social description. As Max Lerner said, the importance of Roosevelt's own responsiveness to public opinion is that he had to educate not only himself, but the whole country, to the forces remaking the world. But in a larger sense Roosevelt was responsive to more than "public opinion." How else are we to understand the world of the thirties that raised him to world leadership, raised him from the amiable but seemingly not too profound land-squire of Hyde Park, the pedestrian Admiralty law specialist, the former vice-president of the Fidelity Deposit Company, the complaisant Governor of New York?

What the documentary literature provided, then, was a register of the learning process, an example of a new social consciousness in America whose greatest distinction was the very fact of that consciousness in itself, the sense of a grim and steady awareness rather than of great comprehension. In this respect none of the devices the documentary and travel reporters used is so significant as their reliance upon the camera. Ever since the daguerreotype had come into American life, writers had been affected by the photographic standard, but now they became curiously abject before it. Nothing in this new literature, indeed, stands out so clearly as its attempt to use and even to imitate the camera. In a whole succession of books—Erskine Caldwell's and Margaret Bourke White's *You Have Seen Their Faces* and *Say, Is This the USA;* Dorothea Lange's and Paul S. Taylor's *An American Exodus;* Archibald MacLeish's *Land of the Free* (pictures by courtesy of the Farm Security Administration); James Agee's and Walker Evans's *Let Us Now Praise Famous Men,* the new genre developed by Pare Lorentz in *The River,* and the rest—the words and pictures were not only mutually indispensable, a kind of commentary upon each other, but curiously interchangeable. In a postscript to his *Land of the Free,* Archibald MacLeish wrote:

> [It] is the opposite of a book of poems illustrated by photographs. It is a book of photographs illustrated by a poem. . . . The book is the result of an attempt to give these photographs an accompaniment of words. . . . The original purpose had been to write some sort of text to which these photographs might serve as commentary. But so great was the power and the stubborn inward livingness of these vivid American documents that the result was a reversal of that plan.

So Dorothea Lange and Paul S. Taylor wrote of their *An American Exodus: A Record of Human Erosion* that it was neither a book of photographs nor an illustrated book, in the traditional sense. "Its particular form is the result of our use of techniques in proportions and relations designed to convey understanding easily, clearly, and vividly. . . . Upon a tripod of photographs, captions, and text we rest themes evolved out of long observations in the field." And even the unillustrated books of social "reportage," like Edmund Wilson's *The American Jitters* and *Travels in Two Democracies,* James Rorty's *Where Life Is Better,* Nathan Asch's *The Road: In Search of America,* Louis Adamic's *My America,* showed that their authors were always seeking to catch reality on the run, as it were; to identify the object seen by etching it sharply on the mind; to give it a kind of wry objective irony or bitterness. Indeed, the technical and psychological fascination of the camera may be considered even to have given a new character to contemporary prose, a transformation which can be appreciated only in terms of its moral example, since it was the camera's essential passiveness that made for its technical influence over so many writers.

As a few great Americans have proved so well, the camera can be an extraordinary medium for the sensitive imagination; but in the crisis-begotten literature of the documentary school it served to give the general appearance of what Lincoln Kirstein described as the function of the candid camera in our time, to make up "in quantitative shock what it lacks in real testimony. . . . Its only inherent characteristic is the accidental shock that obliterates the essential nature of the event it pretends to discover." The photographs in most of the documentary books were anything but candid-camera shots, of course. Few artists today have created anything so rich and meaningful as the photographs Walker Evans contributed to *Let Us Now Praise Famous*

Men and his own volume of *American Photographs,* and the photographs in the documentary books by photographers like Ben Shahn, Dorothea Lange, Carl Mydans, and others were often of extraordinary merit. But the extent to which the camera *as an idea* affected documentary and travel reporters and served them as a prime symbol of a certain enforced simplicity and passivity of mind, is still little appreciated.

Margaret Bourke-White put it with wonderful simplicity when she said: "Whatever facts a person writes have to be colored by his prejudice and bias. With a camera, the shutter opens and closes and the only rays that come in to be registered come directly from the object in front of you." It follows from all that has been said of the documentary reporters that the appeal of the camera was not to their superficiality but to their spiritual fatigue, as it were; to their "not knowing . . . society's not knowing." The "keen historic spasm of the shutter," as James Agee called it, served not only "to portray America," but also to answer subtly to the writer's conscious or unconscious unwillingness or inability to go beyond his material. As Agee put it in that documentary book written to end all documentary books, *Let Us Now Praise Famous Men,*[1] with the camera "everything is to be discerned, for him who can discern it, and centrally and simply, without either dissection into science, or digestion into art . . . all of consciousness is shifted from the imagined, the revisive, to the effort to perceive simply the cruel radiance of what is."

In the vast flood of social reports there were naturally a good many books which merely exploited the camera technique on its lowest level, books as superficial as the average weekly picture magazine or as loud as a tabloid headline. But while there were necessarily a good many books of this order, books which merely pandered to public excitement, the real significance of the literary use of the camera is that many serious writers were so affected by its use—or symbolism—that they

---

[1] Agee's text has a special importance not merely because it is an unusually sensitive document and a work of great moral intensity, but particularly because it represents a revolt against the automatism of the documentary school. It was begun as a typical documentary assignment and ended by being an attack on the facile mechanics and passivity of most documentary assignments. Agee went so far in his revulsion, in fact, that his book even took on the deep personal suffering of Faulkner's novels.

seemed interested only in photographing the country on the run, in giving to the accumulated weight of a thousand different details and impressions of the national texture the solid testimony of their "education." In this respect the camera served to give documentary prose a hard, wry, noncommittal character—a character entirely appropriate to its obsession with the surface drama of the times, its stabbed and stab-like consciousness, its professed contempt for "illusion." What the fascination of the camera represented, in a word, was a kind of sick pride in its fiercely objective "realism." The camera did not fake or gloss over; it told "the truth of the times"; it was at once so aggressive and uncertain that it highlighted an awakened, ironic, militant, yet fundamentally baffled self-consciousness. Most important, the camera reproduced endless *fractions* of reality. In itself so significant a medium of tension, it fastened upon the atmosphere of tension. And if the accumulation of visual scenes seemed only a collection of "mutually repellent particles," as Emerson said of his sentences, was not *that* discontinuity, that havoc of pictorial sensations, just the truth of what the documentary mind saw before it in the thirties?

Reveling in a land so rich in descriptive facts, content with a kind of fever brilliance or anger or wit in the presence of so stupendous and humiliating a disorder as the depression scene provided, the documentary-travel reporter thus had his happiness. America lay all before him, his to choose; and how much there was to see and how little to annotate! The sharecropper, for example, fascinated the writer out to see the country, since he embodied so visual a conception of all that had to be recognized and redeemed in America. He provided an occasion for catharsis; he was a special contemporary phenomenon that fixed the general sense of outrage and quickened the sensibility of fellowship. Yet one had only to look at him (Margaret Bourke-White having taken his picture, imprisoning his agony for all history to gape at) to know how little there was to say. One had only to look at his South to believe that what one saw was the American drama of this day and age, all the pressures of the time brought together at the point of maximum curiosity and rage. Yet having looked, what was there to say that the Farm Security Administration did not have down in its files, the sociologist in his statistics? Here was America, all of it undoubtedly

America—but America in a gallery of photographs, an echo of the people's talk, a storehouse of vivid single impressions.

Here was America—the cars on the unending white ribbon of road; the workers in the mills; the faces of farmers' wives and their children in the roadside camp, a thousand miles from nowhere; the tenant farmer's wife with her child sitting on the steps of the old plantation mansion, where the columns were gray and crumbling with age. Here was the child in the grimy bed, the Okies crossing the desert in their jalopy, the pallor of August in the Dust Bowl, the Baptist service in the old Negro church. Here was the greatest creative irony the reportorial mind of the thirties could establish—a picture of Negro farmers wandering on the road, eating their bread under a billboard poster furnished by the National Association of Manufacturers—"America Enjoys the Highest Standard of Living in the World." Here was the migrant family sleeping on sacks in the roadside grass, above them the railroad legend "Travel While You Sleep." Here was the Negro sitting in the fields near Memphis (more men than jobs at the Bridgehead labor market), saying: "They come off the plantations 'cause they ain't got nothin' to do. . . . They come to town and they *still* got nothin' to do." Here was the treeless landscape in southwestern Oklahoma, a country strewn with deserted and crumbling houses, the farmers driven off by the tractors, a picture of land where the tractors now kneaded the earth right "to the very door of the houses of those whom they replace."

Here, indeed, was an America that could only be quoted and photographed, described in pictures or in words that sought to be pictures. "America today is the scene of a mighty drama," Erskine Caldwell wrote in *Say, Is This the USA*, "the like of which we have never before experienced." There was no audience; everyone was on the stage playing his part. And if there were doubts as to what the play meant, "in the meantime, there is action on top of action, there is action galore. . . . All these people, all this abundance, all these things, is this America we live in; but none of us knows what to do about it. This is us, this is what we have; but nobody knows what to do next." Like Thomas Wolfe, who was reduced to making lists of all those things and scenes in the world he tried vainly to bind together, the documentary reporter, precisely because he was unable or unwilling to bind anything together, was driven to make lists of single impressions, lists of objects and names, above all lists of all those people scattered in the lava flow of the thirties who had stories to tell. America was everywhere, in everything; America was people everywhere; people on farms and on relief; people on the road; farmers in town standing before store windows; the girl on the bus who was going from town to town looking for work; the anonymous sharecropper who told his woes and said sharply, "These things are a pressin' on us in the state of Mississippi"; the migrant farmer in California who said of Oklahoma: "No, I didn't *sell* out back there. I *give* out"; the Negro boy Erskine Caldwell met who built coffins underground because he had served three years on a chain gang in Georgia for owing a white man $11, and had said he would let daylight burn itself out—*he* would never look at it—before he would get caught in such a jam again.

Yes, America lay all before the documentary reporter, his to choose; and what did it matter if the America he saw was often only the America he came prepared to see? He made up his pattern, and the country —so rich in patterns for different minds—always lived up to it. Sherwood Anderson, who early in the thirties published a book appropriately entitled *Puzzled America,* had one pattern. Theodore Dreiser, who published another on *Tragic America,* had his pattern, the Dreiser pattern, always tragic. In *The "Argonauts,"* a book by five leftist college students who went out to see the country "for themselves"—the rootlessness of young people without jobs had long since made a virtue out of necessity—one saw an America that consisted rather exclusively of CIO organizers, chain gangs, sharecroppers, ugly native Fascists, leftist movie stars. In Edmund Wilson's early book of this type—*The American Jitters,* published in the worst year of the depression—all the savagery and inchoate bitterness of 1932 went into coruscating snapshots of police fighting hunger marchers, Tammany Hall, the Fish Committee investigating the Red Menace, suicides in Brooklyn, and the unhappy depositors of the Bank of United States. In his *Travels in Two Democracies* all the nervous brilliance so latent in the travelogue report went into a portrait of extraordinary density, yet one in which everything in America from Hull House to Radio City looked as if it had been photographed on Inauguration Day, 1933, with all the banks closed and the country running a high fever.

From Portland to Portland, from Detroit to the Gulf, from New York to Hollywood, there were patterns for all. In Louis Adamic's *My America,* a sprawling book of impressions by a writer whose immigrant past had given him an outsider's curiosity and a vibrant democratic fraternalism, America appeared as a strange but promising land that was essentially "a process—long and endless." Nathan Asch's highly introspective *The Road* bore no relation to the cautious unpanicky middle-class Indiana of the Lynds' *Middletown in Transition;* Benjamin Appel's studiously leftist *The People Talk* was not the same America that Rollo Brown found in *I Travel by Train;* but it was all America nevertheless. In *Where Life Is Better: An Unsentimental American Journey* (the main title was ironic), James Rorty described an America built on fear and ignorance and hatred, an America "building the stockades of fascism with which to protect what was left of its grandiose acquisitive dream." He saw an America, all retching ugliness and class conflict, that moved him to cry in despair: "What profound failure of American life did this drift of human atoms signify and embody, and to what would it lead? . . . The people had not possessed the landscape, nor had the landscape possessed them. The balance was indeed broken." Yet though what he saw seemed only "some profound profanation of the human spirit," in the end he was moved to confess that he did not know what America was. "I suspect that no one knows. Certainly I am in no position to make any categorical pronouncement."

No. No one knew. The girl in the bus, groping her way in the darkness from job to job; the boy in the road waiting for a lift; the salesman in the store, his baffled eyes belying his professional smile; the hotel clerk who said of the titled refugees from Fascism: "I used to think America would always stay the same, but now with all kinds of people coming here it's bound to change." What were they trying to say that only all America could say for them? Did they know? Did anyone know, when the pictures said so much, when one's whole experience on the road was a succession of pictures on the mind?

3

Yet something always remained: the shadow of the past on the land the Okies had left behind; the land itself that lay everywhere ready to be discovered and reclaimed; the framework of a whole American civilization, richer and more curious than many in the depression generation knew, greater than any crisis, waiting and begging to be known. The paradox of the crisis, as Lewis Mumford said, was that in a period of abnormal stress Americans began for the first time to learn many of the things that should have been normal to them as a people. Playgrounds and schools were built that prosperity could not afford; a new folk art and regionalism, and with it a reawakening to the forgotten cultural resources of the country, were developed out of the make-work programs of the WPA; only when writers had gone on relief was America charted in the great New Deal Baedeker of the states and roads; searching only for facts, a whole army of social reporters and travelers recovered an American sense of history and began to chant the rich diversity and beauty of the country as if America had never been really known before. Reporters of crisis, the documentary and travel writers now stumbled almost unwittingly into history; working and living on the surface of contemporary migration and poverty and unrest, they pieced together the broad outlines of a national civilization.

So Pare Lorentz, preparing his documentary film on floods and erosion in the Mississippi Valley, suddenly caught the image of the river, the spinal cord of the nation, in a chanting litany of American river names, caught it in a burst of celebrant American splendor unparalleled since Whitman. Here was the national center, as Sherman had caught the vision from it of a central union so long before at Vicksburg—here, in the gallery portrait of migration and erosion, the central and symbolic agony of the times. Yet how strange that anything so seemingly "descriptive" could be so beautiful!

> Down the Judith, the Grand, the Osage, and the Platte,
> The Rock, the Salt, the Black and Minnesota,
> Down the Monongahela, the Allegheny, Kanawha and
>   Muskingum,
> The Miami, the Wabash, the Licking and the Green . . .

("Monongahela," Whitman had said admiringly; "it rolls like venison off the tongue.")

So the WPA state guides, seemingly only a makeshift, a stratagem of administrative relief policy to tide a few thousand people along and keep them working, a business of assigning individuals of assorted skills and interests to map the country, mile by mile, resulted in an extraordinary contemporary epic. Out of the need to find something to say about every community and the country around it, out of the vast storehouse of facts behind the guides—geological, geographic, meteorological, ethnological, historical, political, sociological, economic —there emerged an America unexampled in density and regional diversity. Were the state guides, as some felt, only a project for research workers rather than for writers? Perhaps; but the literary merit of some of them was greater than most people have appreciated, and their coverage of the country anything but mechanical. More than any other literary form in the thirties, the WPA writers' project, by illustrating how much so many collective skills could do to uncover the collective history of the country, set the tone of the period. As the first shock and panic of the depression passed, and the social reporters settled down to cover the country with a growing eagerness and interest in the epic unfolding out of their investigations, the WPA guides became something more than a super-Baedeker (America had been too much for the Baedeker industry itself, which had quit after one guide): it became a repository as well as a symbol of the reawakened American sense of its own history.

The facts in the guides were only the underpinning of history, but as they began to pour out of the presses, accompanied by the research notes of the Survey of Federal Archives, the Historical Records Survey, the historical notes of the students collecting American folk songs for the Music Project, they had an extraordinary charm in themselves, and a good many surprises to offer. This, like so much in the descriptive and historical literature of the thirties, was perhaps only the raw stuff of history, America put away into a long succession of files, a formal uninterpreted table of statistics on a civilization. But as Robert Cantwell pointed out, the guides went so far and so deep into every corner of the American land that they uncovered an America that nothing in the academic histories had ever prepared one for, and very little in imaginative writing. Road by road, town by town, down under the alluvia of the industrial culture of the twentieth century, lay an America that belied many of the traditional legends about itself. For here, under the rich surface deposits of the factory and city world, lay the forgotten stories of all those who had failed rather than succeeded in the past, all those who had not risen on the steps of the American dream from work bench to Wall Street, but had built a town where the railroad would never pass, gambled on coal deposits where there was no coal, risked their careers for oil where there was no oil: all the small-town financiers who guessed wrong, all those who groped toward riches that never came. And here, too, was the humorous, the creepy, the eccentric side of the American character: the secret rooms and strange furtive religions; the forgotten enthusiasms and heresies and cults; the relics of fashion and tumbling mansions that had always been someone's folly; the grandiose projects, like the ersatz Venice of so many seaside realtors' dreams in the twenties. Here, as Cantwell said in his essay on the America revealed in the state guides, was a chronicle not of the traditional sobriety and industry and down-to-earth business wit of the American race, but rather of a childlike, fanciful, impulsive, and absent-minded people— "a terrible and yet engaging corrective to the success stories that dominate our literature."

But there was something more than a history of secret failure to be uncovered. Important as the WPA guides were in themselves, they pointed even more significantly to a reawakened interest in the whole of the American past, a need to give the whole spirit of social inventory in New Deal America a basic foundation in the reclaimed American inheritance. Now, as the tide of Fascism mounted higher and higher in Europe, and it looked as if Americans had been thrown back on their own resources as never before, the whole emphasis of the early depression literature on national self-scrutiny became a thundering flood of national consciousness and self-celebration. Suddenly, as if it marked a necessary expiation of too rapid and embittered a disillusionment in the past, American writing became a swelling chorus of national affirmation and praise. Suddenly all the debunkers of the past, who had long since been on relief, became the special objects of revulsion and contempt. Suddenly all the despised catchwords of the democratic rhetoric took on a brilliant radiance in a Hitler world; in the emotional discovery of America the country once more became, as Jefferson had long ago foreseen, "this government: the world's best hope."

No longer could one even believe, as Archibald MacLeish had written in *Land of the Free,* that

> We wonder whether the dream of American liberty
> Was two hundred years of pine and hardwood
> And three generations of the grass
>
> And the generations are up: the years over
>
> We don't know.

No, the dream of American liberty was here; it was now. Americans, MacLeish now let himself go in *The American Cause,* were people "who had the luck to be born on this continent where the heat was hotter and the cold was colder and the sun was brighter and the nights were blacker and the distances were farther and the faces were nearer and the rain was more like rain and the mornings were more like mornings than anywhere else on earth—sooner or sweeter and lovelier over unused hills." *"O my America—my new-found-land . . . / How blest am I in this discovering thee!"* Chanting America, loving it, celebrating it, there was suddenly a whole world of marvels on the continent to possess—a world of rivers and scenes, of folklore and regional culture, of a heroic tradition to reclaim and of forgotten heroes to follow. America was here, now, a continent to be surveyed as Lincoln had surveyed the prairie sod where a civilization would follow, an inheritance to rejoice in and to find strength in. America was, indeed, again what Whitman had seen in the first preface to his great poem:

> The Americans of all nations at any time upon the earth, have probably the fullest poetical nature. The United States themselves are essentially the greatest poem. In the history of the earth hitherto, the largest and most stirring appear tame and orderly to their ampler

largeness and stir. Here at last is something in the doings of man that corresponds with the broadcast doings of the day and night. Here is action untied from strings, necessarily blind to particulars and details, magnificently moving in masses.

After the hard-crusted social novels, the crusading polemics, and the exacerbated social reportage of the thirties, the new nationalism now flowered in a literature of solid and affectionate history and biography. As the great affirmative testaments of this new spirit began to appear in endless anthologies of "the democratic spirit," in Sandburg's Lincoln and Carl Van Doren's Benjamin Franklin, in the lyrical history of the New England nineteenth-century mind produced by Van Wyck Brooks, in the tremendous literature that fought the Civil War over as if it had never been fought before, in hundreds of historical novels, in whole tons of folklore material, the hunger for the past—with all it signified of a yearning for stability in the American tradition—told a story greater and more moving in itself than any of the capacious new biographies and histories and novels could suggest. This was a crisis-begotten nationalism, yes; a fever glow of patriotism, quick to rise and perhaps quick to sicken; an army of open-mouthed tourists who seemed to regard America as one vast national park, full of interesting boulders, quaint bits of Indian folklore, and meteorological wonders. Perhaps. Here, as one liked, was either the ironic epilogue to half a century of critical modernism in America or the happy emergence of a real maturity and profound national allegiance among American writers. Yet whatever its virtues or crudities, historical services or pieties, how great a story it did tell in itself!

"In times of change and danger when there is a quicksand of fear under men's reasoning," John Dos Passos now wrote in his tribute to the democratic tradition, *The Ground We Stand On,* "a sense of continuity with generations gone before can stretch like a lifeline across the scary present." In that contemporary sense of danger and the historical sense it invoked lay the moving force of the new nationalism. There had been a flood of historical novels in the eighteen-nineties, but that had been a purely middle-class romanticism, a desire for sentiment and romance that testified not to an interest in history but to a desire to invest the solidity of the rich self-conscious prosperity of the industrial epoch with the trappings of an adventurous and glorious past. So in the great era of American historical writing represented by Prescott and Parkman, Bancroft and Motley, the pride in the independence and stability of the young republic had led men to look back with a fresh and confident pleasure on its early struggles and on the history of the American continent, cradle of a great civilization. But the historical writing that became so preponderant in the thirties was not so much a self-conscious reading of the past as a supplication to it. All history is self-conscious; all true history, as Croce said, is "contemporary history." But what distinguishes the historical writing of the thirties in most of its forms is its curious solidity, its attempt not to "escape" into the past but to pack the whole of the past into the present. What distinguishes it is a curious literalness, a veneration of the past at once grim and uncritical, a desire actually to use the past as if it had never been used before.

Uncritical *and* unsentimental. Inevitably, some of this historical literature was sentimental, as a good deal of Van Wyck Brooks's New England history, for example, was a sentimental transcription of Concord sights and sounds. Yet the most illuminating quality of this new writing was precisely its objectivity, since its great aim was not to prettify the past but to recover it bodily, as it were; to take possession of it and to enjoy it on the fullest possible scale. The cry now, as in the social journalism of the period, was for facts, facts; but facts on how men *in the past* had lived, on how they had withstood the pressure of their times, on how they had survived. Even the many historical novels, despite their own tradition of romanticism, despite the inevitable confectionery of the sword-and-cape romance, were distinguished by their general tone of sober matter-of-fact realism. In fact, so many of these new historical novels seemed to be written in the best tradition of American scholarship, replete with historical apparatus and bibliographies, that they testified as nothing else could to the demand of the period for solidly grounded and tirelessly accumulated monuments of historical fact. So the new histories and biographies, all so palpably built out of enormous labor and affection, all so objective and massive and even a little pious, revealed the taste for scrupulous and inclusive portraiture of the past.

Nowhere in the enormous descriptive literature of the thirties did this new spirit reveal itself so vividly as in biography, where it had its triumph. Carl Sandburg spoke not only for his fellow craftsmen in the field, but also for a whole generation, when he wrote bitterly of the debunkers that they had written "books where men of shallow wisdom and showman's tricks had subverted and falsified so as to fool young people regarding events and characters where the reality is better than the myth." Odell Shepard, another leading biographer of the period, wrote in reviewing a new, solid, and definitive life of Timothy Dwight (so many of the biographies were now "solid and definitive"):

> During recent years and months . . . we have begun to realize that there was something quite indispensable in those virtues that once seemed parochial and outworn. We are now learning once more to respect those orthodoxies and fidelities which are the products not of ease but of danger. Now and then we look back a little wistfully at the heroes of our national past, wishing that the attitude of hero-worship had not been quite so violently assailed in the presence of those who are now called upon to be themselves heroic. What this amounts to is that our pose of ultra-sophistication, a familiar trait of adolescence, is no longer fashionable. We are now making rapid progress toward the simplicity of really mature minds.

What this "simplicity" meant stood clearly revealed in the foreword that Henry Steele Commager wrote to his glowing biography of Theodore Parker:

> Where [Parker] was vain I have not sought to rebuke his vanity, where he was inconsistent I have not thought it necessary to remark his inconsistency, where he was ungenerous I have not taken him to task, where he was violent I have not tried to abate his violence, where he was mistaken I have not attempted to set him right.

Shades of Joseph Wood Krutch's brilliant psychoanalytical dissection of Poe, of W. E. Woodward's *Meet General Grant,* of Van Wyck Brooks's *The Ordeal of Mark Twain!* The reaction had set in, and with Lytton Strachey departed forever, along with all those easy and deliciously scornful epigrams that had once provoked an irreverent generation to laughter, the taste now was all for an objectivity that not merely fulfilled its function in scholarship but became a search for the very "feel" of the past. It was this pressing need to recover as much of the past as possible, to steep oneself in it, that explains why the staggering detail of these books, with their rich and eagerly proffered accumulation of data, made them seem anything but pedestrian. The stress of biography was no longer on distinction of style, on a calculated evocation of atmosphere and character; given the facts, the biographer seemed to say, the story would tell itself, aided only by common sense, the necessary sympathy for one's subject (this was of the first importance), and a decent respect for the merit and dignity of the world to be described.

With the return of "fat, full, old-fashioned biography, rich in facts and lean in random speculation," the very literary character of modern American biography seemed to change, as indeed it did. But the reaction was not simply a return to the "life-and-letters" school of the Victorian tradition. Books like Carl Van Doren's Franklin, Douglas S. Freeman's Lee, Lloyd Lewis's Sherman, Allan Nevins's Grover Cleveland and Rockefeller and Frémont (among others), Marquis James's Sam Houston and Andrew Jackson, Carl Sandburg's Lincoln, Claude Bowers's Jefferson, were all scholarly books—biography was now nothing if it was not scholarly—but they were books to be read and enjoyed, books that had been written to restore their subjects—"in grand dimensions," as Carl Van Doren wrote of his Franklin—to the world. The "reality was better than the myth," and it had only to be described in all its incomparable fullness. And since there was so much to give back, the writers of these books generally adopted a loose-ranging, convenient bluntness of style that served to shovel the whole of the past into their books. The highest aspiration now was to be as humble and attentive as Boswell; no one ever thought to be as magnificently wrong as Dr. Johnson. A full-dress description of a Civil War battle, as in Douglas S. Freeman's Lee or Lloyd Lewis's Sherman, was now worth a hundred epigrams; a laborious recreation of the subject's background, solidly documented and affectionately written, as in George F. Whicher's notable Emily Dickinson, easily surpassed the most brilliant flights of character speculation. To live with Lincoln in Carl Sandburg's six volumes, face to face with the people he met, the things he saw and wrote, hearing again almost every one of the thousand stories he told, was to know the supreme happiness of being alive again in the past.

The immense distinction of Sandburg's book made it the monument of the new biography, a peculiarly transparent example of a new historical consciousness. Built up through the years like a coral reef, loosely written and at times even slovenly—it was curious to note how the conscious, faintly sentimental lyricism of the early chapters in *The Prairie Years* soon broke into a businesslike trot under the flood of data in *The War Years*—the book revealed a studiously negative artistry. Under the pressure of that whole Civil War world to recreate, the very effort of Sandburg's imagination was subtly transformed into a supreme historical sensitiveness, a capacity for embracing the whole stupendous past. Where in *The Prairie Years* one could still see a certain self-conscious (and appealing) "poetizing" of the facts, with Sandburg, as it were, plotting the chronicle of Lincoln's growth, the measure of Lincoln now became the measure of that whole American civilization that would find its apotheosis in him. The past came rushing back in a torrent, all of it, seemingly; the story began to tell itself. Out of the recovery of a period in time, a period restored day by day, month after month, layer on layer, a mound heap of human stories, Lincoln arose before the reader like a massive shadow of the racked civilization he had held together, a stupendous aggregation of all those American traits that were to find so ambiguous and moving an expression in him. And this was the distinction of Sandburg's portrait: Lincoln did not live in himself, he lived because an epoch had to be pieced together slowly and laboriously to reclaim him; he lived because the very pang of democracy, rising out of so much struggle and aspiration, now resided in him. More than a symbol of a distinct American experience, he had become the propulsion of a great symphonic poem; more than a leader, the people's legend of him now seemed the greatest of all American works of art.

5

Slowly and hopefully, this new historical spirit was now edging its way into the unabashed recovery of an American mythology. The past was not always glorious, but no matter; its glory lay in its being past. A golden haze now lay over "the age of confidence"—a term which Henry Seidel Canby used as the title of his memoir of life in the eighteen-nineties, but which could have been used with equal nostalgia and affection by most of the numerous biographers and historians, autobiographers and historical novelists, who now turned to describe scene after scene out of that past which lay beyond the stain of contemporary instability and terror. Remembering the nineties, Canby wrote of it as a time when "you belonged—and it was up to your own self to find out how and where. There has been no such certainty in American life since." *"In that last epoch of American stability of which I write ..."* Any epoch which a man could remember as different from the present now seemed "the last epoch of American stability." A wave of remembrance had set in, and all the queer country grandfathers, all the joys of life with father, all the solid, folksy virtues came back—less out of a pride in their forbears, as Lewis Gannett suggested, than out of an inferiority complex. So even Harold E. Stearns, who had made a reputation for himself in the twenties by mobilizing contemporary intellectuals in the fashionable expatriate scorn for Babbitt America, now became a heated propagandist of the national virtues. So even H. L. Mencken, who had taken to writing his memoirs, now wrote with an almost touching sentimental pleasure of the great days, the good old days, that lay before. What times! What endless gaiety and confidence!

The past now lay everywhere ready to be reclaimed, waiting to be chanted and celebrated. The old ballads began to come back, all the dear familiar legends, all the fine rawboned heroes of the frontier epic —Davy Crockett and Paul Bunyan, Mike Fink and John Henry, Johnny Appleseed and Daniel Boone, and with them a host of new supermen and gargantuan jokers and work giants—Whiskey Jack, Johnny Inkslinger, Pecos Bill. "From a nation lean in folk annals and too short-lived to boast an heroic age," as one folklore specialist wrote, there had suddenly sprung a knavish, comic, blustering, yet proudly titanic race of superheroes. Often transparently synthetic heroes, they yet all testified to the fascination with the prodigal carelessness, the strong pride in the homemade myths of a lusty day, now felt by their uneasy urbanized descendants. From its first beginnings American folklore had always been the tribute paid in reminiscence by a late generation to an earlier. So even Mike Fink, the Mississippi river god, was supposed to have cried when he was turned out to pasture in a world of canals and factories: "What's the use of improvements? Where's the fun, the frolicking, the fighting? Gone! All gone!" Now the impulse to collect folklore was more poignantly than ever a longing for a heroic tradition, and the stories so many students now begin to pick up were of fabricated giants (what did it matter that they were fabricated?) dreaming and fighting and loving like young gods in the visible Homeric heavens. All other mythical heroes, as Max Eastman said, were serious; ours had come too late to be serious, and that was their charm. They were not plaster casts in a pantheon of greatness; they were the embodiment of a jealous American aspiration, the recovered stuff of a forgotten American laughter. "They were born in laughter," as Eastman said; "they are consciously preposterous; they are cockalorum demi-gods. That is the natively American thing—not that her primitive humor is exaggerative, but that her primitive exaggerations were humorous." And in their humorous strength lay what was wanted.

So the new literature of American folkways, of the river legends and regional cultures, while often shallow enough, was anything but museum-like. Often only too eager to claim a distinctive cultural tradition for every corner of the country, the many descriptive-historical books that now poured out of the presses testified to a need to tag and index and literally possess the country. Everything that lay at hand cried to be photographed and recorded and admired; everything that was past was now interesting and charming and radiantly alive: costumes and houses, manners and people, Benedict Arnold's first great services, cracker-barrel legends, all the stuff of a hundred forgotten political conflicts, *American* conflicts. Even the Loyalists of the Revolutionary period were restored to favor in Kenneth Roberts's slick *Oliver Wiswell*, and everyone sighed over their misfortunes and loved them in the same spirit that they now loved Tom Paine and Sam Adams. Even Ezra Pound, in one of the last cantos he wrote before he went to work for the Axis, paid his tribute to John Quincy Adams. And Daniel Webster, of whom Emerson and Whittier had had another opinion, now appeared in Stephen Vincent Benét's charming story as a *big* man, a pillar of virtue, a gigantic folk hero, fit to rescue Yankee souls from the Devil and beat him easily at his own game. "No American citizen may be forced into the service of a foreign prince."

What all this was leading to, as the trend in biography had shown and the rage of the historical novel now proved, was a desire to enter bodily into the past, to make a great, comforting, yet authentic pageantry out of it. What did it matter that Kenneth Roberts described the Revolutionary patriots as a "rabble," or that Margaret Mitchell won the peace as if the North had never won the Civil War? All the lost causes now came back through the historical novel, that favorite home of lost causes, and no one—least of all the millions of readers in the North and the West gulping up one Confederate romance after another—cared whether the South had lost at all. South or North, West or East, it all added up to everything the contemporary world was not, a kind of seamless web of heroic and exhilarating legend. What the historical novelists now sought was an image of the past made whole, an image of a world modern readers could enter into completely and possess in all its parts; and they generally found it on the basis of an imitative modern realism in the novel. For only a meticulous realism could now reproduce the past as it needed to be reproduced; photographed, as it were, in a succession of glowing scenes. The new historical novel, at once so conscientiously antiquarian and self-consciously contemporary, therefore had no need of the old romantic apparatus of the historical novel; it made a romance out of its recovery of the past. Too deeply interested in their own world to fool with the old conventional idealizations, too sophisticated to want anything less than an authentic transcription of how other people had really lived, the historical novelists were at the same time interested only in making the past come alive, in giving it a realistic quality that would illuminate, rather than deny, the riches of the past it tried to evoke.

It was in this same vein of historical portraiture and pageantry, significantly enough, that popular histories and anthologies of "the American spirit" now began to appear. Even so solidly respectable a historian as Allan Nevins launched an appeal, in *The Gateway to History,* for a more colorful history, a history richer in human interest and literary skill. He paid tribute to the great American historians of the past who had thought of history as the creator and inspirer of nations, and recalled the spirit of Treitschke, who had resolved to revive the national spirit of the Germans by writing history. So even John Dos Passos, sketching the history of the Anglo-American tradition in *The Ground We Stand On,* was moved to a new and startling eloquence in his contemplation of Thomas Jefferson on his hill at Monticello, dreaming the promise of a "future that like a great convex mirror magnified every act and gesture of the men working their fields and building their farms in the tiny settlements along the Eastern seaboard." Describing the lives of Roger Williams and Sam Adams, Tom Paine and Jefferson, of Joel Barlow and Hugh Henry Brackenridge, Dos Passos seemed to recover so exhilarating a sense of pride in the American tradition—"we must never forget that we are heirs to one of the grandest and most nearly realized worldpictures in all history"— that the very writing of history now became for him a series of picturesque and exciting vignettes of the past—Roger Williams bringing the great tradition of Puritan liberalism to New England; Franklin shining in all his natural grace at the French court; Jefferson building his republican projects at Monticello; Sam Adams plotting the Revolution in Boston. Reaching, as it were, for an image of the repose and nobility that so few characters in any Dos Passos novel ever knew, he now found it in the portraiture of the fresh and burgeoning world of eighteenth-century America: the iron forges, the deer in the woods, Jefferson's classic integrity, the moment when the flag was first raised over Fort Pitt at the gateway to the Alleghenies, and it was felt that "the level land of the lakes and rivers would be the nursery of a new century of the young republic."

A golden haze indeed now lay over the past, and with the triumphant popular success of *The Flowering of New England* and *New England: Indian Summer*—the first two volumes in Van Wyck Brooks's projected history of American literature—it became clear that even literary history could now be written with all the ceremonious pageantry of the historical novel. For what was so distinctive about Brooks's loving portrait of the nineteenth-century New England mind was that for all its incidental brilliance of observation, it was the work of a critic who was fundamentally no longer interested in criticism. His history was an affectionate pilgrimage to the great shrines of the past, a radiant and mellifluous avowal of love and pride in a tradition, and it was just Brooks's ability to touch all the departed figures in his work with his own radiance that made his work so eloquent a testament. Where another writer would have described the lives of his characters in an effort to understand their books better, Brooks seemed almost more interested in the authors than in their books. What he was aiming at, as had already been clear in *The Life of Emerson,* was not a desire to meet Emerson—and Emerson's time—as contemporaries, but a sweet and shining epic of a lost heroic tradition, a kind of American Nibelungenlied in which all the gods were literary men and women and all their passions revolved around a distinctive moral idealism. What he was aiming at, in a word, was an epic in heroic tone, an uncovered tradition of ancient dignity and Emersonian sweetness, of aspiration and culture, of a certain delicious quaintness and inspiring integrity, in which author, background, and book were commingled.

So strong was Brooks's desire to make this past come alive in the spirit of the historical novel that he even called his second volume a "sequel" to his first, and wrote in explanation of his emphasis on Boston in that second volume that he had done so partly because he wished to give the book "a unity of place." The writers who streamed through his pages were all characters in a great historical drama, perhaps the noblest and most commanding in American history, and what they had written served to characterize them as actors in it. The emphasis was all on personalities and friendships, the evocation of atmosphere and scenes. One of the chapters in *New England: Indian Summer* was significantly titled "Country Pictures," and all through the two volumes one could see Brooks aiming at "effects" and dramatic revelations and climaxes—a succession of brilliant and often moving scenes, felicitous recreations of lost moments in time, that could be (most explicitly in the chapter on Emily Dickinson) totally unrelated to the writer's work. The scenes, the scenes were the great thing: Washington Allston moving like a great sage through the Boston of 1815; John Quincy Adams remembering proudly that he had said the Lord's

Prayer every night of his life and "had never mumbled it once"; Emerson listening to the Aeolian harp receiving the winds on his porch; Thoreau in the woods; Howells and James walking up and down the streets of Cambridge at night dreaming of future conquests in the novel; Francis James Child, the sailmaker's son, collecting his ballads and tending his roses; Francis Parkman, blind and broken with illness, fighting like a wounded knight to finish his books.

Here, America, here, Brooks seemed to be saying in exultant pride on every page, is your tradition, and what a tradition! What men! What faith! What scholars! In tribute to Emerson's great generation he wrote:

> As heirs of the Revolution they spoke for the liberal world-community. As men who loved the land and rural customs, they shared the popular life in its roots, at its source. As readers and students of the classics, they followed great patterns of behaviour, those that Europeans followed also. . . . If they believed in progress, and felt that America led the way, they professed their faith in a fashion that commanded respect, for they had known doubts and struggles, wars and vigils. . . . They had cultivated their gardens, they knew the country, the seacoast and the homestead, the lakes and mountains.

Lost that great world might be, lost in time; yet by recreating its pageantry, by learning from its accumulated example, there was sustenance for contemporary spirits. What was so moving as the memory of John Quincy Adams (so much a greater man than his querulous grandson Henry), diplomat, scholar, poet, scientist, teacher, Secretary of State, President of the United States, an old Roman who had not been ashamed to return to Congress after leaving the White House, nor too tired to journey to Cincinnati on a flatboat in the dead of winter to dedicate an observatory to the spirit of science that should flourish in the young republic? What heroic example out of the past did any contemporary nation possess as fine as the moral devotion of Wendell Phillips, the purity of Emerson, the courage of Thoreau, the scholarship of Prescott and Parkman, the flinty idealism of Whittier, the radiant spirit of Longfellow?

For Brooks himself, as had been clear ever since he had written his preliminary idyll in *The Life of Emerson,* the wheel had come full circle. In a period of unparalleled crisis of spirit, a period when the whole modern movement he had once helped to shape had reached its climax, he had fashioned for himself a purpose seemingly beyond criticism and even creative literature: he had become, like Fichte or Treitschke, the celebrator of a national tradition, the historian who delved into the past so that he could sustain and arm his countrymen in time of danger. For thirty years and more he had written criticism, as the great nineteenth-century masters he loved had written criticism —as a form of moral instruction, a guide to spiritual fulfillment. For thirty years and more he had lamented the alienation of American writers from their native roots, but had documented and illuminated that rootlessness in a spirit of tragic justification. And all through those years he had been the prophet of only one central, all-pervading idea: that the great writer is only the voice of the culture to which he belongs, the culture in which he is rooted and which he accepts. In the words of D. H. Lawrence, with which Brooks now crowned *The Flowering of New England*: "Men are free when they are in a living homeland . . . free when they are obeying some deep, inward voice of religious belief . . . free when they belong to a living, organic, believing community, active in fulfilling some unfulfilled, perhaps unrealized purpose." Now he had no longer any reason to lament the absence of that spirit in America. He had found it, like buried treasure, under the ground men walked in America, found it in their own past—a standard, an image of belief and security.

Most significantly, out of his rapture in that recovered past Brooks had found a fighting faith for himself, and he now turned it furiously upon all those modern writers in France and England, as well as in America—the Eliots, the Joyces, the Prousts—who had dominated letters in the period between two wars. For it was at this point, with the emergence of so self-consciously contemporary an American mythology, that Brooks passed from his renewal of faith in the native tradition to a bitter attack on all that which in his mind had departed from it and corrupted it, all that which now seemed to impede the mobilization of the democratic spirit at a time when democracy needed every available resource to survive. It was not merely for Brooks himself that the wheel had come full circle; in so unparalleled a crisis the whole tradition of modernism to which Brooks had once contributed was now called into question. Along with writers like Archibald MacLeish, Howard Mumford Jones, Lewis Mumford, Brooks now protested that too many modern writers had failed themselves, failed or even betrayed the democratic hope, failed in their responsibility as humanists and citizens. In the light of the tradition he had recovered Brooks could now see only a degeneracy of will and spirit, an egotism and a subtle corruption, on the part of those who should have been at the very least leaders in the mobilization against Fascism.

Brooks's attack, particularly in such a book as *The Opinions of Oliver Allston,* was primarily a call to arms; but it was significant also because it brought to a head a certain self-disgust that had been evident in contemporary writing. Where Archibald MacLeish fell upon the antiwar novels written in the twenties, and Howard Mumford Jones complained that the irreverence of modern letters had produced a race of young people who had no "mythology" with which to fight the Fascist mythology, Brooks's attack was leveled against what he felt to be the moral irresponsibility of contemporary literature. And it was just here that his stridency exposed him to the charge by T. S. Eliot that he "might have been interested in not merely denouncing modern art, but in enquiring *why* it is what it is." For Brooks's intense personal attacks confused the issue and served no purpose. There is sickness in contemporary literature, a very great sickness; but it is hardly self-willed, and it is bound up with the situation of contemporary humanity. Brooks, by calling some writers "rattlesnakes" in the narrowly censorious fashion with which an Irving Babbitt had so often been moved to call them degenerates, missed the laborious integrity of modern writers, their will to understand, to live, to create insofar as the world will allow them to. He missed, in his attack on Proust, the profound moral structure and genius of Proust's great work; in his attack on Eliot, Eliot's extraordinary services in behalf of the continuity of the Western tradition and of a new language for poetry; in his attack on Joyce, Joyce's passionate devotion to the life of art, to mention nothing more, in a world where art was as never before the embodiment of the life of reason. Brooks saw his own morality and belief in humanity;

he forgot that one does not have to intone a standard to live and write by one, and that those who intone too self-righteously may have nothing left but a standard.

There was nothing in Brooks's attack writers could learn from; he had simply withdrawn his sympathy and understanding from them, and his message was too abstract, too hollow in its evangelicism. The moral paralysis that can be found in certain writers today is real enough, and with it the self-contentment of those who do not know that literature lives by something more than literature. But you cannot relieve that paralysis by calling it wickedness; and Tolstoy and John Greenleaf Whittier, while noble men both, do not mix very well for a writer talking about writing. What was particularly lamentable in Brooks's attack was its essential remoteness from literature. Literature will live fully again when the world is able to live fully again; the "primary" virtues in literature may come back only when men are bound up again in the indivisible moral life of humanity. But if they do come back, it will be not merely because the world has attained some semblance of order, but even more because, in times of terror and human hazard like our own, men have kept their responsibility to literature and to themselves. Literature lives by faith and *works*. Joyce may be the "dead ash of a burnt-out cigar," but the Joyce who worked away at *Ulysses* during the last war kept something alive in the European tradition that those who merely spoke in the name of that tradition did not. Brooks defeated his own best purpose by yielding to an impatience with writers as writers, to the panicky call to action and conformism that had been depressingly familiar in literature after 1930. The pressure of the times was too great for him; it made for so confused a sense of urgency that he forgot that writers are never of any use to themselves, or to society, when they are beaten into shape.

Yes, the pressure of the times is too great; it beats upon all of us. Literature today lives on the narrow margin of security that the democratic West, fighting for its life, can afford; and that margin may grow more narrow every day. The pressure of that struggle beats upon us and all our culture; it beats upon the Hemingways and the Eliots, the Joyces and the Prousts, the wasteland and the grandeur; it beats upon the ardors and accidents, the laborious struggles for realism and realization that make up our modern American literature; it beats equally upon the modernism that dazzled the world between wars and the facile expiation that would wipe it all away. It beats upon us in America as it beats upon all the nations and all the living and the dead; and our whole modern democratic culture is being tried by it. Never was it so imperative as it is now not to sacrifice any of the values that give our life meaning; never was it so imperative for men to be equal to the evil that faces them and not submissive to its terror. The world seems to be waiting, waiting for its new order; everything we do, everything we believe in this moment of climacteric, can help to shape the future toward which men are moving in such agony today. It is not for us, then, but for the Axis Ministers of Culture—the half-men, the death's-heads grinning over their spoil of our time—to impose an external unity upon culture; it is only those who have no culture and no belief in culture who resent differences among men and the explorations of the human imagination. For the rest, the past is what it is; the record of modern literature in America is what men have made it. *They will have seen the new truth in larger and larger degree; and when it shall have become the old truth, they will perhaps have seen it all.* We have seen it become the "old truth." We have not even begun to see it all—and what it may become.

Index

The pages of the main discussion of an author are marked with an asterisk (*). Slight mention is after "ref.," which often means a comparison.

Acknowledgments

For permission to quote from material held under copyright, I am indebted to the following:

D. APPLETON-CENTURY COMPANY. For permission to quote from: *Degeneration*, by Max Nordau; *A Backward Glance*, by Edith Wharton.

JOHN DOS PASSOS. For permission to quote from: *One Man's Initiation*, published by Allen and Unwin, London; *Rosinante to the Road Again*; and *Three Soldiers*.

DOUBLEDAY, DORAN AND COMPANY. For permission to quote from: *Eugene Field's Creative Years*, by C. H. Dennis (Copyright 1924); *Frank Norris*, by Franklin Walker (Copyright 1932); *Leaves of Grass* by Walt Whitman (Copyright 1924); *They Stooped to Folly* (Copyright 1929); *The Miller of Old Church* (Copyright 1911), and *The Romantic Comedians* (Copyright 1926) by Ellen Glasgow.

DUELL, SLOAN & PEARCE, INC. For permission to quote from: *Say, Is This the U.S.A.*, by Erskine Caldwell; *The American Cause*, by Archibald MacLeish; *Butterfield 8*, by John O'Hara.

E. P. DUTTON AND COMPANY. For permission to quote from: *Three Essays on America, New England: Indian Summer*, and *Pilgrimage of Henry James*, by Van Wyck Brooks.

HARCOURT, BRACE AND COMPANY. For permission to quote from: *Main Currents in American Thought*, by Vernon L. Parrington; *Movers and Shakers*, by Mabel Dodge Luhan; *Portrait of the Artist as American*, by Matthew Josephson; *Civilization in the United States*, edited by Harold E. Stearns; Sherwood Anderson's *Memoirs*; *The Modern Temper*, by Joseph Wood Krutch; *The Drama and the Stage*, by Ludwig Lewisohn; *Letters of Lincoln Steffens*, edited by Ella Winter and Granville Hicks; *Principles of Literary Criticism*, by I. A. Richards.

HARPER AND BROTHERS. For permission to quote from: *I'll Take My Stand; With The Procession*, by Henry B. Fuller; *Literary and Social Silhouettes*, by Hjalmar H. Boyesen; *Cities and Men* and *Expression in*

America, by Ludwig Lewisohn; *The Hills Beyond, You Can't Go Home Again* and *The Web and the Rock,* by Thomas Wolfe.

HENRY HOLT AND COMPANY. For permission to quote from: *Democracy,* by Henry Adams; *The Growth and Decadence of Constitutional Government,* by J. Allen Smith.

HOUGHTON MIFFLIN COMPANY. For permission to quote from: *Letters of Charles Eliot Norton,* edited by Mark A. DeWolfe Howe; *The Education of Henry Adams; Autobiography,* by Charles Francis Adams; *Letters of Henry Adams,* 1892-1918, edited by Worthington Chauncey Ford; *My Ántonia,* by Willa Cather; *Literature and the American College, The Masters of Modern French Criticism,* by Irving Babbitt; *Shelburne Essays,* Vol. IX, by Paul Elmer More; *Land of the Free,* by Archibald MacLeish; *Youth and Life,* by Randolph Bourne; *U.S.A.,* by John Dos Passos.

MILDRED HOWELLS and JOHN MEAD HOWELLS. For permission to quote from: *Life in Letters of William Dean Howells,* edited by Mildred Howells; *Criticism and Fiction; A Traveler from Altruria* (Copyright 1894 by Harper & Bros., Copyright 1921 by Mildred Howells and John Mead Howells); *Annie Kilburn; The Quality of Mercy;* and *Through the Eye of the Needle* (Copyright 1907 by Harper & Bros., Copyright 1935 by Mildred Howells and John Mead Howells), by William Dean Howells.

ALFRED A. KNOPF, INC. For permission to quote from: *The Black Riders,* by Stephen Crane; *Prejudices,* by H. L. Mencken; *The Blind Bow-Boy* and *Parties,* by Carl Van Vechten; "The Code of a Critic," by George Jean Nathan; *Linda Condon,* by Joseph Hergesheimer; *Hanna,* by Thomas Beer; *Collected Poems, Jennifer Lorn,* and *The Orphan Angel,* by Elinor Wylie; *Youth and the Bright Medusa* and *A Lost Lady,* by Willa Cather; *The Roving Critic,* by Carl Van Doren.

LIVERIGHT PUBLISHING CORPORATION. For permission to quote from: *The Creative Life* and *Upstream,* by Ludwig Lewisohn; *The Enormous Room,* by E. E. Cummings.

ROBERT M. MCBRIDE AND COMPANY. For permission to quote from: *The Cream of the Jest, Straws and Prayer Books, Beyond Life,* and *Jurgen,* by James Branch Cabell.

THE MACMILLAN COMPANY. For permission to quote from: *The Novel: What It Is,* by F. Marion Crawford; *Degradation of the Democratic Dogma,* by Brooks Adams; *Partial Portraits* and *The Princess Casamassima,* by Henry James; *The Web of Life,* by Robert Herrick; *The Spirit of American Government*, by J. Allen Smith; *Experience and Education* and *Democracy and Education*, by John Dewey; *An Economic Interpretation of the Constitution*, by Charles A. Beard.

HENRY MILLER. For permission to quote from *Tropic of Cancer*, published by the Obelisk Press, Paris.

RANDOM HOUSE. For permission to quote from: *Absalom! Absalom!*, *The Hamlet*, and *The Sound and the Fury*, by William Faulkner.

CHARLES SCRIBNER'S SONS. For permission to quote from: *Essays in Scandinavian Literature*, by Hjalmar H. Boyesen; *Steeplejack*, by James G. Huneker; *This Side of Paradise*, *The Great Gatsby*, and *All the Sad Young Men*, by F. Scott Fitzgerald; *The Fifth Column and the First Forty-Nine Stories*, *Death in the Afternoon*, *In Our Time*, by Ernest Hemingway; *The World's Body*, by John Crowe Ransom; *The Liberation of American Literature*, by V. F. Calverton; *Look Homeward, Angel* and *The Story of a Novel*, by Thomas Wolfe; *The Literary Mind*, by Max Eastman.

FREDERICK A. STOKES COMPANY, INC. For permission to quote from: *The Road to the Temple*, by Susan Glaspell.

THE VIKING PRESS, INC. For permission to quote from: *Essays in Our Changing Order* and *The Place of Science in Modern Civilisation and Other Essays*, by Thorstein Veblen; *Untimely Papers* and *The History of a Literary Radical*, by Randolph Bourne; *A Story-Teller's Story* and *The Triumph of the Egg*, by Sherwood Anderson; *The Grapes of Wrath*, *The Long Valley*, and *In Dubious Battle*, by John Steinbeck.